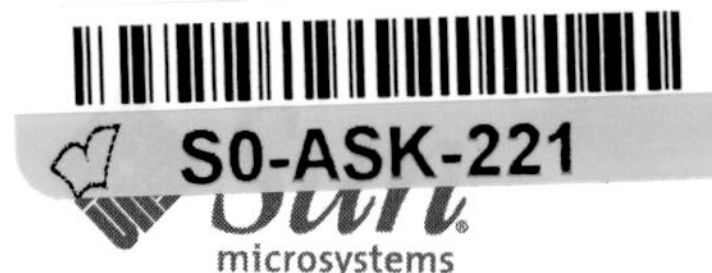

Solaris®

ADVANCED SYSTEM ADMINISTRATOR'S GUIDE, *Second Edition*

Janice Winsor

Associate Publisher, MTP	Jim LeValley
Publisher, Sun Microsystems	Rachel Borden
Marketing Manager, Sun Microsystems	John Bortner
Executive Editor	Julie Fairweather
Acquisitions Editor	Brett Bartow
Development Editor	Lisa Gebken
Managing Editor	Caroline Roop
Project Editor	Brad Herriman
Copy Editors	Leah Williams, Phil Worthington, and Kezia Endsley
Technical Reviewer	Peter Gregory
Proofreader	Pamela Woolf
Book Design	Louisa Klucznik
Page Layout	Aleata Howard, Nicole Ritch
Indexer	Tim Wright

This book was produced on a Macintosh IIfx with the following applications: FrameMaker, Microsoft Word, MacLink *Plus*, Aldus FreeHand, Adobe Photoshop, and Collage Plus.

Sun Microsystems Press
901 San Antonio Rd.
Palo Alto, CA 94303 USA

ISBN 1-57870-039-6
Manufactured in the United States of America
10 9 8

INTRODUCTION

HIS BOOK IS FOR SYSTEM ADMINISTRATORS WHO ARE FAMILIAR WITH BASIC system administration and with the tasks described in the *Solaris System Administrator's Guide*, cited in the bibliography at the end of this book.

A Quick Tour of the Contents

This book is divided into seven parts, two appendixes, a glossary, and a bibliography.

Part 1, "Mail Services," describes the Solaris 2.*x* mail services in four chapters. Refer to the chapters in this part if you need to set up a new mail service or expand an existing one.

Chapter 1, "Understanding Mail Services," describes the components of the mail service, defines mail service terminology, and explains how the programs in the mail service interact.

Chapter 2, "Planning Mail Services," describes several common mail configurations and provides guidelines for setting up each configuration.

Chapter 3, "Setting Up and Administering Mail Services," describes how to set up, test, administer, and troubleshoot mail services.

Chapter 4, "Customizing sendmail Configuration Files," describes the sendmail configuration file and how to customize it if you need a more complex configuration file for your mail system.

Part 2, "NIS+," introduces the NIS+ naming service environment. Refer to the chapters in this part if you want to familiarize yourself with the basics of the NIS+ naming service and its administrative commands. Also refer to these chapters for instructions for setting up an NIS+ client. This part does not provide in-depth information for a system administrator who must set up and support an NIS+ environment.

Chapter 5, "Introducing the NIS+ Environment," provides an overview of NIS+, explains how NIS+ differs from the Solaris 1.*x* NIS naming service, and introduces the NIS+ commands.

Chapter 6, "Setting Up NIS+ Clients," describes how to set up a SunOS 5.*x* system as an NIS+ client when NIS+ servers are set up and running.

Part 3, "Automounter Services," describes the Solaris 2.*x* automount services. Refer to the chapters in this part if you need to set up a new automount service or modify an existing one.

Chapter 7, "Understanding the Automounter," describes automount terminology and the components of automounting, explains how the automounter works, recommends automounting policies, and tells you how to plan your automount services.

Chapter 8, "Setting Up the Automounter," describes how to set up and administer automount maps.

Part 4, “Service Access Facility,” describes the Solaris 2.*x* Service Access Facility (SAF). Refer to the chapters in this part if you need to set up a new SAF service for terminals, modems, or printers or need to modify an existing one.

Chapter 9, “Understanding the Service Access Facility,” provides an overview of the SAF and describes the port monitors and services used by the SAF.

Chapter 10, “Setting Up Modems and Character Terminals,” describes how to set up and administer the SAF for modems and terminals.

Chapter 11, “Setting Up Printing Services,” describes how to set up and administer the SAF for printers and how to troubleshoot printing problems.

Part 5, “Application Software,” describes how to install and delete application software. Refer to this part for guidelines on setting up an application server and for information on installing and removing application software and patches.

Chapter 12, “Installing and Managing Application Software,” provides an overview of the installation process, introduces the package commands and the Software Manager for installation, recommends a policy for installing software on an application server, and describes how to access files from a CD-ROM drive.

Chapter 13, “Package Commands,” describes how to use the package commands to administer application software and how to set up the users’ environment.

Chapter 14, “Admintool: Software Manager,” describes how to use Admintool to administer application software.

Chapter 15, “Installing and Managing System Software Patches,” describes how to use the new `patchadd` and `patchrm` commands.

Part 6, “Introduction to Shell Programming,” familiarizes you with the basics of shell programming. Use the information in this part to decide which shell language you want to use to perform a specific task. This part does not provide in-depth instructions for writing scripts in the three shells.

Chapter 16, “Writing Shell Scripts,” introduces the basic concepts of shell programming and the three shells available with Solaris 2.*x* system software. It describes how shells work and describes the programming elements.

Chapter 17, “Reference Tables and Example Scripts,” provides reference tables comparing shell syntax. It also contains examples of shell scripts.

Part 7, “System Security,” provides information about creating and administering secure systems. Refer to these three chapters if you want to familiarize yourself with the basics of system security and if you want to use authentication services and ASET security.

Chapter 18, “Understanding System Security,” introduces the basic concepts of system security, including file, system, and network security.

Chapter 19, "Using Authentication Services," describes how to use authentication services. It provides an overview of secure RPC and explains how to use pluggable authentication modules (PAM).

Chapter 20, "Using the Automated Security Enhancement Tool (ASET)," describes how to set up and use automated security enhancement tool (ASET).

Refer to these three chapters if you want to familiarize yourself with the basics of system security and if you want to use authentication services and ASET security.

Appendix A, "Volume Management," describes a new feature with Solaris 2.2 system software. Volume management automates the mounting of CD-ROMs and diskettes. You no longer need to have superuser permission to mount a CD-ROM or a diskette.

Appendix B, "Solaris Server Intranet Extension Products," introduces the products available on the Solaris Server Intranet Extension 1.0 CD-ROM and provides brief installation instructions.

The glossary contains basic system administration terms and defines their meanings.

The bibliography contains a list of books on related system administration topics.

Important: Read This Before You Begin

Because you should assume that the root path includes the `/sbin`, `/usr/sbin`, `/usr/bin`, and `/etc` directories, the steps show the commands in these directories without absolute pathnames. Steps that use commands in other, less common directories show the absolute path in the example.

The examples in this book are for a basic Solaris 2.*x* system software installation without the Binary Compatibility Package installed and without `/usr/ucb` in the path.

CAUTION! *If* `/usr/ucb` *is included in a search path, it should always be at the end. Commands such as* `ps` *and* `df` *are duplicated in* `/usr/ucb` *with formats and options that are different than the SunOS 5.*x *commands.*

This book describes six different system administration areas in depth; however, a given section may not contain all of the information you need to administer systems. Refer to the complete system administration documentation set for complete information.

Because the Solaris 2.*x* system software provides the Bourne (default), Korn, and C shells, examples in this book show prompts for each of the shells. The default Bourne and Korn shell prompt is `$`. The default C shell prompt is `system-name%`. The default root prompt for all shells is a pound sign (`#`). In examples that affect more than one system, the C shell prompt (which shows the system name) is used to make it clearer when you change from one system to another.

SPARC and x86 Information

This book provides system administration information for both SPARC and x86 systems. Unless otherwise noted, information throughout this book applies to both types of systems. Table 0-1 summarizes the differences between the SPARC and x86 system administration tasks.

Table 0-1 SPARC and x86 System Administration Differences

Category	SPARC	x86
System operation before kernel is loaded	A programmable read-only memory (PROM) chip with a monitor program runs diagnostics and displays device information. The PROM is also used to program default boot parameters and to test the devices connected to the system.	The basic input/output system (BIOS) runs diagnostics and displays device information. A Solaris Device Configuration Assistant boot diskette with the Multiple Device Boot (MDB) program is used to boot from non-default boot partitions, the network, or the CD-ROM.
Booting the system	Commands and options at the PROM level are used to boot the system.	Commands and options at the MBD, primary, and secondary boot subsystems level are used to boot the system.
Boot programs	bootblk, the primary boot program, loads ufsboot. ufsboot, the secondary boot program, loads the kernel.	mboot, the master boot record, loads pboot. pboot, the Solaris partition boot program, loads bootblk. bootblk, the primary boot program, loads ufsboot. ufsboot, the secondary boot program, loads the kernel.
System shutdown	The `shutdown` and `init` commands can be used without additional operation intervention.	The `shutdown` and `init` commands are used but require operator intervention at the `Type any key to continue` prompt.
Disk controllers	SCSI	SCSI and IDE.
Disk slices and partitions	A disk may have a maximum of eight slices, numbered 0–7.	A disk may have a maximum of four fdisk partitions. The Solaris fdisk partition may contain up to ten slices, numbered 0–9, but only 0–7 can be used to store user data.
Diskette drives	Desktop systems usually contain one 3.5-inch diskette drive.	Systems may contain two diskette drives: a 3.5-inch and a 5.25-inch drive.

Solaris System Software Evolution

Because Solaris 2.*x* system software is evolving, the procedures may differ depending on the system software that is installed on the system you are administering. For example, with the advent of Solaris 2.2 volume management, procedures for accessing files on CD-ROM discs and on diskettes are different for Solaris 2.2 and later releases. The old procedures will not work on the new software. To help you understand how Solaris is evolving, Table 0-1 provides a list of the major system administration feature differences for each release. Table 0-2 describes three new NIS+ scripts.

Table 0-2 Solaris System Software Evolution

Release	New Features
Solaris 1.0	Berkeley (BSD) UNIX with Solaris 4.*x* functionality.
Solaris 2.0 (SunOS 5.0)	A merger of AT&T System V Release 4 (SVR4) and BSD UNIX. To facilitate customer transition, Solaris uses SVR4 as the default environment, with BSD commands and modes as an option. Administration Tool provides a graphical user interface Database Manager and Host Manager. (Refer to the *Solaris System Administrator's Guide.*)
Solaris 2.1 (SunOS 5.1)	Administration Tool adds a graphical user interface Printer Manager and User Account Manager. (Refer to the *Solaris System Administrator's Guide.*)
Solaris 2.2 (SunOS 5.2)	Volume management integrates access to CD-ROM and diskette files with the File Manager and provides a command-line interface. Users no longer need superuser privileges to mount CD-ROMs and diskettes. (Solaris 2.0 and 2.1 procedures do not work with volume management because volume management controls and owns the devices. Refer to Appendix A.)
Solaris 2.3 (SunOS 5.3)	Volume management changes Solaris 2.2 mount point naming conventions. (Refer to Appendix A.)
	Administration Tool adds a graphical user interface Serial Port Manager with templates that provide default settings, which makes adding character terminals and modems much easier. (Refer to Appendix B.)
	The automounter is split into two programs: an automounted daemon and a separate automount program. Both are run when the system is booted. The `/tmp_mnt` mount point is not displayed as part of the pathname, and the local path is displayed as */home/username*. Additional predefined automount map variables are provided. (Refer to Part 3.)
	Online: Backup 2.1 is included with the release. (Not documented in this book.)
	Pluggable Authentication Model (PAM) is included with the release. PAM provides a consistent framework to allow access control applications, such as login, to choose any authentication scheme available on a system without concern for the implementation details of the scheme. (Not documented in this book.)
	C2 Security is included in this release. (Not documented in this book.)
	Format(1) changes for SCSI disks. (Not documented in this book.)
	PPP network protocol product that provides IP network connectivity over a variety of point-to-point connections is included in this release. (Not documented in this book.)

Table 0-2 Solaris System Software Evolution (continued)

Release	New Features
	Cache File System (CacheFS) for NFS is included in this release. CacheFS is a generic, nonvolatile caching mechanism used to improve the performance of certain file systems by using a small, fast, local disk. (Not documented in this book.)
	New NIS+ setup scripts are included in this release. The `nisserver(1M)`, `nispopulate(1M)`, and `nisclient(1M)` scripts described in Table 0-2 let you set up an NIS+ domain much more quickly and easily than if you used the individual NIS+ commands to do so. With these scripts, you can avoid a lengthy manual process.
Solaris 2.4 (SunOS 5.4)	New Motif GUI for Solaris software installation. (Not documented in this book.)
Solaris 2.5 (Solaris 5.5)	New `pax(1M)` portable archive interchange command for copying files and file systems to portable media. (Refer to the *Solaris System Administrator's Guide.*)
	Solstice AdminTools™ utility that is used only to administer local systems.
	Solstice AdminSuite™ product that is available for managing systems in a network for SPARC and x86 systems. (Not documented in this book. Refer to the *Solaris System Administrator's Guide* for a summary of AdminSuite functionality.)
	New process tools are available in `/usr/proc/bin` that display highly detailed information about the active processes stored in the process file system in the `/proc` directory. (Refer to the *Solaris System Administrator's Guide.*)
	Telnet client upgraded to the 4.4 BSD version. rlogin and telnetd remote login capacity improved. (Not documented in this book.)
Solaris 2.5.1 (SunOS 5.5.1)	The limit on user ID and group ID values has been raised to 2147483647, or the maximum value of a signed integer. The nobody user and group (60001) and the no access user and group (60002) retain the same UID and GID as in previous Solaris 2.*x* releases. (Refer to the *Solaris System Administrator's Guide.*)
Solaris 2.6 (SunOS 5.6)	Changes to the Solaris 2.6 printing software provide a better solution than the LP print software in previous Solaris releases. You can easily set up and manage print clients using the NIS or NIS+ name services to enable centralization of print administration for a network of systems and printers. New features include redesign of print packages, print protocol adapter, bundled SunSoft™ Print Client software, and network printer support.
	New `nisbackup` and `nisrestore` commands provide a quick and efficient method of backing up and restoring NIS+ namespaces.
	New patch tools, including `patchadd` and `patchrm` commands, add and remove patches. These commands replace the `installpatch` and `backoutpatch` commands that were previously shipped with each individual patch.
	New `filesync` command for nomadic support ensures that data is moved automatically between a portable computer and a server. (Not documented in this book.)
	Restructuring of the previous `flat/proc` file system into a directory hierarchy that contains additional subdirectories for state information and control functions. It also provides a watchpoint facility to monitor access to and modifications of data in the process address space. The `adb(1)` command uses this facility to provide watchpoints. (Refer to the *Solaris System Administrator's Guide.*)
Release	**New Features**

Table 0-2 Solaris System Software Evolution (continued)

Large files are supported on UFS, NFS, and CacheFS file systems. Applications can create and access files up to one TB on UFS-mounted file systems and up to the limit of the NFS server for NFS- and CacheFS-mounted file systems. A new -mount option is provided to disable the large-file support on UFS file systems. Using the -mount option enables system administrators to ensure that older applications that are not able to safely handle large files do not accidentally operate on large files. (Refer to the *Solaris System Administrator's Guide.*)

NFS Kerberos authentication now uses DES encryption to improve security over the network. The kernel implementations of NFS and RPC network services now support a new RPC authentication flavor that is based on the Generalized Security Services API (GSS-API). This support contains the hooks to add stronger security to the NFS environment.

The PAM authentication modules framework enables you to "plug in" new authentication technologies.

Font Admin enables easy installation and use of fonts for the X Window System™. It supports TrueType, Type0, Type1, and CID fonts for multibyte languages and provides comparative font preview capability. It is fully integrated into the CDE desktop. (Not documented in this book.)

TrueType fonts are supported through X and Display PostScript™. Font Admin enables easy installation and integration of third-party fonts into the Solaris environment. (Not documented in this book.)

The Solaris 2.6 operating environment is year 2000 ready. It uses unambiguous dates and follows the X/Open guidelines where appropriate. (Not documented in this book.)

WebNFS software enables file systems to be accessed through the Web using the NFS protocol. This protocol is very reliable and provides greater throughput under a heavy load. (Not documented in this book.)

The Java Virtual Machine 1.1 integrates the Java platform for the Solaris operating environment. It includes the Java runtime environment and the basic tools needed to develop Java applets and applications. (Not documented in this book.)

For x86 systems, the Configuration Assistant interface is part of the new booting system for the Solaris (Intel Platform Edition) software. It determines which hardware devices are in the system, accounts for the resources each device uses, and enables users to choose which device to boot from. (Not documented in this book.)

For x86 systems, the kdmconfig program is used to configure the mouse, graphics adapter, and monitor. If an `Owconfig` file already exists, kdmconfig extracts any usable information from it. In addition, this updated version of `kdmconfig` also retrieves information left in the devinfo tree by the defconf program and uses that information to automatically identify devices. (Not documented in this book.)

Full X/Open UNIX 95, POSIX 1003.1b and ISO 10646 standards compliance. (Not documented in this book.)

Table 0-3 The NIS+ Scripts

NIS+ Script	What It Does
`nisserver(1M)`	Sets up the root master, nonroot master, and replica servers with level 2 security (DES).
`nispopulate(1M)`	Populates NIS+ tables in a specified domain from their corresponding system files or NIS maps.
`nisclient(1M)`	Creates NIS+ credentials for hosts and users; initializes NIS+ hosts and users; and restores the network service environment.

Refer to the `nisserver`(1M), `nispopulate`(1M), and `nisclient`(1M) manual pages for more information.

Conventions Used in This Book

Commands

In the steps and examples, the commands to be entered are in bold type. For example: "Type **su** and press Return." When following steps, press Return only when instructed to do so, even if the text in the step breaks at the end of a line.

Variables

Variables are in *italic* typeface. When following steps, replace the variable with the appropriate information. For example, to tell a printer to accept a print request, the step instructs you to "type **accept** ***printer-name*** and press Return." To substitute the printer named pinecone for the ***printer-name*** variable, type **accept pinecone** and press Return.

Mouse Button Terminology

This book describes mouse buttons by function. The default mapping of mouse buttons in a three-button mouse is:

- SELECT is left.
- ADJUST is middle.
- MENU is right.

Use the SELECT mouse button to select unselected objects and to activate controls. Use the ADJUST mouse button to adjust a selected group of objects, either adding to the group or deselecting part of the group. Use the MENU mouse button to display and choose from menus.

Storage-Medium Terminology

This book distinguishes among different types of media storage terminology in this way:

- *Disc* is used for an optical disc or CD-ROM.
- *Disk* is used for a hard-disk storage device.
- *Diskette* is used for a floppy diskette storage device. (Note that sometimes screen messages and mount points use the term *floppy*.)

Icons

Marginal icons distinguish between three different types of information:

- The New with SVR4 icon marks material that is new with Solaris 2.*x* system software (not available in Solaris 1.*x*).
- The New with 2.6 icon marks features that are new with Solaris 2.6 system software.
- The New in this edition icon marks new information that has been added to this edition. Some of the new information describes new commands and features that were introduced between the Solaris 2.1 and 2.5.1 releases. Other new information was available in the Solaris 2.0 release but was not included in the first edition. Where possible, the text following the icon indicates the release number in which the command or functionality was added.

ACKNOWLEDGMENTS

ANY PEOPLE CONTRIBUTED TO THE DESIGN, WRITING, AND PRODUCTION OF THE first edition of this book. Sun Microsystems Press would particularly like to acknowledge the following people for their contributions:

Connie Howard and Mike Rogers, SunSoft Information Technology and Products managers, and Bridget Burke for their support and encouragement.

Karin Ellison, SunSoft Press, deserves special thanks for her can-do attitude and her willingness to help out with all kinds of issues related to this book.

Don Charles, SunSoft Engineering Services Organization, for help in setting up a two-SPARC station network for this project, and for general system administration support.

Lori Reid, SunSoft Engineering Services Organization, for providing a Solaris® 2.1 CD-ROM.

Because this book contains so many different subject areas, specific acknowledgments are listed by part.

Part 1: Mail Services

Tom Kessler, SunSoft Engineering, for technical review and helpful discussions about different mail services configurations.

Dave Miner, SunSoft Engineering, for help with information about the Aliases database in Administration Tool.

Mike Gionfriddo, SunSoft Engineering, for answering questions about Administration Tool.

Don Brazell for technical review.

Part 2: NIS+

Rick Ramsey, SunSoft Information Technology and Products, for writing a great book about NIS+, providing me with background information, and answering many questions about NIS+.

Vipin Samar, SunSoft Engineering, for providing the engineering perspective for NIS+ and for technical review.

Saqib Jang, SunSoft Marketing, for providing the marketing perspective and information about the benefits of NIS+.

Bob LeFave, SunSoft Engineering Services Organization, for last-minute technical input and technical review.

John Auer, SMCC Enterprise Information Services, for additional technical review.

Don Brazell for technical review.

Scott Mann and SunU for permission to sit in on lab classes about NIS+.

Part 3: Automounter Services

Brent Callaghan, SunSoft Engineering, for background information and technical review.

Don Brazell for technical review.

Part 4: Service Access Facility

Patrick Moffitt, SunSoft Training, for technical review.

Scott Mann and SunU for permission to sit in on lab classes about the SAF.

Neil Groundwater, SunSoft Engineering, for answering questions about modem connections and for technical review.

Tom Fowler, SunSoft Technical Marketing, for spending lots of time and effort figuring out how printing works in the Solaris 2.*x* releases, and for providing most of the printing troubleshooting examples.

Mary Morris, SunSoft Engineering, for technical review.

Bruce Sesnovich, SunSoft Information Technology and Products, for providing background information about the SAF and modem procedures.

Tom Amiro, SunSoft Information Technology and Products, for providing background information about administering user accounts and printers.

Part 5: Application Software

Steve Shumway, SunSoft Marketing, for technical review.

Davis Weatherby, Sun Information Resources systems engineer, for taking time off from his vacation to provide excellent background information on implementing wrapper-based application servers.

Wayne Thompson, Sun Information Resources systems engineer, for technical review and contributing to the background on application servers.

Rob Goodman, Sun Information Resources software distribution manager, for technical review and for facilitating the quality technical input on Sun's implementation of application servers.

Scott Mann and SunU for permission to sit in on lab classes about pkgadd and Software Manager.

Charla Mustard-Foote, SunSoft Information Technology and Products, for providing me with a CD-ROM of SearchIt™ software to use in the examples, and for answering questions about Software Manager.

MacDonald King Aston and Julie Bettis, SunSoft Information Technology and Products, for patiently answering questions about Software Manager.

Keith Palmby, SunSoft Information Technology and Products, for providing background information about the Online: DiskSuite™ product.

Terry Gibson, SunTech Technical Publications, for providing background information about software licensing.

Dan Larson, SunTech Engineering Support Organization, for discussions about the engineering implementation of application servers.

Bill Petro, SunSoft Marketing, for background information about installing application software.

Linda Ries, SunSoft Engineering, for answering questions about the package commands and Software Manager.

Part 6: Introduction to Shell Programming

Sam Cramer, SunSoft Engineering, for doing two technical reviews of this part, even though his newest family member arrived right in the middle of the review cycle.

Ellie Quigly, Learning Enterprises; Chico, California; for providing me with her class notes for the Bourne, Korn, and C shells, and for permission to use examples from her course notes.

Wayne Thompson, SMCC Sun Information Resources, for technical review and for providing sample scripts for Chapter 16.

Appendix A: Volume Management

Howard Alt, SunSoft Engineering, for background information and for technical review.

Lynn Rohrer, SunSoft Information Technology and Products, for background information and for technical review.

Robert Novak, SunSoft Marketing, for technical review.

Mary Lautner, SunSoft Information Technology and Products, for letting me use her system to test the remote CD-ROM procedures.

Appendix B: Solaris Server Intranet Extension Products

Neil Groundwater, SunSoft Engineering, for background information and for technical review.

Lynn Rohrer, SunSoft Information Technology and Products, for background information and for technical review.

Robert Novak, SunSoft Marketing, for technical review.

Glossary

Craig Mohrman, SunSoft Engineering, for technical review.

Thanks are also due to the following people at Ziff-Davis Press for being so easy to work with: senior development editor Melinda Levine, copy editor Ellen Falk, managing editor Cheryl Holzaepfel, and project coordinator Ami Knox.

The author would like to thank her three cats for lap sitting, keyboard walking, and general company keeping while this book was in progress.

Second Edition

Sun Microsystems Press would like to acknowledge the following people for their contributions to the second edition of this book:

Brett Bartow, Acquisitions Editor, Macmillan Computer Publishing, for his enthusiasm and support on this project.

Mary Lautner, Program Manager, Sun Microsystems, Inc., for her invaluable help and assistance in providing the author with documentation and answers to numerous questions. Without Mary's help and the information she provided, the author would have been unable to complete this project.

Those writers from SunSoft Technical Publications who contributed to the *Solaris System Adminsitration Guide* and the documentation on the Solaris Server Intranet Extension CD-ROM, which were used as technical reference resources.

Lisa Gebken of Macmillan Computer Publishing for editing this manuscript.

Peter Gregory for technical review comments.

Tobin Crockett for networking the author's SPARC station 10 and Macintosh PowerPC and for setting up a network printer.

Rob Johnston, System Support Specialist, Sun Microsystems Computer Company, for installing Solaris 2.6 and troubleshooting hardware and software problems.

Tien Nguyen, System Support Specialist, SunSoft, Inc., for help in troubleshooting hardware and software problems.

Linda Gallops, SunSoft SQA, for help in tracking down information about modems.

Ken Erickson of SunSoft for allowing the author to pester him with occasional technical questions.

The author would especially like to thank Rachel Borden and John Bortner of Sun Microsystems Press for their unfailing enthusiasm, support, and friendship

CONTENTS AT A GLANCE

TABLE OF CONTENTS

Refer to the chapters in this part if you need to set up a new mail service or expand an existing one.

This part describes the Solaris 2.*x* mail services in four chapters. Chapter 1 describes the components of the mail service, defines mail service terminology, and explains how the programs in the mail service interact. Chapter 2 describes several common mail configurations and provides guidelines for setting up each configuration. Chapter 3 describes how to set up and administer mail services. Chapter 4 describes the sendmail configuration file and explains how to customize it if you need a more complex configuration file for your mail system.

PART 1

Mail Services

CHAPTER

1

Understanding Mail Services

Mail Services Terminology

Components of Mail Services

An Overview of the Mail Service

THE SUNOS™ 5.*X* MAIL SERVICES USE THE SUNOS 4.*X* SENDMAIL MAIL-ROUTING PROGRAM—which came from 4.3 BSD UNIX®—with some minor modifications; SunOS 5.*x* does not use the AT&T mail-routing program. If you are familiar with SunOS 4.*x* mail services, you will be able to set up and administer mail services for SunOS 5.*x* system easily. You will also find that it is easy to administer mail services on a network that has some systems running SunOS 4.*x* system software and others running SunOS 5.*x* system software. To help you find the modifications, information that is new to the SunOS 5.*x* sendmail program has an icon in the margin and is labeled SVR4.

As system administrator, you may need to expand an existing mail service or set up a new one. To help you with these tasks, this chapter defines mail services terminology and describes the components of the mail service.

Mail Services Terminology

This section defines the following terms and describes how they are used in the mail services:

- Systems in a mail configuration
  - Relay host
  - Gateway
  - Mailhost
  - Mail server
  - Mail client
- User agent (UA)
- Mail transport agent (MTA)
- Domains
- Mail addressing
- Mailbox
- Aliases

Systems in a Mail Configuration

A mail configuration requires a minimum of three elements, which can be combined on the same system or can be provided by separate systems: a mailhost, at least one mail server, and mail clients. When you want users to be able to communicate with networks outside of your domain, you must also have a relay host or a gateway.

Figure 1–1 shows a typical electronic mail configuration that uses all four elements. Each of these elements is identified and described in the following sections.

Figure 1–1
A typical electronic mail configuration.

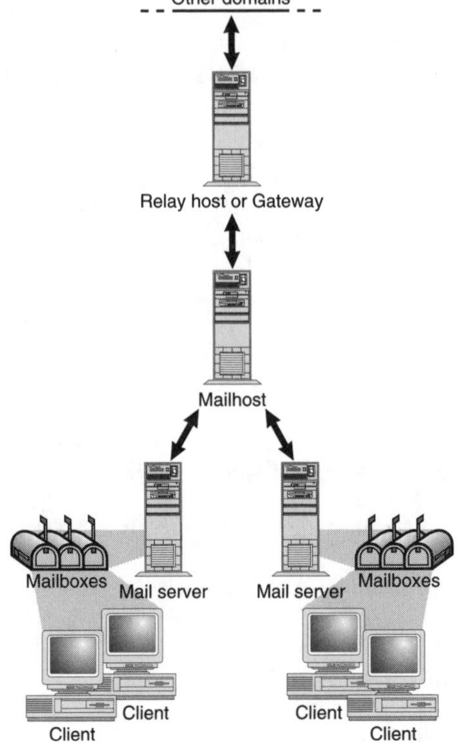

Relay Host

A *relay host* is a system that runs at least one mail-related protocol, which is called a *mailer*. Each mailer specifies a policy and the mechanics to be used when delivering mail. The relay host handles *unresolved mail*—mail with an address for which sendmail could not find a recipient in your domain. If a relay host exists, sendmail uses it for sending and receiving mail outside of your domain.

The mailer on the sending relay host must be compatible with the mailer on the receiving system, as shown in Figure 1–2. You specify the mailer for your domain in the `sendmail.cf` file. The default `sendmail.cf file` defines several *mailer specifications*, such as `smartuucp`, `ddn`, `ether`, and `uucp`. You can define others.

The relay host can be the same system as the mailhost, or you can configure another system as the relay host, as shown in Figure 1–4. You may, in fact, choose to configure more than one relay host for your domain if you have several connections outside of your site. If you have `uucp` or Internet connections, configure the system with those connections as the relay host.

Gateway

A *gateway* is a system that handles connections between networks running different communications protocols, as shown in Figure 1–3. A relay host and the system it is

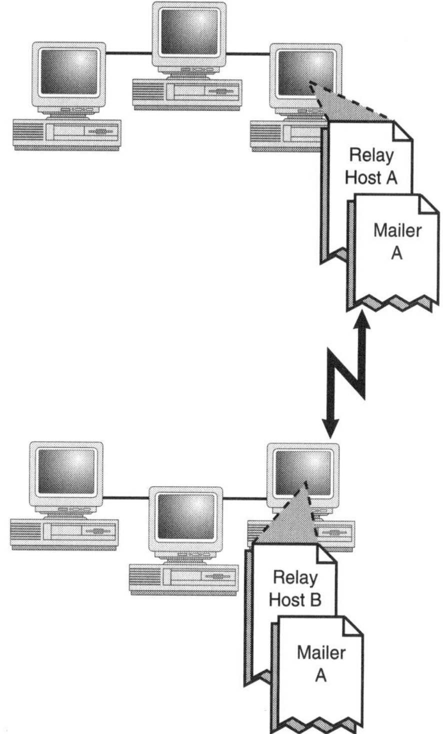

Figure 1–2
Compatible mailers on a relay host and on the receiving system.

connected to must use matching mailers. A gateway can handle connections to systems with unmatched mailers. You must customize the `sendmail.cf` file on the gateway system, which can be a difficult and time-consuming process.

If you have to set up a gateway, find a gateway configuration file that is close to what you need and modify it to fit your situation. For example, you can modify the default `/etc/mail/main.cf` file to use on a gateway system.

Mailhost

A *mailhost* is a system that you designate as the main mail system on your network. The mailhost is the system to which other systems at the site forward mail that they cannot deliver. You designate a system as a mailhost by adding the word **mailhost** to the `Aliases` line for the system entry in the Hosts database or by adding the word **mailhost** to the Internet Protocol (IP) address line in the system's `/etc/hosts` file. You should also use the `main.cf` file as the mail configuration file on the mailhost system.

A good candidate for a mailhost is a system that is attached to an Ethernet and to phone lines or a system configured as a router to the Internet. If you have a standalone system that is not networked but is in a time-sharing configuration, you can treat the standalone as the mailhost of a one-system network. Similarly, if you have several systems on an Ethernet and none have phones, you can designate one as the mailhost.Mail Server

A *mail server* is any system that stores mailboxes in the `/var/mail` directory. The mail server is responsible for routing all of the mail from a client. When a client sends mail, the mail server puts it in a queue for delivery. Once the mail is in the queue, the client can reboot or turn off the system without losing the mail messages. When the recipient gets mail from a client, the path in the From: line of the message contains the name of the mail server. If the recipient chooses to respond, the response goes to the user's mailbox on the server.

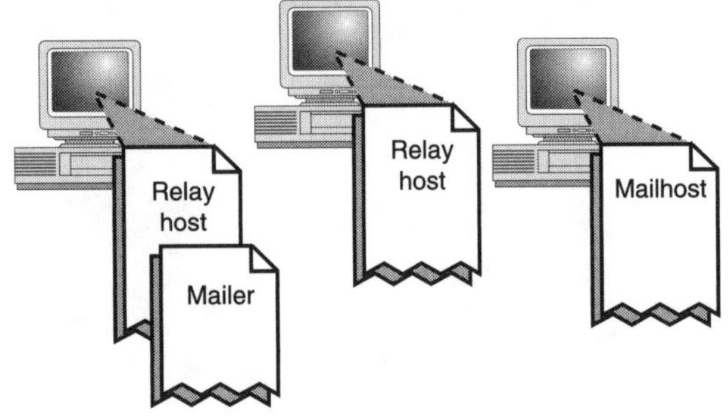

Figure 1–3
A gateway can handle connections between different communications protocols.

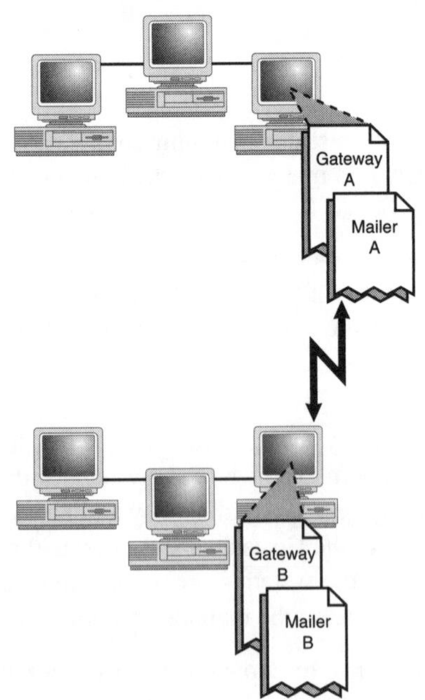

Figure 1–4
The relay host and the mailhost can be on the same system or on different systems.

When the mailbox is on a mail server, messages are delivered to the server, not directly to the client's system. When the mailbox is on the user's local system, the local system acts as its own mail server if it does not mount `/var/mail` from another system.

If the mail server is not the user's local system, users with NFS can mount the `/var/mail` directory in the `/etc/vfstab` file, use the automounter, or log into the server to read their mail.

NOTE. *If you automount the* `/var/mail` *directory, you may have problems with mail on heterogeneous networks that have SunOS 4.*x *mail clients.*

Good candidates for mail servers are systems that provide a home directory for users or that are backed up on a regular basis.

Table 1–1 shows some sample statistics about the size of mail messages and mail traffic at a computer company with about 12,000 employees.

NOTE. *The information in Table 1–1 is valid for ASCII messages only. With the advent of multimedia mail, which lets users transmit any type of data (not just ASCII text), the average size of an email message is likely to grow enormously. In the future, system administrators will need to allocate more spooling space for multimedia mailboxes.*

Table 1–1 Sample Statistics for Mail Messages and Traffic

Statistic	Description
6,500 bytes	Average size of an email message
140 kilobytes	Amount of mail received by an average user in one day
15 kilobytes	Small mailbox size (user reads mail regularly and stores messages elsewhere)
40 megabytes	Large mailbox size (user stores long-term mail in `/var/mail` mailbox)
18,000 messages	Average number of messages per day sent outside of the company
55,000 messages	Average number of messages per day received from outside of the company
2 megabytes	Recommended spooling space to allocate for each user's mailbox, based on the figures in this table

Mail Client

A *mail client* is any system that receives mail on a mail server and does not have a local `/var/mail` directory, but instead mounts `/var/mail` using NFS. You must make sure the mail client has the appropriate entry in the `/etc/vfstab` file and a mount point to mount the mailbox from the mail server.

User Agent

The *user agent* is the program that acts as the interface between the user and the sendmail program. The user agents for SunOS 5.*x* system software are `/usr/bin/mail`, `/usr/bin/mailx`, `$OPENWINHOME/bin/mailtool`, and `/usr/dt/bin/dtmail`.

Mail Transport Agent

The *transport agent* is responsible for actually receiving and delivering messages. The transport agent for SunOS 5.*x* system software is sendmail. The transport agent performs the following functions:

- Accepts messages from the user agent
- Understands destination addresses
- Delivers mail originating on the local system to the proper mailbox(es) if local, or to a delivery agent if not local
- Receives incoming mail from other delivery agents and delivers it to local users

Mailers

A *mailer* is a protocol that specifies the policy and mechanics used by sendmail when it delivers mail. You need to specify a mailer in the `sendmail.cf` file of a relay host or a gateway. The mailer for a relay host must match the mailer on the system outside of your domain. A gateway is a more complicated relay host (alternatively, you can think of a relay host as a simple gateway) that can communicate with more than one type of mailer.

The mailers provided with SunOS 5.*x* system software are as follows:

- `smartuucp` (the default relay mailer) uses `uux` (UNIX-to-UNIX command execution) to deliver messages but formats headers with a domain-style address. The To: and CC: lines are formatted by domain. For example, if `winsor` in the `eng.sun.com` domain sends mail to `guy` at auspex using `smartuucp`, the headers look like this:

  ```
  To: guy@auspex.com
  From: winsor@Eng.Sun.COM
  ```

  Use `smartuucp` for `uucp` mail to systems that can handle and resolve domain-style names. The sender also must be able to handle domain-style names and to receive replies from the Internet.

- uucp uses uux to deliver mail but uses route-based addressing in the headers, in which part or all of the address route is specified by the sender. See "Route-Based Addressing" later in this chapter for more information. For example, if `winsor` in `domain sun.eng.sun.com` sends mail to guy@auspex using the uucp mailer, the headers look like this:

  ```
  To: auspex!guy
  From: sun!winsor
  ```

The exclamation point (bang) in the address means that it is route-based. Use uucp for uucp connections to systems that need a bang-style path.

- ddn uses SMTP (Simple Mail Transport Protocol) on TCP port 25 to connect to the remote host; ddn inverts aliases and adds a domain name. For example, if winsor in domain eng.sun.com sends mail to paul@phoenix.princeton.edu, the headers look like this:

  ```
  To: paul@phoenix.princeton.edu
  From: Janice.Winsor@Eng.Sun.COM
  ```

  If winsor sends mail to irving@sluggo (both are users in the eng.sun.com domain) and is using the main.cf configuration file, the header looks like this:

  ```
  To: Irving.Who@Eng.Sun.Com
  From: Janice.Winsor@Eng.Sun.COM
  ```

  Use ddn for sending mail outside of your domain, especially for mailers that you must reach through a relay.

- ether uses the SMTP protocol on port 25 to connect to the remote host; ether does not invert aliases or append a domain name. Use ether for systems in your dns domain that users can reach directly.

You can define other mailers by providing a mailer specification in the sendmail.cf file. See Chapter 4, "Customizing sendmail Configuration Files," for more information.

Domains

A *domain* is a directory structure for electronic mail addressing and network address naming. The domain address has this format:

```
mailbox@subdomain. . . . . subdomain2.subdomain1.top-level-domain
```

The part of the address to the left of the @ sign is the *local address*, as shown in Figure 1–5. The local address may contain information about routing using another mail transport (for example, bob::vmsvax@gateway or smallberries%mill.uucp@physics.uchicago.edu), an alias (iggy.ignatz), or a token that resolves the name of a mailbox (ignatz--> /var/mail/ignatz). The receiving mailer is responsible for determining what the local part of the address means.

Figure 1–5
Domain address structure.

The part of the address to the right of the @ sign shows the *domain address* where the local address is located. A dot (.) separates each part of the domain address. The domain can be an organization, a physical area, or a geographic region. Domain addresses are case-insensitive. It makes no difference whether you use upper, lower, or mixed case in the domain part of an address.

The order of domain information is hierarchical, with the locations more specific and local the closer they are to the @ sign (although certain British and New Zealand networks reverse the order).

NOTE. *Most gateways automatically translate the reverse order of British and New Zealand domain names into the commonly used order. The larger the number of subdomains, the more detailed the information that is provided about the destination. Just as a subdirectory or a file in a file system hierarchy is inside of the directory above, each subdomain is considered to be inside of the one located to its right.*

Table 1–2 shows the top-level domains in the United States.

Table 1–2 Top-Level Domains in the United States

Domain	Description
.com	Commercial sites
.edu	Educational sites
.gov	Government installations
.mil	Military installations
.net	Networking organizations
.org	Nonprofit organizations

Because of the increasing popularity of the World Wide Web, the International Ad Hoc Committee (IAHC), a coalition of participants from the broad Internet community, has implemented a proposal to add seven new generic top-level domains (gTLDs) to the existing set. The new gTLDs are listed in Table 1–3.

Table 1–3 New Generic Top-Level Domains

Domain	Description
.arts	Entities emphasizing cultural and entertainment activities
.firm	Businesses or firms
.info	Entities providing information services
.nom	Entities who want individual or personal nomenclature
.rec	Entities emphasizing recreation and entertainment activities
.Web	Entities emphasizing activities related to the World Wide Web

In addition to the new gTLDs, up to 28 new registrars will be established to grant registrations for second-level domain names. To guide future registrar developments, under Swiss law a Council of Registrars (CORE) association will be established to create and enforce requirements for registrar operations. The full text of the IAHC report is available at `http://www.iahc.org`.

Table 1–4 shows the top-level domains for the United States and European countries. The book *!%@:: A Directory of Electronic Mail Addressing and Networks,* written by Donnalyn Frey and Rick Adams, contains a complete list of domain addresses and is updated periodically. See the bibliography for a complete reference.

Table 1–4 Top-Level Country Domains

Domain	Description
`.au`	Australia
`.at`	Austria
`.be`	Belgium
`.ch`	Switzerland
`.de`	West Germany
`.dk`	Denmark
`.es`	Spain
`.fi`	Finland
`.fr`	France
`.gr`	Greece
`.ie`	Ireland
`.is`	Iceland
`.it`	Italy
`.lu`	Luxembourg
`.nl`	The Netherlands
`.no`	Norway
`.pt`	Portugal
`.se`	Sweden
`.tr`	Turkey
`.uk`	United Kingdom
`.us`	United States

The following are examples of education, commercial, and government domain addresses:

```
roy@shibumi.cc.columbia.edu
rose@haggis.ssctr.bcm.tmc.edu
smallberries%mill.uucp@physics.uchicago.edu
day@concave.convex.com
paul@basic.ppg.com
angel@enterprise.arc.nasa.gov
```

This is a French domain address:

```
hobbit@ilog.ilog.fr
```

And this is a British address:

```
fred@uk.ac.aberdeen.kc
```

Note that some British and New Zealand networks write their mail addresses from top-level to lower level, but most gateways automatically translate the address into the commonly used order (that is, lower level to higher).

Mail Addressing

The *mail address* contains the name of the recipient and the system where the mail message is delivered. When you are administering a small mail system that does not use a naming service, addressing mail is easy: Login names uniquely identify users.

Mail addressing becomes more complex, however, when you are administering a mail system that has more than one system with mailboxes or one or more domains. It also becomes more complex when you have a `uucp` (or other) mail connection to the outside world. Mail addresses can be route-based, route-independent, or a mixture of the two.

Route-Based Addressing

Route-based addressing requires the sender of an email message to specify not only the local address (typically a username) and its final destination but also the route that the message must take to reach its final destination. Route-based addresses, which are fairly common on `uucp` networks, have this format:

```
host!path!user
```

Whenever you see an exclamation point (bang) as part of an email address, all (or some) of the route was specified by the sender. Route-based addresses are always read from left to right. For example, an email address that looks like

```
castle!sun!sierra!hplabs!ucbvax!winsor
```

is sent to user `winsor` on the system named `ucbvax` by going first from `castle` to the address `sun`, then to `sierra`, then to `hplabs`, and finally to `ucbvax`. (Note that this is an example and not an actual route.) If any of the four mail handlers is out of commission, the message will be delayed or returned as undeliverable.

Route-Independent Addressing

Route-independent addressing requires the sender of an email message to specify the name of the recipient and the final destination address. Route-independent addresses usually indicate the use of a high-speed network, such as the Internet. In addition, newer `uucp` connections frequently use domain-style names. Route-independent addresses have this format:

```
user@host.domain
```

The increased popularity of the domain hierarchical naming scheme for computers across the country is making route-independent addresses more common. In fact, the most common route-independent address omits the host name from the address and relies on the domain-naming service to properly identify the final destination of the email message:

```
user@domain
```

Route-independent addresses are read by searching for the @ sign and then reading the domain hierarchy from the right (the highest level) to the left (the most specific address to the right of the @ sign). For example, an email address such as `winsor@Eng.sun.com` is resolved starting with the `.com` commercial domain, then the `sun` company name domain, and finally the `Eng` department domain.

Mailbox

A *mailbox* is a directory on a mail server that is the final destination for email messages. The name of the mailbox may be the username or a place to put mail for someone with a specific function, such as the postmaster. Mailboxes can be in the `/var/mail/username` directory on the user's local system or on a mail server.

Mail should always be delivered to a local file system so that the user agent can pull mail from the mail spool and store it readily in the local mailbox.

CAUTION! *Do not use NFS-mounted file systems as the destination for a user's mailbox. NFS-mounted file systems cause problems with mail delivery and handling if the server fails.*

The Aliases database, the `/etc/mail/aliases` file, and naming services such as NIS and NIS+ provide mechanisms for creating aliases for electronic mail addresses so that users do not need to know the precise local name of a user's mailbox. Mail aliases provide aliases for names to the left of the `@` sign. Because DNS provides aliases only for systems and domains (for names to the right of the `@` sign), you cannot use DNS to maintain user or mailing list aliases.

Some common naming conventions for special-purpose mailboxes are shown in Table 1–5.

Table 1–5 Conventions for the Format of Mailbox Names

Format	Description
`username`	Usernames are frequently the same as mailbox names.

Table 1–5 Conventions for the Format of Mailbox Names (continued)

Format	Description
`Firstname.Lastname`, `Firstname_Lastname`, `Firstinitial.Lastname`, or `Firstinitial_Lastname`	Usernames may be identified as full names with a dot (or an underscore) separating the first and last names or by a first initial with a dot (or an underscore) separating the initial and the last name.
`postmaster`	Each site and domain is required by Internet standards to have a postmaster mailbox. Users can address questions and report problems with the mail system to the postmaster mailbox.
`MAILER-DAEMON`	Any mail addressed to the `MAILER-DAEMON` is automatically routed to the postmaster by sendmail.
`x-interest`	Names with dashes are likely to be a distribution list or a mailing list. This format is commonly used for net mail groups.
`x-interest-request`	Names ending in `-request` are administrative addresses for distribution lists.
`owner-x-interest`	Names beginning with `owner-` are administrative addresses for distribution lists.
`local%domain`	The percent sign (`%`) shows a local address that is expanded when the message arrives at its destination. Most mail systems interpret mailbox names with `%` characters as full mail addresses. The `%` is replaced with an `@` and the mail is redirected accordingly. Note that although many people use the `%` convention, it is not a formal standard. In the email community, it is referred to as the `%` *hack*.
`usenet`	Required by Internet standards for any domain or system that processes or feeds UseNet news.

Aliases

An *alias* is an alternative name. For electronic mail, you can use aliases to assign additional names to a user, route mail to a particular system, or define mailing lists.

You can create a mail alias for each user at your site to indicate where the mail is stored. Providing a mail alias is like providing a mail stop as part of the address for an individual at a large corporation. If you do not provide the mail stop, the mail is delivered to a central address. Extra effort is required to determine where the mail is to be delivered within the building, and the possibility of error increases. For example, if there are two people named Kevin Smith in the same building, the probability is high that each Kevin will receive mail intended for the other.

Use domains and location-independent addresses as much as possible when you create alias files. To enhance the portability and flexibility of alias files, make your alias entries as generic and system-independent as possible. For example, if you have a user named `ignatz` on a system `oak` in domain `Eng.sun.com`, create the alias as `ignatz` instead of `ignatz@Eng` or `ignatz@oak`. If the user `ignatz` changes the name of the system but remains within the engineering domain, you do not need to update any alias files to reflect the change in the system name.

When creating aliases that include users outside of your domain, create the alias with the username and the domain name. For example, if you have a user named `smallberries` on system `privet` in domain `Corp.sun.com`, create the alias as `smallberries@Corp`.

NOTE. *You can set an option in the* `sendmail.cf` *file to translate the email address to a fully qualified domain name—a domain name that contains all of the elements needed to specify where an electronic mail message should be delivered or where an NIS+ table is located—when mail goes outside of the user's domain. See Chapter 4 for more information.*

Uses for Alias Files

You create mail aliases for global use in the NIS+ *mail_aliases* table, in the NIS *aliases* map, or, if your site does not use a naming service, in local `/etc/mail/aliases` files. You can also create and administer mailing lists using the same alias files.

Depending on the configuration of your mail services, you can administer aliases by using the NIS or NIS+ naming service to maintain a global aliases database or by updating all of the local `/etc/mail/aliases` files to keep them in sync. See Chapter 3, "Setting Up and Administering Mail Services," for information on how to create aliases.

Users can also create and use aliases. They can create aliases either in their local `.mailrc` file, which only they can use, or in their system's local `/etc/mail/aliases` file, which can be used by anyone. Users cannot create or administer NIS or NIS+ alias files. Users cannot administer the local `/etc/mail/aliases` file unless they have access to the root password on their system.

Syntax of Aliases

The following sections describe the syntax of NIS+, NIS, and `.mailrc` aliases.

NIS+ Aliases The NIS+ aliases table contains all of the names by which a system or person is known, except for private aliases listed in users' local `.mailrc` files. The sendmail program can use the NIS+ `Aliases` database instead of the local `/etc/mail/aliases` files to determine mailing addresses. See the `aliasadm`(8) and `nsswitch.conf`(4) manual pages for more information.

The NIS+ aliases table has four columns, as shown in Table 1–6.

Table 1–6 Columns in the NIS+ Aliases Database

Column	Description
`alias`	The name of the alias.
`expansion`	The value of the alias as it would appear in a sendmail `/etc/aliases` file.
`options`	Reserved for future use.

Table 1–6 Columns in the NIS+ Aliases Database (continued)

Column	Description
comments	Can be used to add specific comments about an individual alias.

Aliases use the format of the NIS+ aliases table:

alias: expansion [options# "comments"]

The NIS+ `Aliases` database should contain entries for all mail clients. You list, create, modify, and delete entries in the NIS+ `Aliases` database using the `aliasadm` command. If you are creating a new NIS+ aliases table, you must initialize the table before you create the entries. If the table already exists, no initialization is needed.

When creating alias entries, enter one alias per line. You should only have one entry that contains the user's system name. For example, you could create the following entries for a user named `winsor`:

```
winsor: janice.winsor
jwinsor: janice.winsor
janicew: janice.winsor
janice.winsor: winsor@castle
```

You can create an alias for local names or domains. For example, an alias entry for the user `fred`, who has a mailbox on the system `oak` and is in the domain `Trees`, could have this entry in the NIS+ aliases table:

```
fred: fred@Trees
```

To use the `aliasadm` command, you must be `root`, a member of the NIS+ group that owns the `Aliases` database, or the person who created the database.

NIS Aliases Aliases in the NIS aliases map use this format:

name: name1, name2, . . .

.mailrc Aliases Aliases in a `.mailrc` file use this format:

alias *aliasname name1 name2 name3 . . .*

/etc/mail/aliases Aliases Distribution list formats in a local `/etc/mail/aliases` file use this format:

aliasname: name1,name2,name3 . . .

The aliases in the `/etc/mail/aliases` file are stored in text form. When you edit the `/etc/mail/aliases` file, run the `newaliases` program to rehash the database and make the aliases available to the `sendmail` program in binary form.

See Chapter 3 for information on how to create NIS+ alias tables.

Components of Mail Services

Mail services are composed of a number of programs and daemons that interact with one another. The following sections introduce the programs, along with a number of terms and concepts related to the administration of electronic mail.

The Mail Services Programs

Table 1–7 lists the mail services programs.

Table 1–7 The Components of Mail Services

Command	Description
/usr/bin/mailx	Interactive mail message processing system that is described in the mailx(1) manual page
/usr/bin/mail	Mailer that delivers mail to mailboxes
$OPENWINHOME/bin/mailtool	Window-based interface to the sendmail program
/usr/lib/sendmail	Mail-routing program
/usr/lib/sendmail.mx	Mail-routing program linked with the domain name service resolver
/etc/mail/main.cf	Sample configuration file for main systems
/etc/mail/sendmail.subsidiary.cf	Sample configuration file for subsidiary systems
/etc/mail/sendmail.cf	Configuration file for mail routing
/etc/mail/aliases	Mail-forwarding information
/etc/mail/sendmailvars	Table that stores macro and class definitions for lookup from sendmail.cf file
NEW .sendmailvars.org_dir	NIS+ version of sendmailvars table
/usr/bin/newaliases	Symbolic link to /usr/lib/sendmail that is used to rebuild the database for the mail aliases file
/usr/bin/mailq	Symbolic link to /usr/lib/sendmail that is used to print the headers of messages in the mail queue
/usr/bin/mailstats	File that is used to store mail statistics generated by /etc/mail/sendmail.st (if present)
/usr/bin/mconnect	Command that enables you to connect to the mailer for address verification and debugging
/usr/sbin/in.comsat	Mail notification daemon
/usr/sbin/syslogd	Error message logger that is used by sendmail

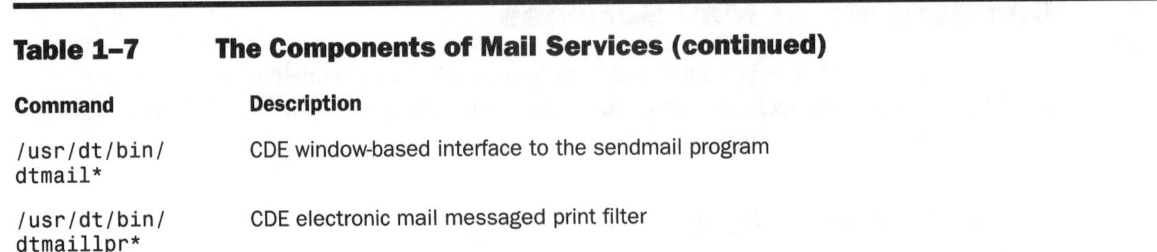

Table 1–7 The Components of Mail Services (continued)

Command	Description
`/usr/dt/bin/dtmail*`	CDE window-based interface to the sendmail program
`/usr/dt/bin/dtmaillpr*`	CDE electronic mail messaged print filter

* CDE mail programs.

NEW

Mail services are provided by a combination of these programs that interact, as shown by the simplified diagram in Figure 1–6.

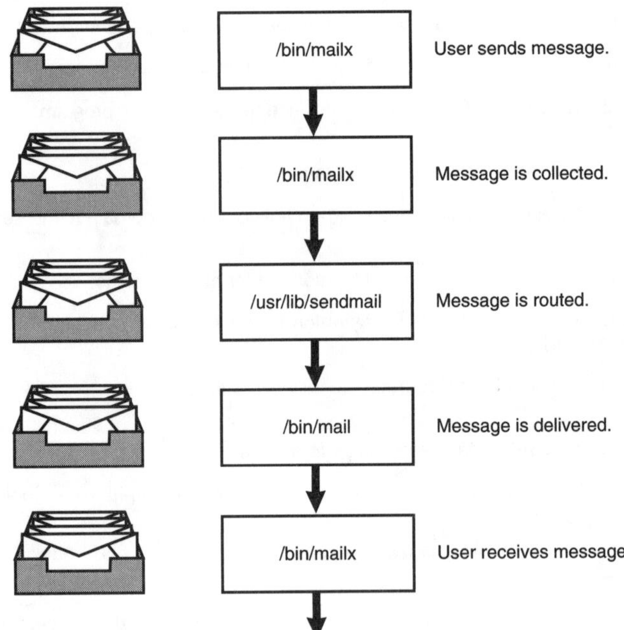

/bin/mailx
User sends message.
/bin/mailx
Message is collected.
/usr/lib/sendmail
Message is routed.
/bin/mail
Message is delivered.
/bin/mailx
User receives message.

Figure 1–6
How mail programs interact.

Users send messages using programs such as `/bin/mailx` or mailtool. See the manual pages for information about these programs.

The message is collected by the program that was used to generate it and is passed to the `sendmail` daemon. The `sendmail` daemon *parses* (divides into identifiable segments) the addresses in the message, using information from the configuration file `/etc/mail/sendmail.cf` to determine network name syntax, aliasing, forwarding information, and network topology. Using this information, sendmail determines the route a message must take to get to a recipient.

The `sendmail` daemon passes the message to the appropriate system. The `/bin/mail` program on the local system delivers the mail to the mailbox in the `/var/mail/`*`username`* directory of the recipient of the message.

The user is notified that mail has arrived and retrieves it using `/bin/mail`, `/bin/mailx`, `mailtool`, `dtmail`, or a similar program.

The sendmail Program

SunOS 5.*x* system software uses `sendmail` as a mail router. The `sendmail` program is responsible for receiving and delivering electronic mail messages. It is an interface between mail-reading programs such as `mail`, `mailx`, `mailtool`, `dtmail`, and mail-transport programs such as `uucp`. The `sendmail` program performs the following functions:

- Controls email messages that users send
- Understands the recipients' addresses
- Chooses an appropriate delivery program
- Rewrites the addresses in a format that the delivery agent understands
- Reformats the mail headers as required
- Passes the transformed message to the delivery agent for delivery

Figure 1–7 shows how sendmail uses aliases. Programs that read mail, such as `/usr/bin/mailx`, can have aliases of their own, which are expanded before the message reaches sendmail.

As system administrator, you should choose a policy for updating aliases and forwarding mail messages. You might set up an aliases mailbox as a place for users to send requests for mail forwarding and changes to their default mail alias. If your system uses NIS or NIS+, you can administer forwarding rather than forcing users to manage it themselves. A common mistake users make is to put a `.forward` file in the home directory of Host A that forwards mail to `user@host-b`. When the mail gets to Host B, sendmail looks up the user in the NIS or NIS+ aliases and sends the message back to `user@host-a`, resulting in a loop and more bounced mail.

The sendmail Configuration File (sendmail.cf)

A *configuration file* controls the way that `sendmail` performs its functions. The configuration file determines the choice of delivery agents, address-rewriting rules, and the format of the mail header.

The sendmail program uses the information from the `/etc/mail/sendmail.cf` file to perform its functions. Each system has a default `sendmail.cf` file installed in the `/etc/mail` directory. You do not need to edit or change the default configuration file for mail servers or mail clients. The only systems that require a customized configuration file are the mailhost, a relay host, or a gateway. See "Mail Services Terminology" earlier in this chapter or the glossary at the back of this book for descriptions of each of these types of systems.

SunOS 5.*x* system software provides two default configuration files, which are also in the `/etc/mail` directory:

- A configuration file named `main.cf` for the system (or systems) you designate as the mailhost, a relay host, or a gateway

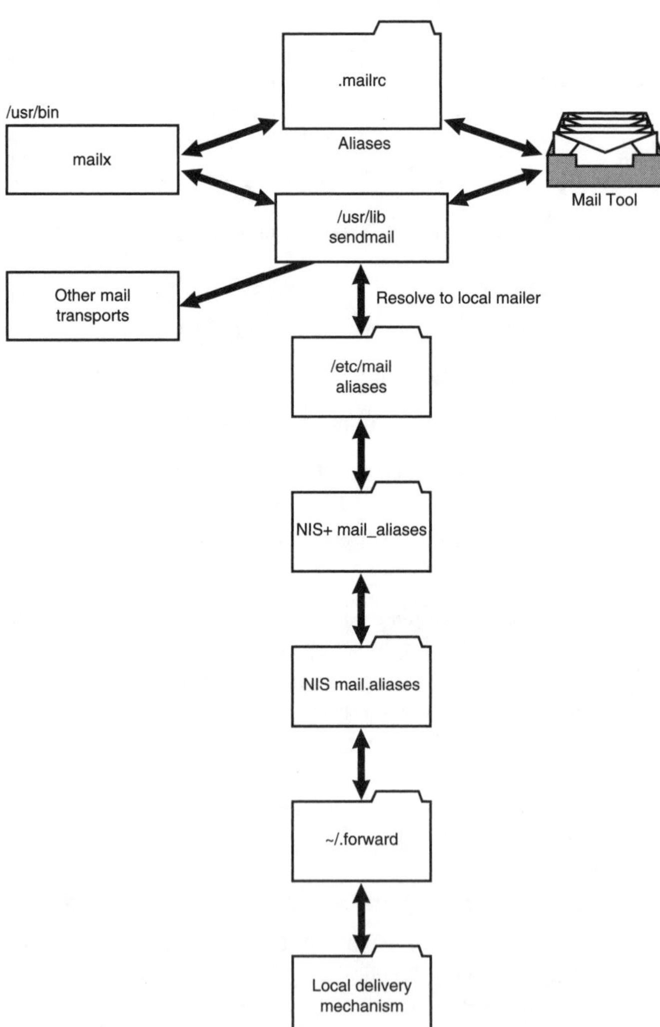

Figure 1–7
How `sendmail` *uses aliases.*

- A configuration file named `subsidiary.cf` (a duplicate copy of the default `sendmail.cf` file)

Which configuration file you use on any individual system depends on the role the system plays in your mail service.

- For mail clients or mail servers, you do not need to do anything to set up or edit the default configuration file.
- To set up a mailhost, a relay host, or a gateway, copy the `main.cf` file and rename it `sendmail.cf` (in the `/etc/mail` directory). Then edit the `sendmail.cf` file to set parameters needed for your mail configuration: relay mailer and relay host. For more information about editing the `sendmail.cf` file, refer to Chapter 4.

The following list describes some configuration parameters you may want to change, depending on the requirements of your site:

- Time values.
  - Specify how often sendmail runs the queue. The interval is typically set to between 15 minutes and 1 hour.
  - Specify read timeouts.
  - Specify how long a message remains in the queue before it is returned to the sender.
- Delivery modes specify how quickly mail will be delivered.
- Load limiting prevents wasted time during loaded periods because it does not attempt to deliver large messages, messages to many recipients, or messages to sites that have been down for a long time.
- Log level specifies what kinds of problems are logged.
- File modes.
  - `setuid` for sendmail
  - Temporary file modes
  - `/etc/mail/aliases` permissions

Refer to Chapter 3 for information on setting up the `sendmail.cf` files. Refer to Chapter 4 for a detailed description of each of these parameters.

The sendmail Configuration Table

The sendmail program can define macros and classes in response to commands from the `sendmail.cf` file by looking up values in the `sendmailvars` configuration table. The `sendmail.cf` file can contain two such commands:

- Lines that begin with the L key letter are *macro definitions*, in which the values assigned to the specified variable are obtained from the configuration table.

- Lines that begin with the G key letter are *class definitions*, in which the values assigned to the specified variable are obtained from the configuration table.

The `L` command has the following syntax:

`LXsearch_key`

For example, in `Lm maildomain`, the search key `maildomain` is used to look up a value in the configuration table to assign to the variable *m*. Most often the single-letter variable name is uppercase, but for internal variables (such as `m` for the mail domain name), it is lowercase.

NOTE. *Lowercase variables are reserved for use by sendmail and may have special meanings to the sendmail program.*

The `G` command, which sets a class, permits multiple entries. It has the following syntax:

`GCsearch_key`

For example, in `GVuucp-list`, the search key `uucp-list` is used to look up a value in the configuration table to assign to the class `V`.

In both cases, matching of the search key is case-sensitive. Both commands have counterparts for defining macros or classes within the `sendmail.cf` file rather than using the lookup table. `D` is the counterpart of `L`; `C` is the counterpart of `G`.

If NIS+ is used to administer the network, you can maintain a global version of the table `sendmailvars.org_dir`. In addition to the NIS+ table (or as an alternative), the table can be maintained in `/etc/mail/sendmailvars` files. The order in which these sources are searched by `sendmail` is controlled by the `sendmailvars` entry in the `/etc/nsswitch.conf file`. By default, the search order is `files nisplus`, which means that sendmail looks for information in the local table before going to the NIS+ table.

Entries in an `/etc/mail/sendmailvars` file have the following format:

`search_key value1 [value2 value3 . . . ]`

The search key may be followed by a Tab or a number of spaces; values are separated by a single space.

The NIS+ `sendmailvars` table has two columns: a Key column and a Value column. The Value column can have one or more values, each separated by a space, as shown in Table 1–8.

The names in the Value column are systems that `uucp` can access.You should define most nondefault mail variables in the NIS+ table. However, in special cases—such as when a system has a local `uucp` connection or is a gateway between two Internet domains—you can override the global setting for a variable on a system by including the variable in the system's local `/etc/mail/sendmailvars` file.

.forward Files

Users can create a `.forward` file in their home directory that `sendmail` uses to temporarily redirect mail or send mail to a custom set of programs without bothering a system

Table 1–8 Examples of Key and Value Columns in an NIS+ sendmailvars Table

Key Column	Value Column
`maildomain`	Eng.Sun.COM
`uucp-list`	castle oak cinderella

administrator with frequent alias change requests. When troubleshooting mail problems, particularly problems of mail not being delivered to the expected address, always check the user's home directory for a `.forward` file.

An Overview of the Mail Service

The following sections describe the directory structure and files of the mail service and explain how the sendmail program and mail addressing work.

The Anatomy of the Mail Service

Files for the mail service are located in three directories: `/bin`, `/etc/mail`, and `/usr/lib`. Users' mailboxes are located in the `/var/mail` directory.

Table 1–9 shows the contents of the `/bin` directory that are used for mail services.

Table 1–9 Contents of the /bin Directory That Are Used for Mail

Name	Type	Description
`mail`	File	A user agent
`mailcompat`	File	A filter to store mail in SunOS 4.*x* mailbox format
`mailq`	Link	Link to `/usr/lib/sendmail`
`mailstats`	File	A file used to store mail statistics generated by the `/etc/mail/sendmail.st` file (if present)
`mailx`	File	A user agent
Name	**Type**	**Description**
`newaliases`	Link	Link to `/usr/lib/sendmail` that is used to rebuild the database for the mail aliases file

Table 1–10 shows the contents of the `/etc/mail` directory.

Table 1–10 Contents of the /etc/mail Directory

Name	Type	Description
mail.rc	File	Default settings for the mailtool user agent
aliases	File	Mail-forwarding information
aliases.dir	File	Binary form of mail-forwarding information (created by running newaliases)
aliases.pag	File	Binary form of mail-forwarding information (created by running newaliases)
mailx.rc	File	Default settings for the mailx user agent
main.cf	File	Sample configuration file for main systems
sendmail.cf	File	Configuration file for mail routing
sendmail.hf	File	Help file used by the SMTP HELP command
sendmail.pid	File	File containing the /usr/lib/sendmail -b -q1h command
sendmail.st	File	The sendmail statistics file (If this file is present, sendmail logs the amount of traffic through each mailer.)
sendmailvars	File	Table that stores macro and class definitions for lookup from sendmail.cf
sendmailvars.org_dir	Table	NIS+ version of sendmailvars table
subsidiary.cf*	File	Sample configuration file for subsidiary systems

*Revised in this edition. Note that the subsidiary.cf file used to be named sendmail.subsuidiary.cf.

Table 1–11 shows the contents of the `/usr/lib` directory.

Table 1–11 Contents of the /usr/lib Directory

Name	Type	Description
newaliases*	File	Command that creates the binary form of the aliases file
sendmail	File	The routing program, also known as the mail transport agent

*The newaliases command used to be located in the /etc/mail directory.

Spooling directories for delivered mail are located in the `/var/mail` directory, as shown in Table 1–12. Mail that has not been delivered is stored in the `/var/spool/mqueue` directory.

Table 1–12 Contents of the /var/mail Directory

Name	Type	Description
mailbox1	File	Mailboxes for delivered mail
mailbox2	File	Mailboxes for delivered mail
mailbox3	File	Mailboxes for delivered mail

How the Mail Service Works

Figure 1–8 shows how sendmail interacts with the other programs in the mail system. The user interacts with a mail-generating and mail-sending program known as a *user agent*. When the mail is submitted, the user agent calls `sendmail`, which routes the message to the correct mailer(s).

How sendmail Works

The sendmail program receives a message from a program such as `mailx`, `mailtool`, or `dtmail`, edits the message header as required by the destination mailer, and calls appropriate mailers to do delivery or queuing for network transmission.

NOTE. *The* `sendmail` *program never edits or changes the body of a message. Any changes that it makes to interpret email addresses are made only in the header of the message.*

Argument Processing and Address Parsing

When sendmail processes a message, it collects recipient names (either from the command line or from the SMTP protocol) and generates two files. One is an envelope that contains a list of recipients and information about delivery. The other file contains the header and the body of the message. The sendmail program expands aliases, including mailing lists, and validates as much as possible the remote recipient; sendmail checks syntax and verifies local recipients. Detailed checking of host names is deferred until delivery. As local recipients are verified, messages are forwarded to them.

After parsing the recipient lists, sendmail appends each name to both the envelope and the header of the message. When a name is aliased or forwarded, it retains the old name in the list and sets a flag to tell the delivery phase to ignore this recipient. The lists are kept free from duplicates, preventing "alias loops" and duplicate messages delivered to the same recipient, which can occur if a recipient is in two different alias groups.

NOTE. *Users may receive duplicate copies of the same message when alias lists contain email addresses for the same person (who is using different syntax). The sendmail program cannot always match the duplicate email addresses.*

Message Collection

The sendmail program then collects the message. The message has a header at the beginning. The header and the body of the message must be separated by a blank line. The only formatting requirement imposed on the message body is that its lines of text must be no greater than 1,024 bytes. The sendmail program stores the header in memory and stores the body of the message in a temporary file. To simplify the program interface, the message is collected even if no names are valid—in which case the message is returned with an error.

NOTE. *Until now, sendmail could not transmit binary data as part of mail messages. With the advent of multimedia mailtool, users can now transmit binary data. It must, however, be encoded by a user agent. Sendmail does not do any automatic encoding of binary data. Refer to the documentation for Mail Tool or* `dtmail` *for information on how to encode and decode electronic mail messages.*

Message Delivery

For each unique mailer and host in the recipient list, sendmail calls the appropriate mailer. Each invocation of a mailer sends a message to all of the users on one host. Mailers that accept only one recipient at a time are handled properly.

The `sendmail` program sends the message to the mailer using one of the same interfaces used to submit a message to `sendmail` (using the conventional UNIX argument vector/return status, speaking over a pair of UNIX pipes, and speaking SMTP over a TCP connection). Each copy of the message has a customized header attached to the beginning of it. The mailer catches and checks the status code, and a suitable error message is given as appropriate. The exit code must conform to a system standard. If a nonstandard exit code is used, the message `Services unavailable` is used.

Queuing for Retransmission

When the mailer returns a status that shows it might be able to handle the mail later (for example, the next host is down, or the phone is busy for `uucp`), sendmail stores it in a queue and tries again later.

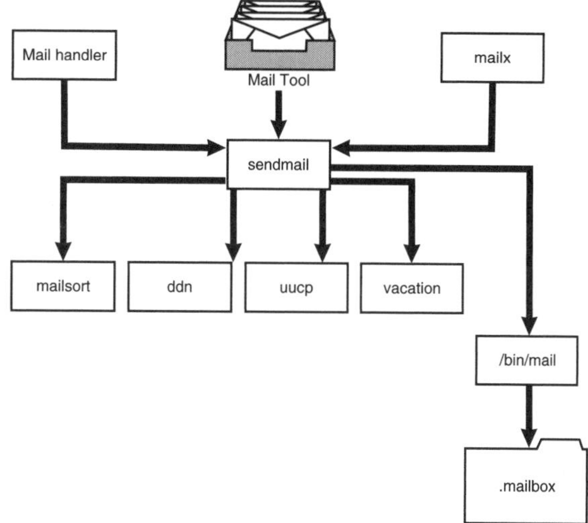

Figure 1–8
How the mail service works.

Return to Sender

If errors occur during processing, sendmail returns the message to the sender for retransmission. The letter may be mailed back or written to the `dead.letter` file in the sender's home directory.

How Mail Addressing Works

Assuming that you use the default rule set in the `sendmail.cf` file, the following examples show the routes an email message may take. The route is determined by how the email is addressed.

- Mail within a domain addressed with only the user's login name goes to the `aliases` file on the mailhost (or to the `Aliases` database) and is sent to the address found in the database. In the example shown in Figure 1–9, mail addressed to the user `winsor` goes to the mailhost and is forwarded to the host named `castle`.

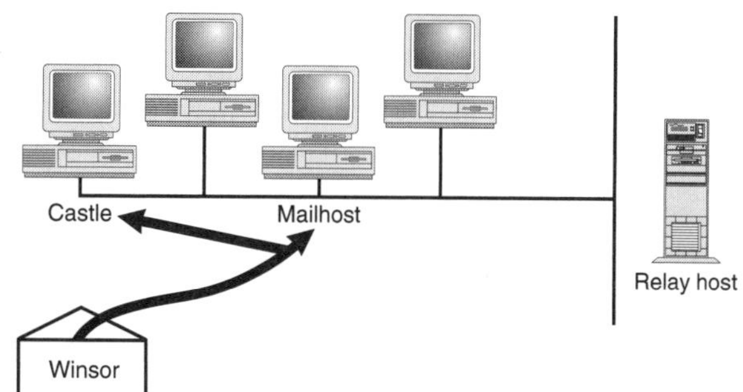

Figure 1–9
Delivery path for mail addressed with a user-name only.

- Mail within a domain addressed with the user's login name and host name goes directly to the host system without any additional processing. In the example shown in Figure 1–10, mail addressed to the user `winsor` at the host named `castle` goes directly to the host named `castle`.
- Mail within a domain addressed with the user's login name and domain name goes to the `aliases` file on the mailhost (or to the `Aliases` database). If the mailhost has an alias, it redirects the message to the host system. In the example shown in Figure 1–11, mail addressed to the user `winsor@Eng` goes to the mailhost and is then forwarded to the host named `castle`.

Figure 1–11
Delivery path for mail addressed with the username and the domain name.

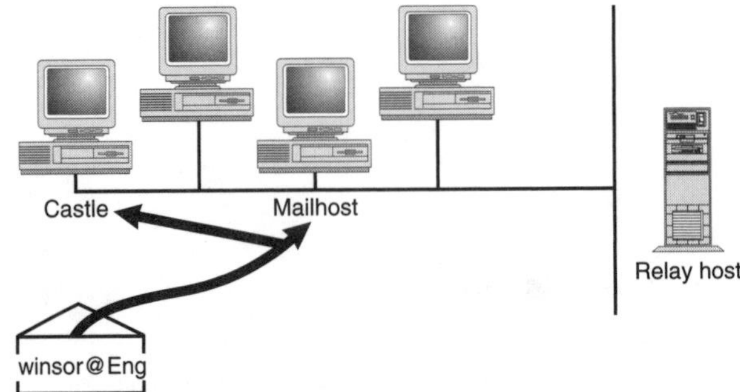

Figure 1–10
Delivery path for mail addressed with the username and the host name.

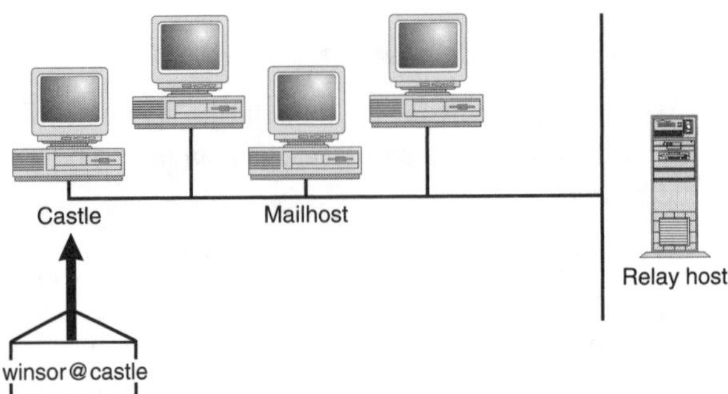

- Mail addressed with the user's name and a fully qualified domain name goes to the mailhost, which sends it to the relay host. The relay host sends the message to the host system. When the mail comes from the recipient's domain, however, the mailhost recognizes the domain name and does not send the message to the relay host. In the example shown in Figure 1–12, mail addressed to the user `ignatz@Eng.sun.com` from outside of the engineering domain goes to the sender's mailhost and then to the sender's relay host. It is then forwarded to the recipient's relay host, the recipient's mail host, and finally to the host named `oak`.

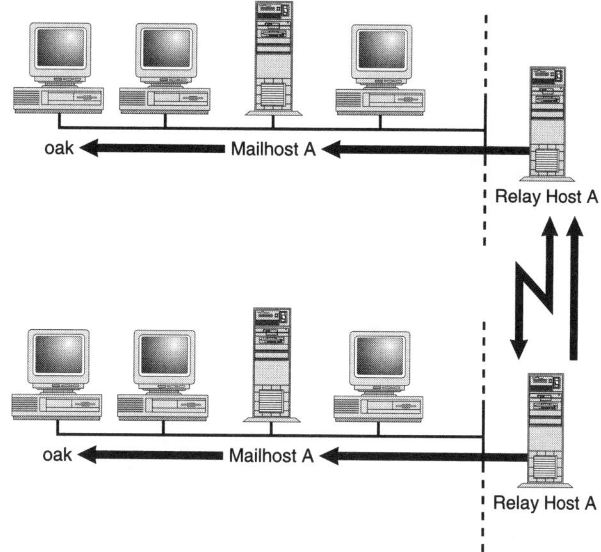

Figure 1–12
Delivery path for mail addressed with a username and a fully qualified domain name.

CHAPTER

Planning Mail Services

THIS CHAPTER DESCRIBES FOUR BASIC MAIL CONFIGURATIONS AND BRIEFLY OUTLINES THE tasks required to set up each configuration. You may find the following sections useful if you need to set up a new mail system or are expanding an existing one. The configurations start with the most basic case (mail completely local, no connection to the outside world) and increase in complexity to a two-domain configuration with a gateway. More complex systems are beyond the scope of this book.

To set up a mail system, regardless of its configuration, you need these elements:

- A `sendmail.cf` configuration file on each system
- Alias files with an alias for each user to point to the place where mail is to be delivered
- A mailbox to store (or spool) mail files for each user
- A `postmaster` alias for the person who administers mail services

See Chapter 3, "Setting Up and Administering Mail Services," for detailed information on how to set up these elements.

How you set up the configuration file and the alias file and where you put the mailboxes depend on the configuration you choose.

Local Mail Only

The simplest mail configuration, shown in Figure 2–1, is one mail server with a number of workstations connected to it. Mail is completely local. One system is both the mail server (providing mail spooling for client mailboxes) and the mailhost. Mail addresses are parsed using the `/etc/mail/aliases` files. No naming service, such as NIS, NIS+, or DNS, is used.

To set up this kind of local mail configuration (assuming that the mail clients mount their mail files from `/var/mail` on the mailhost), you need the following:

- The default `sendmail.cf` file in the `/etc/mail` directory on each system (no editing required).
- A server designated as the mailhost. (Add **mailhost** to the `/etc/hosts` file on the mailhost.)
- The mailhost IP address line added to the `/etc/hosts` file of each mail client.
- Entries in each mail client's `/etc/vfstab` file to mount the `/var/mail` directory when mailboxes are located on the mail server.

See Chapter 3 for detailed information on how to set up mail services.

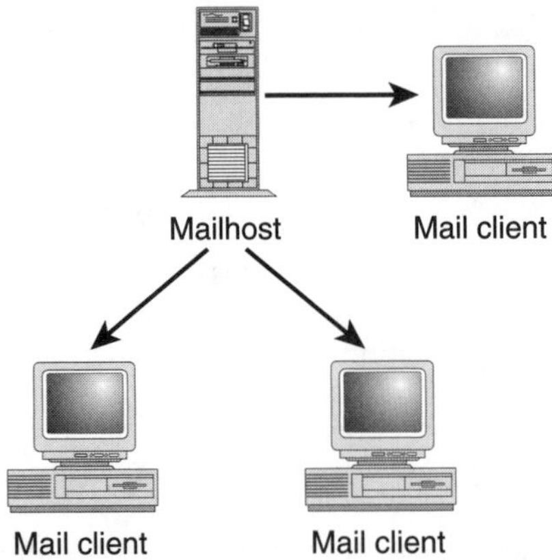

Figure 2–1
Local mail configuration.

Local Mail and a uucp Connection

The most common mail configuration in a small network can be seen in Figure 2–2. One system connects the mail server, the mailhost, and the relay host to the outside world by a `uucp` connection. Mail is distributed using the `/etc/mail/aliases` files. No naming service is required.

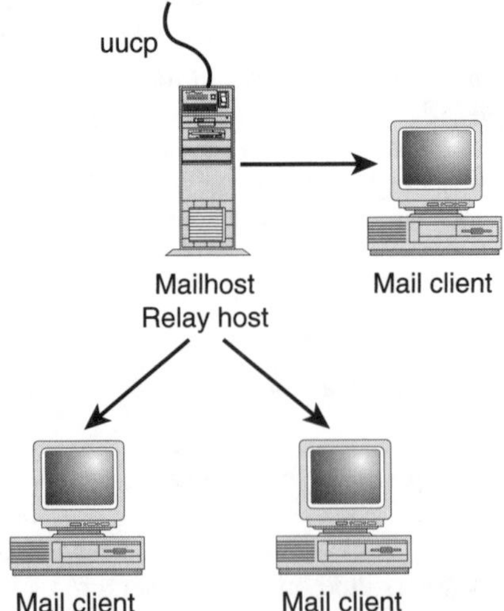

Figure 2–2
Local mail configuration with a `uucp` *connection.*

To set up this kind of mail configuration (assuming that the mail clients mount their mail files from `/var/mail` on the mailhost), you need the following:

- The `main.cf` file on the mailhost. You must edit the file to select a major relay mailer.
- The default `subsidiary.cf` file on each mail client system (no editing required).
- A server designated as the mailhost. (Add **mailhost** to the `/etc/hosts` file on the mailhost; add the mailhost IP address line to the `/etc/hosts` file of all mail clients.)
- Matching `/etc/mail/aliases` files on any system that has a local mailbox.
- Entries in each mail client's `/etc/vfstab` file to mount the `/var/mail` directory when mailboxes are located on the mail server.

See Chapter 3 for detailed information on how to set up mail services.

One Domain, Two Networks, and a Router

The mail configuration shown in Figure 2–3 has one domain, two networks, and a router. In this configuration, the mail server, the mailhost, and the relay host (or hosts) are likely to be different systems. To make administering and distributing mail easier, a naming service is used.

Figure 2–3
One domain, two networks, a router, and multiple uucp connections.

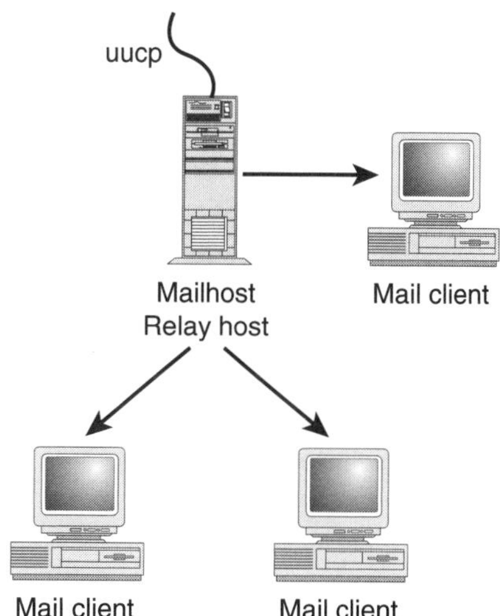

To set up this kind of mail configuration (assuming that the mail clients may have local or remote `/var/mail` files), you need everything that is specified in Table 2–1.

Table 2–1 Requirements for One-Domain, Two-Network Mail Configuration

Category	Requirements
Relay host	The `main.cf` file on the relay hosts—the systems with uucp connections. You must edit the file to select a major relay connector. You may want to define a mail relay host that knows about all of the connections. Special rules added to the `sendmail.cf` file are a good idea but are not mandatory.
Mailhost	One system that is designated as the mailhost. (Add **mailhost** to the `Hosts` database on the mailhost system.)
Mail server	Adequate spooling space for client mailboxes.
Mail client	The `subsidiary.cf` file on each mail client system (no editing required). Entries in each mail client's `/etc/vfstab` file to mount the `/var/mail` directory.
NIS+ tables	`mail_aliases.org_dir` tables for NIS+ with a mail alias entry for all of the users to point to where their mail is stored.

Two Domains and a Gateway

The mail configuration shown in Figure 2–4 has two domains and a gateway. In this configuration, the mail server, the mailhost, and the relay host (or hosts) for each domain are likely to be different systems. To make administering and distributing mail easier, a naming service is used.

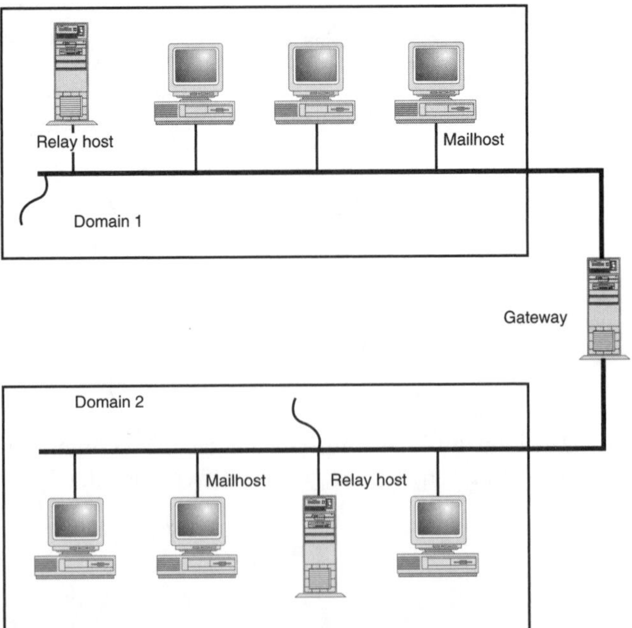

Figure 2–4
Two domains with a gateway.

Table 2–2 lists the requirements for this mail configuration.

Table 2–2 Requirements for Two Domains, One Route Configuration

Category	Requirements
Gateway	Complex gateway systems usually need a customized `sendmail.cf` file with special rules added.
Relay host	The `main.cf` file on the relay hosts—the systems with uucp connections. (You must edit the file to select a major relay mailer.) It might be useful to define a mail relay host that knows about all of the connections. (Special rules added to the `sendmail.cf` file are a good idea but are not mandatory.)
Mailhost	One system designated as the mailhost. (Add **mailhost** to the `Hosts` database on the mailhost system.)
Mail server	Adequate spooling space for client mailboxes.
Mail client	The `sendmail.cf` file on each mail client system (no editing required). Entries in each mail client's `/etc/vfstab` file to mount the `/var/mail` directory.
NIS+ tables	`mail_aliases.org_dir` tables for NIS+ with a mail alias entry for each user to point to the NIS+ tables.

NOTE. *The* `subsidiary.cf` *file has an entry (the CV class) that you can use to define "local"* `uucp` *connections (such as the system at the left of Domain 1 in Figure 2–4). If you define such a local* `uucp` *connection, users must address mail using the format* `uucphost!remote-system!address`.

CHAPTER

Setting Up and Administering Mail Services

Preparing to Set Up Mail Services

Setting Up Mail Services

Testing Your Mail Configuration

Administering Your Mail Configuration

Troubleshooting Your Mail Configuration

THIS CHAPTER DESCRIBES HOW TO SET UP, TEST, ADMINISTER, AND TROUBLESHOOT MAIL services. If you are not familiar with administering mail services, read Chapter 1, "Understanding Mail Services," for an introduction to the terminology and structure of the mail services. Read Chapter 2, "Planning Mail Services," for descriptions of several mail services configurations.

Preparing to Set Up Mail Services

You can set up a mail service relatively easily if your site does not provide connections to electronic mail services outside of your company or if your company is in a single domain. Setting up complicated sites with multiple domains is beyond the scope of this book. Chapter 4, "Customizing sendmail Configuration Files," contains information about how to create the more complicated configuration files required for sites with multiple domains.

Mail requires three types of configurations for local mail and a fourth for communication with networks outside of your domain. These configurations can be combined on the same system or provided by separate systems. A fifth, optional type of mail configuration is called a *gateway*. Table 3–1 describes each of these configurations.

Table 3–1 Mail Configurations

Configuration	Description
Mail server	You need to have at least one mail server. The mail server stores mailboxes in the `/var/mail` directory.
Mailhost	You need at least one mailhost. The mailhost resolves difficult email addresses and reroutes mail within your domain.
Mail client	Mail clients are users who have mailboxes either locally or on a mail server.
Relay host	A relay host manages communication with networks outside of your domain.
Gateway	A gateway is a connection between different communications networks. A relay host may also act as a gateway. You must add rules to the `sendmail.cf` file to set up a gateway. See Chapter 4 for information about adding rules. Another helpful reference is Chapter 15 of the *UNIX System Administration Handbook*, published by Prentice-Hall. (See the bibliography at the end of this book for more information.) If you have to set up a gateway, find a gateway configuration file that is close to what you need and modify it to fit your situation.

Before you begin to set up your mail service, choose the systems that will act as mail servers, mailhosts, and relay hosts. You should also make a list of all of the mail clients you will be providing service for and indicate the location of their mailboxes. This list will help you when you are ready to create mail aliases for your users. See Chapter 1 for more information about the function each of these systems provides. For your convenience, guidelines about which systems are good candidates for mail servers, mailhosts, and relay hosts are described in the following sections.

Setting Up Mail Services

To simplify the setup instructions, the following sections tell you what you need to do to set up individual mail servers, mailhosts, mail clients, and relay hosts. If a system in your mail services configuration is acting in more than one capacity, simply follow the appropriate instructions for each type of system. For example, if your mailhost and mail server are the same system, follow the directions for setting up that system as a mailhost and then follow the directions for setting up the same system as a mail server.

NOTE. *The following procedures for setting up a mail server and a mail client apply when mailboxes are NFS-mounted. You do not need to follow these procedures when mailboxes are maintained in locally mounted* `/var/mail` *directories.*

Setting Up a Mail Server

The *mail server* is responsible for routing all of the mail from a client. The only resource requirement for a mail server is that it have adequate spooling space for client mailboxes. See Chapter 1 for recommendations about spooling space.

To set up a mail server, the `/var` directory must be exported. On SunOS 5.*x* systems, type **share** and then press Return to check whether the `/var` directory is exported. In this example, the `/var/mail` directory is not exported:

```
cinderella% share
cinderella%
```

If the `/var` directory is not exported, become superuser and then type **share -F nfs -o rw /var/mail** and then press Return. You can type **share** with no arguments to verify that the directory is exported. You can also add the line to the `/etc/dfs/dfstab` file so that the file system is shared when the system is rebooted.

```
cinderella% share
cinderella% su
Password:
cinderella# share -F nfs -o rw /var/mail
cinderella# share

-            /var/mail    rw   ""
cinderella# vi /etc/dfs/dfstab
Add the line:
share -F nfs -o rw /var/mail
```

NOTE. *The* `sendmail` *program automatically creates mailboxes in the* `/var/mail` *directory the first time a message is delivered. You do not need to create individual mailboxes for your mail clients.*

Setting Up a Mail Client

A *mail client* is a user of mail services that has a mailbox on a mail server and a mail alias in the Aliases database or local /etc/mail/aliases file. This alias is used to indicate the location of the mailbox.

Follow these steps to set up a SunOS 5.*x* mail client with a mailbox on a mail server. (When instructions for setting up a SunOS 4.*x* mail client are different than those for 5.*x*, the SunOS 4.*x* instructions are included in parentheses.)

1. Become superuser on the mail client's system.
2. Create a /var/mail mount point on the mail client's system.
3. Edit the /etc/vfstab file and add an entry to mount the /var/mail directory from the mail server on the local /var/mail directory—type **<servername>:/var/mail - /var/mail nfs - yes rw** and then press Return. With an entry in the client system's /etc/vfstab file, the client's mailbox is automatically mounted any time that system is rebooted. (To set up a SunOS 4.*x* mail client, edit the client's /etc/fstab file.)
4. Type **mountall** to mount the mailbox. The client's mailbox is mounted. (On SunOS 4.*x* mail clients, type **mount -a** to mount the mailbox.)
5. Use the Solstice AdminSuite Hosts Manager to edit the Hosts database and add an entry for the mail server. (For SunOS 4.*x* systems, edit the /etc/hosts file and add an entry for the mail server.)
6. Add the user accounts for the client system to the Aliases database. See "Creating Mail Aliases" later in this chapter for information on how to create mail aliases for different types of mail configurations. (For SunOS 4.*x* systems, add the client to the /etc/aliases file.)

NOTE. *The sendmail program automatically creates mailboxes in the* /var/mail *directory the first time a message is delivered. You do not need to create individual mailboxes for your mail clients.*

This example sets up the SunOS 5.*x* system newton as a mail client of the system cinderella:

```
newton% su
Password:
newton# mkdir /var/mail
newton# vi /etc/vfstab
Add the line:
cinderella:/var/mail  -  /var/mail  nfs  -  yes  rw
newton# mountall
newton# solstice&
```

If you have Solstice AdminSuite, you can use the Database Manager graphical user interface to add user accounts to the Aliases database.

Setting Up a Mailhost

A mailhost resolves difficult email addresses and reroutes mail within your domain. A good candidate for a mailhost is a system that connects you to the outside world or to a parent domain.

Follow these steps to set up a mailhost:

1. Log into the mailhost system as yourself.
2. Edit the `/etc/hosts` file of the mailhost system and designate the system by typing **mailhost** after the system's IP address. The system is designated as a mailhost. If you are not using NIS+, NIS, or DNS, you must create an entry in the `/etc/hosts` file for each system on the network. The `/etc/hosts` entry should use this format: `IP address mailhost_name` mailhost.
3. Type **cp /etc/mail/main.cf /etc/mail/sendmail.cf** and then press Return. The `main.cf` file is copied to the file `sendmail.cf`.

```
# cp /etc/mail/main.cf /etc/mail/sendmail.cf
#
```

4. Reboot the mailhost and test your mail configuration. See "Testing Your Mail Configuration" later in the chapter for more information.

```
# init 6
```

Setting Up a Relay Host

A *relay host* manages communications with networks outside of your domain that use the same relay mailer. The mailer on the sending relay host must match the mailer on the receiving system.

For example, a good candidate for a relay host is a system attached to an ethernet and to phone lines. Another good candidate is a system configured as a router to the Internet. You may want to configure the mailhost as the relay host or to configure another system as the relay host. You may choose to configure more than one relay host for your domain. Each relay host you configure must use a mailer that matches the mailer on the connecting system. If you have uucp connections, you should configure the system (or systems) that have the uucp connections as the relay host. Follow these steps to set up a relay host:

1. Become superuser on the relay host system.
2. Type **`cp /etc/mail/main.cf /etc/mail/sendmail.cf`** and then press Return. The `main.cf` file is copied and renamed `sendmail.cf`.
3. Edit the `/etc/mail/sendmail.cf` file and make the following changes:
   - If your relay mailer is `uucp`, you do not need to change this entry. If your relay mailer is not `uucp`, change the default entry (`DMsmartuucp`) to the entry that is appropriate for your relay mailer. Available mailers are `smartuucp` (the default), `ddn`, `ether`, and `uucp`.

You can specify a different relay mailer for each relay host (if appropriate). You can define rule sets for other relay mailers in the `sendmail.main.cf` file. See "Mailers" in Chapter 1 for a description of each of the default relay mailers.

- In the entry `DR ddn-gateway`, replace *ddn-gateway* with the name of your relay host. The `DR` entry defines the relay host.
- In the entry `CR ddn-gateway`, replace *ddn-gateway* with the name of your relay host. The `CR` entry defines the class of the relay host. You can designate one or more hosts as a member of this class.
- (Optional) Add a `Dmmail_domain` or `Lmmaildomain` entry to define the mail domain name. If the macro is not defined, the naming service domain name is used, with the first component stripped off. For example, `Ecd.East.Sun.COM` becomes `East.Sun.Com`. If you use the `L` command, sendmail looks up the name to use in the sendmailvars table using `maildomain` as the search key.
- Save the edits.

4. Reboot the mailhost and test your mail configuration.

In this example, the system `oak` is set up as a relay host:

```
castle% rlogin oak
oak% su
Password:
# cp /etc/mail/main.cf /etc/mail/sendmail.cf
# vi /etc/mail/sendmail.cf
Replace DR ddn-gateway and CR ddn-gateway with:
DR oak
CR oak
Save changes and quit.
# init 6
```

Setting Up a Gateway

A *gateway* is a connection between different communications networks. A relay host may also act as a gateway. You must add rules to the `sendmail.cf` file to set up a gateway. Adding rules to the `sendmail.cf` file is beyond the scope of this chapter. See Chapter 4 for information about adding rules. Another helpful reference is the *UNIX System Administration Handbook,* Chapter 15; see the bibliography at the end of this book for the complete reference.

If you have to set up a gateway, your best bet is to find a gateway configuration file that is close to what you need and modify it to fit your situation. Most gateway files must be customized for each site. The `main.cf` file is a good place to start.

Creating Mail Aliases

Use the `aliasadm` command to create, modify, and delete aliases from a command line. See the `aliasadm`(1M) manual page for more information. Alternatively, if you have the Solstice AdminSuite available, you can use the Database Manager to edit the Aliases database.

Setting Up NIS Alias Files

It is likely that you have a network that has a mixture of systems running SunOS 4.*x* and SunOS 5.*x* system software. To help you administer networks with systems running different versions of SunOS system software, this section describes how to set up mail aliases on a SunOS 4.*x* NIS master server.

NOTE. *On SunOS 4.x systems, the aliases file is located in the* `/etc` *directory, not in* `/etc/mail`.

The `/etc/aliases` file on an NIS master contains all of the names by which a system or person is known. The NIS master is searched if there is no match in the local `/etc/aliases` (for SunOS 4.*x* systems) or `/etc/mail/aliases` (for SunOS 5.*x* systems) file. The sendmail program uses the NIS master file to determine mailing addresses. See the `aliases`(5) manual page for more information.

The `/etc/aliases` file on the NIS master should contain entries for all of the mail clients. You can either edit the file on each system or edit the file on one system and copy it to each of the other systems.

Aliases are of the following form:

```
name: name1, name2,...
```

You can alias local names or domains. For example, an alias entry for the user fred, who has a mailbox on the system `oak` and is in the domain `Trees`, would be this entry in the `/etc/aliases` file:

```
fred: fred@Trees
```

Follow these steps to set up NIS mail aliases files:

1. Compile a list of each of your mail clients, the locations of their mailboxes, and the names of the mail server systems.
2. Become superuser on the NIS master server.
3. Edit the `/etc/aliases` file and make the following entries:
   - Add an entry for each mail client.
   - Change the entry `Postmaster: root` to the mail address of the person who is designated as postmaster. See "Setting Up the Postmaster Alias" later in the chapter for more information.
   - If you have created a mailbox for the administration of a mail server, create an entry for **root:** ***mailbox@mailserver.***
   - Save the changes.
4. Edit the `/etc/hosts` file on the NIS master server and create an entry for each mail server.

5. Type **cd /var/yp** and then press Return.
6. Type **make** and then press Return. The changes in the `/etc/hosts` and `/etc/aliases` files are propagated to NIS slave systems. It takes a few minutes, at most, for the aliases to take effect.

Setting Up Local Mail Alias Files

The `/etc/mail` aliases file on a local SunOS 5.*x* system contains all of the names by which a system or person is known. The sendmail program uses this file to look up mailing addresses. See the `aliases`(5) manual page for more information.

The `/etc/mail/aliases` file of each system should contain entries for all mail user accounts. You can either edit the file on each system or edit the file on one system and copy it to each of the other systems.

You can use Admintool to edit local `/etc/mail/aliases` files.

NOTE. *Before you can use Admintool to edit a local* `/etc/mail/aliases` *file, you must either have superuser access to the local system or be a member of the sysadmin group (GID 14).*

It is a good idea to create an administrative account for each mail server. You do this by assigning root a mailbox on the mail server and adding an entry to the `/etc/mail/aliases` file for root. For example, if the system oak is a mailbox server, add the entry **root: sysadmin@oak** to the `/etc/mail/aliases` file.

To set up local mail aliases files:

1. Compile a list of each of your mail clients and the locations of their mailboxes.
2. Become superuser on the mail server.
3. Using the Database Manager's Aliases Database window, make the following entries:
   - Add an entry for each mail user account.
   - Change the entry `Postmaster: root` to the mail address of the person who is designated as postmaster. See "Setting Up the Postmaster Alias" later in the chapter for more information.
   - If you have created a mailbox for the administration of a mail server, create an entry for **root: *mailbox@mailserver***.
   - Save the changes.
4. To re-create the same information on each of the other systems, you can enter it again using the AdminSuite Database Manager. Alternatively, you can copy the `/etc/mail/aliases`, `/etc/mail/aliases.dir`, and `/etc/mail/aliases.pag` files to each of the other systems. You can copy the file by using the `rcp` or `rdist` command or by using a script that you create for this purpose. Remember that you must update all of the `/etc/mail/aliases` files each time you add or remove a mail client.

Setting Up DNS Alias Files

The DNS naming service does not use aliases for individuals. It does use aliases for hosts or domains, which are called *Mail Exchange (MX) records*. The `/etc/named.boot` file on the DNS server(s) for the domain or subdomain contains a list of other configuration files in DNS, one of which contains MX host information. You can specify host names or domain names in this file. Domain names can contain wildcards; for example, `*.sun.com` is an acceptable domain name.

You must use the `sendmail.mx` program with the DNS naming service. When you use the `sendmail.mx` program, the `${name}` rule, which creates fully qualified host names, is activated in the `sendmail.cf` file. You do not need to edit the configuration file to activate this rule.

Follow these steps to set up the `sendmail.mx` program:

1. Type **mv /usr/lib/sendmail /usr/lib/sendmail.nomx** and then press Return. The current sendmail program is renamed.
2. Type **mv /usr/lib/sendmail.mx /usr/lib/sendmail** and then press Return. The `sendmail.mx` file gets host names directly from DNS.
3. Make sure there is an entry for mailhost in the DNS `/etc/named.boot` file on the DNS server.

Setting Up the Postmaster Alias

Every system should be able to send mail to a postmaster. You can create an NIS or NIS+ alias for postmaster or create one in each local `/etc/mail/aliases` file. This is the default `/etc/mail/aliases` entry:

```
# Following alias is required by the mail protocol, RFC 822
# Set it to the address of a HUMAN who deals with this system's mail problems.
Postmaster: root
```

To create the `postmaster` alias, edit each system's `/etc/mail/aliases` file and change root to the mail address of the person who will act as the postmaster.

You may want to create a separate mailbox for the postmaster to keep postmaster mail separate from personal mail. If you create a separate mailbox, use the mailbox address instead of the postmaster's mail address when you edit the `/etc/mail/aliases` files.

Follow these steps to create a separate mailbox for the postmaster:

1. Create an account named postmaster and put an asterisk (*) in the password field of the `/etc/shadow` file.
2. Type **mail -f postmaster** and then press Return. Mail will be able to read and write to the mailbox name.

Follow these steps to add the postmaster mailbox to the alias:

1. Become superuser and edit the `/etc/mail/aliases` file on each system. If your network runs NIS or NIS+, use the AdminSuite Database Manager to edit the Aliases database.
2. Change the postmaster alias from root to postmaster:

   postmastermailbox@postmasterhost

   Save the changes.
3. On the postmaster's local system, create an entry in the `/etc/mail/aliases` file that defines the name of the alias (postmaster, for example) and includes the path to the local mailbox.
4. Type **newaliases** and then press Return.

Alternatively, you could change the "postmaster:" entry in the aliases file to **postmaster:** ***/usr/somewhere/somefile***.

Testing Your Mail Configuration

When you have all of the systems in your mail configuration set up, use the suggestions in this section to test the setup to make sure mail messages can be sent and received.

1. Reboot any system for which you have changed a configuration file.
2. Send test messages from each system by typing **/usr/lib/sendmail -v </dev/null** ***names*** and then press Return. Specify a recipient's email address in place of the *names* variable. This command sends a null message to the specified recipient and displays messages while it runs.
3. Run the following tests:
   - Send mail to yourself or to other people on the local system by addressing the message to a regular username.
   - If you are on an ethernet, send mail to someone on another system. Do this in three directions: from the main system to a subsidiary system, from a subsidiary system to the main system, and from a subsidiary system to another subsidiary system.
   - If you have a relay host, send mail to another domain from the mailhost to ensure that the relay mailer and host are configured properly.
   - If you have set up an `uucp` connection on your phone line to another host, send mail to someone at that host and have that individual send mail back or call you when the message is received.
   - Ask someone to send you mail over the `uucp` connection. The sendmail program cannot tell whether the message gets through because it hands the message to `uucp` for delivery.

- Send a message to the postmaster on different systems and make sure that it comes to your postmastesr's mailbox.

Administering Your Mail Configuration

The following sections describe how to keep mail services running smoothly.

Duties of Postmaster

Your responsibilities for administering mail include the following tasks:

- Check the mail queues to make sure that mail is flowing in and out.
- Check any downed systems where mail is backing up. If the system is not needed, delete it from the mail system or bring it up to keep mail moving.
- Fix personal aliases, as requested.
- Administer Aliases databases as people move in and out of the domain.
- Set up temporary forwarding files.
- Contact owners of mailing lists and help them fix mailing list problems.
- Go through postmaster mail daily and look for problems, broken `.forward` files, and mail alias loops. Fix the problem or tell people how to fix it.
- Answer questions about mail delivery problems from outside of the company.
- Truncate log files periodically.

The Mail Queue

Under high load or temporary failure conditions, sendmail puts a message into a job queue in the `/var/spool/mqueue` directory instead of delivering it immediately. Ordinarily, the mail queue is processed automatically. Sometimes, however, you may have to intervene manually. For example, if a major host is down for a period of time, the queue may become clogged. Although sendmail ought to recover gracefully when the host comes up, you may find performance unacceptable in the meantime.

Printing the Mail Queue

You can print the contents of the queue by specifying the `-bp` flag to sendmail. Type **/usr/lib/sendmail -bp | more** and then press Return. A list of the queue IDs, the size of the message, the date the message entered the queue, the message status, and the sender and recipients are displayed. You can also type **mailq** and then press Return to print the contents of the mail queue.

Format of Queue Files

The sendmail program stores temporary queue files in `/var/spool/mqueue`. All such queue files have the form *xfAA99999,* where *AA99999* is the ID for the file and *x* is the type. Table 3–2 shows the types of queue files.

Table 3–2 Types of Queue Files

Type	Description
d	A data file. The message body (excluding the header) is kept in this file.
l	A lock file. If this file is present, the job is currently being processed, and running the queue will not process it. For this reason, an extraneous lock file can make a job seem to disappear.
n	This separate file is created whenever an ID is created. It ensures that no mail can ever be destroyed because of a race condition. This file should not exist for more than a few milliseconds at any given time.
q	The queue control file. This file contains the information needed to process the job.
t	A temporary file. This file is an image of the qf file when it is being rebuilt. When the rebuild is complete, the file is renamed qf.
x	A transcript file that exists during the life of a session and shows everything that happens during that session.

The qf file contains a series of lines, each beginning with a code letter, as shown in Table 3–3. See Chapter 4 for more information about qf file codes.

Table 3–3 Codes for the qf File

Code	Description
P	The current message priority, which is used to order the queue. The higher the number, the lower the priority. The priority increases as the message sits in the queue. The initial priority depends on the message class and the size of the message.
T	The job creation/submission time in seconds, which is used to compute when the job times out.
D	The name of the data file.
M	A message. This line, which is printed by using sendmail with the `-bp` flag, is generally used to store status information. It can contain any text.
S	The sender name.
E	Error recipient name. Error messages are sent to this user instead of to the sender. This line is optional.

Table 3–3 Codes for the qf File (continued)

Code	Description
H	A header definition. There may be any number of these lines. The order is important: It represents the order in the final message. The syntax is the same as in the header definitions in the configuration file.
R	A recipient name. There is one line for each recipient. The recipient name normally is completely aliased, but it is actually re-aliased when the job is processed. The recipient name must be at the end of the qf file.

The queue is automatically run at the interval specified in the `sendmail.cf` file. (The default is every hour.) The queue is read and sorted by message priority, and then sendmail tries to process all jobs in order. The sendmail program first checks to see if a job is locked. If locked, it skips the job; if not locked, sendmail processes it.

If a major host goes down for several days, the queue may become prohibitively large, and sendmail will spend lots of time sorting the queue. You can fix this by moving the queue to a temporary place and creating a new queue. You can run the old queue later, when the host is returned to service.

Forcing the Queue

Follow these steps to force the queue to process mail in the queue now:

1. Become superuser on the mailhost.
2. Type **ps -el | grep sendmail** and then press Return. Note the PID for sendmail; you will use it in the next step.
3. Type **kill *PID*** and then press Return. The old sendmail daemon is killed to keep it from trying to process the old queue directory.
4. Type **cd /var/spool** and then press Return.
5. Type **mv mqueue omqueue; mkdir mqueue** and then press Return. These commands move the directory mqueue and all of its contents to the directory omqueue and then create a new empty mqueue directory.
6. Type **chmod 755; chown daemon; chgrp daemon; mqueue** and then press Return. These commands set the permissions of the directory to read/write/execute by others and read/execute by group and by others. They also set the owner and group to daemon.
7. Type **/usr/lib/sendmail -bd -q1h** and then press Return. A new sendmail daemon is started, with a queue runtime of one hour.

Running the Old Mail Queue

Follow these steps to run the old mail queue:

1. Type **/usr/lib/sendmail -oQ/var/spool/omqueue -q** and then press Return. The `-oQ` flag specifies an alternate queue directory, and the `-q` flag says to run every job in the queue. Use the `-v` flag if you want to see the verbose output displayed on the screen.
2. When the queue is finally emptied, type **rmdir /var/spool/omqueue** and then press Return. The empty directory is removed.

You can run a subset of the queue at any time with the `-R`*`string`* option (run queue where any recipient name matches *string*) or with the `-M`*`nnnnn`* option to sendmail. (Run just one message with queue ID *nnnnn*.)

To run a subset of the mail queue, type **/usr/lib/sendmail -R*string*** and then press Return. In this example, everything in the queue for recipient wnj is processed:

```
oak% /usr/lib/sendmail -Rwnj
```

The System Log

The mail services log most errors using the `syslogd` program. The default is for `syslogd` to send messages to a system identified as the loghost.

Just as you define a system called mailhost to handle mail relaying, you can define a system called loghost in the `/etc/hosts` file to hold all logs for an entire NIS domain. The system log is supported by the syslogd program. You can specify a loghost in the Hosts database. If no loghost is specified, then error messages from syslogd are not reported.

This is the default `/etc/syslog.conf` file:

```
#ident  "@(#)syslog.conf        1.4     96/10/11 SMI"   /* SunOS 5.0 */
#
# Copyright (c) 1991-1993, by Sun Microsystems, Inc.
#
# syslog configuration file.
#
# This file is processed by m4 so be careful to quote (`') names
# that match m4 reserved words.  Also, within ifdef's, arguments
# containing commas must be quoted.
#
*.err;kern.notice;auth.notice                   /dev/console
*.err;kern.debug;daemon.notice;mail.crit        /var/adm/messages

*.alert;kern.err;daemon.err                     operator
*.alert                                         root

*.emerg                                         *

# if a non-loghost machine chooses to have authentication messages
# sent to the loghost machine, un-comment out the following line:
#auth.notice                    ifdef(`LOGHOST', /var/log/authlog, @loghost)

mail.debug                      ifdef(`LOGHOST', /var/log/syslog, @loghost)

#
```

```
# non-loghost machines will use the following lines to cause "user"
# log messages to be logged locally.
#
ifdef(`LOGHOST', ,
user.err                                        /dev/console
user.err                                        /var/adm/messages
user.alert                                      `root, operator'
user.emerg                                      *
)
castle% more /etc/syslog.conf
#ident  "@(#)syslog.conf       1.4     96/10/11 SMI"   /* SunOS 5.0 */
#
# Copyright (c) 1991-1993, by Sun Microsystems, Inc.
#
# syslog configuration file.
#
# This file is processed by m4 so be careful to quote (`') names
# that match m4 reserved words.  Also, within ifdef's, arguments
# containing commas must be quoted.
#
*.err;kern.notice;auth.notice                   /dev/console
*.err;kern.debug;daemon.notice;mail.crit        /var/adm/messages

*.alert;kern.err;daemon.err                     operator
*.alert                                         root

*.emerg                                         *

# if a non-loghost machine chooses to have authentication messages
# sent to the loghost machine, un-comment out the following line:
#auth.notice                    ifdef(`LOGHOST', /var/log/authlog, @loghost)

mail.debug                      ifdef(`LOGHOST', /var/log/syslog, @loghost)

#
# non-loghost machines will use the following lines to cause "user"
# log messages to be logged locally.
#
ifdef(`LOGHOST', ,
user.err                                        /dev/console
user.err                                        /var/adm/messages
user.alert                                      `root, operator'
user.emerg                                      *
)
```

You can change the default configuration by editing the `/etc/syslog.conf` file.

When the syslogd daemon starts up, it creates the file `/etc/syslog.pid`, which contains its process ID number. This is an example of a `syslog.pid` file:

```
oak% more /etc/syslog.pid
166
oak%
```

This is an example of a system log file:

```
oak% tail /var/log/mailog
Apr  4 09:47:41 oak sendmail[14192]: AA14190: to=<uucp>, delay=00:00:01, stat=Sent
Apr  4 09:47:50 oak sendmail[14195]: AA14195: message-id=<9304041647
.AA195@oak.Eng.Sun.COM>
Apr  4 09:47:50 oak sendmail[14195]: AA14195: from=<uucp>, size=378, class=0,
received from ignatz (129.144.52.69)
Apr  4 09:47:51 oak sendmail[14197]: AA14195: to=<uucp>, delay=00:00:01, stat=Sent
Apr  4 10:44:27 oak sendmail[14280]: AA14280: message-
id=<93040401748.AA06975@castle.Eng.Sun.COM>
Apr  4 10:44:27 oak sendmail[14280]: AA14280: from=<winsor@castle>, size=892,
class=0, received from zigzag (129.144.1.38)
Apr  4 10:44:27 oak sendmail[14282]:AA14280: to=lautner@oak, delay=00:00:01,
stat=Sent
Apr  4 10:52:43 oak sendmail[14307]: AA14307: message-
id=<9304041753.AA05638@pigglet.Eng.Sun.COM>
Apr  4 10:52:43 oak sendmail[14307]: AA14307: from=<nixed@pigglet>,
size=918,class=0, received from piglet (129.144.154.7)
Apr  4 10:52:44 oak sendmail[14309]: AA14307: to=lautner@ oak, delay=00:00:01,
stat=Sent
oak%
```

NOTE. *Because of the length of each entry, space has been added between entries in this example to improve readability.*

Each line in the system log contains a timestamp, the name of the system that generated it, and a message. A large amount of information can be logged by syslog. The log is arranged as a succession of levels. At the lowest level, only unusual occurrences are logged. At the highest level, even the most mundane and uninteresting events are recorded. As a convention, log levels under 10 are considered useful. Log levels higher than 10 are usually used for debugging.

Troubleshooting Your Mail Configuration

The following sections provide some tips and tools that you can use for troubleshooting the mail.

Checking Aliases

To verify aliases and determine whether mail can be delivered to a given recipient, type **/usr/lib/sendmail -v -bv *recipient*** and then press Return. The command displays the aliases and identifies the final address as deliverable or not. Here is an example of the output:

```
% /usr/lib/sendmail -v -bv shamira@raks
shamira... aliased to   mwong
mwong... aliased to             shamira@raks
shamira@raks... deliverable
%
```

CAUTION! *Take extra care to avoid loops and inconsistent databases when both local and domain-wide aliases are used. Be especially careful when you move a user from one system to another to avoid creating alias loops.*

Testing sendmail

Follow these steps to run sendmail in test mode:

1. Type **/usr/lib/sendmail -bt** and then press Return. Information is displayed.
2. At the last prompt (>), type **0 *e-mail-address*** and then press Return. See Chapter 4 for a complete description of the diagnostic information.

Verifying Connections to Other Systems

To verify connections to other systems, you can use the `mconnect` program to open connections to other sendmail systems over the network. The `mconnect` program runs interactively. You can issue various diagnostic commands. See the `mconnect`(1) manual page for a complete description.

If you cannot use mconnect to connect to an SMTP port, check these conditions:

- Is the system load too high?
- Is the sendmail daemon running?
- Does the system have the appropriate `/etc/mail/sendmail.cf` file?
- Is TCP port 25 (the port that sendmail uses) active?
- Is the network connection down?
- Is a firewall blocking the connection?

Other Diagnostic Information

For other diagnostic information, check the following sources:

- Look at the received lines in the header of the message. These lines trace the route the message took as it was relayed, reading from the bottom up. Note that in the `uucp` network many sites do not update these lines, and in the Internet the lines often get rearranged. To straighten them out, look at the date and time in each line. Do not forget to account for time zone differences, and beware of clocks that have been set incorrectly.
- Look at messages from MAILER-DAEMON. These messages typically report delivery problems.
- Check the system log that records delivery problems for your group of workstations. The sendmail program always records what it is doing in the system log. You may want to modify the `crontab` file to run a shell script nightly that searches the log for `SYSERR` messages and mails any that it finds to the postmaster.
- Use the `mailstats` program to test mail types and determine the number of messages coming in and going out.

CHAPTER

4

Customizing sendmail Configuration Files

THE SENDMAIL PROGRAM IS A MAIL-TRANSPORT AGENT AND MESSAGE ROUTER THAT USES A configuration file to provide aliasing and forwarding, automatic routing to network gateways, and flexible configuration. The Solaris environment supplies the standard configuration files that most sites can use. Chapter 3, "Setting Up and Administering Mail Services," explains how to set up an electronic mail system using the standard configuration files. This chapter explains how to customize sendmail configuration files if you need to tailor them to fit your site's needs.

Sections in this chapter describe the following subjects:

- Command-line arguments to sendmail.
- sendmail parameters that you can alter.
- In-depth information on the configuration file. This section provides information for those sites that need to write their own configuration file.
- Brief explanations of several lesser-used features of sendmail.

The sendmail program can accept domain-based naming, as well as arbitrary (older) name syntaxes—resolving ambiguities using heuristics that you specify. The sendmail program can also convert messages between a pair of disparate naming schemes.

Certain special cases can be handled by ad hoc techniques, such as when providing network names that appear local to hosts on other networks. For example, user@host is left-to-right syntax, and host!user is right-to-left syntax.

Overview of sendmail Functions

The sendmail program is a message router that calls administrator-selected mailer programs to deliver messages. It collects a message from a program such as mail, edits the header of the message as required by the destination mailer, and calls appropriate mailers to do delivery or queueing for network transmission. When mailing to a file, however, sendmail delivers directly. New mailers, which increase heterogeneity and convenience, can be added at minimal cost.

Interfaces to the Outside World

The sendmail program can communicate with the outside world in three ways:

- Using the conventional argument vector/exit status
- Using pairs of pipes
- Using SMTP over a TCP connection

Argument Vector/Exit Status

The standard way to communicate with a process is using the *argument vector* (command name and arguments). The argument vector sends a list of recipients, and the message body is sent on the standard input. If problems occur, anything that the mailer prints is collected and returned to the sender. After the message is sent, the exit status from the mailer is collected, and a diagnostic is printed, if appropriate.

SMTP over Pipes

The SMTP protocol can be used to run an interactive lock-step interface with the mailer. A subprocess is still created, but no recipient names are passed to the mailer from the argument list. Instead, the names are passed one at a time in commands sent to the standard input of the processes. Anything appearing on the standard output must be a standard SMTP reply code.

SMTP over a TCP Connection

This technique is similar to SMTP over pipes, except that it uses a TCP connection. SMTP over a TCP connection is normally used to connect to a sendmail process on another system. This method is exceptionally flexible because the mailer need not reside on the same machine.

How the sendmail Program Works

The following sections describe in detail how the sendmail program works. When a sender wants to send a message, the program issues a request to sendmail using one of the three methods previously described. The sendmail program then goes through these steps, which are described in detail in the following sections:

1. Arguments are processed and then the address is parsed.
2. The message is collected.
3. The message is delivered.
4. If instructions are received from the mailer, the message is queued for retransmission.
5. If errors occur during processing, the message is returned to the sender.

Argument Processing and Address Parsing

If sendmail is called by using the argument vector or is connected to via a pipe, the arguments are first scanned and option specifications are processed. Recipient names are then collected, either from the command line or from the SMTP command, and a list of recipients is created. Aliases are expanded at this step, including mailing lists. As much validation as possible of the remote recipient is done at this step: Syntax is checked and local recipients are verified, but detailed checking of host names is deferred until delivery. Forwarding is also performed as the local recipients are verified.

The sendmail program appends each name to the recipient list after parsing. When a name is aliased or forwarded, the old name is retained in the list and then a flag is set that tells the delivery phase to ignore this recipient. This list is kept free from duplicates, thus preventing alias loops and duplicate messages from being delivered to the same recipient, as might occur when a person is in two groups.

NOTE. *Users may receive duplicate copies of the same message when alias lists contain email addresses for the same person using different syntaxes. The sendmail program cannot always identify the email addresses as duplicates of one another.*

Message Collection

The sendmail program then collects the message, which has a header at the beginning. The message body does not need to be formatted in any special way except that it must be composed of lines of text. (In other words, binary data is not allowed.) The header is stored in memory, and then the body of the message is saved in a temporary file.

To simplify the program interface, the message is collected even if no names were valid. The message subsequently is returned with an error.

Message Delivery

For each unique mailer and host in the recipient list, sendmail calls the appropriate mailer. Each mailer invocation sends the message to all users receiving it on one host. Mailers that accept only one recipient at a time are handled properly.

The message is sent to the mailer using one of the same three interfaces used to submit a message to sendmail. Each copy of the message has a customized header added to the beginning of the message. The mailer status code is caught and checked and a suitable error message is given, if appropriate. The exit code must conform to a system standard or the generic message `Service unavailable` is given.

Retransmission Queuing

When the mailer returns a status indicating that it might be able to handle the mail later, sendmail queues the mail and tries again later.

Return to Sender

When errors occur during processing, sendmail returns the message to the sender for retransmission. The letter can be mailed back (when the mail comes from a different site) or written to the dead.letter file in the sender's home directory.

Message-Header Editing

The sendmail program does some editing of the message header automatically. Header lines can be inserted under control of the configuration file. Some lines may be merged; for example, a From: and a Full-name: line may be merged under certain circumstances. A Received header is added to the header lines.

Configuration File

Almost all configuration information is read at runtime from a text file:

- Macro definitions (defining the value of macros used internally) are encoded.
- Header declarations (the format of header lines that are specially processed, and lines that are added or reformatted) are embedded.
- Mailer definitions (with information such as the location and characteristics of each mailer) are included.
- Name-rewriting rules (a limited pattern-matching system used to rewrite names) are defined.

How sendmail Is Implemented

The following sections provide an overview of the syntax used in sendmail and describe some implementation details.

You can follow flag arguments with recipient name arguments unless you run in SMTP mode. In brief, the format of recipient names is

- Anything in parentheses is thrown away (as a comment).
- Anything in angle brackets (< >) is preferred over anything else. This rule implements the Internet standard that writes names in the form of *username* *<system-name>* and sends to the electronic *system-name* rather than to the human *username*.
- Double quotes (") denote phrases; backslashes (\) denote characters. Backslashes cause otherwise equivalent phrases to compare differently—for example, *user* and *"user"* are equivalent, but *user* is different from either of them.

Parentheses, angle brackets, and double quotes must be properly balanced (that is, used in pairs) and nested. The rewriting rules control the rest of the needed processing.

Mail to Files and Programs

Files and programs are legitimate message recipients. Files provide archival storage of messages, which are useful for project administration and history. Programs are useful as recipients in a variety of situations—for example, to use `mailsort` to sort mail or to have the `vacation` program respond with an informational message when users are away.

Any name passing through the initial parsing algorithm as a local name is scanned for two special cases:

- If the prefix is a vertical bar (|), the rest of the name is processed as a shell command.

- If the username begins with a slash (/), the name is used as a filename, instead of a login name.

Message Collection

After all of the recipient names are parsed and verified, the message is collected. The message comes in two parts: a message header and a message body. The header and the body are separated by a blank line. The header is formatted as a series of lines of the form:

```
field-name: field-value
```

For example, a sample header might be

```
From: John Smith <Smith@Podunk.edu>
```

Field-value can be split across lines by starting the subsequent lines with a space or a Tab. Some header fields have special internal meaning and have appropriate special processing. Other headers are simply passed through. Some header fields, such as time stamps, may be added automatically.

The body is a series of text lines. It is completely uninterpreted and untouched, except that lines beginning with a dot have the dot doubled when transmitted over an SMTP channel. This extra dot is then stripped by the receiver.

Message Delivery

The send queue is grouped by the receiving host before transmission to implement message batching. An argument list is built as the scan proceeds. Mail to files is detected during the scan of the send list. The interface to the mailer is performed using one of the techniques described in "Overview of sendmail Functions," earlier in this chapter.

After a connection is established, sendmail makes the per-mailer changes to the header and sends the result to the mailer. If any mail is rejected by the mailer, a flag is set to invoke the return-to-sender function after all delivery is complete.

Queued Messages

If the mailer returns a `Temporary failure` exit status, the message is queued. A control file describes the recipients as well as various other parameters. This control file is formatted as a series of lines, each describing a sender, a recipient, the time of submission, or some other parameter of the message. The header of the message is stored in the control file so that the associated data file that is in the queue is simply the original temporary file.

Configuration Overview

Configuration is controlled primarily by a configuration file read at startup. Adding mailers or changing the rewriting or routing information does not require that you recompile sendmail. The configuration file encodes macro definitions, header declarations, mailer definitions, rewriting rules, and options.

Macros

Macros can be used in various ways. Certain macros transmit unstructured textual information into the mail system, such as the name that sendmail uses to identify itself in error messages. Other macros are unused internally and can be used as shorthand in the configuration file.

Header Declarations

Header declarations inform sendmail of the format of known header lines. Knowledge of a few header lines is built into sendmail, such as the From: and Date: lines.

Most configured headers are automatically inserted in the outgoing message if they don't exist in the incoming message. Certain headers are suppressed by some mailers.

Mailer Declarations

Mailer declarations specify the internal name of the mailer, some flags associated with the mailer, and an argument vector used on the call. This vector is expanded by a macro before use.

Name-Rewriting Rules

Name-rewriting rules are the heart of name parsing in sendmail. They are an ordered list of pattern-replacement rules, which are then applied to each name. In particular, ruleset 0 determines which mailer to use. The name is rewritten until it is either rewritten into a special canonical form—for example, a {*mailer, host, user*} triplet, such as {ddn, isi.edu, postel}, representing the name "postel@isi.edu"—or until it falls off the end. When a pattern matches, the rule is reapplied until it fails.

The configuration file also supports the editing of names into different formats. For example, a name of the form

```
ucsfcgl!tef
```

might be mapped into

```
tef@ucsfcgl.UUCP
```

to conform to the internal syntax. Translations can also be performed in the other direction for particular mailers.

Option Setting

Several options can be set from the configuration file. These options include the pathnames of various support files, timeouts, default modes, and so on.

Introducing Arguments to sendmail

The complete list of arguments to sendmail is described in detail in the sections "Command-Line Arguments" and "Configuration Options" later in the chapter. Arguments used to set the queue interval, daemon mode, and debugging flags, as well as for using an alternative configuration file, are described in the following sections.

Queue Interval

The `-q` flag defines how often sendmail runs the queue. If you run in mode `b` (the default) or `i`, you can set a relatively long time interval, because it is only used when a host that was down comes back up. If, however, you run in mode `q`, set a relatively short time, because the `q` flag defines the maximum amount of time that a message may sit in the queue. Typically, queue time is set between 15 minutes (`-q15m`) and one hour (`-q1h`).

Daemon Mode

If you allow incoming mail over a TCP connection, make sure a daemon is running. Set the `-bd` flag in your `/etc/rc3.d/S88sendmail` file.

You can combine the `-bd` flag and the `-q` flag in one call. In this example, the daemon is specified along with a queue interval of 30 minutes:

```
# /usr/lib/sendmail -bd -q30m
```

An Alternative Configuration File

You can specify an alternative configuration file by using the `-C` flag. For example,

```
# /usr/lib/sendmail -Ctest.cf
```

uses the configuration file `test.cf` instead of the default `/etc/mail/sendmail.cf`. If you do not define a value for the `-C` flag, it uses the `sendmail.cf` file in the current directory.

Tuning Configuration Parameters

You can tune several configuration parameters, depending on the requirements of your site. Most of these parameters are set using an option in the configuration file. For example, the line `OT3d` sets option `T` to the value `3d` (three days).

Time Values

All time intervals use a syntax of numbers and letters. For example, `10m` is 10 minutes, and `2h30m` is two and a half hours. The full set of time symbols is shown in Table 4–1.

Table 4–1 Time Syntax Options

Code	Description
s	seconds
m	minutes
h	hours
d	days
w	weeks

Queue Interval

The argument to the `-q` flag specifies how often sendmail runs the queue. It is usually set between 15 minutes (`-q15m`) and one hour (`-q1h`).

Read Timeouts

The `Or` option in the configuration file sets the read timeout. The default read timeout is `Or15m`. The sendmail program may time out when reading the standard input or when reading from a remote SMTP server. If your site has problems with read timeouts, set the read timeout to a larger value, such as one hour (`Or1h`), to reduce the chance of several idle daemons accumulating on your system.

Message Timeouts

The `OT` option in the configuration file sets the message timeout. The default message timeout is three days (`OT3d`). To inform the sender that a message cannot be delivered, it should be returned after sitting in the queue for a few days.

You can flush messages that have been hanging for a short period by running the queue with a short message timeout. For example,

```
# /usr/lib/sendmail -oT1d -q
```

runs the queue and flushes anything that is one day old or older.

Delivery Mode

The `Od` option in the configuration file sets the delivery mode. The default delivery mode is `Odbackground`. Delivery modes, shown in Table 4–2, specify how quickly mail is delivered.

Table 4–2 Delivery Mode Options

Code	Description
i	Deliver interactively (synchronously)

Table 4–2 Delivery Mode Options (continued)

b	Deliver in background (asynchronously)
q	Queue only (do not deliver)

There are trade-offs. Mode `i` passes the maximum amount of information to the sender, but is hardly ever necessary. Mode `q` puts the minimum load on your machine, but means that delivery may be delayed for up to the queue interval. Mode `b`, the default, is probably a good compromise.

Load Limiting

The goal of load limiting is to prevent wasted time during loaded periods. This is done by attempting to deliver large messages, messages to many recipients, or messages to sites that have been down for a long time.

Central mail machines often can be overloaded. Of course, the best solution is to dedicate a more powerful machine to handling mail, but the load almost always expands to consume whatever resources are allocated.

Use the `Ox` and `OX` options to limit the load caused by sendmail. The default sets no load limits if no options are used. Both of these configuration options take an argument that is an integer-load average. For example, if you specify `Ox4` and `OX8`, the `x` load limiting will be used when the load is above four, and the `X` load limiting will be used when the load is above eight. When the load is above the value specified in the `X` option, the SMTP server does not accept connections from the network. (Locally originated mail and other mail such as uucp are not affected.) The `x` option has a more subtle effect, controlling whether messages are queued for later delivery or are delivered immediately. The general idea is to deliver small messages immediately and to defer large messages for delivery during off-peak periods.

The `Oq` option specifies the maximum size of messages to be delivered immediately. The size of the message includes not only the number of bytes in the message, but also includes assigned penalties for a large number of recipients and for unsuccessful delivery attempts. The penalty per recipient is option value `y`, by default set to 1000. The penalty per delivery attempt is the option value `z`, by default set to 9000. The size limit also depends on current load, so that more and more messages are queued as the load goes higher. If the load is one above the `x` threshold, the limit is halved; if the load is two above the threshold, the limit is divided by three, and so forth. Note that this limit also applies to messages that are delivered when running the queue, in contrast to earlier versions of sendmail.

Log Level

You can adjust the level of logging for `sendmail`. The default log level is `9`. The levels are shown in Table 4–3.

Table 4–3 Log Level Codes

Level	Description
0	No logging
1	Major problems only
2	Message collections and failed deliveries
3	Successful deliveries
4	Messages being deferred (due to a host being down and so forth)
5	Normal message queue-ups
6	Unusual but benign incidents (for example, trying to process a locked queue file)
9	Log internal queue ID to external message ID mappings, which can be useful for tracing a message as it travels between several hosts
12	Several messages that are basically of interest only when debugging
16	Verbose information regarding the queue
22	All of the above

File Modes

Certain files can have a number of modes. The following sections describe the modes that you can control from the `sendmail.cf` file. The modes you use depend on what functionality you want and the level of security you require.

setuid

By default, sendmail is executed with the user ID set to `0` (setuid to root) so that it can deliver to programs that might write in a user's home directory. When sendmail is ready to execute a mailer program, sendmail checks to see whether the user ID is 0; if so, it resets the user ID and group ID to the values set by the `u` and `g` options in the configuration file. By default, these values are `Ou1` and `Og1`, which set both the user ID and the group ID to `1`, which is daemon. You can override these values by setting the `S` flag to the mailer for mailers that are trusted and must be called as root. In this case, mail processing is accounted to root rather than to the user sending the mail.

Temporary File Modes

The `OF` option sets the mode of all temporary files that sendmail uses. The default is `OF0600`. The numbers stand for the usual octal values for file permissions. Thus, `0600` is for secure mail (`-rw-------`) and `0644` for permissive (`-rw-r--r--`). If you use the more permissive mode, you do not need to run sendmail as root (even when running the queue). Users can read mail in the queue.

Aliases Database Permissions

You can control access to the Aliases database. Many sites permit only accredited users to make modifications to the Aliases database or to create new ones.

If you use the local `/etc/mail/aliases` file to control mail aliases, you can use UNIX file permissions to restrict or permit write access. Default permissions on the `/etc/mail/aliases` are set to `644` with root as the owner. If you want to permit other users to be able to control mail aliases, you can use ACLs to enable specific individuals to write to the file or set up a group that contains members who can change mail aliases.

The Configuration File

The following sections describe the configuration file in detail, including hints for writing your own file.

The syntax of the configuration file is parsed every time sendmail starts up. This syntax is optimized for speed of processing, but can be mastered with the information that follows. The sendmail file uses single letters for several different functions:

- Command-line flags
- Configuration options
- Queue file line types
- Configuration file line types
- Mailer field names
- Mailer flags
- Macro names
- Class names

The following sections provide an overview of the configuration file and details of its semantics.

Parts of the sendmail Configuration File

The sendmail configuration file has three parts:

- Definition of symbols, classes, options, and parameters
- Definitions of mailers and delivery programs
- Rulesets that determine the rules for rewriting addresses

You define symbols, classes, options, and parameters to set up the environment for sendmail. You define your mailers and delivery programs so that sendmail knows the protocols to use and the delivery programs with which to interact.

You define rewriting rules, grouped into rulesets, to transform addresses from one form to another. In general, each rule in a ruleset is applied to a particular address. An address might be rewritten several times within a ruleset.

There are eight standard rulesets; these are applied in the order shown in Table 4–4.

Table 4–4 Order of Application of Rulesets

Ruleset	Description
Ruleset 3	The first ruleset applied; tries to put the address into the canonical form local-address@host-domain.
Ruleset 0	Determines what the destination is, as well as which mailer program to use in order to send mail. It resolves the destination into a triplet (*mailer, host, user*).
Ruleset D	Appends sender domain information to addresses that have no domain specified.
Ruleset 1	Rewrites the sender address.
Ruleset S	Each mailer can specify additional rulesets for the sender addresses to perform final mailer-specific cleanup. These rulesets have different names for each mailer. In this example, *S* stands for a generic "sender."
Ruleset 2	Rewrites the recipient address.
Ruleset R	Each mailer can specify additional rulesets for the recipient addresses to perform final mailer-specific cleanup. These rulesets have different names for each mailer. In this example, *R* stands for a generic "recipient."
Ruleset 4	Rewrites all addresses for the final time, usually from internal to external form.

NOTE. *Rulesets D, S, and R represent rulesets that are specified in one of the mailer configuration statements. For example, R and S might be ruleset 22.*

Ruleset 0 must resolve to the internal form, which in turn is used as a pointer to a mailer descriptor. The mailer descriptor describes the interface requirements of the mailer.

Rewriting names in the message typically is completed in two phases. The first phase uses ruleset 3 to map names in any format into a canonical form. The second phase maps the canonical form into the syntax appropriate for the receiving mailer. Names are rewritten by sendmail in three subphases. Rulesets 1 and 2 are applied to all sender and recipient names, respectively. You may specify mailer-specific rulesets in ruleset 3 for both sender and recipient names. Finally, ruleset 4 is applied to do any conversion to external form.

RFC 822 describes the format of the mail message itself. The sendmail program follows this RFC closely, to the extent that many of the standards described in this document cannot be changed without changing the code. In particular, the following characters have special interpretations:

```
< > ( ) " \
```

CAUTION! *Use the RFC 822 special characters < > ( ) " \ only for their designated purposes. Information between parentheses, ( ), is reserved for comments and personal names. Information between angle brackets, < >, is reserved for canonical addresses. The " sign is used to quote strings in an address or identifier. For example, ":sysmail"@somewhere.domain.com. The string is treated literally so that nothing inside it is considered an address until it reaches the system in somewhere.domain.com. The \ is used to escape a single character.*

A Sample sendmail Configuration File

Following is an example of the default main.cf file. Subsequent sections describe the syntax and semantics used in this file.

```
#############################################################
#
#Sendmail configuration file for "MAIN MACHINES"
#
#You should install this file as /etc/mail/sendmail.cf
#if your machine is the main (or only) mail-relaying
#machine in your domain.  Then edit the file to
#customize it for your network configuration.
#
#@(#)main.mc1.2497/06/05 SMI
#

###local info

# delete the following if you have no sendmailvars table
Lmmaildomain

# my official hostname
# You have two choices here.  If you want the gateway machine to identify
# itself as the DOMAIN, use this line:
Dj$m
# If you want the gateway machine to appear to be INSIDE the domain, use:
#Dj$w.$m
# if you are using sendmail.mx (or have a fully-qualified hostname), use:
#Dj$w

# major relay mailer - typical choice is "ddn" if you are on the
# Defense Data Network (e.g. Arpanet or Milnet)
DMsmartuucp

# major relay host: use the $M mailer to send mail to other domains
DR ddn-gateway
CR ddn-gateway

# If you want to pre-load the "mailhosts" then use a line like
```

```
# FS /usr/lib/mailhosts
# and then change all the occurrences of $%y to be $=S instead.
# Otherwise, the default is to use the hosts.byname map if NIS
# is running (or else the /etc/hosts file if no NIS).

# valid top-level domains (default passes ALL unknown domains up)
CT arpa com edu gov mil net org
CT us de fr jp kr nz il uk no au fi nl se ca ch my dk ar

# options that you probably want on a mailhost:

# checkpoint the queue after this many recipients
OC10

# refuse to send tiny messages to more than these recipients
Ob10

#################################################
#
#General configuration information

# local domain names
#
# These can now be determined from the domainname system call.
# The first component of the NIS domain name is stripped off unless
# it begins with a dot or a plus sign.
# If your NIS domain is not inside the domain name you would like to have
# appear in your mail headers, add a "Dm" line to define your domain name.
# The Dm value is what is used in outgoing mail.  The Cm values are
# accepted in incoming mail.  By default Cm is set from Dm, but you might
# want to have more than one Cm line to recognize more than one domain
# name on incoming mail during a transition.
# Example:
# DmCS.Podunk.EDU
# Cm cs cs.Podunk.EDU
#
# known hosts in this domain are obtained from gethostbyname() call

# Version number of configuration file
#ident"@(#)version.m41.1792/07/14 SMI"/* SunOS 4.1*/
#
#
#Copyright Notice
#
#Notice of copyright on this source code product does not indicate
#publication.
#
#(c) 1986,1987,1988,1989  Sun Microsystems, Inc
#          All rights reserved.

DVSMI-SVR4


###   Standard macros

# name used for error messages
```

```
DnMailer-Daemon
# special user
CDMailer-Daemon root daemon uucp
# UNIX header format
DlFrom $g  $d
# delimiter (operator) characters
Do.:%@!^=/[]
# format of a total name
Dq$g$?x ($x)$.
# SMTP login message
De$j Sendmail $v/$V ready at $b

###   Options

# Remote mode - send through server if mailbox directory is mounted
OR
# Turn on the DNS name look up
OI
# location of alias file
OA/etc/mail/aliases
# default delivery mode (deliver in background)
Odbackground
# rebuild the alias file automagically
OD
# temporary file mode -- 0600 for secure mail, 0644 for permissive
OF0600
# default GID
Og1
# location of help file
OH/etc/mail/sendmail.hf
# log level
OL9
# default messages to old style
Oo
# Cc my postmaster on error replies I generate
OPPostmaster
# queue directory
OQ/var/spool/mqueue
# read timeout for SMTP protocols
Or15m
# status file -- none
OS/etc/mail/sendmail.st
# queue up everything before starting transmission, for safety
Os
# return queued mail after this long
OT3d
# default UID
Ou1

###   Message precedences
Pfirst-class=0
Pspecial-delivery=100
Pjunk=-100

###   Trusted users
T root daemon uucp
```

```
###   Format of headers
H?P?Return-Path: <$g>
HReceived: $?sfrom $s $.by $j ($v/$V)
id $i; $b
H?D?Resent-Date: $a
H?D?Date: $a
H?F?Resent-From: $q
H?F?From: $q
H?x?Full-Name: $x
HSubject:
H?M?Resent-Message-Id: <$t.$i@$j>
H?M?Message-Id: <$t.$i@$j>
HErrors-To:

###########################
###   Rewriting rules   ###
###########################


#  Sender Field Pre-rewriting
S1
# None needed.

#  Recipient Field Pre-rewriting
S2
# None needed.

# Name Canonicalization

# Internal format of names within the rewriting rules is:
# anything<@host.domain.domain...>anything
# We try to get every kind of name into this format, except for local
# names, which have no host part.  The reason for the "<>" stuff is
# that the relevant host name could be on the front of the name (for
# source routing), or on the back (normal form).  We enclose the one that
# we want to route on in the <>'s to make it easy to find.
#
S3

# handle "from:<>" special case
R$*<>$*$@@turn into magic token

# basic textual canonicalization
R<$*<@$+>>$@$1<@$2>
R$*<$+>$*$2basic RFC822 parsing

# make sure <@a,@b,@c:user@d> syntax is easy to parse -- undone later
R@$+,$+:$+@$1:$2:$3change all "," to ":"
R@$+:$+$@$>6<@$1>:$2src route canonical

R$+:$*;@$+$@$1:$2;@$3list syntax
R$+@$+$:$1<@$2>focus on domain
R$+<$+@$+>$1$2<@$3>move gaze right
R$+<@$+>$@$>6$1<@$2>already canonical
```

```
# convert old-style names to domain-based names
# All old-style names parse from left to right, without precedence.
R$-!$+$@$>6$2<@$1.uucp>uucphost!user
R$-.$+!$+$@$>6$3<@$1.$2>host.domain!user
R$+%$+$@$>3$1@$2user%host

#  Final Output Post-rewriting
S4
R$+<@$+.uucp>$2!$1u@h.uucp => h!u
R$+$: $>9 $1Clean up addr
R$*<$+>$*$1$2$3defocus


#  Clean up a name for passing to a mailer
#  (but leave it focused)
S9
R$=w!@$@$w!$n
R@$@$nhandle <> error addr
R$*<$*LOCAL>$*$1<$2$m>$3change local info
R<@$+>$*:$+:$+<@$1>$2,$3:$4<route-addr> canonical


#######################
#   Rewriting rules

# special local conversions
S6
R$*<@$*$=m>$*$1<@$2LOCAL>$4convert local domain

# Local and Program Mailer specification

Mlocal,P=/usr/lib/mail.local, F=flsSDFMmnP, S=10, R=20, A=mail.local -d $u
Mprog,P=/bin/sh,   F=lsDFMeuP,  S=10, R=20, A=sh -c $u

S10
# None needed.

S20
# None needed.

#ident"@(#)etherm.m41.1695/12/01 SMI"/* SunOS 4.1*/
#
#Copyright Notice
#
#Notice of copyright on this source code product does not indicate
#publication.
#
#(c) 1986,1987,1988,1989  Sun Microsystems, Inc
#          All rights reserved.

############################################################
#####
#####Ethernet Mailer specification
#####
#####Messages processed by this configuration are assumed to remain
#####in the same domain.  This really has nothing particular to do
```

```
#####   with Ethernet - the name is historical.

Mether,P=[TCP], F=msDFMuCX, S=11, R=21, A=TCP $h, E=\r\n
S11
R$*<@$+>$*$@$1<@$2>$3already ok
R$=D$@$1<@$w>tack on my hostname
R$+$@$1<@$k>tack on my mbox hostname

S21
R$*<@$+>$*$@$1<@$2>$3already ok
R$+$@$1<@$k>tack on my mbox hostname




############################################################
#  General code to convert back to old style UUCP names
S5
R$+<@LOCAL>$@ $w!$1name@LOCAL => sun!name
R$+<@$-.LOCAL>$@ $2!$1u@h.LOCAL => h!u
R$+<@$+.uucp>$@ $2!$1u@h.uucp => h!u
R$+<@$*>$@ $2!$1u@h => h!u
# Route-addrs do not work here.  Punt til uucp-mail comes up with something.
R<@$+>$*$@ @$1$2just defocus and punt
R$*<$*>$*$@ $1$2$3Defocus strange stuff

#UUCP Mailer specification

Muucp,P=/usr/bin/uux, F=msDFMhuU, S=13, R=23,
A=uux - -r -a$f $h!rmail ($u)

# Convert uucp sender (From) field
S13
R$+$:$>5$1convert to old style
R$=w!$+$2strip local name
R$+$:$w!$1stick on real host name

# Convert uucp recipient (To, Cc) fields
S23
R$+$:$>5$1convert to old style


#ident"@(#)ddnm.m41.893/06/30 SMI"/* SunOS 4.1*/
#
#
#Copyright Notice
#
#Notice of copyright on this source code product does not indicate
#publication.
#
#(c) 1986,1987,1988,1989  Sun Microsystems, Inc
#          All rights reserved.

############################################################
#
#DDN Mailer specification
```

```
#
#Send mail on the Defense Data Network
#   (such as Arpanet or Milnet)

Mddn,P=[TCP], F=msDFMuCX, S=22, R=22, A=TCP $h, E=\r\n

# map containing the inverse of mail.aliases
# Note that there is a special case mail.byaddr will cause reverse
# lookups in both Nis+ and NIS.
# If you want to use ONLY Nis+ for alias inversion comment out the next line
# and uncomment the line after that
DZmail.byaddr
#DZREVERSE.mail_aliases.org_dir

S22
R$*<@LOCAL>$*$:$1
R$-<@$->$:$>3${Z$1@$2$}invert aliases
R$*<@$+.$*>$*$@$1<@$2.$3>$4already ok
R$+<@$+>$*$@$1<@$2.$m>$3tack on our domain
R$+$@$1<@$w.$m>tack on our full name


# "Smart" UUCP mailer: Uses UUCP transport but domain-style naming
Msmartuucp, P=/usr/bin/uux, F=CmsDFMhuU, S=22, R=22,
A=uux - -r $h!rmail ($u)


###########################################################
#
#RULESET ZERO
#
#This is the ruleset that determines which mailer a name goes to.

# Ruleset 30 just calls rulesets 3 then 0.
S30
R$*$: $>3 $1First canonicalize
R$*$@ $>0 $1Then rerun ruleset 0

S0
# On entry, the address has been canonicalized and focused by ruleset 3.
# Handle special cases.....
R@$#local $:$nhandle <> form

# resolve the local hostname to "LOCAL".
R$*<$*$=w.LOCAL>$*$1<$2LOCAL>$4thishost.LOCAL
R$*<$*$=w.uucp>$*$1<$2LOCAL>$4thishost.uucp
R$*<$*$=w>$*$1<$2LOCAL>$4thishost

# Mail addressed explicitly to the domain gateway (us)
R$*<@LOCAL>$@$>30$1strip our name, retry
R<@LOCAL>:$+$@$>30$1retry after route strip

# For numeric spec, you can't pass spec on to receiver, since old rcvr's
# are not smart enough to know that [x.y.z.a] is their own name.
R<@[$+]>:$*$:$>9 <@[$1]>:$2Clean it up, then...
R<@[$+]>:$*$#ether $@[$1] $:$2numeric internet spec
```

```
R<@[$+]>,$*$#ether $@[$1] $:$2numeric internet spec
R$*<@[$+]>$#ether $@[$2] $:$1numeric internet spec

# deliver to known ethernet hosts explicitly specified in our domain
R$*<@$%y.LOCAL>$*$#ether $@$2 $:$1<@$2>$3user@host.sun.com
# deliver to hosts in our domain that have an MX record
R$*<@$%x.LOCAL>$*$#ether $@$2 $:$1<@$2>$3user@host.sun.com

# etherhost.uucp is treated as etherhost.$m for now.
# This allows them to be addressed from uucp as foo!sun!etherhost!user.
R$*<@$%y.uucp>$*$#ether $@$2 $:$1<@$2>$3user@etherhost.uucp

# Explicitly specified names in our domain -- that we've never heard of
R$*<@$*.LOCAL>$*$#error $:Never heard of host $2 in domain $m

# Clean up addresses for external use -- kills LOCAL, route-addr ,=>:
R$*$:$>9 $1Then continue...

# resolve UUCP-style names
R<@$-.uucp>:$+$#uucp  $@$1 $:$2@host.uucp:...
R$+<@$-.uucp>$#uucp  $@$2 $:$1user@host.uucp

# Pass other valid names up the ladder to our forwarder
#R$*<@$*.$=T>$*$#$M    $@$R $:$1<@$2.$3>$4user@domain.known

# Replace following with above to only forward "known" top-level domains
R$*<@$*.$+>$*$#$M    $@$R $:$1<@$2.$3>$4user@any.domain

# if you are on the DDN, then comment-out both of the lines above
# and use the following instead:
#R$*<@$*.$+>$*$#ddn $@ $2.$3 $:$1<@$2.$3>$4user@any.domain

# All addresses in the rules ABOVE are absolute (fully qualified domains).
# Addresses BELOW can be partially qualified.

# deliver to known ethernet hosts
R$*<@$%y>$*$#ether $@$2 $:$1<@$2>$3user@etherhost
# deliver to known ethernet hosts that have an MX record
R$*<@$%x>$*$#ether $@$2 $:$1<@$2>$3user@etherhost

# other non-local names have nowhere to go; return them to sender.
R$*<@$+.$->$*$#error $:Unknown domain $3
R$*<@$+>$*$#error $:Never heard of $2 in domain $m
R$*@$*$#error $:I don't understand $1@$2

# Local names with % are really not local!
R$+%$+$@$>30$1@$2turn % => @, retry

# everything else is a local name
R$+$#local $:$1local names
```

Configuration File Syntax

The configuration file is organized as a series of lines, each of which begins with a single character defining the semantics for the rest of the line. Lines beginning with a space or a Tab are continuation lines (although in many places the semantics are not well defined). Blank lines and lines beginning with a pound sign (#) are comments.

D and L (Define Macro)

Macros are named with a single character. Although a macro can be defined with any character from the complete ASCII set, use only uppercase letters for macros that you define. However, do not use characters such as M, R, L, G, and V, which are already used in the default `sendmail.cf` file. Lowercase letters and special symbols are used internally. You can define macros in two ways:

- `D` assigns the value directly specified.
- `L` assigns the value looked up in the sendmailvars database (either the NIS+ table or the `/etc/mail/sendmailvars` file). The `L` command is classified as an uncommitted interface.

The syntax for `D` macro definitions is

```
DXval
```

in which *X* is the name of the macro and *val* is the value it should have. Spaces are not allowed. Macros can be inserted in most places using the escape sequence `$X`.

An example of `D` macro definitions from the configuration file follows:

```
DRmailhost
DmEng.Sun.COM
```

The variable *`R`* is set to contain the value `mailhost` and the internal variable *`m`* is set to contain the value `Eng.Sun.COM`.

The `m` macro defines the mail domain. If it is not defined, the name service domain name is used with the first component stripped off. For example, `Ecd.East.Sun.COM` becomes `East.Sun.COM`.

The syntax for an `L` macro definition, which is an even more flexible way to define the mail domain name, is

```
LXsearch_key
```

in which *`X`* is the name of the macro and *`search_key`* is searched in the sendmailvars database. The value found in the entry located by the search key is assigned to *`X`*.

An example of an internal `L` macro definition from the configuration file follows:

```
Lmmaildomain
```

The variable *`m`* is set to the value found in the sendmailvars database using maildomain as the search key. If the entry in the sendmailvars database looks like this example:

```
maildomain        Eng.Sun.COM
```

the value of *`m`* becomes `Eng.Sun.COM`.

NOTE. *The sendmail program uses the* `sendmailvars` *entry in the* `/etc/nsswitch.conf` *file to determine the order in which it searches the NIS+ database and the* `/etc/mail/sendmailvars` *database.*

C, F, and G (Define Classes)

You can define classes of words to match on the left side of rewriting rules. For example, you might create a class of all local names for this site so that you can eliminate attempts to send to yourself.

Classes may be named from the set of uppercase letters. Lowercase letters and special characters are reserved for system use. You can define classes in three ways:

- `C` assigns the value(s) specified directly.
- `F` reads in the value(s) from another file or from another command.
- `G` assigns the value(s) looked up in the sendmailvars database (either the NIS+ database or the `/etc/mail/sendmailvars` file). The `G` command is classified as an uncommitted interface.

The syntax of the different forms of class definition is

```
CC word1 word2
FC file
FC ¦ command
GCsearch_key
```

The first form defines the class `C` to match any of the named words. The second form reads words from the file into the class `C`, for example, `FC /.rhosts`. The format is used with `scanf` to read from the file; otherwise, the first word from each line is used. The third form executes the given command and reads the elements of the class from standard output of the command. For example,

```
FC ¦ awk '{print $2}' /etc/hosts
```

The fourth form reads the elements of the class from the entry in the `sendmailvars` database pointed to by the search key. For example,

```
GVuucp-list
```

gets the definition of class `V` from the `uucp-list` entry in the `sendmailvars` database. If the entry in the `sendmailvars` database looks like this:

```
uucp-list            castle oak cinderella
```

the value of `V` becomes `castle oak cinderella`.

NOTE. *The sendmail program uses the* `sendmailvars` *entry in the* `/etc/nsswitch.conf` *file to determine the order in which it searches the NIS+ database and the* `/etc/mail/sendmailvars` *database.*

You can split class definitions among multiple lines. For example,

```
CHmonet ucbmonet
```

is equivalent to

```
CHmonet
CHucbmonet
```

O (Set Option)

You can set several options (not to be confused with mailer flags or command-line arguments) from a configuration file. Options are also represented by single characters. The syntax of this line is

```
OC ovalue
```

Option `C` is set to *`value`*. Depending on the option, *`value`* may be a string, an integer, a boolean (with legal values `t`, `T`, `f`, or `F`—the default is true), or a time interval. See the section "Configuration Options" later in this chapter for the list of options.

P (Precedence Definitions)

You can define values for the Precedence: field using the `P` control line. The syntax of this field is

```
Pname=num
```

When the *`name`* is found in a Precedence: field, the message class is set to *`num`*. Higher numbers mean higher precedence. Numbers less than zero have the special property in which error messages are not returned. The default precedence is zero. For example,

```
Pfirst-class=0
Pspecial-delivery=100
Pjunk=-100
```

T (Define Trusted Users)

Trusted users are those users who are permitted to override the sender name using the `-f` flag. These users typically are root, uucp, daemon, and network. For some sites, it may be convenient to extend this list to include other users, perhaps to support a separate uucp login for each host. The syntax of this line is

```
T user . . .
```

You can use more than one line to define trusted users.

H (Define Header)

The format of the header lines is defined by the `H` line. The syntax of this line is

```
H[c ?c mflagsc ?]c hnamec :c htemplate
```

Continuation lines in this specification are inserted directly into the outgoing message. The *`htemplate`* is macro-expanded before it is inserted into the message. If the expansion is empty, the header line is not included. If the `mflags` (surrounded by question marks) are specified, at least one of the specified flags must be stated in the mailer definition for this header to be automatically output. If one of these headers is in the input, it is directed to the output regardless of these flags.

Special Header Lines

Several header lines have special interpretations defined by the configuration file. Others have interpretations built into sendmail that cannot be changed without changing the code. The built-in features are described in the following list:

- Return-Receipt-To: If this header is sent, a message will be sent to any specified names when the final delivery is complete. The mailer must have the `l` flag (local delivery) set in the mailer descriptor.
- Errors-To: If errors occur anywhere during processing, this header sends error messages to the listed names rather than to the sender. Use this header line for mailing lists so that errors are returned to the list administrator.
- To: If a message comes in with no recipients listed in the message (in a To:, CC:, or BCC: line), sendmail adds an Apparently To: header line for each recipient specified on the sendmail command line.

S and R (Rewriting Rules)

Address parsing is performed using the rewriting rules, which are a simple pattern-matching system. Scanning through the set of rewriting rules, sendmail looks for a match on the left-hand side (LHS) of the rule. When a rule matches, the name is replaced by the right-hand side (RHS) of the rule.

There are several sets of rewriting rules. Some of the rewriting sets are used internally and must have specific semantics. Other rewriting sets do not have specifically assigned semantics and may be referenced by the mailer definitions or by other rewriting sets. For example,

```
Sn
```

sets the current ruleset being collected to *n*. If you begin a ruleset more than once, it deletes the old definition.

`R` is used to define a rule in the ruleset. The syntax of the `R` line is

```
Rlhs            rhs             comments
```

An example of how a rule definition might look follows:

```
# handle "from:<>" special case
R<>             $@@             turn into magic token
```

The fields must be separated by at least one Tab character; you may use embedded spaces in the fields. The `lhs` is a pattern that is applied to the input. If it matches, the input is rewritten to the rhs. The comments are ignored.

M (Define Mailer)

Programs and interfaces to mailers are defined on this line. The format is

```
Mname, P=, F=, S=, R=, A=, and so on
{c field=c value}*
```

in which `name` is the name of the mailer (used in error messages) and the `field=value` pairs define attributes of the mailer. The fields are shown in Table 4–5. (Only the first character of the field name is checked.)

Table 4–5 Mailer Definition Fields

Field	Description
P[ath]	The pathname of the mailer
F[lags]	Special flags for this mailer
S[ender]	A rewriting set for sender names
R[ecipient]	A rewriting ruleset for recipient names
A[rgv]	An argument vector to pass to this mailer
E[ol]	The end-of-line string for this mailer
M[axsize]	The maximum message length to this mailer
L[ength]	The maximum length of the argument vector (argv) for this mailer

Address Rewriting Rules

The following sections describe the details of rewriting rules and mailer descriptions.

Special Macros, Conditionals

Macros are referenced using the format `$c x`, in which *x* is the name of the macro to be matched (LHS) or inserted (RHS). Lowercase letters are reserved for special semantics, and some special characters are reserved to provide conditionals.

The macros shown in Table 4–6 *must* be defined to transmit information into sendmail.

Table 4–6 Required sendmail Macros

Macro	Description
e	The SMTP entry message
j	The official domain name for this site
l	The format of the UNIX From line

Table 4–6 Required sendmail Macros (continued)

Macro	Description
n	The name of the daemon (for error messages)
o	The set of separators in names
q	The default format of sender names

The `$e` macro is printed when SMTP starts. The first word of `$e` is the `$j` macro. The `$j` macro needs to be in domain-name format. The `$o` macro is a list of characters treated as tokens. This list separates the tokens when scanning. For example, if `y` is in the `$o` macro, the input `xyzzy` is scanned as four tokens: `x`, `y`, `zz`, and `y`. Finally, the `$q` macro specifies how a sender name must appear in a message when it is created. For example, the SunOS 5.*x* default special macros are as follows:

```
De$j Sendmail $v ready at $b*
DnMAILER-DAEMON
DlFrom $g $d
Do.:%@!^=/
Dq$g$?x ($x)$.¦
Dj$H.$D
```

You do not need to change any of these macros except under unusual circumstances. For example, you might want to change the banner asterisk (*) for security. You might want to change ¦ or to make several hosts look like one host.

An acceptable alternative for the `$q` macro is

```
$?x$x $.<$g>
```

These correspond to the following two formats:

```
nowicki@sun.COM (Bill Nowicki)
Bill Nowicki <nowicki@sun.COM>
```

Some macros are defined by sendmail for use in mailer arguments or for other contexts. These macros are shown in Table 4–7.

Table 4–7 Additional sendmail Macro Definitions

Macro	Description
a	The origination date in ARPANET format
b	The current date in ARPANET format
c	The hop count
d	The date in UNIX (`ctime`) format

Table 4–7 Additional sendmail Macro Definitions (continued)

Macro	Description
f	The sender (`from`) name
g	The sender name relative to the recipient
h	The recipient host
i	The queue ID
m	The domain name
p	Sendmail's process ID
r	Protocol used
s	Sender's host name
t	A numeric representation of the current time
u	The recipient user
v	The version number of sendmail
w	The host name of this site
x	The full name of the sender
z	The home directory of the recipient

You can use three types of dates. The `$a` and `$b` macros are in ArpaNet format; `$a` is the time as extracted from the Date: line of the message (if there was one), and `$b` is the current date and time (used for postmarks). If no Date: line is found in the incoming message, `$a` is set to the current time as well. The `$d` macro is equivalent to the `$a` macro in UNIX (`ctime`) format.

The `$f` macro is the ID of the sender as originally determined; when mailing to a specific host, the `$g` macro is set to the name of the sender relative to the recipient. For example, suppose the sender eric sends to bollard@matisse from the machine ucbarpa. In this case, the `$f` macro is eric and the `$g` macro is eric@ucbarpa.

The `$x` macro is set to the full name of the sender, which can be determined in several ways:

- Can be passed as a flag to sendmail.
- Can use the value of the Full-name: line in the header if it exists.
- Can use the comment field of a From: line.
- If all of these fail—and if the message is being originated locally—the full name is searched in the `/etc/passwd` file. It can also be read from the `NAME` environment variable.

When sending, the $h, $u, and $z macros get set to the host, user, and home directory (if local) of the recipient. The first two are set from the $@ and $: part of the rewriting rules, respectively.

The $p and $t macros create unique strings (for example, for the Message-Id: field). The $i macro is set to the queue ID on this host; if put into the timestamp line, it can be useful for tracking messages. The $v macro is the version number of sendmail; this normally is placed in timestamps and can be extremely useful for debugging. Some people feel, however, that it is a security risk, as it may provide outsiders with information about your network setup. The $w macro is set to the primary name of this host as given by the Host table for NIS+, or gethostname(1) and gethostbyname(3) for NIS. The $c field is set to the *hop count*—that is, the number of times this message has been processed—which can be determined by the -h flag on the command line or by counting the timestamps in the message.

The $r and $s fields are set to the protocol used to communicate with sendmail and the sending host name. You can specify conditionals by using the syntax:

```
$?x text1 $¦ text2 $
```

This syntax inserts text1 if the macro $x is set, and text2 otherwise. The else (c $¦) clause may be omitted.

Special Classes

The class $=w is the set of all names by which this host is known. It can be used to delete local host names. The class $=m is set to the list of domain names to which this host belongs.

The Left Side

The left side of rewriting rules contains a pattern. Normal words are simply matched directly. Dollar signs introduce *metasymbols*, which match units other than simple words, such as macros or classes. The metasymbols are shown in Table 4–8.

Table 4–8 Left-Side Metasymbols for sendmail

Symbol	Description
$*	Match zero or more tokens
$+	Match one or more tokens
$-	Match exactly one token
$=x	Match any string in class x
$~x	Match any token not in class x
$%x	Match any token in NIS map or NIS+ table $x
$!x	Match any token not in NIS map or NIS+ table $x
$x	Match macro x

If any of the patterns match, the match is assigned to the symbol `$c` *n* for replacement on the right side, in which *n* is the index in the LHS. For example, if the LHS

```
$-:$+
```

is applied to the input

```
UCBARPA:eric
```

the rule will match, and the values passed to the RHS will be

```
$1 UCBARPA
$2 eric
```

The `$%x` uses the macro `x` to specify the name of an NIS map or NIS+ table. The special form `$%y` matches any host name in the Hosts database for NIS+, in `hosts.byname` map for NIS, or in `/etc/hosts` if NIS or NIS+ is not running.

Right-Side Address Rewriting Rules

When the left side of a rewriting rule matches, the input is replaced by the right side. Tokens are copied directly from the right side unless they begin with a dollar sign. Metasymbols for more complicated substitutions are shown in Table 4–9.

Table 4–9 Right-Side Metasymbols for sendmail

Symbol	Description
`$x`	Expand macro x
`$`*n*	Substitute indefinite token *n* from LHS
`$>`*n*	Call ruleset *n*
`$#mailer`	Resolve to *mailer*
`$@`*host*	Specify *host* (+ `prefix?` ruleset return)
`$:`*user*	Specify *user* (+ `prefix` rule limit)
`$[`*host*`$]`	Map to primary host name
`${x` *name*`$}`	Map name through NIS map or NIS+ table $x. If the map name begins with REVERSE, it will look things up in reverse to invert aliases

The `$c` *n* (*n* being a digit) syntax substitutes the corresponding value from a `$+`, `$-`, `$*`, `$=`, or `$@` match on the LHS. It may be used anywhere.

The `$>c` *n* syntax substitutes the remainder of the line as usual and then passes it to ruleset *n*. The final value of ruleset *n* then becomes the substitution for this rule (such as a procedure or function call).

Use the `$#` syntax only in ruleset 0. Evaluation of the ruleset stops immediately and signals to sendmail that the name has completely resolved. The complete syntax is

```
$#mailer$@host$:user
```

This syntax specifies the {*mailer, host, user*} triplet necessary to direct the mailer. More processing may then take place, depending on the mailer. For example, local names are aliased.

A right side may also be preceded by a `$@` or a `$:` to control evaluation. A `$@` prefix returns the remainder of the right side as the value. A `$:` prefix terminates the rule immediately, but the ruleset continues; thus, it can be used to limit a rule to one application. Neither prefix affects the result of the right side expansion.

The `$@` and `$:` prefixes can precede a `$>` specification. For example,

```
R$+                $:$>7$1
```

matches anything, passes that to ruleset 7, and continues; the `$:` is necessary to avoid an infinite loop. The `$[host]$` syntax replaces the host name with the "official" or primary host name—the one listed first in the `hosts.byname` NIS map, NIS+ table, DNS, or local `/etc/hosts` file. It is used to eliminate nicknames for hosts. The `${x name $}` syntax replaces the string by the result of the `nis_map_name` indicated in macro `$x`.

Semantics of Rewriting Rulesets

Five rewriting sets have specific semantics, as shown in Figure 4–1.

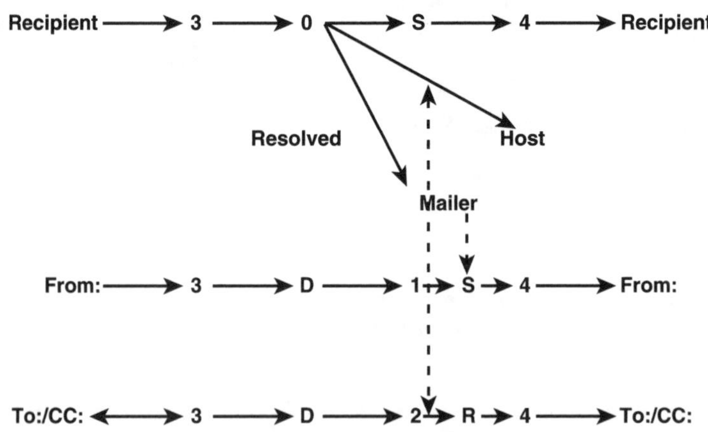

Figure 4–1 *Semantics of rewriting rulesets.*

Ruleset 3 is applied by sendmail before it does anything with any name. That ruleset should turn the name into canonical form, with the basic syntax

```
local-part@host-domain-spec
```

If no `@` sign is specified, the *`host-domain-spec`* may be appended from the sender name (if the `C` flag is set in the mailer definition corresponding to the sending mailer).

Ruleset 0 is applied after ruleset 3 to names that actually specify recipients. It must resolve to a {*mailer*, *host*, *user*} triplet. The mailer must be defined in the mailer definitions from the configuration file. The host is defined into the `$h` macro for use in the argument expansion of the specified mailer; the user is defined into `$u`.

Rulesets 1 and 2 are applied to all From:, To:, and CC: recipient names, respectively. The rulesets specified in the mailer definition line (and `R=`) are then applied. Note that this process is completed many times for one message, depending on how many mailers the message is routed to by ruleset 0.

Ruleset 4 is applied last to all names in the message. It is typically used to translate addresses from internal to external form.

The error Mailer

You can use this mailer with the special name error in ruleset 0 to generate a user error message. The user field is a message to be printed. For example, the entry

```
$#error$:Host unknown in this domain
```

on the RHS of a rule generates the specified error if the LHS matches.

Semantics of Mailer Descriptions

Each mailer has an internal name. It can be arbitrary, except that the names *local* and *prog* must be defined first and second, respectively. Ruleset 0 resolves names to this mailer name (and a host and a username).

Give the pathname of the mailer in the P field. If this mailer will be accessed via a TCP connection, use the string `[TCP]` instead.

Define the mailer flags in the F field. Specify an `f` or an `r` flag to pass the name of the sender as `-f` or `-r` flags, respectively. These flags are passed only if they were passed to `sendmail`, so that mailers that give errors under some circumstances can be placated. If the mailer is not picky, you can just specify `-f$g` in the `argv` template. If the mailer must be called as root and if sendmail is running setuid to root, use the `S` flag; it will not reset the user ID before calling the mailer. If this mailer is local (that is, will perform final delivery rather than another network hop), use the flag. Quote characters (backslashes and double quotes) can be stripped from names if the `s` flag is specified; if it is not specified, they are passed through. If the mailer is capable of sending to more than one user on the same host in a single transaction, the `m` flag should be used. If this flag is `on`, the `argv` template containing `$u` is repeated for each unique user on a given host. The `e` flag marks the mailer as being "expensive," and then sendmail defers connection until a queue run. Note that the `c` configuration option must also be set.

The `C` flag is an unusual case. It applies to the mailer that the message is received from, rather than the mailer being sent to. If this flag is set, the domain specification of the sender (that is, the `@host.domain` part) is saved and is appended to any names in the message that do not already contain a domain specification. For example, a message of the form

```
From: eric@ucbarpa
To: wnj@monet, mckusick
```

is modified to

```
From: eric@ucbarpa
To: wnj@monet, mckusick@ucbarpa
```

if and only if the `C` flag is defined in the mailer corresponding to `eric@ucbarpa`.

The `S` and `R` fields in the mailer description are rewriting sets specific to a mailer and must be applied to sender and recipient names, respectively. These are applied after the sending domain is appended and the general rewriting set (ruleset 1 or 2) is applied, but before the output rewrite (ruleset 4) is applied. A typical use is to append the current domain to names that do not already have a domain. For example, a header of the form

```
From: eric@host
```

might be changed to be

```
From: eric@host.Podunk.EDU
```

or

```
From: ucbvax!eric
```

depending on the domain it is being shipped to. These sets can also be used to perform special-purpose output rewriting in cooperation with ruleset 4. The `E` field defines the string to use as an end-of-line indication.

A string containing return and newline is the default if you are using TCP; otherwise a newline indicates end of line. You can use the `printf` backslash escapes (`\r`, `\n`, `\f`, `\b`).

Use the `A` field to specify an argument vector template. It may have embedded spaces. The template is expanded by a macro before being passed to the mailer. Useful macros include `$h` (the host name resolved by ruleset 0) and `$u` (the username or names resolved). If there is no argument with a $u macro in it, sendmail uses SMTP to communicate with the mailer. If the pathname for this mailer is `[TCP]`, use the argument vector

```
TCP $h [ port ]
```

in which *`port`* is the optional port number to connect to.

If an `L` field exists, it specifies the maximum length of the `$u` macro passed to the mailer. To make UUCP mail more efficient, the `L` field can be used with the `m` flag to send multiple recipients with one call to the mailer, while avoiding mailer limitations on argument length. Even if that recipient exceeds the `L=` limit, `$u` always expands to at least one recipient.

For example, the specification

```
Mlocal, P=/bin/mail, F=flsSDFMmnP, S=10, R=20, A=mail -d $u
Mether,  P=[TCP],   F=msDFMuCX,  S=11, R=21, A=TCP $h
```

names a mailer to do local delivery and a mailer for ethernet delivery. The first mailer is called local and is located in the file `/bin/mail`. It takes the `-f` flag, performs local delivery, strips quotes from names, and delivers multiple users at once. It applies ruleset 10 to sender names in the message and applies ruleset 20 to recipient names. The argument vector to send to a message is the word `mail`, the letter `-d`, and words containing the name of the receiving user. If the -r or -f flag is inserted, it is between `mail` and `-d`.

The second mailer is called ether. It is connected via TCP and can handle multiple users at once. It defers connections and appends any domain from the sender name to any receiver name without a domain. Sender names are processed by ruleset 11 and recipient names by ruleset 21. Messages passed through this mailer have a 100,000-byte limit.

Building a New Configuration File

Building a configuration file from scratch is a complex task. Fortunately, you can accommodate almost every situation by changing an existing file. In any case, it is critical that you understand what it is that you are trying to do and come up with a policy statement for the delivery of mail. The following sections explain the purpose of a configuration file and provide some ideas for what your policy might be.

Domains and Policies

RFC 1006 describes domain-based naming. RFC 822 touches on this issue as well. Essentially, each host is given a name that is a right-to-left dot-qualified pseudopath from a distinguished root. The elements of the path are organizational entities, not physical networks.

RFC 822 and 976 specify how certain sorts of addresses are parsed. You can configure sendmail to either follow or ignore these rules.

How to Proceed

After you have established a policy, it is worth examining the available configuration files to decide if any of them are close enough so that you can use major parts of them. Almost always, a fair amount of boilerplate code can be reused.

NOTE. *Always keep a backup copy of your configuration files to protect against accidental deletion.*

The next step is to build ruleset 3, which specifies a ruleset for your individual mailers. Building ruleset 3 is the hardest part of the job. Here are some guidelines:

- Beware of doing too much to the name in this ruleset, because anything you do reflects through to the message.

- Do not strip local domains in this ruleset. This can leave you with names with no domain spec. Because sendmail likes to append the sending domain to names with no domain, the semantics of names can change.
- Do not provide fully qualified domains in this ruleset. Although technically legal, fully qualified domain names can lead to unpleasantly and unnecessarily long names reflected into messages. The SunOS configuration files define ruleset 9 to qualify domain names and strip local domains. Ruleset 9 is called from ruleset 0 to get all names into a cleaner form.

After you have ruleset 3 finished, the other rulesets are relatively simple. If you need hints, examine the supplied configuration files.

To turn on fully qualified domain names, use the `sendmail.mx` file and replace `Mether` with `Mddn`. Another way to turn on fully qualified domain names is to duplicate the `Mddn` mailer and change its name to `Mether`.

Testing the Rewriting Rules—the -bt Flag

When you build a configuration file, you can perform a certain amount of testing using the test mode of sendmail. For example, you can invoke sendmail as

```
% sendmail -bt -Ctest.cf
```

which then reads the configuration file `test.cf` and enters test mode. For example,

```
ADDRESS TEST MODE
Enter <ruleset> <name>
>
```

In this mode, you enter lines of the form

```
ADDRESS TEST MODE
Enter <ruleset> <name>
> rwset name
```

in which *rwset* is the rewriting set you want to use and *name* is a name to which the set is applied. Test mode shows you the steps it takes as it proceeds, finally showing you the name it ends up with. You may use a comma-separated list of *rwsets* for sequential application of rules to an input; ruleset 3 is always applied first. For example,

```
ADDRESS TEST MODE
Enter <ruleset> <name>
> 1,21,4 monet:bollard
```

first applies ruleset 3 to the input `monet:bollard`. Ruleset 1 is then applied to the output of ruleset 3, followed similarly by rulesets 21 and 4.

If you need more detail, you can also use the `-d21.99` flag to turn on more debugging. For example,

```
% sendmail -bt -d21.99
```

turns on an incredible amount of information; a single word name may result in several pages of information.

Command-Line Arguments

The following sections describe the arguments for sendmail that you can use on the command line. The arguments are briefly described in Table 4–10.

Table 4–10 Command-Line Arguments for sendmail

Argument	Description
`-r` *name*	The sender's name is *name.* This flag is ignored unless the real user is listed as a "trusted user" or if *name* contains an exclamation point (because of certain restrictions in UUCP).
`-f` *name*	An obsolete form of `-r`.
`-h cnt`	Sets the hop count to `cnt`. It shows the number of times this message has been processed by sendmail (to the extent that it is supported by the underlying networks). During processing, `cnt` is incremented; if it reaches the value of configuration option `h`, sendmail returns the message with an error.
`-F`*name*	Sets the full name of this user to *name.*
`-n`	Does not do aliasing or forwarding.
`-t`	Reads the header for To:, CC:, and BCC: lines, and sends to everyone listed in those lists. The BCC: line is deleted before sending. Any names in the argument vector are deleted from the send list.
`-bx`	Sets operation mode to `x`. Operation modes are `m` Deliver mail (default). `a` Run in ArpaNet mode. `s` Speak SMTP on input side. `d` Run as a daemon. `t` Run in test mode. `v` Just verify recipients. `i` Initialize the Aliases database. `p` Print the mail queue. `z` Freeze the configuration file.

Table 4–10 Command-Line Arguments for sendmail (continued)

Argument	Description
-q*time*	Tries to process the queued-up mail. If the time is given, sendmail repeatedly runs through the queue at the specified interval to deliver queued mail; otherwise, it runs only once.
-C*file*	Uses a different configuration file.
-d*level*	Sets debugging level.
-ox*value*	Sets configuration option x to the specified *value.*
-M msgid	Runs given message ID from the queue.
-R *recipient*	Runs messages for given recipient only from the queue.

These arguments are described in the next section.

You can specify several configuration options as primitive flags. These are the c, e, i, m, T, and v arguments. Also, you can specify the f configuration option as the -s argument.

Configuration Options

You can set the options shown in Table 4–11 using either the -o flag on the command line or the O line in the configuration file.

Table 4–11 Configuration Options for sendmail

Option	Description
A*file*	Use the named *file* as the alias file instead of /etc/mail/aliases. If no file is specified, use aliases in the current directory.
A*time*	If set, time to wait for an @:@ entry to exist in the Aliases database before starting up. If it does not appear after that time, rebuild the database.
B*value*	Blank substitute. Default is the dot (.) character.
b*n*	Disallow empty messages to more than *n* recipients.
c	If an outgoing mailer is marked as being expensive, do not connect immediately. A queue process must be run to actually send the mail.
c*n*	Checkpoint after *n* recipients.
D	If set, rebuild the Aliases database if necessary and possible. If this option is not set, sendmail never rebuilds the Aliases database unless explicitly requested using -bi.
d*x*	Deliver in mode x. Legal modes are i Deliver interactively (synchronously). b Deliver in background (asynchronously).

Table 4–11 Configuration Options for sendmail (continued)

Option	Description
	q Just queue the message (deliver during queue run).
`e`*x*	Dispose of errors using mode *x*. The values for *x* are
	p Print error messages (default).
	q No messages, just give exit status.
	m Mail back errors to sender.
	w Write back errors (mail if user is not logged in).
	e Mail back errors and give zero exit status always.
`f`	Save UNIX-style From lines at the front of headers. Normally, they are assumed redundant and are discarded.
`F`*n*	The temporary queue file mode, in Octal. Good choices are 644 (rw-r--r--) and 600 (rw-------).
`g`*n*	Set the default group ID for mailers to run in to *n*.
`H`*file*	Specify the help file for SMTP [Postel82].
`h` *n*	Set maximum hop count to *n*.
`i`	Ignore dots in incoming messages.
`L`*n*	Set the default log level to *n*.
`m`	Send to me too, even if I am in an alias expansion.
`Mx`*value*	Set the macro x to *value*. This is intended for use only from the command line.
`o`	Assume that the headers may be in old format; that is, spaces delimit names. This flag actually turns on an adaptive algorithm. If any recipient name contains a comma, parentheses, or angle brackets, it is assumed that commas already exist. If this flag is not on, only commas delimit names. Headers are always output with commas between the names.
`P`*name*	The name of the local postmaster. If defined, error messages from the MAILER-DAEMON send the header to this name.
`Q`*dir*	Use the directory named in the `dir` variable as the queue directory.
`q`*limit*	Size limit of messages to be queued under heavy load. Default is 10,000 bytes.
`R`*server*	Remote mode. Deliver through remote SMTP server. Default is location of `/var/mail`.
`r`*time*	Timeout reads after *time* interval.
`s`	Be super-safe when running things; that is, always create the queue file, even if you are going to try immediate delivery. The sendmail program always creates the queue file before returning control to the client under any circumstances.
`S`*file*	Save statistics in the named file.

Table 4–11 Configuration Options for sendmail (continued)

Option	Description
T*time*	Set the queue timeout to *time*. After this interval, messages that have not been sent successfully are returned to the sender.
u*n*	Set the default user ID for mailers to *n*. Mailers without the S flag in the mailer definition run as this user.
v	Run in verbose mode.
X*n*	Set the load average value so that the sendmail daemon refuses incoming SMTP connections to reduce system load. Default is zero, which disables this feature.
x*n*	Set the load average value so that sendmail simply queues mail (regardless of the d*x* option) to reduce system load. Default is zero, which disables this feature.
y*n*	Recipient factor. Lower the delivery priority of messages with the specified number of bytes per recipient.
Y*name*	NIS map name to be used for aliases. Default is `mail.aliases`.
Z*n*	Time factor. Lower the delivery priority of messages with the specified number of bytes per delivery attempts.
z*n*	Message class factor. Lower the delivery priority of messages with the specified number of bytes per class.

Mailer Flags

The flags you can set in the mailer description are described in Table 4–12.

Table 4–12 Flags You Can Set in the Mailer Description for sendmail

Flag	Description

C	If mail is received from a mailer with this flag set, any names in the header that do not have an at sign (@) after being rewritten by ruleset 3 have the `@domain` clause from the sender tacked on. This flag allows mail with headers of the form:
	`From: usera@local`
	`To: userb, userc@remote`
	to be automatically rewritten as:
	`From: usera@local`
	`To: userb@local, userc@remote`

D	This mailer wants a `Date:` header line.
E	Escape From lines to be `>From` (usually specified with U).
e	This mailer is expensive to connect to, so try to avoid connecting normally; any necessary connection occurs during a queue run.

Table 4–12 Flags You Can Set in the Mailer Description for sendmail (continued)

Flag	Description
F	This mailer wants a `From:` header line.
f	This mailer wants the `-f` from flag, but only if this is a network forward operation. (That is, the mailer gives an error if the executing user does not have special permissions.)
h	Preserve uppercase in host names for this mailer.
L	Limit the line lengths as specified in RFC 821.
l	This mailer is local (that is, final delivery will be performed).
M	This mailer expects a `Message-Id:` header line.
m	This mailer can send to multiple users on the same host in one transaction. When a $u macro occurs in the `argv` part of the mailer definition, that field is repeated as necessary for all qualifying users. The L= field of the mailer description can be used to limit the total length of the $u expansion.
n	Do not insert a UNIX-style From line on the front of the message.
P	This mailer expects a `Return-Path:` line.
p	Always add local host name to the `MAIL From:` line of SMTP, even if there already is one.
r	Same as `f`, but sends the `-r` flag.
S	Do not reset the user ID before calling the mailer. This flag is used in a secure environment in which sendmail ran as root. This flag can be used to avoid forged names.
s	Strip quote characters from the name before calling the mailer.
U	This mailer wants UNIX-style From lines with the UUCP-style remote from `<host>` on the end.
u	Preserve uppercase in usernames for this mailer.
X	This mailer uses the *hidden dot* algorithm as specified in RFC 821; basically, any line beginning with a dot will have an extra dot inserted at the front (to be stripped at the other end). This flag ensures that lines in the message containing a dot do not terminate the message prematurely.
x	This mailer expects a `Full-Name: header` line.

This part introduces the NIS+ naming service environment. Chapter 5 provides an overview of NIS+, explains how NIS+ differs from the Solaris 1.*x* NIS naming service, and introduces the NIS+ commands. Chapter 6 describes how to add a system as an NIS+ client in an existing NIS+ environment.

Refer to the chapters in this part if you want to familiarize yourself with the basics of the NIS+ naming service and its administrative commands and for instructions on how to set up an NIS+ client.

PART

NIS+

CHAPTER

Introducing the NIS+ Environment

Comparison of NIS and NIS+

The NIS+ Namespace

NIS+ Security

The NIS+ Updating Model

NIS and NIS+ Compatibility

The Name Service Switch

NIS+ Administration

NIS+ IS A NETWORK INFORMATION SERVICE THAT IS NEW WITH SOLARIS 2.*x*. NIS+ IS A repository of administrative information, the foundation for the Solaris 2.*x* AdminSuite applications, and a storage place for network resource information that users can access without knowing the specific location of the resource. NIS+ is a component of ONC+™. ONC+ consists of a set of new and enhanced core services for enterprise-wide distributed computing. ONC+ services—including NIS+, TI-RCP (transport-independent RPC), and enhanced NFS—are completely compatible and will interoperate with the installed base of ONC (open network computing) services, including NFS, NIS, and RPC services. NIS+, which replaces Solaris 1.*x* NIS, is compatible with it. When run in compatibility mode, NIS+ serves NIS requests as well as NIS+ requests. NIS+ is designed to manage resources for distributed systems, make it easier to administer in complex organizations, and provide more security than was possible with NIS.

The main function of NIS+ is to simplify system and network administration, including tasks such as adding and relocating systems and users. A second function is to act as directory assistance for the network by allowing users and applications to find other network entities easily. For example, when using NIS+, you can easily locate other users and resources in the corporate network, regardless of the actual physical location of the entity.

One important benefit of NIS+ is scalability: NIS+ simplifies the administration of both small and large networks. As organizations grow and decentralize, NIS+ continues to provide administrative efficiency. Another key enhancement in NIS+ is update performance. Changes made to the NIS+ information base are automatically and instantaneously propagated to replica servers across the network. You can implement tasks such as adding new systems and users much more rapidly than with NIS. NIS+ provides improved security over NIS. NIS+ lets you flexibly control access to network resources by preventing unauthorized sources from reading, changing, or destroying naming service information.

This chapter describes the differences between NIS and NIS+; how NIS+ information is organized, stored, and distributed; how NIS+ security mechanisms work; and how NIS+ information is updated. It also describes a new feature of Solaris 2.*x* system software (the name service switch file) and introduces the NIS+ commands. Chapter 6, “Setting Up NIS+ Clients,” describes how to set up an NIS+ client system on a network where NIS+ is already installed and configured. Describing NIS+ completely and providing installation and setup instructions for master and replica servers are beyond the scope of this book.

Comparison of NIS and NIS+

To help you understand the differences between NIS and NIS+, Table 5–1 compares the features of the two programs.

Table 5–1 Comparison of NIS and NIS+ Features

Capability	NIS Features	NIS+ Features
Namespace	Flat.	Hierarchical.
Database	Centralized for each independent network domain.	Partitioned into directories to support each network subset or autonomous domain.
Data storage	Multiple bi-column maps with key-value pairs.	Multicolumn tables with multiple searchable columns.
Replication	Minimum of one replica server per IP subnetwork.	Each replica server can serve clients on multiple IP subnets.
Update privileges	Requires superuser privileges on the master server.	Performed remotely by authorized administrators; no superuser privileges required.
Update propagation	Initiated by administrator; whole maps transferred.	Automatic and high-performance updating using only updated information.
Authorization	Anyone can read all of the information stored in the NIS database.	Access control to individual elements within the NIS+ directories, tables, columns, and entries.
Resource access across domains	Not supported.	Permitted for authorized users.

The NIS+ Namespace

The *NIS+ namespace* is the arrangement of information stored by NIS+. You can arrange the information in the namespace in a variety of ways to suit the needs of your organization. The hierarchical namespace of NIS+ is similar to that used by DNS and by the UNIX file system. With a hierarchical namespace, you can decentralize administration and improve security. When Solaris 1.*x* NIS was developed, the basic assumption was that the network and organization-wide namespace would be small enough for one person to administer. The growth of networked computing has resulted in a need to change this assumption.

NIS+ is designed to work best when the information in the NIS+ namespace is arranged into configurations called *domains*. An NIS+ domain is a collection of information about the systems, users, and network services in a portion of an organization. In the sample network shown in Figure 5–1, the domains for a fictitious company, Starlight Corporation, are organized by division.

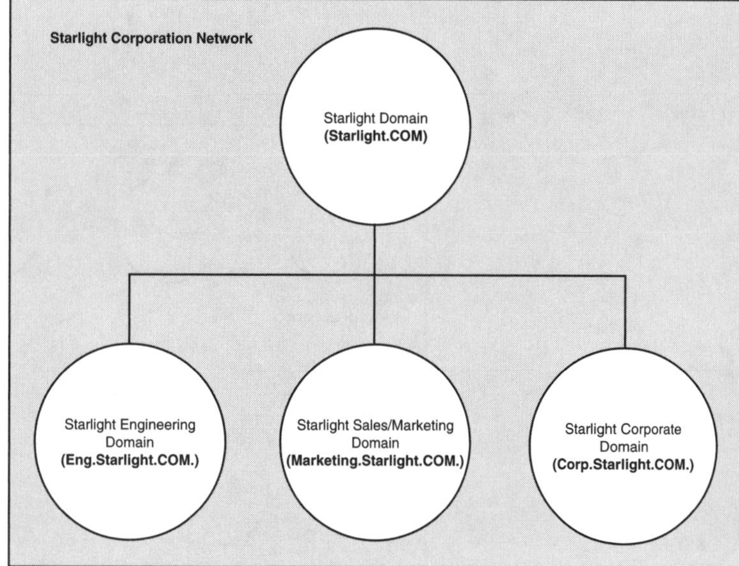

Figure 5–1
Creation of administrative domains.

As Starlight Corporation grows beyond a few hundred systems, the corresponding growth of its NIS+ directory begins to affect manageability and performance. Functional groups, such as Engineering and Sales/Marketing, may choose to create local subdomains and appoint (or hire) autonomous system administrators for these subdomains. These local administrators take responsibility for administering their own subdomains, thus relieving the central administration group of some of its workload.

As Starlight Corporation continues to grow, further decentralized administrative requirements may emerge. Administrators will be able to continue to subdivide the domains along functional groups or other natural administrative lines, such as by location or by building. Figure 5–2 shows how the Starlight network has decentralized the Sales domain.

Each domain can be administered either locally or centrally. Alternatively, some portions of domain administration can be performed locally, while others remain under the control of a central administrator. A domain can even be administered from within another domain. As more domains are created, NIS+ clients will continue to have the same access to the information in other NIS+ domains of the company.

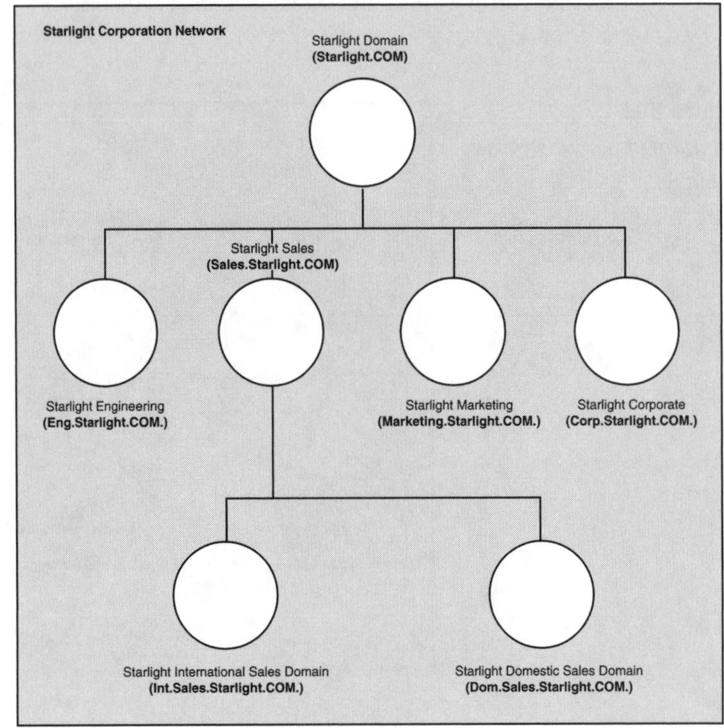

Figure 5–2
Hierarchical domains.

AdminSuite's Database Manager and the NIS+ commands allow authorized administrators to interactively administer and add, delete, or change information in NIS+ servers from systems across the domain or enterprise network. Administrators do not need to remotely log into or have superuser privileges on these servers to be able to perform administrative functions. The following sections describe the components of the NIS+ namespace. NIS+ security is discussed later in this chapter.

Components of the NIS+ Namespace

The NIS+ namespace contains the following components:

- Directory objects
- Table objects
- Group objects

- Entry objects
- Link objects

Directory, table, and group objects are organized into NIS+ domains. Entry objects are contained in tables. Link objects provide connections between different objects. Directory and table objects are described in detail in the following sections.

Directory Objects

Directory objects, which are the framework of the namespace, divide it up into separate parts. Each domain consists of a directory object; its two administrative directories, `org_dir` and `groups_dir`; and a set of NIS+ tables, as shown in Figure 5–3.

Figure 5–3
The `org_dir` *and* `groups_dir` *directories for two domains.*

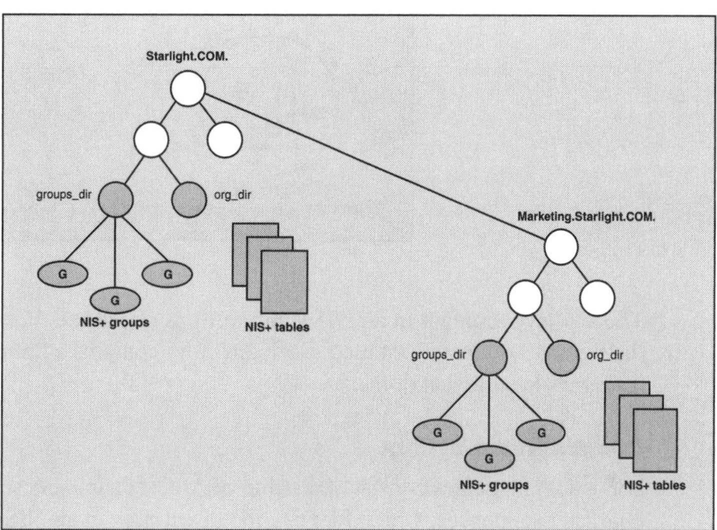

The `org_dir` directory contains NIS+ tables that are used for storing information about users and systems on your network. The tables are described in the section "Table Objects." The `groups_dir` directory stores information about the NIS+ groups for the domain. A directory object is considered a domain only if it contains its own administrative tables in the `org_dir` and `groups_dir` subdirectories. The NIS+ scripts that are run when NIS+ is set up create these two default directories. Figure 5–4 shows the contents of the `org_dir` directory for the Starlight Corporation top-level domain and two subdomains.

Figure 5–4
An example of the domains, directories, and tables in an NIS+ namespace.

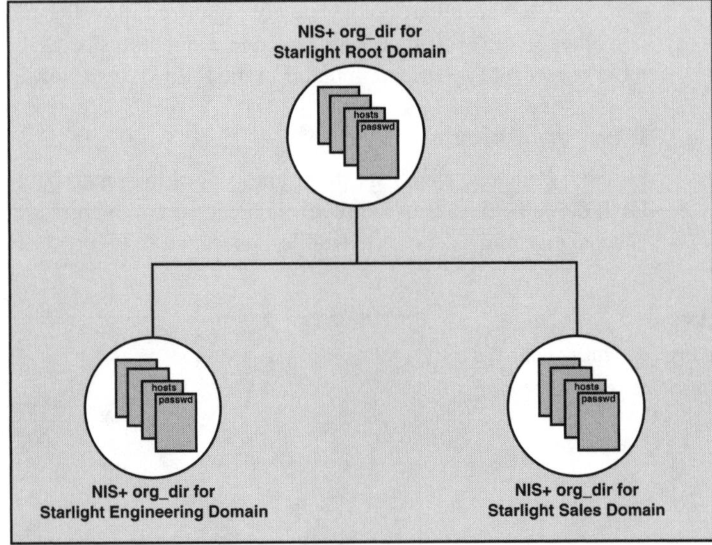

The top-level domain in an NIS+ hierarchy is called the *root domain*. The root domain is the first NIS+ domain installed. Each directory contains administrative information on resources local to that domain.

Domain Name Syntax

NIS+ domain names consist of a string of ASCII characters separated by a dot (.). These character sequences, which identify the directories in an NIS+ domain, are called *labels.* The order of labels is hierarchical. The directory at the left of the sequence is the most local, and the directories identifying the parts of the domain become more global the closer they are to the right, as is the convention for most email domain addresses. Unlike email domain addresses, you must use a dot at the end of a fully qualified NIS+ domain name. The dot identifies the global root of the namespace. NIS+ names are fully qualified when the name includes all of the labels that identify all of the directories. Figure 5–5 shows examples of some fully qualified names in an NIS+ namespace. Note that an *NIS+ principal* is a user or system whose credentials have been stored in the NIS+ namespace. See "NIS+ Security" later in this chapter for more information.

NOTE. *If an NIS+ command requires a fully qualified domain name and you omit the global root dot from the end of the name, a syntax error message is displayed.*

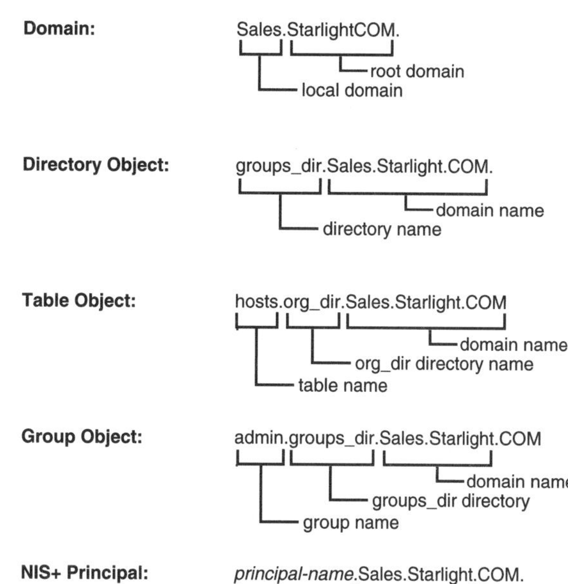

Figure 5–5
Fully qualified names of NIS+ namespace components.

Names without a trailing dot are called *partially qualified.* For example, `hosts.org_dir` is a partially qualified domain name that specifies the hosts table in the `org_dir` directory of the default domain.

Figure 5–6 shows a more detailed example of a hierarchical namespace. In Figure 5–6, `Starlight.Com` is the root domain, `Sales` and `Corp` are subdomains of the root domain, `Int` is a subdomain of `Sales`, and `hostname.int.sales.starlight.com` is a client system in the `int.sales.starlight.com.` domain. The system `hostname.corp.starlight.com.` is a client of the Corp domain

NOTE. *Domain names for NIS+ are not case-sensitive. You do not need to type the names with exact capitalization. The names* `esg.eng.starlight.com.` *and* `ESG.Eng.Starlight.COM.` *are identical for NIS+.*

Table Objects

NIS+ table objects use columns and entries (rows) to store information for NIS+ domains. NIS+ tables provide two major improvements over the maps used by NIS.

- First, you can access any searchable column in an NIS+ table; with NIS maps you could search in the first column only. Duplicate maps (which were used by NIS) are unnecessary. Instead of providing NIS `hosts.byname` and `hosts.byaddr` as separate maps, NIS+

commands can search any column (name or address) marked searchable in the hosts.org_dir table.

Figure 5–6
An example of the directories and domains in an NIS+ namespace.

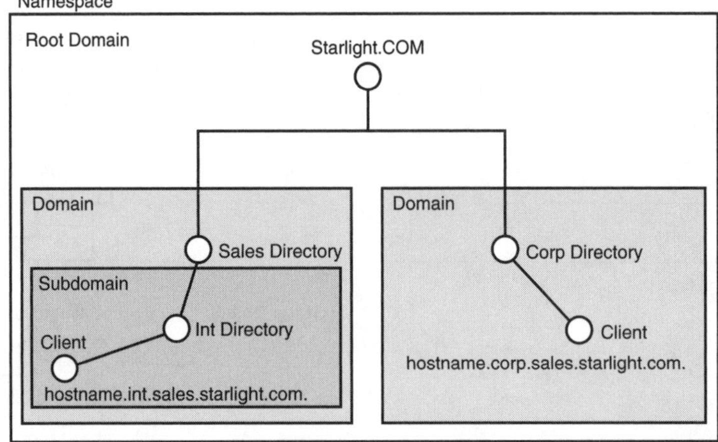

- Second, an NIS+ principal's access to NIS+ tables can be controlled at three levels: at the object level of the table itself, at the column level, and at the row or entry level. If access is given at the table level, it cannot be restricted at the column or entry level. Any access granted at the column level cannot be taken away at the entry level.

In addition, you can specify a search path for each table, and you can create symbolic links between table objects and entries using the nisln command. See the nisln(1) manual page for more information about creating links.

Each table object has its own access security information that controls whether a principal has access to the table object itself. Table security is similar to UNIX file security. See "NIS+ Security" later in this chapter for more information.

NIS+ org_dir Tables

The tables in org_dir provide much of the functionality that you need to administer your network. Although you can create your own tables, you will do most of the standard NIS+ table administration using the tables in the org_dir.

Table 5–2 lists the tables in the org_dir directory in alphabetical order and briefly describes the contents of each table.

Table 5–2 NIS+ org_dir Tables

Table	Description
aliases	Information about the email aliases in the domain.
auto_home	The location of automounted home directories in the domain.
auto_master	The master automount map.
bootparams	Location of the root, swap, and dump partitions of every diskless client in the domain.
cred	NIS+ credentials for principals who have permission to access the information or objects in the domain.
ethers	The ethernet address for systems in the domain.
group	Group password, group ID, and the list of members for every UNIX group in the domain. Note that the group table is for UNIX groups and should not be confused with the NIS+ groups in the groups_dir directory.
hosts	Network address and hostname of every system in the domain.
netgroup	The netgroups to which systems and users in the domain may belong.
netmasks	The networks in the domain and their associated netmasks.
networks	The networks in the domain and their canonical names.
passwd	Password information about every user in the domain.
protocols	The list of IP protocols used in the domain.
RPC	The RPC program numbers for RPC services available in the domain.
services	The names of IP services used in the domain and their port numbers.
timezone	The timezone of the domain.

See the section "Table Information Display" at the end of this chapter for a brief explanation of how to display information about these tables.

The following sections briefly describe how the `org_dir` tables are created and populated. Creating and populating these tables is part of the procedure for setting up NIS+.

As part of setting up NIS+, a set of empty tables is created in the `org_dir` directory. Once the tables are created, authorized principals can add information from existing NIS maps or text files by using the `nisaddent` command or the `nistbladm` command, or by using the AdminSuite Database Manager to edit the contents of NIS+ databases. If NIS+ entries already exist in the table, authorized principals can use the `nisaddent` command to merge NIS map information with existing NIS+ information. See the `nisaddent`(1) manual page for more information.

NIS+ Security

NIS+ is designed to protect the information in its directories and tables from unauthorized access. For example, an authorized user can create a table listing the home telephone number and address of members of the Starlight Engineering domain as part of the domain's NIS+ directory. Access to this table can be limited to all or part of the Engineering organization. In another example, a desktop application can create NIS+ tables of application-specific information that must be available to the entire network. In a third example, confidential personnel information, such as the company identification number and job category for employees, can be stored in an NIS+ table with access only authorized on a very selective basis.

NIS+ controls access to servers, directories, and tables in two ways:

- Authentication verifies the identity of a system or a user of NIS+.
- Authorization controls access to information stored in NIS+.

In addition to authentication and authorization of access rights, you can run the NIS+ daemon, `rpc.nisd`, at three different levels of security, as described in Table 5–3.

Table 5–3 Levels of NIS+ Security

Security Level	Description
0	Does not check the principal's credentials at all. Any client is allowed to perform any operation. Level 0 is designed for testing and setting up the initial NIS+ root domain.
1	Checks the principal's credentials and accepts any authentication. Because some credentials are easily forged, do not use this level on networks to which untrusted servers may have access. Level 1 is recommended for testing only.
2	Checks the principal's credentials and accepts only DES authentication (described in the next section). Level 2 is the highest level of security currently provided and is the default level assigned to an NIS+ server.

You control the level of security using the `-S` option when you start the rpc.nisd daemon. If a system is configured as an NIS+ server, the `rpc.nisd` daemon is automatically started when a system boots. When rpc.nisd is started with no arguments, the default security level is 2. To start the daemon with security level 0, use `rpc.nisd-S 0`. To start the daemon with security level 1, use `rpc.nisd -S 1`.

NIS+ Authentication

Every request to an NIS+ server is made by an *NIS+ principal*. An NIS+ principal can be a user or a workstation. *Authentication* is the process of identifying the principal who made a request to the NIS+ server by checking the principal's credentials. These credentials are based on encrypted verification information stored in the NIS+ `cred` table.

The purpose of authentication is to obtain the principal's name so that access rights to information in the name server can be looked up and verified. All interactions that an NIS+ principal has with an NIS+ server are authenticated.

The benefit of authentication is the protection of NIS+ information from access by untrusted clients, which provides more flexible and secure administration of NIS+ servers.

NOTE. *Protection of resource information in NIS+ does not imply protection of the resource itself. For example, protecting information about a server does not protect the server itself.*

Principals can have two types of credentials: LOCAL and DES. A LOCAL credential consists of the UID of an NIS+ principal. An NIS+ server uses the LOCAL UID credential to look up the identity of the principal who sent the request so that the NIS+ server can determine the principal's rights to access the requested object.

A DES credential is more complicated, and both users and systems can have such credentials. The DES credential consists of the principal's secure RPC netname and a verification field.

Table 5–4 shows the columns in the `cred` table and describes the type of information stored for LOCAL and DES authentication.

The first column, cname, contains the fully qualified credential name of an NIS+ principal. When the authentication type is LOCAL, the first column can only contain usernames because client systems cannot have LOCAL credentials. When the authentication type is DES, the principal name can be either a username or a system name.

Table 5–4 Columns in the cred Table

cname	auth_type	auth_name	public_data	private_data
NIS+ principal name of a client user	LOCAL	UID	GID list	None
NIS+ principal name of a client user or client system	DES	Secure RPC netname	Public key	Encrypted Private key

The following example shows the contents of the `cred` table on the system named `oak`. The fields are separated by colons.

```
oak% niscat -h cred.org_dir
# cname:auth_type:auth_name:public_data:private_data
oak.ESG.Eng.sun.COM.:DES:unix.oak@ESG.Eng.sun.COM:5c8349c1e0eb851a17170efb5a8dd63e4
47210341e565eaf::f8f133ebb68679c958ea4c5e43d61aad5b76c17bba4ffdefad27edc2fcd89cc0
winsor.ESG.Eng.sun.COM.:LOCAL:6693:1,14:
winsor.ssi.eng.sun.com.:DES:unix.6693@esg.eng.sun.com:aacf4fcdc47811b2550f443bca4d2
8c1a8fcf287e81dec24::b11a448a04877fd3dfc48c599fa18cad3d7e7431ebaac7492d731dc2f60517
61
```

```
ignatz.DGDO.Eng.sun.COM.:LOCAL:6694:1:
oak%
```

The first entry shows the names of the columns in the `cred` table. The second entry is the DES authentication for the system `oak`. The third and fourth entries are LOCAL and DES authentication entries for the user `winsor`. The fifth entry is LOCAL authentication for user `ignatz`, who has an account on the system. User `ignatz` does not have DES authentication credentials in the local domain. Only a LOCAL cred entry is needed if the user's home domain is not the local one.

NIS+ security privileges are assigned in two stages: The principal is authenticated (identified) as an authorized user, and the access rights are checked.

Figure 5–7 shows a simplified view of how NIS+ security works.

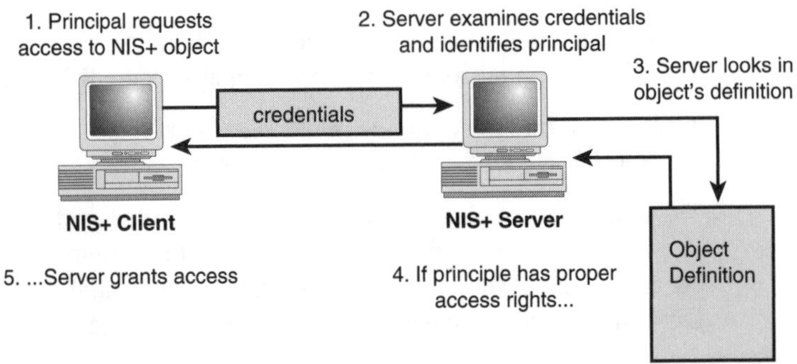

Figure 5–7
How NIS+ security works.

NIS+ classifies NIS+ principals into four authorization categories, as shown in Table 5–5.

Table 5–5 NIS+ Authorization Categories

Abbreviation	Authorization	Description
n	Nobody	A category reserved for unauthenticated requests.
o	Owner	A single NIS+ principal, who was the creator of the object. You can change the ownership of existing objects using the `nischown` command.
g	Group	A collection of NIS+ principals, grouped together to provide access to the namespace. When an object is created, it is by default assigned to the NIS+ principal's default group. NIS+ group information is stored in the NIS+ group object in the `groups_dir` subdirectory of every NIS+ domain.

Table 5–5 NIS+ Authorization Categories (continued)

Abbreviation	Authorization	Description
w	World	All NIS+ principals that are authenticated by NIS+.

Access Rights

Access rights are granted not to specific NIS+ principals, but to four categories of NIS+ principals: Nobody, Owner, Group, and World, as previously described. The four types of NIS+ access rights are Read, Modify, Create, and Destroy, as shown in Table 5–6.

Table 5–6 NIS+ Access Rights

Abbreviation	Access Right	Description
r	Read	Principal can read the contents of the object.
m	Modify	Principal can modify the contents of the object.
c	Create	Principal can create new objects in a table or a directory.
d	Destroy	Principal can destroy objects in a table or a directory.
–	No access	Principal cannot access the object.

Each object grants access rights to the four categories of NIS+ principals: Nobody, Owner, Group, and World. Access rights for each object consist of a string of 16 characters, 4 for each principal category. In the example shown in Figure 5–8, all access rights are permitted for each authentication category.

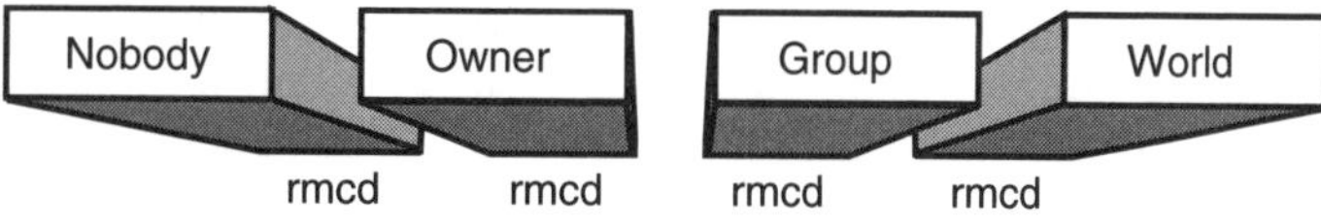

Figure 5–8
NIS+ authentication categories and access rights.

In the following example, Nobody has read permission (`r---`); Owner has read, modify, create, and destroy permissions (`rmcd`); Group has read and modify permissions(`rm--`), and World has read permission (`r---`).

```
r---rmcdrm--r---
```

An NIS+ table or directory can grant one or more access rights to one or more categories of clients. For example, a directory could grant Read access to the World category but only Modify access to the Group and Owner. NIS+ authorization supports flexible and secure administration. For example, the Group access right allows finer control for NIS+ administration. It can be used to maintain security and control as administrative authority becomes more decentralized. When NIS+ domains are first created, a group consisting of central administrative personnel could have only Modify and Create access rights to directories across the network. As the domain evolves and decentralizes, directories could grant these access rights to new groups that contain both local and central administrative personnel. Expanding access rights while maintaining access to existing administrators permits the smooth transition of control.

When you create an object, NIS+ assigns the object a default owner, group, and set of access rights. The default owner is the NIS+ principal who creates the object (in this case, you). The default group is the group named in the `NIS_GROUP` environment variable. The default set of access rights is:

```
----rmcdr---r---
```

You can change these default values in several different ways. One way to change the access rights of an NIS+ object or table entry is to use the `nischmod` command. To use the `nischmod` command, you must already have Modify rights to the object or entry. The `nischmod` command syntax is much like the syntax for the `chmod` command. You add access rights using the + operator and remove access rights using the - operator. For example, you would use the following syntax to add Read and Modify rights to the Group of the `esg.eng.starlight.com.` directory:

```
oak% nischmod g+rm esg.eng.starlight.com.
```

See the manual page for `nischmod`(1) for more information. See the section "NIS+ Commands" on page 115 for a list of the NIS+ commands.

Once they are set, the access rights for a table object define the level of security for that table object. The only way to make entries or columns in a table more secure is to change the access rights for the table object itself. You can, however, provide additional access to the information stored in a table object by extending the rights to additional principals or by providing additional access rights to existing principals.

For example, your company may have a policy that permits anybody in the company to create, modify, or delete entries for a particular email alias. Access to all other aliases is restricted to the owner of the `aliases` table. To implement this policy, you would create the most restrictive rights for the `aliases` table object itself (`----rmcdr---r---`) and grant free access to the entry that contains the particular alias (`rmcdrmcdrmcdrmcd`).

You can use the `nistbladm` command to set access rights to a table when it is created, to set access rights to an entry and a column when you create the entry, or to modify the access rights of an existing table. See the `nistbladm`(1) manual page for more information.

The NIS+ Updating Model

The NIS+ updating model is more reliable and efficient than the NIS updating model. NIS+ stores a primary copy of a directory on a master server. Zero or more replica servers store replicas of the primary copy. When you use AdminSuite or the NIS+ commands to administer NIS+, changes are made only to the directory on the master server. When a master server receives an update to an object—whether a directory, group, link, or table—the server waits about two minutes for other updates so that it can batch the updates. When the waiting period is complete, the server stores the updates on disk and in a transaction log, along with a timestamp, and propagates the changes to its replica servers. In contrast to NIS updates, which usually take a day or more to propagate in large organizations, NIS+ incremental updates are automatically and quickly propagated to the replicas.

The NIS+ updating model allows for more efficient use of network bandwidth because only the changes are transmitted from the master to the replica servers. In addition, replica servers are contacted only once, with an aggregate update to all tables occurring within a short time. If replicas are out-of-date, they ask for updated information.

The NIS+ transaction log model provides rollback recovery and consistency of NIS+ databases, even when a server fails during an update. NIS+ master and replica servers can use the transaction log to automatically repair databases to their state before the failure occurred.

NIS and NIS+ Compatibility

NIS+ provides an NIS compatibility mode. This mode lets an NIS+ server running Solaris 2.*x* system software answer requests from NIS as well as NIS+ clients. When the NIS+ server is set up, the NIS compatibility mode can be selected. You do not need to do any additional setup or changes for the NIS client. The NIS+ compatibility mode is one way that you can gradually make the transition from NIS to NIS+.

Another way that you can ease the transition is to set up a Solaris 1.*x* server to act as an NIS+ server. To accomplish this task, you must install the NIS+ SunOS 4.1 distribution on the Solaris 1.*x* server. The NIS+ SunOS 4.1 distribution permits Solaris 1.*x* servers to act as NIS+ servers without an upgrade to Solaris 2.*x*. The Solaris 2.*x* CD-ROM contains a complete set of SunOS 4.1.*x* NIS+ executables that you can install on a SunOS 4.1.*x* system. The executables are in a separate tar file in the root directory of the Solaris 2.*x* CD-ROM. You must manually install the NIS+ files, following the instructions in the `readme` file provided on the CD-ROM. You cannot install the NIS+ files on a SunOS 4.1.*x* system using SunInstall.

Table 5–7 shows a matrix of possible configurations between clients and servers. The additional rows and columns for ONC NIS systems are included because many customers have ONC NIS name servers from vendors other than SunSoft.

Table 5–7 NIS/NIS+ Compatibility

Server / Client	NIS+	NIS+	NIS
	SunOS 5.*x*	**SunOS 4.*x***	**Any ONC NIS**
SunOS 5.*x*	Supported	Supported	Supported*
SunOS 4.*x*	Supported**	Supported**	Supported
Any ONC NIS	Supported**	Supported**	Supported

*client must specify nis in the /etc/nsswitch.conf file. The SunOS client system can run ypbind and access the ONC NIS system.

** NIS+ server must run in NIS compatibility mode (-Y option).

The comparison between master servers and slave servers is as follows: NIS master servers know about NIS slave servers only; NIS does not know about NIS+. NIS+ master servers interact with NIS+ replica servers only. NIS+ does not convert NIS+ tables into maps and push them to NIS slave servers.

The Name Service Switch

Solaris 2.*x* provides a new name service switch file, `/etc/nsswitch.conf`, that you can use to tailor the name service policy of individual systems to use multiple name services in the Solaris 2.*x* environment. With the `/etc/nsswitch.conf` file, you can specify the following:

- Which name service(s) is used for each type of configuration information, such as password or host IP address
- The order in which the different name services are used for each type of information
- The criteria for search continuation if information is not found or if a name service is not available

You can use the `/etc/nsswitch.conf` file to set flexible policies for name service use and to describe and change these policies after site requirements change. For example, a system running the Solaris 2.*x* environment could obtain its host's information from an NIS+ table, its group information from NIS maps, and its password information from a `local /etc` file.

The `/etc/nsswitch.conf` file also simplifies migration from NIS to NIS+, as both Solaris 1.*x* and Solaris 2.*x* systems can be clients of Solaris 1.*x* NIS servers. In addition, Solaris 2.*x* systems can be clients of both NIS and NIS+, which allows the two name services to coexist during the transition. If you combine NIS and NIS+ domains, make sure that they both use the same domain name.

When you install Solaris 2.*x* system software, the `/etc` directory contains a default `nsswitch.conf` file and the files `nsswitch.files`, `nsswitch.nis`, and `nsswitch.nisplus`, which provide default settings for each of these possible sources of name service information: files, NIS, and NIS+, respectively. An example of the default `nsswitch.nisplus` file is included in Chapter 6.

When you set up an NIS+ server or client system, you must copy the `/etc/nsswitch.nisplus` file to `/etc/nsswitch.conf`. After you have copied the file, you can either use the default file or customize it to suit the needs of your site. SunSoft suggests that you start by using the default file and customize it only if you need to do so.

Table 5–8 lists the locations that the `/etc/nsswitch.conf` file can search for information:

Table 5–8 Location of Name Service Information

Location	Description
files	File on the client's local system
nisplus	An NIS+ table
nis	An NIS map
compat	Supports old-style "+" syntax for passwd and group
dns	Applies only to the hosts entry

When NIS+ searches one or more of these locations, it returns one of the four status messages listed in Table 5–9.

Table 5–9 Name Service Switch Status Messages

Status Message	Description
SUCCESS	Found a valid result
UNAVAIL	Could not use the source
NOTFOUND	Information not in the source
TRYAGAIN	Source returned an "I'm busy, try later" code

In the `/etc/nsswitch.conf` file, you can specify what action NIS+ should take when it returns one of these status messages. The actions you can specify are the following:

- `continue`—try the next source
- `return`—stop trying, and return this result

If no action is specified in the `/etc/nsswitch.conf` file, NIS+ uses the default value `[NOTFOUND=continue]`.

The entries in the /etc/nsswitch.conf file use the following syntax:

table: *location* [*location*...] [*status*=*action*] [*location*]

The *table* variable contains the name of the NIS map, the NIS+ table, or the /etc file. The *location* variable specifies the first place for the system to search, using any of the locations shown in Table 5–8. If you want, you can specify additional locations to search. You can also specify an *action* (continue or return) if one of the status messages shown in Table 5–9 is encountered. An example of the default /etc/nsswitch.nisplus file is shown in Chapter 6.

In the default NIS+ file, local /etc files are not consulted for hosts, services, networks, protocols, rpc, ethers, netmasks, and bootparams unless NIS+ is down. If the entry is not found, the [NOTFOUND=return] entry prevents NIS+ from consulting the /etc files. If you want NIS+ to consult the appropriate /etc file on the local system when an entry is not found in the NIS+ table, edit the default file and remove the [NOTFOUND=return] entries.

NIS+ Administration

When NIS+ is configured on the network, you can use either Solstice AdminSuite's Database Manager or the NIS+ commands to administer NIS+. SunSoft recommends that at least one administrator be familiar with all of the NIS+ commands.

AdminSuite

You can use the unbundled AdminSuite Database Manager to administer most of the tables in the org_dir directory. Consult the *Solstice AdminSuite 2.3 Administration Guide* for information about using AdminSuite.

NOTE. *If you have a large site, you may want to use the NIS+ commands instead of Admin-Suite; displaying large databases can be time-consuming.*

NIS+ Commands

A major advantage of NIS+ over NIS is that you have direct read-write access to information served by NIS+ through the command-line and programmatic interface. You can further fine-tune control of this access using the NIS+ security authentication and access mechanisms.

The command-line interface lets you change NIS+ tables and directories on servers significantly more easily and quickly without first creating text files and converting them into databases.

Tasks such as adding users and systems to a domain require changing information only in that domain's NIS+ directory. You can also perform these operations remotely—from systems around the domain—without needing superuser privileges or rlogin access to the NIS+ master servers.

Because you have read-write programmatic access to NIS+ information, you can develop interactive and innovative system administration applications on top of NIS+. NIS+ is used by all Solaris distributed system management applications as the storage facility for administrative data.

Figure 5–9 introduces the NIS+ commands. It also shows which NIS commands are available for compatibility with NIS+ and which NIS commands are not available with Solaris 2.*x* system software.

Figure 5–9
Overview of name services commands.

Solaris 1.x

NIS commands

ypmake
ypserv
ypupdated
ypxfrd

NIS commands

ypcat
ypbind
ypwhich
ypinit
ypmatch
ypxfr
ypset
yppoll
yppasswd

/var/yp
/var/yp/aliases
/var/yp/Makefile

DNS
in.named
/usr/lib/libresolve
/etc/resolv.conf

Solaris 2.x

Name service switch
/etc/nsswitch.conf

NIS+ commands

nisaddcred
nesaddent
nis_cachemgr
niscat
nischgrp
nischmod
nischown
nischtti
nisdefaults
nisgrep
nisgrpadm
nisinit
nisln
nisls

nismatch
nismkdir
nispasswd
nisping
nisrm
nisrmdir
nissetup
nisshowcache
nisbladm
nisupdkeys

rpc.nisd

Commands available for compatibility with NIS

Table 5–10 alphabetically lists the NIS+ commands, shows the NIS equivalent command (if appropriate) and where the command can be used, and describes how the command is used. See the appropriate manual pages for more information about these commands.

Because NIS+ uses a completely different way to propagate new information, no NIS+ equivalents to the `ypbind`, `ypwhich`, `ypxfr`, and `ypset` NIS commands exist.

Refer to Chapter 6 for examples of how to use NIS+ commands to set up an NIS+ client. Refer to Chapter 8 for examples of how to use NIS+ commands to administer automount maps.

For some NIS+ commands, such as `nistbladm -m` (used to modify a specific entry in an existing entry), you must identify information in the table by using a format called an *indexed name*. An indexed name uses this syntax:

```
'[column=value,column=value]'table-name.directory-name
```

You must include the indexed name in single quotes (`'`) to prevent the shell from interpreting the information between the square brackets as wild-card characters for expansion.

Table 5-10 NIS and NIS+ Commands

NIS+ Command	NIS Command	Used For	Description
nisaddcred*	N/A	Authentication	Maintain credentials for NIS+ principals and store them in the Cred table.
nisaddent	N/A	Tables	Put information from ASCII files or NIS maps into NIS+ tables.
nisbackup	N/A	Back up NIS+ master server	Back up NIS+ master server running Solaris 2.5 release or later.
nis_cachemgr	N/A	NIS+ directories	Start the NIS+ cache manager on an NIS+ client.
niscat*	ypcat	Tables	Display the format or the content of NIS+ tables and directory objects.
nischgrp	N/A	Objects	Change the NIS+ group owner of an NIS+ object.
nischmod	N/A	Objects	Change the access rights that an NIS+ object grants. Access can be changed for four categories of NIS+ principal: Nobody, Owner, Group, and World.
nischown	N/A	Objects	Change the owner of an NIS+ object.
nischttl	N/A	Objects	Change the time-to-live value for an NIS+ object.
nisdefaults	N/A	Objects	Show the default values for an NIS+ principal: domain name, group name, system name, NIS+ principal name, access rights, directory search path, and time to live.
nisgrep*	ypmatch	Tables	Search for entries in an NIS+ table.
nisgrpadm	N/A	Administration	Use to display information for, create, or destroy an NIS+ group; also use to add, remove, or test for members of existing groups.
nisinit	ypinit	Administration	Initialize an NIS+ client or server.

Table 5–10 NIS and NIS+ Commands (continued)

NIS+ Command	NIS Command	Used For	Description
`nisln`	N/A	Objects	Create a symbolic link between two NIS+ objects.
`nisls`*	N/A	NIS+ directories	List the contents of an NIS+ directory.
`nismatch`*	`ypmatch`	Tables	Search for entries in an NIS+ table.
`nismkdir`	N/A	NIS+ directories	Create an NIS+ directory and specify its master and replica servers.
`nispasswd`*	`yppasswd`	Authentication	Change NIS+ password information.
`nisping`*	`yppush yppoll`	NIS+ directories	Update or checkpoint updates to domain replicas.
`nisrestore`	N/A	Restore NIS+ master server	Restore NIS+ master server running Solaris 2.5 release or later.
`nisrm`	N/A	Objects	Remove NIS+ objects from the namespace.
`nisrmdir`	N/A	NIS+ directories	Remove NIS+ directories from the namespace.
`nissetup`	N/A	Domains	Create `org_dir` and `groups_dir` directories and a complete set of standard, unpopulated NIS+ tables for an NIS+ domain.
`nisshowcache`	N/A	Administration	List the contents of the NIS+ shared cache that the NIS+ cache manager maintains.
`nistbladm`*	N/A	Tables	Create or delete NIS+ tables and modify or delete entries in an existing NIS+ table.
`nisupdkeys`	N/A	Directories	Update the public keys stored in an NIS+ directory object.

*An asterisk means that the NIS+ command is one that you are likely to use frequently.

NOTE. *The old NIS+ manual pages incorrectly show a comma after the final bracket and before the table name.*

For example, if you want to change only one column for an existing entry, you can use the `nistbladm -m` command. To change just the IP address for a system in the hosts table, first you specify the new IP address you want, then you provide an indexed name for the current entry. In the following example, the IP address for cinderella is changed from 129.144.52.75 to 129.144.52.80.

```
oak% nistbladm -m addr=129.144.52.80 '[addr=129.144.52.75]'hosts.org_dir
oak%
```

Table Information Display

This section describes several ways that you can use NIS+ commands to display information about table objects and view the contents of the tables.

The NIS+ commands require either a directory name or a fully qualified name to follow the name of the table in the argument. The fully qualified name is the name of the table, followed by the directory where the NIS+ tables are stored and the domain name, respectively.

NOTE. *With NIS+ commands, a fully qualified name has a period at the end of the domain name. For example,* `auto_master.org_dir.Sun.COM.` *is the fully qualified name for the* `auto_master` *table, which is in the directory* `org_dir` *in the domain* `Sun.COM.`

If you use the name of the table only, the NIS+ commands use the information from the `NIS+` `NIS_PATH` environment variable to complete the name. You set the `NIS_PATH` environment variable just as you set any other shell environment variable—from a shell for the current session, or in the user's `.cshrc` file (C shell) or `.profile` file (Bourne or Korn shell). For example, to set the `NIS_PATH` environment variable to `org_dir.ESG.Eng.Sun.COM` for the C shell, type **setenv NIS_PATH org_dir.ESG.Eng.Sun.COM** and press Return. The examples in this chapter assume that the `NIS_PATH` environment variable is set; only the directory name for each command is used.

You can display the contents of the `org_dir` directory using the `nisls` command. When you type **nisls *directory-name***, the directory and domain name are displayed followed by a list of the contents of the directory. In the following example, the client is in the domain `esg.eng.sun.com.`:

```
oak% nisls org_dir
org_dir.esg.eng.sun.com.:
auto_home
auto_master
bootparams
cred
ethers
group
hosts
mail_aliases
sendmailvars
netgroup
netmasks
networks
passwd
protocols
rpc
services
```

```
timezone
oak%
```

The `nisls -l` command displays a long listing of the contents of the directory. In the next example, the client is in the domain `esg.eng.sun.com`. The `T` in the left column identifies each entry as a table object. The second column displays the access rights for the table; the third column displays the owner of the table; the fourth through eighth columns display the date the tables were created; and the ninth column displays the name of the table.

```
oak% nisls -l org_dir
org_dir.esg.eng.sun.com.:
T ----rmcdrmcdr--- oak.ESG.Eng.sun.COM. Sun Feb 28 21:24:46 1993 auto_master
T ----rmcdrmcdr--- oak.ESG.Eng.sun.COM. Sun Feb 28 21:24:48 1993 auto_home
T ----rmcdrmcdr--- oak.ESG.Eng.sun.COM. Sun Feb 28 21:24:49 1993 bootparams
T r---rmcdrmcdr--- oak.ESG.Eng.sun.COM. Sun Feb 28 21:24:51 1993 cred
T ----rmcdrmcdr--- oak.ESG.Eng.sun.COM. Sun Feb 28 21:24:53 1993 ethers
T ----rmcdrmcdr--- oak.ESG.Eng.sun.COM. Sun Feb 28 21:24:55 1993 group
T ----rmcdrmcdr--- oak.ESG.Eng.sun.COM. Sun Feb 28 21:24:56 1993 hosts
T ----rmcdrmcdr--- oak.ESG.Eng.sun.COM. Sun Feb 28 21:24:58 1993 mail_aliases
T ----rmcdrmcdr--- oak.ESG.Eng.sun.COM. Sun Feb 28 21:25:00 1993 sendmailvars
T ----rmcdrmcdr--- oak.ESG.Eng.sun.COM. Sun Feb 28 21:25:01 1993 netmasks
T ----rmcdrmcdr--- oak.ESG.Eng.sun.COM. Sun Feb 28 21:25:03 1993 netgroup
T ----rmcdrmcdr--- oak.ESG.Eng.sun.COM. Sun Feb 28 21:25:05 1993 networks
T ----rmcdrmcdr--- oak.ESG.Eng.sun.COM. Sun Feb 28 21:25:07 1993 passwd
T ----rmcdrmcdr--- oak.ESG.Eng.sun.COM. Sun Feb 28 21:25:08 1993 protocols
T ----rmcdrmcdr--- oak.ESG.Eng.sun.COM. Sun Feb 28 21:25:10 1993 rpc
T ----rmcdrmcdr--- oak.ESG.Eng.sun.COM. Sun Feb 28 21:25:12 1993 services
T ----rmcdrmcdr--- oak.ESG.Eng.sun.COM. Sun Feb 28 21:25:13 1993 timezone
oak%
```

You can display information about each table object using the `niscat -o` *`table-name.directory-name`* command. Information about the hosts table object is displayed in the following example:

```
oak% niscat -o hosts.org_dir
Object Name   : hosts
Owner         : oak.ESG.Eng.sun.COM.
Group         :
Domain        : org_dir.ESG.Eng.sun.COM.
Access Rights : ----rmcdrmcdr---
Time to Live  : 12:0:0
Object Type   : TABLE
Table Type          : hosts_tbl
Number of Columns   : 4
Character Separator :
Search Path         :
Columns             :
        [0]     Name          : cname
                Attributes    : (SEARCHABLE, TEXTUAL DATA, CASE INSENSITIVE)
                Access Rights : ----------------
        [1]     Name          : name
                Attributes    : (SEARCHABLE, TEXTUAL DATA, CASE INSENSITIVE)
                Access Rights : ----------------
        [2]     Name          : addr
                Attributes    : (SEARCHABLE, TEXTUAL DATA, CASE INSENSITIVE)
```

```
        Access Rights : ---------------
[3]     Name          : comment
        Attributes    : (TEXTUAL DATA)
        Access Rights : ---------------
oak%
```

The access rights for the table object are displayed on the fifth line. This table has four named columns: `cname`, `name`, `addr`, and `comment`. Each column has its own access rights, which are displayed after the name and attributes of the column. In this example, no additional access to the columns has been granted, and owner and group have read, modify, create, and delete permissions for the table object.

If you have read permission, you can display the values for a table using the `niscat` *`table-name.directory-name`* command. In the next example, the `auto_master.org_dir` map has two entries:

```
oak% niscat auto_master.org_dir
/bin  auto_local
/-    auto_direct
oak%
```

You can display the names of the columns and the contents using the `niscat -h` *`table-name.directory-name`* command. In the following example, the auto_master table has two columns, named `key` and `value`, and the separator is a space. The `auto_master.org_dir` map has two entries:

```
oak% niscat -h auto_master.org_dir
# key value
/bin  auto_local
/-    auto_direct
oak%
```

NOTE. *When an NIS+ table has many entries, the output of the* `niscat` *command can be quite long. If you're searching for specific entries, you may want to use* `nismatch` *or* `nisgrep` *instead.*

You can create or delete tables using the `nistbladm` command. You can also use the `nistbladm` command to create and modify entries. See the `nistbladm(1)` manual page for more information. You can also look in Chapter 8, "Setting Up the Automounter," for examples of how to use the `nistbladm` command to create and edit automount maps.

CHAPTER

6

Setting Up NIS+ Clients

Security Considerations

Prerequisites

Steps for Setting Up NIS+ Client Credentials

Steps for Setting Up an NIS+ Client

Verification of the Setup

THIS CHAPTER DESCRIBES HOW TO SET UP A SUNOS 5.*X* SYSTEM AS AN NIS+ CLIENT WHEN NIS+ servers are running. To set up an NIS+ client, you first must create DES credentials for the client in the domain. Then, on the client system, you perform these tasks as the superuser:

1. Assign the client its new domain name.
2. Set up the nsswitch.conf file.
3. Install the `/etc/resolv.conf` file if you are using DNS.
4. Check the `/var/nis` directory to make sure it's empty.
5. Run the `nisinit` script to initialize the client.
6. Kill and restart the keyserv daemon.
7. Run `keylogin -r` to load root private key into /etc/.rootkey.
8. Reboot the client.

These tasks are described in detail later in this chapter.

Security Considerations

Both the administrator and the client must have the proper credentials and access rights. The administrator can have either:

- DES credentials in the client's home domain.
- A combination of DES credentials in the administrator's home domain and LOCAL credentials in the client's domain.

See Chapter 5, "Introducing the NIS+ Environment," for more information about DES and LOCAL credentials.

After you create the client's credentials in the NIS+ domain, you can complete the setup process on the client system. The directory object for its home domain on the NIS+ server must have Read access for the World and Nobody categories. If you are adding a client to an NIS+ domain that has existing clients, the directory object probably has the proper access permissions.

You can check the access rights for the directory object with the `niscat -o` command. The access rights are displayed on the fifth line of the output. In this example, the World category has Read access, as shown by the `r---` at the end of the access rights string:

```
rootmaster# niscat -o ESG.Eng.sun.COM.
Object Name    : ESG
Owner          : oak.ESG.Eng.sun.COM.
Group          : admin.ESG.Eng.sun.COM.
```

```
Domain        : Eng.sun.COM.
Access Rights : r---rmcdrmcdr---
Time to Live  : 12:0:0
Object Type   : DIRECTORY
Name : 'ESG.Eng.sun.COM.'
Type : NIS
Master Server :
        Name       : oak.ESG.Eng.sun.COM.
        Public Key : None.
        Universal addresses (6)
        [1] - udp, inet, 127.0.0.1.0.111
        [2] - tcp, inet, 127.0.0.1.0.111
        [3] - -, inet, 127.0.0.1.0.111
        [4] - -, loopback, oak.rpc
        [5] - -, loopback, oak.rpc
        [6] - -, loopback, oak.rpc
Time to live : 12:0:0
Default Access rights :
```

If you have Modify rights, you can change the access rights for the directory object using the `nischmod` command. See the `nischmod`(1) manual page for more information.

Prerequisites

Before you set up a SunOS 5.*x* system as an NIS+ client, the client's domain must be set up and running NIS+. If you need help setting up NIS+, refer to *All About Administering NIS+* by Rick Ramsey.

Before you start the setup procedure, check the items on the following list:

- You must have valid DES credentials and Modify rights to the Cred table in the client's home domain. Use either the `nisls -l cred.org_dir` or the `niscat -o cred.org_dir` command to check the access rights for the Cred table.
- The client must have Read rights to the directory object of its home domain. Use either the `nisls -l` *`domain-name`* or the `niscat -o` *`domain-name`* command to check the access rights for the domain.
- The master server for the domain must recognize the IP address for the client system. To recognize the client's IP address, you must have an entry for the client in either the `/etc/hosts` file or the NIS+ Hosts table for the domain. Use AdminSuite's Database Manager to display the contents of the Hosts database and, if needed, add the client name and IP address to the Hosts table.
- The client must be able to resolve the IP address of the domain master or local NIS+ replica. One or both of these host names and IP addresses must be in the client's `/etc/hosts` file because the client cannot use NIS+ to find the domain master until after it is running.

Steps for Setting Up NIS+ Client Credentials

This section provides the steps needed for setting up NIS+ client credentials from the master server. Before you start performing the steps in this section, you need the following information:

- The name of the master server for the client's domain.
- The name of the client system; valid DES credentials.
- Modify rights to the Cred table.

Follow these steps to set up the credentials for an NIS+ client on the master server:

1. Log on to the master server.
2. Type **nisaddcred -p unix.*client-name@net-name* -P *client-name.domain-name.* des *domain-name*** and then press Return. The first argument is the secure RPC name of the principal. Note that you do not type a dot (.) following the RPC net-name. The second argument associates the NIS+ principal name with the client system.
3. When prompted, type the root login password for the client.
4. When prompted, retype the root login password for the client.

In this example, credentials are added to the master server named oak for a client named seachild in the domain `ESG.Eng.sun.COM`.

```
oak% nisaddcred -p unix.seachild@esg.eng.sun.com -P seachild.esg.eng.sun.com. des
esg.eng.sun.com.
Adding key pair for unix.seachild@esg.eng.sun.com (seachild.esg.eng.sun.com.).
Enter login password: <enter-root-password>
Retype password: <enter-root-password>
```

Steps for Setting Up an NIS+ Client

This section provides the steps needed for setting up an NIS+ client after the client credentials have been created on the master server. You need the name of the master server, the domain name, and the superuser password for the client system in order to perform the steps in this section. Follow these steps to set up an NIS+ client:

1. Make sure that credentials for the client system have been added to the master server. To verify the values in the Cred table, type **nisgrep *hostname* cred.org_dir** and then press Return.
2. Become the superuser on the client system.
3. Follow these steps if you need to assign a new domain name to the client system. If the domain name for the client system is correct, skip to Step 4.

- Type **domainname *domainname*** and then press Return. You have changed the name of the domain for the client system. Note that you do not include a dot (.) at the end of the domain name. In this example, the domain name is changed to esg.eng.sun.com:

```
# domainname esg.eng.sun.com
#
```

- Type ***domainname*** and then press Return. The current domain name is displayed. Check to make sure you entered it correctly. If you need to make any changes, redo the previous step.

```
# domainname
esg.eng.sun.com
```

- Type ***domainname* > /etc/*defaultdomain*** and then press Return. You have redirected the domain name into the `/etc/defaultdomain` file so that the proper domain name is used when the system is rebooted. To ensure that all processes use the new domain name, you must reboot the system at some point.

4. Type **more /etc/nsswitch.conf** and then press Return. The contents of the default `/etc/nsswitch.conf` file are displayed. You want to use the NIS+ version of the `nsswitch.conf` file. If the `/etc/nsswitch.conf` file on the client system looks like the following example, skip to Step 7.

```
# more /etc/nsswitch.conf
#
# /etc/nsswitch.nisplus:
#
# An example file that could be copied over to /etc/nsswitch.conf; it
# uses NIS+ (NIS Version 3) in conjunction with files.
#
# "hosts:" and "services:" in this file are used only if the /etc/netconfig
# file contains "switch.so" as a nametoaddr library for "inet" transports.

# the following two lines obviate the "+" entry in /etc/passwd and /etc/group.
passwd:     files nisplus
group:      files nisplus

# consult /etc "files" only if nisplus is down.
hosts:      nisplus [NOTFOUND=return] files
#Uncomment the following line, and comment out the above, to use both DNS and
NIS+
#hosts:      nisplus dns [NOTFOUND=return] files

services:   nisplus [NOTFOUND=return] files
networks:   nisplus [NOTFOUND=return] files
protocols:  nisplus [NOTFOUND=return] files
rpc:        nisplus [NOTFOUND=return] files
ethers:     nisplus [NOTFOUND=return] files
netmasks:   nisplus [NOTFOUND=return] files
bootparams: nisplus [NOTFOUND=return] files

publickey:  nisplus
```

```
netgroup:   nisplus

automount:  files nisplus
aliases:    files nisplus
```

5. If you need to change to the NIS+ `/etc/nsswitch.conf` file, type **cp /etc/nsswitch.nisplus /etc/nsswitch.conf** and then press Return.

6. If the system was configured as an NIS+ server or client, you need to remove any files in the `/var/nis` directory and kill the cache manager.

   - Type **ls /var/nis** and then press Return.
   - If any files exist, type **rm -rf /var/nis/*** and then press Return.
   - Type **ps -ef | grep nis_cachemgr** and then press Return. Take note of the PID for `nis_cachemgr`. You use it in the next step.
   - Type **kill *PID*** and then press Return. In this example, the client system already has a coldstart file and a directory cache file:

   ```
   # ls /var/nis
   NIS_COLD_START     NIS_SHARED_CACHE
   # rm -rf /var/nis/*
   # ps -ef | grep nis_cachemgr
      root  295   260 10 15:26:58 pts/0  0:00 grep nis_cachemgr
      root  286     1 57 15:21:55 ?      0:01 /usr/sbin/nis_cachemgr
    # kill 286
    #
   ```

7. Type **nisinit -cH *master-server*** and then press Return. The initialization should take only a few seconds. In the following example, oak is the master server. If this step does not work, check to make sure that the master server name and IP address are in the /etc/hosts file. In this example, the initialization is successful.

```
# nisinit -cH oak
This machine is in the ESG.Eng.sun.COM. NIS+ domain.
Setting up NIS+ client ...
All done.
#
```

8. Type **ps -ef | grep keyserv** and then press Return. Take note of the process ID for the keyserv daemon. You use it in the next step.

9. Type **kill *PID*** and then press Return. You have killed the keyserv daemon.

10. Type **keyserv** and then press Return. You have restarted the keyserv daemon so that it re-reads the public key entry in the /etc/nsswitch.conf file, as shown in the following example:

```
# ps -ef | grep keyserv
root  145    1  67  16:34:44   ?   keyserv
# kill 145
# keyserv
#
```

11. Type **keylogin -r** and then press Return.

12. When prompted, type the root password for the client system. This password must be the same one that created the client's DES credentials. The password decrypts the client's private key and is stored in the /etc/.rootkey file.

```
client1# keylogin -r
Password: <enter-root-password>
Wrote secret key into /etc/.rootkey
```

13. Type **init 6** and then press Return. The system is rebooted and the NIS+ configuration is complete.

Verification of the Setup

The following sections describe some ways to verify that the system has been properly configured as an NIS+ client.

Verify That the Cache Manager Is Running

Check to see whether nis_cachemgr is running. Type **ps -ef | grep nis_cachemgr** and then press Return. In this example, the cache manager is running:

```
seachild% ps -ef ¦ grep nis_cachemgr
    root   105      1 51 16:52:17 ?        0:01 /usr/sbin/nis_cachemgr
  winsor   251    240 15 20:11:07 pts/1    0:00 grep nis_cachemgr
seachild%
```

Check the Contents of the /var/nis Directory

When an NIS+ client is set up properly, the /var/nis directory has one or more files. Type **ls /var/nis** and then press Return. The contents of /var/nis should look like this example:

```
seachild% ls /var/nis
NIS_COLD_START
NIS_SHARED_DIRCACHE
seachild%
```

Verify That the NIS+ Commands Succeed

When an NIS+ client is set up properly, you can use the NIS+ commands. For example, type **nisls org_dir** and then press Return. When the command is successful, a list of the tables in the org_dir directory is displayed, as shown in this example:

```
seachild% nisls org_dir
org_dir.ESG.Eng.sun.COM.:
auto_master
auto_home
bootparams
cred
```

```
ethers
group
hosts
mail_aliases
sendmailvars
netmasks
netgroup
networks
passwd
protocols
rpc
services
timezone
seachild%
```

This part describes the Solaris 2.*x* automounter services in two chapters.

Chapter 7 describes automount terminology and the components of automounting, explains how the automounter works, recommmends automounting policies, and tells you how to plan your automounter services. Chapter 8 describes how to set up and administer automounter maps.

Refer to the chapters in this part if you need to set up a new automount service or modify an existing one.

PART

3

Automounter Services

CHAPTER

Understanding the Automounter

NFS Terminology

NIS+ Terminology

Automount Terminology

Automount Maps and Mount Points

How the Automounter Works

How to Plan for Automounting

THE AUTOMOUNTER WORKS WITH THE NFS (NETWORK FILE SYSTEM) TO AUTMATICALLY mount and unmount directories from other systems on the network as they are needed. The automounter supplements the virtual file system table (`/etc/vfstab`) and manual mount and unmount activities with an automatic, on-demand facility. When the user types a command that accesses a remote file or directory, the automounter consults a series of *maps*—described in detail later in this chapter—to determine which directories to mount, which system to mount them from, which mount parameters to use, and where to mount them on the user's local system. The directory remains mounted as long as it is in use. When the user exits from the file or the directory, the resource is automatically unmounted if it has not been accessed for 5 minutes.

Although you could administer the automounter by editing local automount maps in the `/etc` directory, SunSoft recommends that you use the NIS+ naming service with the automounter. Using NIS+ creates a consistent global namespace for your users and a centralized control model for your administrators, and it provides a consistent automounter configuration throughout the domain. The instructions in this chapter and in Chapter 8, "Setting Up the Automounter," are for the recommended configuration, which is using the automounter with NIS+. (*All About Administering NIS+,* by Rick Ramsey, offers complete instructions for setting up and administering NIS+; see the bibliography at the end of this book for the complete reference.)

SunOS 5.*x* system software uses the SunOS 4.*x* automount program with some minor modifications. If you are familiar with SunOS 4.*x* automount services, you can easily set up and administer the automounter for SunOS 5.*x* systems. You will find that it is easy to administer automounting on a network in which some systems run SunOS 4.*x* and others run SunOS 5.*x* system software.

This chapter describes some automount terminology, the automount maps and mount points, and how automounting works. It also provides some example maps and suggests policies you can use to implement automounting in your network environment. (How to create and edit automount maps is discussed in the next chapter.)

NFS Terminology

NFS, which is the SunOS 5.*x* distributed network file system, is the industry's most widely available file-sharing system, which has been adopted and shipped by more than 300 vendors. The terms in this discussion are commonly used to describe how resources are shared using NFS and how these terms relate to the automounter.

Server and Client Systems

The terms *server* and *client* are used to describe the roles that systems perform when they interact to share resources. These terms are part of general distributed computing terminology and are not specific to either NFS or the automounter.

- A *server* is a system that shares (exports) file systems so that they are accessible to other systems on the network.
- A *client* is a system that accesses some or all of its files from one or more servers.

You do not need to set up server file systems in a special way for access by the automounter. As long as the file systems are shared for NFS access, the automounter software can mount and unmount them.

Mount Points

Mount points are directories on a client system that are used as places to attach (or mount) other file systems. When you mount or automount a file system on a mount point, any files or directories that are stored locally in the mount point directory are hidden and inaccessible as long as the file system is mounted. These files are not permanently affected by the mounting process, and they become available again when the file system is unmounted. However, mount directories are usually empty so that existing files are not obscured.

The Virtual File System Table

Each system has a virtual file system table (`/etc/vfstab`) that specifies which file systems are mounted by default at system boot. Local ufs (UNIX file system) and NFS that are mounted automatically when a system boots are specified in this file. The `/etc/vfstab` file has additional entries for file systems, such as swap and proc, that are used by the system. In addition, the `/etc/vfstab` file may have entries for pcfs (personal computer file system) and cdrom file systems.

The automounter does not use the `/etc/vfstab` file to specify which file systems to mount and unmount. It uses maps instead because they are more flexible and they enable a consistent network-wide view of all filenames.

You can mount some file systems using the `/etc/vfstab` file and other files, using the automounter without any conflict. In fact, some file systems—such as local file systems and file systems exported with the `share` command from a server—must not be automounted.

CAUTION! *Do not create entries in the* `/etc/vfstab` *file for file systems that will be automounted. Conversely, do not put file systems that are included in the* `/etc/vfstab` *file into any of the automount direct maps. These redundant entries can seriously degrade system performance and generate much unnecessary network traffic.*

Mount and Unmount

User file systems are mounted when the system boots using entries in the `/etc/vfstab` file. When file systems are not automounted, users employ the `mount` and `umount` commands—which require superuser privileges—if they need to mount any additional file systems or unmount a mounted file system. The `mount` command is used to mount a file system. The umount command is used to unmount a file system. When file systems are automounted, users do not need to use the mount and umount commands.

For a description of the types of file systems and for information on how to share, mount, and unmount files, refer to *Solaris System Administrator's Guide,* by Janice Winsor. (See the bibliography at the end of this book.)

The Mount Table (/etc/mnttab)

The SunOS 5.*x* system software uses a mount table, which is maintained in the /etc/mnttab file, to keep track of currently mounted file systems. Whenever users mount or unmount a file system using either the mount/umount commands or the automounter, the system modifies the /etc/mnttab file to list the currently mounted file systems.

NIS+ Terminology

NIS+ is the SunOS 5.*x* enterprise naming service. Information used by NIS+ is stored in tables, also called *databases*, which can be administered using the nistbladm (NIS+ table administration) command. You can administer some of the NIS+ tables using Solstice AdminSuite's Database Manager. NIS+ implementations of automount maps also are called databases or *tables*. For example, you administer the NIS+ Auto_home database using the Database Manager. You administer the NIS+ auto_master table, and any other NIS+ auto_variable tables you create, using the nistbladm command.

Automount Terminology

This section describes terms that are specific to the automounter.

Automounter

The automounter (also referred to as the *automount program* and *AutoFS*), a daemon that is started at boot time by the rc2 script, runs in the background. It automatically mounts and unmounts NFS file systems as needed. Information provided in maps in the /etc directory have the prefix auto_ and are used to mount and unmount directories and subdirectories that are listed in the automount maps. The term *automounter* in this context refers to the automount program and the functionality that it provides, and the term *automounting* describes the activities of the automount program.

Since the Solaris 2.3 system software release, the automount program has split into two programs: an automount daemon and a separate automount program. Both are run when the system is booted. See "How the Automounter Works" later in this chapter for more information.

Automount Maps

The automounter uses maps to determine which file systems to mount and where to mount them. There are three kinds of automount maps: master, indirect, and direct. Map names must always have `auto_` as a prefix.

NOTE. *SunOS 4.*x *automount maps used the* `auto.` *prefix naming convention. You do not need to rename your SunOS 4.*x *automount maps for them to be compatible with the SunOS 5.*x *automounter. The SunOS 5.*x *automounter looks first for files with an* `auto_` *prefix. If none are found, it looks for files with an* `auto.` *prefix.*

The Master Map

The *master map*, named `auto_master`, is the master file consulted by the automounter when the system starts up. It contains the default mount points `/net` and `/home` and the names of the direct or indirect maps that the automounter consults.

Indirect and Direct Maps

The indirect and direct maps contain detailed information that the automounter uses to mount and unmount the file systems. You can specify indirect maps by using a simple pathname; you can specify direct maps by using an absolute pathname. See "Indirect Maps' and "Direct Maps" on page 141 for more information.

The most commonly used indirect map is the *home directory map*, which contains the mount point and the names of the home directories that are to be mounted automatically. You can use the AdminSuite's Database Manager to administer the automounter's home directory database.

Automount Maps and Mount Points

The following sections describe the syntax of automount maps, the `auto_master` default mount points, and the mount point required for direct maps.

The Default Automount Maps

SunOS 5.*x* system software provides you with two default automounter maps: `auto_master` and `auto_home`.

The Master Map

The master map is located in the `/etc` directory. As indicated earlier, this map contains the default mount points `/net` and `/home`. These default mount points are new with SVR4. Use them as a convenient way to maintain a consistent namespace.

The syntax of the entries in the `auto_master` map is:

```
mount-point      map-name      [mount-options]
```

The full pathname of a directory is `mount-point`. If the directory does not exist, the automounter creates it, if possible. The map used by the automounter to find the mount points and locations of the server's file systems is named `map-name`. Finally, `mount-options` is an optional list of comma-separated options that control the mounting of the entries specified by `map-name`. Options specified in the `map-name` map take precedence over options specified in the `auto_master` map. The `mount-options` used by the automounter are the same mount-options used in the `/etc/vfstab` file. Table 7–1 shows the most common mount options. See the `mount_nfs`(1M) manual page for a complete list of NFS mount options.

Table 7–1 Mount Options

Option	Description
`rw`	Resource is mounted read-write. If no option is specified, the resource is mounted `rw`.
`ro`	Resource is mounted read-only.
`suid`	Set user ID execution is allowed. If no option is specified, the resource is mounted `suid`.
`nosuid`	Set user ID is not allowed.
`soft`	Return an error if the server does not respond.
`hard`	Continue retrying the mount request until the server responds.
`intr`	Allow keyboard interrupts to kill a process that is hung while waiting for a response on a hard-mounted file system. The default is `intr`.
`nointr`	Do not allow keyboard interrupts to kill a process that is hung while waiting for a response on a hard-mounted file system.

Here is the default `auto_master` map:

```
# Master map for automounter
#
+auto_master
/net         -hosts        -nosuid,nobrowse
/home         auto_home    -nobrowse
/xfn         -xfn
```

Each client system has a copy of the default `/etc/auto_master` map. The `+auto_master` entry provides a link to the NIS or NIS+ `auto_master` map. This entry is the first entry in the file in order to ensure that the NIS or NIS+ `auto_master` map overrides information that is specified locally. The `/xfn` entry provides a way for the federated name service to map composite names to a reference. For more information on `xfn`, refer to the `xfn`(3N) manual page.

NOTE. *NIS+ provides backward compatibility with SunOS 4.*x `auto.master` *and other* `auto.` *files. If the automounter does not find any maps with an* `auto_` *prefix, it searches for maps with the* `auto.` *prefix.*

The default `auto_master` map contains a `/net` mount point as part of an entry that automatically includes all of the systems under the special map `-hosts`. This built-in map uses the NIS+ hosts.org_dir map to locate exported file systems on a remote host system when the user specifies a system by name. What this means to users is that they can gain access to any files on systems that are listed in the NIS+ Hosts database by using the usual SunOS commands. For example, suppose that Fred sends an email telling you that a document is available on his system for review. Fred includes the system name—oak—and the path to the document—/export/home/fred/Newprojects/review.doc—in the email message. He may show the path as /net/oak/export/home/fred/Newprojects/review.doc. To print the file without copying it to your local system, you would type the following:

```
castle% lp /net/oak/export/home/fred/Newprojects/review.doc
castle%
```

To copy the file to your current working directory on your local system, you would type the following:

```
castle% cp /net/oak/export/home/fred/Newprojects/review.doc .
castle%
```

If you know that the file is somewhere on the system named oak, but you are not sure of the complete pathname, you can work your way down through the file system, as shown in this example:

```
castle% cd /net/oak
castle% ls
export
castle% cd export;ls
home
castle% cd home;ls
fred ignatz newton magic
castle% cd fred;ls
Newprojects Status Oldprojects
castle% cd Newprojects;ls
review.doc
castle% pwd
/tmp_mnt/net/oak/export/home/fred/Newprojects
castle%
```

If NIS+ is not running, the -hosts map consults the /etc/hosts file. For example, if a user types **cd /net/castle** and the system named castle is in the Hosts database, castle is mounted on /net as /tmp_mnt/net/castle. The -nosuid option prevents users from running setuid programs that are a security threat on the /net mount point.

The default auto_master map also contains a /home mount point and the auto_home map name so that you do not need to make a special entry in the auto_master map for auto_home. SunSoft recommends that you use /home/*user-name* as your naming convention instead of the SunOS 4.*x* naming convention of /home/*system-name*/*user-name*.

The auto_master map is parsed from top to bottom. The top entry takes precedence. Consequently, when you use NIS+ maps to set up a global namespace, the local /etc/auto_master maps should always have the +auto_master entry at the top of the file.

You can add new entries to the NIS+ `auto_master` map and take them away, although you should be careful when you delete entries from the NIS+ `auto_master` map. If you want to change the default mount point, change the `/net -hosts` entry to `/net -null` and define your new mount point. For example, to change the mount point to `/foo`, you would add the entry:

```
/foo    -hosts    -setuid
```

NOTE. *Although you can change the default* `/net` *mount point, SunSoft recommends that you use the* `/net` *mount point to make the automounter easier to administer, to provide a consistent namespace for your users, and to ensure compatibility with future automounter releases. If you have a different default mount point, consider gradually making the transition toward the recommended default.*

When you create new indirect or direct maps, you must add the mount points and map names to the NIS+ `auto_master` table so that the automounter knows to look for them. If you create a direct map, use `/-` as the mount point. The automounter recognizes this mount point as an instruction to not associate the entries in the `auto_direct` map with any directory. See Chapter 8 for step-by-step instructions for creating indirect and direct maps and updating the `auto_master` map.

The Home Directory Map

The home directory map, located in the `/etc` directory, is named `auto_home`. The default map contains a `+auto_home` link to the NIS+ auto_home database.

The syntax of entries in the `auto_home` map is:

```
user-name    [mount-options]    server:pathname
```

The user's login name is `user-name`, which is used as the mount point for the home directory. An optional, comma-separated list of options, [*`mount-options`*], controls the mounting of the user's home directory. If no options are specified, the home directory is mounted read-write. The `server:pathname` variable specifies the name of the server and the path to the user's home directory.

This is the default `auto_home` map:

```
# Home directory map for automounter
#
+auto_home
```

Each system has a copy of the default `/etc/auto_home` map. The `+auto_home` entry tells the client to use the NIS or NIS+ `Auto_home` database. SunSoft recommends that you use the Solstice AdminSuite's Database Manager to administer the NIS+ Auto_home database.

With Solaris 2.3 system software and later, the `/tmp_mnt` mount point is not displayed as part of the pathname, and the local path is displayed as `/home/`*`username`*.

Indirect Maps

In an *indirect map*, you can specify a simple name as the mount point (no slashes). The auto_home map is a good example of an indirect map that mounts a resource from a single server. You can create as many other indirect maps as you like so that you can provide users access to files exported from one or more servers.

The simple syntax for indirect maps is the same as for the auto_home map:

```
key      [mount-options]      server:pathname
```

The simple pathname is *key*, which is used as the mount point for the resource. An optional, comma-separated list of options, [*mount-options*], controls the mounting of the resource. If no options are specified, the resource is mounted read-write. The name of the server and the path to the resource is *server:pathname*.

Map entries can describe any number of resources—from different locations and with different mount options. For example, in this auto_local file, FrameMaker and OpenWindows are made available from different servers:

```
# Indirect map for executables: auto_local
#
openwin      -ro  oak:/usr/openwin
frame-3.1    ash:/usr/local/frame.3.1
```

You could include an integer in parentheses to specify more than one server location, use shortcuts and wildcard characters to shorten entries with similar characteristics, and set weighting factors for each server named. The most likely to be selected is (0); progressively higher values decrease the chance of being selected. For more information, see "Syntax and Shortcuts for Map Entries" on page 143.

Direct Maps

In *direct maps*, you can specify an absolute pathname as the mount point. Use a direct map only if you cannot create the map indirectly.

The simple syntax for a direct map is as follows:

```
key      [mount-options]      server:pathname
```

The absolute pathname, *key*, is to be used as the mount point. An optional, comma-separated list of options, [*mount-options*], controls the mounting of the resource. If no options are specified, the resource is mounted read-write. The name of the server and the path to the resource are *server:pathname*.

By convention, create only one direct map, named auto_direct, and use it for all of the file systems you want to mount using an absolute pathname.

Manual pages are a good example of an entry you might want to automount in a direct map. To show you the difference between indirect and direct maps for manual pages, let's first see how an indirect map would look. If you created an indirect map named auto_man to automount man pages from a server named `oak` on mount point `/usr/man`, it would look like this:

```
# Indirect map for man pages: auto_man
#
man1     oak:/usr/share/man/man1
man1b    oak:/usr/share/man/man1b
man1c    oak:/usr/share/man/man1c
man1f    oak:/usr/share/man/man1f
man1m    oak:/usr/share/man/man1m
man1s    oak:/usr/share/man/man1s
man2     oak:/usr/share/man/man2
man3     oak:/usr/share/man/man3
man3b    oak:/usr/share/man/man3b
man3c    oak:/usr/share/man/man3c
man3e    oak:/usr/share/man/man3e
man3g    oak:/usr/share/man/man3g
man3i    oak:/usr/share/man/man3i
man3k    oak:/usr/share/man/man3k
man3m    oak:/usr/share/man/man3m
man3n    oak:/usr/share/man/man3n
man3r    oak:/usr/share/man/man3r
man3s    oak:/usr/share/man/man3s
man3x    oak:/usr/share/man/man3x
man4     oak:/usr/share/man/man4
man4b    oak:/usr/share/man/man4b
man5     oak:/usr/share/man/man5
man6     oak:/usr/share/man/man6
man7     oak:/usr/share/man/man7
man9     oak:/usr/share/man/man9
man9e    oak:/usr/share/man/man9e
man9f    oak:/usr/share/man/man9f
man9s    oak:/usr/share/man/man9s
manl     oak:/usr/share/man/manl
mann     oak:/usr/share/man/mann
```

You must also create a corresponding entry named `auto_man` in the NIS+ `auto_master` map so that the automounter knows to look for the `auto_man` map.

If you do not want to create directories for each manual group, you can instead create a direct map with a single entry to automount manual pages. The manual page direct map entry might look like this:

```
# Direct map: auto_direct
    #
# Entry for automounting manual pages
#
/usr/man    oak:/usr/share/man
```

This map creates a direct association between the shared directory and the mount point.

You must also create a corresponding entry with the mount point `/-` and the `auto_man` map name in the NIS+ `auto_master` map so that the automounter knows to look for the `auto_man` map and to use as the mount point the absolute pathname from the direct map. In this case, you can clearly see the benefits of using a direct map.

CAUTION! *Be sparing in your use of direct maps. Using direct maps can generate a lot of network traffic because of unnecessary mounting. For example, in the preceding manual page example, all of the manual pages are mounted from the direct map any time any manual page is accessed. From the indirect map, only the individual section containing the manual page is mounted.*

Syntax and Shortcuts for Map Entries

These sections describe the syntax and shortcuts you can use for map entries. The examples show indirect maps, but you can also use these same shortcuts for the `mount-options` and `server:pathname` fields of direct maps.

Specifying Multiple Servers

You can specify more than one server as the resource for one mount point. If you specify more than one server in the `server:pathname` field, the automounter mounts the file system from the first server that replies to the mount request from the local net or subnet. If no server responds, all of the servers on the list are retried.

Following is the syntax for multiple locations for the same mount point.

```
key     [mount-options]      server:pathname \
        [mount-options]      server:pathname \
        [mount-options]      server:pathname
```

The backslash at the end of each line tells the automounter to consider the entire entry as one line, and it makes the entry easier for administrators to read. The last entry line does not have a backslash because it ends the sequence. For example, to mount the OpenWindows executable from three servers, the map entry might look like this:

```
openwin     -ro    oak:/usr/openwin \
            -ro    ash:/usr/openwin \
            -ro    elm:/usr/openwin
```

In this entry, each server specifies the same `mount-options`. You can combine them after the key by using this syntax:

```
key     [mount-options]\
            server:pathname \
            server:pathname \
            server:pathname
```

When you use the syntax that combines `mount-options` for all servers, the entry looks like this:

```
openwin      -ro\
                oak:/usr/openwin\
                ash:/usr/openwin\
                elm:/usr/openwin
```

This example works in exactly the same way as the preceding `openwin` example.

Specifying Multiple Servers with the Same Path

You can shorten the previous example because each of the locations uses the same path. Combine the server names on one line and separate them with commas, using this syntax:

```
key  [mount-options] server1,server2,server3:pathname
```

When you use the syntax that combines `mount-options` for all servers and the names of the servers, the entry looks like this:

```
openwin     -ro   oak,ash,elm:/usr/openwin
```

This example works in exactly the same way as the previous two examples.

Specifying Weighting Factors for Each Server

You can specify weighting factors for each server in the list by putting a number in parentheses after the name of the server. `Server(0)` is most likely to be selected, with progressively higher values decreasing the chance of being selected. If you do not specify a number, the automounter assumes the server to have a `(0)` weighting, and thus the highest priority.

NOTE. *Some older versions of the automounter do not recognize the server-weighting values. When the automounter does not recognize the weighting values, servers with such values are ignored. Consequently, if you want to share automount maps among systems of various release levels, do not use the weighting factors.*

This is the syntax for weighting factors:

```
key      [mount-options]\
            server1(n),server2(n),server3(n):pathname
```

When you use the syntax that combines `mount-options` for all servers and combines the names of the servers with weighting factors, the entry looks like this:

```
openwin      -ro\
                oak,ash(1),elm(2):/usr/openwin
```

In this example, the server `oak` has the highest priority, (`0`), the server `ash` has the second highest priority, and the server `elm`, the third.

You can use the weighting factor for any list of servers, whether they are on individual lines or are combined on the same line. Just place the weighting factor number in parentheses after the name of the server.

NOTE. *Server proximity takes precedence over the weighting value. For example, a server on a local subnet is chosen even if it has a higher weighting value than a server on a different subnet. The weighting value is used to choose between servers that have the same network proximity.*

Using Map Variables

The automounter provides predefined map variables, similar to environment variables, that you can use in defining paths. In Solaris 2.0 and 2.1, the map variables are `ARCH` and `CPU`.

NOTE. *The* `$ARCH` *variable is obsolete. It uses the output of the* `/usr/kvm/arch` *command, which is provided for compatibility. Use the* `$CPU` *variable instead.*

When you include `$CPU` as part of the path, the map variable returns the name of the system architecture as it would be returned by the `uname -p` command.

```
oak% uname -p
sparc
oak%
```

In this example, the `uname -p` command returns the architecture `sparc`.

If you have a server exporting binaries for both `SPARC` and Intel 486 architectures from `/usr/local/bin/sparc` and `/usr/local/bin/i486`, respectively, you can use the `$CPU` command to create a map entry that mounts the binaries appropriate for each system's architecture. The entry would look like this:

```
bin     -ro     server:/usr/local/bin/$CPU
```

With this entry, the map can be used for clients running all architectures.

The Solaris 2.3 system software and later provide additional predefined map variables, as described in Table 7–2.

Table 7–2 Solaris 2.3 Predefined Map Variables

Variable	Means	Command	Example
ARCH	architecture type	`/usr/kvm/arch`	sun4, i486pc
CPU	processor type	`uname -p`	sparc, i486
HOST	hostname	`uname -n`	castle
OSNAME	operating system name	`uname -s`	SunOS
OSREL	operating system release	`uname -r`	5.2
OSVERS	operating system version	`uname -v`	Generic

How the Automounter Works

These sections provide an overview of how the automounter works. When a system is booted, the automounter daemon is started from the `/etc/init.d/nfs.client` script. With Solaris 2.3 system software and later, the boot procedure is split into two programs: an `automount` command and an `automountd` daemon. The startup script for Solaris 2.3 system software is `/etc/init.d/autofs`.

The automounter checks for the local `auto_master` map. When the first entry in the local `auto_master` map is `+auto_master`, the automounter consults the NIS+ `auto_master` table, builds a list of the specified mount points, and consults the `auto_variable` maps it finds listed there. When the first entry in the local `auto_master` map is not `+auto_master`, the automounter consults the local `auto_variable` maps. The startup procedure for Solaris 2.0, 2.1, and 2.2 system software is shown in Figure 7–1. If no NIS+ `auto_master` map is found, NIS+ searches for an NIS `auto.master` map.

Figure 7–1
Starting the automounter.

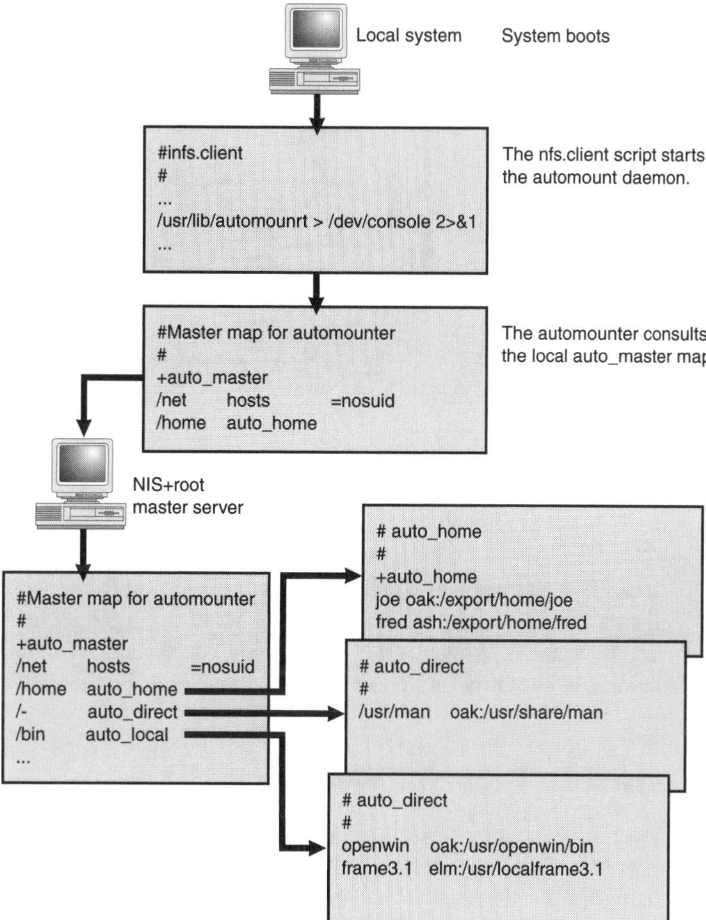

When a user changes to a directory that has a mount point controlled by the automounter, the automounter intercepts the request and mounts the remote file system in the `/tmp_mnt` directory if it is not already mounted.

On the other hand, when a user changes out of a directory controlled by the automounter, the automounter waits a predetermined amount of time (the default is 5 minutes) and unmounts the file system if it has not been accessed during that time. Figure 7–2 shows how the automounter works.

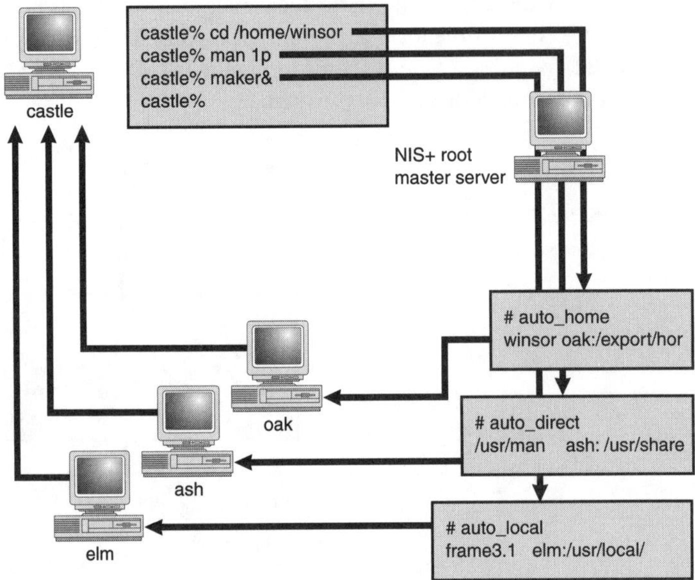

Figure 7–2
How the automounter works.

In Figure 7–2, when the user types **cd**, the automounter looks in the table that was created at boot time from the NIS+ `auto_master` map and NIS+ `auto_home` map and mounts the user's home directory from the server named `oak`. When the user types **man lp**, the automounter looks in the table that was created at boot time, mounts the manual pages on `/usr/man`, and displays the manual page for the `lp` command. After 5 minutes of inactivity, the manual pages are unmounted. When the user types **maker&**, the automounter looks in the table that was created at boot time and mounts the executable for FrameMaker on `/bin/frame3.1`.

How to Plan for Automounting

In these discussions about the automounter, it is assumed that you are administering a network of systems running SunOS 4.*x* and SunOS 5.*x* system software and that you are using NIS on the 4.*x* systems and NIS+ on the 5.*x* systems. This configuration provides you with a global namespace so that you can mount file systems that are exported from any server on the network. It also creates host-independent resources so that you can specify a list of servers from which file systems can be mounted, and it allows you to relocate resources from one server to another without disrupting the user environment.

NOTE. *Although you can set up the automounter using local maps (*`auto_master` *files on a local system instead of on an NIS+ root master server), SunSoft strongly recommends that you do not do so. Decentralized and local maps are more complicated and expensive to main-*

tain, and they are difficult to update consistently. SunSoft is implementing many new automount features in future versions of Solaris system software. Some of these new features will work only with maps stored in NIS+.

Recommended Automounting Policies

Before you begin planning your automounting, review the list of recommended policies in the following sections. They may affect how you set up your automount maps.

- Use the default mount points `/net` and `/home`. If your site uses a different mount point naming scheme, convert your site gradually to use the default mount point names to ensure compatibility with future releases.
- Always use the NIS+ (or NIS) maps. Discourage the use of local maps.
- Use indirect maps as much as you can to minimize the excessive network traffic that can be generated by direct maps.
- Use direct maps only when absolutely necessary.
- Use two-level home directory names (`/home/username`) instead of the SunOS 4.*x* three-level home directory names (`/home/server/username`).
- Because the automounter uses the `/home` directory as a mount point, do not use just `/home` as the top-level directory name on the servers that contain users' home directories. Create a user's home directories as a three-level path (`/export/home/username`). Most importantly, make sure that user disk partitions are not mounted on or under `/home`. Multiple partitions may require separate mount points—for example, `/export/home1`, `/export/home2`, and so on.
- Never use the `share` command to automount local file systems or systems that are exported from a server. Mount them from the system's local `/etc/vfstab` file.
- Do not put entries that are already in the `/etc/vfstab` file into automount direct maps.
- If your site has a mixture of systems running SunOS 4.*x* and SunOS 5.*x*, you do not need to change the names of your SunOS 4.*x* automount maps from `auto.`*`variable`* to `auto_`*`variable`*. NIS searches for `auto.master` if it cannot find an `auto_master` map.

CAUTION! *You should never change the SunOS 4.x* `auto.master` *map name; this name is required by the SunOS 4.*x *automounter.*

Prerequisites for Using the Automounter

These sections describe the prerequisites for using the automounter. Before creating automount maps, the network should be up and running NIS+ on SunOS 5.*x* systems and NIS on SunOS 4.*x* systems.

Each system on the network should have the default auto_master and auto_home maps in its local /etc directory. These maps are automatically installed with the system software.

Servers and the Automounter

Automounter use is completely transparent to servers. A server has no way of telling whether files it shares are accessed using the mount command or using the automounter. As long as you set up your server file systems and share (export) them, you do not need to do any additional administration to plan for or set up the automounter.

When planning for automounter setup, you need a list of servers that have the file systems you want to automount and the path to the resources.

If servers are accessible to user logins, you should set them up like clients. The automounter on a server handles references to local file systems correctly. You must not mount local file systems at automount mount points.

Clients and the Automounter

As long as you use NIS+ to store automount maps, you do not need to do anything special to administer client systems of the automounter. If you use local /etc/auto_* maps, you must manually update them using editors, rcp, or rdist.

NIS+ Maps

When you use NIS+ with the automounter, all you need to do to set up and administer the automounter is to create and modify NIS+ automount maps. Chapter 8 describes how to create, modify, and delete entries in NIS+ automount maps.

The auto_master map must contain a list of mount points, optional mount options, and the names of the maps. The auto_home map must contain a list of usernames and the server and the path to each user's home directory.

You can create additional maps, both indirect and direct, to provide access to executables, manual pages, source files, project files, or any other set of files that are made available from a server.

CHAPTER

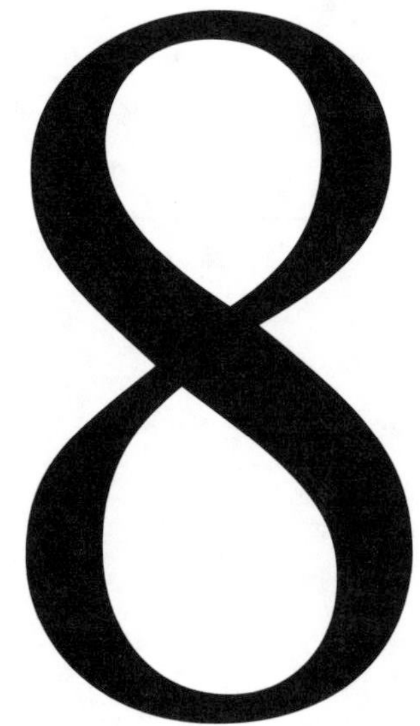

Setting Up the Automounter

Setting Up Automount Server Systems

Setting Up Automount Client Systems

Displaying Information about NIS+ Automount Maps

Setting Up NIS+ Automount Maps

THIS CHAPTER DESCRIBES HOW TO SET UP THE AUTOMOUNTER ON A NETWORK THAT IS running NIS+ on SunOS 5.*x* systems and NIS on SunOS 4.*x* systems. If you need help setting up NIS+, refer to *All About Administering NIS+* by Rick Ramsey. (See the bibliography at the end of this book.)

Setting Up Automount Server Systems

A system that is an NFS server shares one or more of its file systems over the network. A server keeps a list of currently exported file systems and their access restrictions (such as read-write or read-only). You can share a resource by adding an entry to the `/etc/dfs/dfstab` (distributed file system table) on the server and then typing **shareall**. See the `dfstab`(4) and the `share`(1M) manual pages for more information.

You do not need to perform any additional steps on the NFS server to make the shared file systems available to the automounter.

Setting Up Automount Client Systems

Client systems that use the automounter need to have the default `auto_master` and `auto_home` maps in their local `/etc` directory. These default files are included in the system software installation. You should not need to edit these default files.

If you have problems with automounting from a system, check to make sure that it has the default `auto_master` and `auto_home` maps and that they are in the `/etc` directory. If the maps are there, check to make sure that the `auto_master` map contains the `+auto_master` entry and that the `auto_home` map contains the `+auto_home` entry. These entries tell the automounter to use the NIS+ automounter maps. If the entries are not present, the automounter uses only the information from the local `/etc` automount maps.

Displaying Information about NIS+ Automount Maps

The following sections describe how to use the `-o` and the `-v` options to the `niscat` command to display information about the format and the content of NIS+ automount maps. You do not need to be root or be a member of the sysadmin group (GID 14) to display information using the `niscat` command. You do need to have at least read permission for the NIS+ automount tables. See Chapter 5, "Introducing the NIS+ Environment" for more information about NIS+. For complete information about how to set up and administer NIS+, refer to *All About Administering NIS+*, which is referenced earlier in this chapter.

Displaying the Format of NIS+ Automount Maps

Information used by NIS+ is stored in tables on the NIS+ root master server. Copies of these tables are stored on NIS+ replica servers. The automount maps are instances of NIS+ tables. You can display the format of any existing NIS+ automount map by using the `niscat -o` command. The format shows information about the NIS+ table; its ownership and permissions; and the names, attributes, and access rights of each column. Use the `niscat -o` command for information such as the permissions for the map and the names of the columns.

The syntax of the `niscat -o` command is the following:

```
niscat -o table-name.directory.domain-name.
```

For NIS+ automount tables, the more specific syntax is the following:

```
niscat -o auto_name.org_dir.domain-name.
```

NOTE. *NIS+ tables require a fully qualified domain name—the name of the map, the directory where the map is stored (*`org_dir`*), and the domain name, which must be followed by a dot (.). If you omit the trailing dot, a syntax error is displayed. If the* `NIS_PATH` *environment variable is set, then you do not have to specify the complete path to the* `org_dir` *directory. You can type* ***table-name.directory*** *(with no trailing dot) and press Return. The examples in this book use the fully qualified domain name. See Part 2 for more information about NIS+.*

Format information about the NIS+ `auto_home` map in the `sun.COM.` domain is displayed in the following example:

```
oak% niscat -o auto_home.org_dir.sun.COM.
Object Name   : auto_home
Owner         : oak.sun.COM.
Group         : admin.sun.COM
Domain        : org_dir.sun.COM.
Access Rights : ----rmcdrmcdr---
Time to Live  : 12:0:0
Object Type   : TABLE
Table Type          : automount_map
Number of Columns   : 2
Character Separator :
Search Path         :
Columns             :
        [0]     Name          : key
                Attributes    : (SEARCHABLE, TEXTUAL DATA, CASE SENSITIVE)
                Access Rights : ----------------
        [1]     Name          : value
                Attributes    : (TEXTUAL DATA)
                Access Rights : ----------------
oak%
```

See Part 2 for more information on NIS+ security and on how to interpret that information.

Displaying the Contents of NIS+ Automount Maps

You can display the content (or value) of any existing NIS+ automount map's columns by using the `niscat -v` command. Use this command when you want to determine the values set for an automount map or to verify that an entry has been created successfully.

The syntax of the `niscat -v` command is as follows:

```
niscat -v table-name.directory.domain-name.
```

For NIS+ automount tables, the more specific syntax is the following:

```
niscat -v auto_name.org_dir.domain-name.
```

In the following example, the NIS+ `auto_home` map for the `domain sun.COM.` contains only one entry; the user `winsor` automounts a home directory from `oak:/export/home/winsor`.

```
oak% niscat -v auto_home.org_dir.sun.COM.
winsor  oak:/export/home/winsor
oak%
```

NOTE. *The* `niscat` *command displays the values for the NIS+ table you specify as the argument to the command. The output lists the file systems that can be mounted but does not indicate whether the file systems are mounted.*

Setting Up NIS+ Automount Maps

The setup and administration of automounting on a network—running NIS+ on SunOS 5.*x* systems and NIS on SunOS 4.*x* systems—involves creating and maintaining NIS+ automount maps. The steps in the following sections describe how to create these maps on the NIS+ root master server. See "Administering NIS+ Automount Maps" later in this chapter for information on how to modify existing maps.

Setting Up the auto_home Map

The `auto_home` map is created when you set up the NIS+ root master server. You do not need to create it separately. If you have AdminSuite's Database Manager, you can use it to read or edit the contents of this map and to set up home directory information for your users.

Follow these steps to set up your initial entries in the Auto_home database:

1. Make a list of all of the usernames. For each username, indicate the server used and the path to the user's home directory.
2. Type **solstice &** and press Return to start the AdminSuite. The AdminSuite window is displayed.
3. Click SELECT on the Database Manager icon. The Load Database window is displayed.
4. Choose the name service used on your network.

5. Check to see if the domain or the host name is correct. If not, type the domain or host name you want to access.
6. Choose the `Auto_home` file.
7. Click on the OK button. The Database Manager main window is displayed.
8. For each user account:
   a. Type the name of the user in the User Name text field.
   b. Type ***server-name:pathname*** in the Path text field.
   c. Click SELECT or OK.

NOTE. *You do not need to make an entry for the* `auto_home` *map in the NIS+* `auto_master` *map. The entry is already included in the default* `auto_master` *map. Consult* All About Administering NIS+ *(mentioned earlier) for information on how to set up NIS+ and how to convert the contents of NIS maps into NIS+ tables.*

Setting Up Indirect Maps

Use the NIS+ command `nistbladm` to create and edit indirect maps on the NIS+ root master server.

NOTE. *The* `nistbladm` *command requires a fully qualified name for the table—that is, the name of the table, followed by the directory where the NIS+ tables are stored and the domain name, respectively. Note that for NIS+ commands, the domain name of a fully qualified name ends in a period. For example,* `auto_master.org_dir.Sun.COM.` *is the fully qualified name for the* `auto_master` *table, which is in the directory* `org_dir` *in the domain* `Sun.COM.`

1. Decide which indirect maps you want to create. Make a list of the mount points, the servers, and the pathnames for each indirect map.
2. Log on to the NIS+ root master server. If you are a member of the group that has permission to edit NIS+ automount tables, you can edit the tables as yourself. Otherwise, you must become superuser on the NIS+ root master.
3. For each indirect map you want to create, type

   ```
   nistbladm -c automount_map key=S value=S auto_table-name.org_dir.domain-name.
   ```

   and then press Return. The -c option creates the table, assigns it the table type automount, creates two columns named key and value—which are searchable—and assigns the table name auto_table-name. Note that any mount options you specify are part of the value.
4. For each entry in the table, type

   ```
   nistbladm -a key=mount-point value=options,pathname
   auto_table-name.org_dir.domain-name.
   ```

and then press Return. The `-a` option adds the entry to the table you specify, and the values are assigned to the columns.

5. To display the values in the table, type

   `niscat -v auto_table-name.org_dir.domain-name.`

   and then press Return.

6. For each map you create, you must add an entry to the `auto_master` map.

   a. To display the names of the columns in the `auto_master` map, type

      `niscat -o auto_master.org_dir.`*`domain-name`***`.`**

      and then press Return.

   b. For each entry, type

      `nistbladm -a key=mount-point value=map-name auto_master.org_dir.domain-name.`

      and then press Return.

The `auto_master` map is only read at boot time or when the automounter is started. After you have completed creating new maps and have added the mount point and map name to the `auto_master` map, you must stop the automounter and restart it. With Solaris 2.3 and newer, you do not need to stop and restart the automounter. Instead, just run the `automount` command.

NOTE. *For Solaris 2.2 and later, you can restart the automounter and read the* `auto_master` *map by booting the system. To avoid interrupting services, however, I suggest that you restart the automounter from the command line.*

Follow these steps to stop the automounter and restart it:

1. Become superuser on the system on which you changed the `auto_master` map.
2. Type **ps -ef | grep automount** and then press Return.
3. Type **kill -1** PID and then press Return. Note the PID of the process. It will be used in the next step.
4. Type **/usr/lib/nfs/automount** and then press Return.

CAUTION! *Never use the* `-9` *option to kill the automounter.*

In the following example, I create an indirect `automount_map` named `auto_local` in the `org_dir` domain for `sun.COM`. We enter two rows in the table, add the indirect map to the NIS+ `auto_master` table, and stop and restart the automounter.

```
oak% su
Password:
oak# nistbladm -c automount_map key=S value=S auto_local.org_dir.sun.COM.
oak# nistbladm -a key=openwin value=oak:/usr/openwin auto_local.org_dir.sun.COM.
oak# nistbladm -a key=frame3.1 value=ash:/usr/local/frame3.1
auto_local.org_dir.sun.COM.
```

```
oak# niscat -v auto_local.org_dir.sun.COM.
openwin  oak:/usr/openwin
frame3.1  ash:/usr/local/frame3.1
oak# niscat -o auto_master.org_dir.sun.COM.
Object Name   : auto_master
Owner         : oak.sun.COM.
Group         : admin.sun.COM
Domain        : org_dir.sun.COM.
Access Rights : ----rmcdrmcdr---
Time to Live  : 12:0:0
Object Type   : TABLE
Table Type          : automount_map
Number of Columns   : 2
Character Separator :
Search Path         :
Columns             :
        [0]     Name          : key
                Attributes    : (SEARCHABLE, TEXTUAL DATA, CASE SENSITIVE)
                Access Rights : ----------------
        [1]     Name          : value
                Attributes    : (TEXTUAL DATA)
                Access Rights : ----------------
oak# nistbladm -a key=/bin value=auto_local auto_master.org_dir.sun.COM.
oak# niscat -v auto_master.org_dir.sun.COM.
/bin auto_local
oak# ps -ef ¦ grep automount
 root  131   1 16  21:18:47 ?      0:00  /usr/lib/nfs/automount
 root  407 398 14  23:14:00 pts/3 0:00 grep automount
oak# kill -1 131
oak# /usr/lib/nfs/automount
oak#
```

Setting Up a Direct Map

You can set up a direct map in the same way that you set up indirect maps—using the NIS+ `nistbladm` command. The only differences are that, by convention, the direct map is named `auto_direct` and you use the complete pathname in the key field. By convention, all direct mounts are included in the map named `auto_direct`.

See the section "Setting Up Indirect Maps" earlier in the chapter for complete instructions.

The following example sets up a direct map named `auto_direct`—with one entry for automounting manual pages—and adds it to the `auto_master` map. At the end of the example, the automounter is stopped and then restarted.

```
oak% su
Password:
oak# nistbladm -c automount_map key=S value=S auto_direct.org_dir.sun.COM.
oak# nistbladm -a key=/usr/man value=-ro,oak:/usr/share/man
auto_direct.org_dir.sun.COM.
oak# niscat -v auto_local.org_dir.sun.COM.
/usr/man  -ro  oak:/usr/share/man
oak# niscat -o auto_master.org_dir
Object Name   : auto_master
```

```
Owner          : oak.sun.COM.
Group          : admin.sun.COM
Domain         : org_dir.sun.COM.
Access Rights  : ----rmcdrmcdr---
Time to Live   : 12:0:0
Object Type    : TABLE
Table Type           : automount_map
Number of Columns    : 2
Character Separator  :
Search Path          :
Columns              :
        [0]     Name           : key
                Attributes     : (SEARCHABLE, TEXTUAL DATA, CASE SENSITIVE)
                Access Rights  : ----------------
        [1]     Name           : value
                Attributes     : (TEXTUAL DATA)
                Access Rights  : ----------------
oak# nistbladm -a key=/- value=auto_direct auto_master.org_dir.sun.COM.
oak# niscat -v auto_master.org_dir.sun.COM.
/bin auto_local
/- auto_direct
oak# ps -ef ¦ grep automount
 root  138    1 16  21:18:47 ?      0:00  /usr/lib/nfs/automount
 root  412 398 14  23:14:00 pts/3 0:00 grep automount
oak# kill -1 138
oak# /usr/lib/nfs/automount
oak#
```

Setting Up the Master Map

When the NIS+ root master server is configured, the NIS+ `auto_master` map is created automatically. You do not need to create it as a separate step.

You do, however, need to provide an entry in the NIS+ `auto_master` map for each direct map and indirect map that you create.

The section "Setting Up Indirect Maps" contains information on how to edit the NIS+ `auto_master` map. That information is summarized here for your reference.

Follow these steps to add an entry to the NIS+ `auto_master` map:

1. Display the names of the columns in the `auto_master` map by typing **niscat -o auto_master.org_dir.*domain-name*.** and then pressing Return.
2. To add each entry, type **nistbladm -a key=*mount-point* value=*map-name* auto_master.org_dir.*domain-name***. and then press Return.
3. Stop and restart the automounter. (Remember that you do not need to do this for Solaris 2.3 and later releases—just run the `automount` command.)

Administering NIS+ Automount Maps

The following sections describe how to modify entries in existing automount maps and how to delete entries from NIS+ automount maps.

Modifying NIS+ Automount Maps

You can use the -A option for nistbladm to force an overwrite of information in an existing NIS+ automount map.

The syntax for the nistbladm -A option follows. You must specify a value for each of the columns in the table.

```
nistbladm -A column= ... table-name.domain-name.
```

For NIS+ automount tables, the more specific syntax is the following:

```
nistbladm -A key= value= auto_name.org_dir.domain-name.
```

In the next example, the administrator typed ***key=bin*** instead of ***key=/bin*** for the auto_local entry in the auto_master table. When the system booted, the automounter displayed an error message informing the administrator that the name bin in the auto_master table needed to be changed to /bin.

This is how the administrator changed the entry using the nistbladm -A command:

```
oak% nistbladm -A key=/bin value=auto_local auto_master.org_dir.sun.COM.
oak%
```

Deleting Entries from NIS+ Automount Maps

You can delete rows from NIS+ automount maps by using the nistbladm -r command and specifying one of the columns.

This is the syntax for the nistbladm -r option:

```
nistbladm -r column= table-name.domain-name.
```

For NIS+ automount tables, the more specific syntax is the following:

```
nistbladm -r column= auto_name.org_dir.domain-name.
```

If you create an incorrect entry, you can delete it. The administrator who created the key=bin value=auto_local entry in the NIS+ auto_master map could have deleted the entry as follows and then created a new one:

```
oak% niscat -v auto_master.org_dir.sun.COM.
bin  auto_local
/-  auto_direct
oak% nistbladm -r key=bin auto_master.org_dir.sun.COM.
oak% niscat -v auto_master.org_dir.sun.COM.
/-  auto_direct
oak% nistbladm -a key=/bin value=auto_local auto_master,org_dir.sun.COM.
oak% niscat -v auto_master.org_dir.sun.COM.
bin  auto_local
/-  auto_direct
oak%
```

This part describes the Solaris 2.*x* Service Access Facility (SAF) in three chapters.

Chapter 9 provides an overview of the SAF and describes the port monitors and services used by the SAF. Chapter 10 describes how to set up and administer the SAF for modems and terminals. Chapter 11 describes how to set up and administer the SAF for printers and how to troubleshoot printing problems.

Refer to the chapters in this part if you need to set up a new SAF service for terminals, modems, or printers or to modify an existing one.

PART

4

Service Access Facility

CHAPTER

Understanding the Service Access Facility

THE SERVICE ACCESS FACILITY (SAF) IS A GROUP OF DAEMONS AND ADMINISTRATIVE commands that provide a flexible administrative framework for managing service requests in an open-systems environment. You can use the SAF to set up and administer port monitors so that users can log in from a terminal or a modem and can use network printing resources. The SAF replaces the SunOS 4.*x* `getty`, `login`, and `stty` commands and the `/etc/gettytab` and `/etc/ttytab` files. SAF controls and configures terminals and printers using the terminfo database.

You can use the Admintool: Serial Ports graphical user interface to the SAF to set up and configure modems and character terminals on a local system. See "Admintool: Serial Ports and SAF" on page 183 for more information. If you have Solstice AdminSuite available, you can use its Serial Port Monitor graphical user interface to set up and configure modems and character terminals remotely.

Benefits of the SAF

The SAF is an open-systems solution that controls how users access their UNIX system through TTY devices and local area networks. The SAF offers well-defined interfaces so that customers and value-added resellers can easily add new features and configure existing ones.

Flexibility is an important requirement in an open-systems environment. Service of incoming connection requests must be available regardless of the location or connection path of the requester. Both local and remote requests must be handled, as much as possible, independently of the available network transports.

Restrictions in previous System V and BSD-based versions of UNIX prevented this type of open-systems computing environment. Those restrictions included:

- Lack of selective access control.
- Inflexible `getty` process. Only the login service was provided because it was hard-wired in.
- Difficulty in selectively disabling/enabling login service.
- Impossibility of scaling an increasing number of ports because of the model of one `getty` per potential access port.
- Inaccuracy of `/etc/utmp` in accounting for remote services.
- Mixed or no authentication for non-RPC and TCP/IP requests.

You can use the Solaris 2.*x* SAF framework if you want to create a complex application, such as the banking database service shown in Figure 9–1.

Figure 9–1
A typical bank database server.

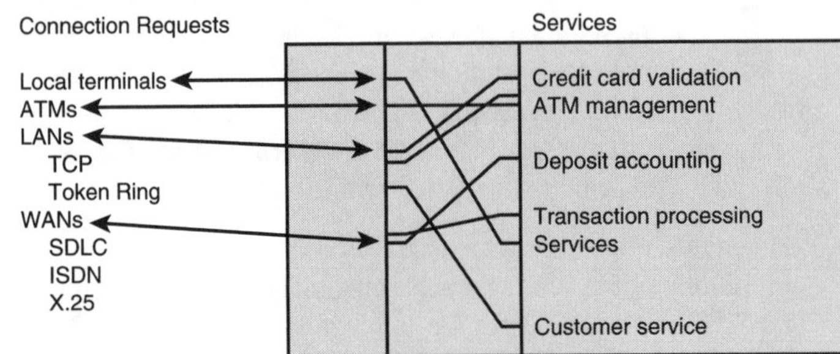

The left side of the figure shows incoming connection requests for services—some from local terminals, others from automatic teller machines (ATMs). The right side shows the service that is provided. Many requests come from local area networks that are running a variety of different transport protocols. Bank networks usually have wide-area network connections over a variety of datalink layers, such as X.25, SDLC, frame relay, and ISDN.

The SAF Daemons

The SAF uses the Service Access Controller daemon (sac) to oversee all of the SAF port monitors. The sac daemon is started at boot time at run level 2 by `init`.

The following two port monitors watch for activity on a port:

- The ttymon port monitor handles requests for login services. Solaris 2.*x* provides a default set of ttymon services for use with a standalone system. You need to set up a ttymon port monitor to process login requests from modems and additional terminals (such as Wyse or VT terminals) if you configure them for a system.
- The listen port monitor handles requests for network services, such as remote printing and remote file access. You need to set up a listen port monitor to provide remote printing services.

After the ports are configured, the port monitors are automatically started any time a system is running in multiuser mode. The ttymon and listen port monitors are described in more detail in "Port Monitors" on page 167.

The SAF Commands

You can use three SAF commands to administer modems and alphanumeric terminals—`sacadm`, `pmadm`, and `ttyadm`. You can also use three SAF commands to administer printing—`sacadm`, `pmadm`, and `nlsadmin`.

Use the `sacadm` command to add and remove port monitors. This command is your main link with the Service Access Controller (SAC) and its administrative files `/etc/saf/_sactab`, `/etc/saf/_safconfig`, and `/etc/saf/pmtag/_config`.

NOTE. *Although these configuration files are ASCII text and can be edited, the SAC may not be aware of the changes. SunSoft recommends that you do not edit these files directly. Instead, you should use the* `sacadm` *and* `pmadm` *commands to make changes to the SAF administrative files.*

Use the `pmadm` command to add or remove a service and to associate a service with a particular port monitor. Each port monitor has its own administrative file.

You can use two additional commands, `ttyadm` and `nlsadmin`, as part of the command-line arguments to `pmadm` to provide input specific to a port monitor. The `ttyadm` command provides information for the ttymon port monitor; the `nlsadmin` command provides information for the listen port monitor. SAF commands, which use many options and arguments, can be quite lengthy. See the section "Reference to SAF Commands, Tasks, and Options" on page 180 for more information.

SAF Architecture

Figure 9–2 shows the architecture of SAF. Each of the architectural elements is described in the following paragraphs.

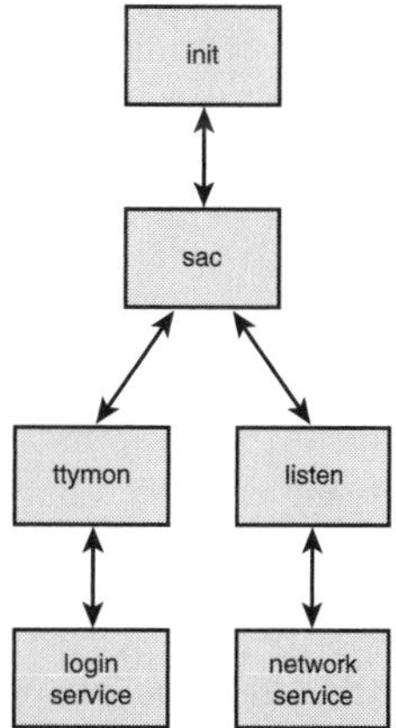

Figure 9–2
Service Access Facility architecture.

The init Process

The init process controls the overall state of the UNIX operating system and creates processes by using the information stored in the `/etc/inittab` file. The init process monitors the sac. The `/etc/inittab` file has an entry that restarts the `sac` process if `init` receives a signal indicating that the `sac` process has died.

Service Access Controller

The `sac` daemon controls the overall state of arbitrary processes that are started in response to connection requests. The sac daemon receives all of the requests to enable, disable, start, or stop port monitors and takes the appropriate action. If port monitor processes are terminated, `sac` is responsible for restarting them.

The `sac` is started from this entry in the `/etc/inittab` file:

```
sc:234:respawn:/usr/lib/saf/sac -t 300
```

NOTE. *The* `rc` *scripts do not start or control the* `sac` *process.*

When `sac` is started, it first customizes its own environment by reading the `/etc/saf/_sysconfig` configuration file. Each system has one `/etc/saf/_sysconfig` file. When the `sac` process is started, this file is interpreted and used for all of the port monitors on the system. Modifications to the environment from this file are inherited by all of sac's child processes.

Then `sac` starts all of the designated port monitors using information from the `/etc/saf/_sactab` file. For each port monitor to be started, `sac` forks a port monitor child process. The ttymon port monitor reads its configuration information from the `/etc/saf/pmtag/_pmtab` port monitor table. If configured, the listen port monitor reads its configuration information from the `/etc/saf/ pmtag/_pmtab` file. You set the value of the `pmtag` variable when you use the `sacadm` command to create the port monitor. The default name for the ttymon port monitor for serial ports is `zsmon`; the default name for the listen port monitor is `tcp`.

Once the port monitors are running, sac polls them periodically for status information. If a port monitor that should be running has stopped, `sac` restarts it if a non-zero restart count was specified using the `-n` *`count`* option to the `sacadm` command when the port monitor was created.

Port Monitors

Port monitors monitor a set of homogeneous incoming requests on a system port, detect incoming requests, and connect them to the appropriate service process. As already mentioned, Solaris 2.*x* system software provides a TTY port monitor daemon named `ttymon`, and a network port monitor daemon named `listen`.

To find out which port monitors are running and to show their status, type **sacadm -l** and press Return.

```
oak% /usr/sbin/sacadm -l
PMTAG          PMTYPE         FLGS RCNT STATUS      COMMAND
zsmon          ttymon         -    Ø    ENABLED     /usr/lib/saf/ttymon #
oak%
```

In this example, only the `ttymon` monitor, which is identified by the default port monitor tag of `zsmon`, is started, and the status is `ENABLED`. Table 9–1 describes the fields shown in the output of the `sacadm -l` command.

Table 9–1 Fields in the sacadm -l Output

Field	Description
PMTAG	A unique tag that identifies a particular port monitor. The system administrator assigns the name of the port monitor. The `pmtag` is used by the sac to identify the port monitor for all of the administration. Use the default `ttymon` pmtag, `zsmon`, for ttymon ports A and B; use the listen pmtag, `tcp`, for listen ports in the United States. PMTAG can contain up to 14 alphanumeric characters. The default `ttymon` pmtag, `zsmon`, was chosen because SPARCstation serial port chips are made by Zilog. In practice, a server may have hundreds of serial ports. If so, SunSoft recommends creating one port monitor for each serial port device. For example, consider a server that has two built-in serial ports and two add-in serial port boards, known as *asynchronous line multiplexers*, or *ALMs*. You could set up three port monitors and name them `zsmon`, `alm1`, and `alm1`. The service tag, `svctag`, could be named a and b for `zsmon`, and `0-7` for `alm1` and `alm2`. (An `alm` usually has eight ports, numbered 0 through 7.) The default `listen` pmtag, `tcp`, was chosen because the device associated with it is the network. In the United States, the network is usually `tcp`. In Europe, the network is usually `X.25`. Always create the `pmtag listen` variable in such a way that it describes the network.
PMTYPE	The type of the port monitor: `ttymon` or `listen`.
FLGS	If no flag is specified, the port monitor is started and enabled. The d flag specifies that when the port monitor is started, it is not enabled. The x flag specifies that the port monitor is not to be started.
RCNT	Retry count specifies the number of times a port monitor can fail before its state is changed to `FAILED`. If no count is specified, the field is set to 0 and the port monitor is not restarted if it fails.
STATUS	The status of activity for the port monitor. Possible states are `STARTING`, `ENABLED`, `DISABLED`, `STOPPING`, `NOTRUNNING`, and `FAILED`. The `FAILED` message is displayed if the SAC cannot start the port monitor after the number of tries specified by RCNT.
COMMAND	The complete pathname of the command that starts the port monitor, which is followed by a # and any comment that was entered when the port monitor was configured.

Refer to Chapter 10, "Setting Up Modems and Character Terminals," for information about how to configure, start, and enable the ttymon port monitor. Refer to Chapter 11, "Setting Up Printing Services," for information about how to configure, start, and enable the listen port monitor.

To view the contents of the port monitor administrative file, type **pmadm -l** and press Return.

```
oak% /usr/sbin/pmadm -l
PMTAG          PMTYPE         SVCTAG         FLGS ID       <PMSPECIFIC>
zsmon          ttymon         ttya           u    root     /dev/term/a I -
➥/usr/bin/login - 9600 ldterm,ttcompat ttya login:  - tvi925
y  #
zsmon          ttymon         ttyb           u    root     /dev/term/b I -
➥/usr/bin/login - 9600 ldterm,ttcompat ttyb login:  - tvi925
y  #
oak%
```

In this example, the ttymon ports /dev/term/a and /dev/term/b show the default Solaris 2.*x* configuration. Table 9–2 describes the fields shown in the output of the pmadm -l command.

Table 9–2 Fields in the pmadm -l Output

Field	Description
PMTAG	A unique tag that identifies a particular port monitor. The system administrator assigns the name of the port monitor. The pmtag is used by the sac to identify the port monitor for all of the administration. Use the default pmtag zsmon for ttymon ports; use the pmtag tcp for listen ports. PMTAG can contain up to 14 alphanumeric characters.
PMTYPE	The type of the port monitor: ttymon or listen.
SVCTAG	A tag unique to the port monitor that identifies a service. The service tags for the serial ports are ttya and ttyb. A service requires both a service tag and a port monitor tag to uniquely identify it.
FLGS	If no flag is specified, the port is enabled and no utmp entry is created for the service. The x flag specifies that the port should not be enabled; the u flag specifies that a utmp entry should be created for this service. Some services, such as login, will not start unless a utmp entry has been created.
ID	The login name of the person who starts the service, typically root.
PMSPECIFIC	The address, name of a process, name of a STREAMS pipe, or baud rate and configuration for a login port.

The ttymon Port Monitor

The ttymon STREAMS-based port monitor performs the functions provided by the getty process in SunOS 4.*x* system software. In addition, ttymon initializes and monitors tty ports, sets terminal modes and line speeds, invokes service on serial ports when it receives a connection request, and idles while a service is connected.

NOTE. *In Solaris 2.*x, *the serial ports* /dev/term/a *and* /dev/term/b *are provided with a default configuration for the ttymon port monitor with a* pmtag *of* zsmon.

Each instance of ttymon can monitor multiple ports, as specified in the port monitor's administrative file. You configure the administrative file using the pmadm and ttyadm commands.

When an instance of ttymon is started by the sac daemon, ttymon starts to monitor the daemon's ports. For each port, it first initializes the line disciplines, if specified, and the speed and terminal settings. The values it uses for terminal initialization are taken from the appropriate entry in the tty settings file, which is maintained by the sttydefs command. Default line disciplines on ports are set up by the autopush(1M) facility. You do not need to do anything to configure autopush.

The listen Port Monitor

The listen process "listens" for network service requests, accepts requests when they arrive, and starts services in response to the requests.

NOTE. *No* listen *processes are started by default in Solaris 2.*x *system software.*

The listen process provides services similar to those provided by the traditional Internet Services daemon, inetd. In Solaris 2.*x* system software, the inetd daemon is started with the -s option to run standalone outside of the SAF.

CAUTION! *Solaris 2.*x *does not support running* inetd *under SAF. Be sure that the* -s *option is always present.*

Service Invocations

A *service invocation* is a process that provides the requested service to the incoming connection request. A service invocation can be a process such as login or lp. The ttymon port monitor works only with the login process, and the listen port monitor works only with the LP print service. The SAF architecture is structured so that programmers can write new port monitors to support other processes specified by the port monitor.

Port Monitor States

Once added, port monitors can be operational, transitional, or inactive in one of the six states shown in Figure 9–3.

Operational States

Port monitor operational states are ENABLED and DISABLED. Port monitors are started and enabled by default when you add them. Port monitors are stopped and disabled by default when you remove them. When a port monitor is enabled, it accepts requests for service. When a port monitor is disabled, existing services continue, but new service requests are refused. When a port monitor service is killed, all of its services are terminated.

Transitional States

A port monitor may be STARTING or STOPPING. When a port monitor is in the process of starting, it is in an indeterminate state in the process of becoming either ENABLED or DISABLED. When a port monitor is stopping, it has been terminated manually but has not yet completed its shutdown procedure. Consequently, it is in an indeterminate state in the process of becoming NOTRUNNING.

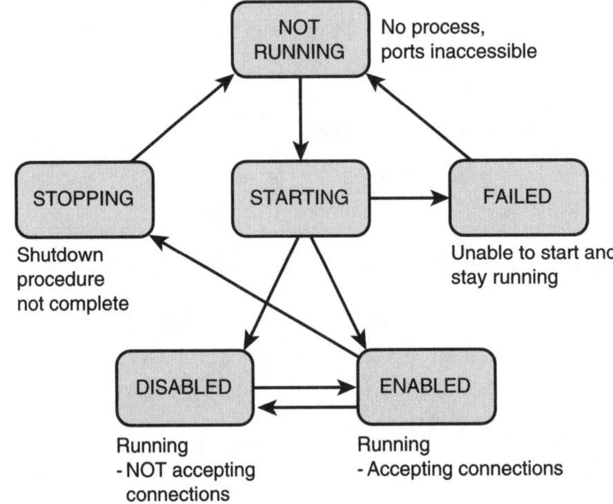

Figure 9–3
Port monitor state model.

Inactive States

An inactive port monitor is either NOTRUNNING or has FAILED. A failed port monitor is unable to start and remain running. When a port monitor is not running, it has been killed. All ports it was monitoring are inaccessible. Unlike the disabled state, when a port monitor is not running, the system cannot write a message on the inaccessible port telling the user that it is disabled. If the message option is not used, an external user cannot determine whether a port is disabled or not running.

The Line Control Model

The line control model for Solaris 2.*x* system software is different from that of Solaris 1.*x* releases. The files /etc/gettytab and /etc/ttytab have been removed. Line settings are now stored in the /etc/ttydefs file and in the ttymon configuration files. Table 9–3 compares the Solaris 1.*x* and Solaris 2.*x* line control models.

Table 9–3 Comparison of Solaris 1.*x* and Solaris 2.*x* Line Control Models

Feature	Solaris 1.*x* File	Solaris 2.*x* File
Database descriptor	/etc/termcap /etc/terminfo	/etc/terminfo
Set terminal I/O operation	stty (BSD)	stty (SVR4)

Table 9–3 Comparison of Solaris 1.*x* and Solaris 2.*x* Line Control Models

Feature	Solaris 1.*x* File	Solaris 2.*x* File
Line settings and sequences	`/etc/gettytab /etc/ttytab`	`/etc/ttydefs`
Administer tty definitions		`ttydef(1M)`

Figure 9–4 shows how the terminal control and the SAF interact. The init program starts sac, which controls the ttymon port monitor. In turn, `ttymon` monitors serial port devices. It connects incoming requests to services, which are usually login processes. Port monitors keep a close watch over the device or network transport, add and delete services, and start and stop services at the appropriate time. You can use the `stty` and `tput` commands to configure the terminal I/O settings to match the characteristics of the terminal. When `ttymon` gets a character from the terminal, it starts a login to the terminal. When the user logs out, `ttymon` hangs up to recycle the serial port and waits for another service request.

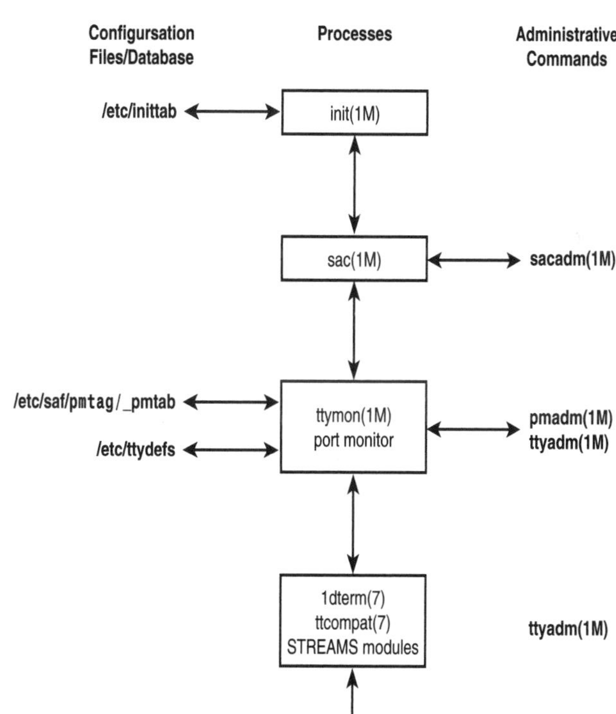

Figure 9–4
Terminal control architecture.

The /etc/ttydefs File

The /etc/ttydefs file defines baud rates and terminal settings for tty ports. When you set up modems, you use the ttyadm -l *ttylabel* argument as part of the pmadm command-line argument in order to specify information about the baud rate and the modem settings. The ttylabel variable specifies the first field for an entry in the /etc/ttydefs file. When ttymon initializes a port, it uses the information from the /etc/saf/pmtag/_pmtab file to search the /etc/ttydefs file for an entry that contains the ttylabel that matches the ttylabel for the port. The ttydefs file is similar to the old gettydefs file. Each entry in the /etc/ttydefs file has five fields, which are separated by colons.

ttylabel:initial-flags:final-flags:autobaud:nextlabel

- The ttylabel field contains the ttylabel that matches the port.
- The initial-flags field contains the initial terminal input and output settings.
- The final-flags field contains the terminal input and output values set by ttymon after a connections request is made but before the port service is started.
- The autobaud field allows ttymon to determine the line speed of the TTY port by analyzing the first Return received and setting the speed accordingly. To enable autobaud, the field must contain the character *A*. If the field is empty, autobaud is disabled.
- The nextlabel field is used to specify a hunt sequence that links speeds together in a closed set. For example, 4800 may be linked to 1200, which is linked to 2400, which is linked to 4800. If the current ttydefs entry does not provide a compatible line speed, the next speed in the sequence is tried. The default /etc/ttydefs file follows:

NEW

```
castle% more /etc/ttydefs
# VERSION=1
460800:460800 hupcl:460800 hupcl::307200
307200:307200 hupcl:307200 hupcl::230400
230400:230400 hupcl:230400 hupcl::153600
153600:153600 hupcl:153600 hupcl::115200
115200:115200 hupcl:115200 hupcl::76800
76800:76800 hupcl:76800 hupcl::57600
57600:57600 hupcl:57600 hupcl::38400
38400:38400 hupcl:38400 hupcl::19200
19200:19200 hupcl:19200 hupcl::9600
9600:9600 hupcl:9600 hupcl::4800
4800:4800 hupcl:4800 hupcl::2400
2400:2400 hupcl:2400 hupcl::1200
1200:1200 hupcl:1200 hupcl::300
300:300 hupcl:300 hupcl::460800

460800E:460800 hupcl evenp:460800 evenp::307200
307200E:307200 hupcl evenp:307200 evenp::230400
230400E:230400 hupcl evenp:230400 evenp::153600
153600E:153600 hupcl evenp:153600 evenp::115200
115200E:115200 hupcl evenp:115200 evenp::76800
76800E:76800 hupcl evenp:76800 evenp::57600
57600E:57600 hupcl evenp:57600 evenp::38400
38400E:38400 hupcl evenp:38400 evenp::19200
```

```
19200E:19200 hupcl evenp:19200 evenp::9600
9600E:9600 hupcl evenp:9600 evenp::4800
4800E:4800 hupcl evenp:4800 evenp::2400
2400E:2400 hupcl evenp:2400 evenp::1200
1200E:1200 hupcl evenp:1200 evenp::300
300E:300 hupcl evenp:300 evenp::19200

auto:hupcl:sane hupcl:A:9600

console:9600 hupcl opost onlcr:9600::console
console1:1200 hupcl opost onlcr:1200::console2
console2:300 hupcl opost onlcr:300::console3
console3:2400 hupcl opost onlcr:2400::console4
console4:4800 hupcl opost onlcr:4800::console5
console5:19200 hupcl opost onlcr:19200::console

contty:9600 hupcl opost onlcr:9600 sane::contty1
contty1:1200 hupcl opost onlcr:1200 sane::contty2
contty2:300 hupcl opost onlcr:300 sane::contty3
contty3:2400 hupcl opost onlcr:2400 sane::contty4
contty4:4800 hupcl opost onlcr:4800 sane::contty5
contty5:19200 hupcl opost onlcr:19200 sane::contty


4800H:4800:4800 sane hupcl::9600H
9600H:9600:9600 sane hupcl::19200H
19200H:19200:19200 sane hupcl::38400H
38400H:38400:38400 sane hupcl::2400H
2400H:2400:2400 sane hupcl::1200H
1200H:1200:1200 sane hupcl::300H
300H:300:300 sane hupcl::4800H

conttyH:9600 opost onlcr:9600 hupcl sane::contty1H
contty1H:1200 opost onlcr:1200 hupcl sane::contty2H
contty2H:300 opost onlcr:300 hupcl sane::contty3H
contty3H:2400 opost onlcr:2400 hupcl sane::contty4H
contty4H:4800 opost onlcr:4800 hupcl sane::contty5H
contty5H:19200 opost onlcr:19200 hupcl sane::conttyH
```

Figure 9–5 shows how the `ttylabel` entry in the `/etc/saf/zsmon/_pmtab` file matches an entry in the `/etc/ttydefs` file. In this example, the `ttylabel` is part of the default entry provided by Solaris 2.*x* system software for serial port B

The `/etc/ttydefs` file also contains information about speed and terminal settings for the TTY ports on a system. You can use the `sttydefs`(1M) administrative command to create new entries in the `/etc/ttydefs` file. See the sttydefs(1M) manual page for information on how to configure the `/etc/ttydefs` file.

The terminfo Database

The `terminfo` database describes the characteristics of TTY devices. The source files in terminfo specify a set of capabilities for a device by quantifying certain aspects of the device and by specifying character sequences that control particular results. This database is often used by applications such as vi and curses, as well as by the `ls` and `more` commands.

Information in the terminfo database is stored in a compiled binary format. The terminfo compiler, `tic`(1M), translates a `terminfo` file from source format to the required compiled binary format that applications use..

Figure 9–5
How `ttymon` identifies the `ttylabel` in the `/etc/ttydefs` file.

```
38400:38400 hupcl:38400 hupcl::19200
19200:19200 hupcl:19200 hupcl::9600
9600:9600 hupcl:9600 hupcl::4800
4800:4800 hupcl:4800 hupcl::2400
2400:2400 hupcl:2400 hupcl::300
300:300 hupcl:300 hupcl::38400
```

If you have site-specific `termcap` entries for devices, you can use the `captoinfo` utility to convert those entries into terminfo source format. Then use the tic compiler to translate the data into compiled format. See the `captoinfo`(1M) and `tic`(1M) manual pages for more information.

The tput Utility

Use the `tput`(1M) utility to initialize or reset the terminal or to make terminal-dependent capabilities and information available to the shell. The `tput` command sets terminal characteristics using data in the terminfo database. The `tput` utility is similar to the SunOS 4.*x* `tset`(1B) utility, which is provided in the SunOS/BSD Compatibility Package. The `tput` utility uses the following syntax:

```
tput [-Ttype] init
tput[-Ttype] reset
```

The stty Command

The `/usr/bin/stty` command is the SVR4 version of the SunOS 4.*x* `stty` command. The old `/usr/ucb/stty` command is available in the SunOS/BSD Compatibility Package. Use of the options varies, depending on which version of `stty` you are using. The `stty` command uses this syntax:

```
stty [-a] [-g] [options]
```

The `-a` flag lists current options using their `termio` names. The `-g` flag lists the same information in a format that can be used as an argument to another `stty` command.

The following examples show the default line settings using first the `/usr/bin/stty` command and then the `/usr/ucb/stty` command.

```
oak% /usr/bin/stty
speed 9600 baud; evenp hupcl
rows = 66; columns = 80; ypixels = 508; xpixels = 61289;
swtch = <undef>;
brkint -inpck icrnl -ixany imaxbel onlcr
echo echoe echok echoctl echoke iexten
oak% /usr/ucb/stty
speed 9600 baud; evenp hupcl
rows = 66; columns = 80; ypixels = 508; xpixels = 61289;
swtch = <undef>;
-inpck imaxbel
crt iexten
oak%
```

Table 9–4 compares the default line settings for SunOS 4.*x* and Solaris 2.*x*. Note that the dash means not to set the value.

Table 9–4 Default Line Settings

SunOS 4.*x*	Solaris 2.*x*	Description
9600	9600	Baud rate.
evenp	-parity	Even parity/disable parity.
	hupcl	Hang up connection on close.
	rows=X, columns=X, ypixels=0	Set number of rows, columns, and ypixels.
xpixels=0		Set `xpixels` to 0.
	swtch=<undef>, dsusp=<undef>	Set control character assignments.
	brkint	Signal `INTR` on break.
-inpck	-inpck	Disable input parity checking.
	icrnl	Map `CR` to `NL` on input.
	-ixany	Do not allow only DC1 to restart output.
imaxbel	imaxbel	Echo `BEL` when the input line is too long.
	onlcr	Map `NL` to `CR-NL` on output.
	tab3	Select style of delay for horizontal tabs.
	echo	Echo back every character typed.
	echoe	Echo `ERASE` character as a backspace-space-backspace string.
	echok	Echo `NL` after `KILL` character.
	echoctl	Echo control characters as `^char`, delete as `^?`.

Table 9–4 Default Line Settings (continued)

SunOS 4.*x*	Solaris 2.*x*	Description
	echoke	BS-SP-BS erase entire line.
iexten	iexten	Enable extended functions for input data.

UUCP Files

To use uucp, tip, or cu with modems and terminals, you must use information from or add information to the /etc/uucp/Dialers and /etc/uucp/Devices files. Each of these files is described in the following sections.

The /etc/uucp/Dialers File

The /etc/uucp/Dialers file contains information that specifies the initial conversation that takes place on a line before it can be made available for transferring data. This conversation is usually a sequence of character strings that is transmitted and expected. The string often contains a telephone number that is dialed using an *automatic call unit (ACU)*. Each entry in /etc/uucp/Dialers begins with a label identifying the type of the modem. The Solaris 2.*x* /etc/uucp/Dialers file contains support for many different modem types. Each type of caller included in the /etc/uucp/Devices file should be contained in the /etc/uucp/Dialers file except for built-in callers. You probably do not need to create an entry in this file. You do need to look in this file to verify that it contains an entry appropriate for your modem and to determine the *type* to use when you edit the /etc/uucp/Devices file.

Each line consists of three parts: the name of the caller, the table that translates the phone number into the code for the particular device, and a chat script to establish the connection. Comments at the beginning of the /etc/uucp/Dialers file explain the codes shown in the brief excerpt that follows:

```
penril  =W-P     "" \d > Q\c : \d- > s\p9\c )-W\p\r\ds\p9\c-) y\c : \E\TP > 9\c OK
ventel--=&-%     "" \r\p\r\c $ <K\T%%\r>\c ONLINE!
vadic   =K-K     "" \005\p *-\005\p-*\005\p-* D\p BER? \E\T\e \r\c LINE
develcon ""      "" \pr\ps\c est:\007 \E\D\e \n\007
micom   ""       "" \s\c NAME? \D\r\c GO
direct
##########
#       The following entry is for use with direct connections
#       using ttymon with the -b and -r options on both ends,
#       or the old uugetty with the -r option.
##########
uudirect ""      "" \r\d in:--in:

#  Rixon Intelligent Modem -- modem should be set up in the Rixon
#  mode and not the Hayes mode.
#
rixon   =&-%     "" \r\r\d $ s9\c )-W\r\ds9\c-) s\c : \T\r\c $ 9\c LINE
```

```
#   Hayes Smartmodem -- modem should be set with the configuration
#   switches as follows:
#
#       S1 - UP         S2 - UP         S3 - DOWN       S4 - UP
#       S5 - UP         S6 - DOWN         S7 - ?          S8 - DOWN
#
hayes   =,-,    "" \dA\pTE1V1X1Q0S2=255S12=255\r\c OK\r \EATDT\T\r\c CONNECT
```

The /etc/uucp/Devices File

The /etc/uucp/Devices file contains information for all of the devices that may be used to establish a link to remote systems. Provisions are made for several types of devices, such as ACUs, direct links, and network connections. You need to add an entry to the /etc/uucp/Devices file if you want to set up support for a bidirectional modem. Each entry in the Devices file has the following format:

```
type line line2 class dialer-token-pairs
```

The excerpt from the /etc/uucp/Devices file that follows shows the default:

```
TCP,et - - Any TCP -

ACU cua/b - Any hayes
Direct cua/b - Any direct
```

The type argument you supply when editing the /etc/uucp/Devices file is the name of the modem as displayed at the end of the entry from the /etc/ uucp/Devices file. It points to an entry in /etc/uucp/Dialers.

SAF Log Files

The SAF records port monitor behavior in the /var/saf/_log file. In addition, each ttymon port monitor has its own log file, /var/saf/pmtag/log, in which it records information, such as messages that it receives from sac and the services that it starts.

An example of the end of the /var/saf/_log file follows. This information shows that the system was rebooted three times and that the ttymon port monitor zsmon was started and enabled successfully each time.

```
oak% tail /var/saf/_log
Mon Mar 15 14:23:12 1993; 199; port monitor <zsmon> changed state from STARTING to
➥ENABLED
Fri Mar 19 09:43:18 1993; 199; *** SAC starting ***
Fri Mar 19 09:43:19 1993; 203; starting port monitor <zsmon>
Fri Mar 19 09:43:19 1993; 199; port monitor <zsmon> changed state from STARTING to
➥ENABLED
Wed Mar 24 15:24:24 1993; 437; *** SAC starting ***
Wed Mar 24 15:24:25 1993; 443; starting port monitor <zsmon>
Wed Mar 24 15:24:25 1993; 437; port monitor <zsmon> changed state from STARTING to
➥ENABLED
Thu Mar 25 20:36:11 1993; 201; *** SAC starting ***
Thu Mar 25 20:36:12 1993; 208; starting port monitor <zsmon>
```

```
Thu Mar 25 20:36:13 1993; 201; port monitor <zsmon> changed state from STARTING to
➥ENABLED
oak%
```

Following is an example of the /var/saf/_log file from another system that has a listen tcp port monitor configured.

```
seachild% tail /var/saf/_log
Wed Mar 24 12:06:19 1993; 176; *** SAC starting ***
Wed Mar 24 12:06:20 1993; 181; starting port monitor <tcp>
Wed Mar 24 12:06:20 1993; 182; starting port monitor <zsmon>
Wed Mar 24 12:06:21 1993; 176; port monitor <zsmon> changed state from STARTING to
➥ENABLED
Wed Mar 24 12:06:22 1993; 176; port monitor <tcp> changed state from STARTING to
➥ENABLED
Thu Mar 25 20:47:44 1993; 177; *** SAC starting ***
Thu Mar 25 20:47:44 1993; 183; starting port monitor <tcp>
Thu Mar 25 20:47:45 1993; 184; starting port monitor <zsmon>
Thu Mar 25 20:47:45 1993; 177; port monitor <zsmon> changed state from STARTING to
➥ENABLED
Thu Mar 25 20:47:46 1993; 177; port monitor <tcp> changed state from STARTING to
➥ENABLED
seachild%
```

An example of the end of the /var/saf/zsmon/log file is given next. This information shows more detailed information about how the ttymon port monitor zsmon was initialized successfully.

```
oak% tail /var/saf/zsmon/log
Thu Mar 25 20:36:13 1993; 208; PMTAG: zsmon
Thu Mar 25 20:36:13 1993; 208; Starting state: enabled
Thu Mar 25 20:36:13 1993; 208; Got SC_ENABLE message
Thu Mar 25 20:36:13 1993; 208; max open files = 1024
Thu Mar 25 20:36:13 1993; 208; max ports ttymon can monitor = 1017
Thu Mar 25 20:36:13 1993; 208; *ptr == 0
Thu Mar 25 20:36:13 1993; 208; SUCCESS
Thu Mar 25 20:36:13 1993; 208; *ptr == 0
Thu Mar 25 20:36:13 1993; 208; SUCCESS
Thu Mar 25 20:36:13 1993; 208; Initialization Completed
oak%
```

An example of the end of the /var/saf/tcp/log file follows:

```
seachild% tail /var/saf/tcp/log
04/06/93 15:11:10; 183; Connect: fd 7, svctag lpd, seq 117, type passfd
04/06/93 15:11:12; 183; Connect: fd 7, svctag lpd, seq 118, type passfd
04/06/93 15:26:12; 183; Connect: fd 7, svctag lpd, seq 119, type passfd
04/06/93 15:26:13; 183; Connect: fd 7, svctag lpd, seq 120, type passfd
04/06/93 15:34:02; 183; Connect: fd 6, svctag 0, seq 41, type exec
04/06/93 15:34:03; 3391; NLPS (lp) passfd: /var/spool/lp/fifos/listenS5
04/06/93 15:50:10; 183; Connect: fd 7, svctag lpd, seq 121, type passfd
04/06/93 15:50:11; 183; Connect: fd 7, svctag lpd, seq 122, type passfd
04/06/93 16:05:12; 183; Connect: fd 7, svctag lpd, seq 123, type passfd
04/06/93 16:05:12; 183; Connect: fd 7, svctag lpd, seq 124, type passfd
seachild%
```

NOTE. *You should periodically clear out or truncate these log files. If you want cron to do the cleanup for you, create cron jobs by using the* `crontab(1)` *command. Refer to the* `crontab(1)` *manual page for more information.*

Reference to SAF Commands, Tasks, and Options

The following sections provide a quick reference to the variables used in SAF commands; tasks performed with the `sacadm` and `pmadm` commands; and options for the `sacadm`, `pmadm`, `ttyadm`, and `nlsadmin` commands. Refer to Chapter 10 for step-by-step instructions on how to use the SAF commands to set up modems and terminals. Refer to Chapter 11 for step-by-step instructions on how to use the SAF commands to set up printers.

Quick Reference to SAF Variables

Table 9–5 describes the variables used with the SAF commands.

Table 9–5 Variables Used with the SAF Commands

Variable	Example	Description
`pmtag`	`zsmon`	The name of a specific instance of a port monitor.
`svctag`	`b`	The name of the port in the `/dev/term` directory.
`dev-path`	`/dev/term/b`	The full name of the `tty` port device file.
`ttylabel`	`2400H`	The baud rate and line discipline from the `/etc/ttydefs` file.
`type`	`ventel`	The type of the modem, as specified in the `/etc/uucp/Devices` file.

Quick Reference to Service Access Control (sacadm)

Table 9–6 provides a task-oriented quick reference to the tasks you perform using the `sacadm` command.

Table 9–6 Quick Reference to the Service Access Controller

Task	Command Syntax
Add a port monitor	`sacadm -a -p` *`pmtag`* `-t ttymon -c /usr/lib/saf/ttymon -v `ttyadm -V` -y "comment"`

Table 9–6 Quick Reference to the Service Access Controller (continued)

Disable a port monitor	`sacadm -d -p` *pmtag*
Enable a port monitor	`sacadm -e -p` *pmtag*
Kill a port monitor	`sacadm -k -p` *pmtag*
List status information for a port monitor	`sacadm -l -p` *pmtag*
Remove a port monitor	`sacadm -r -p` *pmtag*
Start a port monitor	`sacadm -s -p` *pmtag*
Add a listen port monitor	`sacadm -a -p` *pmtag* `-t listen -c /usr/lib/saf/listen -v` `` `ttyadm -V` `` `-y "comment"`

Table 9–7 describes the options to the `sacadm` command.

Table 9–7 Options to sacadm Command

Option	Description
a	Add a port monitor.
p	Specify an identifying port monitor tag (`pmtag`) for the port monitor.
t	Specify the type of the port monitor—either `ttymon` or `listen`.
c	Specify the commands used to start a port monitor.
v	Specify the version number of the port monitor. Use `ttyadm -V` to find out the version number to use, or use `` `ttyadm -V` `` as an argument to the `-v` option.
f	Specify one or both flags. The d flag specifies that the port monitor is not enabled. The x flag specifies that the port monitor is not started.

Quick Reference to Port Monitor Administration (pmadm)

Table 9–8 provides a quick reference to the tasks you perform using the `pmadm` command.

Table 9–8 Quick Reference to Port Monitor Administration (pmadm)

Task	Command Syntax
Add a standard terminal service	`pmadm -a -p` *pmtag* `-s svctag -i root -v` `` `ttyadm -V` `` `-m "`ttyadm -i 'terminal disabled.' -l contty -m ldterm,ttcompat -d` *dev-path* `-s /usr/bin/login`"`

Table 9–8 Quick Reference to Port Monitor Administration (pmadm) (continued)

Task	Command Syntax
Disable a ttymon port monitor	`pmadm -d -p` *pmtag* `-s svctag`
Enable a ttymon port monitor	`pmadm -e -p` *pmtag* `-s svctag`
List all services	`pmadm -l`
List status information for one ttymon port monitor	`pmadm -l -p` *pmtag* `-s svctag`
Add a listen service	`pmadm -a -p` *pmtag* `` -s lp -i root -v `nlsadmin -V` -m "`nlsadmin -o /var/spool/lp/fifos/listenS5`" ``
Disable a listen port monitor	`pmadm -d -p` *pmtag* `-s lp`
Enable a listen port monitor	`pmadm -e -p` *pmtag* `-s lp`
List status information for one ttymon port monitor	`pmadm -l -p` *pmtag*

Table 9–9 describes the options to the `pmadm` command.

Table 9–9 Options to the pmadm Command

Option	Description
a	Add a service.
p	Specify the port monitor tag (*pmtag*)—for example, zsmon.
s	Specify the service tag associated with a given service (*svctag*)—for example, ttya for serial port A.
i	Specify the identity assigned to the service when it is started.
f	Specify one or both flags. The x flag does not enable the specified service. The u flag creates a utmp entry for the service.
v	Specify the port monitor version number. Use `ttyadm -V` to find the version number, or use `` `ttyadm -V` `` as an argument to the -v option.
m	Identify port monitor-specific options to be included on the -a command line.

Table 9–10 shows the options to the `ttyadm` command. You usually include the `ttyadm` command and its options in backquotes (` `) as part of the `pmadm` command.

Table 9–10 Options to the ttyadm Command

Option	Description
d	Specify the full pathname of the device file for the tty port—for example, `/dev/term/a` for serial port A.
l	Specify the ttylabel from the `/etc/ttydefs` file that the port monitor uses to set the proper baud rate—for example, 9600.
s	Specify the service pathname to be used when a connection request is received—for example, `/usr/bin/login`.
V	Display the version number of the SAF.

Table 9–11 shows only the options to the `nlsadmin` command that can be included as part of the command-line argument for the `sacadm` and `pmadm` commands. See the `nlsadmin`(1M) manual page for further information.

Table 9–11 Options to the nlsadmin Command

Option	Description
A	Interpret the address as private for the server. The listener monitors this address and dispatches all calls arriving on this address directly to the designated service. This option may not be used with the `-D` option.
`c "cmd"`	Specify the full pathname of the server and its arguments. Use double quotes around the pathname to ensure that it is interpreted as a single word by the shell.
D	Dynamically assign a private address that is selected by the transport provider. This option is frequently used with the `-R` option for RPC services. This option may not be used with the `-A` option.
`o streamname`	Specify the full pathname of a FIFO or named STREAM through which a server is receiving the connection.
`p modules`	If this option is specified, the modules are interpreted as a list of STREAMS modules for the listener to push before starting the service. Modules are pushed in the order they are specified. Specify the modules as a comma-separated list with no spaces.
R	Register an RPC service whose address, program number, and version number are registered with the rpcbinder for this transport provider.
V	Display the version number of the SAF.

Admintool: Serial Ports and SAF

You can configure a serial port for use with a modem or terminal on a local system using either the Admintool: Serial Ports graphical user interface or the SAF commands described in Part 4 of this book. SunSoft recommends that you use the Admintool: Serial Ports graphical user interface for these tasks. If you have Solstice AdminSuite available, you can use AdminSuite's Serial Port Manager to configure serial ports on remote systems.

Admintool: Serial Ports and AdminSuite's Serial Port Manager both use the `pmadm` command to configure the serial port software to work with terminals and modems. They provide templates for common terminal and modem configurations and provide a quick visual status of each port. You can also set up multiple ports, modify them, or delete port services.

Once a serial port is configured, use the SAF commands to administer the port.

Templates

The Serial Port Manager provides five templates for the most common terminal and modem configurations, which you can then modify for a particular device.

- Terminal—hardwired
- Modem—dial-in only
- Modem—dial-out only
- Modem—bidirectional
- Initialize Only—no connection

When you choose one of these templates from the Use Template menu, a set of default values is displayed that are optimized for the service that you selected.

Starting Admintool: Serial Ports

You can use the Admintool: Serial Ports graphical user interface for the following tasks on a local system:

- Initialize a port without configuring the service
- Add a service
- Modify a service
- Disable a service
- Delete a service

You perform each task by clicking SELECT on the name of each port you want to configure and then choosing an item from the Edit menu. You choose Modify Service for the first four tasks and Delete Service if you want to delete the service for the selected port(s). Use the following steps to access the Admintool: Serial Ports graphical user interface.

1. Type **/usr/bin/admintool &** and press Return. The Admintool: Users window is displayed, as shown in Figure 9–6.

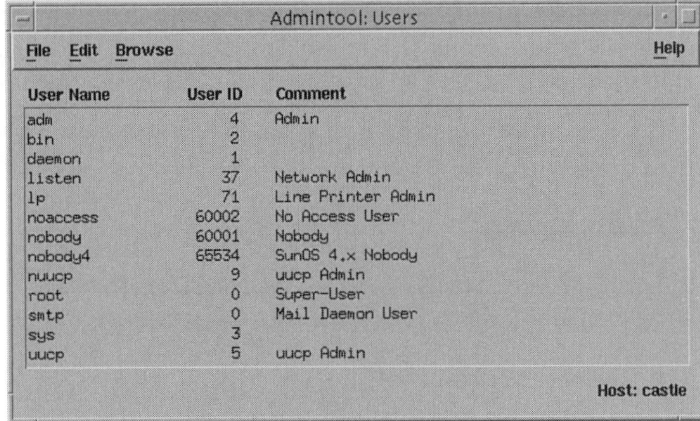

Figure 9–6
Admintool: Users base window.

2. From the Browse menu, choose Serial Ports. The Modify Serial Port window is displayed, as shown in Figure 9–7.

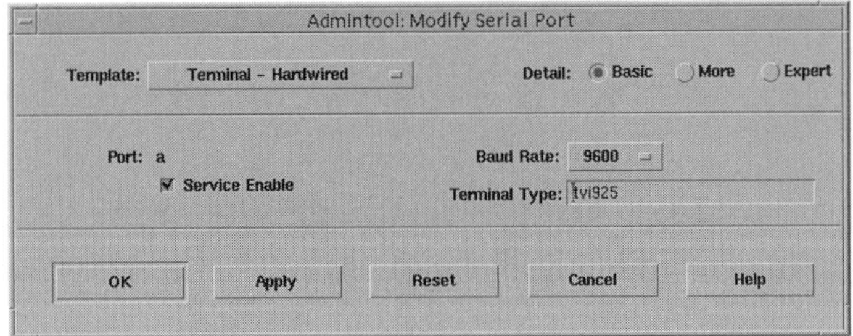

Figure 9–7
Admintool: Modify Serial Port window.

3. Click the port you want to modify and choose Modify from the Edit menu. The Modify Serial Port window is displayed, as shown in Figure 9–8.

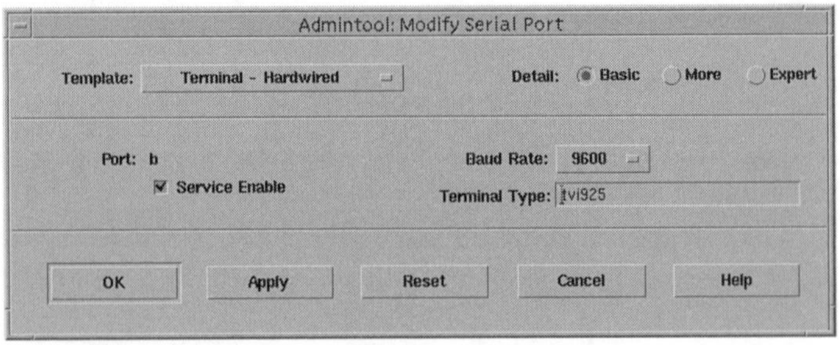

Figure 9–8
Admintool: Modify Serial Port window.

The Modify Serial Port window displays three levels of information about the port. When the window is first displayed, only Basic information is displayed. You can click the More radio button to display more information. Clicking the Expert radio button shows all of the possible settings.

For information on how to set up modems and character terminals, see Chapter 10.

CHAPTER

10

Setting Up Modems and Character Terminals

Tools for Setting Up Modems and Character Terminals

Using Variables in SAF Commands

Setting Up Modems

Setting Up the SAF for Character Terminals

THIS CHAPTER DESCRIBES HOW TO USE THE TTYMON PORT MONITOR TOSET UP THE SERVICE Access Facility (SAF) for modems and character terminals. See Chapter 11, "Setting Up Printing Services," for information on how to use the SAF to set up printers.

Tools for Setting Up Modems and Character Terminals

You perform three basic tasks to set up a serial port device, such as a modem or a character terminal:

1. Use the `sacadm` command to add a port monitor (if one is not already configured).
2. Use the `pmadm` command to designate a service to be associated with the new port monitor.
3. Edit one or more communications-related files as needed.

The Solaris environment now provides you with two additional tools that provide a graphical user interface to the SAF to manage terminals and modems:

- Admintool graphical user interface. Use this bundled tool to manage terminal and modem setup for local systems only.
- Serial Port Manager in the unbundled Solstice AdminSuite provides a graphical user interface that you can use to manage terminals and modems in a networked, name-service environment.

Table 10–1 describes three tasks that are not supported in the Solstice Serial Port Manager. You must use SAF commands to perform these tasks.

Table 10–1 Tasks Not Supported by the Solstice Serial Port Manager

Task	SAF Command	Description
Inform users that a port is disabled	`ttyadmin -i`	This command specifies the inactive (disabled) response message. The message is sent to a terminal or modem when a user logs in when the port is disabled. This functionality is not provided when you disable a port using Solstice Serial Port Manager.
Keep the modem connected when a user logs off a host	`ttyadmin -h`	This command specifies that the system does not hang up on a modem before setting or resetting to the default or specified value. If `ttyadmin -h` is not used, the host hangs up the modem when the user logs out of that host.

Table 10–1 Tasks Not Supported by the Solstice Serial Port Manager (continued)

Task	SAF Command	Description
Require the user to type a character before the system displays a prompt	`ttyadmin -r`	This command specifies that `ttymon` requires the user to type a character or press Return a specified number of times before the login prompt is displayed. When `-r` is not specified, pressing Return one or more times prints the prompt anyway. This option prevents a terminal server from issuing a welcome message that the Solaris host might misinterpret to be a user trying to log in. Without the `-r` option, the host and terminal server might begin looping and printing prompts to each other.

Using Variables in SAF Commands

The following sections describe the variables used in the SAF commands in this chapter. When using SAF commands, you supply arguments to specify one (or more) of the variables described in Table 10–2. These variable names were chosen to match the names of the fields used to display the output of SAF commands. These variables and the files they use are described in the following sections.

Table 10–2 Variables Used with the SAF Commands

Variable	Example	Description
`pmtag`	`zsmon`	The name of a specific instance of a port monitor.
`svctag`	`ttyb`	The name of the port.
`dev-path`	`/dev/term/b`	The full name of the tty port device file.
`ttylabel`	`2400H`	The baud rate and line discipline from the `/etc/ttydefs` file.
`type`	`hayes`	The type of the modem, as specified in the `/etc/uucp/Devices` file.

The Port Monitor Tag (pmtag)

You can use the `pmtag` variable to specify the name you assign to a specific instance of a port monitor. You can give port monitors any name you like, provided the name is unique and contains no more than 14 alphanumeric characters. The default `pmtag` variable for Solaris 2.*x* system software is `zsmon` for serial ports A and B. If you install a multiplexer, serial ports are automatically configured as part of the installation process and are given the `pmtag` variable `ttymon0`. SunSoft suggests that you use the system-defined `pmtag` variables.

The Service Tag (svctag)

Each port assigned to a port monitor has its own service tag. By convention, `svctag` is `tty` followed by the name of the port in the `/dev/term` directory. For example, for device `/dev/term/b`, the corresponding `svctag` is `ttyb`. For `/dev/term/7`, the `svctag` is `tty7`.

NOTE. *You can assign any* `svctag` *name that you like, as long as you use it consistently.*

To display a list of currently active services, type **pmadm -l** and press Return. You do not need to be superuser to display a list of currently active services. In the following example, the first three entries are defined for printing services. The last two entries define the default zsmon services for serial ports A and B.

```
castle% /usr/sbin/pmadm -l
PMTAG          PMTYPE         SVCTAG         FLGS ID       <PMSPECIFIC>
tcp            listen         lp             -    root     - - p -
➥/var/spool/lp/fifos/listenS5 #
tcp            listen         lpd            -    root
➥\x00020203000000000000000000000000 - p - /var/spool/lp/fifos/listenBSD #
tcp            listen         0              -    root
➥\x00020ACE000000000000000000000000 - c - /usr/lib/saf/nlps_server #
zsmon          ttymon         ttya           u    root     /dev/term/a I -
➥/usr/bin/login - 9600 ldterm,ttcompat ttya login:  - tvi925 y  #
zsmon          ttymon         ttyb           u    root     /dev/term/b I -
➥/usr/bin/login - 9600 ldterm,ttcompat ttyb login:  - tvi925 y  #
castle%
```

In the preceding example, the `pmtag` is `zsmon`; the `pmtype` is `ttymon`; the `svctag` is `ttya` and `ttyb`; the `flag` is `u` (which creates a utmp directory for the service); and the `ID`, `root`, is the user identity that is assigned to the service tag when it is started. The port monitor-specific information includes the device path, `I` (initialize only), a login account, 9600 baud rate, terminal configuration information, and the `login:` prompt.

NOTE. *A single port monitor can handle multiple requests for the same service concurrently, so it is possible for the number of active login services to exceed the number of ttymon port monitors.*

The Device Path (dev-path)

You use the `dev-path` variable to specify the full name of the tty port device file to which the modem or character terminal is connected. For example, the pathname for a character terminal or modem connected to serial port A is `/dev/term/b`. A terminal attached to the first port of a serial port adapter board or multiplexer would be `/dev/term/00`.

CAUTION! *Do not use* `/dev/cua/*` *device names to set up the SAF. The* `tip`, `cu`, *and* `uucp` *commands should, however, be set up to call out on* `/dev/cua/*`, *not* `/dev/term/*` *devices. If you call out on* `/dev/term` *with the* `tip` *command, the message link down is displayed, and the* `cu` *command times out.*

The Baud Rate and Line Discipline (ttylabel)

You can use the `ttylabel` variable to specify which entry in the `/etc/ttydefs` file is used when the SAF searches for the proper baud rate and line discipline. The following example shows the first group of settings from the `/etc/ttydefs` file.

```
460800:460800 hupcl:460800 hupcl::307200
307200:307200 hupcl:307200 hupcl::230400
230400:230400 hupcl:230400 hupcl::153600
153600:153600 hupcl:153600 hupcl::115200
115200:115200 hupcl:115200 hupcl::76800
76800:76800 hupcl:76800 hupcl::57600
57600:57600 hupcl:57600 hupcl::38400
38400:38400 hupcl:38400 hupcl::19200
19200:19200 hupcl:19200 hupcl::9600
9600:9600 hupcl:9600 hupcl::4800
4800:4800 hupcl:4800 hupcl::2400
2400:2400 hupcl:2400 hupcl::1200
1200:1200 hupcl:1200 hupcl::300
300:300 hupcl:300 hupcl::460800
```

Type of Modem

The type of modem you use is discussed later in this chapter in the section "Modem Connection and Switch Settings."

Comments

You can add comments (in double quotes) to both the `pmadm` and `sacadm` comments after the `-y` flag when you add a port monitor or service. Any comments you add are displayed when you use the `-l` option to the `sacadm` or `pmadm` command to display port monitors or services.

Use comments to specify the ports with which the various port monitors are associated.

Setting Up Modems

You can set up a modem in three ways:

- Dial-out service. You can access other systems, but other systems cannot call your system.
- Dial-in service. Other systems can call your system through the modem, but you cannot call other systems.
- Bidirectional service. This service provides both dial-in and dial-out capabilities.

Using any one of these modem services, you can `tip` or `cu` to a remote system.

Hardware Carrier Detect Setting

You must disable hardware carrier detect. On Sun systems, you can do this in two ways. One way is to do the following:

1. Become superuser.
2. Type **eeprom ttyb-ignore-cd=false** and press Return.

Alternatively, follow these steps to disable hardware carrier detect on Sun systems:

1. Halt the system.
2. At the `ok PROM` prompt, type **setenv ttyb-ignore-cd=false** and press Return.
3. Type **boot** and press Return to reboot the system.

Modem Connection and Switch Settings

Connect the modem to a serial port with an RS-232-C cable that has pins 2 through 8 and pin 20 wired straight through. You may also use a full 25-pin cable to connect the modem to the system. Ensure that all of the connections are secure.

SunOS 5.*x* system software supports many popular modems. The following modems have been tested and qualified for use with Solstice PPP:

- AT&T DataPort Express
- BocaModem V.34 DataFax
- Cardinal V.34/V.FC 28.8 data/fax
- Cardinal MVP288I 28.8 Kbps V.34 Fax Modem
- Hayes Accura 144B and 288V.FC
- Megahertz XJ2288 PCMCIA
- Motorola Codex 326X V.34
- MultiModem MT2834BLF
- MultiModem MT1432BF
- Olitec 288
- Practical 14400 V32bis
- SupraFaxModem 288
- USRobotics Sporter 14400
- USRobotics Sporter 288

- USRobotics Courier V.34
- Zoom V34

NOTE. *This information does not imply a support contract or warranty from Sun Microsystems, Inc. for any of the listed devices.*

Hayes-compatible Modem Settings

Hayes-compatible modems that use the Hayes `AT` command set may work with cu and uucp software. Use the following configurations:

- Use hardware data terminal ready (DTR). When the system drops DTR (for example, when someone logs off), the modem should hang up.
- Use hardware carrier detect (CD). The modem raises the CD line only when there is an active carrier signal on the phone connection. When the carrier drops, either because the other end of the connection is terminated or the phone connection is broken, the system is notified and acts appropriately. The CD signal is also used for coordinating dial-in *and* dial-out use on a single serial port and modem.
- Respond with numeric result codes.
- Send result codes.
- Do not echo commands.

Variables Used to Set Up Modems

To set up a dial-in or a bidirectional modem, you need information for the following variables:

- `svctag` The name of the port the modem is connected to (typically `ttya` or `ttyb`).
- `pmtag` The name of the port monitor service (for Sun Microsystems, `zsmon`).
- `dev-path` The name of the device for the port (typically `/dev/term/a` or `/dev/term/b`).
- `ttylabel` The entry in the `/etc/ttydefs` file that is used to set the proper baud rate and line discipline.
- `type` The type of the modem from the `/etc/uucp/Dialers` file—for example, the type for a Hayes modem is hayes.

SAF Configuration for Modems

To configure the SAF for modems, you must use the `pmadm` and `ttyadm` commands. You can use the Admintool: Serial Ports graphical user interface to configure SAF for modems on a local system. See "Using Admintool: Serial Ports to Configure Modems" on page 197 for more information.

Follow the steps in this section to set up the SAF to use a modem for dial-in or bidirectional service.

1. Become superuser.
2. Type **pmadm -l** and press Return. A list of all of the available port monitors is displayed. Note the `PMTAG`, `PMTYPE`, and `SVCTAG` values for the modem port. Substitute these values for the appropriate variables in the next steps.
3. Type **pmadm -r -p *pmtag* -s *svctag*** and press Return. You must remove the existing configuration for the service tag before you can create a new one. If the message `Invalid request, pmtag: not found` comes up, then the port monitor is not configured. Continue to the next step.
4. To set up the port monitor for use with the modem, type **pmadm -a -p *pmtag* -s *svctag* -i root -fu -v `ttymon -V` -m "`ttyadm -t *terminfo-type* -b -d *dev-name* -l *ttylabel* -m ldterm,ttcompat -s /usr/bin/login -S n`"** and press Return. The `-a` option adds the service, the `-p` option specifies the port monitor tag, the `-s` option specifies the service tag, and the `-i` option sets root as the ID of the owner. The `-fu` option creates a utmp directory for the service, the `-v` option specifies the version number, and the `-m` option specifies the information specific to the port monitor using input from the `ttyadm` command. The `ttyadm -t` option specifies the type of the terminal, as specified by the terminfo database; the `-b` option specifies that the service is bidirectional; and the `-d` option specifies the device name. The `-l` option specifies the tty label; the `-m ldterm,ttcompat` command specifies the STREAMS modules to be pushed; the `-s` option specifies a login service; and the `-S n` option sets the hardware carrier on.
5. Type **pmadm -l** and press Return. Check the output to ensure that you configured the port monitor service properly.
6. Type **grep cua*n* /etc/remote**. This entry in the `/etc/remote` file sets the correct baud rate for the port. In this example, the information for cuab is correct:

```
# grep cuab /etc/remote
cuab:dv=/dev/cua/b:br#2400
#
```

If the entry is not in the `/etc/remote` file, edit the file and add it.

7. If using the port for uucp, edit the `/etc/uucp/Devices` file and add the following entry, where *n* is the name of the device in the `/dev/term directory` (for example, b for `/dev/term/b`):

```
ACU term/n,M - ttylabel type
```

NOTE. *If you are setting up service on a bidirectional port, you must enable login individually for each port. To enable logins, type* ***pmadm -e -p pmtag -s svctag*** *and press Return.*

In the following example, a Hayes-compatible 2400 baud modem is configured for bidirectional service on serial port_B. Note that the `contty3H` entry is an entry for a 2400 baud modem.

```
oak# pmadm -l
PMTAG          PMTYPE         SVCTAG         FLGS ID       <PMSPECIFIC>
zsmon          ttymon         ttya           u    root     /dev/term/a I -
➥/usr/bin/login - 9600 ldterm,ttcompat ttya login:  - tvi925
y  #
zsmon          ttymon         ttyb           u    root     /dev/term/a I -
➥/usr/bin/login - 9600 ldterm,ttcompat ttyb login:  - tvi925
y  #
oak# pmadm -r -p zsmon -s ttyb
oak# pmadm -a -p zsmon -s ttyb -i root -fu -v `ttyadm -V` -m "`ttyadm -t tvi925 -b
➥-d /dev/term/b -l contty3H -m ldterm,ttcompat -s /usr/bin/login -S n`"
oak# pmadm -l
PMTAG          PMTYPE         SVCTAG         FLGS ID       <PMSPECIFIC>
zsmon          ttymon         ttya           u    root     /dev/term/a I -
➥/usr/bin/login - 9600 ldterm,ttcompat ttya login:  - tvi925
y  #
zsmon          ttymon         ttyb           u    root     /dev/term/b b -
➥/usr/bin/login - contty3H ldterm,ttcompat login:  - - n  #
oak# sacadm -l
PMTAG          PMTYPE         FLGS RCNT STATUS     COMMAND
zsmon           ttymon          -    0    ENABLED    /usr/lib/saf/ttymon #
oak# grep cuab /etc/remote
cuab:dv=/dev/cua/b:br#2400
oak# vi /etc/uucp/Devices
If using the port for uucp, add the following line to the end of the file:
ACU cua/b,M - contty3H hayes
```

Dial-Out Modem Service Configuration

If you want to dial out on the modem, you do not need to configure SAF files. Once the modem is connected to the system and its switches are properly set, follow these steps to configure dial-out service:

1. Edit the `/etc/uucp/Devices` file and add the following line, where *n* is the name of the device in the `/dev/cua` directory. Use the type `hayes` for Hayes-compatible modems.

   ```
   ACU cua/n,M - ttylabel type
   ```

2. Type **pmadm -d -p *pmtag* -s *svctag*** and press Return. Login service is disabled. (Permitting logins for a modem that is set up to provide dial-out service only is a security hole.)

Modem Connection Troubleshooting

When troubleshooting problems with modem connections, first check the following list with the user:

- Was the correct login ID or password used?
- Is the terminal waiting for xon flow control key?
- Is the serial cable loose or unplugged?

- Is the serial cable verified to work properly?
- Is the terminal configuration correct?
- Is the terminal turned off?

Continue troubleshooting by checking the configuration of the terminal or the modem.

- Was the proper `ttylabel` used?
- Does the `ttylabel` setting of the modem match the `ttylabel` of the SAF?
- If you have changed any modem switches, turn the power to the modem off, wait a few seconds, and turn it on again.

If the problem persists, check the system software.

- Was the port monitor configured to service the modem?
- Does it have the correct `ttylabel` associated with it?
- Does the `type` definition match a setting in the `/etc/ttydefs` file?
- Is the port monitor enabled? (Use the `sacadm -l -p` *`pmtag`* command.)
- Is the service enabled? (Use the `pmadm -l -p` *`pmtag`* command.)

If the SAC is starting the ttymon port monitor, the service is enabled, and the configuration matches the port monitor configuration, continue to search for the problem by checking the serial connection. A serial connection consists of serial ports, cables, modems, and terminals. Test each of these parts by using it with two other parts that are known to be reliable.

To check for cable problems, a breakout box is helpful. It plugs into the RS-232-C cable. A patch panel lets you connect any pin to any other pins. A breakout box often contains light-emitting diodes that show whether a signal is present on each pin.

Continue troubleshooting by checking each of the following:

- If you cannot access a port, and the `ps` command shows that a process is running on it, make sure that pin 8 in the cable is connected. If that does not work, check that the device driver is configured properly to set the correct flag for the line to Off.
- If the error message `can't synchronize with hayes` is displayed when using a Hayes-compatible modem, check the `/etc/remote` file and make sure that you have changed `at=ventel` to `at=hayes`.
- If the message `all ports busy` is displayed, the port may actually be busy running a dial-in user. Use the `ps` command to see what is running. You should also check to ensure that the carrier detect is set up properly. Type **pmadm -l** and press Return. If the last flag in the `PMSPECIFIC` field is `y`, delete the entry and reconfigure it, making sure that you use `-S n` (not `-S y`) as the last argument for ttymon. If the port still shows as busy, check the

/var/spool and /var/spool/locks directories for leftover lock files. A lock file would have a name like LCK.cua0. If you find a lock file, remove it.

Using Admintool: Serial Ports to Configure Modems

You can use the Admintool: Serial Ports graphical user interface to configure SAF for modems on a local system. You can also use the Solstice AdminSuite Serial Port Manager to configure SAF for modems.Table 10–3 shows the Admintool default values for a dial-in modem.

Table 10–3 Modem—Dial-In Only Default Values

Item	Default Value
Port	a ¦ b ¦ other port identifier*
Service	enabled
Baud rate	9600
Terminal type	tvi925
Option: Initialize only	no*
Option: Bidirectional	no
Option: Software carrier	no
Login prompt	ttyn login:*
Comment	Modem—Dial-In Only
Service tag	ttyn*
Port monitor tag	zsmon
Create utmp entry	yes
Connect on carrier	no
Service	/usr/bin/login
Streams modules	ldterm,ttcompat
Timeout (secs)	never

* Revised in this edition.

Table 10–4 shows the Admintool default values for a dial-out modem.

* Revised in this edition.

Table 10–4 Modem—Dial-Out Only Default Values

Item	Default Value
Port	a ¦ b ¦ other port identifier*
Service	enabled
Baud rate	9600
Terminal type	tvi925*
Option: Initialize only	yes*
Option: Bidirectional	no
Option: Software carrier	no
Login prompt	ttyn login:*
Comment	Modem—Dial-Out Only
Service tag	ttyn*
Port monitor tag	zsmon
Create utmp entry	yes
Connect on carrier	no
Service	/usr/bin/login
Streams modules	ldterm,ttcompat
Timeout (secs)	never

Table 10–5 shows the Admintool default settings for bidirectional modem service.

Table 10–5 Modem—Bidirectional Default Values

Item	Default Value
Port	a ¦ b ¦ other port identifier*
Service	enabled
Baud rate	9600
Terminal type	tvi925*
Option: Initialize only	no
Option: Bidirectional	yes
Option: Software carrier	no
Login prompt	ttyn login:*

Table 10–5 Modem—Bidirectional Default Values (continued)

Item	Default Value
Comment	`Modem—Bidirectional`
Service tag	`ttyn*`
Port monitor tag	`zsmon`
Create utmp entry	`yes`
Connect on carrier	`no`
Service	`/usr/bin/login`
Streams modules	`ldterm,ttcompat`
Timeout (secs)	`never`

* Revised in this edition.

Use the following steps to configure SAF for a modem from the Admintool Serial Ports window:

1. In the Admintool: Serial Ports window, click the port that will be used with the modem.
2. From the Edit menu, choose Modify. The Admintool: Modify Serial Port window is displayed, as shown in Figure 10–1.

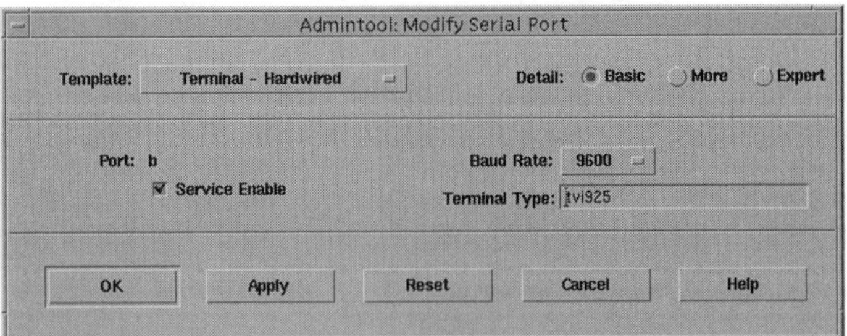

Figure 10–1
Admintool: Modify Serial Port window.

3. Click the Expert radio button to display all of the settings, as shown in Figure 10–2.
4. Choose the modem configuration from the Template menu that meets or most closely matches your modem service.
5. Change the values of template entries if desired. If you change the values, make sure that you change the comment field so that other users know that you have changed the default values.
6. Click OK to configure the port.

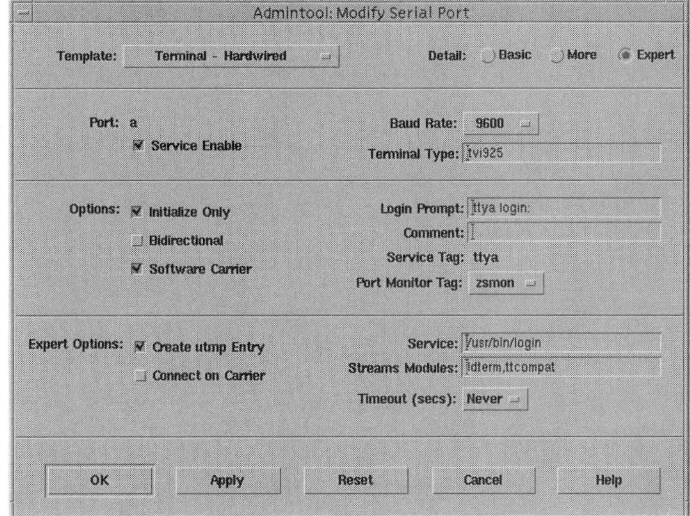

Figure 10–2
Admintool: Modify Serial Port window with Expert options.

Setting Up the SAF for Character Terminals

The Solaris 2.*x* system software is automatically configured to work properly with Sun graphics display monitors. You do not need to do any additional SAF configuration to use them. The word *terminal* is used in this chapter to describe a *character terminal*—a serial port device that displays only letters, numbers, and other characters, such as those produced by a typewriter. The VT100 model, for example, is a popular type of character terminal that many other terminals can emulate.

Not all systems require character terminals. You may want to attach a character terminal to a server as an inexpensive control console or to a malfunctioning system's serial port to use for diagnostics.

If you do attach a character terminal to a system, you need to use the SAF to set it up. See Chapter 9, "Understanding the Service Access Facility," for background information about terminal control.

Terminal Connection

Use a null modem cable to connect a character terminal to serial ports on Sun systems. A null modem cable swaps lines 2 and 3 so that the proper transmit and receive signals are communicated between two DTE devices. Line 7 goes straight through, connecting pin 7 of the devices at each end of the null modem cable.

SAF Configuration for Character Terminals

Solaris 2.*x* systems come with a ttymon port monitor named `zsmon` and with serial ports A and B already configured with default settings for terminals, as shown in the following example:

```
castle% /usr/sbin/sacadm -l
PMTAG          PMTYPE         FLGS RCNT STATUS     COMMAND
tcp            listen         -    999  ENABLED    /usr/lib/saf/listen tcp #
zsmon          ttymon         -    0    ENABLED    /usr/lib/saf/ttymon #
castle% /usr/sbin/pmadm -l
PMTAG          PMTYPE         SVCTAG          FLGS ID       <PMSPECIFIC>
tcp            listen         lp              -    root     - - p -
➥/var/spool/lp/fifos/listenS5 #
tcp            listen         lpd             -    root
➥\x00020203000000000000000000000000 - p - /var/spool/lp/fifos/listenBSD #
tcp            listen         0               -    root
➥\x00020ACE000000000000000000000000 - c - /usr/lib/saf/nlps_server #
zsmon          ttymon         ttya            u    root     /dev/term/a I -
➥/usr/bin/login - 9600 ldterm,ttcompat ttya login:  - tvi925 y  #
zsmon          ttymon         ttyb            u    root     /dev/term/b I -
➥/usr/bin/login - 9600 ldterm,ttcompat ttyb login:  - tvi925 y  #
castle%
```

The `I` in the second field of the `<PMSPECIFIC>` column means that the service is initialized for the hardware configuration, but connection to the service is not enabled.

You probably only need to add a login service to configure an existing port. Follow these steps to configure the SAF for a character terminal:

1. Become superuser.
2. Type **sacadm -l** and press Return. Check the output to make sure that a ttymon port monitor is configured. It is unlikely that you will need to add a new port monitor. If you do need to add one, type **sacadm -a -p** ***pmtag*** **-t ttymon -c /usr/lib/saf/ttymon -v \`ttymon -V\`** and press Return.
3. Type **pmadm -a -p** ***pmtag*** **-s** ***svctag*** **-i root -fu -v \`ttymon -V\` -m "\`ttyadm -t** ***terminfo-type*** **-d** ***dev-path*** **-l** ***ttylabel*** **-s /usr/bin/login\`"** and press Return. The port is configured for a login service.
4. Attach all of the cords and cables to the terminal and turn it on.

In this example, a ttymon port monitor called `ttymon0` is created and a login is enabled for serial port `/dev/term/00`:

```
oak% su
Password:
# sacadm -l
PMTAG          PMTYPE         FLGS RCNT STATUS     COMMAND
zsmon          ttymon         -    0    ENABLED    /usr/lib/saf/ttymon #
# sacadm -a -p ttymon0 -t ttymon -c /usr/lib/saf/ttymon -v `ttyadm -V`
# sacadm -l
PMTAG          PMTYPE         FLGS RCNT STATUS     COMMAND
ttymonm0        ttymon         -    0    STARTING   /usr/lib/saf/ttymon #
zsmon          ttymon         -    0    ENABLED    /usr/lib/saf/ttymon #
```

```
# pmadm -a -p ttymonØ -s ttyØØ -i root -fu -v `ttyadm -V` -m "`ttyadm -t tvi925 -d
➥/dev/term/ØØ -l 96ØØ -s
/usr/bin/login`"
# pmadm -l
PMTAG           PMTYPE          SVCTAG          FLGS ID       <PMSPECIFIC>
zsmon           ttymon          ttya            u    root     /dev/term/a I -
➥/usr/bin/login - 96ØØ ldterm,ttcompat ttya login:  - tvi925 y  #
zsmon           ttymon          ttyb            u    root     /dev/term/b I -
➥/usr/bin/login - 96ØØ ldterm,ttcompat ttyb login:  - tvi925 y  #
ttymonØ        ttymon          ttyØØ           u    root     /dev/term/ØØ - - -
➥/usr/bin/login - 96ØØ login: - tvi925 - #
#
```

Terminal Connection Troubleshooting

When troubleshooting problems with terminal connections, first check the following list with the user:

- Was the correct login ID or password used?
- Is the terminal waiting for the xon flow control key?
- Is the serial cable loose or unplugged?
- Is the serial cable verified to work properly?
- Is the terminal configuration correct?
- Is the terminal turned off?

Continue troubleshooting by checking the configuration of the terminal.

- Was the proper `ttylabel` used?
- Does the `ttylabel` setting of the modem match the `ttylabel` of the SAF?

If the problem persists, check the system software.

- Was the port monitor configured to enable logins?
- Does it have the correct `ttylabel` associated with it?
- Is the port monitor enabled? (Use the `sacadm -l -p` *pmtag* command.)
- Is the service enabled? (Use the `pmadm -l -p` *pmtag* command.)

If the SAC is starting the ttymon port monitor, the service is enabled, and the configuration matches the port monitor configuration, continue to search for the problem by checking the serial connection. A serial connection consists of serial ports, cables, and terminals. Test each of these parts by using it with two other parts that are known to be reliable.

To check for cable problems, a breakout box is helpful. It plugs into the RS-232-C cable. A patch panel lets you connect any pin to any other pins. A breakout box often contains light-emitting diodes that show whether a signal is present on each pin.

If you cannot access a port, and the `ps` command shows that a process is running on it, make sure that pin 8 in the cable is connected. If that does not work, check that the device driver is configured properly to set the correct flag for the line to Off.

Using Admintool: Serial Ports to Add a Character Terminal

You can use the Admintool: Serial Ports graphical user interface to add a character terminal. Table 10–6 shows the Admintool default settings for adding a character terminal.

Table 10–6 Terminal—Hardwired Default Values

Item	Default Value
Port	a | b | other port identifier*
Service	enabled
Baud rate	`9600`
Terminal type	`tvi925*`
Option: Initialize only	`no`
Option: Bidirectional	`no`
Option: Software carrier	`yes`
Login prompt	`login:`
Comment	Terminal—Hardwired
Service tag	`ttyn*`
Port monitor tag	`zsmon`
Create utmp entry	`yes`
Connect on Carrier	`no`
Service	`/usr/bin/login`
Streams modules	`ldterm,ttcompat`
Timeout (secs)	`never`

* Revised in this edition.

Use the following steps to configure SAF for a character terminal:

1. In the Admintool: Serial Ports window, click the port that will be used with a terminal.
2. From the Edit menu, choose Modify. The Admintool: Modify Serial Port window is displayed showing the Basic settings. Click either More or Expert to display more settings.
3. Terminal—Hardwired is the default choice from the Template menu. If it is not displayed, choose it. Admintool: Modify Serial Port window displays default settings for the Terminal—Hardwired template shown in Table 10–6.
4. Change values of template entries if desired. If you change the values, make sure that you change the comment field so that other users know that you have changed the default values.
5. Click OK to configure the port.

Initializing Ports Without Configuring

The Admintool: Modify Serial Port window enables you to initialize a port without configuring it. Table 10–7 shows the Admintool default values for initializing a port without configuring it.

Table 10–7 Initialize Only—No Connection Default Values

Item	Default Value
Port	a | b | other port identifier*
Service	enabled
Baud rate	9600
Terminal type	tvi925*
Option: Initialize only	yes
Option: Bidirectional	no
Option: Software carrier	no
Login prompt	ttyn login:*
Comment	Initialize Only—No Connection
Service tag	ttyn*
Port monitor tag	`zsmon`
Create utmp entry	yes
Connect on carrier	no
Service	`/usr/bin/login`

Table 10–7 Initialize Only—No Connection Default Values (continued)

Item	Default Value
Streams modules	ldterm,ttcompat
Timeout (secs)	never

* Revised in this edition.

To initialize ports without configuring for a specific device, follow these steps:

1. From the Admintool: Serial Ports window, click the port you want to initialize.
2. From the Edit menu, choose Modify. The Admintool: Modify Serial Port window is displayed.
3. Click Expert to display all of the settings.
4. Choose Initialize Only—No Connection from the Template menu.
5. Change values of template entries if desired. If you change the values, make sure that you change the comment field so that other users know that you have changed the default values.
6. Click OK to initialize the port.

Removing Port Services

To delete services on configured ports using Admintool, follow these steps:

1. In the Admintool: Serial Ports window, click the port that you want to delete.
2. From the Edit menu, choose Delete. A confirmation window is displayed asking if you really want to delete the service for the specified port.
3. Click Cancel to stop the operation or Delete to delete the port.

CHAPTER

11

Setting Up Printing Services

What's New in Printing

Print Administration Tools in the Solaris 2.6 Environment

System Requirements for a Print Server

Printer Configuration Information

Local PostScript Printer Setup

Print Server Setup

Print Client Setup

Using the SunSoft Print Client

Printing Problems

UNSOFT RECOMMENDS THAT YOU USE ADMINTOOL: PRINTERS WINDOW OR SOLSTICE AdminSuite to set up printing on systems running Solaris 2.1 (or later) system software. Consult the *Solaris System Administrator's Guide* for information on how to use the Admintool: Printers window and for information on how to use printing commands. See the bibliography at the back of this book for a complete reference.

This chapter describes how to set up network printing services from a command line using SAF commands and the listen port monitor.

The network at your site may comprise many systems—some may be running Solaris 2.*x* system software, and others may be running SunOS 4.*x*. You need to decide which systems will have local printers directly cabled to them and which systems will connect to printers over the network. The system that has the printer connected to it and makes the printer available to other systems is called a *print server*. The system that has its printing needs met by a print server is called a *print client*.

You perform three basic tasks to set up printing services:

- Setting up local printers
- Setting up print servers
- Setting up print clients

You can have the following client-server combinations:

- SunOS 5.*x* print clients with a SunOS 5.*x* print server
- SunOS 5.*x* and SunOS 4.*x* print clients with a SunOS 5.*x* print server
- SunOS 5.*x* and SunOS 4.*x* print clients with a SunOS 4.*x* print server

This chapter describes how to set up printing services using the SunOS 5.*x* LP print service. Refer to your SunOS 4.*x* documentation for information on how to set up SunOS 4.*x* print servers and print clients.

What's New in Printing

The Solaris 2.6 print software provides better centralized print administration than does the LP print software in previous Solaris releases. With the Solaris 2.6 release, you can easily set up and manage print clients using the NIS or NIS+ name services.

Solaris 2.6 print software features include:

- Redesign of print packages
- Print protocol adaptor

- SunSoft print client
- Network printer support

The Solaris 2.6 print software limitations do not include:

- Support for print servers defined as s5 (the System V print protocol) in previous Solaris 2.*x* releases.
- Print filtering on print clients.

Redesign of Print Packages

The Solaris 2.6 print packages have been redesigned to provide greater flexibility and modularity of print software installation and to enable installation of a print client that takes up less disk space.

In the Solaris 2.6 redesign, the default is to install all of the packages. Print servers require installation of all packages, including both client and server. For print clients, you can choose to install only the print client packages. PostScript filter software is provided in its own print package, which provides client configuration files and utilities for the print service. Table 11–1 describes the new set of print packages.

Table 11–1 Solaris 2.6 Print Packages

Package	Base Directory	Description
SUNWpcr	root (/)	SunSoft Print-Client
SUNWpcu	usr	SunSoft Print-Client
SUNWpsr	root (/)	SunSoft Print-LP Server
SUNWpsu	usr	SunSoft Print-LP Server
SUNWpsf	usr	PostScript Filters
SUNWscplp	usr	SunSoft Print-Source Compatibility

The following print packages have been removed from the Solaris 2.6 release:

- SUNWlpr - LP print service, (root)
- SUNWlpu - LP print service-Client, (usr)
- SUNWlps - LP print service-Server, (usr)

Print commands from SUNWscpu have been moved into the SUNWscplp (SunSoft Print-Source Compatibility) package.

Print Protocol Adaptor

The Solaris 2.6 print protocol adaptor replaces the Service Access Facility (SAF), the network listener, and `lpNet` on the inbound side of the LP spooler with a more modular and modern design.

The print protocol adaptor provides the following features:

- Implementation of the complete BSD print protocol plus extended Solaris functionality.
- Multiple spooling systems can coexist on the same host and have access to the BSD print protocol.
- Third-party application developers can extend the print protocol adaptor to support other printing protocols such as Apple and Novell.

The new print protocol adaptor is compatible with print clients set up in previous Solaris 2.*x* releases if the "BSD" protocol was used to configure these clients. If the "BSD" protocol was not used, you must modify the previous Solaris 2.*x* print client configuration to use the "BSD" protocol using Admintool™, Solstice Printer Manager, or the `lpsystem` command.

SunSoft Print Client

The SunSoft Print Client software is bundled with the Solaris 2.6 release as packages SUNWpcr and SUNWpcu. This software was previously released as an unbundled product. It was available on the Solaris Migration CD-ROM and as part of the AdminSuite 2.*x* suite of administration products.

The SunSoft Print Client software uses an NIS map, NIS+ table, or a single file to provide centralized client administration in the Solaris 2.6 release. Features of the Print Client software include:

- Replacing the `/etc/lp` directory structure with a configuration database that can be stored in a user file (`$HOME/.printers`), a system file (`/etc/prints.conf`), an NIS map (`printers.conf.byname`), or an NIS+ FNS context.
- Using a more streamlined implementation that provides reduced client overhead and quicker, more accurate responses to print status requests.
- Using the `lpset(1M)` command to create the `printers.conf` file.
- Reducing the size of the package from previous Solaris releases.
- Providing interoperability with the BSD protocol available with SunOS 4.*x*, Solaris 2.*x*, HPUX, and other systems as described in RFC-1179.

Enhanced Network Printer Support

The Solaris 2.6 print software provides better support for network printers than in previous Solaris releases, including the following features:

- A new interface script, `/usr/lib/lp/model/netstandard`, which is specifically designed to support network printers. This script collects the spooler and print database information necessary for performing network printing and passes that information to the print output module.
- A new print output module, `netpr`, is called from the `netstandard` interface script to print the print job. It opens a network connection to the printer, creates the correct protocol instructions, and sends the data to the printer. The `netpr` program currently supports two protocols: BSD print protocol and a TCP pass-through.
- New arguments to the `lpadmin -o` command are available for specifying destination name, protocol, and time-out values for the network printer.
- Solstice AdminSuite 2.3 Printer Manager can be used to set up and manage network printers.

Print Administration Tools in the Solaris 2.6 Environment

The Solaris 2.6 printing software provides an environment for setting up and managing client access to printers on a network. The Solaris 2.6 printing software contains the following components:

- SunSoft Print Client software, previously available only with the Solstice™ AdminSuite™ set of administration tools, enables you to make printers available to print clients by using a name service.
- Admintool, a graphical user interface, enables you to manage printing on a local system.
- The LP print service commands, a command-line interface, enables you to set up and manage printers that provide additional functionality that is not available with the other print management tools.
- The Solstice AdminSuite Printer Manager, a graphical user interface that lets you manage printers in a name service environment and over the network, is available with the Solaris 2.6 server products.

NOTE. *If you do not use the Solstice AdminSuite Print Manager to set up and manage printing, you must use some combination of the other components to completely manage printing in the Solaris 2.6 environment.*

Table 11–2 summarizes the features of the Solaris 2.6 printing components.

Table 11–2 Solaris 2.6 Printing Component Features

Component	Graphical User Interface	Set Up Print Clients	Manage Print Clients and Servers	NIS or NIS+
SunSoft Print Client	No	Yes	No	Yes
Admintool	Yes	Yes	Yes	No
LP commands	No	Yes	Yes	No
Solstice AdminSuite	Yes	Yes	Yes	Yes

Choosing a Method to Manage Printers

As you can see from the list of features in Table 11–2, the printing components provide quite a bit of overlapping functionality. Your site requirements and needs for centralized or decentralized printer administration will determine the optimum combination of tools you use for print administration.

The Solaris 2.6 print client software and the Printer Manager application in Solstice AdminSuite offer a graphical solution for setting up and managing printers on a network. The advantage of the Solaris 2.6 print client software is that it supports a name service (NIS or NIS+), which enables you to centralize print administration for a network. You can also use the `lpadmin` command to configure printers on individual systems.

You must run Admintool on the system to which the printer is connected. When you set up a printer, Admintool makes the appropriate changes in the `/etc/printers.conf` file and `/etc/lp` directories on the system as required. You can use Admintool to set up a system as a print server or print client only if it is running the SunOS 5.*x* operating system.

Admintool should meet most of your needs for setting up printing services. However, if you have special needs, such as writing scripts, you may want to use the LP print service commands directly.

System Requirements for a Print Server

You can attach a printer to a standalone system or to any system on the network. You can make any networked system that has a printer and adequate system resources into a print server.

Each print server should have the following system resources:

- Spooling directory space of 8MB (or more)
- Hard disk strongly recommended (not required)

- Memory of 12MB (or more)
- Swap space of 20 to 24MB (or more)

If the print server has a `/var` directory that resides in a small partition, and if a large amount of disk space is available elsewhere, you can use that space as spooling space by mounting it on the `/var` directory on the print server. Consult the *Solaris 2.6 System Administrator's Guide* for information about mounting file systems and editing the `/etc/vfstab` file.

Table 11–3 provides some common disk configuration information and recommendations for the average number of users that the configuration can serve.

Table 11–3 Typical Disk Configuration Information

Disk Size (MB)	/var Partition (MB)	Spooling Space (MB)	Number of Users
104	8	4	1– 3
207	16	12	1–16
424	212	206	1–32
669	335	328	1–64
991	500	490	1–64 or more
1360	335	206	1–32

Printer Configuration Information

To configure a printer on the network, you need the following configuration information:

- The serial (or parallel) device name (required), for example `/dev/xxx`.
- A unique name for the printer (required).
- The printer type (required).
- The type of file content (required), for example, PS for PostScript, simple for ASCII, or both.
- The filter names for your printer (required).
- The print server's Internet Protocol (IP) address in universal address format (output by the `lpsystem -A` command), required for printing between systems (required).
- The description of the printer to convey to users (recommended, optional)
- The default printer for each system (recommended, optional).

Configuration information is stored in the LP configuration files in the `/etc/lp` directory.

Printer Device Name

The *printer device name* identifies the port to which the printer is connected. When you use the `-v` option to identify the port, the `lpadmin` command uses the stty settings from the standard printer interface program to initialize the printer port.

Printer Name

Choose a *printer name* for the printer you are adding to a system. A printer name must be unique among all printers known to the system, and can contain a maximum of 14 alphanumeric characters and underscores. When you administer printers in a complex network, keep printer names unique.

You should also establish conventions when naming printers. Make your printer names meaningful and easy to remember. A printer name can identify the type of printer, its location, or the print server name. Establish a naming convention that works for your site. If you have different types of printers on the network, for example, including the printer type as part of the printer name can help users choose an appropriate printer. You could identify, for instance, PostScript printers with the letters `PS`. If all of the printers at your site are PostScript printers, however, you do not need to include `PS` as part of the printer name.

You use printer names to perform the following tasks:

- Add the printer to the LP print service
- Change the configuration of the printer
- Monitor the print queue
- Check the status of the printer
- Accept or cancel print requests for the printer
- Enable or disable the printer
- Specify a default printer
- Submit a print job to a particular printer

Printer Port

When you install a printer or later change its setup, you can specify the device, or the printer port, to which the printer is connected by using Admintool or the `lpadmin -p` *`printer-name`* `-v` *`device-name`* command.

Most systems have two serial ports and a parallel port. Unless you add ports, you cannot connect more than two serial printers and a parallel printer to one system.

With Admintool, you can choose either `/dev/term/a` or `/dev/term/b` for the serial port, or choose Other and specify any port name that the print server recognizes. These options give you as much flexibility as the `lpadmin` command.

The LP print service initializes the printer port using the settings from the standard printer interface program. If you have a parallel printer or a serial printer for which the default settings do not work, you need to adjust the printer port characteristics to use a custom setting.

NOTE. *If you use multiple ports on an x86 microprocessor-based system, only the first port is enabled by default. To use more than one port, you must manually edit the device driver port configuration file for each additional asy (serial) port or lp (parallel) port. Here are the pathnames for the x86 port configuration files:*

```
/platform/i86pc/kernel/drv/asy.conf
/platform/i86pc/kernel/drv/lp.conf
```

Refer to your x86 documentation for information about configuring serial and parallel ports on x86 systems.

Printer Type

A `printer type` is the generic name for a printer. By convention, it is often derived from the manufacturer's name. For example, the printer type for the Digital Equipment Corporation LN03 printer is `ln03`. However, one common printer type—PS, for PostScript laser printer—does not follow this convention. PS is used for many different models of PostScript printers.

For a local PostScript printer, use either `PS` or `PSR` (which reverses the pages) as the printer type. `PSR` works reliably only with PostScript files that conform to the standards in Appendix C of the *PostScript Language Reference Manual*. Refer to the bibliography at the back of this book for a complete reference.

The printer type must match an entry in the terminfo database. The LP print service uses the printer type to extract information about the capabilities of the printer from the terminfo database, as well as the control data, to initialize a particular printer before printing a file.

You specify the printer type with the `-T` option of the `lpadmin` command, where *`printer-type`* matches the name of a file in the `terminfo` database, which contains compiled terminal information files. These files are located in the `/usr/share/lib/terminfo/*` directories. For example, the `terminfo` file for the type name `PS` is `/usr/share/lib/terminfo/P/PS`.

If a printer can emulate more than one kind of printer, you can assign it several types. If you specify more than one printer type, the LP print service uses one of the types as appropriate for each print request.

If you don't specify a type, the default type is `unknown`, and the local printer does not get initialized before printing a file. When specifying the printer type on a SunOS 5.*x* print client, the default type `unknown` is desirable.

File Content Type

The *file content type* tells the LP print service what types of files you can print directly on each printer. Print requests can ask for a type, and the LP print service uses this type to match jobs to printers. Most printers can print two types of files:

- The same type as the printer type (for example, `PS` for PostScript)
- The type `simple` (an ASCII file)

Some printers can accept and print several types of files. You can specify the names of the content types as a list. Table 11–4 lists some common file content types for local printers.

Table 11–4 Common File Content Types for Local Printers

Type	Description
`any`	Accepts any file content type
`cif`	Output of BSD cifplot
`daisy`	Daisy wheel printer
`dmd`	DMD
`fortran`	ASA carriage control format
`otroff`	Cat typesetter instructions generated by BSD or pre-System V `troff` (old `troff`)
`plot`	Plotting instructions from Tektronix displays and devices
`PS`	PostScript language
`raster`	Raster bitmap format for Varian raster devices
`simple`	ASCII file
`tex`	DVI format files
`troff`	Device-independent output from `troff`

NOTE. *If you specify more than one printer type, you must specify* `simple` *as one of the content types.*

Content type names may look like printer names, but you are free to choose content type names that are meaningful to you and the users of the printers. You use the following command to specify the file content type:

```
lpadmin -p printer-name -I file-content-type
```

The content types to use for a Solaris 2.*x* print client are `any`, `simple`, and `PS`. If you omit the content type, the default is `any`, which filters files on the print server. The type `PS` filters files on the client.

Table 11–5 lists the printer type and content type for frequently used PostScript printers.

NOTE. *The name* `simple` *means ASCII file, and* `any` *means any file content type. Be sure to use them consistently. The name* `terminfo` *is reserved as a reference to all types of printers.*

All printers in Table 11–5 are either `PS` or `PSR`. `PS` prints a banner page first, and prints the document from front to back. `PSR` reverses the pagination, printing the pages in reverse order, with the banner page last. File content type is `PS` for all these models.

Table 11–5 Frequently Used PostScript Printers

Manufacturer	Model
Apple	Personal LW II LaserWriterII LaserWriter IINT LaserWriter IINTX
Canon	BJ-10 BJ-130e LBP-4 LBP-8
Epson	all
GammaData	System300
Hewlett Packard	II, IIP, IID III, IIIP, IIID Deskjet+
Mitsubishi Electric	G650 G370 S340
Pacific	Rim Data Sciences
QMS	PS 410 PS 810
Raster Graphics	ColorStation
Seiko	5504 5514
Sharp	JX-730
Shinko	CHC-635 CHC-645-2 CHC-645-4 CHC-345 CHC-445 CHC-445-4 CHC-745-2
Talaris/Ricoh	1590, 1590-T
Talaris/Xerox	2492-B

Table 11–5 Frequently Used PostScript Printers (continued)

Manufacturer	Model
Talaris	2090
Talaris/Olympus	3093 5093
Tektronix	Phaser DXN Phaser SXS
Versatec	8836 C25*xx* series CE3000 series 7000 series V-80 series 8200 series 8500 series CADMate series 8600 series 8900 series

Table 11–6 lists additional non-PostScript printers and shows the printer type to use for configuring each printer. The file content type is simple for all these printers.

Table 11–6 Non-PostScript Printers

Printer	Printer Type
Daisy	daisy
Datagraphix	datagraphix
DEC LA100	la100
DEC LN03	ln03
DECwriter	decwriter
Diablo	diablo diablo-m8
Epson 2500 variations	epson2500 epson2500-80 epson2500-hi epson2500-hi80
Hewlett Packard HPCL printer*	hplaser
IBM Proprinter	ibmproprinter

*New in this edition.

Print Filters

Print filters are programs that convert print requests from one format to another. The LP print service uses filters to perform the following tasks:

- Convert a file from one data format to another so that you print it properly on a specific type of printer
- Handle the special modes of printing, such as two-sided printing, landscape printing, or draft- or letter-quality printing
- Detect printer faults and notify the LP print service of them so that the print service can alert users and system administrators

Not every print filter can perform all these tasks. Because each task is printer-specific, you can implement each one separately.

Solaris 2.*x* system software provides a default set of PostScript filters. Some of the TranScript filters used with SunOS 4.*x* have Solaris 2.*x* equivalents, and some do not. Table 11–7 lists and describes the default PostScript filters and identifies the TranScript filters, when applicable.

Table 11–7 PostScript Filters

Filter	Action	TranScript Equivalent
`download`	Download fonts	
`dpost`	`ditroff` to PostScript	`psdit`
`postdaisy`	`daisy` to PostScript	
`postdmd`	dmd to PostScript	
`postio`	Communicate with printer	`pscomm`
`postior`	Communicate with printer	
`postmd`	Matrix gray scales to PostScript	
`postplot`	`plot` to PostScript	`psplot`
`postprint`	`simple` to PostScript	`enscript`
`postreverse`	Reverse or select pages	`psrev`
`posttek`	TEK4014 to PostScript	`ps4014`

Solaris 2.*x* system software does not provide the following filters:

- TEX
- oscat (NeWSprint™ opost)
- Enscript

Universal Address for the Print Server

The *universal address* is required for setting up both print servers and print clients. As part of configuring the network listen process to listen for print requests from other systems, you must provide the universal address—the IP address of the print server in hexadecimal form—to the LP print service. You use the `lpsystem -A` command to find the universal address. The universal address has four parts, as shown in Figure 11–1. The last part, RFU, means Reserved for Future Use, and you could use it for other families of addresses (for example, Open Systems Interface) in the future.

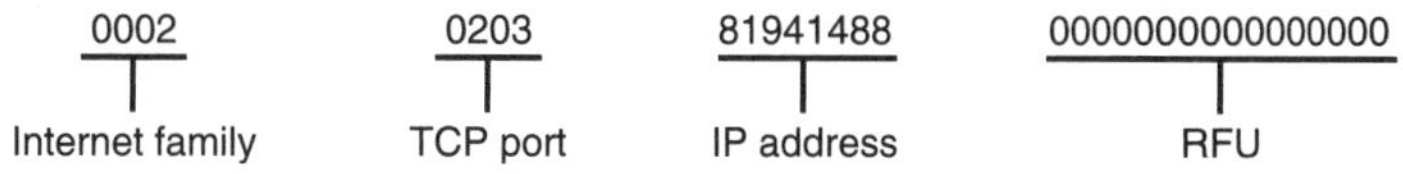

Figure 11–1
Parts of the universal address.

0002	0203	81941488	0000000000000000
Internet family	TCP port	IP address	RFU

Printer Description (Optional)

You can define a *printer description* for a printer. The description can contain any helpful information that might benefit its users. For example, the description could say where the printer is located, or whom to call when the printer has problems.

Users can display the printer's description by typing the command:

```
% lpstat -D -p printer-name
```

Default Printer (Optional)

You can specify a *default printer* for each system, even if it is the only printer connected to the system. When you specify a default printer, users do not need to type the default printer name when they use LP print service commands. However, they can override the default by explicitly naming a printer or setting the `LPDEST` environment variable. Before you can designate a default printer, it must be known to the LP print service on the system.

Local PostScript Printer Setup

The first task in setting up a print server is to set the printer up as a local Solaris 2.*x* printer. You generally perform the following tasks to set up a local printer:

- Connect the printer to the system.
- Set the printer switches or configure baud rate, port, and other settings.
- Plug the printer into a power outlet.
- Define the characteristics of the printer to the LP print service (using the `lpadmin` command).

You need the following information to set up a local printer:

- System's superuser password
- Device name (typically, `/dev/term/a` or `/dev/term/b`)
- Unique printer name
- Printer type
- Printer file content type
- Printer description (optional)

Refer to the section "Printer Configuration Information" on page 213 if you need more information. Follow these steps to configure a local printer:

1. Connect the printer to the system and turn on the power to the printer. See the printer manual for setup information. Printer cables usually are connected to a serial port.
2. Become superuser.
3. Type **chown lp /dev/term/*address*** and press Return. The lp user now owns the port device to which the printer is connected. For a serial port, *address* is usually `a` or `b`.
4. Type **chmod 600 /dev/term/*address*** and press Return. Now only lp can access the printer port device.
5. Type **lpadmin -p *printer-name* -v /dev/term/*address*** and press Return. The printer is registered with the LP print service.
6. Type **lpadmin -p *printer-name* -T *printer-type*** and press Return. Use `PS` for PostScript or `PSR` for PostScript reverse (to reverse the order of the pages) as the printer type for a PostScript printer. The printer type is registered with the LP print service.

NOTE. *If you specify printer type PS and pages print in reverse order, try printer type PSR.*

7. Type **lpadmin -p *printer-name* -I *file-content-type*** and press Return. The file-content type is specified. If you specify more than one type, separate the names with commas. Alternatively, you can enclose the list in double quotes and separate the names with spaces.
8. Type **cd /etc/lp/fd** and press Return. You are in the directory that contains the print filter descriptor files.

9. Type the following script to install the PostScript filters:

```
# sh
# for f in download dpost postio postior postprint postreverse
> do
> lpfilter -f $f -F $f.fd
> done
#
```

10. Type **accept** ***printer-name*** and press Return. The printer is now ready to begin accepting (queuing) print requests.

11. Type **enable** ***printer-name*** and press Return. The printer is now ready to process print requests in the print queue.

12. (Optional) Type **lpadmin -p** ***printer-name*** **-D "*comment*"** and press Return. Attaching a description can give users helpful information, such as where the printer is located. The comment is displayed as part of the printer status.

13. (Recommended) Type **lpadmin -d** ***printer-name*** and press Return. The printer you specify is established as the default printer for the system.

14. Type **lpstat -t** and press Return. Check the messages displayed to verify that the printer is accepted and enabled.

15. Type **lp** ***filename*** and press Return. If you specified a default printer in step 13, you do not need to include the printer destination (`-d` *`printer-name`*). The file you choose is sent to the default printer.

16. If the file does not print correctly or is not printed on the correct printer, see the section "Printing Problems" later in this chapter for help.

After you have set up the local printer, you can set the system up to become a print server. See "Print Server Setup" for instructions.

The following example is based on a network of five systems. You have one PostScript printer on the network. You designate `pine` as the print server, because it can support printing for all five systems.

The following characteristics are established for this printer:

- Printer name: `pinecone`
- Printer type: `PS`
- File content type: `PS`
- Device name: `/dev/term/b` (the port used to connect the printer)

```
pine% su
# lpstat -r
scheduler is running
# chown lp /dev/term/b
# chmod 600 /dev/term/b
```

```
# lpadmin -p pinecone -v /dev/term/b
# lpadmin -p pinecone -T PS
# lpadmin -p pinecone -I PS
# cd /etc/lp/fd
# lpfilter -f download -F download.fd
# lpfilter -f dpost -F dpost.fd
# lpfilter -f postio -F postio.fd
# lpfilter -f postior -F postior.fd
# lpfilter -f postprint -F postprint.fd
# lpfilter -f postreverse -F postreverse.fd
# accept pinecone
destination "pinecone" now accepting requests
# enable pinecone
printer "pinecone" now enabled
# lpadmin -p pinecone -D "PostScript Laser printer in Building 5, Room 262"
# lpadmin -d pinecone
# lpstat -t
scheduler is running
system default destination: pinecone
device for pinecone: /dev/term/b
pinecone accepting requests since Mon Mar 4 14:37:55 PST 1991
printer pinecone is idle. enabled since Mon Mar 4 14:37:59 PST 1991. available.
# lp -d pinecone /etc/passwd
request id is pinecone-1 (1 file)
#
```

Print Server Setup

After you set up a local printer, you need to perform the following tasks to set up a Solaris 2.*x* system (with its printer) to act as a print server:

- Configure the port monitor.
- Register the network listen service.
- Identify the print clients.

Before you set up a system as a print server, you should first add and configure a local printer. See "Local PostScript Printer Setup" for instructions. The system also should be connected to a network.

You need the following information:

- The superuser password for the print server system.
- The name of the printer.
- The name of the print server.
- The names of the systems that will be print clients.

Adding the listen Service

For print clients to access a print server running Solaris 2.*x* system software, you must configure the listen port monitor on the print server to accept service requests and to notify the LP print service of such requests. In addition, you must configure the listen port monitor on each Solaris 2.*x* print client.

Follow these steps to add the listen port monitor:

1. If you haven't done so already, set up the local printer.
2. Become superuser on the server system.
3. Type **sacadm -a -p tcp -t listen -c "/usr/lib/saf/listen tcp" -v `nlsadmin -V` -n 9999** and press Return. The `-a` option adds the port specified by the `-p` option. The `-t` option identifies the type of service. The `-c` option specifies which command starts the port monitor, the `-v` option specifies the version of the network listen process, and the `-n` option specifies the number of times SAC will restart the process if it dies. The listen port monitor is configured.
4. Type **sacadm -l** and press Return. When the network listen service is started and enabled, the following information appears on-screen:

```
# sacadm -l
PMTAG       PMTYPE    FLGS RCNT STATUS     COMMAND
tcp         listen     -    9999 ENABLED    /usr/lib/saf/listen tcp #
```

NOTE. *It may take several minutes for the network listen service to become enabled.*

Creating the listen Services

The LP print service uses a connection-oriented protocol to establish connections for incoming requests from remote systems. When the port monitor is configured, you register the following listen services:

- Service 0
- listenS5
- listenBSD

These services "listen" for print requests from print clients, or confirmations from the server. When the service detects a communication, it hands the process over to the lpsched daemon.

You use the universal address, or a modified version of it, to set up the listen port monitors. The first four digits identify the Internet family. The fifth through eighth digits identify the TCP port. (For the modified version, replace port number 0203 with 0ACE. The first digit is a zero.) To display the universal address, type **lpsystem -A** and press Return. The system's universal address appears, as shown in the following example:

```
# lpsystem -A
00020203819418 0e0000000000000000
#
```

Table 11–8 lists the variable input to the `pmadm` command used to configure the three listen port monitors.

Table 11–8 Variable Input to the pmadm Command Options

type Value	*nlscmd* Value
`lp`	`nlsadmin -o /var/spool/lp/fifos/listenS5`
`lpd`	`nlsadmin -o /var/spool/lp/fifos/listenBSD -A '\xaddress'`
`0`	`nlsadmin -c /usr/lib/saf/nlps_server -A '\xmodified_address'`

NOTE. *Type* **\x** *at the beginning of the universal (or modified universal) address exactly as shown. In addition, the address must be enclosed in single quotation marks so that the back-slash is not stripped off.*

The following steps describe how to create the three listen port monitors:

1. Type **pmadm -a -p tcp -s type -i root -m `*nlscmd*` -v `nlsadmin -V`** and press Return. Repeat this step for each of the three service types. The listen port monitor is configured to listen to requests from the LP print service for both Solaris 2.*x* and SunOS 4.*x* print clients.
2. Type **cat /var/saf/tcp/log** and press Return. Examine the messages to make sure that the services are enabled and initialized.

The following example registers all three network listen services for the print server `pine`:

```
# lpsystem -A
00020203819418 0e0000000000000000
# pmadm -a -p tcp -s lp -i root -m `nlsadmin -o /var/spool/lp/fifos/listenS5`
-v `nlsadmin -V`
# pmadm -a -p tcp -s lpd -i root -m `nlsadmin -o /var/spool/lp/fifos/listenBSD
-A '\x00020203819418 0e0000000000000000'` -v `nlsadmin -V`
# pmadm -a -p tcp -s 0 -i root -m `nlsadmin -c /usr/lib/saf/nlps server -A
'\x00020ACE8194180e0000000000000000'` -v `nlsadmin -V`
pine# cat /var/saf/tcp/log
10/28/91 10:22:51; 178; @(#)listen:listen.c     1.19.9.1
10/28/91 10:22:51; 178; Listener port monitor tag: tcp
10/28/91 10:22:51; 178; Starting state: ENABLED
10/28/91 10:22:51; 178; Service 0: fd 6 addr \x00020ACE8194180e0000000000000000
10/28/91 10:22:51; 178; Service lpd: fd 7 addr \x00020203819418 0e0000000000000000
10/28/91 10:22:52; 178; Net opened, 2 addresses bound, 56 fds free
10/28/91 10:22:52; 178; Initialization Complete
#
```

Specifying the Print Client Systems

For print client systems to access a Solaris 2.*x* print server, you must tell the print server which systems can send print requests. In effect, you have to register the names of the print clients with the LP print service on the server. This information is stored in the file `/etc/lp/Systems`.

To configure print client systems, type **lpsystem client-system1 client-system2...** and press Return. The print client systems that are designated to use the print server are identified. You can specify more than one system name, as long as you separate them with spaces. You can add print clients at any time by using the command in this step.

The following example shows how to identify the print clients `oak`, `ash`, `elm`, and `maple`.

```
# lpsystem oak ash elm maple
"oak" has been added.
"ash" has been added.
"elm" has been added.
"maple" has been added.
```

NOTE. *The Solaris 2.1 release provides a patch so that any client can print on any print server. This feature is useful for cutting down on print client administration in large corporations.*

You can perform additional optional setup steps, depending on the type of printer and the printing policies you want to set for your site. For example, you may want to create a class of printers and include the printer in that class, or you may want to set up the printer to use a certain form.

The next task, after you set up the print server, usually is to set up print clients. It is difficult to tell whether you have set up the print server correctly until you set up a print client and try to print from it.

Print Client Setup

On each Solaris 2.*x* print client, you need to complete the following tasks so that the print client can use the printer that is connected to the print server:

- Start the LP print service scheduler.
- Identify the printer and server system to which the printer is connected.
- Define the characteristics of the printer.
- Configure the port monitor and register the listen services with the port monitor.

Setting up print servers and clients presumes that you have a network that enables access between systems. If your network is running NIS+, you already should have enabled access between systems. If your network is not running NIS or NIS+, you must add the Internet address and system name for each client system to the `/etc/hosts` file on the print server *before* you set up print servers and print clients. You must also include the Internet address and system name for the print server in the /etc/hosts file of each print client system.

Before you can set up print clients, the print server must be installed and configured and the systems must be able to access one another over the network.

You need the following information to configure print clients:

- Superuser password of the print server
- Superuser password for each print client system
- Names of printer, server, and clients
- Printer type (optional; if you do not specify a printer type, unknown is used by default.)
- Printer file content type (optional; if you do not specify a file content type, any is the default.)

Follow these steps on the Solaris 2.*x* print server.

NOTE. *If the print clients are going to use a SunOS 4.1 print server, skip steps 1, 2, and 3.*

1. Become superuser.
2. Type **lpstat -p** ***printer-name*** **-l** and press Return. The type, file content, and class of the printer appear. Write down this information; you need it in subsequent steps.
3. If you have not already identified the print clients to the print server, type **lpsystem** ***client-system1 client-system2...*** and press Return.

On each Solaris 2.*x* print client:

1. Become superuser.
2. Specify the type of print server system:
   - For Solaris 2.*x* print servers, type **lpsystem -t s5** ***server-system-name*** and press Return. The print server system is identified as a Solaris 2.*x* print server. The information is added to the /etc/lp/Systems file on the print client.
   - For SunOS 4.*x* print servers, type **lpsystem -t bsd** ***server-system-name*** and press Return. The print server system is identified as a SunOS 4.*x* print server. The information is added to the /etc/lp/Systems file on the print client.
3. Type **lpadmin -p** ***printer-name*** **-s** ***server-system-name*** and press Return. The printer on the print server is identified.
4. (Optional) Type **lpadmin -p** ***printer-name*** **-T unknown** and press Return. If you omit this step, the printer type unknown is used by default.
5. (Optional) Type **lpadmin -p** ***printer-name*** **-I** ***file-content-type*** and press Return. Specify the file content type as simple, any, or PS. If you omit this step, a file content type of any

is used by default. The name simply means ASCII file. Use `any` when you want files to be filtered on the print server. Use `PS` to indicate that the print server supports PostScript and to have the files filtered on the print client.

6. Type **cd /etc/lp/fd** and press Return. You are in the directory that contains the print filter descriptor files.
7. Type the following script to install the PostScript filters:

```
# sh
# for f in download dpost postio postior postprint postreverse
> do
> lpfilter -f $f -F $f.fd
> done
#
```

8. Type **accept** ***printer-name*** and press Return. The LP print system now accepts print requests.
9. Type **enable** ***printer-name*** and press Return. The printer is enabled and can process print requests.
10. (Optional) Type **lpadmin -p** ***printer-name*** **-D "*comment*"** and press Return. Attaching a description can give the user helpful information, such as where the printer is located. The comment is displayed as part of the printer status.
11. (Recommended) Type **lpadmin -d** ***printer-name*** and press Return. The printer you specify is configured as the default printer for the client system.
12. Type **lpstat -t** and press Return. Check the messages on-screen to verify that the printer has been accepted and enabled.
13. Type **lp -d** ***printer-name filename*** and press Return. The file you choose is sent to the printer. If the file does not print correctly or does not print on the right printer, see "Printing Problems" later in this chapter for help.

Follow these additional steps on Solaris 2.*x* print clients only if you want to set up the SAF. You do not need to do any additional configuration for a SunOS 4.*x* print client.

1. Type **sacadm -a -p tcp -t listen -c "/usr/lib/saf/listen tcp" -v `nlsadmin -V` -n 9999** and press Return. The network listen service that listens for TCP/IP requests is started.
2. Type **sacadm -l** and press Return. When the network listen service is starting, the following information appears:

```
# sacadm -l
PMTAG        PMTYPE    FLGS RCNT STATUS      COMMAND
tcp          listen     -    9999 ENABLED    /usr/lib/saf/listen tcp #
```

NOTE. *It may take several minutes before the network listen service is enabled.*

3. Type **lpsystem -A** and press Return. The system's universal address appears. You use the universal address, or a modified version of it, to configure the port monitors. The first

four digits identify the Internet family. The fifth through eighth digits identify the TCP port. For the modified version, replace port number 0203 with 0ACE. (The first digit is a zero.)

Table 11–9 lists the variable input to the `pmadm` command used to configure the three listen port monitors.

Table 11–9 Variable Input to the pmadm Command Options

type Value	*nlscmd* Value
`lp`	`nlsadmin -o /var/spool/lp/fifos/listenS5`
`lpd`	`nlsadmin -o /var/spool/lp/fifos/listenBSD -A '\xaddress'`
`0`	`nlsadmin -c /usr/lib/saf/nlps server -A '\xmodified address'`

NOTE. *Type* **\x** *at the beginning of the universal (or modified universal) address in the next step exactly as shown. In addition, be sure to enclose the address in single quotation marks so as to avoid stripping off the backslash.*

4. Type **pmadm -a -p tcp -s *type* -i root -m `*nlscmd*` -v `nlsadmin -V`** and press Return. Repeat the command for each of the three types. The port monitor is configured to listen to requests from the LP print service.
5. Type **cat /var/saf/tcp/log** and press Return. Examine the messages on-screen to make sure that the services have been enabled and initialized.

The following example shows the steps for setting up a Solaris 2.*x* print client `oak` to print on `pinecone`, which is connected to the Solaris 2.*x* print server pine. Beginning with the `lpsystem` command, you would perform the same steps on other print clients such as `ash`, `elm`, and `maple` to let them become print clients of `pine`. You must tell each client system about the print server and the characteristics of its printer.

```
oak% rlogin pine
pine% lpstat -p pinecone -l
printer pinecone is idle. enabled since Wed Jan 2 18:20:22 PST 1991. available.
        Content types: PS
        Printer types: PS
        Description:
        Users allowed:
                (all)
        Forms allowed:
                (none)
        Banner not required
        Character sets:
                (none)
        Default pitch:
        Default page size:
pine% su
# lpsystem -t s5 oak
```

```
"oak" has been added.
pine% logout
oak% su
# lpsystem -t s5 pine
"pine" has been added.
# lpadmin -p pinecone -s pine -T PS -I PS
# cd /etc/lp/fd
# lpfilter -f download -F download.fd
# lpfilter -f dpost -F dpost.fd
# lpfilter -f postio -F postio.fd
# lpfilter -f postior -F postior.fd
# lpfilter -f postprint -F postprint.fd
# lpfilter -f postreverse -F postreverse.fd
# accept pinecone
destination "pinecone" now accepting requests
# enable pinecone
printer "pinecone" now enabled
# lpadmin -p pinecone -D "PostScript Laser printer in Building 5, Room 262"
# lpadmin -d pinecone
# lpstat -t
scheduler is running
system default destination: pinecone
system for pinecone: pine
pinecone accepting requests since Mon Mar 4 15:15:21 PST 1991
printer pinecone is idle. enabled since Mon Mar 4 15:15:26 PST 1991. available.
# lpsystem -A
000202038194180e0000000000000000
# pmadm -a -p tcp -s lp -i root -m `nlsadmin -o /var/spool/lp/fifos/listenS5`
-v `nlsadmin -V`
# pmadm -a -p tcp -s lpd -i root -m `nlsadmin -o /var/spool/lp/fifos/listenBSD
-A
'\x000202038194180e0000000000000000'` -v `nlsadmin -V`
# pmadm -a -p tcp -s 0 -i root -m `nlsadmin -c /usr/lib/saf/nlps_server -A
'\x00020ACE8194180e0000000000000000'` -v `nlsadmin -V`
pine# cat /var/saf/tcp/log
10/28/91 10:22:51; 178; @(#)listen:listen.c     1.19.9.1
10/28/91 10:22:51; 178; Listener port monitor tag: tcp
10/28/91 10:22:51; 178; Starting state: ENABLED
10/28/91 10:22:51; 178; Service 0: fd 6 addr \ \x00020ACE8194180e0000000000000000
10/28/91 10:22:51; 178; Service lpd: fd 7 addr \x000202038194180e0000000000000000
10/28/91 10:22:52; 178; Net opened, 2 addresses bound, 56 fds free
10/28/91 10:22:52; 178; Initialization Complete
# lp /etc/passwd
request id is pinecone-23
```

Using the SunSoft Print Client

This section describes how the SunSoft Print Client works. The SunSoft Print Client is now provided as part of the Solaris 2.6 release. It was available previously only as an unbundled product.

A system becomes a SunSoft print client when you install the SunSoft print client software and enable access to remote printers on the system. The SunSoft print client commands have the same names and produce the same output as the print commands of the previous Solaris releases.

The Solaris 2.6 SunSoft print client commands use a greater number of options to locate printer configuration information than in the previous Solaris operating environment and the client communicates directly with the print server.

The print command locates a printer and printer configuration information in the following sequence:

- It checks to see if the user specified a destination printer name or printer class in one of the three valid styles—atomic, POSIX, or context-based. See "Submitting Print Requests" on page 232 for more information.
- If the user did not specify a printer name or class in a valid style, the command checks the user's `PRINTER` or `LPDEST` environment variable for a default printer name.
- If neither environment variable for the default printer is defined, the command checks the `.printers` file in the user's home directory for the `_default printer` alias.
- If the command does not find a `_default printer` alias in the `.printers` file, it then checks the SunSoft print client's `/etc/printers.conf` file for configuration information.
- If the printer is not found in the `/etc/printers.conf` file, the command checks the name service (NIS or NIS+) if any.

The client does not have a local print queue. The SunSoft print client sends its requests to the queue on the specified print server. The client writes the print request to a temporary spooling area only if the print server is not available or if an error occurs. This streamlined path to the server decreases the print client's use of resources, reduces the chance for printing problems, and improves performance.

Printer Configuration Resources

This section describes the resources that the SunSoft print client commands use to locate printer names and printer configuration information.

The SunSoft print client commands can use a name service, which is a shared network resource, for storing printer configuration information for all printers on the network. The name service (either NIS or NIS+) simplifies the maintenance of printer configuration information. When you add a printer in the name service, all SunSoft print clients on the network can access it.

The SunSoft print client software locates printers by checking the following resources:

- Atomic, POSIX, or context-based printer name or class (see "Submitting Print Requests" on page 232 for more information)
- User's `PRINTER` or `LPDEST` environment variable for the default printer

- User's `.printers` file for a printer alias
- SunSoft print client's `/etc/printers.conf` file
- Name service (NIS or NIS+)

Submitting Print Requests

Users submit a print request from a SunSoft print client by using either the `lp` or `lpr` command. The user can specify a destination printer name or class in any of three styles:

- Atomic style, which is the print command and option followed by the printer name or class and the filename: **lp -d** ***<printer-name> <filename>***
- POSIX style, which is the print command and option followed by server:printer and the filename: **lpr -P** ***<server-name:printer-name> <filename>***
- Context-based style, as defined in the *Federated Naming Service Guide* in the *Solaris 2.6 Software Developer AnswerBook*: **lpr -d** ***<department-name/service-name/ printer-name> <filename>***

Summary of the SunSoft Print Client Process

This section summarizes the SunSoft print client process.

1. A user submits a print request from a SunSoft print client by using a SunSoft print client command (`lp` or `lpr`).
2. The print client command checks a hierarchy of print configuration resources to determine where to send the print request.
3. The print client command sends the print request directly to the appropriate print server. A print server can be any server that accepts BSD printing protocol, including SVR4 (LP) print servers and BSD print servers such as the SunOS 4.*x* BSD print server.
4. The print server sends the print request to the appropriate printer.
5. The print request is printed.

Setting Up a Print Client by Using Admintool

You can use Admintool to set up access to a network printer or to configure a local printer. To use the Admintool: Printers windows, you must be a member of the UNIX sysadmin group (GID 14).

To set up a print client, you need this information:

- Printer name
- Print server name

- Description
- Whether this is the default printer for the print client system

Use the following steps to access a network printer:

1. (If necessary) Type **admintool&** and press Return to start Admintool.
2. From the Browse menu, choose Printers. The Admintool: Printers window appears as shown in Figure 11–2.

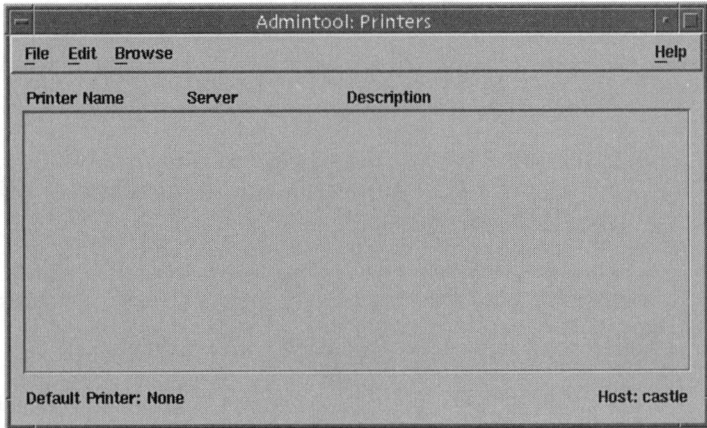

Figure 11–2
The Admintool: Printers window.

3. From the Edit menu, choose Add and Access to Printer. The Admintool: Add Access to Printer window appears, as shown in Figure 11–3.

Figure 11–3
The Admintool: Add Access To Printer window.

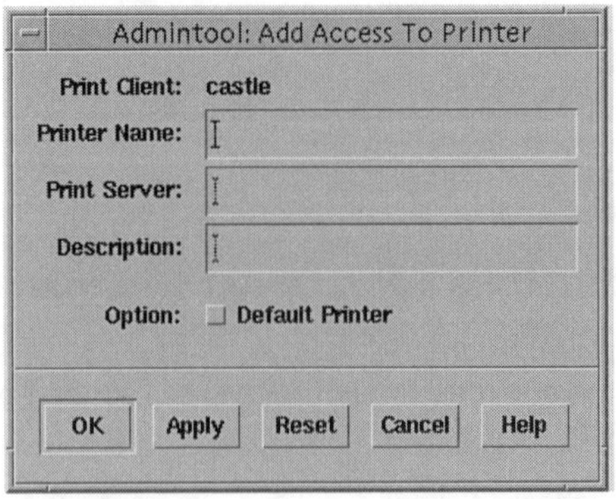

4. Enter the Printer Name, Print Server Name, and Description.
5. If you want this printer to be the default printer, click the Default Printer checkbox.

6. Click OK. The printer is configured and the printer information is added to the list in the Admintool: Printers window.

Setting Up a Local Printer by Using Admintool

To set up a local printer, you need this information:

- Printer name
- Print server name
- Description
- Printer port
- Printer type
- File contents
- Type of fault notification
- Whether this is the default printer for the print client system
- Whether you want to always print a banner page
- Whether to specify a custom user access list

Use the following steps to add a local printer:

1. (If necessary) Type **admintool&** and press Return to start Admintool.
2. From the Browse menu, choose Printers.
3. From the Edit menu, choose Add and Local Printer. The Admintool: Add Local Printer window appears, as shown in Figure 11–4.
4. Enter the Printer Name and Description.
5. Choose the Printer Port, Printer Type, File Contents, and Fault Notification.
6. If you want to specify this printer as the default printer, click the Default Printer checkbox.
7. If you want to always print the banner, click the Always Print Banner checkbox.
8. (If necessary) Modify the User Access List.

Figure 11–4
The Admintool: Add Local Printer window.

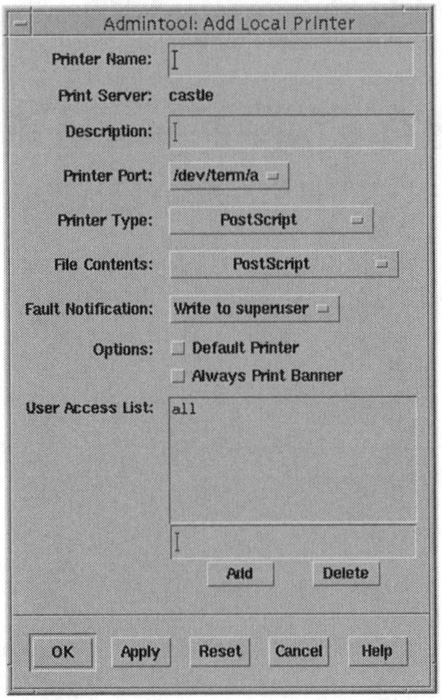

9. After you complete all of the setup steps, click OK. The printer is configured and the printer information is added to the list in the Admintool Printers window, as shown in Figure 11–5.

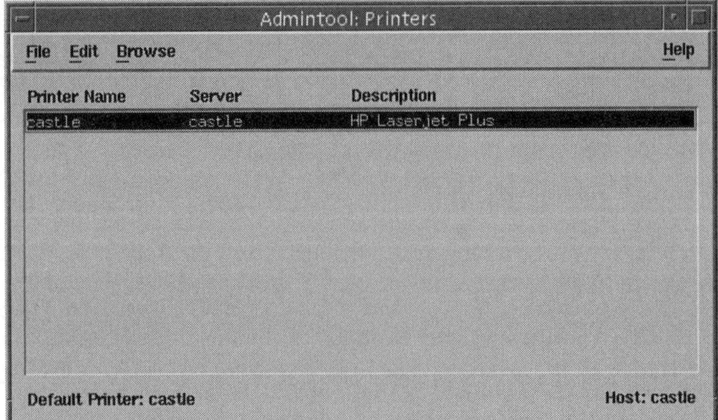

Figure 11–5
The Admintool: Printers window.

Printing Problems

When you set up a printer, you may find that nothing prints the first time you try to print a file. Or you may get a little farther: Something prints, but it is not what you expect—the output is incorrect or illegible. Then, when you get past these problems, you may encounter other problems, such as the following:

- LP commands hang
- Printers become idle
- Users get conflicting messages

NOTE. *Although many of the suggestions in this chapter are relevant to parallel printers, they are specific to the more common serial printers.*

No Output (Nothing Prints)

When nothing prints, you want to check three basic areas:

- The printer hardware
- The network
- The LP print service

Check the Hardware

The hardware is the first thing to check. As obvious as it sounds, make sure that the printer is plugged in, turned on, and online. In addition, refer to the manufacturer's documentation for information about hardware settings. Some computers use hardware switches that change the characteristics of a printer port.

The printer hardware includes the printer, the cable that connects it to the computer, and the ports at each end of the cable. As a general approach, work your way from the printer to the system.

Use the following checklist to troubleshoot hardware problems:

1. Check that the printer is plugged in, turned on, and online.
2. Check that the cable is connected to the correct port on the printer and to the correct port on the workstation or server.
3. Check that the cable is the correct cable and that it is not defective.
4. Refer to the manufacturer's documentation.
5. Check that hardware switches for the ports are set properly.
6. Check that the printer is operational. Use the printer's self-test feature if the printer has one. (Check the printer documentation for information about printer self-testing.)
7. (If applicable) Check that the baud settings for the computer and the printer are correct. If the baud settings are not the same for both the computer and the printer, sometimes nothing prints, but more often you get incorrect output.

Check the Network

Problems with remote jobs—those going from a print client to a print server—are common. Make sure that network access between the print clients and the print server is enabled.

If the network is running NIS+, check NIS+ configurations and credentials. If the network is not running NIS or NIS+, check to make sure that names and IP addresses of each client are correctly entered in the `/etc/hosts` file on the print server. Also check to be sure that the name and IP address of the print server are correctly entered in the `/etc/hosts` file of each print client system.

Use the following steps to check for problems with the network:

1. On a print client or server, type **ping** ***system-name*** and press Return. This command helps you check that the network link between the print server and print clients is set up correctly.

```
elm% ping maple
maple is alive
elm% ping oak
oak not available
elm%
```

   If the system is alive (answers the `ping`), the network connection is probably all right. Either a naming service or the local `/etc/hosts` file has successfully translated the host (system) name you entered into an IP address.

   If the system is not available, check the NIS or NIS+ setup at your site. You may need to take additional steps so that print servers and print clients can communicate with one another. If your site is not running NIS or NIS+, make sure that you have entered the IP address for the print server in the `/etc/hosts` file for each print client, and that you have entered all of the names and IP addresses of the client systems in the `/etc/hosts` file of the print server.

2. Check that the port monitor is configured correctly on the print server. For more information refer to "Print Server Setup" on page 223.

3. Check that the network listen services are registered with the port monitor on the print server. For more information refer to "Print Server Setup" on page 223.

Check the LP Print Service

For printing to work, the LP scheduler must be running on both the print server and print clients. In addition to the scheduler running, a printer must be enabled and accepting requests before it can produce output. If the LP print service is not accepting requests for a printer, the submitted jobs (print requests) are rejected. Usually, in that instance, the user receives a warning message when a job is submitted. If the LP print service is not enabled for a printer, jobs remain queued on the system until the printer is enabled. In general, analyze a printing problem as follows:

1. Follow the path of the print request step by step.
2. Examine the status of the LP print service at each step.
3. Is the configuration correct?
4. Is the printer accepting requests?
5. Is the printer enabled to process requests?
6. If the request is hanging on transmission, examine the `lpsched` log (`/var/lp/logs/lpsched`).

7. If the request is hanging locally, have notification of the printer device errors (faults) mailed to you, and re-enable the printer.

Following are a couple other questions to ask:

- Did the printer ever work?
- Was something changed recently that might affect printing?

How to Check and Start the Scheduler

The print scheduler must be running both on the print server and on each print client system. On the print server and on each print client, type **lpstat -r** and press Return. Check the output of the command to make sure that the LP print service is running.

```
elm% lpstat -r
scheduler is running
elm%
```

If the scheduler is not running, become superuser, type **/usr/lib/lp/lpsched**, and press Return.

How to Enable Printers and Accept Print Requests

You must enable printers and tell them to accept print requests.

Follow these steps both on the print server and on each print client to make sure that the printer is enabled and is accepting print requests:

1. Type **lpstat -a** and press Return to make sure that the printer is accepting requests.

   ```
   elm% lpstat -a
   oak accepting requests since Wed Mar 13 20:37:07 PST 1991
   pinecone not accepting requests since Wed Apr 17 19:10:55 PDT 1991 unknown
   reason
   elm%
   ```

   - If the printer is not accepting requests, become superuser and then type **accept *printer-name*** and press Return. The printer you specify should now accept requests. Type **lpstat -a** and press Return again to make sure that the printer is accepting requests.

2. Type **lpstat -p *printer-name*** and press Return to make sure that the printer is enabled to print requests. In the following example, the printer `pinecone` is disabled.

```
elm% lpstat -p pinecone
printer pinecone disabled since Wed Apr 17 19:13:33 PDT 1991. available.
unknown reason
elm%
```

If the printer is disabled, become superuser, then type **enable** ***printer-name*** and press Return. The printer you specify should be enabled. Type **lpstat -p** ***printer-name*** and press Return again to make sure the print is enabled.

```
pine% su
Password:
# enable pinecone
printer "pinecone" now enabled.
#
```

How to Check the Port Connection

Make sure that the cable is connected to the port that the LP print service is using. To find out which port is configured for the LP print service, type **lpstat -t** on the print server and press Return. In the following example, the printer is connected to `/dev/term/a`.

```
elm% lpstat -t
scheduler is running
system default destination: pinecone
device for pinecone: /dev/term/a
elm%
```

If the cable is connected to the right port, type **ls -l /devices** and press Return to check whether the device is owned by lp and that the permissions are set to 600. In the following example, the port is configured correctly.

```
oak% ls -l /devices
total 12
crw-rw-rw-   1 root     sys      28,  0 Mar 24 10:22 audio@1,f7201000:sound,audio
crw-rw-rw-   1 root     sys      28,128 Mar 24 10:22 audio@1,f7201000:sound,
➥audioctl
crw-------   1 root     sys      68, 11 Mar 24 09:39 eeprom@1,f2000000:eeprom
brw-rw-rw-   1 root     sys      36,  0 Mar 24 09:39 fd@1,f7200000:a
crw-rw-rw-   1 root     sys      36,  0 Mar 24 09:39 fd@1,f7200000:a,raw
brw-rw-rw-   1 root     sys      36,  1 Mar 24 09:39 fd@1,f7200000:b
crw-rw-rw-   1 root     sys      36,  1 Mar 24 09:39 fd@1,f7200000:b,raw
brw-rw-rw-   1 root     sys      36,  2 Mar 24 09:39 fd@1,f7200000:c
crw-rw-rw-   1 root     sys      36,  2 Mar 24 09:39 fd@1,f7200000:c,raw
drwxr-xr-x   2 root     sys        4608 Mar 24 10:22 pseudo
drwxr-xr-x   3 root     sys         512 Mar 24 11:41 sbus@1,f8000000
crw-------   1 lp       sys      29,  0 Mar 24 09:39 zs@1,f1000000:a
crw-rw-rw-   1 root     sys      29,131072 Mar 24 09:39 zs@1,f1000000:a,cu
crw-rw-rw-   1 root     sys      29,  1 Mar 24 09:39 zs@1,f1000000:b
crw-rw-rw-   1 root     sys      29,131073 Mar 24 09:39 zs@1,f1000000:b,cu
oak%
```

If you are not certain which device is the serial port, you can type **ls -l /dev/term** and press Return to display the link to the `/devices` file.

```
oak% ls -l /dev/term
total 4
```

```
lrwxrwxrwx   1 root     root          29 Mar 24 10:23 a ->
➥../../devices/zs@1,f1000000:a
lrwxrwxrwx   1 root     root          29 Mar 24 10:23 b ->
➥../../devices/zs@1,f1000000:b
oak%
```

Use the following steps if you need to change the ownership or permissions for the device:

1. Become superuser.
2. Type **chown lp** ***device-name*** and press Return. The lp process now owns the port device file, and no other processes can use it.
3. Type **chmod 600** ***device-name*** and press Return. Only lp or root can access the printer port device file.

How to Check Printer Configurations

Check to make sure the printer type and file content type are configured properly on the print server and on each print client. Type **lpstat -p** ***printer-name*** **-l** and press Return. In the following example, a remote printer is configured properly and is available to process print requests:

```
castle% lpstat -p seachild -l
printer seachild is idle. enabled since Sep 26 12:24 1997. available.
        Remote Name: seachild
        Remote Server: seachild
        Content types: PS
        Printer types: PS
castle%
```

If the printer type or file content type is incorrect, type **lpadmin -p** ***printer-name*** **-T** ***printer-type*** **-I** ***file-content-type*** and press Return. On the print client, try setting the print type to `unknown` and the content type to `any`.

How to Check for Printer Faults on the Print Server

Print jobs may be waiting in the queue because of a printer fault on the print server. Use the following steps to make sure that the printer is not waiting because of a printer fault:

1. On the print server, become superuser.
2. Type **lpadmin -p** ***printer-name*** **-F continue** and press Return. You have instructed the LP print service to continue if it is waiting because of a fault.
3. Type **enable** ***printer-name*** and press Return. This command forces an immediate retry.
4. (Optional) Type **lpadmin -p** ***printer-name*** **-A 'write root'** and press Return. You have instructed the LP print service to set a default policy of sending the printer fault message to the terminal on which root is logged in if the printer fails. This policy may help you to get quick notification of faults as you try to fix the problem.

It is easy to set up a printer port as a login terminal by mistake. To check that the printer port is not incorrectly set up as a login terminal, type **ps -ef** and press Return. Look for the printer port entry. In the example, port `/dev/term/a` is incorrectly set as a login terminal. You can tell by the `"passwd\n##` information at the end of the line.

```
pine% ps -ef
 root   169   167  Ø   Apr Ø4 ?        Ø:Ø8 /usr/lib/saf/listen tcp
    root   939     1  Ø 19:3Ø:47 ?        Ø:Ø2 /usr/lib/lpsched
    root   859   858  Ø 19:18:54 term/a   Ø:Ø1 /bin/sh -c /etc/lp/interfaces/
pinecone pinecone-294 pine!winsor "passwd\n##
pine%
```

If the port is set up as a login port, follow these steps to disable the login:

1. Become superuser.
2. Type **cancel *request-id*** and press Return. The request ID is shown in the output of the `ps -ef` command. In the following example, `request-id pinecone-294` is cancelled:

   ```
   pine% su
   # cancel pinecone-294
   request "pinecone-294" cancelled
   #
   ```

3. Type **lpadmin -p *printer-name* -h** and press Return. The printer port is set to be a non-login device.
4. Type **ps -ef** and press Return. Verify that the printer port is no longer a login device.

If you do not find the source of the printing problem in the basic LP print service functions, use one of the following procedures for the specific client or server case that applies.

How to Check Printing from a Solaris 2.*x* Client to a Solaris 2.*x* Print Server

Before you follow the steps in this section, you should already have checked the basic functions of the LP print service on both the print server and the print client. Make sure that the printer works locally before trying to diagnose problems with a print client.

On the print client, type **ping *print-server-name*** and press Return. This command checks to make sure that the systems are connected and available on the network.

```
oak% ping pine
pine is alive
oak% ping elm
elm not available
oak%
```

If you receive the message *`system`* `not available`, you have a network connection problem.

To check the print server type for a Solaris 2.*x* client with a Solaris 2.*x* print server:

1. On the print client, become superuser.

2. Type **lpsystem -l** and press Return. Check the output to make sure that the print server is identified as type s5 (for Solaris 2.*x*). In the following example, the print server `oak` is properly identified as type `s5`:

```
# lpsystem -l
System:                      oak
Type:                        s5
Connection timeout:          never
Retry failed connections:    after 10 minutes
Comment:                     none
#
```

If the print server is not identified correctly, type **lpsystem -t S5 *print-server-name*** and press Return, as follows:

```
# lpsystem -t S5 oak
#
```

Use the following steps to check the print queue on the print client:

1. Type **cd /var/spool/lp/requests/*system-name*** and press Return. This directory contains a record of print requests still in the queue.
2. Type **ls -l** and press Return. A list of the print jobs appears on-screen.
3. For the print job you want to check, type **lpstat -o *request-id*** and press Return. In the following example, the job is queued successfully:

```
# cd /var/spool/lp/requests/clobber
# ls -l
total 12
-rw-rw----    1 lp       lp             43 May 22 19:44 11-0
# lpstat -o pinecone-11
pinecone-11              root                 364   May 22 19:59
#
```

If the job is not queued successfully, the client-server connection may be faulty. Use the following steps to make sure that the client-server connection is not faulty:

1. On the print client, type **tail /var/lp/logs/lpsched** and press Return. The output of this command shows whether `lpsched` can connect to the print server. In the following example, the log does not indicate any problems:

```
# tail /var/lp/logs/lpsched
09/24 14:53:53: Print services started.
09/24 18:05:40: build info: 07/15/97:21:39:52
09/24 18:05:40: Print services started.
09/25 08:19:53: build info: 07/15/97:21:39:52
09/25 08:19:53: Print services started.
09/25 09:09:28: build info: 07/15/97:21:39:52
09/25 09:09:28: Print services started.
09/25 17:04:34: Print services stopped.
09/26 08:52:57: build info: 07/15/97:21:39:52
09/26 08:52:57: Print services started.
#
```

2. If the connection is not being made, on the print server, type **lpstat -t** and press Return. The output of this command shows you whether the print server is operating properly. In the following example, printers `pinecone` and `red` are up and running on the print server:

```
pine% lpstat -t
scheduler is running
system default destination: pinecone
device for pinecone: /dev/term/a
pinecone accepting requests since Thu May 23 20:56:26 PDT 1991
printer red is idle. enabled since Sun May 19 17:12:24 PDT 1991. available.
printer pinecone now printing pinecone-314. enabled since Fri May 24 16:10:39
PDT 1991. available.
pinecone-129          root              488    May 23 20:43 filtered
pine%
```

3. On the print server, type **tail /var/lp/logs/lpsched** and press Return. Examine the `lpsched` log to see if the print server is connecting to the client. If there is no entry, or if the server cannot complete the connection to the print client, `lpsched` is not transmitting correctly. The following example shows the log for two jobs. The first job, from the system `elm`, completed successfully. The second job could not complete because the print server could not connect to the system `opus`.

```
papers% tail /var/lp/logs/lpsched
05/17/93 09:39 c   834 elm Starting.
05/17/93 09:39 c   834 elm Normal process termination.
05/17/93 09:41 p   162 <none> Started child for elm, pid = 902
05/17/93 09:41 c   902 elm Starting.
05/17/93 09:41 c   902 elm Connected to remote child.
05/17/93 09:41 c   341 opus Could not connect to remote child.
05/17/93 09:51 c   341 opus Could not connect to remote child.
05/17/93 10:01 c   341 opus Could not connect to remote child.
05/17/93 10:11 c   341 opus Could not connect to remote child.
05/17/93 10:21 c   341 opus Could not connect to remote child.
papers%
```

4. On the print server, type **lpsystem -l** and press Return. Check the output to make sure that the print client is correctly identified as type `s5`. In the following example, the print client `oak` is configured correctly:

```
# lpsystem -l
System:                     clobber
Type:                       s5
Connection timeout:         never
Retry failed connections:   after 10 minutes
Comment:                    none
```

If the print client configuration is incorrect, type **lpsystem -t s5** ***client-system-name*** and press Return, as follows:

```
# lpsystem -t s5 oak
```

5. On the print server, type **sacadm -l** and press Return. Make sure that the port monitor and network listen service are set up properly. The following example shows a print server that is configured correctly:

```
# sacadm -l
PMTAG          PMTYPE         FLGS RCNT STATUS     COMMAND
tcp       listen         -    9999 ENABLED    /usr/lib/saf/listen tcp #
#
```

6. Type **pmadm -l** and press Return. The following example shows a print server that is configured for all three types of services:

```
# pmadm -l
PMTAG          PMTYPE         SVCTAG         FLGS ID       <PMSPECIFIC>
tcp      listen   lp      - root    - - p - /var/spool/lp/fifos/listenS5 #
tcp            listen         lpd            -    root
\x00020203819414 3a0000000000000000 - p -
/var/spool/lp/fifos/listenBSD #
tcp            listen         0              -    root
\x00020ACE8194143a0000000000000000 - c -
/usr/lib/saf/nlps_server #
#
```

If the service and port monitors are not configured correctly, refer to the instructions earlier in this chapter for how to configure SAF for printers.

How to Check Printing from a Solaris 2.*x* Client to a SunOS 4.*x* Print Server

The steps in this section describe how to check printing services if the Solaris 2.*x* client is receiving printing services from a SunOS 4.*x* print server. Before you use the steps in this section, you should already have checked the basic functions of the LP print service. Refer to "Check the LP Print Service" on page 237 for more information.

Use the following steps to make sure the print server is accessible:

1. On the print client, type **ping** ***print-server-name*** and press Return. If you receive the message `system not available`, you have a network problem.
2. On the print server, type **ps -ax | grep lpd** and press Return. If the lpd daemon is running, you see a line, as shown in the following example. If it is not running, no process information is shown, although you still get the `grep lpd` line.

```
maple% ps -ax | grep lpd
  126 ?  IW    0:00 /usr/lib/lpd
  200 p1 S     0:00 grep lpd
maple%
```

3. If lpd is not running on the print server, become superuser and type **/usr/lib/lpd &** and press Return. The lpd daemon starts.

Use the following steps to make sure that the remote lpd daemon is configured properly:

1. On the print server, become superuser.
2. Type **/usr/etc/lpc** and press Return. The line printer control `lpc>` prompt shows up on-screen.

3. Type **status** and press Return. Status information is displayed. In the following example, the daemon is not running and needs to be restarted:

```
maple% su
Password:
# /usr/etc/lpc
lpc> status
red:
queuing is enabled
printing is enabled
no entries
no daemon present
lpc>
```

4. If no daemon is present, at the `lpc>` prompt, type **restart** and press Return. The daemon restarts.
5. Type **status** and press Return. Verify that the lpd daemon has started.
6. Type **quit** and press Return. You are returned to the shell prompt.

Try printing from the print server. If the job does not print properly, the problem is with the server's local LP spooler. If the job prints properly, the problem is with the network or the print client.

If you get this far without pinpointing the problem, the SunOS 4.*x* system is working properly.

To make sure that the connection to the remote lpd print daemon from the print client is made correctly, type **ps -ef | grep lp** and press Return. One lpsched daemon should be running, as shown in the following example:

```
# ps -ef | grep lp
   root   154      1 80   Jan 07 ?        0:02 /usr/lib/lpsched
#
```

NOTE. *The Solaris 2.6 printing implementation does not include the lpNet daemon.*

If the lpsched daemon is not running, follow these steps to start it:

1. Become superuser.
2. Type **lpshut** and press Return. The LP print service stops.
3. Type **/usr/lib/lp/lpsched** and press Return. The LP print service restarts.

Use the following steps to make sure that the remote print server is identified correctly as a SunOS 4.*x* system:

1. On the print client, become superuser.
2. Type **lpsystem -l** and press Return. In the following example, a SunOS 4.*x* print server (maple) is specified correctly, as shown by Type being set to `bsd`.

```
elm% su
Password:
# lpsystem -l
System:                      maple
Type:                        bsd
Connection timeout:          never
Retry failed connections:    after 10 minutes
Comment:                     none
#
```

3. If the print server is identified incorrectly, type **lpsystem -t bsd *print-server-name*** and press Return.

Use the following steps to check the print logs on the print client:

1. Type **tail -100 /var/lp/logs/lpsched** and press Return. The last 100 lines of the log file are displayed. By examining the `lpsched` log, you can tell if the print client (castle in the following example) is connecting properly to the print server. The following example shows a few typical lines from the `/var/lp/logs/lpsched` log file when connections are being made properly:

```
castle% tail -100 /var/lp/logs/lpsched
09/24 14:53:53: Print services started.
09/24 18:05:40: build info: 07/15/97:21:39:52
09/24 18:05:40: Print services started.
09/25 08:19:53: build info: 07/15/97:21:39:52
09/25 08:19:53: Print services started.
09/25 09:09:28: build info: 07/15/97:21:39:52
09/25 09:09:28: Print services started.
09/25 17:04:34: Print services stopped.
09/26 08:52:57: build info: 07/15/97:21:39:52
09/26 08:52:57: Print services started.
castle%
```

   The following example shows a few lines from a log file that show that a connection has not been successful. Usually, if there is a problem you will see retries to the `BSD` system.

```
oak% tail -10 /var/lp/logs/lpsched
05/23/91 14:39 c   120 oak lpd retrying connection to oak
05/23/91 14:51 c   120 oak lpd retrying connection to oak
05/23/91 15:02 c   120 oak lpd retrying connection to oak
oak%
```

2. On the print client, become superuser.
3. Type **lpsystem -l *print-server-name*** and press Return. You see the current retry and time-out parameters.
4. Type **lpsystem -T n | 0 | N -R n | 0 | N *print-server-name*** and press Return. The `-T` option specifies the length of time a network connection can be idle before it is dropped. Choose either `n` (never time out) or `0` (drop immediately), or enter a number (wait *N* minutes, then drop connection). The default is `n`. The `-R` option specifies the length of time to wait before trying to reestablish a connection. Choose either `n` (do not retry until there is more work) or `0` (try to reconnect immediately), or enter a number

(wait *N* minutes before trying to reconnect). The default is to wait 10 minutes before trying to reconnect. In the following example, the network connection is specified to never time out, and the retry time is specified to reconnect immediately.

```
elm% su
Password:
# lpsystem -T n -R Ø maple
"maple" has been modified.
#
```

Incorrect Output

If the printer and the print service software are not configured correctly, the printer may print, but it may provide output that is not what you expect.

Check the Printer Type

If you used the wrong printer type when you set up the printer with the LP print service, inappropriate printer control characters may be sent to the printer. The results are unpredictable: Nothing may print, output may be illegible, or output may be printed in the wrong character set or font.

Use the following steps to check the printer type:

1. Become superuser.
2. Type **lpstat -p** ***printer-name*** **-l** and press Return. A list of the printer characteristics appears.

```
elm% lpstat -p pinecone -l
printer pinecone is idle. enabled since Wed Jan  2 18:2Ø:22 PST 1991.
➥available.
        Content types: PS
        Printer types: PS
        Description:
        Users allowed:
                (all)
        Forms allowed:
                (none)
        Banner not required
        Character sets:
                (none)
        Default pitch:
        Default page size:
elm%
```

If the printer type is not correct, become superuser and type **lpadmin -p** ***printer-name*** **-T** ***printer-type*** and press Return.

Check the stty Settings

Many formatting problems can result when the default stty (standard terminal) settings do not match the settings required by the printer. The following sections describe what happens when some of the settings are incorrect. Read the printer documentation to determine the correct stty settings for the printer port.

NOTE. *If a printer is connected by a parallel port, the baud setting is irrelevant.*

To display the current stty settings for the printer port, type **stty -a <** ***device-name*** and press Return. The current stty settings for the printer port are displayed.

```
elm# stty -a < /dev/term/a
speed 9600 baud;
rows = 0; columns = 0; ypixels = 0; xpixels = 0;
eucw 1:0:0:0, scrw 1:0:0:0
intr = ^c; quit = ^ |; erase = ^?; kill = ^u;
eof = ^d; eol = <undef>; eol2 = <undef>; swtch = <undef>;
start = ^q; stop = ^s; susp = ^z; dsusp = ^y;
rprnt = ^r; flush = ^o; werase = ^w; lnext = ^v;
parenb -parodd cs7 -cstopb -hupcl cread -clocal -loblk -parext
-ignbrk brkint -ignpar -parmrk -inpck istrip -inlcr -igncr icrnl -iuclc
ixon -ixany -ixoff imaxbel
isig icanon -xcase echo echoe echok -echonl -noflsh
-tostop echoctl -echoprt echoke -defecho -flusho -pendin iexten
opost -olcuc onlcr -ocrnl -onocr -onlret -ofill -ofdel tab3
elm#
```

To change the stty settings, type **lpadmin -p** ***printer-name*** **-o "stty=*options*"** and press Return.

You can change more than one option setting by including the options in single quotation marks and separating them by spaces. For example, suppose the printer requires you to enable odd parity and set a 7-bit character size. You would type a command such as the following:

```
# lpadmin -p clobber -o "stty='parenb parodd cs7'"
```

The stty option `parenb` enables parity checking/generation, `parodd` sets odd parity generation, and `cs7` sets the character size to 7 bits.

To send a document to the printer, type **lp -d** ***printer-name filename*** and press Return. Look at the document to verify that it is printing correctly.

Table 11–10 shows the default stty options used by the LP print service's standard printer interface program.

Table 11–10 Default stty Settings Used by the Standard Interface Program

Option	Meaning
`9600`	Set baud rate to 9600.
`cs8`	Set 8-bit bytes.
`-cstopb`	Send 1 stop bit per byte.
`-parity`	Do not generate parity.
`ixon`	Enable XON/XOFF (also known as START/STOP or DC1/DC3).

Table 11–10 Default stty Settings Used by the Standard Interface Program

Option	Meaning
opost	Do "output post-processing."
-olcuc	Do not map lowercase to uppercase.
onlcr	Change line feed to carriage return/line feed.
-ocrnl	Do not change carriage returns into line feeds.
-onocr	Output carriage returns even at column 0.
nl0	No delay after line feeds.
cr0	No delay after carriage returns.
tab0	No delay after tabs.
bs0	No delay after backspaces.
vt0	No delay after vertical tabs.
ff0	No delay after form feeds.

Use Table 11–11 to choose stty options to correct various problems affecting print output.

Table 11–11 stty Options to Correct Print Output Problems

stty Values	Result	Possible Problem from Incorrect Setting
300, 600, 1200, 1800, 2400, 4800, 9600, 19200, 38400	Sets baud rate to the specified value (enter only one baud rate)	Random characters and special characters may be printed and spacing may be inconsistent.
oddp	Sets odd parity	Characters are randomly missing or appear incorrectly.
evenp	Sets even parity	
-parity	Sets no parity	
-tabs	Sets no tabs	Text is jammed against right margin.
tabs	Sets tabs every eight spaces	Text has no left margin, is run together, or is jammed together.
-onlcr	Sets no return at the beginning of lines	Text has incorrect double spacing.
onlcr	Sets return at beginning of lines	Zigzags print down the page.

Check the Baud Settings

When the baud setting of the computer does not match the baud setting of the printer, you usually get some output, but it does not look like what you submitted for printing. Random characters show up, with an unusual mixture of special characters and undesirable spacing. The default for the LP print service is 9600 baud.

NOTE. *If a printer is connected by a parallel port, the baud setting is irrelevant.*

Check the Parity Setting

Some printers use a parity bit to ensure that data received for printing has not been garbled during transmission. The parity bit settings for the computer and for the printer must match. If they do not match, some characters do not print at all or are replaced by other characters. The output will look only approximately correct, with the word spacing all right and many letters in their correct place. The LP print service does not set the parity bit by default.

Check the Tab Settings

If tabs are set but the printer expects no tabs, the printed output may contain the complete contents of the file, but the text may be jammed against the right margin. Also, if the tab settings for the printer are incorrect, the text may not have a left margin, may run together, may be concentrated in a portion of the page, or may be incorrectly double-spaced. The default is for tab settings every eight spaces.

Check the Return Setting

If the output is double-spaced but should be single-spaced, either the tab settings for the printer are incorrect or the printer is adding a line feed after each Return. The LP print service adds a Return before each line feed, so the combination causes two line feeds.

If the print zigzags down the page, the stty option `onlcr`, which sends a Return before every line feed, is not set. The `stty=onlcr` option is set by default, but you may have cleared it while trying to solve other printing problems.

Hung LP Print Service Commands

If you type any of the lp commands (`lpsystem`, `lpadmin`, `lpstat`, `lpshut`) and nothing happens (you get no error message, status information, or prompt), chances are that something is wrong with the LP scheduler. You usually can resolve such a problem by stopping and restarting the LP scheduler.

Use the following steps to free hung lp commands:

1. Become superuser.
2. Type **lpshut** and press Return. If this command hangs, press Control-C and proceed to the next step. If this command succeeds, skip to step 5.
3. Type **ps -e | grep lpsched** and press Return. Note the process ID numbers (PID) from the first column. You use these PID numbers in the next step.

```
# ps -e | grep lpsched
134 term/a   0:01 lpsched
```

```
#
```

4. Type **kill -9 *pid*** and press Return. All the lp processes are terminated.

```
# kill -9 134
#
```

5. Type **rm /usr/spool/lp/SCHEDLOCK** and press Return. You have removed the SCHEDLOCK file so that you can restart the LP print service.

6. Type **/usr/lib/lp/lpsched** and press Return. The LP print service restarts.

Idle (Hung) Printers

You may find a printer that is idle even though print requests have been queued to it. A printer may seem idle when it shouldn't be for one of the following reasons:

- The current print request is being filtered.
- The printer has a fault.
- Networking problems may be interrupting the printing process.

Check the Print Filters

Slow print filters run in the background to avoid tying up the printer. A print request that requires filtering will not print until it has been filtered. To check the print filters, type **lpstat -o *printer-name*** and press Return. See if the first waiting request is being filtered. If the output looks like the following example, the file is being filtered. The printer is not hung; it just is taking a while to process the request.

```
pine% lpstat -o pinecone
pinecone-10          fred          1261    Mar 12 17:34 being filtered
pinecone-11          iggy          1261    Mar 12 17:36 on pine
pinecone-12          jack          1261    Mar 12 17:39 on pine
pine%
```

Check Printer Faults

When the LP print service detects a fault, printing resumes automatically, but not immediately. The LP print service waits about five minutes before trying again, and continues trying until a request is printed successfully. You can force a retry immediately by enabling the printer.

Use the following steps to resume printing after a printer fault:

1. Look for a message about a printer fault and try to correct the fault if you find one. Depending on how printer fault alerts have been specified, messages may be sent to root by email or may be written to a terminal on which you (root) are logged in.

2. Type **enable** ***printer-name*** and press Return. If a request was blocked by a printer fault, this command will force a retry. If this command doesn't work, continue with other procedures in this section.

Check Network Problems

When printing files over a network, you may encounter the following types of problems:

- Requests sent to print servers may back up in the client system (local) queue.
- Requests sent to print servers may back up in the print server (remote) queue.

Use the following steps to check that the printer is ready to print:

1. Type **lpstat -p** ***printer-name*** and press Return. The information that comes up tells you whether the printer is idle or active, enabled or disabled, or available or not accepting print requests. If everything looks all right, continue with other procedures in this section.
2. If the printer is not available (is not accepting requests), become superuser and type **accept** ***printer-name*** and press Return. The printer begins to accept requests to its print queue.
3. If the printer is disabled, type **enable** ***printer-name*** and press Return. This command re-enables the printer so that it can act on the requests in its queue.

Check for Jobs Backed Up in the Local Client Queue

Jobs earmarked for a print server may back up in the client system queue for the following reasons:

- The print server is down.
- The printer is disabled on the print server.
- The network between the print client and print server is down.
- Underlying Solaris 2.*x* network software was not set up properly.

While you are tracking down the source of the problem, use the disable command on the print server to stop new requests from being added to the queue.

Check for Jobs Backed Up in the Remote Server Queue

If jobs back up in the print server queue, the printer probably has been disabled. When a printer is accepting requests but not processing them, the requests are queued to print. After you enable the printer, the print requests in the queue should print—unless there is an additional problem.

Use the following steps to send jobs to a remote printer when they back up in the local queue:

1. On the print client, type **reject** ***printer-name*** and press Return. Additional queuing of print requests from the print client to the print server ceases.
2. Type **ping** ***print-server-name*** and press Return to check that the print server and the network between the print client and the print server is up.
3. Type **tail /var/lp/logs/lpsched** and press Return. The resulting information may help you pinpoint what is preventing the transmission of print requests from the print client to the print server.
4. After you fix the problem, on the print client, type **accept** ***printer-name*** and press Return. New jobs can begin to queue.
5. (If necessary) On the print client type **enable** ***printer-name*** and press Return. The printer is enabled.

Use the following steps to free jobs from a print client that back up in the print server queue:

1. On the print server, type **reject** ***printer-name*** and press Return. Additional print requests are not queued.
2. Type **tail /var/lp/logs/lpsched** and press Return. The information that appears on-screen may help you pinpoint what is preventing the print requests that have been transmitted from the print client to the print server from being printed.
3. After you fix the problem, on the print server type **accept** ***printer-name*** and press Return. The printer accepts new jobs in the print queue.
4. (If necessary) On the print server, type **enable** ***printer-name*** and press Return. The printer is enabled.

Conflicting Status Messages

A user may enter a print request and be notified that the client system has accepted it, then receive mail from the print server that the job has been rejected. These conflicting messages may occur for the following reasons:

- The print client may be accepting requests, but the print server is rejecting requests.
- The definition of the printer on the print client might not match the definition of that printer on the print server. More specifically, the definitions of the print job components, such as filters, character sets, print wheels, and forms, are not the same on the client and server systems.

Make sure that identical definitions of these job components are registered on both the print clients and print servers so that local users can access printers on the print servers.

Use the following steps to resolve conflicting status messages:

1. Type **lpstat -p** ***printer-name*** and press Return. Check that the printer connected to the print server is enabled and accepting requests. Users see conflicting status messages when the print client accepts requests but the print server rejects them.
2. On the print server and on each print client, type **lpstat -p -l** ***printer-name*** and press Return. Check that the definition of the printer on the print client matches the definition of the printer on the print server. Look at the definitions of the print job components, such as print filters, character sets, print wheels, and forms, to be sure they are the same on both the client and server systems, so that local users can access printers on print server systems.

The four chapters in this part describe how to install and delete application software and how to install system software patches.

Chapter 12 provides an overview of the installation process, introduces the package commands and the Software Manager for installation, recommends policy for installing software on an application server, and describes how to access files from a CD-ROM drive.

Chapter 13 describes how to use the package commands to administer application software and how to set up the users' environment.

Chapter 14 describes how to use the Software Manager to administer application software.

Chapter 15 describes how to use the `patchadd` and `patchrm` commands that are now bundled with the Solaris 2.6 system software to administer system software patches.

PART

5

Application Software

CHAPTER

12

Installing and Managing Application Software

HEN YOU SUPPORT A NETWORK THAT PROVIDES APPLICATION SOFTWARE TO users, your responsibilities include the following tasks:

- Setting up the software installation environment
- Installing the software on a server or on the users' local system
- Setting up the users' environment to access software
- Removing software that is obsolete or no longer used

This chapter introduces the package commands and Admintool—two alternative ways to install and manage application software. It also describes how to set up an application server and access files from a remote and a local CD-ROM drive. Chapter 13 describes how to use the package commands. Chapter 14 describes how to use Admintool. Although you can install application software on a user's local system, the information in this chapter describes how to set up the software on an application server and share the files so that they are available over the network to make software administration and upgrades easier.

Overview of Installing and Managing Application Software

With Solaris 2.*x* system software, installation is managed by packages of information. A software package contains the components of a software product that are delivered on the CD-ROM installation medium. The components typically contain groups of files such as compiled programs, files, and installation scripts.

Software packages are installed from the CD-ROM onto a system, and are removed from a system, in one of the following ways:

- Using the package commands from a command line.
- Using Admintool™ (which calls the package commands).
- Using an installation script provided by the application vendor (which calls the package commands). Some vendors may also provide a deinstallation script.

NOTE. *Before the Solaris 2.5 release, Software Manager, accessed with the* `swmtool` *command, provided the graphical tool for adding and removing software. With Solaris 2.5 and 2.6 releases, Admintool, accessed by using the* `admintool` *command, provides the same capability. If you use the* `swmtool` *command on a Solaris 2.5 or 2.6 system, it starts Admintool.*

You can use the package commands and Admintool interchangeably. For example, you can install software by using Admintool and remove the software by using the `pkgrm`(1M) command. Alternatively, you can install software by using the `pkgadd(1M)` command and remove that software by using Admintool.

In the Solaris 2.6 release, new `patchadd` and `patchrm` commands are provided to support adding and removing patches from a Solaris 2.*x* system. You cannot use these commands to manage patches on a Solaris 1.*x* system. For more information about these commands, see Chapter 15, "Installing and Managing System Software Patches."

Using Package Commands

You manage software from a command line by using the commands shown in Table 12–1.

Table 12–1 Package Commands

Task	Command
Set installation defaults	`vi(1) admin(4)`
Create a script to define installation parameters	`pkgask(1M)`
Install software package or store files for installation at a later time	`pkgadd(1M)`
Check accuracy of installation	`pkgchk(1M)`
List installed packages	`pkginfo(1M)`
Remove packages	`pkgrm(1M)`

These tasks are described in detail in Chapter 13.

Using Admintool

Admintool is a graphical user interface tool that you can use to perform the same tasks that you would perform from a command line by using the package commands. You can group packages that are slated for install using Admintool into clusters for easier administration. Admintool calls the package commands to perform the requested functions. Figure 12–1

shows the Admintool: Software window. Refer to Chapter 14 for instructions on how to use this tool.

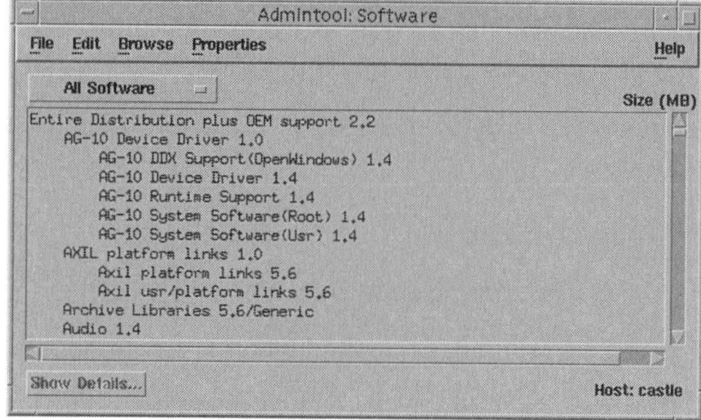

Figure 12–1

The Admintool: Software window.

You can view more detailed information about each package by clicking on a package to highlight it and then clicking on the Show Details button. Figure 12–2 shows the details for the SUNWpcr package, which is part of the new SunSoft Print Client software available in the Solaris 2.6 release.

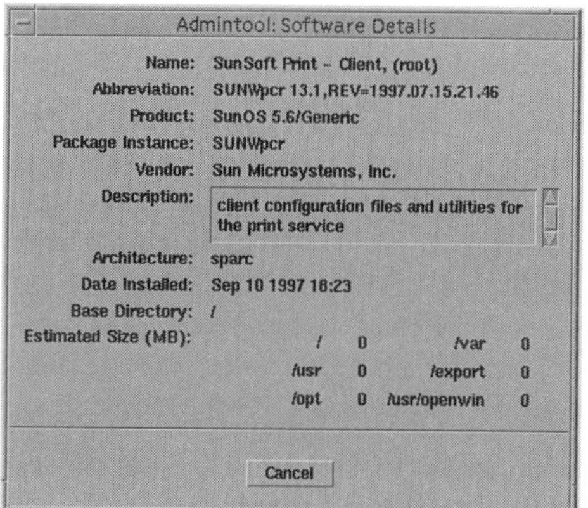

Figure 12–2

Package details for the SUNWpcr package.

Using Installation Scripts

Although SunSoft recommends a policy on how to create packages for installation, some software products from application vendors provide their own installation scripts. The installation scripts may call the package commands to perform setup and installation of the software. Always read the installation instructions from the vendor to make sure that you follow the vendor's recommended installation procedure.

User Access to Applications

Making applications available to users is a major task for system administrators. Most users depend on reliable access to application software to get their jobs done. The demands of creating and maintaining user access to application software can easily consume a quarter or more of system administration time.

You may need to perform any or all of the following tasks to administer user access to applications:

- Acquire software.
- Locate space for the software.
- Install the software on multiple local systems, or on a server.
- Set up user environments, such as paths, links, and environment variables.
- Revise user environments each time the software version changes or new software is added.

Anything that you can do to leverage these tasks will increase productivity.

You can use a variety of creative approaches to managing software access. One existing approach uses the automounter extensively to match up users with the proper binary version of applications. The principal drawback to using only an automounter approach is that it does not manage the environmental setup that most packages require.

Another existing approach uses scripts that are run once on each system to set up the user environment for an application. Subsequently, when the user starts the application, the environment is already properly prepared. A disadvantage to this approach is that it introduces additional command names that users have to learn to prepare for running an application. An additional drawback is that some programs use the same environment variable names as other programs with different values. When users run a script for a specific application but do not start the application until later, other packages that use the same environment variable may be affected. (See "Wrappers and Dot Files" later in this chapter for an example.)

Another approach is to have user `.login` or `.profile` files "source" a global configuration file that sets up the user's environment.

Another approach uses *wrappers* to manage access to software. Wrappers are tailored application startup scripts. These scripts set up the user's environment at runtime and start the application. Wrappers perform the setup that you would otherwise have to hard-code in individual users' dot files.

Using wrappers together with standard application server layouts and simplified user mount and path setups can produce an environment in which you need to do very little, if any, administrative maintenance of the end user environment. Users can have as few as one software access mount and one software access path component.

Most application access at Sun is based on this last approach, which was developed by Sun Information Resources. SunSoft recommends that you consider dedicating servers to provide access to application software over the network, in the manner proposed in the following sections.

NOTE. *A comprehensive description of how to configure and manage application servers is beyond the scope of this book. However, the approaches and examples cited here provide you with a foundation based on sound principles and real-world experience.*

Automating Your Application Environment

The information in the following sections provides suggestions for ways that you can automate your application environment. The key technologies and techniques are introduced in Table 12–2 and described in the following sections.

Table 12–2 Key Elements for an Application Server

Element	Used to
NFS/automounter	Share application file systems across the network; guarantee consistency and integrity with read-only access
Online: DiskSuite™	Permit file systems larger than individual disks; enable a single mount to access a huge distribution
wrappers	Remove setup requirements from the end-user environment; provide all users with consistent behavior
symbolic links	Allow one executable to have many startup names; permit generic path references to version-named locations; control default application versions
common command directory	Make all commands accessible with a single path component
`rdist`	Facilitate replication of file systems across application servers
NIS/NIS+	Facilitate sharing files in a network environment

When you set up an application server, you dedicate a single slice (partition) to contain the applications and wrappers. You create two (or more) directories in the slice. The *application directory* contains the applications and wrappers, as well as a symbolic link directory that you can use to determine the default version of the application. The *common command directory* contains symbolic links in the form of command names that link to the wrappers for each application. You can use a product such as SunSoft Online: DiskSuite™ to create a large file system that spans more than one slice or disk. When you have installed the application packages, you write a wrapper that sets up the environment for the application. If you want to copy the setup to another server, you can do so by using the `rdist` command. Refer to "Designing an Application Server" later in this chapter for a detailed description of these tasks.

Benefits of a Standardized Application Server Setup

The information in the following sections describe the administrative benefits that you gain from a standardized application server setup.

Use NFS Installing the same application for multiple users on local disks uses extra disk space, requires more time, and becomes a support burden. You must perform upgrades at multiple locations. When problems arise, you may have to deal with multiple versions of the same application.

When you provide an NFS-shared installation, you reduce local disk installations. You save time by reducing the number of systems that you must support. When multiple users share access to a single read-only copy of an application, you perform fewer installations and upgrades, and simplify troubleshooting by assuring that users are executing the same code.

Consolidate Your Installations Even NFS-shared applications can be difficult to maintain if they are scattered among too many locations. Sometimes applications have been installed on a user's system or on a server. As demand for the application develops, users share it from the original location. Users frequently pass the word to other users about where they can mount the application from. In such a situation, users may draw on inconsistent or unreliable sources and experience confusion regarding where they should get applications.

To solve this problem, designate dedicated application servers. Sharing all standard applications from the same server offers users a reliable source and lets you keep track of where maintenance is needed.

Hopefully, you are already using NFS and dedicated application servers in your application environment.

Standardize Server Layouts Your environment, like that at Sun, may require many application servers to service different networks, buildings, and regions. If so, commit to using the same file system layout on all application servers. Although the contents of different application servers may vary from one server to another, the locations of individual applications should be consistent. A unified file system naming scheme simplifies user paths and reduces the updates required when user moves dictate their change from one application server to another. This approach also simplifies the process of copying (distributing) applications from a master installation server to production servers, since the destination file system is the same.

Sometimes in comparing two locations where a product has been installed, you cannot tell whether the contents of like-named directories are intended to be the same or different; you have no outward clue. SunSoft recommends that you install applications in directories with names that identify both the product and the version. That lets you and others know what the directories contain. In addition, you can maintain multiple versions of an application at the same directory level.

In some environments, you must perform maintenance at numerous locations for each change. Using wrappers and a common command directory reduces the number of locations where attention is needed, limits them to servers, and leverages the results for all users.

Synchronize Version Cutovers In the traditional UNIX environment, you may find it difficult to convert to a new application version quickly because of the number of changes to the user environment that may be required. Using symbolic links to control all the versioning at this level, and using wrappers that immediately provide any necessary user setups, can help to speed up, and to synchronize, cutovers. It can be difficult to know who is using particular applications, or whether some applications are being used at all.

Wrappers can increase usage visibility if you code them to report to a central location by email each time the product starts up.

Benefits of a Standardized User Environment

The information in these sections describes the administrative benefits you gain from a standardized user environment setup.

Simplify User Mount Points When users access applications from a variety of locations or even from multiple file systems on a dedicated server, they need a variety of mount points. You, as system administrator, probably have to maintain the information that supports these mounts. Regardless of whether you perform this maintenance on individual user systems or by using automounter maps, the fewer times you need to update the user environment, the more time you save.

Simplify User Path Requirements When you configure dedicated application servers so that all applications are accessible from a single file system, users need only one mount, which may not need to be updated. Even when the contents of the file system that users are mounting change, the mount point remains the same.

Maintaining path updates for users may be an unnecessary burden. If users have the "right" path, you do not need to change it. The *right path* is one whose standard component(s) provide ongoing access to all applications.

Reduce Runtime Conflicts The settings that some applications need at runtime may be in conflict with those needed by others. Wrappers tailor one process environment without affecting others.

Simplify User Relocations User moves can impose a tremendous burden, because many user setups in a nonstandard environment are customized. Using wrappers and simplified user mounts and paths can drastically reduce the updates required to reinstate application service after a move. In some cases, you need change only the server name for the user's mount.

Using Wrapper Technology

Wrappers are custom startup scripts for applications, and have been used for quite some time. Many application vendors, such as Frame Technology, use wrappers to tailor their application startup.

Vendors cannot, however, anticipate the full range of startup decisions and settings that will be needed in every customer environment. You can add value by developing wrappers that are truly customized to your own end-user environment. It may be worth writing your own wrapper—even to front end an application vendor-designed wrapper. Wrappers can leverage your system administration expertise and hard-won knowledge of the application requirements in a consistent way, to the benefit of all your users.

Wrappers and Dot Files

Ordinarily, user dot files (for example, `.login` and `.cshrc` for the C shell or `.profile` for the Bourne shell) try to provide for what users may do after they log in. The goal is to define a comprehensive environment that supports all requests to access applications. It is not only difficult, but in some cases impossible, to provide for all cases: Some applications need a different value for an environment variable than do other applications that use the same variable name.

For example, to run a given Sybase application, the users may need to set the `DSQUERY` variable to identify the back-end database server for the application. If this variable is set from dot files at login time, it extends throughout subsequent shell environments. However, other Sybase applications may require different `DSQUERY` values. If `DSQUERY` is set, instead, by a wrapper for the Sybase application, the `DSQUERY` value applies only to the application, and may be set to different values by other wrappers for other applications.

When you use wrappers, the environment for each application is set up as needed. Wrappers construct the needed environment at runtime, before executing the application. In addition, the settings are visible to the resulting application process only; they do not interact with the rest of the user's environment. This encapsulation of runtime environment is a significant advantage of wrappers.

Likewise, users' paths frequently must be updated as applications come and go, in an effort to provide for what the user may decide to run.

Consider this analogy: In a given year, you plan to go running, hiking, skating, scuba diving, and snow skiing. (Forget for a moment that, as a system administrator, you're too busy.) Doesn't it seem more practical to don the special equipment for each activity just before you need it (and take it off when you're done), rather than trying to put it all on at the beginning of the year, "just so you'll be ready"? Clearly, the latter approach can generate conflicts. And in choosing where to go skiing, for instance, you probably would prefer to choose your destination based on where the snow is at the time you are ready to go.

Additional Wrapper Advantages

With wrappers, you can provide sensible default values for variables, while still allowing users the option to override those settings. You can automate user installation steps that some applications require when first run, and know that you are producing consistent results. You can also generate usage information about the application.

Wrapper Overhead and Costs

Some administrators question whether the merits of a wrapper approach justify the overhead imposed each time an application starts up. After all, an additional shell script runs ahead of the normal application startup. Several years of experience with complex wrappers at Sun have shown that the delay in startup time is trivial and the benefits overwhelming.

The biggest cost to consider is the flip side of the greatest benefit—wrappers are powerful, so they require care. Wrappers present consistent behavior to large numbers of users. If wrappers are well produced and maintained, they deliver gratifyingly reliable service and prevent many problems. On the other hand, if wrappers are broken, service to large numbers of users may be impacted.

Introduction of Wrappers into an Existing Environment

One of the great advantages of wrappers is that you can introduce them immediately into almost any application environment. Once you develop a wrapper for a given application, if the command names that link to it are installed in a location already in the users' paths (for example, `/usr/local/bin`), you can make the application immediately available without needing to do anything to set up the user environment.

To provide a limited implementation, you can decide how many wrappers you want to provide, and for which applications. You can write wrappers as you add new packages, and you can write wrappers for older applications as well. You can create links to the wrappers in a directory already in the users' paths. Alternatively, you can create a new directory that contains the links to the wrappers.

The tasks involved in setting up a limited implementation of an application server with wrappers include the following:

- Installing packages using vendor instructions
- Creating a value-added subhierarchy within each package
- Creating wrappers for applications, to eliminate or minimize any requirement for hard-coded setup by individual users
- Installing wrappers into their respective application value-added subhierarchy
- Creating all application command names as symbolic links in a directory that is already on the users' path (or in a new directory to be added to their paths)
- Creating symbolic links to point to the application wrapper

Designing an Application Server

To provide a complete implementation of these techniques throughout an environment, the tasks on the server include the following:

- Identifying servers to specialize in providing application access
- Implementing the fewest possible slices (partitions) to contain the software packages
- Performing software installations on these servers in a consistent file system layout
- Sharing the application server file system read-only to users
- Naming package directories in a way that reflects both the application name and the version
- Installing packages initially per vendor instructions and then (if necessary) adjusting them to simplify and encapsulate their structure
- Creating a value-added subhierarchy within each application
- Creating wrappers for applications, to eliminate or minimize any requirement for hard-coded setup on the part of individual users
- Installing wrappers into their respective application value-added subhierarchy
- Creating all application command names as symbolic links in a common directory, and creating symbolic links to point to the application wrapper
- As applications are added to a server, updating other servers appropriately, using `rdist`
- Separating servers for network services (NIS/NIS+, DNS, NTP, mail, and so on) from application servers in all but the smallest environments

The tasks in the user environment include:

- Setting up users with the appropriate mount point and mount to access the application server
- Setting up users with a path that includes the common command directory

The following sections describe in greater detail the basic tasks involved in a general implementation. However, coverage of many topics necessarily is superficial, and the overall model is simplified.

Server Configuration

Consider the following points when designating servers to act as application servers:

- Choose server configurations that you believe to be robust. Consolidating applications into one location simplifies life only to the extent that the system provides ongoing, reliable service. Typically, when application service is down, users are down.

- Choose servers that can retain their identities for reasonable lengths of time. Hostname changes require mount maintenance, and hostid changes can make licensed passwords obsolete.

User Capacity

It is impossible to offer specific guidelines concerning the number of servers you will require. Your goal is to provide reasonable NFS response time to all clients served. The user ratio you can support depends on many factors, such as the server characteristics, network characteristics, the types of applications being served, and the number of clients.

Try to locate application servers on the same network segments as the bulk of their clients. As a rule, you obtain the best response if you minimize NFS traffic through routers and other store-and-forward network devices.

Automounter maps for application directories are especially useful when applications are moved from one server to another.

Compatible Services

It is probably simplest to dedicate a server exclusively as an application server. If, however, it is impossible or impractical to do so in your environment, you may need to implement a multipurpose server.

Certain services present little conflict with NFS service because of their light weight or typical scheduling. Examples include license service and backup service. Additional, nonapplication NFS roles, such as sharing client root or home directory file systems, may have some impact on application response time.

NOTE. *For its role as an NFS server, a platform need not be typical of the user base platforms. However, if an application server is also to act as a license server, it must be capable of running the license support binaries provided by the application vendors.*

Other functions are incompatible with optimum NFS performance because they make heavy CPU and I/O demands. Examples of incompatible functions include back-end database engine, development activity, and routing.

Disk Allocation

You need to allocate adequate space for applications on the server, allowing ample space to accommodate future additions. Also remember that you may need space for multiple versions of some applications as you transition users to newer versions.

As noted earlier, you want to serve applications from a single file system to minimize user mounts. If your overall application space requirements exceed the size of your largest disk, you may want to use the Solstice DiskSuite product. This product lets you concatenate (group together) multiple physical disk slices into one logical metaslice. DiskSuite offers other performance and high-availability enhancements, such as striping, mirroring and “hot spare” capability. For more information about the Solstice DiskSuite product, refer to“DiskSuite” on page 510 of Appendix B.

Contrary to system defaults, put /, /usr, and /opt into a single partition large enough to hold dozens or hundreds of patches as well as providing enough room for an OS upgrade.

File System Configuration

The following sections suggest a basic file system configuration for application servers. When you create one or more application servers, you generally provide a single file system with a consistent directory hierarchy. In that way, you create an environment that is consistent throughout your organization.

Base Directories When you have a server with a disk slice (partition) that you consider adequate for long-term use as an application server, you can begin to implement the file system itself. As a foundation, SunSoft recommends that you create a minimum of two standard directories, which, in this model, we name `/usr/apps/exe` and `/usr/apps/pkgs`, respectively.

You install symbolic links or wrappers that represent all the available commands used to execute applications in the `/usr/apps/exe`, the common command directory. You install all of the applications in the `/usr/apps/pkgs` directory.

Parallel Hierarchies You may want to create one or more parallel file systems. For example, you might want to make a distinction between packages implemented by central administration and packages introduced by regional administration. You also might want to distinguish between production and beta versions of software.

If you want to create such parallel hierarchies, you could designate them as follows:

```
/usr/apps/local/pkgs
/usr/apps/local/exe
```

The `/usr/apps/local/pkgs` directory contains the applications, and the corresponding `/usr/apps/local/exe` directory would contain the symbolic links to the wrappers for those applications. Under this type of arrangement, you need to add a second path (`/usr/apps/local/exe`) to the users' environment. If you arrange the directory as a parallel hierarchy instead of a separate file system, you could use a single mount point. If you create a separate file system, users would need to have a second mount point.

Clearly there are more variations not presented here. It is important for you to determine your needs. Try to plan for the long term, and try to keep your setup as simple and as consistent as possible. At Sun it has, indeed, been possible to provide most application services through a single mount.

Transitory Names If you use wrappers, avoid the temptation to create a file system with directories that are named after architectures or other transitory distinctions; for example, `/usr/apps/sun3`. Packages are always present, but other distinctions come and go. Confine file system distinctions to individual application directories (which come and go themselves) where the changes impact only the wrapper.

Permissions Unless you have good reasons not to do so, permissions should be mode 755 for directories you create and for those within applications, so that they are writable by owner, with read and execute for group and world. Sometimes vendors ship nonwritable directories that interfere with your ability to transfer the contents to another system. In general, make other files writable by owner, and readable by all, and leave execute permissions intact. You can use the following commands to change a directory hierarchy to the recommended permissions:

```
$ /usr/bin/find directory-name -type d -exec /usr/bin/chmod 755 {} \;
$ /usr/bin/chmod -R u+w directory-name
$ /usr/bin/chmod -R ugo+r directory-name
$
```

CAUTION! *Do not execute these commands from the root (/) directory.*

Ownership If you set up or maintain an extensive network of application servers and update them using trusted host relationships, consider what account should own the software distribution. In general, you do not need to have root be the owner. You may find some security advantages to creating a special, nonprivileged ownership account for managing application servers.

File System Sharing

Before users can access files on the application server, you must share (export) the file system to make it available to other systems on the network. SunSoft strongly recommends that you share the application's file system read-only.

Follow these steps on the application server to share the file system:

1. Become superuser.
2. Edit the `/etc/dfs/dfstab` file and add the following line:

   ```
   share -F nfs -o ro pathname
   ```

3. Type **share** ***pathname*** (or **shareall**) and press Return.

In the following example, the pathname `/usr/apps` is shared:

```
oak% su
Password
# vi /etc/dfs/dfstab
[Add the following line]
share -F nfs -o ro /usr/apps
[Quit the file and save the changes]
# share /usr/apps
#
```

If you must start the NFS service manually, use the following steps. Otherwise, the services will start up at boot time.

1. Type **/usr/lib/nfs/nfsd 8** and press Return. You have started the NFS daemons.
2. Type **/usr/lib/nfs/mountd** and press Return. You have started the mount daemon.
3. Type **share -F nfs -o ro** ***pathname*** and press Return.

The *pathname* is the name of the mount point file system. For example, if you have mounted the partition as `/usr/apps`, type **share -F nfs -o ro /usr/apps** and press Return.

Installing and Configuring Packages

If you want to install the application in the `/usr/apps` directory rather than `/opt`, you need to set up either the package commands or Admintool to install the software in a different directory, and then install the software.

SunSoft suggests that you use a name for the application directory that reflects the actual product name (in lowercase for simplicity), with some sort of version suffix. For example, following the proposed naming convention, you might install version 2.0 of FooTool in the directory `/usr/apps/pkgs/footool,v2.0`.

Follow the vendor's directions to install the software. If the vendor's or developer's install procedure does not use the package commands, you may need to rename the directory after completing the vendor installation process. See Chapter 13 for instructions on how to use the package commands. See Chapter 14 for instructions on how to use Admintool.

Normally you should minimize any changes that you make to the original installed software. The flexibility of the wrapper helps you adapt to unusual requirements. You do, however, typically want to add some things to the package—at least, the wrapper itself. Create a subdirectory at the top level of the package to contain the wrapper and other possible additions. Such additions might include site-specific README files, announcements, and scripts that complete server-specific setup for the package. In the following example, the subdirectory is called `dist`.

```
$ cd /usr/apps/pkgs/footool,v2.0
$ /usr/bin/mkdir dist
$
```

Determine whether you think this directory requires additional subdivision. If so, be sure to use a consistent naming convention. The location of the wrapper determines the form of the command name links that must connect to it. For the purpose of this example, refer to the wrapper as being in the top level of this subdirectory and name it simply `wrapper`; in other words:

```
/usr/apps/pkgs/footool,v2.0/dist/wrapper
```

In many application packages, you must configure some of the files before the package can be run. If you are maintaining multiple application servers, consider the following:

- Once you modify the original files, you may not have generic copies left. If you copy the package to another server, you may want the original files to match the vendor's setup documentation.
- If you synchronize the package between servers after setup, be careful not to overwrite the server-specific setups with those from another server.

Consider how you want to handle such files. One way is to identify the files that are candidates for modification and to make copies of them where they reside, using a suffix such as ".orig." This convention preserves generic copies. You still must avoid shipping the modified versions of these files to other servers so that you do not overwrite local configurations that are already established.

Changes to the Default Package Version

Applications are installed into directories that identify their versions. Multiple versions can thus coexist at the same directory level. To identify the default version of a given application, create a generic directory name as a symbolic link pointing to the version-named directory that you want to serve as the default.

In the following example, the `/usr/apps/pkgs` directory contains two versions of FooTool and a generic footool name link:

```
$ cd /usr/apps/pkgs
$ ls -ld footool*
lrwxrwxrwx   1 nobody   nobody     12 Jun 19  1992 /usr/apps/pkgs/footool ->
footool,v1.0
drwxr-xr-x   9 nobody   nobody    512 Jun 18  1992 /usr/apps/pkgs/footool,v1.0
drwxr-xr-x   9 nobody   nobody    512 May  3 21:23 /usr/apps/pkgs/footool,v2.0
$
```

The default version is footool,v1.0. If you want to change the default version to 2.0, remove the existing link and create a new link to version 2.0, as shown in the following example:

```
$ /usr/bin/rm footool
$ /usr/bin/ln -s footool,v2.0 footool
$ ls -ld footool*
lrwxrwxrwx   1 nobody   nobody     12 Jul 19 07:32 /usr/apps/pkgs/footool ->
footool,v2.0
drwxr-xr-x   9 nobody   nobody    512 Jun 18  1992 /usr/apps/pkgs/footool,v1.0
drwxr-xr-x   9 nobody   nobody    512 May  3 21:23 /usr/apps/pkgs/footool,v2.0
$
```

The version footool,v2.0 is the default for all users, because the symbolic links in `/usr/apps/exe` point to a wrapper using a path that refers to the directory named `footool`. This path now leads to the wrapper in `footool,v2.0`.

Developing Wrappers

The information in the following sections describe some basic information about how to develop wrappers. Refer to Part 6 of this book for an introduction to shell programming.

Interpreter Choice

You typically write wrapper scripts in an interpreted language so that they can execute on the various platform configurations in the environment. If you are going to write wrappers, you must decide which interpreter to use. Solaris 2.*x* provides three shells that make suitable interpreters for wrappers, as noted in Table 12–3.

Table 12–3 Available Shells

Shell	Description
`/usr/bin/sh`	Bourne shell
`/usr/bin/ksh`	Korn shell
`/usr/bin/csh`	C shell

SunSoft recommends that you use the Bourne shell to write wrappers. The Korn shell may not be available on some systems in the environment. Although the C shell is popular for interactive use, the Bourne shell is more advanced as a programming language. The C shell is also less portable because there are more feature variations between UNIX platforms. The Bourne shell supports functions—which result in code that is reusable in other wrappers—and the ability to pipe into and out of control constructs. The examples in this chapter use Bourne shell syntax.

NOTE. *In an environment that is so heterogeneous that even the Bourne shell is not universally available, you would have to seek yet another interpreter, possibly perl.*

This is the first line in a Bourne shell wrapper script:

```
#!/bin/sh
```

Wrapper Directory and Naming

Create a subdirectory in the application directory, for example, `/usr/apps/_pkgs/application-name/dist`. Within that directory, create a wrapper that has the same name as the other wrappers. For example, name each wrapper "`wrapper`" (for example, `/usr/apps/pkgs/application-name/dist/wrapper`). When you use the same name for each application wrapper, it simplifies administration because you do not need to remember a host of different wrapper names. You can easily create links to any wrapper.

Command Name Evaluation

One of the first things a wrapper must do is evaluate the name that was used to invoke it. The wrapper has its own name. The wrapper name is different from any of the application command names, but the wrapper must know which command name it is being asked to represent.

For example, for package `footool,v2.0`, commands `foo` and `bar` each are links to the script called `wrapper` that is located in the `/usr/apps/pkgs/footool,v2.0/dist` directory. When a user types **foo**, the wrapper learns the name used to invoke it from the construct `$0`. In this case, `$0` is `/usr/apps/exe/foo`. The `/bin/basename` command is used to strip the leading path, and `foo` is assigned to the variable `cmd`, as follows:

```
cmd=`/bin/basename $0`
```

Environment Variables

Many applications require that you assign environment variables before you can execute them. Environment variables usually are values that cannot be reliably predicted by the compiled code, such as the directory where the application is installed. Such variables must be set and exported to be available to subsequently executing processes, just as they would be from a user's dot files. In Bourne shell format, the syntax is as follows:

```
export FOOHOME
FOOHOME=/usr/apps/pkgs/footool,v2.0
```

NOTE. *You can export the environment variable either before or after you assign it a value.*

Platform Evaluation

Not all applications support all combinations of hardware platforms and operating systems that may be in your environment. Therefore, you need to evaluate the user's platform to see if service can be provided.

For example, if footool,v2.0 supports only the Sun4 platform, the code shown here declines service (politely) to all other platforms:

```
case $arch in
      sun4)
                ;;
      *)
                echo >&2 "Sorry, $cmd not available for $arch architecture."
                exit 1
                ;;
esac
```

Command Path Construction

Next, you define the variable command in terms of code that will yield the complete execution path to the application binary.

NOTE. *The wrapper may not, in fact, execute the binary itself, but rather, may invoke a link that the vendor has routed through its own wrapper, as is the case with the product FrameMaker.*

In the `footool,v2.0` wrapper, you might write a command path definition, as shown here:

```
command=$FOOHOME/bin.$arch/$cmd
```

The command path definition could be more complex, or it could be as simple as that shown here:

```
command=$FOOHOME/bin/$cmd
```

Exec/Argument Passing

The wrapper has now made its assignments and calculations and has determined that the service is available for this user. It is time to hand off execution to the application and get out of the way, via the `exec` statement. The wrapper process has navigated to the correct binary and passed on the necessary environment. It then vanishes and imposes no further burden.

The last action of the wrapper is to make sure that any arguments the user included on the original command line get through exactly as expressed, which is the purpose of the `${1+"$@"}` construct at the end of the `exec` statement shown below:

```
exec $command ${1+"$@"}
```

A Basic Wrapper

At this point, the wrapper looks like this:

```
#!/bin/sh
        cmd=`/bin/basename $0`
        export FOOHOME
        FOOHOME=/usr/apps/pkgs/footool,v2.0
        case $arch in
              sun4)
                      ;;
              *)
                      echo >&2 "Sorry, $cmd not available for $arch
                      architecture."
                      exit 1
                      ;;
        esac
        command=$FOOHOME/bin/$cmd
        exec $command ${1+"$@"}
```

The wrapper example is not quite complete; it does not consider how `$arch` gets defined. The code necessary to assess architecture varies depending on the mix of platforms in the environment. However, in a given environment, you would need to use this same code for many wrappers. You can create the code as a Bourne shell function that can be replicated in as many wrappers as necessary.

In fact, for ease of maintenance, you might choose to make this code one function among others in a library external to the wrappers themselves. The wrappers requiring this function then merely source it from the library and execute it at the appropriate point in the wrapper. In this way, you often can carry out maintenance required by the wrappers by updating the library that supports all the wrappers. See Chapter 17 for some examples of wrapper functions.

If you provide a function library, be sure to use a consistent naming convention so that the wrappers can access and source the wrapper functions. You may want to apply the version-naming convention to this directory as well. For example, you might create a directory named `/usr/apps/library,v1.0`.

When a function library exists, you use the functions in scripts by defining the library location and sourcing the function script at the beginning of the wrapper. Then, before you use the `$arch` variable, you set it, as defined in the wrapper function. Next, you would execute the function at the appropriate point in the wrapper to return the values required. Remember, our wrapper example here is intentionally basic. The bold lines in the following example show the additions made to the basic script. See Chapter 17 for an example of the function `arch.sh.fctn`.

```
#!/bin/sh
library=/usr/apps/pkgs/library,v1.0
. $library/sh/arch.sh.fctn
cmd=`/bin/basename $0`
export FOOHOME
FOOHOME=/usr/apps/pkgs/footool,v2.0
arch=`Arch`
case $arch in
      sun4)
          ;;
     *)
          echo >&2 "Sorry, $cmd not available for $arch architecture."
          exit 1
          ;;
esac
command=$FOOHOME/bin/$cmd
exec $command ${1+"$@"}
```

Using a Common Command Directory

You want to create symbolic links for all application command names in the `/usr/apps/exe` directory. When you do so, users can access all of the software in the distribution with a single, unchanging path component.

If you choose to have a common command directory for a parallel hierarchy, as mentioned previously, two path components are sufficient to access the entire distribution.

The command names are symbolic links that point to the location of the wrapper for their application. For example, if the package FooTool 2.0 has the commands `foo` and `bar`, create these names as symbolic links in `/usr/apps/exe`, as follows:

```
$ cd /usr/apps/exe
$ /usr/bin/ln -s /usr/apps/pkgs/footool/dist/wrapper foo
$ /usr/bin/ln -s /usr/apps/pkgs/footool/dist/wrapper bar
$ ls -l foo bar
lrwxrwxrwx   1 nobody   nobody        35 Apr  6  1992 foo ->
                                            /usr/apps/pkgs/footool/dist/wrapper
lrwxrwxrwx   1 nobody   nobody        35 Apr  6  1992 bar ->
                                            /usr/apps/pkgs/footool/dist/wrapper
```

Notice that the link destinations refer to the generic directory name link, footool, rather than explicitly to the `footool,v2.0` directory. Use the generic directory name link for each package in this way to determine the version of the package to which the commands are connected. The users start the default version of the software, and you can change the default version simply by changing the link that determines it.

You could link the command names via the specific version-named directory instead, but you would find that changing from one version to another, when that time inevitably arrives, requires more work and more exposure. This extra work might not be obvious when packages have only one or two commands, but some applications have many. FrameMaker, for instance, has more than 80 commands!

Setting User Configurations

The following sections describe what you need to do to set up the user environment to access files on the application server.

Mount Points

In a general implementation, each user system needs to have a mount point directory; for example, `/usr/apps`.

Mounts

You can mount files from an application server when you use NFS. You can mount files either by editing the `/etc/vfstab` or by using the automounter.

If you use the `/etc/vfstab` file, edit it on each user's system and add a line that looks like the following:

```
#device      device       mount       FS      fsck    mount     mount
#to mount    to fsck      point       type    pass    at boot   options
#
server-name:/usr/apps -  /usr/apps   nfs     -       yes       ro
```

For example, to mount from an application server named `oak`, become superuser and add the following line to the user's `/etc/vfstab` file:

```
oak:/usr/apps   -   /usr/apps  nfs  -  yes  ro
```

Refer to Part 3 of this book for information about setting up the automounter.

Path

Each user typically needs either one or two path components to access applications, depending on whether you implement a parallel hierarchy. The name of the second component depends on the naming scheme applied to the parallel hierarchy. Suppose the path components are as follows:

```
/usr/apps/exe
/usr/apps/local/exe
```

The order in which you put the directories in the path is up to you. If you have applications that share the same name in both directories, you may want priority applied to either the global or the local distribution. The placement in the path relative to the standard OS directories is significant only if you expect to encounter name conflicts with commands in those locations.

A path for Solaris 2.*x* users could conceivably be as simple as the following:

```
/usr/openwin/bin /usr/bin /usr/sbin /usr/apps/exe /usr/apps/local/exe
```

Migration Considerations

In migrating existing users to a new software scheme, you must (carefully) simplify their existing setups. Of course, they need the mount point and mount, and the path component(s). Beyond these, you must remove most of the other hard-coded settings, to allow the dynamic connections to operate. There are always exceptions, though, and some hard-coded setups remain appropriate.

Understanding Distribution Issues

If you must maintain multiple application servers and need to copy application packages (or entire file systems) from one to another, you probably want to become familiar with the `rdist`(1) command. It is a standard utility specially designed for synchronizing file systems or portions of file systems between remote hosts. One of `rdist`'s great advantages is that it compares the status of files between the source and destination systems and copies only those files that need updating. This procedure is more efficient in many cases than using `tar`, for example, which copies all files unconditionally.

Unfortunately, the manual page for `rdist` does not provide clear guidelines for how to begin simply and scale to more sophisticated formats. The following paragraphs provide some suggestions for how to begin.

NOTE. *Be sure to begin with controlled experimentation in a test environment and study of the `rdist` manual page so that you are not unpleasantly surprised by unexpected results.*

To be able to `rdist` from one system to another depends on some level of trusted host relationship. (That is, the UID using `rdist` must be able to log in to the remote system without a password.) You may want this account to be owned by a UID other than root.

Once this privilege exists, you can `rdist` a hierarchy from the local system to the same destination on the remote system with a command as simple as the following:

```
$ rdist -c /usr/apps remote-system
```

Perhaps the most common form of `rdist` is to refer to a file that lists the target host systems and the pathnames to be synchronized. When the file has been created, use the following syntax:

```
$ rdist -f distfile
```

You may encounter limitations because `rdist` distfiles cannot use actual shell variables for flexibility. You can work around this limitation, however, by creating a script in which the shell expands variables before feeding the resulting syntax to `rdist`. The format of such a script, shown here, is the beginning of the power needed to use `rdist` to perform flexible, selective updates.

```
#!/bin/sh
files="
pathname1
pathname2
. . .
"
hosts="
host1
host2
. . .
"
rdist -f - <<-EOrdist
("$files")
-> ("$hosts")
EOrdist
```

NOTE. *Beware of using* `rcp -r` *to copy hierarchies. In the process, symbolic links get converted to actual copies of their destination files. This conversion not only can affect the amount of space occupied, but can produce unexpected behavior. You may later make changes to link destination files, such as wrappers, not realizing that command names have become outdated copies of the script itself. Also,* `rcp` *does not replicate UID, GID, or permissions.*

Licensing

Many SunSoft unbundled products and application software packages require software licenses that control the number of users who can access the product at the same time. If the application software has a floating license system, you can also designate the application server as a license server. Alternatively, a single license server can manage licenses for multiple application servers, provided the license server is accessible to all the application servers across an existing network.

A full description of all the available types of licenses and license servers is beyond the scope of this book. Following are three possible configurations for setting up license servers:

- Single independent license server: All licenses are handled by a single server.
- Multiple independent license servers: You can have as many independent license servers as you have systems on the network. Each license server is configured independently, and you must obtain individual license passwords for each independent server system.
- Multiple redundant license servers: You can define a set of servers that operate together to emulate a single independent license server configuration. A redundant license server configuration improves the stability of a license system and ensures that licensed products will not shut down as long as the majority of your license servers are running. You must obtain a license password for each set of redundant license servers. When you define a set of redundant license servers, you must administer them as a set. If you add a license password to one of the servers in the set, you must add it to all other license servers in the set.

CD-ROM Mounts

The following sections describe how to access files on a CD-ROM from a local drive on a system running Solaris 2.2 (and later) system software, from a local drive on a system running Solaris 2.0 and 2.1, and from a remote drive.

Using a Local CD-ROM Drive (Solaris 2.2 and Later System Software)

With Solaris 2.2 system software (and later), the CD-ROM is automatically mounted for you when you insert a CD-ROM caddy into the CD-ROM drive. Use the following procedures if you are running Solaris 2.2 system software or later. (If you are running Solaris 2.0 or 2.1 system software, use the procedures described in the section "Using a Local CD-ROM Drive (Solaris 2.0 or 2.1 System Software).")

NOTE. *Diskettes are also automatically mounted using the Solaris 2.2 volume management software. See Appendix A for more information.*

To access files from a local CD-ROM drive with Solaris 2.2 (and beyond) system software, you do not need to have superuser privileges or to create a mount point. Simply insert the CD-ROM disc into the disc caddy and insert the disc caddy into the CD-ROM drive. The `/cdrom` mount point is created and the files are mounted. The `/cdrom` directory contains a `cdrom0` subdirectory that is a symbolic link to the volume name of the CD-ROM. You can type either **cd /cdrom/cdrom0** or **cd /cdrom/*cdrom-name*** to access the files.

Using a Local CD-ROM Drive (Solaris 2.0 or 2.1 System Software)

Follow these procedures to mount a CD-ROM from a command line.

1. Become superuser.
2. Insert the CD-ROM into the caddy and insert the caddy into the CD-ROM drive.
3. Type **mkdir /cdrom** and press Return. You have created a mount point directory named `/cdrom`.
4. Type **mount -F *file-system-type* -o ro /dev/dsk/c0t6d0s2 /cdrom** and press Return. For UNIX file system type, use `-F ufs`; for High Sierra file system type, use `-F hsfs`. The files are mounted on the `/cdrom` mount point.

If you want to simplify the mount process, you can add an entry to the `/etc/vfstab` file, as shown in the following steps:

1. Become superuser.
2. Edit the `/etc/vfstab` file and add the following entry. If the ***`file-system-type`*** is UNIX, use `ufs`; if the ***`file-system-type`*** is High Sierra, use `hsfs`.)

```
/dev/dsk/c0t6d0s2  -  /cdrom   file-system-type  -  no  ro
```

Alternatively, you can specify:

```
/dev/dsk/c0t6d0s2  -  /cdrom-hsfs hsfs -  no  ro
/dev/dsk/c0t6d0s2  -  /cdrom-ufs  ufs  -  no  ro
```

3. Insert the CD-ROM into the caddy and insert the caddy into the CD-ROM drive.
4. Type **mount /cdrom** and press Return. The CD-ROM files are mounted. If you use the alternative `/etc/vfstab` file format, you would type **mount /cdrom-hsfs**, or **mount /cdrom-ufs**, and then press Return.

Accessing Files from a Remote CD-ROM

These sections tell you how to set up a Solaris 2.*x* system with a remote CD-ROM drive to share files. The following procedure for sharing files works for Solaris 2.2 releases or greater.

How to Share CD Files from a Remote CD-ROM Drive

Before you can share CD-ROM files from a command line, the `mountd` daemon must be running. To find out if the `mountd` daemon is running, and to start it, you must do the following:

1. On the system that has the CD-ROM drive attached, type **ps -ef | grep mountd** and press Return. If the `mountd` daemon is running, other systems can access shared files. However, if the `mountd` daemon is not running, you will need to stop NFS services and restart them. Be sure to notify any users of the system that NFS services will momentarily be interrupted.
2. Become superuser.
3. Type **/etc/rc3.d/S15nfs.server stop** and press Return. The NFS services come to a halt.
4. Type **/etc/rc3.d/S15nfs.server start** and press Return. The NFS services restart and the CD files are exported.

Use the following steps to share CD files from a remote CD-ROM drive:

1. Insert the CD-ROM into the caddy and insert the caddy into the drive. The CD-ROM is mounted.
2. Become superuser on the Solaris 2.2 system with the CD-ROM drive attached.
3. Type **share -F nfs -o ro /cdrom/cdrom0** and press Return.

CAUTION! *Volume management does not recognize entries in the* `/etc/dfs/dfstab` *file. With Solaris 2.3 and later volume management, you can set up remote CD-ROM mounts by editing the* `/etc/rmmount.conf` *file. Refer to the* `rmmount.conf` *manual page for more information.*

```
oak% ps -ef ¦ grep mountd
    root  4571  4473  5 12:53:51 pts/3    0:00 grep mountd
oak% su
```

```
Password:
# /etc/rc3.d/S15nfs.server stop
# /etc/rc3.d/S15nfs.server start
# share -F nfs -o ro /cdrom/cdrom0
# ps -ef ¦ grep mountd
    root  4655  4473  6 12:56:05 pts/3    0:00 grep mountd
    root  4649     1 47 12:55:25 ?        0:00 /usr/lib/nfs/mountd
```

How to Access Shared CD-ROM Files

You can use the `/mnt` directory as the mount point for the CD-ROM files, or you can create another directory.

NOTE. *Do not use the `/cdrom` mount point to mount local files. Volume management may interfere with accessing files on the volume management `/cdrom` mount point.*

Once the CD-ROM is in the remote drive and the files are shared, follow these steps to access the shared files on a local system:

1. On the local system, become superuser.
2. Type **mount *remote-system-name*:/cdrom/cdrom0 */mount-point*** and press Return. The files from the remote system directory `/cdrom/cdrom0` are mounted on the `/mount-point` directory. The `cdrom0` subdirectory is symbolically linked to the actual name of the CD-ROM, which has a name assigned by the application vendor.

In the following example, the files from the remote system `castle` are mounted on the `/mnt` mount point.

```
oak% su
Password:
# mount castle:/cdrom/cdrom0 /mnt
# cd /mnt
# ls
SUNWssser  SUNWsssra  SUNWsssrb  SUNWsssrc  SUNWsssrd  SUNWssstr
#
```

How to Unmount Shared CD-ROM Files

When you are through using the CD-ROM files, use the following steps to unmount the remote CD-ROM:

1. On the local system, become superuser.
2. Type **cd** and press Return.
3. Type **umount */mount-point*** and press Return. The files from the remote system directory `/cdrom/cdrom0` are unmounted.

CHAPTER

13

Package Commands

Package Command-Line Utilities

Setting Up Package Configuration Files

Adding Packages

Checking the Installation of a Package

Listing Packages

Removing Packages

Package System Log File

HIS CHAPTER DESCRIBES HOW TO USE THE SOLARIS 2.*X* PACKAGE COMMANDS TO INSTALL, remove, and administer software.

Package Command-Line Utilities

You manage software from a command line by using the commands shown in Table 13–1.The package commands are located in the `/usr/sbin` directory. You must have superuser privileges to use the `pkgadd` and `pkgrm` commands.

Table 13–1 Package Commands

Task	Command
Set installation defaults	`vi(1) admin(4)`
Create a script to define installation parameters	`pkgask(1M)`
Install software package or store files for installation at a later time	`pkgadd(1M)`
Check accuracy of installation	`pkgchk(1M)`
List installed packages	`pkginfo(1M)`
Remove packages	`pkgrm(1M)`

Before adding a package, insert the CD-ROM into its caddy and mount the CD-ROM, following the instructions at the end of Chapter 12.

NOTE. *You may experience problems with adding and removing some packages that were developed before the Solaris 2.5 release. If adding or removing a package fails during user interaction or if you are prompted for user interaction and your responses are ignored, set the following environment variable to:*

```
NONABI_SCRIPTS=TRUE
```

Setting Up Package Configuration Files

The `pkgadd` and `pkgrm` files, by default, use information from the `/var/sadm/install/admin/default` file, as shown here:

```
oak% more /var/sadm/install/admin/default
#ident      "@(#)default1.492/12/23 SMI"/* SVr4.0  1.5.2.1*/
mail=
instance=unique
partial=ask
runlevel=ask
idepend=ask
rdepend=ask
space=ask
setuid=ask
conflict=ask
action=ask
basedir=default
oak%
```

The parameters in this file are a set of *parameter=value* pairs, each on a separate line. If you do not want to use the default values, you can create an admin file and set different values. Table 13–2 lists and describes the parameters and shows the available values.

Table 13–2 Package Administration Options

Parameter	Description	Possible Value
mail	Who will receive mail about installation or removal?	*user-name*
instance	Package already installed.	ask
		overwrite
		unique*
		quit
partial	Partial package installed.	ask*
		nocheck
		quit
runlevel	Is run level correct?	ask*
		nocheck
		quit
idepend	Are package dependencies met?	ask*
		nocheck
		quit
rdepend	Is there a dependency on other packages?	ask*
		nocheck
		quit

Table 13–2 Package Administration Options (continued)

Parameter	Description	Possible Value
space	Is disk space adequate?	ask*
		nocheck
		quit
setuid	Ask permission to setuid?	ask*
		nocheck
		quit
		nochange
conflict	Will overwriting a file cause conflict with other packages?	ask*
		nocheck
		quit
		nochange
action	Check for security impact?	ask*
		nocheck
		quit
basedir	Set base install directory. ($PKGINST creates a default directory with the same name as the package.)	default*
		$PKGINST
		/path
		/path/$PKGINST

* Indicates the default value.

CAUTION! *Do not edit the* /var/sadm/install/admin/default *file. If you want to change the defaults, create your own admin file.*

If you create a custom admin file and specify it from the command line using the -a admin option, the pkgadd and pkgrm commands automatically look for the file first in the current working directory and then in the /var/sadm/install/admin directory. If you put the admin file in another directory, you must specify the absolute pathname for the file as part of the command-line argument. The following example specifies an admin file in the /var/tmp directory:

```
# pkgadd -a /var/tmp/admin -d /cdrom/cdrom0
```

To create an admin file, use any editor. Define each *parameter=value* pair on a single line. You do not need to assign values to all 11 parameters. If you do not assign a value and *pkgadd* needs one, it uses the default value ask.

CAUTION! *You cannot define the value ask in an admin file for use with noninteractive installation. Installation will fail when a problem occurs.*

The following example shows an admin file created to automatically install files in the /usr/apps/pkgs directory and to use the default values for other parameters:

```
oak% more /var/sadm/install/admin/admin
mail=
instance=unique
partial=ask
runlevel=ask
idepend=ask
rdepend=ask
space=ask
setuid=ask
conflict=ask
action=ask
basedir=/usr/apps/pkgs/$PKGINST
oak%
```

Setting Up the Installation Base Directory

Before you begin software installation, decide where you want to install the software. If you want to install in a directory other than /opt, create an admin file in the /var/sadm/install/admin directory and set the basedir parameter to the directory where you want to install the software. If basedir is the only parameter you want to change, you can create an admin file that contains only one parameter. All other parameters use the default values. Refer to Table 13–2 on 285–286 for a description of the other parameters you can customize.

The following steps show how to create an admin file that installs files in the /usr/apps/pkgs directory and uses the name of the package as the directory name, and how to use the admin file to control installation:

1. Become superuser.
2. Type **cd /var/sadm/install/admin** and press Return.
3. Use any editor to create a file. Assign the file any name you like, other than the name "default." A suggested filename is "admin."
4. Type **basedir=/usr/apps/pkgs/$PKGINST** to the file.
5. Save the changes and quit.

Installing a Package with an Alternative Admin File

Unless you specify a different administrative file, the `pkgadd` command uses the `/var/sadm/install/admin/default` file, which specifies the base directory as `/opt`. To use an alternative admin file, use the following syntax:

```
pkgadd -d device -a admin-file pkgid
```

The following example installs the package SUNWssser from the CD-ROM device using an admin file named `admin`:

```
# pkgadd -d /cdrom/cdrom0 -a admin SUNWssser
```

Adding Packages

Use the `pkgadd` command to install software packages. The default `pkgadd` command is interactive and can inform you of potential problems in the installation as they occur.

NOTE. *You must have superuser privileges to use the* `pkgadd` *command.*

The syntax of the `pkgadd` command is as follows:

```
pkgadd -d device-name [ -a admin-file ] pkgid
```

For example, to interactively install a software package named SUNWpkgA from a directory named `/cdrom/cdrom0`, you would type **/usr/sbin/pkgadd -d /cdrom/cdrom0 SUNWssser** and press Return. To install the same software package using an alternative administrative file named admin, type **/usr/sbin/pkgadd -d /cdrom/cdrom0 -a admin SUNWssser** and press Return. See "Setting Up Package Configuration Files" on page 284 for information about package administrative files.

You can install multiple packages from the command line by typing a list of *pkgids* separated by spaces. The following example shows an edited example of installation of SearchIt 2.0 software from the `/cdrom/cdrom0` directory:

```
# pkgadd -d /cdrom/cdrom0 SUNWssser SUNWsssra SUNWsssrb SUNWsssrc SUNWsssrd
SUNWssstr

Processing package instance <SUNWssser> from </cdrom/cdrom0>

SearchIt Text Messages and Handbook
(sparc) 2.0

(C) 1992, 1993 Sun Microsystems, Inc. Printed in the United States of America. 2550
Garcia Avenue, Mountain View, California, 94043-1100
U.S.A.

(Additional copyright information not shown)

Using </opt> as the package base directory.
## Processing package information.
## Processing system information.
## Verifying package dependencies.
```

```
WARNING:
    The <SUNWsssra> package "SearchIt Runtime 1 of 3" is a prerequisite package and
    should be installed.

Do you want to continue with the installation of this package [y,n,?] y
## Verifying disk space requirements.
## Checking for conflicts with packages already installed.

The following files are already installed on the system and are being
used by another package:
    /opt <attribute change only>

Do you want to install these conflicting files [y,n,?,q] y
## Checking for setuid/setgid programs.

Installing SearchIt Text Messages and Handbook as <SUNWssser>

## Installing part 1 of 1.
/opt/SUNWssoft/SearchIt/share/locale/C/LC_HELP/Home.info
/opt/SUNWssoft/SearchIt/share/locale/C/LC_HELP/Index.info
/opt/SUNWssoft/SearchIt/share/locale/C/LC_HELP/Search.info
/opt/SUNWssoft/SearchIt/share/locale/C/LC_HELP/SearchIt.handbook
/opt/SUNWssoft/SearchIt/share/locale/C/LC_HELP/SearchIt.info
/opt/SUNWssoft/SearchIt/share/locale/C/LC_HELP/Viewer.info
/opt/SUNWssoft/SearchIt/share/locale/C/LC_MESSAGES/SUNW_SEARCHIT_LABELS.po
/opt/SUNWssoft/SearchIt/share/locale/C/LC_MESSAGES/SUNW_SEARCHIT_MESSAGES.po
/opt/SUNWssoft/SearchIt/share/locale/C/LC_MESSAGES/SUNW_SEARCHIT_XVBROWSER.po
[ verifying class <none> ]

Installation of <SUNWssser> was successful.

Processing package instance <SUNWsssra> from </cdrom/cdrom0>

SearchIt Runtime 1 of 3
(sparc) 2.0

(Copyright information not shown)

Using </opt> as the package base directory.
## Processing package information.
## Processing system information.
   3 package pathnames are already properly installed.
## Verifying package dependencies.
WARNING:
    The <SUNWsssrb> package "SearchIt Runtime 2 of 3" is a prerequisite package and
    should be installed.
WARNING:
    The <SUNWsssrc> package "SearchIt Runtime 3 of 3" is a prerequisite package and
    should be installed.

Do you want to continue with the installation of this package [y,n,?] y
## Verifying disk space requirements.
## Checking for conflicts with packages already installed.
## Checking for setuid/setgid programs.

Installing SearchIt Runtime 1 of 3 as <SUNWsssra>
```

```
## Installing part 1 of 1.
/opt/SUNWssoft/SearchIt/README
/opt/SUNWssoft/SearchIt/bin/auto_index
/opt/SUNWssoft/SearchIt/bin/browseui
/opt/SUNWssoft/SearchIt/bin/catopen
/opt/SUNWssoft/SearchIt/bin/collectionui
(Additional files not shown)
[ verifying class <none> ]

Installation of <SUNWsssra> was successful.

Processing package instance <SUNWsssrb> from </cdrom/cdromØ>

SearchIt Runtime 2 of 3
(sparc) 2.Ø

(Copyright information not shown)

Using </opt> as the package base directory.
## Processing package information.
## Processing system information.
   4 package pathnames are already properly installed.
## Verifying package dependencies.
## Verifying disk space requirements.
## Checking for conflicts with packages already installed.
## Checking for setuid/setgid programs.

Installing SearchIt Runtime 2 of 3 as <SUNWsssrb>

## Installing part 1 of 1.
/opt/SUNWssoft/SearchIt/lib/fultext/fultext.ftc
/opt/SUNWssoft/SearchIt/lib/fultext/fultext.stp
/opt/SUNWssoft/SearchIt/lib/libft.so.1
[ verifying class <none> ]

(Additional package installations not shown)
```

The `pkgadd` command, by default, looks for packages in the `/var/spool/pkg` directory. In this context, any packages that you have copied into that directory are "spooled" and waiting for installation. If there are no packages in the `/var/spool/pkg` directory, installation fails, as shown in the following example:

```
castle# pkgadd
pkgadd: ERROR: no packages were found in </var/spool/pkg>
castle#
```

To install packages directly from media, such as from a CD-ROM, you must use the `-d` option to specify a full (absolute) pathname to the directory on the device that contains the packages that you want to install.

If `pkgadd` encounters a problem, information about the problem appears along with the prompt `Do you want to continue with this installation of the package?`. Type **yes**, **no**, or **quit** and press Return.Typing **yes** continues with the installation. If you have specified more than one package, typing **no** stops the installation of the package that failed, but does not stop the installation of the other packages. Typing **quit** stops installation of all packages.

In the following example, although the command-line argument specifies a valid directory on the CD-ROM, that directory contains no packages and the `pkgadd` command returns an error message:

```
castle# pkgadd -d /cdrom/sol_2_6_sparc/s0/Solaris_2.6
pkgadd: ERROR: attempt to process datastream failed
    - open of </cdrom/sol_2_6_sp1arc/s0/Solaris_2.6> failed, errno=2
pkgadd: ERROR: could not process datastream from </cdrom/sol_2_6_sp1arc/s0/
Solaris_2.6>
castle#
```

In the following example, the command-line argument specifies a path to a valid directory on the CD-ROM that contains packages:

```
castle# pkgadd -d /cdrom/sol_2_6_sparc/s0/Solaris_2.6/Product

The following packages are available:
  1  AXILvplr.c      Axil platform links
             (sparc.sun4c) 5.6,REV=96.01.21.22.49
  2  AXILvplr.m      Axil platform links
             (sparc.sun4m) 5.6,REV=96.01.21.22.50
  3  AXILvplr.u      Axil platform links
             (sparc.sun4u) 5.6,REV=96.01.21.22.49
  4  AXILvplu.c      Axil usr/platform links
             (sparc.sun4c) 5.6,REV=96.01.21.22.51
  5  AXILvplu.m      Axil usr/platform links
             (sparc.sun4m) 5.6,REV=96.01.21.22.51
  6  AXILvplu.u      Axil usr/platform links
             (sparc.sun4u) 5.6,REV=96.01.21.22.51
  7  FJSVvplr.u      Fujitsu platform specific symlinks (Root)
             (sparc.sun4u) 1.0,REV=97.05.26.01
  8  FJSVvplu.u      Fujitsu platform specific symlinks (user)
             (sparc.sun4u) 1.0,REV=97.05.26.01
  9  PFUaga.m        AG-10 Device Driver
             (sparc.sun4m) 1.4.0,REV=0.0.3
 10  PFUaga.u        AG-10 Device Driver
             (sparc.sun4u) 1.4.0,REV=0.0.3

... 298 more menu choices to follow;
<RETURN> for more choices, <CTRL-D> to stop display:The following packages are
available:
```

Alternatively, you can use the `cd` command to change to the directory that contains the packages, and then type **pkgadd -d .** and press Return to proceed with installation, as shown in the following example:

```
castle# cd /cdrom/sol_2_6_sparc/s0/Solaris_2.6/Product
castle@ pkgadd -d .

The following packages are available:
  1  AXILvplr.c      Axil platform links
             (sparc.sun4c) 5.6,REV=96.01.21.22.49
  2  AXILvplr.m      Axil platform links
             (sparc.sun4m) 5.6,REV=96.01.21.22.50
  3  AXILvplr.u      Axil platform links
             (sparc.sun4u) 5.6,REV=96.01.21.22.49
```

```
  4 AXILvplu.c      Axil usr/platform links
             (sparc.sun4c) 5.6,REV=96.01.21.22.51
  5 AXILvplu.m      Axil usr/platform links
             (sparc.sun4m) 5.6,REV=96.01.21.22.51
  6 AXILvplu.u      Axil usr/platform links
             (sparc.sun4u) 5.6,REV=96.01.21.22.51
  7 FJSVvplr.u      Fujitsu platform specific symlinks (Root)
             (sparc.sun4u) 1.0,REV=97.05.26.01
  8 FJSVvplu.u      Fujitsu platform specific symlinks (user)
             (sparc.sun4u) 1.0,REV=97.05.26.01
  9 PFUaga.m        AG-10 Device Driver
             (sparc.sun4m) 1.4.0,REV=0.0.3
 10 PFUaga.u        AG-10 Device Driver
             (sparc.sun4u) 1.4.0,REV=0.0.3

... 298 more menu choices to follow;
<RETURN> for more choices, <CTRL-D> to stop display:The following packages are
available:
```

Checking the Installation of a Package

You can use the pkgchk command to check the completeness, specific pathname, file contents, and file attributes of an installed package.

The syntax of the pkgcheck command follows:

```
pkgchk pkgid
```

For example, to check the package SUNWman, the online manual pages, type **pkgchk SUNWman** and press Return. If the prompt comes up without any messages, the package has installed properly.

```
oak% pkgchk SUNWman
oak%
```

If you do get messages, however, the package has not installed properly, as shown in the following example:

```
oak% pkgchk SUNWssoft
WARNING: no pathnames were associated with <SUNWssoft>
oak%
```

You can specify more than one package identifier by typing a list separated by spaces. If you do not specify a *pkgid*, the complete list of packages on a system is checked.

You can check the installation completeness of a specific pathname by using the -p option with pkgchk, using the following syntax:

```
pkgchk -p pathname
```

If you want to check more than one path, provide the paths as a comma-separated list.

You can check the installation completeness of just the file attributes by using the -a option with the pkgchk command. You can check the installation completeness of just the file contents by using the -c option with the pkgchk command. Here is the appropriate syntax:

```
# /usr/sbin/pkgchk [ -a ¦ -c ] pkgid
```

To check the completeness of a spooled package, use the -d option with the pkgchk command. This option looks in the specified directory or on the specified device and performs a check of the package; for example:

```
# /usr/sbin/pkgchk -d spool-dir pkgA
```

In this example, the pkgchk command looks in the spool directory *spool-dir* and checks the completeness of the package named pkgA.

NOTE. *Spooled package checks are limited because not all information can be audited until a package is installed.*

Listing Packages

If you need to check which packages are installed on a system, use the pkginfo command. By default, it displays information about currently installed packages. You can also use the pkginfo command to display packages that are on mounted distribution media.

Use the command pkginfo with no arguments to list all installed packages. The following example shows the first few packages from a system:

```
[48]castle{winsor}% pkginfo
system      SUNWadmap     System & Network Administration Applications
system      SUNWadmfw     System & Network Administration Framework
system      SUNWadmr      System & Network Administration Root
system      SUNWarc       Archive Libraries
system      SUNWaudio     Audio Applications
system      SUNWbcp       Binary Compatibility
system      SUNWbtool     CCS tools bundled with SunOS
system      SUNWcar       Core Architecture, (Root)
(Additional packages not shown in this example)
```

You can display information about a single package by using the following syntax:

```
pkginfo pkgid
```

In the following example, information is displayed for the SUNWsteNP package:

```
oak% pkginfo SUNWsteNP
application SUNWsteNP     NeWSprint
oak%
```

To display information about packages on a CD-ROM, mount the CD-ROM (see the instructions at the end of Chapter 12). Then use the following syntax to display a complete list of packages on the CD-ROM:

```
oak% pkginfo -d /cdrom/cdrom-name
```

You can display information about single packages on a CD-ROM using the following syntax:

```
oak% pkginfo -d /cdrom/cdrom-name pkgid
```

Removing Packages

Under previous releases of SunOS, you could remove unbundled software packages using the `rm(1)` command. With Solaris 2.*x* system software, you should always use the `pkgrm` command to remove packages. The `pkgrm` command makes administration easier by removing a complete unbundled package with a single command.

Use the following syntax to remove a package in interactive mode:

```
# /usr/sbin/pkgrm pkgid
```

In the following example, the package SUNWdiag is removed:

```
oak% su
Password:
# pkgrm SUNWdiag

The following package is currently installed:
   SUNWdiag        Online Diagnostics Tool
         (sparc) 2.1

Do you want to remove this package [y,n,?,q] y

## Removing installed package instance <SUNWdiag>
## Verifying package dependencies.
## Processing package information.
## Removing pathnames in <none> class
/opt/SUNWdiag/lib/libtest.a
/opt/SUNWdiag/lib
/opt/SUNWdiag/include/sdrtns.h
/opt/SUNWdiag/include
/opt/SUNWdiag/bin/what_rev
/opt/SUNWdiag/bin/vmem
/opt/SUNWdiag/bin/tapetest
/opt/SUNWdiag/bin/sunlink
/opt/SUNWdiag/bin/sundials
/opt/SUNWdiag/bin/sundiagup
/opt/SUNWdiag/bin/sundiag.info
/opt/SUNWdiag/bin/sundiag
/opt/SUNWdiag/bin/sunbuttons
/opt/SUNWdiag/bin/sptest
/opt/SUNWdiag/bin/revision_ref_file
/opt/SUNWdiag/bin/rawtest
/opt/SUNWdiag/bin/prp
/opt/SUNWdiag/bin/probe
/opt/SUNWdiag/bin/pmem
/opt/SUNWdiag/bin/nettest
/opt/SUNWdiag/bin/music.au
/opt/SUNWdiag/bin/mptest
/opt/SUNWdiag/bin/lpvitest
```

```
/opt/SUNWdiag/bin/isdntest
/opt/SUNWdiag/bin/gttest.data
/opt/SUNWdiag/bin/gttest
/opt/SUNWdiag/bin/fstest
/opt/SUNWdiag/bin/fputest
/opt/SUNWdiag/bin/fbtest
/opt/SUNWdiag/bin/dispatcher
/opt/SUNWdiag/bin/diagscrnprnt
/opt/SUNWdiag/bin/cg6test
/opt/SUNWdiag/bin/cg12.data.gsxr
/opt/SUNWdiag/bin/cg12.data
/opt/SUNWdiag/bin/cg12
/opt/SUNWdiag/bin/cdtest
/opt/SUNWdiag/bin/cbrtest
/opt/SUNWdiag/bin/bpptest
/opt/SUNWdiag/bin/autest.data
/opt/SUNWdiag/bin/autest
/opt/SUNWdiag/bin/audbri
/opt/SUNWdiag/bin/57fonts.400
/opt/SUNWdiag/bin/57fonts.300
/opt/SUNWdiag/bin
/opt/SUNWdiag
## Updating system information.

Removal of <SUNWdiag> was successful.
#
```

To remove a package in noninteractive mode, use the `-n` option with the `pkgrm` command, as shown here:

```
# /usr/sbin/pkgrm -n pkgid
```

To remove a package that was spooled to a directory, use the `-s` option with the `pkgrm` command, as shown here:

```
# /usr/sbin/pkgrm -s spooldir [ pkgid ]
```

In this example, *spooldir* is the name of the spool directory to which the unbundled package was spooled and *pkgid* is the name of the package specified for removal. When you do not supply a package identifier, `pkgrm` interactively prompts you to remove or preserve each package listed in the spool directory.

Package System Log File

The package commands maintain a list of installed packages in the `/var/sadm/install/contents` file. No tools are available to list the files contained in a package. The following example shows the first ten lines of the `/var/sadm/install/contents` file:

```
oak% head contents
/bin=./usr/bin s none SUNWcsr
/dev d none 0775 root sys SUNWcsr SUNWcsd
/dev/conslog=../devices/pseudo/log:conslog s none SUNWcsd
/dev/console=../devices/pseudo/cn:console s none SUNWcsd
/dev/dsk d none 0775 root sys SUNWcsd
```

```
/dev/fd d none 0775 root sys SUNWcsd
/dev/ie=../devices/pseudo/clone:ie s none SUNWcsd
/dev/ip=../devices/pseudo/clone:ip s none SUNWcsd
/dev/kmem=../devices/pseudo/mm:kmem s none SUNWcsd
/dev/ksyms=../devices/pseudo/ksyms:ksyms s none SUNWcsd
oak%
```

If you need to determine which package contains a particular file, you can use the `grep` command to search the package system file. In the following example, using the `grep` command to search for information about the `pkgadd` command shows that the command is part of the SUNWcsu package and is located in `/usr/sbin`. A manual page for the `pkgadd` command is part of the SUNWman package, and is located in `/usr/share/man/man1m`.

```
oak% grep pkgadd /var/sadm/install/contents
/usr/sbin/pkgadd f none 0500 root sys 77472 53095 733241518 SUNWcsu
/usr/share/man/man1m/pkgadd.1m f none 0444 bin bin 3784 63018 732833371 SUNWman
# Last modified by pkgadd for SUNWsteNP package
oak%
```

CHAPTER

14

Admintool: Software Manager

Starting Admintool

Customizing Installation

Installing Software

Removing Software

DMINTOOL IS A GRAPHICAL USER INTERFACE TO THE PACKAGE COMMANDS THAT YOU can use to install and remove unbundled software packages on a Solaris 2.*x* system.

This chapter replaces the Software Manager chapter in the first edition because, starting with the Solaris 2.5 system software release, the Admintool: Software functionality replaces Software Manager (`swmtool`).

Software that is designed to be managed using Admintool groups the packages into a set of clusters to make software management easier. Admintool calls the package commands. You can use the package commands and Admintool interchangeably. For example, you can install software by using Admintool and remove the software by using the `pkgrm` command. Alternatively, you can install software by using the `pkgadd` command and remove that software by using Admintool. Admintool displays all packages installed on a system, regardless of how they were installed.

Admintool provides the following functionality:

- Displays a list of the software packages installed on a local system, showing the full title, package names, icons, and the size of each package
- Installs and removes software on a local or a remote Solaris 2.*x* system
- Lets you specify the directory from which to install the software

It is easy to use Admintool to add and remove software from a local system. Admintool provides a graphical user interface to the `pkgadd` and `pkgrm` commands. It also includes online help that provides general information on using the tool. Admintool enables you to view a descriptive list of software that is already installed on a system or of the software on the installation media. It also enables you to view detailed information about each package, including the package name.

Admintool does not enable you to add packages to a spool directory or to eliminate user interaction by using an administration file. You must use `pkgadd` command to access these tasks.

NOTE. *Before the Solaris 2.5 release, Software Manager (accessed with the* `swmtool` *command) was the graphical tool for adding and removing software. With Solaris 2.5 and later releases, Admintool (accessed by using the* `admintool` *command) provides that capability. The* `swmtool` *command in the Solaris 2.5 and 2.6 releases is linked to the* `admintool` *command.*

Starting Admintool

Admintool executable, `admintool`, is located in the `/bin` directory. The obsolete Software Manager executable, `swmtool` (located in the `/usr/sbin` directory) is linked to the

`/bin/admintool` command. If you type **swmtool&**, the Admintool window opens. Use the following steps to start Admintool.

NOTE. *You must run Admintool as superuser to install or remove software or be a member of the UNIX sysadmin group (GID 14).*

1. Log in as root, or become superuser, if you have not done so already.

```
oak% su
Password: <your root password>
oak#
```

2. Type **admintool &** and press Return. The Admintool: Users window opens, as shown in Figure 14–1

```
# /bin/admintool &.
```

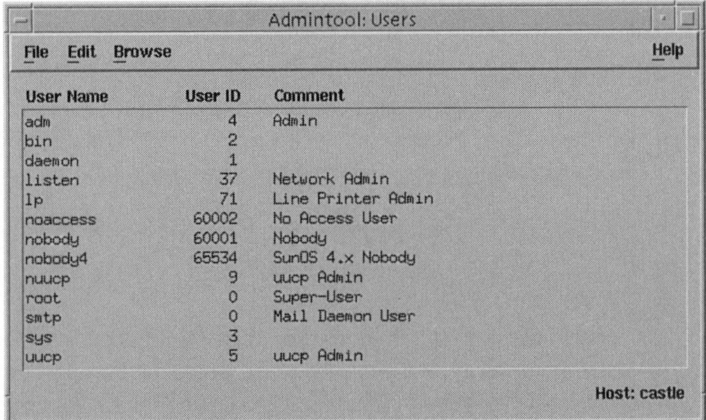

Figure 14–1
Admintool: Users window.

3. From the Browse menu, choose Software. The Admintool: Software window appears, as shown in Figure 14–2.

Installing Software

The following sections describe how to access files from a local CD-ROM, how to set up custom installation, and how to choose an alternative location for installation.

Accessing Files from a Local CD-ROM Drive

Use the following steps to access software from a local CD-ROM:

1. Insert the CD in the CD-ROM drive. After a few moments, a File Manager window displays the contents of the CD-ROM.

Figure 14–2
Admintool:Software window.

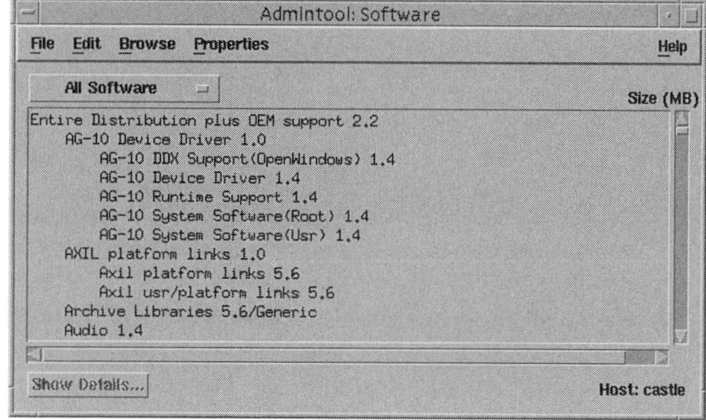

2. From the Edit menu, choose Add. If volume management can read the CD-ROM and the packages are at the top level of the CD-ROM, the Admintool: Add Software window appears, as shown in Figure 14–3.

Figure 14–3
Admintool: Add Software window.

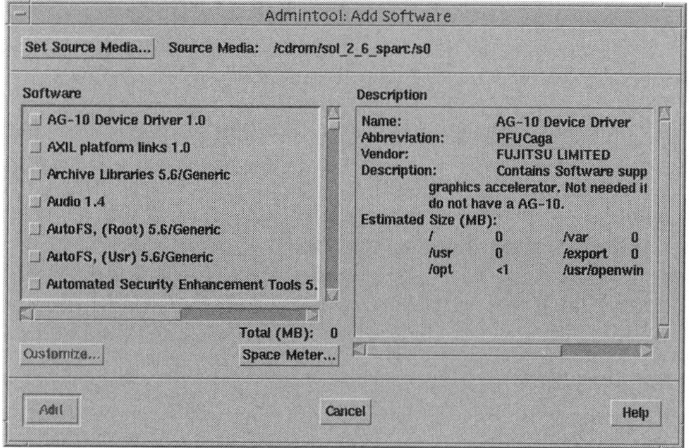

3. If Admintool cannot find any packages at the top level of the hierarchy of the CD-ROM, or if volume management is not running, the Admintool: Set Source Media window opens, as shown in Figure 14–4. In this window, you can choose an alternative media or specify a different path.

4. (If necessary) From the Software Location list, choose Hard Disk or CD without Volume Management. CD with Volume Management is the default.

5. (If necessary) In the CD Path field, type the path to the subdirectory that contains the packages on the media.

Figure 14–4
Admintool: Set Source Media window.

6. Click the OK button. If Admintool cannot locate any packages, an Admintool: Error window opens, as shown in Figure 14–5, telling you that no packages can be found at the path you specified.

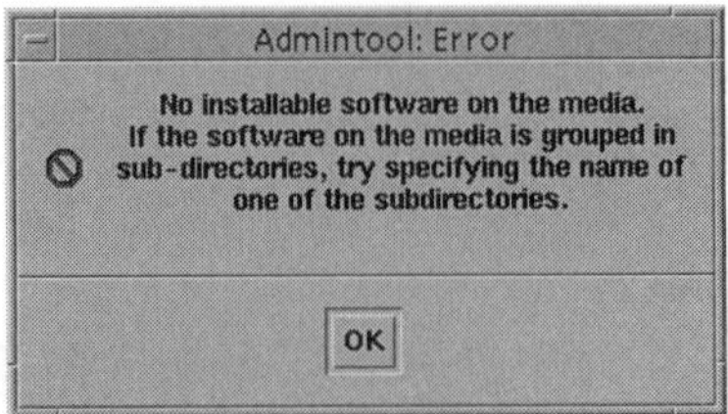

Figure 14–5
Admintool: Error window.

7. Adjust the path until you find the subdirectory that contains the packages you want to add.

Customizing Installation

Before you begin installing software, you can customize some of the installation parameters to minimize or maximize the amount of operator intervention required during installation.

Use the following steps to customize installation:

1. Click the package you want to customize. The package name is highlighted and the Customize button is activated.
2. Click the Customize button. The Admintool: Customize Installation window appears, as shown in Figure 14–6.
3. By default, all packages are selected. Click individual packages to deselect them or use the Deselect All button to deselect all of the packages.
4. The default location for installing packages is the `/opt` directory. If you want to specify an alternative location for installation, type it into the Installation Directory text field.
5. When all of the settings are correct, click OK. The Customize Installation window closes.

Figure 14–6
Admintool: Customize Installation window.

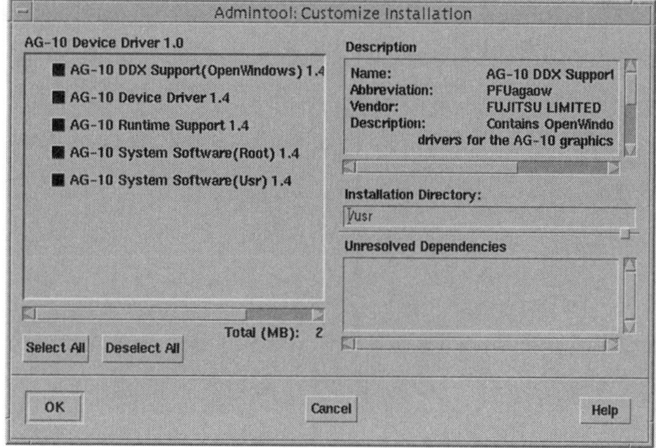

Beginning Installation

Before you follow the steps in this section, check to make sure that you have done the following:

- Set the source media properties to the CD-ROM mount point directory
- Specified a base directory for installation (if you do not want to use the default installation directory)

After you set up all properties and specify the base directory (if desired), you are ready to install software. Use the following steps to install software:

1. In the Admintool: Add Software window, click the Add button. A terminal window opens, revealing additional instructions. Figure 14–7 shows instructions for the SUNWsadma package.
2. Answer the questions generated by the package you are installing. When the installation is complete, the packages are installed and listed in the Admintool: Software window. When you press Return in the Admintool: Add Software terminal window, the window closes.

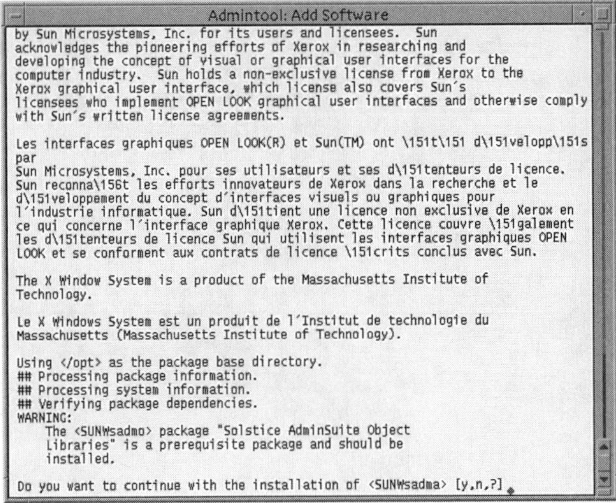

Figure 14–7
Admintool: Add Software window.

Removing Software

You can use the Admintool: Software window to display installed packages and to remove software from a system.

Use the following steps to remove software from a system:

1. Become superuser.
2. If Admintool is not running, type **admintool&** and press Return.
3. From the Browse menu, choose Software.
4. In the Admintool: Software window, click the package you want to remove. The package becomes highlighted.
5. From the Edit menu, choose Delete. An Admintool: Warning window appears, asking you to confirm the delete, as shown in Figure 14–8.

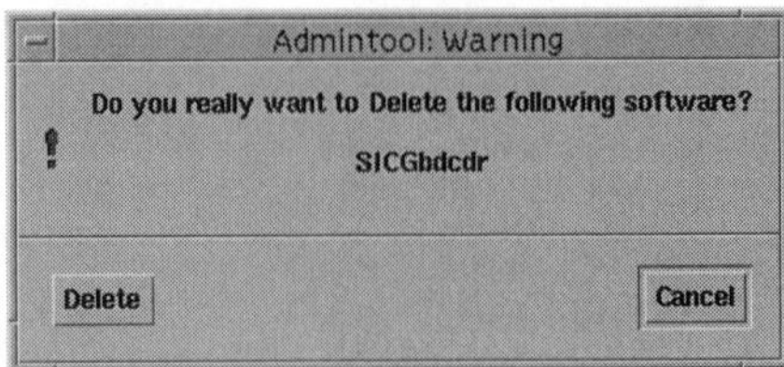

Figure 14–8
Admintool: Warning window.

6. Click the Cancel button to cancel, or click the Delete button to delete the package. The Admintool: Delete Software terminal window comes up, as shown in Figure 14–9.

Figure 14–9
Admintool: Delete Software window.

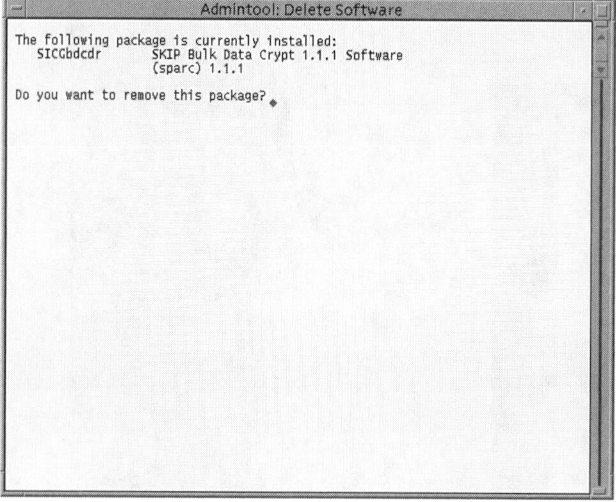

7. To delete, type **Y** and press Return. Continue to answer any additional questions that the package displays.

8. When you press Return after the delete is complete, the Admintool: Delete Software window closes.

CHAPTER

15

Installing and Managing System Software Patches

Patch Distribution

Patch Numbering

Installing Patches

Removing Patches

ATCH ADMINISTRATION INVOLVES INSTALLING OR REMOVING SOLARIS PATCHES FROM A running Solaris system. It may also involve removing or backing out unwanted or faulty patches.

A *patch* is a collection of files and directories that replaces or updates existing files and directories to facilitate proper execution of the software. The existing software is derived from a specific package format, which conforms to the Application Binary Interface. For more information about packages, see Chapter 13, "Package Commands."

The Solaris 2.6 release bundles the following two commands for administering patches.

- `patchadd`: Use to install directory-format patches to a Solaris 2.*x* system.
- `patchrm`: Use to remove patches installed on a Solaris 2.*x* system. This command restores the file system to its state before a patch was applied.

These commands replace the `installpatch` and `backoutpatch` commands that previously shipped with each individual patch.

Detailed information about how to install and back out a patch is provided in the `Install.info` file that accompanies each patch. Each patch also contains a `README` file that contains specific information about the patch.

Before installing patches, you need to know what patches have previously been installed on the system. Table 15–1 shows commands that provide useful information about existing patches.

Table 15–1 Useful Commands for Patch Administration

Command	Description
`showrev -p`	Shows all patches applied to a system.
`pkgparam` *pkgid* `PATCHLIST`	Shows all patches applied to the package identified by `pkgid`.
`pkgparam` *pkgid* `PATCH_INFO_`*patch-number*	Shows the installation date and time of the host from which the package was applied. `pkgid` is the name of the package; for example, SUNWadmap.
`patchadd -R` *client_root_path* `-p`	Shows all patches applied to a client from the server's console.
`patchadd -p`	Shows all patches applied to a system.

Patch Distribution

All Sun customers can access security patches and other recommended patches from the World Wide Web or via anonymous `ftp`. Sun customers who have purchased a service contract can access an extended set of patches and a complete database of patch information. This information is available on the World Wide Web or by anonymous `ftp`, and is regularly distributed on a CD-ROM. Table 15–2 summarizes customer access to patch information.

Table 15–2 Customer Access to Patch Information

Status	Patch Access
Sun Service customer	The SunSolve database provides access to patch information. Patches are available from the Web or by anonymous `ftp`.
Not a Sun Service customer	Customers can access a general set of security patches and other recommended patches from the Web or by anonymous `ftp`.

Requirements to Access Sun Patches

You can access Sun patches from the World Wide Web or by anonymous `ftp`. If you have purchased a Sun service contract, you also can get patches from the regularly distributed patch CD-ROM.

To access patches from the Web, you need a system that is connected to the Internet and capable of running Web browsing software such as Mosaic or Netscape.

To access patches by anonymous `ftp`, you need a system that is connected to the Internet and capable of running an `ftp` program.

Accessing Patches from the Web

To access patches from the Web, use the following URL:

`http://www.sun.com/`

1. After you reach the Sun home page, click on the Sales and Service button and navigate your way to the SunSolve patch database, shown in Figure 15–1.

The patch database for publicly available patches is labeled `Public patch access`. The patch database for the comprehensive set of patches and patch information available to contract customers is labeled `Contract customer patch access`. You are prompted for a password to access the contract customer database.

You also can use the following URL to access publicly available patches:

`http://sunsite.unc.edu/`

Figure 15–2 shows the Sun Site Web page.

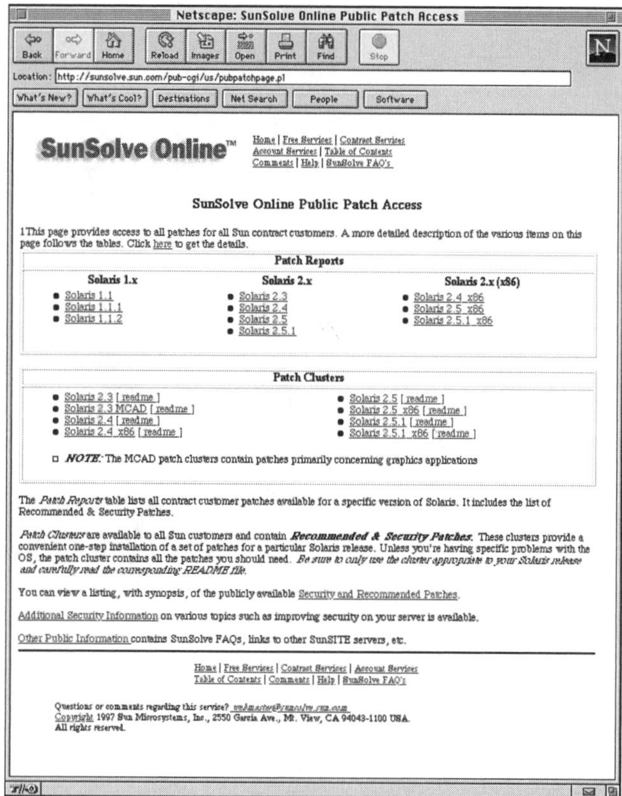

Figure 15–1
The SunSolve Online Public Patch Access Web page.

Accessing Patches by ftp

To access patches by `ftp`, use the `ftp` command to connect to either of the following:

- `sunsolve1.sun.com` (provided by Sun Service)
- `sunsite.unc.edu` (maintained by the University of North Carolina)

When `ftp` prompts you for a login, enter **anonymous** as the login name. When prompted for a password, enter your complete email address. After login is complete, you can find publicly available patches in the `/pubs/patches` directory.

NOTE. *You must transfer patches in binary mode. To change to binary mode, at the ftp prompt, type* ***bin*** *and press Return.*

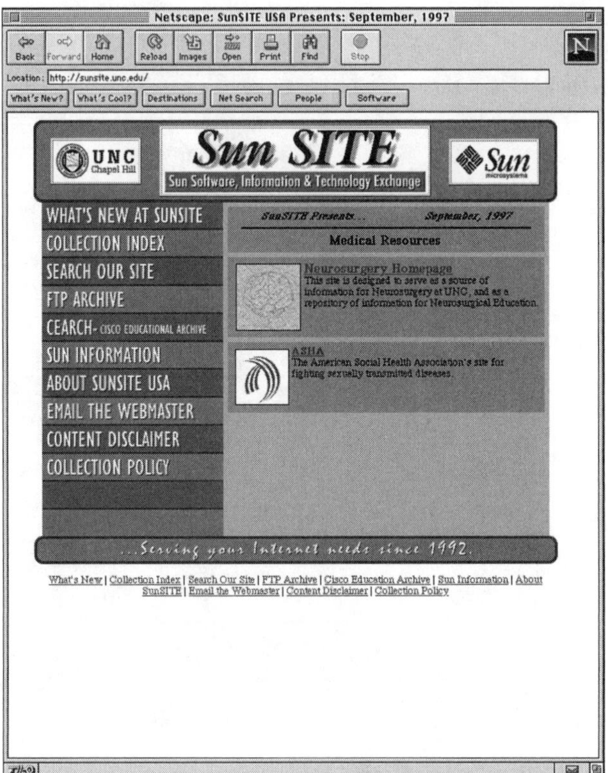

Figure 15–2

The Sun Site Web page.

Patch Numbering

Patches are identified by unique alphanumeric strings with the patch base code first, a hyphen, and a number that represents the patch revision number. For example, patch 101977-02 is a Solaris 2.4 patch to correct the `lockd` daemon. 101988 is the number for the `lock` daemon patch. "-02" indicates that this is the second release of the patch.

Installing a Patch

When you install a patch, the `patchadd` command copies files from the patch directory to a local system disk. The `patchadd` command does the following:

- Determines the Solaris version number of the managing host and the target host.
- Updates the `pkginfo` file of the patch package with information about patches that are rendered obsolete by the patch being installed, other patches required by this patch, and patches that are incompatible with this patch.

During patch installation, the patchadd command keeps a log of the patch installation in /var/sadm/patch/*patch-number*/log for the Solaris 2.4 and earlier operating environments. The Solaris 2.5 and 2.6 releases also store log files in this location, but only in the event of installation errors.

The patchadd command does not install a patch under the following conditions:

- The package is not fully installed on the host.
- The patch architecture differs from the system architecture.
- The patch version does not match the installed package version.
- A patch is already installed with the same base code and a higher version number.
- The patch is incompatible with another, already installed patch. (This information is stored in the pkginfo file for each patch.)
- The patch being installed requires another patch that is not installed.

The following example installs a patch to a standalone system:

```
# patchadd /var/spool/patch/104945-02
```

The following example installs a patch to a client system, client1, from the server's console:

```
# patchadd -R /export/root/client1 /var/spool/patch/104945-02
```

The following example installs a patch to a service from the server's console:

```
# patchadd -S Solaris_2.3 /var/spool/patch/104945-02
```

The following example installs multiple patches in a single patchadd invocation:

```
# patchadd -M /var/spool/patch 104945-02 104946-02 102345-02
```

The following example installs multiple patches, specifying a file that contains the list of patches to install:

```
# patchadd -M /var/spool/patch patchlist
```

The following example installs multiple patches to a client and saves the backout data to a directory other than the default:

```
# patchadd -M /var/spool/patch -R /export/root/client1 -B /export/backoutrepository
104945-02 104946-02 102345-02
```

The following example installs a patch to a Solaris 2.6 or later Net Install Image:

```
# patchadd -C /export/Solaris_2.6/Tools/Boot /var/spool/patch/104945-02
```

The following example installs a patch to a Solaris 2.6 or later Net Install Image, but instructs the patchadd command not to save copies of files that are updated or replaced:

```
# patchadd -d /export/Solaris_2.6/Tools/Boot /var/spool/patch/104945-02
```

CAUTION! *Never use the* `-d` *option because it makes it difficult to remove or back out patches that become obsolete.*

Removing Patches

When you remove, or back out, a patch, the `patchrm` command restores all files modified by that patch, unless any of the following are true:

- The patch was installed with `patchadd -d`, which instructs `patchadd` not to save copies of files that are updated or replaced.
- The patch has been obsoleted by a later patch.
- The patch is required by another patch.

The `patchrm` command calls `pkgadd` to restore packages that were saved from the initial patch installation.

During the patch installation, `patchrm` keeps a log of the patch installation in `/tmp/backoutlog.`*`pid`*. This log is removed if the patch backs out successfully.

The following example removes a patch from a standalone system:

```
# patchrm 104945-02
```

The following example removes a patch from a client's system from the server's console:

```
# patchrm -R /export/root/client1 104945-02
```

The following example removes a patch from a server's service area:

```
# patchrm -S Solaris_2.3 104945-02
```

The following example removes a patch from a Net Install Image:

```
# patchrm -C /export/Solaris_2.6/Tools/Boot 104945-02
```

This part introduces shell programming in two chapters: Chapter 16 introduces the basic concepts of shell programming and the three shells available with Solaris 2.*x* system software. It describes how shells work, describes the programming elements, and provides reference tables comparing shell syntax. Chapter 17 contains examples of shell scripts.

Understanding shell programs can help you interpret system scripts, such as the run control (rc) scripts, and write your own scripts to automate system administration tasks. Refer to these two chapters if you want to familiarize yourself with the basics of shell programming and to decide which shell language you want to use to perform a specific task. This book does not provide in-depth instructions for writing scripts in the Bourne, Korn, and C shell programming languages. Refer to one of the many books that have been written on the subject for complete instructions on how to use any of the shell programming languages. Refer to the Bibliography at the end of this book for a partial list of references.

PART

6

Introduction to Shell Programming

CHAPTER

16

Writing Shell Scripts

Basic Concepts

Variables

Input and Output

Testing Conditions

Controlling the Flow

Exit Status

Mathematical Operations

User-Defined Functions

Debugging Shell Scripts

SOLARIS 2.X SYSTEM SOFTWARE INCLUDES THREE SHELLS: BOURNE, KORN, AND C. EACH shell has its own high-level programming language that you can use to execute sequences of commands, select among alternative operations, perform logical tests, and repeat program actions. The Bourne and Korn shells use almost identical syntax, although the Korn shell is a superset of the Bourne shell and provides more functionality. The Bourne shell is used for most scripts that are distributed with Solaris 2.*x* system software. The C shell uses a syntax that is similar to C programming language syntax, and it has built-in capabilities not provided with the Bourne shell, such as history and array capability.

This chapter introduces the basic concepts of shell programming and the three shells, describes how shells work, and compares the syntax of the three shells; reference tables are provided throughout this chapter and are repeated in Chapter 17.

Basic Concepts

A *shell* is a specialized Solaris 2.*x* utility that provides an interface between the user and the operating system kernel. The *kernel* is the central core of the operating system and controls all basic aspects of a computer's operation. The kernel coordinates all of the executing utilities and manages the system's resources. The shell is a special command interpreter that invokes and interacts with the kernel to provide a way for users to execute utilities and other programs.

Each user is assigned a default shell that starts each time the user logs in to a system or opens a new Command Tool or Shell Tool window. The shell interprets the commands that it reads. You can type those commands directly into the shell at the prompt, or the shell can read the commands from a file. A file that contains shell commands is called a *shell program* or *shell script.*

Shell programs are interpreted, not compiled: The commands are read and executed one by one, in sequence. A compiled program, on the other hand, is initially read and converted to a form that can be directly executed by the CPU, and thereafter executed all at once. Because shell scripts are interpreted, even the fastest shell script always runs more slowly than an equivalent program written in a compiled language such as C.

Introducing Bourne, Korn, and C Shells

The Bourne, Korn, and C shells each have their own environment and syntax. Table 16–1 compares the initialization files that define the shell environment at startup.

Table 16–1 Shell Initialization Files

Feature	Bourne	Korn	C
Read at login	`.profile`	`.profile`	`.login`
Read at invocation of shell	N/A	Any file specified in `.profile` with ENV=.*file*	`.cshrc`

The initialization files contain environment variables and other settings that configure the user's environment when a shell starts. Refer to the section "Environment Variables" on page 329 for more information. The `.profile` (Bourne and Korn shells) and `.login` (C shell) files execute when a user logs in to a system. The Korn shell and `.cshrc` (C shell) environment files execute each time a new shell starts. Use these environment files to define aliases and functions for interactive use, and to set variables that you want to apply to the current shell.

Bourne Shell

The Bourne shell, written by Steve Bourne when he was at AT&T Bell Laboratories, is the original UNIX shell. This shell is preferred for shell programming because of its programming capabilities and its universal availability. It lacks features for interactive use, such as built-in arithmetic and the capability to recall previous commands (history). The Bourne shell is the default login shell for the root account, and it serves as the default user login shell if you do not specify another shell in the user's `passwd` file. The Bourne shell is used for all system-supplied administration scripts.

The Bourne shell command is `/bin/sh`. The default prompt for the Bourne shell is a dollar sign (`$`). The root prompt is a pound sign (`#`).

Korn Shell

The Korn shell, written by David Korn of AT&T Bell Laboratories, was designed to be compatible with the Bourne shell and to offer interactive features comparable to the C shell. The Korn shell includes convenient programming features such as built-in integer arithmetic, arrays, and string-manipulation facilities. The Korn shell runs faster than the C shell, and runs virtually all scripts that are written for the Bourne shell.

The Korn shell command is `/bin/ksh`. The default prompt for the Korn shell is a dollar sign (`$`). The root prompt is a pound sign (`#`).

C Shell

The C shell, written by Bill Joy when he was at the University of California at Berkeley, was designed to incorporate features such as aliases and command history for interactive use. The syntax for its programming features is similar to that for the C programming language.

The C shell command is `/bin/csh`. The default prompt for the C shell is the system name followed by a percent sign (`%`). The root prompt is the system name followed by a pound sign (`#`).

Understanding How Shells Process Commands

Each shell creates *subshells* and *child processes*—subordinate shells and processes that are executed within the originating, or *parent,* shell—to interpret and execute commands. For example, the following list shows a simplified version of the order in which the Korn shell processes commands:

1. Parses (divides up) the command into units separated by the fixed set of metacharacters: Space Tab Newline ; ( ) < > | &. Types of units include words, keywords, I/O redirectors, semicolons, and others.
2. Checks the first part of each unit for shell keywords, such as `function` or `if` statements, with no quotes or backslashes. When it finds a keyword, the shell processes the compound command.
3. Searches the list of aliases.
4. Expands any tilde (~) expressions.
5. Substitutes variables.
6. Substitutes commands.
7. Substitutes arithmetic expressions.
8. Splits the items that result from parameter, command, and arithmetic substitution and splits them into words again.
9. Expands wildcards.
10. Looks up built-in commands, functions, and executable files.
11. Sets up I/O redirection.
12. Runs the command.

The Bourne shell interprets commands similarly, but does not check for aliases, tildes, or arithmetic. The C shell interprets commands in a different order.

Naming Shell Scripts

When you assign a name to a shell script, follow the general rule for naming Solaris 2.*x* files. Make a script name as descriptive as possible so that you can easily remember its designated function. Be careful to avoid names that Solaris 2.*x* itself uses for its own programs unless you intend to replace those utilities with your own scripts.

Each shell has a list of built-in commands. You should also avoid using built-in shell commands as script names. If you name a file with one of the shell built-in commands—such as `alias`, `break`, `case`, `cd`, `continue`, `echo`, `else`, `exit`, or `history` for the C shell—the shell interprets the script name as a built-in shell command and tries to execute it instead of executing the script. For example, with the Bourne or Korn shell, you will run into trouble if you name a script "test," which you might easily do if you are testing something out, because `test` is a built-in Bourne and Korn shell command. Refer to the shell syntax sections in Chapter 17 and to the `sh`(1), `ksh`(1), and `csh`(1) manual pages for a complete list of built-in commands.

Identifying the Shell

The first line of each shell script determines the shell that runs—or interprets—the program. Always identify the interpreting shell on the first line of the script, using the information from Table 16–2.

Table 16–2 First Line of Script

Shell	Syntax
Bourne	`#!/bin/sh`
Korn	`#!/bin/ksh`
C	`#!/bin/csh -f`

The `-f` (fast) option to `/bin/csh` runs the script without sourcing the `.cshrc` file.

If you do not specify the shell in the first line of the script, and it is an executable script, the current shell interprets the contents of the script.

After the first line of a script, any line beginning with a pound sign (#) is treated as a comment line and is not executed as part of the script.

Making Scripts Executable

Before you can run a shell script, it is customary to change its permissions so that it has at least read and execute permissions (`chmod 555`). When you write and debug the script, give yourself write permission to the file (`chmod 755`) so that you can edit it. When assigning permissions to a completed shell script, consider the scope of access that you want to permit to this script. Use restrictive permissions if the script is proprietary or individual, and use more relaxed permissions if many users who are not in the same group will use the script.

Storing Shell Scripts

After you create a shell script, you can execute it only from the directory in which it resides or by using the full pathname, unless you set your `PATH` variable to include the directory that contains the script.

If you write many scripts, you may want to create a `~/bin` directory in your home directory and update your search path to include this directory. In this way, your scripts are available regardless of where you are in the directory hierarchy. If you provide scripts for more general use, be sure to debug them before you put them in a directory where they are more accessible.

Writing Shell Scripts: The Process

The following checklist describes the process to follow when writing any shell script:

1. Decide what you want the script to do. Establish a list of the commands you need to use to accomplish the desired task.
2. Use an editor to put the commands into a file. Give the file a name that indicates what the script does.
3. Identify the shell in the first line of the script.
4. Include comments at the beginning of the script to describe its purpose and to annotate each individual part of the script. These comments can be useful when you debug the script and to interpret a script that may be used only occasionally. Comments are also invaluable in helping others to interpret scripts that you have written.
5. Save the file and quit the editor.
6. Change the permissions so that the file has, at a minimum, read and execute permissions.
7. Check your path, or the `PATH` variable, to make sure that the directory that contains the script is in the search path.
8. Type the name of the script as a command. The script executes one line at a time.
9. If errors occur, debug the script.
10. When the script is complete, decide where you want to store the command (for example, in your home directory, your local `~/bin` directory, or in a more globally available directory).

Variables

A *variable* is a name that refers to a temporary storage area in memory. A variable holds a value. Changing a variable's value is called *assigning* a value to the variable. Shell programming uses two types of variables: shell variables and environment variables. By convention, you write shell variables in lowercase and environment variables in uppercase.

Shell Variables

Shell variables are maintained by the shell and are known only to the shell. Shell variables are always local and are not passed on from parent to child processes.

Displaying Variables from a Command Line

You use the `set` command with no arguments to display a list of current shell and environment variables. The Bourne and Korn shells display variables in the format shown in the following example:

```
$ set
CALENDAR=/home/winsor
DVHOME=/home/winsor/docudisc/dd.alpha
DVPATH=/home/winsor/docudisc/dd.alpha
ERRNO=10
FCEDIT=/bin/ed
FMHOME=/home2/frame
HELPDIR=$SUNDESK/help
HOME=/home1/winsor
HZ=100
IFS=

LD_LIBRARY_PATH=/usr/openwin/lib:/usr/lib:/usr/ucblib
LINENO=1
LOGNAME=winsor
MAIL=/var/mail/winsor
MAILCHECK=600
MANSECTS=\1:1m:1c:1f:1s:1b:2:\3:3c:3i:3n:3m:3k:3g:3e:3x11:3xt:3w:3b:9:4:5:7:8
OPENWINHOME=/usr/openwin
OPTIND=1
PATH=.:/home1/winsor:/usr/openwin:/usr/openwin/bin/xview:/home2/frame/bin:/usr/dist
/local/exe:/usr/dist/exe:/home1/winsor/bin:/etc:/usr/etc:/usr/sbin:/usr/bin:/usr/ucb:.
PPID=9139
PS1=$
PS2=>
PS3=#?
PS4=+
PWD=/home1/winsor
RANDOM=23592
SECONDS=1
SHELL=/bin/csh
TERM=sun
TMOUT=0
TZ=US/Pacific
USER=winsor
$
```

The C shell displays its variables in the following format:

```
[26]castle{winsor}% set
argv    ()
cwd     /home1/winsor
history 25
home    /home1/winsor
ignoreeof
```

```
noclobber
noglob
path    (. /home1/winsor /usr/openwin /usr/openwin/bin/xview /home2/frame/bin
/usr/dist/local/exe /usr/dist/exe /home1/winsor/bin /etc /usr/etc /usr/sbin
/usr/bin /usr/ucb .)
prompt  [!]castle{winsor}%
savehist        25
shell   /bin/csh
status  Ø
term    sun
time    15
user    winsor
[27]castle{winsor}%
```

Setting and Displaying Shell Variables

To create a Bourne or Korn shell variable, you simply assign the value of the variable to the name. If the value contains spaces or characters that the shell interprets in a special way, you must enclose the value in quotes. Refer to the section "Quoting" on page 338 for more information. Use the following syntax to assign the value of the variable to a name:

```
variable=value
```

In the following Bourne or Korn shell example, the variable `today` is set to display the output of the `date` command:

```
$ today=Tuesday
$ echo $today
Tuesday
$
```

To display the value for a variable for any shell, type **echo *$variable***. Although the Korn shell recognizes the `echo` command, `print $variable` is the preferred syntax. Optionally, you can enclose the name of the variable in curly braces ({}). You may want to use curly braces if you are concatenating strings together and want to separate the name of the variable from the information that follows it. In the following example, a variable named `flower` is set to `rose`. If you want to add an "s" at the end of the variable name when appears on-screen, you must enclose the variable in curly braces.

```
$ flower=rose
$ echo $flower
rose
$ echo $flowers

$ echo ${flower}s
roses
$
```

You can set local variables from the command line, as shown in the previous examples, or within a script.

Use the following syntax to set a C shell variable. If the value contains spaces or characters that the shell interprets in a special way, you must enclose the value in quotes. Refer to the section "Quoting" on page 338 for more information.

```
set variable=value
```

You can also set the value of a variable to return the output of a command. To do so, enclose the name of the command in backquotes (` `). The Korn shell also supports the notation `$(command)`. The following C shell example sets the variable *today* to display the output of the `date` command:

```
oak% set today = `date`
oak% echo $today
Thu Jul 8 12:41:27 PDT 1993
oak%
```

Refer to the section "Quoting" on page 338 for more information.

Unsetting Shell Variables

You can use the `unset` command to remove any shell variable, as shown in the following Bourne shell example:

```
$ unset today
$ echo $today

$
```

Stripping Filenames

Sometimes you want to modify a pathname to strip off unneeded parts. With the Bourne shell, you can use the `basename`(1) utility to return only the filename, and the `dirname`(1) utility to return only the directory prefix. The Korn and C shells provide a built-in way for you to modify path names.

Korn Shell Path Stripping

The Korn shell provides pattern-matching operators, shown in Table 16–3, that you can use to strip off components of pathnames.

Table 16–3 Korn Shell Pattern-Matching Operators

Operator	Description
${*variable*# *pattern*}	Deletes the shortest part at the beginning of the variable that matches the pattern and returns the rest.
${*variable*## *pattern*}	Deletes the longest part at the beginning of the variable that matches the pattern and returns the rest.
${*variable*% *pattern*}	Deletes the shortest part at the end of the variable that matches the pattern and returns the rest.
${*variable*%% *pattern*}	Deletes the longest part at the end of the variable that matches the pattern and returns the rest.

The following example shows how all of the operators work, using the pattern `/*/` to match anything between two slashes, and `.*` to match a dot followed by anything:

```
$ pathname=/home/winsor/Design.book.new
$ echo ${pathname#/*/}
winsor/Design.book.new
$ echo ${pathname##/*/}
Design.book.new
$ echo ${pathname%.*}
/home/winsor/Design.book
$ echo ${pathname%%.*}
/home/winsor/Design
$
```

C Shell Path Stripping

The C shell provides a set of modifiers that you can use to strip off unneeded components. These modifiers are quite useful in stripping pathnames, but can also be used to modify variable strings. Table 16–4 lists the C shell variable modifiers.

Table 16–4 C Shell Filename Modifiers

Modifier	Description
`:e`	Extension—remove prefix ending with a dot.
`:h`	Head—remove trailing pathname components.
`:r`	Root—remove trailing suffixes beginning with a dot.
`:t`	Tail—remove all leading pathname components.
`:q`	Quote—force variable to be quoted. (Used to quote `$argv`.)
`:x`	Like `q`, but break into words at each space, tab, or newline.

The following example shows the results of the first four variable modifiers:

```
oak% set pathname = /home/winsor/Design.book
oak% echo $pathname:e
book
oak% echo $pathname:h
/home/winsor
oak% echo $pathname:r
/home/winsor/Design
oak% echo $pathname:t
Design.book
```

Built-In Shell Variables

All three shells have a set of single-character variables that are set initially by the shell, as shown in Table 16–5. You can use these variables to access words in variables and return other information about the variable. These variables are used differently in the C shell than they are in the Bourne and Korn shells.

Table 16–5 Variables Initialized by Shell

Variable	Explanation
$*	Bourne or Korn shell: List the value of all command-line parameters. This variable is useful only in scripts because the login shell has no arguments associated with it.
	C Shell: Not used. Use `$argv` instead.
$#	Bourne or Korn shell: Return the number of command-line arguments (in decimal). Useful only in scripts.
	C shell: Count the number of words (in decimal) in a variable array.
$?	Bourne or Korn shell: Return the exit status (in decimal) of the last command executed. Most commands return a zero exit status if they complete successfully; otherwise a non-zero exit status is returned. This variable is set after each command is executed.
	C shell: Check to see if a variable of that name has been set.
$$	All shells: Return the process ID (PID) number of the current shell (in decimal).
$!	Bourne or Korn shell: Return the process number (in decimal) of the last process run in the background.

For the Bourne and Korn shells, you can use the `$*` variable to list the values of command-line arguments within a script, and the `$#` variable to hold the number of arguments. In the following example, the shell expands the `$*` variable to list all of the command-line arguments to the script:

```
#!/bin/sh


echo $#
for var in $*
do
        echo $var
done
```

If you named the script **tryit** and executed it with three arguments, it would echo the value of arguments from `$#`, and then display the list of arguments from `$*`, one on each line. The input string may contain quotes. Refer to the `sh`(1) manual page for information about how quoted strings are interpreted.

```
$ tryit one two three
3
one
two
three
$
```

For the C shell, the `$#variable` command holds the number of words in a variable array, as shown in the following example:

```
oak% set var = (a b c)
oak% echo $#var
3
oak%
```

For the Bourne shell, the `$?` variable displays exit status for the last command executed; it displays this information in the same way that the C shell status variable does. Refer to the section "Exit Status" on page 349 for an example.

For the C shell, you can use the variable `$?variable` to test whether a variable is set. `$?variable` returns a `1` if a named variable exists, or `0` if the named variable does not exist.

```
oak% set var="a b c"
oak% echo $?var
1
oak% unset var
oak% echo $?var
0
oak%
```

NOTE. *The numbers returned by* `$?variable` *are the opposite from status numbers, where 0 is success and 1 is failure.*

For all shells, the `$$` variable returns the PID number of the current shell process, as shown in the following examples. Because process numbers are unique, you can use this string to generate unique temporary file names. For example, when a script assigns a filename of `tmp.$$`, that file rarely is confused with another file.

NOTE. *If you are concerned about generating unique filenames, you can use the format feature of the* `date`(1) *command to generate a temporary filename that includes both a process ID and a time and date stamp.*

```
oak% echo $$
364
oak% sh
$ echo $$
392
$
```

Each shell also includes built-in commands for efficiency. Table 16–6 lists the built-in commands. The Bourne shell relies more on using external commands to do the work, and thus has the fewest built-in commands. The additional built-in commands for the Korn shell are shown by (K) following the command name. The job control variant of the Bourne shell, `jsh`, has the same job control features as the Korn shell.

CAUTION! *Do not use any of the built-in commands as names for shell scripts. If you use one of the built-in commands as a shell script name, the shell will execute the built-in command instead of running the script.*

Table 16–6 Shell Built-In Commands

Purpose	Bourne or Korn Shell	C Shell
Null command	:	:
Create a command name alias	alias (K)	alias
Run current command in background	bg (K)	bg
Exit enclosing for or while loop	break	break
Break out of a switch	N/A	breaksw
Change directory	cd	cd
Continue next iteration of for or while loop	continue	continue
Default case in switch	N/A	default
Print directory stack	N/A	dirs
Write arguments on stdout	echo, print (K)	echo
Evaluate and execute arguments	eval	eval
Execute the arguments	exec	exec
Return or set shell variables	N/A	@
Exit shell program	exit	exit
Create an environment variable	export	setenv
Bring a command into foreground	fg (K)	fg
Execute foreach loop	for	foreach
Perform filename expansion	N/A	glob
Go to label within shell program	N/A	goto
Display history list	fc (K)	history
If-then-else decision	if	if
List active jobs	jobs (K)	jobs
Send a signal	kill	kill

Table 16–6 Shell Built-In Commands (continued)

Purpose	Bourne or Korn Shell	C Shell
Set limits for a job's resource use	`ulimit`	`limit`
Terminate login shell and invoke login	N/A	`login`
Terminate a login shell	N/A	`logout`
Change to a new user group	`newgrp (K)`	N/A
Change priority of a command	N/A	`nice`
Ignore hangup	N/A	`nohup`
Notify user when job status changes	N/A	`notify`
Control shell processing on receipt of a signal	`trap`	`onintr`
Pop the directory stack	N/A	`popd`
Push a directory onto the stack	N/A	`pushd`
Read a line from stdin	`read`	`$<`
Change a variable to read-only	`readonly`	N/A
Repeat a command *n* times	N/A	`repeat`
Set shell environment variables	=	`setenv`
Set a local C shell variable	N/A	`set`
Shift positional parameters $* or $argv	`shift`	`shift`
Read and execute a file	`.` (dot)	`source`
Stop a background process	N/A	`stop`
Stop the shell	suspend (K)	`suspend`
CASE statement	`case ... esac`	`switch ... endsw`

Table 16–6 Shell Built-In Commands (continued)

Purpose	Bourne or Korn Shell	C Shell
Evaluate conditional expressions	`test`	N/A
Display execution times	`times`	`time`
Set default security for creation of files and directories	`umask`	`umask`
Discard aliases	`unalias` (K)	`unalias`
Remove limitations on resources	`ulimit`	`unlimit`
Unset a variable	`unset`	`unset`
Unset an environment variable	N/A	`unsetenv`
`UNTIL` loop	`until`	N/A
Wait for background process to complete	`wait`	N/A
`WHILE` loop	`while`	`while`

Environment Variables

Environment variables are often used to define initialization options such as the default login shell, user login name, search path, and terminal settings. Some environment variables are set for you each time you log in. You can also create your own variables and assign values to them. By convention, environment variable names are in capital letters.

Environment variables are passed on from parent to child processes. For example, an environment variable set in a shell is available to any program started in that shell, to any additional program started by the initial program, and so on. In other words, environment variables are inherited from parent to child, from child to grandchild, and so on. They are not inherited backward from parent to grandparent or child to parent.

Use the `env` command to display a list of current environment variables. Consult the *Solaris System Administrator's Guide* for more information about environment variables.

For the Bourne and Korn shells, use the following syntax to assign environment variables and export them. You must export the variable before it can be put into the environment of child processes.

```
VARIABLE=value;export VARIABLE
```

For the Korn shell, you can also use the following syntax:

```
export VARIABLE=value
```

For the C shell, use the `setenv` command with the following syntax to assign environment variables:

```
setenv VARIABLE value
```

Use the `unsetenv` command with the following syntax to remove the environment variable:

```
unsetenv VARIABLE
```

Input and Output

When you write shell scripts, you want to be able to obtain input from sources outside your scripts; for example, from another file or from keyboard input. You also want to be able to generate output both for use within the script and for display on-screen.

The following sections describe how to control input and output of a shell script using standard input, output, error, and redirection; how to accept user input (input from the keyboard) to a script; how to create "here" documents; and how to generate output to the screen.

Standard In, Standard Out, and Standard Error

When writing shell scripts, you can control input/output redirection. *Input redirection* is the ability to force a command to read any necessary input from a file instead of from the keyboard. *Output redirection* is the ability to send the output from a command into a file or pipe instead of to the screen.

Each process created by a shell script begins with three file descriptors associated with it, as shown in Figure 16–1.

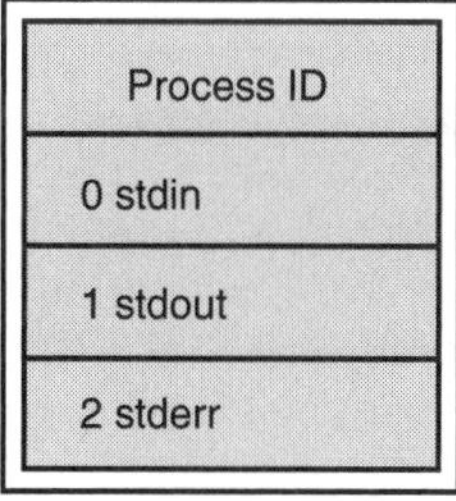

Figure 16–1
File descriptors.

These file descriptors—*standard input*, *standard output*, and *standard error*—determine where input to the process comes from, and where the output and error messages are sent.

Standard input (STDIN) is always file descriptor 0. Standard input is the place where the shell looks for its input data. Usually data for standard input comes from the keyboard. You can specify standard input to come from another source using input/output redirection.

Standard output (STDOUT) is always file descriptor 1. Standard output (default) is the place where the results of the execution of the program are sent. Usually, the results of program execution are displayed on the terminal screen. You can redirect standard output to a file, or suppress it completely by redirecting it to `/dev/null`.

Standard error (STDERR) is always file descriptor 2. Standard error is the place where error messages are sent as they are generated during command processing. Usually, error messages are displayed on the terminal screen. You can redirect standard error to a file, or suppress it completely by redirecting it to `/dev/null`.

You can use the file descriptor numbers 0 (standard input), 1 (standard output), and 2 (standard error) together with the redirection metacharacters to control input and output in the Bourne and Korn shells. Table 16–7 shows the common ways you can redirect file descriptors.

Table 16–7 Bourne and Korn Shell Redirection

Description	Command
Take STDIN from file	<*file*, or 0<*file*
Redirect STDOUT to file	> *file*, or 1> *file*
Redirect STDERR to file	2> *file*
Append STDOUT to end of file	>> *file*
Redirect STDERR to STDOUT	2>&1
Pipe standard output of cmd1 as standard input to *cmd2*	*cmd1* | *cmd2*
Use *file* as both STDIN and STDOUT	<> *file*
Close STDIN	<&-
Close STDOUT	>&-
Close STDERR	2>&-

When redirecting STDIN and STDOUT in the Bourne and Korn shells, you can omit the file descriptors 0 and 1 from the redirection symbols. You must always use the file descriptor 2 with the redirection symbol.

The 0 and 1 file descriptors are implied, and not used explicitly for the C shell, as shown in Table 16–8. The C shell representation for standard error (2) is an ampersand (&). STDERR can only be redirected when redirecting STDOUT.

Table 16–8 C Shell Redirection Metacharacters

Description	Command
Redirect STDOUT to file	> *file*
Take input from file	< *file*
Append STDOUT to end of file	>> *file*
Redirect STDOUT and STDERR to file	>& *file*
Append STDOUT and STDERR to file	>>& *file*

Command-Line Input

You can ask users to provide input to a script as part of the command-line argument when the script is run. All three shells use the positional parameter $*n* to specify as many as nine command-line arguments (for example, $1, $2, $3, and so on). $0 is a legitimate variable, and returns the name of the command. Consider the following Bourne shell script, named tryit:

```
#!/bin/sh

echo $#
for var in $*
do
        echo $var
done
```

NOTE. *With the Korn shell, you can use* ${10}, ${11} . . . *notation to recognize more than nine command-line arguments.*

You can rewrite the tryit script in the following way to work with any of the three shells. You can use each of these command-line arguments to pass filenames or other information into a shell script from a command line.

NOTE. *For the C shell, you cannot use the echo* $# *statement in the script. Instead, you can use* $#argv *to hold the number of command-line arguments.*

Instead of using $#argv, which is shown in later examples, echo $0 (which displays the name of the script) is substituted in the following example:

```
echo $0
echo $1
```

```
echo $2
echo $3
```

The resulting screen display lists the command-line arguments, as shown below:

```
oak% tryit one two three
tryit
one
two
three
oak%
```

NOTE. *The* `$n` *notation does not return an error if no parameters are provided as part of the command. Users do not need to supply command-line arguments, so you cannot be sure that* `$n` *will contain a value unless you check the number of positional parameters using* `$#` *for the Bourne and Korn shells.*

The C shell provides additional syntax for positional parameters, as shown in Table 16–9.

Table 16–9 C Shell $argv Notation

Notation	Description
`$#argv`	Counts the number of command-line arguments.
`$*`	Returns the value of all arguments.
`$argv`	Returns the value of all arguments.
`$argv[1-3]`	Returns the value of arguments 1 through 3.
`$0`	Returns the command used to run the shell script.
`$argv[n]`	Returns the *n*th argument.
`$argv[$#argv}`	Returns the last argument.

The shell performs range checking on the `$argv[n]` syntax, but it does not on the `$n` syntax. If the shell does not find the word, you get the message `Subscript out of range.`

NOTE. `$argv[0]` *is not defined and does not return the name of the script as* `$0` *does.*

Table 16–10 shows an example script and the output.

Table 16–10 A Sample $argv Script and Its Output

Notation	Description
`#!/bin/csh -f`	oak$ **argdemo one two three four**

Table 16–10 A Sample $argv Script and Its Output (continued)

Notation	Description
`echo Number of args = $#argv`	Number of args = 4
`echo All args = $*`	All args = one two three four
`echo All args = $argv`	All args = one two three four
`echo Args 1-3 = $argv[1-3]`	Args 1-3 = one two three
`echo Name of script file = $0`	Name of script file = argdemo
`echo Script file\ ? = $argv[0]`	Script file? =
`echo Second arg = $argv[2]`	Second arg = two
`echo Last arg = $argv[$#argv]`	Last arg = four
`echo Fifth arg = $5`	Fifth arg =
`echo Fifth arg = $argv[5]`	Subscript out of range

Shifting Command-Line Arguments

You can use the `shift` command, which is built into all three shells, to manipulate the positional parameters in a script. The `shift` command moves each argument from `$1` through `$n` to the left, changing the previous argument list. The `shift` command is particularly useful in processing positional parameters in `while` loops; you can use these commands together to process each positional parameter in turn.

In the following Bourne shell example, each argument is displayed in turn. The `shift` command shifts the list to the left, removing the leftmost value in the list, as shown in the following script:

```
#!/bin/sh
while [ $# -ne 0 ]
do
    echo argument: $1
    shift
done
```

The following example shows the output of this script:

```
$ tryit one two three
argument: one
argument: two
```

```
argument: three
$
```

Because the `shift` command shifts the positional parameters, you need to use `$1` in the script only if you want to display (or process) the command-line arguments. The following example shows how to shift positional parameters from a Bourne shell command line:

```
$ set a b c d e f g h i
$ while [ $# -gt Ø ]; do
> echo $*
> shift
> done
a b c d e f g h i
b c d e f g h i
c d e f g h i
d e f g h i
e f g h i
f g h i
g h i
h i
i
$
```

Refer to the section "Using while Loops" on page 346 for more information about `while` loops.

Interactive Input

You can ask the user to type a single line of input anywhere in a script. For the Bourne and Korn shells, use the `read` command followed by a variable name for interactive input.

NOTE. *You do not need to assign the variable before you use it as an argument to the* `read` *command. The following example shows the Bourne and Korn shell syntax for interactive input.*

NOTE. *To suppress the newline at the end of the prompt so that users type the input on the same line as the string that is displayed, use* `\c` *at the end of the string when* `/usr/bin` *is in the path before* `/usr/ucb`. *The SunOS 4.*x `echo -n` *command works only if you have* `/usr/ucb` *in the path before* `/usr/bin`. *Otherwise, the script uses the Solaris 2.*x *version of the echo command. Refer to the* `echo`(1) *manual page for more information.*

```
#!/bin/sh

echo "Enter search pattern and press Return: \c"
read filename
```

When the prompt appears, the script waits for input from the keyboard. When the user types input and presses Return, the input is assigned to the variable and the script continues to execute.

NOTE. *Be sure to always include a descriptive screen prompt as part of the script before you request input so that users know that the script is waiting for screen input before it continues.*

For the C shell, the special variable `$<` waits for a value from `STDIN`. You can use `$<` anywhere you would use a variable.

For the C shell, use `$<` as a value to a variable, as shown below:

```
#!/bin/csh -f
echo "Enter search pattern and press Return: \c"
set pattern = $<
```

When the prompt appears, the script waits for input from the keyboard. When the user types input and presses Return, the input is assigned to the variable and the script continues to execute.

Here Documents

Sometimes a shell script requires data. Instead of having the data in a file somewhere in the system, you can include the data as part of the shell script. Including the data in the script makes it simpler to distribute and maintain the script. Such a collection of data is called a *here document*—the data (document) is right here in the shell script. Another advantage of a here document is that shell parameters can be substituted in the document as the shell is reading the data.

The general format of a *here document* is shown as follows. The format is the same for all three shells.

```
   lines of shell commands
   ...
command << delimiter
lines of data belonging
to the here document
delimiter
   ...
   more lines of shell commands
```

The here document operator `<<` signals the beginning of the here document. The operator must be followed by a special string that delimits the input, for example `<<DONE`. Follow the here document operator with the list of input you want to use. The input can consist of any text, and may include variables because the shell does variable substitution on a here document. At the end of the here document, you must include the delimiter at the left margin on a single line. The shell sends everything between the two delimiters to be processed as standard input.

In the following example, the mail message specified in the here document is sent to members of the staff whose names are contained in a file named `stafflist`, which invites them to a party. The delimiter used is the string `EOF`.

```
#!/bin/sh

time="7:00 p.m."
mail -s "staff party" `cat stafflist` << EOF
```

```
Please come to our staff party being held
in the cafeteria at $time tomorrow night
EOF
```

Generating Output

The following sections describe how to use the echo command, quoting, and command substitution.

NOTE. *Although the* echo *command works in Korn shell scripts, the* print *command is preferred. The syntax for the* print *command is the same as for the* echo *command.*

The Echo and Print Commands

Use the echo command to generate messages to display on a terminal screen. You have already seen some examples of using the echo command to display the value for a variable. You can also use the echo command to display text messages, as shown in the following portion of an interactive Bourne shell script:

```
#!/bin/sh
echo "Enter a pathname and press Return:"
read pathname
```

If you want to echo more than one message on the same line, use the \c string at the end of the line to leave the cursor at the end of the output line and to suppress the newline. The following example modifies the previous Bourne shell script so that the user types the input following the colon, instead of on the line beneath the prompt message:

```
#!/bin/sh
echo "Enter a pathname and press Return: \c"
read pathname
```

If you need to display control characters or metacharacters, you can *escape* them (that is, get the shell to interpret the character literally) by putting a backslash (\) in front of the character. Refer to the echo(1) manual page for information about special backslash characters (for example, \c, \n).

The Bourne and Korn shell echo command has fewer restrictions on quoting metacharacters than does the C shell echo command. The following Bourne shell script displays an error message only for the parentheses in the last line, which are not escaped with backslashes. Note that the dollar sign ($) followed by a space does not need to be escaped.

```
$ more echodemo
#!/bin/sh

echo Type a pathname and press Return:
echo You owe me \$35 \(Please pay\).
echo This is a $ sign (not a variable)
$ echodemo
Type a pathname and press Return:
You owe me $35 (Please pay).
This is a $ sign (Not a variable).
anything: syntax error at line 6: `(' unexpected
$
```

Quoting

All three shells use the same syntax for quoting, as shown in Table 16–11. Quoting a string incorrectly can cause many unexpected results.

Table 16–11 Quoting

Character	Term	Description
\	Backslash	Nullifies the special meaning of any shell metacharacter, including another backslash.
` `	Backquotes	Substitutes the output as if it were typed in place of the command. Refer to the shell manual pages for more information.
' '	Single quotes	Nullifies the special meaning of all characters except bang (!), the backslash (\), and the single quote itself ('). Single quotes are more restrictive than double quotes and do not permit variable or backquote expansion.
" "	Double quotes	Nullifies the special meaning of all special characters except bang (!), backquote (` `), and dollar sign ($). Permits variable and backquote expansion.

NOTE. *The bang (!) is not used as a metacharacter in the Bourne and Korn shells. If it is not quoted properly, it is likely to cause problems mostly in the C shell.*

The following examples demonstrate the result of different forms of quotation:

```
$ name=Fred
$ echo "My name is $name"
My name is Fred
$ echo 'My name is $name'
My name is $name
$ echo "Today is `date`"
Today is Fri Jul  9 12:12:35 PDT 1993
$ echo 'Today is `date`'
Today is `date`
$ echo 'Use metacharacters * ? < > ¦ & and $ often'
Use metacharacters * ? < > ¦ & and $ often
$ echo "It's hard to turn off"!
It's hard to turn off!
```

Command Substitution

You can substitute the output of the command in place of the command itself. This process is called *command substitution*. Use backquotes (` `) to surround the desired command. You can use command substitution to return the output of the command, or to use it as the value for a variable.

NOTE. *In the Korn shell, you can use the* `$(command)` *syntax instead of backquotes.*

In the first example following, the output of the `date` command is used as part of a larger output string, and the output of the `who` command is filtered through `wc`, which counts the number of lines in the output of `who` to determine how many users are logged in. The second example pipes the output of the `who` command to the `cut` command to display only the list of usernames and uses the `uname -n` command to display the name of the system.

```
$ echo Today is `date` and there are `who ¦ wc -l` users logged in
Today is Fri Jul 9 13:12:41 PDT 1993 and there are 5 users logged in

$ echo `who ¦ cut -f1 -d" "` logged onto `uname -n`
winsor newton fred george anna logged onto seachild
$
```

Testing for Conditions

When writing scripts, you frequently want to test for conditions. The simplest test is to determine whether a condition is true or false. If the expression is true, execute any subsequent commands (shown indented in Table 16–12); if not, continue with the script. Table 16–12 shows the syntax for conditional tests.

Table 16–12 Conditional Test Syntax

Bourne and Korn Shells	C Shell
`if` *command*	`if (`*cond*`) then`
`then`	*commands*
commands	`else if (`*cond*`) then`
`elif` *command*	*commands*
commands	`else`
`elsefi`	*commands*
commands	`endif`
fi	

if-then-else-elif

For the Bourne and Korn shells, use the `if-then-else-elif-fi` syntax to test for conditions. You can follow the `if` statement with the `test` command and its argument(s) to test for conditions. As an alternative to typing the `test` command, you can enclose the test condition in square brackets `[ ]`. You must put a space after the first bracket and before the last one for the characters to be interpreted correctly—for example:

```
if [ -r filename ]
then
```

The results of test `-r filename` and `[ -r filename ]` are identical. Refer to the section "Test and C Shell Built-in Test" in Chapter 17 for test command options.

The Bourne shell fragment shown next uses the simplest form of the `if` statement to test whether a user has entered at least one command-line argument following the name of the script:

```
#!/bin/sh
#
# Test for at least one command-line argument
#
if test $# -lt 1
then
    echo Usage: $0 name requires one command-line argument
    exit 1
fi
```

If you want the script to perform additional actions if the first conditional test fails, use the `else` clause, as shown in the following Bourne shell fragment:

```
#!/bin/sh

if test $# -lt 1
then
    echo Usage: $0 name requires one command-line argument
    exit 1
else
    echo "Thank you for entering arguments"
    echo "You entered $# arguments"
fi
```

You can use the `elif` conditional (a combination of `else` and `if`) to test for additional conditions within the `if` statement . The `elif` clause is performed if only if the previous `if` or `else` fails. Each `elif` clause lists another command to be tested. The following Bourne shell example has one `elif` and one `else` clause:

```
#!/bin/sh
#
# Time of day greetings
#
hour=`date +%H`

if [ $hour -H 12 ]
then
    echo "Good Morning!"
elif [ $hour -H 17 ]
then
    echo "Good Afternoon!"
else
    echo "Good Night!"
fi
```

if-else-else if-endif

The C shell has built-in constructs that you can use to test conditions. Refer to the section "Test and C Shell Built-in Test" in Chapter 17 for C shell test command options.

The C shell fragment shown next tests whether a user has entered one or more command-line arguments following the name of the script:

```
#!/bin/csh -f

if ($#argv == 0) then
    echo Usage: $0 name requires one command-line argument
    exit 1
endif
```

NOTE. *The* `then` *statement for the C shell, if present, must be positioned at the end of the* `if` *line.*

If you want the script to perform additional actions if the first conditional test fails, use the `else` clause, as shown in the following C shell fragment:

```
#!/bin/csh -f

if ($#argv == 0) then
    echo Usage: $0 requires command-line arguments
    exit 1
else
    echo "Thank you for entering arguments"
    echo "You entered $# arguments"
endif
```

You can use the `else if` conditional to test for additional conditions within the `if` statement. The `else if` clause is performed only if the previous `if` or `else if` fails (is false). Each `else if` statement lists another command to be tested. The following C shell example has one `else if` and one `else` statement:

```
#!/bin/csh -f
#
# Time of day greetings
#
set d=`date +%H`
set hour = $d[4]

if ($hour < 12) then
    echo "Good Morning\!"
else if ($hour < 17) then
    echo "Good Afternoon\!"
else
    echo "Good Night\!"
endif
```

Nested if Constructs

`If` statements can contain additional `if` statements. When you write a script that contains nested `if` statements, be sure to indent the statements to make it easier to follow the logic of the statements and to check that you have included all the required elements.

Here is the syntax for nesting `if` statements in the Bourne and Korn shells:

```
if command
then
    if command
    then
        command
        ...
    else
        command
        ...
    fi
elif command
then
    command
    ...
else
    command
    ...
fi
```

The syntax for nesting `if` statements in the C shell follows:

```
if (expression) then
    if (expression) then
        if (expression) then
            command
            ...
        else
            command
            ...
        endif
    else if (expression) then
        command
        ...
    else
        command
        ...
    endif
endif
```

Multi-Branching

You may want to take several different types of action depending on the value of a variable or a parameter. Although you can use conditional testing to test each value and take action, you can more easily perform such tests using the `case` statement or the C shell `switch` statement, as shown in Table 16–13.

Table 16–13 Switch and Case Syntax

Bourne and Korn Shells	C Shell
`case` *value* `in`	`switch (`*value*`)`
pattern1`)`	`case` *pattern*:
command	*commands*
command ;;	`breaksw`
pattern2)	`default:`
command ;;	*commands*
`*)`	`breaksw`
default action	`endsw`
`;;`	
`esac`	

The value of the variable is successively compared against patterns until a match is found. The commands immediately following the matching pattern are executed until finding `;;` (for the Bourne and Korn shells) or `breaksw` (for the C shell). The last test `*)` (Bourne or Korn shell) or default: (C shell) is a default action. If no other values match, the shell executes the default action. In many scripts, the default action displays an error message and exits from the shell.

Case statements can be especially helpful for processing parameters to a function.

The following Bourne script example sets the terminal type:

```
#!/bin/sh
#
# Set the terminal type
#
case $TERM in
    tvi???)
        echo $TERM
        echo Probably the system console ;;
    vt[12][02]0)
        echo A VT terminal ;;
    Wyse40 ¦ Wyse75)
        echo A Wyse terminal ;;
    sun)
        echo Aha!! a workstation ;;
    *)
        echo surprise! it's a $TERM
esac
```

The following example shows an interactive C shell script to set the terminal type:

```
#!/bin/csh -f
#
```

```
# Set the terminal type
#
echo "Do you want to see the present setting? \c"
set input = $<
switch ("$input")
    case [Yy]*:
        echo "term =" $TERM
        breaksw
endsw
echo "Terminal type? \c"
set term = $<
switch ($term)
    case tvi950:
    case vt100:
    case sun:
        setenv TERM $term
        breaksw
    default:
        echo "I don't know that one."
        breaksw
endsw
```

Controlling the Flow

You can use loops to control the flow of execution in a script. A *loop* is an iterative mechanism that repeats a sequence of instructions until a predetermined condition is met. You can use different forms of loops. The `for/foreach` loop executes a list of commands one time for each value of a loop variable. The `while` loop repeatedly executes a group of commands within the body of the loop until the test condition in the expression is no longer true. The Bourne and Korn shells provide an `until` loop that continues to execute until a command executes successfully. Table 16–14 shows the syntax for `for/foreach`, `while`, and `until` loops.

Table 16–14 Looping Syntax

Feature	Bourne/Korn Shell	C Shell

`for/foreach` loops	`for` *variable* `in` *list*
	`do`
	commands
	`done`
		`foreach` *variable* (*list*)
		commands
		`end`

`while` loops	`while` *command*
	`do`
	commands
	`done`
		`while` (*cond*)
		commands
		`end`

`until` loops	`until` *command*
	`do`
	commands
	`done`	

Using for/foreach Loops

Use the `for` loop to process items from a fixed list or from a command-line argument. The Bourne and Korn shell `for` loop executes the commands between the `do` and the `done` statement as many times as there are words or strings listed after "in."

The `for` loop's basic syntax follows:

```
for variable in word1 word2 word3 . . . wordn
    command $variable
    command
done
```

A special format of the first line of the `for` loop, `for variable`, uses the values of positional parameters `$1`, `$2`, and so on, and is equivalent to using for variable in `$@` as the first line of the for loop.

The following Bourne shell script contains two examples of `for` loops. The first example copies files into a backup directory. The second removes all files that contain a `.o` suffix.

```
#!/bin/sh
#
# Backup files
#
dir=/home/winsor/backup
for file in ch1 ch2 ch3 ch4
do
    cp $file $dir/${file}.back
    echo $file has been backed up in directory $dir
done

for file in *.o
do
    echo removing $file
    rm $file
done
```

In the C shell, use the `foreach` loop to process items from a fixed list or to execute commands interactively from a command line. In the C shell, the `foreach` construct executes a list of commands one time for each value specified in the (*list*).

The following C shell script contains two examples of `foreach` loops. The first example copies `$file` into a backup directory. The second example removes all files that contain a `.o` suffix.

```
#!/bin/csh -f
#
# Backup files
#
set dir=/home/winsor/backup
foreach file (ch1 ch2 ch3 ch4)
    cp $file $dir/${file}.back
    echo $file has been backed up in directory $dir
end

foreach file (*.o)
```

```
    echo removing $file
    rm $file
end
```

You can type the `foreach` loop statement at the command-line prompt. The secondary prompt (`?`) appears. At the prompt, type the commands you want to execute in the loop. After you complete the list of commands, type **end**. The commands are executed in sequence and the C shell prompt reappears. The following example displays and compiles the name of each C source file in the directory and renames the binary output file. The `:r` modifier removes the `.c` extension. If there are 10 source files in the current working directory, the loop executes 10 times. When there are no more C source files, the loop ends.

```
oak% foreach file (*.c)
? echo $file
? cc -o $file:r $file
? end
oak%
```

The following example converts raster files to GIF format, strips off the `.rs` suffix, and adds a `.gif` suffix:

```
oak% foreach file (*.rs)
? cat $file | rasttoppm | ppmtogif > ${file:r}.gif
? end
oak%
```

Using while Loops

Use `while` loops to repeatedly execute a group of commands within the body of a loop until the test condition in the expression is no longer true. In other words, the `while` loop says, "While the expression is true, execute these commands."

For the Bourne and Korn shells, the `while` loop executes the commands between the `do` and the `done` statements as long as the initial command exits with a status of zero.

The basic syntax for the `while` loop follows:

```
while command
do
    command
    command
done
```

In the following Bourne shell script, the first example sets the variable `num` equal to 0 and adds 1 to it as long as the number is less than or equal to 4.

```
#!/bin/sh

num=0
while [ $num -le 4 ]
do
        num=`expr $num + 1`
        echo number: $num
done
```

Refer to "Mathematical Operations" on page 349 for information on how to use the expr commmand.

The next example displays the command-line arguments in sequence when any arguments are given. Refer to the section "Shifting Command-Line Arguments" earlier in this chapter for information about the shift command.

```
#!/bin/sh

while [ $# -ne 0 ]
do
        echo argument: $1
        shift
done
```

For the C shell, the while loop executes the commands between the while and the end statement as long as the expression evaluates to true.

The basic syntax for the while loop follows:

```
while (expression)
    command
    command
end
```

In the following C shell script, the first example sets the variable num equal to 0 and adds 1 to it as long as the number is less than or equal to 4:

```
#!/bin/csh -f

@ num = 0
while ($num <= 4)
    @ num++
    echo "number: $num"
end
```

The output of this script follows:

```
oak% tryit
number: 0
number: 1
number: 2
number: 3
number: 4
```

The next example displays the command-line arguments in sequence when any arguments are given:

```
#!/bin/csh -f
#
while ($#argv != 0)
        echo "argument: $1"
        shift
end
```

Using Until Loops

Use Bourne or Korn shell `until` loops to test an expression until the command returns a successful status. The syntax for the `until` loop is similar to the `while` loop:

```
until command
do
    command
    command
done
```

NOTE. *The* `until` *condition is checked at the top of the loop, not at the bottom.*

The following example prints out the numbers 1 through 5:

```
#!/bin/sh

num=0
until [ $num -gt 4 ]
do
        num=`expr $num + 1`
        echo number: $num
done
```

The results of this script are the same as the example shown using the `while` loop. Refer to the section "Mathematical Operations" on page 349 for a description of the `expr` command used in the preceding example.

Breaking Loops

All three shells have built-in `break` and `continue` commands that you can use to break out of a `for/foreach`, `while`, or `until` loop. The `break` command forces premature termination of the loop and transfers control to the line after the `done` (for the Bourne and Korn shells) or `end` (for the C shell) statement. In the following C shell example, the script continues running the `while` loop until the user answers Yes (or yes, y, or Y). When the user does answer yes, the break terminates the `while` loop and, in this case, exits because there are no additional commands to execute.

```
#!/bin/csh -f
#
while (1)
        echo "Finished yet? \c"
        set answer = $<
        if ($answer =~ [Yy]*) break
end
```

You can use the `continue` command in a similar way to control `for/foreach` and `while` loops. The `continue` command operates on the innermost loop with which it is associated. The `continue` statement transfers execution immediately back to the `while` test, skipping all subsequent commands in the innermost loop. If continue is used with a `foreach` loop, the continue statement quits the current iteration of the loop and processes the next item in the list.

Exit Status

When a command or shell function terminates, it returns an exit status to the invoking shell. The *exit status* is a numeric value that indicates whether the program ran successfully and whether certain events occurred in the command.

Every command that runs has an exit status, which is set by the programmer when writing the command. Usually, an exit status of 0 means that the program executed successfully. Any non-zero value (usually 1 or -1) means that the program failed. Programmers may not always follow this convention. Check the manual page for a given command to determine its exit status. For example, the grep command returns one of three exit status values: 0 means that the search pattern was found, 1 means that the pattern could not be found, and 2 means that the grep command could not open or find the file(s) to be searched.

For the Bourne shell, the $? variable holds exit status for the last command executed in the same way that the C shell status variable does. Usually, 0 indicates success and 1 indicates failure.

```
$ pwd
/home/seachild/winsor
$ echo $?
0
$ cd /home3
/home3: bad directory
$ echo $?
1
$
```

The C shell variable status is automatically set by the shell to the exit status of the last command executed. You can use the echo command to display the exit status at the prompt.

```
oak% grep root /etc/passwd
root:x:0:1:0000-Admin(0000):/:/sbin/sh
oak% echo $status
0
oak% grep anthonly /etc/passwd
oak% echo $status
1
oak% grep root /etc/password
grep: can't open /etc/password
oak% echo $status
2
oak%
```

When writing shell scripts, you can add an exit 0 to the end of the script to indicate successful completion. Exiting with any other value shows that something went wrong.

Mathematical Operations

You can do mathematical operations only on integers (whole numbers) for all three shells. If you want to do more complicated arithmetic, you can use the awk command.

To perform mathematical operations in the Bourne shell, you can use the `expr` command. Here is the syntax:

```
expr arguments
```

You must separate the mathematical operators (shown in Table 16–15) and the operand with white space.

Table 16–15 Mathematical Operators

Operator	Description
+	Addition
-	Subtraction
*	Multiplication
/	Division
%	Remainder

The multiplication, division, and remainder operators have higher precedence than do the addition or subtraction operators. Use parentheses for grouping.

The following example uses the `expr` command:

```
$ i=4
$ expr $i + 1
5
$ expr $i - 1
3
$ expr $i \* 2
8
$ expr $i / 2
2
$ expr $i % 2
0
$ j=2
$ expr $i + $j
6
$
```

The Korn shell has `let` and built-in `$(())` expressions for doing arithmetic.

The C shell `@` command is similar to the Bourne and Korn shell `expr` command. The `@` command evaluates an expression mathematically and then assigns the resulting value to a shell variable, as shown in Table 16–16.

The expressions can be mathematical or logical. Mathematical expressions typically use the operators shown in Table 16–15. Logical expressions typically use one of the following operators, and yield a `1` (true) or `0` (false) value:

```
> < >= <= == !=
```

The following example shows C shell numeric values:

```
oak% @ total = 5 + 3
oak% echo $total
8
oak% @ total++
oak% echo $total
9
oak% @ total += 4
oak% echo $total
13
oak% @ newtotal = ($total > 5)
oak% echo $newtotal
1
oak%.
```

Table 16–16 C Shell Mathematical Operators

Syntax	Description
@ *variable* = (*expression*)	Sets value of variable equal to the expression.
@ *variable* += (*expression*)	Performs addition.
@ *variable* -= (*expression*)	Performs subtraction.
@ *variable* *= (*expression*)	Performs multiplication.
@ *variable* /= (*expression*)	Peforms division.
@ variable ++	Adds 1.
@ variable --	Subtracts 1.

User-Defined Functions

You can write your own functions in the Bourne and Korn shells and use them as part of other scripts.

NOTE. *Not all Bourne shells support functions. However, the Solaris 2.*x *Bourne shell supports functions.*

User-defined functions are useful if you have a series of commands that you want to use repeatedly. The functions written for an application server are an example of user-defined functions. Some examples of functions are provided in the section "Example Scripts" in

Chapter 17. When you define a function, you use the name of the function at the place where you want to execute the series of commands contained in the function.

Typically, you define functions at the beginning of a script, but you can define them in separate files and share them between scripts. Once the function has been defined, you can use it any number of times.

Use the following syntax to define functions:

```
function_name() {
    (body of the function)
}
```

Shell functions use positional parameters and special variables such as * and # in the same way that shell scripts do. Typically, you define several shell functions within a single shell script. Each function receives arguments as positional parameters. These positional parameters "overlay" command-line parameters.

To call the function, use the *function_name* as if it were a normal command at the place in the script where you want to use the function. The following Bourne shell script defines and uses a simple function:

```
#!/bin/sh
#
printlist() {
        echo The current list of arguments is:
        echo $*
}
while [ $# -gt 0 ]
do
        printlist $*
        shift 2
done
```

The following example shows the result of running this script:

```
oak% doit one two three four
The current list of arguments is:
one two three four
The current list of arguments is:
three four
oak%
```

Debugging Shell Scripts

The following sections provide some suggestions for debugging shell scripts.

Using Debugging Flags

A common problem when writing shell scripts is that the shell does not interpret the command in exactly the way that you expect. When the shell interprets a command line, it substitutes variables with values, replaces filename wildcards with the appropriate file names, and performs command substitution. If the interpretation transforms a command line into something unexpected, the command most likely will not execute the way you intend for it to.

All three shells provide -x (echo) and -v (verbose) options that you can use to help pinpoint where problems are occurring in a script. The -v option displays each line of the script as it is read from the file. The -x option shows each line after it has been processed by the shell and is ready for execution. The combination of these two options provides you with much useful information for debugging your scripts.

You can use the options from the command line, as shown:

```
oak% csh -xv script-name
$ sh -xv script-name
$ ksh -xv script-name
```

Alternatively, you can set the flag options in the first line of the script, as follows:

```
#!/bin/sh -xv
#!/bin/csh -f -xv
#!/bin/ksh -xv
```

The following example shows the time-of-day greeting script with the -x option in the command line, followed by the screen output:

```
#!/bin/sh -x
#
# Time of day greetings
#
hour=`date +%H`

if [ $hour -le 12 ]
then
        echo "Good Morning!"
elif [ $hour -le 17 ]
then
        echo "Good Afternoon!"
else
        echo "Good Night!"
fi

$ greetings
+ date +%H
hour=11
+ [ 11 -le 12 ]
+ echo Good Morning!
Good Morning!
$
```

The following example shows the output for the same script with the -v option set:

```
$ greetings
#!/bin/sh -v
#
# Time of day greetings
#
```

```
hour=`date +%H`

if [ $hour -le 12 ]
then
        echo "Good Morning!"
elif [ $hour -le 17 ]
then
        echo "Good Afternoon!"
else
        echo "Good Night!"
fi
Good Morning!
$
```

The following example shows the screen output of the same script with `-xv` set:

```
$ greetings
#!/bin/sh -xv
#
# Time of day greetings
#
hour=`date +%H`
+ date +%H
hour=11

if [ $hour -le 12 ]
then
        echo "Good Morning!"
elif [ $hour -le 17 ]
then
        echo "Good Afternoon!"
else
        echo "Good Night!"
fi
+ [ 11 -le 12 ]
+ echo Good Morning!
Good Morning!
$
```

Understanding Shell Parsing Order

Each shell analyzes commands, whether from the command line or in a script, and then parses them (divides them up) into recognizable parts. Shells can perform many kinds of substitutions and expansions. These operations are carried out in a very specific order for each shell. The parsing order for a shell can have a definite impact on shell programs that you write. Understanding the parsing order can help you determine where a script may be broken. Figure 16–2 shows a simplified version of Korn shell parsing order. When a command or string is quoted, the parsing order is affected. It can be difficult to understand exactly how the evaluation process works. Nevertheless, sometimes understanding the order in which a shell performs its operation can provide some insight into a problem. The Bourne shell parses in a similar order to the Korn shell, omitting history and alias substitution.

Figure 16–3 shows a simplified version of C shell parsing order.

The Bourne shell script that follows fails because variable expansion occurs *after* redirection:

```
$ moreit='¦ more'
$ cat   /etc/passwd $moreit
ppp:x:12881:1:PPP:/tmp:/usr/etc/ppp-listen
root:x.:Ø:1:Operator:/:/bin/csh
nobody:x:65534:65534::/:
(Lines omitted from example)
+::Ø:Ø:::
cat: ¦: No such file or directory
cat: more: No such file or directory
```

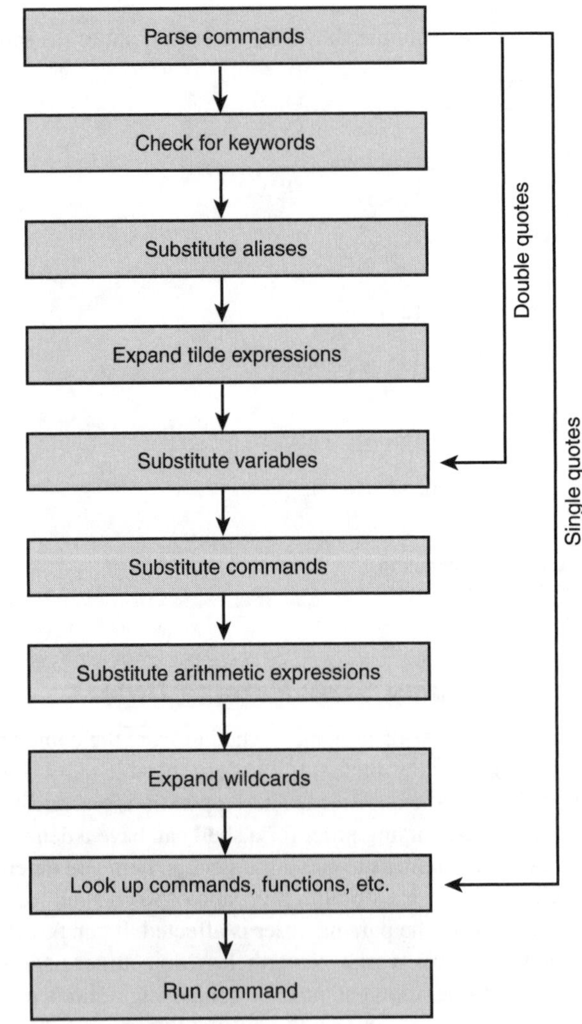

Figure 16–2
Korn shell parsing order.

Figure 16–3
C shell parsing order.

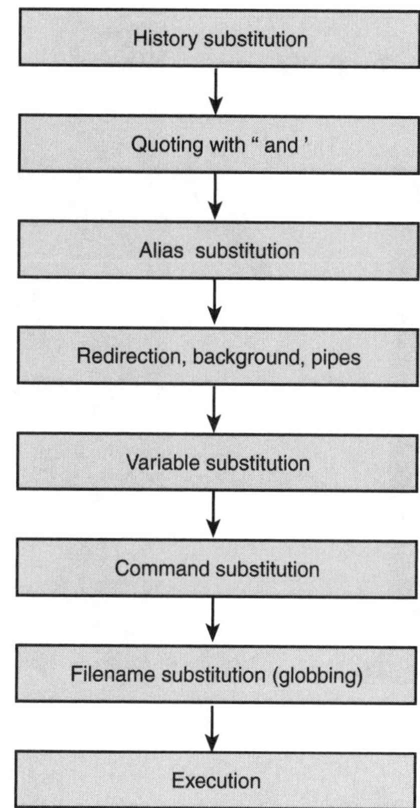

See Chapter 17 for shell programming reference tables and for examples of more complex shell scripts.

CHAPTER

17

Reference Tables and Example Scripts

Reference Tables
Example Scripts

Reference Tables

THIS CHAPTER CONTAINS TABLES OF SYNTAX ELEMENTS FOR ALL THREE SHELLS AND examples of shell scripts.

Environment Files

Feature	Bourne	Korn	C
Read at login	`.profile`	`.profile`	`.login`
Read at invocation of shell		Any file specified in `.profile` with ENV=.*file*	`.cshrc`

First Line of Script

Shell	Syntax
Bourne	`#!/bin/sh`
Korn	`#!/bin/ksh`
C	`#!/bin/csh -f`

Korn Shell Path Operators

Operator	Description
${*variable*#*pattern*}	Delete the shortest part at the beginning of the variable that matches the pattern and return the rest.
${*variable*##*pattern*}	Delete the longest part at the beginning of the variable that matches the pattern and return the rest.
${*variable*%*pattern*}	Delete the shortest part at the end of the variable that matches the pattern and return the rest.
${*variable*%%*pattern*}	Delete the longest part at the end of the variable that matches the pattern and return the rest.

C Shell Path Modifiers

Modifier	Meaning	Description
:e	Extension	Remove prefix ending with a dot.
:h	Head	Remove trailing pathname component.
:r	Root	Remove suffixes beginning with a dot (.).
:t	Tail	Remove all leading pathname components.
:q	Quote	Force variable to be quoted. Used to quote `$argv`.
:x		Like q, but break into words at each space, tab, or newline.

Variables Initialized by Shell

Variable	Explanation
`$*`	Bourne or Korn shell: List the value of all command-line parameters. This variable is useful only in scripts because the login shell has no arguments associated with it. C shell: Not used. Use `$argv` instead.
`$#`	Bourne or Korn shell: Return the number of command-line arguments (in decimal). Useful only in scripts. C shell: Count the number of words (in decimal) in a variable array.
`$?`	Bourne or Korn shell: Return the exit status (in decimal) of the last command executed. Most commands return a zero exit status if they complete successfully; otherwise, a non-zero exit status is returned. This variable is set after each command is executed. C shell: Check to see if a variable of that name has been set.
`$$`	All shells: Return the process ID (PID) number of the current shell (in decimal).
`$!`	All shells: Return the process number (in decimal) of the last process run in the background.

Shell Built-In Commands

The (K) in the Bourne or Korn Shell column indicates commands that are available only with the Korn shell.

Purpose	Bourne or Korn Shell	C Shell
Null command	`:`	`:`
Create a command name alias	`alias` (K)	`alias`
Run current command in background	`bg` (K)	`bg`
Exit enclosing `for` or `while` loop	`break`	`break`
Break out of a switch		`breaksw`
Change directory	`cd`	`cd`
Continue next iteration of `for` or `while` loop	`continue`	`continue`
Default case in switch	N/A	`default`
Print directory stack	N/A	`dirs`
Write arguments on STDOUT	`echo`, `print` (K)	`echo`
Evaluate and execute arguments	`eval`	`eval`
Execute the arguments	`exec`	`exec`
Return or set shell variables	`set`	`@`
Exit shell program	`exit`	`exit`

Purpose	Bourne or Korn Shell	C Shell
Create an environment variable	`export`	`setenv`
Bring a command into foreground	`fg` (K)	`fg`
Execute `foreach` loop	`for`	`foreach`
Perform filename expansion	N/A	`glob`
Go to label within shell program	N/A	`goto`
Display history list	`fc` (K)	`history`
If-then-else decision	`if`	`if`
List active jobs	`jobs` (K)	`jobs`
Send a signal	`kill`	`kill`
Set limits for a job's resource use	`ulimit`	`limit`
Terminate login shell and invoke login	N/A	`login`
Terminate a login shell	`exit`	`logout`
Change to a new user group	`newgrp`	N/A
Change priority of a command	N/A	`nice`
Ignore hangup	N/A	`nohup`
Notify user when job status changes	N/A	`notify`
Control shell processing on receipt of a signal	`trap`	`onintr`
Pop the directory stack	N/A	`popd`
Push a directory onto the stack	N/A	`pushd`
Read a line from stdin	`read`	`$<`
Change a variable to read-only	`readonly`	N/A
Repeat a command *n* times		`repeat`
Set shell environment variables	=	`setenv`
Set a local C shell variable		`set`
Shift positional parameters `$*` or `$argv`	`shift`	`shift`
Read and execute a file	`.` (dot)	`source`

Purpose	Bourne or Korn Shell	C Shell
Stop a background process	N/A	`stop`
Stop the shell	`suspend` (K)	`suspend`
CASE statement	`case`	`switch`
Evaluate conditional expressions	`test`	N/A
Display execution times	`times`	`time`
Set default security for creation of files and directories	`umask`	`umask`
Discard aliases	`unalias` (K)	`unalias`
Remove limitations on resources	`ulimit`	`unlimit`
Unset a variable	`unset`	`unset`
Unset an environment variable	N?A	`unsetenv`
`UNTIL` loop	`until`	N/A
Wait for background process to complete	`wait`	N/A
`WHILE` loop foreground	`while`	`while`

Bourne and Korn Shell Redirection

Description	Command
Take standard input from file	<*file*, or 0< *file*
Redirect STDOUT to file	> *file*, or 1> *file*
Redirect STDERR to file	2> *file*
Append STDOUT to file	>> *file*
Redirect STDERR to stdout	2>&1
Pipe standard output of *cmd1* as standard input to *cmd2*	*cmd1* ¦ *cmd2*
Use file as both STDIN and STDOUT	<> *file*
Close STDIN	<&-
Close STDOUT	>&-

C Shell Redirection Metacharacters

Description	Command
Redirect STDOUT to file	> *file*
Take input from file	< *file*
Append STDOUT to end of file	>> *file*
Redirect STDOUT and STDERR to file	>& *file*
Append STDOUT and STDERR to file	>>& *file*
Close STDERR	27&-

C Shell $argv Notation

Notation	Description
$#argv	Count the number of command-line arguments.
$*	Display all arguments.
$argv	Display all arguments.
$argv[1-3]	Display arguments 1 through 3.
$0	Display the command used to run the shell script.
$argv[n]	Display the *n*th argument.
$argv[$#argv}	Display the last argument.

Quoting

Character	Term	Description
\	Backslash	Nullifies the special meaning of the following shell metacharacter, including another backslash.
``	Backquotes	The output is substituted as if it were typed in place of the command. Refer to the shell manual pages for more information.
''	Single quote	Nullifies the special meaning of all characters except bang (!), the backslash (\), and the single quote itself ('). Single quotes are more restrictive than double quotes and do not permit variable or backquote expansion.
""	Double quotes	Nullifies the special meaning of all special characters except bang (!), backquote (``), and dollar sign ($). Permits variable and back-quote expansion.

Metacharacter Shell Syntax

Feature	Bourne and Korn	C
Single-character wildcard	?	?
Any number of characters	*	*
Set of single characters	[abc]	[abc]
Range of single characters	[a-c]	[a-c]
Inverse range of single characters	[!a-c]	N/A

Variable Shell Syntax

Feature	Bourne	Korn	C
Assigning regular variables	`x=1`	`x=1`	`set x = 1`
Accessing regular variables	`echo $x`	`echo $x`	`echo $x`
Assigning arrays	N/A	`y[0]=1; y[1]=2`	`set y=(1 2)`
Accessing array elements	N/A	`echo $y` `echo ${y[1]}`	`echo $y[1] $y[2]`
Accessing entire array	N/A	`echo ${y[*]}`	`echo $y`
Exporting variables (make global)	`export var`	`export var`	`use setenv` *command*
Command-line arguments	N/A	N/A	`$argv, $#argv, $argv[1]`
Positional parameters	`$*, $#, $1`	`$*, $#, $1`	`$*, $1`
Setting positional parameters	`set a b c`	`set a b c`	N/A

I/O Redirection and Piping

Feature	Bourne	Korn	C
STDOUT to file	> *filename* or 1> *filename*	> *filename* or 1> *filename*	> *filename*
STDIN from file	< *filename* or 0< *filename*	< *filename* or 0< *filename*	< *filename*
STDERR to file	2> *filename*	2> *filename*	N/A
Output and errors to file	2>&1	2>&1	>& *filename*
Output to next command	¦ cmd	¦ cmd	¦ cmd
Output and errors to next command	2>&1 ¦	2>&1 ¦	¦&

Printing to the Screen

Feature	Bourne	Korn	C
Display text and variables	echo	print or echo	echo

Reading from the Keyboard

Feature	Bourne	Korn	C
Read keyboard input	read *name1 name2* . . .	read *name1 name2* . . .	set var = $<

Math and Calculations

Feature	Bourne	Korn	C
Perform a calculation	var=`expr a + b`	let var= a + b	@ var = (a + b)
Test a relational condition	var=`expr a < b`	let var=a < b	@ var = (a < b)

Command Substitution

Feature	Bourne	Korn	C
Command substitution	`*command*`	$(*command*) or `*command*`	`*command*`

Tilde Expansion

Feature	Korn	C
Tilde represents user's home directory	~ ~~loginid	~ ~loginid
Tilde represents current and previous directories	~+ ~- -	N/A

Alias Syntax

Feature	Korn	C
Create new alias	alias name=value	alias name value
Display current list of values	alias	alias
Remove alias from list	unalias name	unalias name

History Syntax

Feature	Korn	C
Turn on history	`automatic`	`set history = num`
Display history list	`history` or `fc`	`history`
Display partial listing	`history` *n m*	`history` *n*
	`history -`*n*	
Reexecute a command	`r` *string*	`!`*string*
	`r` *number*	`!`*number*
	`r`	`!!`

Function Syntax

Feature	Bourne and Korn	C
Create a function	`func() {`*commands*`}`	`func() {`*commands*`}`
	`function func {`*commands*`}`	
Use a function	Use `func` as a command	Use `func` as a command

Programming Statement Syntax

Feature	Bourne and Korn	C

`If` conditional	`if` *command*
	`then`
	  commands
	`elif` *command*
	commands
	`else`
	  commands
	`fi`
		`if (`*cond*`) then`
		  commands
		`else if (`*cond*`) then`
		  commands
		`else`
		  commands
		`endif`

`Switch` and `case pattern`	`case` *variable* `in`
	  pattern`)`
	    commands`;;`
	`*)`
	    commands`;;`
	`esac`
		`switch (`*variable*`)`
		  `case` *pattern*`:`
		    commands
		  `default:`
		    commands
		`endsw`

`While loops`	`while` *command*
	`do`
	  commands
	`done`
		`while (`*cond*`)`
		  commands
		`end`

`For/foreach loops`	`for` *variable* `in` *list*
	`do`
	  commands
	`done`
		`foreach` *variable* `(`*list*`)`
		  commands
		`end`

Test and C Shell Built-In Test

What Is Tested	Test Command	csh Built-In
file is block device	`-b` *file*	N/A

What Is Tested	Test Command	csh Built-In
file is character device	-c *file*	N/A
file is directory	-d *file*	-d *file*
file or directory exists	N/A	-e *file*
file is *file*	-f *file*	-f *file*
file has *set-group-id* bit set	-g *file*	N/A
file has sticky bit set	-k *file*	N/A
file is owned by executing user	N/A	-o *file*
file is a named pipe	-p *file*	N/A
current user can read *file*	-r *file*	-r *file*
file exists and has size >0	-s *file*	N/A
n is a terminal file descriptor	-t *n*	N/A
file has set-user-id bit set	-u *file*	N/A
current user can write to *file*	-w *file*	-w *file*
current user can execute *file*	-x *file*	N/A
file has zero size	N/A	-z *file*
string is NULL	-z *string*	*string* == ""
string is NOT NULL	*string* != ""	-n *string*, *string*
strings are equal	*string* = *string*	*string* == *string*
strings are not equal	*string* != *string*	*string* != *string*
string matches filename wildcard pattern	N/A	*string* =~ *pattern*
string does not match filename wildcard pattern	N/A	*string* !~ *pattern*
num1 is equal to *num2*	*num1* -eq *num2*	*num1* == *num2*
num1 is not equal to *num2*	*num1* -ne *num2*	*num1* ¦= *num2*
num1 is less than *num2*	*num1* -lt *num2*	*num1* < *num2*
num1 is less than or equal to *num2*	*num1* -le *num2*	*num1* <= *num2*
num1 is greater than *num2*	*num1* -gt *num2*	*num1* > *num2*
num1 is greater than or equal to *num2*	*num1* -ge *num2*	*num1* >= *num2*

What Is Tested	Test Command	csh Built-In
logical AND	-a	&&
logical OR	-o	||
logical NEGATION	!	!!

Bourne Shell Mathematical Operators

Operator	Description
+	Addition
-	Subtraction
*	Multiplication
/	Division
%	Remainder

C Shell Mathematical Operators

Syntax	Description
`@ variable = (expression)`	Set value of `variable` equal to the `expression`.
`@ variable += (expression)`	Addition.
`@ variable -= (expression)`	Subtraction.
`@ variable *= (expression)`	Multiplication.
`@ variable /= (expression)`	Division.
`@ variable ++`	Add 1.
`@ variable --`	Subtract 1.

Example Scripts

These sections contain some examples of Bourne shell scripts.

Anonymous ftp Script

A script named `fez` performs an anonymous `ftp get` or `list`.

```
#!/bin/sh
#
#     @(#)fez,v1.Ø                          (me@anywhere.EBay.Sun.COM) 08/29/92
#
PATHNAME=anywhere.EBay:/home/me/bin/fez
MYNAME=`basename $Ø`
#
# Author:
#     Wayne Thompson
#
# Synopsis:
usage=`/bin/sed -e "s/^ *//" << endusage
```

```
      usage: $MYNAME [-h] [-abfglmprR] [[login@]hostname:[sourcepath]]
endusage`
#
# Description:
#       This script will perform an anonymous ftp get or list.
#
#       If the hostname is not specified on the command line, then
#       it is derived from the basename(1) of the current directory.
#       This provides for a hierarchy of hostnames within which to
#       get files or directory listings.
#
#       If no flags and arguments are given or a single argument of
#       the form "hostname:" is given, the default action will be
#       to retrieve a recursive directory listing from the remote
#       host into the file "./ls-lR.".
#
#       Directory listings are named in the following manner:
#           <the command used to produce the listing w/spaces collapsed>
#           followed by the path it was produced from with slashes(/)
#           transliterated to dots(.). e.g.
#               ls-l.           (ls -l /)
#               ls-lR.a.b       (ls -lR /a/b)
#
#       When mirroring is enabled (default), the directory listing
#       "ls-lR.a.b" would be placed in the directory "./a/b" which
#       would be created if necessary.
#       Likewise, "fez export.lcs.mit.edu:/contrib/3dlife.c" would
#       get "/contrib/3dlife.c" from "export.lcs.mit.edu" and place
#       it into "./contrib/3dlife.c".
#       An alternative behavior is provided by the "-f" flag, which
#       serves to flatten the destination hierarchy.
#       "fez -f export.lcs.mit.edu:/contrib/3dlife.c" would get
#       "/contrib/3dlife.c" into "./3dlife.c"
#
#       The default user is "anonymous".
#       The default password is one of:
#           internal to Sun = $USER@hostname
#           external to Sun = $USER@Sun.Com
#       You may override these in $HOME/.netrc (see netrc(5))
#       or from the command line.
#
# Options:
#       -a          ascii mode
#       -b          binary mode                     (default)
#       -f          flatten hierarchy
#       -g          get                             (default w/arg)
#       -h          print command description.
#       -l          list                            (default w/o arg)
#       -m          mirror hierarchy                (default)
#       -p passwd   password
#       -(r¦R)      recursive                       (default w/o arg)
#
# Environment:
#
# Files:
#       $HOME/.netrc            file for ftp remote login data
```

```
#
# Diagnostics:
#     Exit Status:
#         Ø     normal termination
#         1     abnormal termination
#
#     Errors (stderr):
#         usage
#
#     Warnings (stderr):
#
#     Info (stdout):
#
# Dependencies:
#     Fez only knows how to talk to UNIX(R) hosts.
#
# Caveats:
#     A recursive directory get will not fetch subdirectories unless
#     they already exist.
#
# Bugs:
#

# >> BEGIN parse options >>>>>>>>>>>>>>>>>>>>>>>>>>>>>>>>>>>>>>>>>>>> #

while [ $# -gt Ø ]
do
    case $1 in
        -??*)                                       # bundled options
            opts=$1
            while [ $opts ]
            do
                opts=`/bin/expr $opts : '.\(.*\)'`
                case $opts in
                    a*)                             # ascii mode
                        mode=asci
                        ;;

                    b*)                             # binary mode
                        mode=binary
                        ;;

                    f*)                             # flatten remote hierarchy
                        flat=true
                        ;;

                    g*)                             # get
                        ;;

                    l*)                             # list
                        list=true
                        ;;

                    p)
                        passflg=true
                        shift
```

```
                    if [ $# -eq Ø ]
                    then
                        echo >&2 "$MYNAME: error: no passwd"
                        echo >&2 "usage"
                        exit 1
                    fi
                    passwd=$1
                    ;;

                p*)
                    echo >&2 "$MYNAME: error: p: must be last element of
                     bundled options"
                    exit 1
                    ;;

                [rR]*)                          # recursive
                    recurse=true
                    ;;

                ?*)
                    echo >&2 "$MYNAME: error: -`/bin/expr $opts : '\(.\)'`:
                     unknown option."
                    echo >&2 "$usage"
                    exit 1
                    ;;
            esac
        done
        shift
        ;;

    -a)                                         # ascii mode
        mode=ascii
        shift
        ;;

    -b)                                         # binary mode
        mode=binary
        shift
        ;;

    -f)                                         # flatten remote hierarchy
        flat=true
        shift
        ;;

    -g)                                         # get
        shift
        ;;

    -h)                                         # help
        /bin/awk '
            /^$/ {
                exit;
            }

            /^[# :]/ && NR > 1 {
```

```
                print substr ($Ø, 3);
            }
        ' $Ø ¦
        /bin/sed "
            /^$/{
                N
                /^\n$/D
            }
            s/\$MYNAME/$MYNAME/
        "
        exit Ø
        ;;

    -l)                                         # list
        list=true
        shift
        ;;

    -m)                                         # mirror remote hierarchy
        mirror=true
        shift
        ;;

    -p)
        passflg=true
        shift
        if [ $# -eq Ø ]
        then
            echo >&2 "$MYNAME: error: no passwd"
            echo >&2 "usage"
            exit 1
        fi
        passwd=$1
        shift
        ;;

    -[rR])                                      # recursive
        recurse=true
        shift
        ;;

    --)                                         # end of options
        shift
        break
        ;;

    -*)
        echo >&2 "$MYNAME: error: $1: unknown option."
        echo >&2 "$usage"
        exit 1
        ;;

    *)                                          # end of options
        break
        ;;
esac
```

```
done

# << END parse options <<<<<<<<<<<<<<<<<<<<<<<<<<<<<<<<<<<<<<<<<<<<<<<< #

# >> BEGIN parse arguments >>>>>>>>>>>>>>>>>>>>>>>>>>>>>>>>>>>>>>>>>>>>> #

case $# in
    Ø)
        list=true
        recurse=true
        ;;

    1)
        case $1 in
            *:)
                list=true
                recurse=true
                ;;
        esac
        ;;

    *)
        echo >&2 "$MYNAME: error: unexpected argument(s)."
        echo >&2 "$usage"
        exit 1
        ;;
esac

# << END parse arguments <<<<<<<<<<<<<<<<<<<<<<<<<<<<<<<<<<<<<<<<<<<<<< #

# >> BEGIN initialization >>>>>>>>>>>>>>>>>>>>>>>>>>>>>>>>>>>>>>>>>>>>> #

[ umask -ge 700 ] && umask `/bin/expr \`umask\` - 0700`

# return unrooted dirname
dirname () {
    expr \
    './'${1-.}'/' : '\(\.\)/[^/]*/$' \
    \¦ ${1-.}'/' : '/*\(.*[^/]\)//*[^/][^/]*//*$' \
    \¦ .
}
[ ${1-.} = / ] && set .
host=`/bin/expr \
    "$1" : '[^@]*@\(.*\):' \
    \¦ "$1" : '\(.*\):' \
    \¦ \`/bin/basename \\\`pwd\\\`\`
`
path=`/bin/expr "$1" : '[^:]*:\(.*\)' \¦ $1. : '[^:]*:\(.*\)' \¦ ${1-.}`
dir=`dirname $path`
file=`/bin/basename $path`
login=`/bin/expr "$1" : '\([^@]*\)@' \¦ anonymous`
if /bin/ypmatch $host hosts.byname 2>&- 1>&- ¦¦
    /bin/ypmatch $host hosts.byaddr 2>&- 1>&-
then
    port=21
    passwd=${passwd-USER@`hostname`}
```

```
else
    port=4666
    passwd=${passwd-USER@Sun.COM}
    machine=$host
    host=sun-barr.EBay
fi

if [ $list ]
then
    cmd="ls -l${recurse+R}"
    file=ls-l${recurse+R}`expr \
        $path : '\(\.\)$' \
        \¦ $dir$file : '\(\..*\)' \
        \¦ /$dir/$file ¦ tr / .
    `
    dir=$path
else
    cmd=${recurse+m}get
    [ $recurse ] && dir=$path && file=\*
fi

case $1 in
    *@*:*)
        ;;
    *)
        [ $passflg ] ¦¦
        eval `
            /bin/awk '
                /machine *'"${machine-$host}"'/ {
                    for (i = 1; i <= NF; i++) {
                        if ($i == "login") print "login="$++i";";
                        if ($i == "password") print "passwd="$++i";";
                    }
                    exit;
                }
            ' $HOME/.netrc 2>&-
        `
        ;;
esac

# << END initialization <<<<<<<<<<<<<<<<<<<<<<<<<<<<<<<<<<<<<<<<<<<<<<<<< #

# >> BEGIN verify prerequisites >>>>>>>>>>>>>>>>>>>>>>>>>>>>>>>>>>>>>>>> #

if [ ! "$flat" ]
then
    /bin/mkdir -p $dir 2>&-
    cd $dir
fi

# << END verify prerequisites <<<<<<<<<<<<<<<<<<<<<<<<<<<<<<<<<<<<<<<<<< #

# >> BEGIN main >>>>>>>>>>>>>>>>>>>>>>>>>>>>>>>>>>>>>>>>>>>>>>>>>>>>>>>> #

/usr/ucb/ftp -i -n -v $host $port << EOFTP
    user $login${machine+@$machine} $passwd
```

```
    ${mode-binary}
    cd $dir
    $cmd $file
    quit
EOFTP
echo ""

# << END main <<<<<<<<<<<<<<<<<<<<<<<<<<<<<<<<<<<<<<<<<<<<<<<<<<<<<<<<<<<<<<< #
```

arch.sh.fctn Function

The `arch.sh.fctn` script emulates SunOS 4.*x* system architecture.

```
#
#  %M%:    Version:  %I%    Date:     %G%
#

[ $_Arch_loaded ] || {


# Function:
#     @(#)Arch                         (Wayne.Thompson@Sun.COM) 05/14/92
#
# Description:
#     This function emulates 4.x arch(1).
#
# Variables:
#
# Usage:
#     Arch
#     Arch -k
#     Arch archname
#
# Return:
#     0 success
#     1 non-success
#
# Dependencies:
#     This function works under SunOs 3.x - 5.x.
#
# Bugs:
#

Arch () {
    case $1 in
        '')
            /bin/arch $* 2>&- || /bin/expr `/bin/uname -m` : '\(sun[0-9]*\)'
            ;;

        -k)
            /bin/arch $* 2>&- || /bin/uname -m
            ;;

        *)
            if [ -x /bin/arch ]
            then
```

```
                /bin/arch $*
            else
                [ $* = `/bin/expr \`/bin/uname -m\` : '\(sun[Ø-9]*\)'` ]
            fi
            ;;
    esac
}

_Arch_loaded=1
}
```

array.sh.fctn Function

The following function extends the functionality of the Bourne shell to include associative arrays:

```
## >> BEGIN package: arrays >>>>>>>>>>>>>>>>>>>>>>>>>>>>>>>>>>>>>>>> ##

# Package:
#     @(#)arrays,v1.Ø                    (Wayne.Thompson@Sun.COM) 05/02/93
#
# Description:
#     This package contains functions that emulate associative arrays.
#     Keys are limited to letters, digits, underscores, hyphens and periods.
#
# Variables:
#     __array_size_<array>
#     __array_keys_<array>
#     __array__<array>_<key>
#     __array_filename
#     __array_name
#     __array_key
#     __array_keys
#     __array_cell
#
# Usage:
#     setarray array key [value ...]
#     getarray array key
#     unsetarray array [key ...]
#     keys array
#     sizearray array
#     defined array [key]
#     dumparray pathname [array ...]
#
# Dependencies:
#     Array names and keys are combined to form strings which are
#     evaluated as parameters.
#
# Bugs:
#

### >> BEGIN function: setarray >>>>>>>>>>>>>>>>>>>>>>>>>>>>>>>>>> ###

# Function:
#     @(#)setarray,v1.Ø                  (Wayne.Thompson@Sun.COM) 05/16/93
```

```
#
# Description:
#     This function assigns values to array elements. If more than one
#     value is provided and the key is an integer, values will be
#     assigned to successive elements beginning with the initial key.
#
# Variables:
#     __array_size_<array>
#     __array_keys_<array>
#     __array__<array>_<key>
#     __array_name
#     __array_key
#     __array_cell
#
# Usage:
#     setarray array key [value ...]
#     setarray pathname
#
# Return:
#
# Dependencies:
#
# Bugs:
#

setarray () {
    case $# in
        0)
            echo >&2 setarray: error: "$@"
            echo >&2 usage: setarray array key '[value ...]'
            exit 1
            ;;

        1)
            if [ -f $1 ]
            then
                while read __array_name __array_key __array_value
                do
                    setarray $__array_name $__array_key $__array_value
                done < $1
                return
            else
                echo >&2 setarray: error: $1: no such file
                exit 1
            fi
            ;;

        2|3)
            ;;

        *)
            case $2 in
                [0-9]*)
                    ;;

                *)
```

```
                    echo >&2 setarray: error: "$@"
                    echo >&2 setarray: error: 2nd argument must be an integer
                    exit 1
                    ;;
            esac
            ;;
    esac
    __array_name=$1
    __array_key=$2
    case $2 in
        *[-.]*)
            __array_cell=`echo $2 ¦ /bin/tr '[-.]' __`
            shift 2
            set $__array_name $__array_cell "$@"
            ;;
    esac
    eval "
        if [ \${__array_size_$1+1} ]
        then
            [ \${__array__$1_$2+1} ] ¦¦ {
                __array_size_$1=\`/bin/expr \$__array_size_$1 + 1\`
                __array_keys_$1=\"\$__array_keys_$1 \$__array_key \"
            }
        else
            __array_size_$1=1
            __array_keys_$1=\$__array_key
        fi
        __array__$1_$2=\$3
    "
    case $# in
        2)
            shift 2
            ;;

        *)
            shift 3
            ;;
    esac
    while [ $# -gt Ø ]
    do
        __array_key=`/bin/expr $__array_key + 1`
        eval "
            [ \${__array__${__array_name}_$__array_key+1} ] ¦¦ {
               __array_size_$__array_name=\`/bin/expr \$__array_size_$__array_name
+ 1\`
                __array_keys_$__array_name=\"\$__array_keys_$__array_name
\$__array_key\"
            }
            __array__${__array_name}_$__array_key=\$1
        "
        shift
    done
}

### << END function: setarray <<<<<<<<<<<<<<<<<<<<<<<<<<<<<<<<<<<<<<<< ###
```

```
### >> BEGIN function: getarray >>>>>>>>>>>>>>>>>>>>>>>>>>>>>>>>>>> ###

# Function:
#     @(#)getarray,v1.Ø                    (Wayne.Thompson@Sun.COM) 05/02/93
#
# Description:
#     This function prints array values.
#
# Variables:
#     __array__<array>_<key>
#     __array_name
#
# Usage:
#     getarray array [key ...]
#
# Return:
#
# Dependencies:
#
# Bugs:
#

getarray () {
    case $# in
        Ø)
            echo >&2 getarray: error: "$@"
            echo >&2 usage: getarray array '[key ...]'
            exit 1
            ;;

        1)  # entire array
            set $1 `keys $1`
            ;;
    esac
    __array_name=$1
    shift
    while [ $# -gt Ø ]
    do
        case $1 in
            *[-.]*)
                eval echo \$__array__${__array_name}_`echo $1 ¦
                /bin/tr '[-.]' __`
                ;;

            *)
                eval echo \$__array__${__array_name}_$1
                ;;
        esac
        shift
    done
}

### << END function: getarray <<<<<<<<<<<<<<<<<<<<<<<<<<<<<<<<<<<<<<<<< ###

### >> BEGIN function: unsetarray >>>>>>>>>>>>>>>>>>>>>>>>>>>>>>>>> ###
```

```
# Function:
#     @(#)unsetarray,v1.Ø               (Wayne.Thompson@Sun.COM) 05/02/93
#
# Description:
#     This function unsets (undefines) one or more array elements
#     or an entire array.
#
# Variables:
#     __array_size_<array>
#     __array_keys_<array>
#     __array__<array>_<key>
#     __array_name
#     __array_key
#     __array_keys
#
# Usage:
#     unsetarray array [key ...]
#
# Return:
#
# Dependencies:
#
# Bugs:
#

unsetarray () {
    case $# in
        Ø)
            echo >&2 unsetarray: error: "$@"
            echo >&2 usage: unsetarray array '[key ...]'
            exit 1
            ;;

        1)  # entire array
            set $1 `keys $1`
            ;;
    esac

    __array_name=$1
    shift

    while [ $# -gt Ø ]
    do
        eval "
            __array_keys=
            [ \${__array__${__array_name}_$1+1} ] &&
            for __array_key in \$__array_keys_$__array_name
            do
                case \$__array_key in
                    \$1)
                        case \$1 in
                            *[-.]*)
                                unset __array__${__array_name}_\`echo \$1 ¦
                                /bin/tr '[-.]' __\`
                                ;;
```

```
                        *)
                            unset __array__${__array_name}_$1
                            ;;
                    esac
                    __array_size_$__array_name=\`/bin/expr
                     \$__array_size_$__array_name - 1\`
                    ;;

                *)
                    case \$__array_keys in
                        '')
                            __array_keys=\$__array_key
                            ;;

                        *)
                            __array_keys=\"\$__array_keys \$__array_key\"
                            ;;
                    esac
                    ;;
            esac
        done
        __array_keys_$__array_name=\$__array_keys
    "
    shift
  done
  eval "
    case \$__array_size_$__array_name in
        Ø)
            unset __array_size_$__array_name __array_keys_$__array_name
            ;;
    esac
  "
}

### << END function: unsetarray <<<<<<<<<<<<<<<<<<<<<<<<<<<<<<<<<<<< ###

### >> BEGIN function: keys >>>>>>>>>>>>>>>>>>>>>>>>>>>>>>>>>>>>>>>>>> ###

# Function:
#     @(#)keys,v1.Ø                      (Wayne.Thompson@Sun.COM) 05/02/93
#
# Description:
#     This function prints the keys of an array.
#
# Variables:
#     __array_keys_<array>
#
# Usage:
#     keys array
#
# Return:
#
# Dependencies:
#
# Bugs:
#
```

```
keys () {
    case $# in
        1)
            eval echo \$__array_keys_$1
            ;;

        *)
            echo >&2 keys: error: "$@"
            echo >&2 usage: keys array
            exit 1
            ;;
    esac
}

### << END function: keys <<<<<<<<<<<<<<<<<<<<<<<<<<<<<<<<<<<<<<<<<<< ###

### >> BEGIN function: sizearray >>>>>>>>>>>>>>>>>>>>>>>>>>>>>>>>>>> ###

# Function:
#     @(#)sizearray,v1.Ø                (Wayne.Thompson@Sun.COM) Ø5/Ø2/93
#
# Description:
#     This function prints the number of defined array elements.
#
# Variables:
#     __array_size_<array>
#
# Usage:
#     sizearray array
#
# Return:
#
# Dependencies:
#
# Bugs:
#

sizearray () {
    case $# in
        1)
            eval echo \${__array_size_$1:-Ø}
            ;;

        *)
            echo >&2 sizearray: error: "$@"
            echo >&2 usage: sizearray array
            exit 1
            ;;
    esac
}

### << END function: sizearray <<<<<<<<<<<<<<<<<<<<<<<<<<<<<<<<<<<<<< ###

### >> BEGIN function: defined >>>>>>>>>>>>>>>>>>>>>>>>>>>>>>>>>>>>> ###
```

```
# Function:
#     @(#)defined,v1.Ø                   (Wayne.Thompson@Sun.COM) 05/02/93
#
# Description:
#     This function returns whether an array element or array is defined.
#
# Variables:
#     __array_size_<array>
#     __array__<array>_<key>
#
# Usage:
#     defined array [key]
#
# Return:
#     Ø         defined
#     1         undefined
#
# Dependencies:
#
# Bugs:
#

defined () {
    case $# in
        1)
            eval set \${__array_size_$1+Ø} 1
            ;;

        2)
            case $2 in
                *[-.]*) set $1 `echo $2 | /bin/tr '[-.]' __`;;
            esac
            eval set \${__array__$1_$2+Ø} 1
            ;;

        *)
            echo >&2 defined: error: "$@"
            echo >&2 usage: defined array '[key]'
            exit 1
            ;;
    esac
    return $1
}

### << END function: defined <<<<<<<<<<<<<<<<<<<<<<<<<<<<<<<<<<<<<<<<< ###

### >> BEGIN function: dumparray >>>>>>>>>>>>>>>>>>>>>>>>>>>>>>>>>> ###

# Function:
#     @(#)dumparray,v1.Ø                 (Wayne.Thompson@Sun.COM) 05/02/93
#
# Description:
#     This function dumps arrays in file in a format readable by
#     shell dot (.) command.
#
# Variables:
```

```
#     __array_filename
#
# Usage:
#     dumparray pathname [array ...]
#
# Return:
#     Ø         success
#     1         failure
#
# Dependencies:
#
# Bugs:
#     Since this depends on the output of set, and set does not preserve
#     quoting, the resultant file may be unusable. Use of
#     storearray/setarray is safer, albeit slower.
#

dumparray () {
    case $# in
        Ø)
            echo >&2 dumparray: error: "$@"
            echo >&2 usage: dumparray pathname '[array ...]'
            exit 1
            ;;
    esac

    __array_filename=$1
    shift

    set ¦
    /bin/awk '
        /\(\){$/ { exit }               # functions follow parameters

        /^__array_(filename¦name¦key¦keys¦cell)=/ { next }      # temp storage

        /^__array_(size¦keys)*_('`echo ${*:-.\*} ¦ /bin/tr " " \¦`')(_¦=)/ {
            if (NF > 1) {
                n = index($Ø, "=");
                print substr($Ø , 1, n)"'\''"substr($Ø, n+1)"'\''";
            }
            else {
                print;
            }
        }
    ' > $__array_filename
}

### << END function: dumparray <<<<<<<<<<<<<<<<<<<<<<<<<<<<<<<<<<<<<<<<<<<< ###

## << END package: arrays <<<<<<<<<<<<<<<<<<<<<<<<<<<<<<<<<<<<<<<<<<<<<<<<<<<< ##
```

The function scripts `arch.sh.fctn` (displayed earlier in this chapter), `hostname.sh.fctn`, `osr.sh.fctn`, and `whoami.sh.fctn` are used to help in the transition from SunOS 4.*x* to Solaris 2.*x*.

hostname.sh.fctn Function

The `hostname.sh.fctn` script emulates the SunOS 4.*x* `hostname` command:

```
#
#  %M%:    Version:  %I%    Date:     %G%
#

[ $_Hostname_loaded ] || {


# Function:
#     @(#)hostname                   (Wayne.Thompson@Sun.COM) 02/15/92
#
# Description:
#     This function emulates 4.x hostname(1) given no arguments.
#
# Variables:
#
# Usage:
#     Hostname
#
# Return:
#
# Dependencies:
#     This funcion works under SunOs 3.x - 5.x.
#
# Bugs:
#

Hostname () {
    /bin/hostname 2>&- || /bin/uname -n
}

_Hostname_loaded=1
}
```

osr.sh.fctn Function

The `osr.sh.fctn` script outputs the numeric portion of the current operating system release—for example, 5.2 for Solaris 5.2 system software:

```
#
#  %M%:    Version:  %I%    Date:     %G%
#

[ $_Osr_loaded ] || {

# Function:
#     @(#)Osr                        (Wayne.Thompson@Sun.COM) 02/08/92
#
# Description:
#     This function outputs the numeric portion of the current OS release.
#
# Variables:
```

```
#
# Usage:
#     os=`Osr`
#
# Return:
#     Ø success
#     1 non-success
#
# Dependencies:
#     This funcion works under SunOs 3.x - 5.x.
#
# Bugs:
#

Osr () {
    /bin/expr `
        {
            /bin/uname -r ¦¦
            /bin/cat /usr/sys/conf*/RELEASE
        } 2>&- ¦¦
        /etc/dmesg ¦
        /bin/awk '
            BEGIN { status = 1 }
            /^SunOS Release/ { print $3; status = Ø; exit }
            END { exit status }
        ' ¦¦
        /bin/expr "\`
            /usr/ucb/strings -50 /vmunix ¦
            /bin/egrep '^SunOS Release'
        \`" : 'SunOS Release \([^ ]*\)'
    ` : '\([.Ø-9]*\)'
}

_Osr_loaded=1
}
```

whoami.sh.fctn Function

The `whoami.sh.fctn` emulates the SunOS 4.*x* `whoami` command:

```
#
#  @(#)  whoami.sh.fctn      1.2    Last mod: 6/4/93
#

[ $_Whoami_loaded ] ¦¦ {

# Function:
#     @(#)whoami                   (Wayne.Thompson@Sun.COM) Ø3/2Ø/92
#
# Description:
#     This function emulates 4.x whoami(1).
#
# Variables:
#
# Usage:
#     whoami
```

```
#
# Return:
#
# Dependencies:
#     This funcion works under SunOs 3.x - 5.x.
#
# Bugs:
#

Whoami () {
    /usr/ucb/whoami 2>&- ||
    /bin/expr "`/bin/id`" : '[^(]*(\([^)]*\)'
}

_Whoami_loaded=1
}
```

This part introduces system security in three chapters. Chapter 18 introduces the basic concepts of system security, including file, system, and network security. Chapter 19 describes how to use authentication services. It provides an overview of secure RPC and explains how to use pluggable authentication modules (PAM). Chapter 20 describes how to set up and use Automated Security Enhancement Tool (ASET).

Refer to these three chapters if you want to familiarize yourself with the basics of system security and if you want to use authentication services and ASET security.

PART

7

System Security

CHAPTER

18

Understanding System Security

New Security Features in the Solaris 2.6 Release

Overview of System Security

File Security

Network Security

ANAGING SYSTEM SECURITY IS AN IMPORTANT PART OF SYSTEM ADMINISTRATION. THIS chapter provides information about managing system security at the file, system, and network level.

At the file level, the Solaris 2.*x* operating system provides some standard security features that you can use to protect files, directories, and devices. At the system and network levels, the security issues are similar. In the workplace, a number of systems connected to a server can be viewed as a large, multifaceted system. When you are responsible for the security of this larger system or network, it is important for you to defend the network from outsiders trying to gain access. In addition, it is important to ensure the integrity of the data on the systems within the network.

New Security Features in the Solaris 2.6 Release

The Solaris 2.6 release provides two new features to enhance security:

- The Pluggable Authentication Module (PAM) framework.
- A `noexec_user_stack` variable, set in the `/etc/system` file, which enables you to specify whether stack mappings are executable or not.

Pluggable Authentication Module (PAM)

PAM enables you to plug in new authentication technologies without changing the login, ftp, or telnet commands. You can also use PAM to integrate UNIX login with other security mechanisms, such as data encryption standard (DECS) or Kerberos. You can also plug in mechanisms for account, session, and password management using this framework. For more information, see Chapter 19, "Using Authentication Services."

Executable Stacks and Security

A number of security bugs are related to default executable stacks when permissions are set to read, write, and execute. Although the SPARC and Intel application binary interface (ABI) mandates that stacks have execute permissions, most programs can function correctly without using executable stacks.

The Solaris 2.6 release provides a `noexec_user_stack` variable, which enables you to specify whether stack mappings are executable or not. By default, the value for the variable is zero, which provides ABI-compliant behavior. If the variable is set to non-zero, the system marks the stack of every process in the system as readable and writable but not executable.

Disabling Programs from Using Executable Stacks

Use the following steps to disable programs from using executable stacks:

1. Become superuser.
2. Add the line **set noexec_user_stack=1** to the `/etc/system` file.
3. Type **init 6** to reboot the system.

When the variable is set to a non-zero value, programs that execute code on their stack are sent a SIGSEGV signal, which usually terminates the program with a core dump. Such programs also generate a warning message, which includes the name of the program, the PID, and the UID of the user who ran the program, as shown in the following example:

```
a.out[347] attempt to execute code on stack by uid 555
```

The message is logged by the `syslogd`(1M) daemon when the syslog kern facility is set to notice level. This logging is set by default in the `syslog.conf`(4) file, which means that the message is sent to both the console and to the `/var/adm/messages` file.

When you have set the `noexec_user_stack` variable, you can monitor these messages to observe potential security problems. You can also monitor the messages to identify valid programs that depend on executable stacks and have been prevented from correct operation.

You can explicitly mark program stacks as executable by using the `mprotect`(2) function. See the `mprotect`(2) manual page for more information.

NOTE. *Because of hardware limitations, executable stack problems can be caught and reported only on sun4m, sun4d, and sun4u platforms.*

Disabling Executable Stack Message Logging

If you do not want to log executable stack messages, you can set the `noexec_user_stack_log` variable to zero in the `/etc/system` file. Note that even if you disable executable stack message logging, the SIGSEGV signal may continue to dump core for the executing program.

Use the following steps to disable executable stack message logging:

1. Become superuser.
2. Add the line **set noexec_user_stack_log=0** to the `/etc/system` file.
3. Type **init 6** to reboot the system.

Overview of System Security

The first line of security defense is to control access to systems. You can control and monitor system access in the following ways:

- Maintain physical site security
- Maintain login control
- Restrict access to data in files
- Maintain network control
- Monitor system use
- Set the path variable correctly
- Monitor setuid programs
- Track superuser (root) login
- Install a firewall
- Use the Automated Security Enhancement Tool (ASET)

Maintaining Physical Site Security

To control access to systems, your company must maintain the physical security of the computer environment. For instance, if a user logs on to a system and leaves it unattended, anyone who can use that system can gain access to the operating system and the network. Be aware of your users' surroundings and educate them to physically protect the computers from unauthorized access.

Maintaining Login and Access Control

Use password and login control to restrict unauthorized logins to a system or to the network. All accounts on a system should have a password. A single account without a password makes your entire network accessible to anyone who knows or can guess a username.

Solaris 2.*x* system software restricts control of certain system devices to the user login account. Only a process running as superuser or console user can access a system mouse, keyboard, frame buffer, or audio device unless `/etc/logindevperm` is edited. See the `logindevperm`(4) manual page for more information.

Restricting Access to Data in Files

Use UNIX directory and file permissions to control access to the data on your users' systems. You may want to enable some people to read certain files and grant other people permission to change or delete certain files. You may have data that you do not want anyone else to see. See "File Security" on page 394 for information on how to set file permissions.

Maintaining Network Control

Computers are often part of a configuration of systems called a network. A *network* enables connected systems to exchange information and access data and other resources that are available from systems connected to the network. Networking has created a powerful and sophisticated way of computing. However, networking introduces the opportunity for breaches in computer security.

For example, within a network of computers, individual systems are open to enable sharing of information. Because many people have access to the network, the opportunity for unwanted access is increased, especially through user error, such as a poor choice of passwords.

Monitoring System Use

Be aware of all aspects of the systems that are your responsibility, including the following:

- What is the normal load?
- Who has access to the system?
- When do individuals access the system?

Use the available tools to audit system use and monitor the activities of individual users. Monitoring is useful when you suspect a breach in security.

Setting the Correct Path

Path variables are important. They can prevent users from accidentally running a program introduced by someone else that harms data on a system. A program that creates a security hazard is referred to as a *Trojan horse*. For example, a substitute switch user (`su`) program could be placed in a public directory where you, as system administrator, might run it. Such a script would look like the regular `su` command that you use to gain superuser access. Because it removes itself after execution, it is difficult to tell that you have actually run a Trojan horse.

The path variable is automatically set at login time through the `.login`, `.profile`, and `.cshrc` startup files. Setting up the user search path so that the current directory (`.`) comes last prevents you or your users from running this type of Trojan horse. Never include a publicly writable directory in root's search path. The path variable for superuser should not include the current directory at all. The ASET utility examines the startup files to ensure that the path variable is set up correctly and that it does not contain a dot (`.`) entry. For more information about ASET, see Chapter 20, "Using the Automated Security Enhancement Tool (ASET)."

Monitoring setuid Programs

Many executable programs must be run as `root` or superuser to work properly. These executables run with the UID set to 0 (`setuid=0`). Anyone running these programs runs them with the root ID, which creates a potential security problem if the programs are not written with security in mind.

You should not allow the use of setuid programs except for executables shipped with setuid to root. At the least, you should restrict and keep these programs to a minimum.

Installing a Firewall

Another way to protect your network is to use a firewall or secure gateway system. A *firewall* is a dedicated system that separates two networks, each of which approaches the other as untrusted. Consider a firewall setup as mandatory between your internal network and any external networks, such as the Internet, with which you want internal network users to communicate.

A firewall can also be useful between some internal networks. For example, the firewall or secure gateway computer does not send a packet between two networks unless the gateway computer is the origin or the destination address of the packet. Set up a firewall to forward packets for particular protocols only. For example, you may allow packets for transferring mail, but not for telnet or rlogin. The ASET utility, when run at high security, disables the forwarding of Internet Protocol (IP) packets. For more information about ASET, see Chapter 20.

Reporting Security Problems

If you experience a suspected security breach, you can contact the Computer Emergency Response Team/Coordination Center (CERT/CC), which is a Defense Advanced Research Projects Agency (DARPA) funded project located at the Software Engineering Institute at Carnegie Mellon University. It can assist you with any security problems you are having. It can also direct you to other CERTs that may be more appropriate for your particular needs. You can contact them in the following ways:

- CERT/CC 24-hour hotline: 412-268-7090
- Email: `cert@cert.sei.cmu.edu`
- URL: `http://www.cert.org/`

File Security

All of the users logged into the SunOS 5.*x* operating system can read and use files belonging to one another as long as they have permission to do so. UNIX file security is based on a combination of user classes and file and directory permissions, as described briefly in the following sections.

NOTE. *In most cases, you can keep sensitive files in an inaccessible directory (700 mode) and make the file unreadable by others (600 mode). However, anyone who guesses your password or has access to the root password can read and write to that file. In addition, the sensitive file is preserved on backup tapes every time you back up the system.*

*All Solaris 2.*x *system software users in the United States have an additional layer of security available—the optional file encryption kit. The encryption kit includes the* `crypt` *command, which scrambles the data to disguise the text.*

In addition to basic UNIX file security, you can implement Access Control Lists (ACLs, pronounced "ackkls") to provide greater control over file permissions. For more information about ACLs, see "Access Control Lists (ACLs)" on page 406.

User Classes

Each UNIX file has three classes of users:

- Users
- Members of a group
- All others who are not the file or group owner

Only the owner of the file or root can assign or modify file permissions

File Permissions

File permissions, listed in Table 18–1, apply to regular files and to special files, such as devices, sockets, and named pipes (FIFOs). When a file is a symbolic link, the permissions that apply are those of the file that the link points to.

Table 18–1 File Permissions

Symbol	Permission	Description
r	Read	Can open and read the contents of a file.
w	Write	Can write to the file (modify its contents), add to it, or delete it.
x	Execute	Can execute the file (if it is a program or shell script) or run it with one of the `exec(1)` system calls.
-	Denied	Cannot read, write, or execute the file.

Directory Permissions

Directory permissions listed in Table 18–2 apply to directories.

Table 18–2 Directory Permissions

Symbol	Permission	Description
r	Read	List the files in the directory.
w	Write	Add or remove files or links in the directory.

Table 18–2 Directory Permissions (continued)

Symbol	Permission	Description
x	Execute	Open or execute files in the directory.
-	Denied	Cannot list, write, or open the files in the directory.

You can protect the files in a directory and its subdirectories by denying access to that directory. Note, however, that superuser has access to all files and directories on the system, regardless of permission settings. Other permission values and their meanings are discussed in the section "Special File Permissions (setuid, setgid, and Sticky Bit)" on page 402.

Octal Values for Permissions

Instead of using the letter symbol, you can use a numeric argument for file and directory permissions. Table 18–3 shows the octal values for setting file permissions. You can use these numbers in sets of three to set permissions for owner, group, and other. For example, the value 644 sets permissions to rw-r--r--: read/write permissions for owner, and read-only permissions for group and other.

Table 18–3 Octal Values for File and Directory Permissions

Value	Permissions	Description
0	---	No permissions
1	--x	Execute-only
2	-w-	Write-only
3	-wx	Write, execute
4	r--	Read-only
5	r-x	Read, execute
6	rw-	Read, write
7	rwx	Read, write, execute

Default umask

When a user creates a file or directory, it is created using a default set of permissions. These default permissions are determined by the value of `umask` that is set in the `/etc/profile` system file or in the user's `.cshrc`, `.login` or `.profile` file. If no umask is set, the system sets the default permissions on a text file to 666, granting read and write permission to user, group, and other, and to 777 on a directory or executable file.

```
 777 full permissions
-022 umask
 755 allowed permissions
```

The value assigned by umask is subtracted from the default. It denies permissions in the same way that the `chmod` command grants them. For example, while the command `chmod 022` grants write permission to group and others, `umask 022` denies write permission for group and others.

Table 18–4 shows some typical umask settings and describes the effect on an executable file.

Table 18–4 umask Settings for Different Security Levels

Security Level	umask	Disallows
744 (Permissive)	022	Write for group and others
740 (Moderate)	027	Write for group; read, write, execute for others
741 (Moderate)	026	Write for group; read, write for others
700 (Severe)	077	Read, write, execute for group and others

File Types

A file can be one of the six types listed in Table 18–5.

Table 18–5 File Types

Symbol	Description
-	Text or program
d	Directory
b	Block special file
c	Character special file
p	Named pipe (FIFO)
L	Symbolic link

File Administration Commands

Table 18–6 lists the file administration commands that you can use on files or directories.

Displaying File Information

Use the `ls` command to display information about files in a directory. The `-l (long)` option to the `ls` command displays the following information:

Table 18–6 File Administration Commands

Command	Description
ls(1)	List the files in a directory and display information about them.
chown(1)	Change the ownership of a file.
chgrp(1)	Change the group ownership of a file.
chmod(1)	Change permissions on a file.

- Type of file and its permissions
- Number of hard links
- Owner of the file
- Group of the file
- Size of the file, in bytes
- Date the file was created or the last date it was changed
- Name of the file

The -a option to the ls command displays all files, including hidden files that begin with a dot (.). To display information about files, type the following:

```
castle% ls -la
```

The following example shows a partial listing of the files in the root directory (/).

```
castle% cd /
castle% ls -la
total 140
drwxr-xr-x  31 root     root        1024 Sep 30 13:26 .
drwxr-xr-x  31 root     root        1024 Sep 30 13:26 ..
-rw-------   1 root     other        205 Sep 23 10:02 .Xauthority
-rw-------   1 root     root        1028 Oct  2 08:47 .cpr_config
-rw-rw-rw-   1 root     other         52 Sep 26 12:19 .cshrc
drwxr-xr-x  12 root     other        512 Sep 23 10:02 .dt
-rwxr-xr-x   1 root     other       5111 Sep 11 10:21 .dtprofile
drwxr-xr-x   2 root     root         512 Sep 11 10:21 TT_DB
-rw-r--r--   1 root     other         11 Sep 24 14:46 awk
lrwxrwxrwx   1 root     root           9 Sep 10 17:58 bin -> ./usr/bin
drwxr-xr-x   5 root     nobody       512 Oct  2 08:47 cdrom
drwxrwxr-x  18 root     sys         4096 Oct  2 08:46 dev
drwxrwxr-x   5 root     sys          512 Sep 10 18:38 devices
dr-xr-xr-x   2 root     root         512 Sep 11 09:05 doe
(More information not shown)
```

Changing File Ownership

Use the chown command to change file ownership. Only the owner of the file or superuser can change the ownership of a file. Use the following steps to change file ownership:

1. If you are not the owner of the file or directory, become superuser.
2. Type **chown *<username>* *<filename>*** and press Return.
3. Type **ls -l *<filename>*** and press Return to verify that the owner of the file has changed.

You can change ownership on groups of files or on all of the files in a directory by using metacharacters such as * and ? in place of filenames or in combination with them.

You can change ownership recursively by use the chown -R option. When you use the -R option, the chown command descends through the directory and any subdirectories setting the ownership ID. If a symbolic link is encountered, the ownership is changed only on the target file itself.

The following example changes the ownership of the file local.cshrc from root to winsor:

```
castle% ls -l local.cshrc
-rw-r--r--   1 root     other        124 Sep 12 10:32 local.cshrc
castle% su
Password:
# chown winsor local.cshrc
# ls -l local.cshrc
-rw-r--r--   1 winsor   other        124 Sep 12 10:32 local.cshrc
# exit
castle%
```

NOTE. *You can also change file ownership by specifying the UID number as the first argument to the* chgrp *command.*

Changing Group Ownership of a File

Only the owner of the file or superuser can change the group ownership of a file. Use the chgrp command to change group ownership of a file or directory:

1. If you are not the owner of the file or directory, become superuser.
2. Type **chgrp *<groupname>* *<filename>*** and press Return.
3. Type **ls -l *<filename>*** and press Return to verify that the group owner of the file is changed.

NOTE. *You can also change group ownership by specifying the group number as the first argument to the* chgrp *command.*

You can change group ownership on a set of files or on all of the files in a directory by using metacharacters such as * and ? in place of filenames or in combination with them.

You can change group ownership recursively by using the chgrp -R option. When you use the -R option, the chgrp command descends through the directory and any subdirectories setting the group ownership ID. If a symbolic link is encountered, the group ownership is changed only on the target file itself.

The following example changes the group ownership of the file `local.cshrc` from `other` to `staff`:

```
castle% ls -l local.cshrc
-rw-r--r--   1 winsor   other        124 Sep 12 10:32 local.cshrc
castle% chgrp staff local.cshrc
castle% ls -l local.cshrc
-rw-r--r--   1 winsor   staff        124 Sep 12 10:32 local.cshrc
castle%
```

Changing File Permissions

Use the `chmod` command to change the permissions on a file or directory. Only the owner of a file or superuser can change file and directory permissions.

You can set permissions with the `chmod` command in one of two ways:

- Absolute mode—Use numbers to represent file permissions. When you change permissions by using the absolute mode, you represent permissions by specifying an octal mode triplet, such as 700 or 666.
- Symbolic mode—Use combinations of letters and symbols to add or remove permissions.

Refer to Table 18–3 on page 416 for the octal values used to set file permissions in absolute mode.

Table 18–7 lists the symbols for setting file permissions in symbolic mode. You can use symbols to specify whose permissions are to be set or changed, the operation to be performed, or the permissions being assigned or changed.

Table 18–7 Symbolic Values for File and Directory Permissions

Symbol	Function*	Description
u	Who	User (owner)
g	Who	Group
o	Who	Others
A	Who	All
=	Operation	Assign
+	Operation	Add
-	Operation	Remove
r	Permission	Read
w	Permission	Write

Table 18–7 Symbolic Values for File and Directory Permissions (continued)

Symbol	Function*	Description
x	Permission	Execute
l	Permission	Mandatory locking, setgid bit is on, group execution bit is off
s	Permission	setuid or setgid bit is on
S	Permission	suid bit is on, user execution bit is off
t	Permission	Sticky bit is on, execution bit for others is on
T	Permission	Sticky bit is on, execution bit for others is off

* The who, operator, and permissions designations in the function column specify the symbols that change the permissions on the file or directory.

Use the following steps to change permissions in absolute mode:

1. If you are not the owner of the file or directory, become superuser.
2. Type **chmod <*nnn*> <*filename*>** and press Return.
3. Type **ls -l <*filename*>** and press Return to verify that the permissions of the file have changed.

Use the following steps to change permissions in symbolic mode:

1. If you are not the owner of the file or directory, become superuser.
2. Type **chmod <*who*> <*operator*> <*permission*> <*filename*>** and press Return.
3. Type **ls -l <*filename*>** and press Return to verify that the permissions of the file have changed.

The following example changes permissions in absolute mode for the file `local.cshrc` to 666.

```
castle% chmod 666 local.cshrc
castle% ls -l local.cshrc
-rw-rw-rw-   1 winsor   staff        124 Sep 12 10:32 local.cshrc
castle%
```

The following example removes read permission from others for the file `filea`:

```
castle% chmod o-r filea
```

The following example adds read and execute permissions for user, group, and others for the file `fileb`.

```
castle% chmod a+rx fileb
```

The following example adds read, write, and execute permissions for group for the file `filec`.

```
castle% chmod g=rwx filec
```

Special File Permissions (setuid, setgid, and Sticky Bit)

Three special types of permissions are available for executable files and public directories.

- `setuid` permission
- `setgid` permission
- Sticky bit

When these permissions are set for an executable file, any user who runs that file assumes the permissions of the owner or group of the executable file.

CAUTION! *Be extremely careful when setting special permissions because they constitute a security risk. For example, a user can gain superuser permission by executing a program that sets the UID to root.*

Monitor your system for any unauthorized use of the setuid and setgid permissions to gain superuser privileges. See "Searching for Files with Special Permissions" for information on how to search for file systems and print out a list of all of the programs using these permissions. A suspicious listing would be one that grants ownership of such a program to a user rather than to bin or sys. Only superuser can set these permissions.

setuid Permission

When `setuid` (set-user identification) permission is set on an executable file, a process that runs this file is granted access based on the owner of the file (usually root), rather than the user who created the process. This permission enables a user to access files and directories that are normally available only to the owner.

The `setuid` permission is shown as an `s` in the file permissions. For example, the setuid permission on the `passwd` command enables a user to change passwords, assuming the permissions of the root ID are the following:

```
castle% ls -l /usr/bin/passwd
-r-sr-sr-x   3 root     sys         96796 Jul 15 21:23 /usr/bin/passwd
castle%
```

NOTE. *Using* `setuid` *permissions with the reserved UIDs (0–99) from a program may not set the effective UID correctly. Instead, use a shell script to avoid using the reserved UIDs with* `setuid` *permissions.*

You `setuid` permissions by using the `chmod` command to assign the octal value 4 as the first number in a series of four octal values. Use the following steps to `setuid` permissions:

1. If you are not the owner of the file or directory, become superuser.
2. Type **chmod <4*nnn*> <*filename*>** and press Return.
3. Type **ls -l <*filename*>** and press Return to verify that the permissions of the file have changed.

The following example sets `setuid` permission on the `myprog` file:

```
# chmod 4555 myprog
-r-sr-xr-x   1 winsor    staff     12796 Jul 15 21:23 myprog
#
```

To minimize setuid problems, minimize the number of local setuid programs. If you write a setuid program, use the following guidelines to minimize security problems:

- Do not write setuid shell scripts for any shell.
- Do not use library routines that start slave shells.
- Do not use `execlp`(3) and `execvp`() routines that duplicate the path-searching functionality of a shell.
- Use full pathnames to identify files.
- Only `setuid` to root when you need to.
- Use the set effective user ID function, `seteuid`(2), to control setuid use.
- Keep permissions on setuid programs restrictive.
- Avoid secret back-door escapes in your code.

setgid Permission

The setgid (set-group identification) permission is similar to `setuid`, except that the effective group ID for the process is changed to the group owner of the file and a user is granted access based on permissions granted to that group. The `/usr/bin/mail` program has `setgid` permissions:

```
castle% ls -l /usr/bin/mail
-r-x--s--x   1 bin      mail        64376 Jul 15 21:27 /usr/bin/mail
castle%
```

When `setgid` permission is applied to a directory, files subsequently created in the directory belong to the group the directory belongs to, not to the group the creating process belongs to. Any user who has write permission in the directory can create a file there; however, the file does not belong to the group of the user, but instead belongs to the group of the directory.

You can set `setgid` permissions by using the `chmod` command to assign the octal value 2 as the first number in a series of four octal values. Use the following steps to set `setgid` permissions:

1. If you are not the owner of the file or directory, become superuser.
2. Type **chmod <*2nnn*> <*filename*>** and press Return.
3. Type **ls -l <*filename*>** and press Return to verify that the permissions of the file have changed.

The following example sets setuid permission on the `myprog2` file:

```
# chmod 2551 myprog2
# ls -l myprog2
-r-xr-s--x   1 winsor    staff  26876 Jul 15 21:23 myprog2
#
```

Sticky Bit

The sticky bit on a directory is a permission bit that protects files within that directory. If the directory has the sticky bit set, only the owner of the file, the owner of the directory, or root can delete the file. The sticky bit prevents a user from deleting other users' files from public directories, such as `uucppublic`:

```
castle% ls -l /var/spool/uucppublic
drwxrwxrwt   2 uucp     uucp         512 Sep 10 18:06 uucppublic
castle%
```

When you set up a public directory on a TMPFS temporary file system, make sure that you set the sticky bit manually.

You can set sticky bit permissions by using the `chmod` command to assign the octal value 1 as the first number in a series of four octal values. Use the following steps to set the sticky bit on a directory:

1. If you are not the owner of the file or directory, become superuser.
2. Type **chmod <1*nnn*> <*filename*>** and press Return.
3. Type **ls -l <*filename*>** and press Return to verify that the permissions of the file have changed.

The following example sets the sticky bit permission on the `pubdir` directory:

```
castle% chmod 1777 pubdir
castle% ls -l pubdir
drwxrwxrwt   2 winsor    staff    512 Jul 15 21:23 pubdir
castle%
```

Searching for Files with Special Permissions

You should monitor your systems for any unauthorized use of the `setuid` and `setgid` permissions to gain superuser privileges. A suspicious listing would be one that grants ownership of a setuid or setgid program to a user other than bin or sys.

You can use the permissions (`-perm`) option to the find command to search for files with `setuid`, `setgid`, or sticky bit permissions. Use the following steps to search for files with `setuid` permissions:

1. Become superuser.
2. Type **find <*directory*> -user root -perm -4000 -print** and press Return.

The following example lists the system files that have setuid permissions.

```
castle% find / -user root -perm -4000 -print
/usr/lib/lp/bin/netpr
/usr/lib/fs/ufs/quota
/usr/lib/fs/ufs/ufsdump
/usr/lib/fs/ufs/ufsrestore
/usr/lib/exrecover
/usr/lib/pt_chmod
/usr/lib/sendmail
/usr/lib/utmp_update
/usr/lib/acct/accton
/usr/openwin/lib/mkcookie
/usr/openwin/bin/xlock
/usr/openwin/bin/ff.core
/usr/openwin/bin/kcms_configure
/usr/openwin/bin/kcms_calibrate
/usr/openwin/bin/sys-suspend
/usr/dt/bin/dtaction
/usr/dt/bin/dtappgather
/usr/dt/bin/sdtcm_convert
/usr/dt/bin/dtprintinfo
/usr/dt/bin/dtsession
/usr/bin/at
/usr/bin/atq
/usr/bin/atrm
/usr/bin/crontab
/usr/bin/eject
/usr/bin/fdformat
/usr/bin/login
/usr/bin/newgrp
/usr/bin/passwd
/usr/bin/ps
/usr/bin/rcp
/usr/bin/rdist
/usr/bin/rlogin
/usr/bin/rsh
/usr/bin/su
/usr/bin/uptime
/usr/bin/w
/usr/bin/yppasswd
/usr/bin/admintool
/usr/bin/ct
/usr/bin/chkey
/usr/bin/nispasswd
/usr/bin/cancel
/usr/bin/lp
/usr/bin/lpset
/usr/bin/lpstat
/usr/bin/volcheck
/usr/bin/volrmmount
/usr/sbin/allocate
/usr/sbin/mkdevalloc
/usr/sbin/mkdevmaps
/usr/sbin/ping
/usr/sbin/sacadm
```

```
/usr/sbin/whodo
/usr/sbin/deallocate
/usr/sbin/list_devices
/usr/sbin/ffbconfig
/usr/sbin/m64config
/usr/sbin/lpmove
/usr/sbin/pmconfig
/usr/sbin/static/rcp
/usr/ucb/ps
/proc/216/object/a.out
/proc/388/object/a.out
castle%
```

Access Control Lists (ACLs)

Access Control Lists (ACLs, pronounced "ackkls") can provide greater control over file permissions when traditional UNIX file permissions are not enough. UNIX file protection provides read, write, and execute permissions for three user classes: owner, group, and other. An ACL provides better file security by enabling you to define file permissions for the owner, owner's group, others, specific users, and groups. It also enables you to define default permissions for each of these categories.

For example, you might have two groups that need permission to access a file, one to read it and one to write to it. Alternatively, you might have a file that you wanted everyone in a group to be able to read, so you would give group read permissions on that file. Suppose that you want only two people in the group to be able to write to that file. With standard UNIX permissions, you cannot give write permission to only two members of a group. You can, however, set up an ACL for that file to grant only two people in the group write permissions on that file.

ACLs are extensions to standard UNIX file permissions. The ACL information is stored and associated with each file individually.

ACL Commands

You define an ACL for a file or directory by using the ACL commands and options listed in Table 18–8.

Table 18–8 ACL Commands and Options

Command/Option	Description
getfacl	Displays ACL entries.
-a	Displays the filename, owner, group, and ACL of the file.
-d	Displays the filename, owner, and group of the file. The information is displayed even if the file does not have an ACL.
setfacl	Sets, adds, modifies, and deletes ACL entries.

Table 18–8 ACL Commands and Options (continued)

Command/Option	Description
-s *acl_entries*	Sets the ACL for the file, removing all old entries and replacing them with the newly specified ACL.
-m *acl_entries*	Adds one or more new ACL entries to the file or modifies one or more existing ACL entries for the file. If an entry already exists, the specified permissions replace the current permissions. If no entry exists, a new entry is created.
-d *acl_entries*	Deletes one or more entries from the file. You cannot delete entries for the file owner, the owning group, and other. Note that deleting an entry does not necessarily have the same result as removing all permissions from the entry.
-f *acl_file*	Specifies a file containing the ACL entries to be used as arguments to the `setfacl` command.
-r	Recalculates permissions for the ACL mask. Permissions specified in the mask are ignored and replaced by the maximum permissions needed to give access to any additional user, owning group, and additional group entries in the ACL.

Each ACL entry consists of the following fields, which are separated by colons:

<entry-type>:[*<UID>*] ¦ [*<GID>*]:*<perms>*

Table 18–9 explains each of the elements of the syntax for ACL commands.

Table 18–9 ACL Argument Syntax

Argument	Description
<entry-type>	Type of ACL entry on which to set file permissions. For example, *<entry_type>* can be user (the owner of a file) or mask (the ACL mask).
<UID>	Username or identification number.
<GID>	Group name or identification number.
<perm>	Permissions set for the *<entry-type>*. Permissions can be set symbolically using the characters r, w, x, and - or by using octal values from 0 to 7.

NOTE. *ACLs are supported in UFS file systems only. If you restore or copy files with ACL entries in the* `/tmp` *directory, which is usually mounted as a TMPFS file system, the ACL entries are lost. If you need to temporarily store UFS files containing ACLs, use the* `/var/tmp` *directory instead.*

ACL Permissions for Files

You can set the following permissions for UFS files:

- u[ser]::*<perm>* Sets the permissions for the owner of the file.

- g[roup]::<*perm*> Sets the permissions for the owner's group.
- o[ther]::<*perm*> Sets the permissions for users other than the owner or members of the owner's group.
- m[ask]::<*perm*> Sets the ACL mask. The mask entry indicates the maximum permissions allowed for users other than the owner and for groups. Using the mask is a quick way to change permissions on all of the users and groups. For example, the mask:r-- and mask:4 entry indicates that users and groups cannot have more than read permissions, even though they may have write/execute permissions.
- u[ser]:<*UID*> ¦ <*username*>:<*perm*> Sets the permissions for a specific user.
- g[roup]:<*GID*> ¦ <*groupname*>:<*perm*> Sets the permissions for a specific group.

ACL Permissions for Directories

You can set default ACL entries on a directory that apply to files subsequently created within the directories. Files created in a directory that has default ACL entries will have the same ACL entries as the directory.

When you set default ACL entries for specific users and groups on a directory for the first time, you must also set default ACL entries for the owner, owner's group, others, and the mask.

- d[efault]:u[ser]::<*perm*> Sets the default permissions for the owner of the directory.
- d[efault]:g[roup]::<*perm*> Sets the default permissions for the owner's group.
- d[efault]:o[ther]::<*perm*> Sets the default permissions for users other than the owner or members of the owner's group.
- d[efault]:m[ask]::<*perm*> Sets the default ACL mask.
- d[efault]:u[ser]:<UID>:<*perm*> Sets the default permissions for a specific user.
- d[efault]:g[roup]:<GID>:<*perm*> Sets the default permissions for a specific group.

Determining If a File Has an ACL

You can determine if a file has an ACL in one of two ways:

- By using the ls -l command
- By using the getfacl command

When you use the ls -l command, any file that has an ACL displays a plus (+) sign to the right of the mode field.

NOTE. *If you define an ACL for a file and do not specify any additional users or groups, the plus sign is not displayed to the right of the mode field even though the file has a basic ACL. The plus sign is displayed only if additional users or groups are included in the ACL.*

In the following example, the file `foo` has an ACL and at least one entry in the list:

```
castle% ls -l foo
-rwxrw----+  1 winsor   staff          0 Oct  3 14:22 foo
castle
```

When you use the `getfacl <filename>` command with no options, the ACL information for the file is displayed in the following format:

```
# file: filename
# owner: uid
# group: gid
user::perm
user:uid:perm
group::perm
group:gid:perm
mask:perm
other:perm
default:user::perm
default:user:uid:perm
default:group::perm
default:group:gid:perm
```

The ACL for the file `foo` in the following example gives the owner of the file `rwx` permissions and user `ray` read-only permissions:

```
castle% getfacl foo

# file: foo
# owner: winsor
# group: staff
user::rwx
user:ray:r--              #effective:r--
group::rw-                #effective:rw-
mask:rw-
other:---
castle%
```

NOTE. *You can use the* `getfacl` *command to display permissions on any UFS file or directory in the same format. The file does not need to have an ACL.*

For comparison, the following example shows the output of the `ls -l` and `getfacl` commands for the file `bar`, which does not have an ACL.

```
castle% ls -l bar
-rwxrw----    1 winsor   staff          0 Oct  3 14:22 bar
castle% getfacl bar

# file: bar
# owner: winsor
# group: staff
user::rwx
group::rw-                #effective:rw-
mask:rw-
other:---
castle%
```

Setting ACL File Permissions

Use the `setfacl` command to set ACL permissions on a file. You can set the permissions for a file or a group of files from a command line or by listing the permissions in a file and using the file as an argument to the `setfacl` command. You can specify the permissions with the following syntax:

```
u[ser]::<perm>
u[ser]:uid:<perm>
g[roup]::<perm>
g[roup]:gid:<perm>
m[ask]:<perm>
o[ther]:<perm>
d[efault]:u[ser]::<perm>
d[efault]:u[ser]:uid:<perm>
d[efault]:g[roup]::<perm>
d[efault]:g[roup]:gid:<perm>
d[efault]:m[ask]:<perm>
d[efault]:o[ther]:<perm>
```

NOTE. *You can use either octal or symbolic values to set permissions.*

On a command line, use a comma to separate each permission statement. In an ACL file, put each statement on a separate line. The statements do not need to be in any particular order.

Setting Permissions for a File from a Command Line

To set ACL permissions from a command line, you must specify at least the basic set of user, group, other, and mask permissions. Type the following command to set ACL permissions: **setfacl -s u::<*perm*>,g::<*perm*>,o:<*perm*>, m:<*perm*>, [u:<UID>:<*perm*>], [g:<GID>:<*perm*>**

You can set users by using either their username or their UID number. Note that before you can use the username argument, the user account must already exist in the Passwd database or in the local `/etc/passwd` file. You can assign permissions to any UID by number, regardless of whether a user account exists.

In the same way, you can set group names by using either the group name or the GID number.

The following example assigns all of the permissions to the user, restricts group permissions to read-only, and denies permissions to other. The default mask sets read-write permissions, and user `ray` is assigned read-write permissions to the file `foo`.

First, take a look at the current permissions for the file:

```
castle% ls -l foo
-rw-rw-rw-   1 winsor   staff          0 Oct  3 14:22 foo
```

Then set permissions for user, group, owner, and the mask and add one user to the ACL:

```
castle% setfacl -s u::rwx,g::r--,o:---,mask:rw-,u:ray:rw- foo
```

Using octal values, as shown in the following example, gives you the same result:

```
castle% setfacl -s u::7,g::4,o:0,mask:6,u:ray:6 foo
```

Next, verify that the permissions have been set and that the file has an ACL:

```
castle% ls -l foo
-rwxrw----+  1 winsor   staff          0 Oct  3 14:22 foo
```

As you can see, the permissions for the file are changed and the plus sign after the permission field shows that the file has an ACL. Last, use the `getfacl` command to verify that everything has been set correctly:

```
castle% getfacl foo

# file: foo
# owner: winsor
# group: staff
user::rwx
user:ray:rw-            #effective:rw-
group::rw-              #effective:rw-
mask:rw-
other:---
castle%
```

The `getfacl` command always displays ACL permissions symbolically, regardless of how you specify the values from the command line.

Using an ACL Configuration File to Set Permissions

You can create an ACL configuration file that contains a list of the permissions you want to set and then use that filename as an argument to the `setfacl -s` command.

NOTE. *You can use a configuration file only with the* `-s` *option to the* `setfacl` *command.*

Use the following steps to set up the ACL configuration file:

1. Use any editor to create a file.
2. Edit the file to include the permissions you want to set, putting each statement on a separate line. Be sure to include permissions for user, group, other, and mask as a minimum set.
3. Save the file by using any filename you choose.
4. Type **setfacl -f *<acl_filename>* *<filename1>* [*<filename2>*] [*<filename3>*]** and press Return.
5. Type **getfacl *<filename1>* [*<filename2>*] [*<filename3>*]** and press Return to verify that the permissions are set correctly.

NOTE. *If you make typographical errors in the configuration file, the command might return a prompt without displaying any error messages. If you make syntax errors, the* `setfacl` *command might display an error message. Be sure to use the* `getfacl` *command to check that the permissions are set properly.*

In the following example, the owner has `rwx` permissions, group has `rw-`, other has `---`, and the mask is `rw-`. Three users with different permissions are also granted access to the file. The acl_file (named `anything`) contains the following access list:

```
u::rwx
g::rw-
o:---
m:rw-
u:ray:rwx
u:des:rw-
u:rob:r--
```

Once you have set up the ACL for the file named `anything`, you can use the `setfacl -f` option to assign those same permissions to one more file. In the following example, the file named `anything` is used as the argument to the `-f` option to change ACLs for the files `foo` and `bar` so that they match the file `anything`:

```
castle% setfacl -f anything foo bar
castle% getfacl foo bar

# file: foo
# owner: winsor
# group: staff
user::rwx
user:ray:rwx            #effective:rwx
user:des:rw-            #effective:rw-
user:rob:r--            #effective:r--
group::rw-              #effective:rw-
mask:rw-
other:---

# file: bar
# owner: winsor
# group: staff
user::rwx
user:ray:rwx            #effective:rwx
user:des:rw-            #effective:rw-
user:rob:r--            #effective:r--
group::rw-              #effective:rw-
mask:rw-
other:---
castle%
```

Adding and Modifying ACL Permissions

You can add and modify ACL permissions for a file that already has an ACL or for any existing UFS file or directory by using the `setfacl -m` command. Arguments to the `setfacl -m` command use the same syntax and structure as arguments to the `setfacl -s` command.

Because each file already has a default owner, group, other, and mask setting, you can use the `setfacl -m` command on any UFS file without first using the `setfacl -s` command to specify an owner, group, other, or mask setting. If the file already has the permissions you want to use, you can simply use the `setfacl -m` command to modify (and create) the ACL for any file or directory.

When you use the `-m` option, if an entry already exists for a specified UID or GID, the permissions you specify replace the current permissions. If an entry does not exist, it is created.

Type the following syntax to add and modify permissions for a file or files and press Return:

setfacl -m <acl_entry_list><*filename1*> [<*filename2*>] [<*filename3*>]

In the following example, permissions for user `ray` are modified from `rwx` to `rw-` for the file `foo`.

```
castle% setfacl -m u:ray:rw- foo
castle% getfacl foo

# file: foo
# owner: winsor
# group: staff
user::rw-
user:ray:rw-            #effective:rw-
group::rw-              #effective:rw-
mask:rw-
other:rw-
castle%
```

Deleting an ACL Entry

Use the `setfacl -d` command to delete an ACL entry. To delete the entry, you can specify the entry type and the UID or GID. You do not need to include the permissions as part of the argument to the `-d` option.

Type the following syntax to delete an ACL entry and then press Return:

setfacl -d <*entry_type*>:<*UID*> | <*GID*> <*filename1*> [<filename2>] [<filename3>]

In the following example, user `ray` is deleted from the ACL of the file `foo`.

```
castle% setfacl -d u:ray foo
castle% getfacl
usage: getfacl [-ad] file ...
castle% getfacl foo

# file: foo
# owner: winsor
# group: staff
user::rw-
group::rw-              #effective:rw-
mask:rw-
other:rw-
castle%
```

Copying ACL File Permissions

You can copy ACL file permissions from one file to another without specifying them on the command line by piping the output of `getfacl <filename>` to another file by typing the following syntax and pressing Return:

getfacl <*filename1*> | setfacl -f - <*filename2*>

In the following example, the ACL for file `foo` is used as the template for the ACL for file `bar`.

First, verify that the files have different ACL permissions:

```
castle% getfacl foo bar

# file: foo
# owner: winsor
# group: staff
user::rw-
user:ray:rwx            #effective:rw-
group::rw-              #effective:rw-
mask:rw-
other:rw-

# file: bar
# owner: winsor
# group: staff
user::rw-
group::rw-              #effective:rw-
mask:rw-
other:rw-
```

Then list the ACL using the `getfacl` command and pipe the output to the `setfacl -f` command. The dash (`-`) tells the `setfacl` command to use the output from the file specified for the getfacl command as input to the second file.

```
castle% getfacl foo | setfacl -f - bar
```

Finally, use the `getfacl` command to verify that both files now have the same ACL permissions:

```
castle% getfacl foo bar

# file: foo
# owner: winsor
# group: staff
user::rw-
user:ray:rwx            #effective:rw-
group::rw-              #effective:rw-
mask:rw-
other:rw-

# file: bar
# owner: winsor
# group: staff
user::rw-
user:ray:rwx            #effective:rw-
group::rw-              #effective:rw-
mask:rw-
other:rw-
castle%
```

Network Security

Networks create an interesting access and security paradox. Users on a network almost always push for freer access to information and files. System administrators almost always push for more restrictive access to information and files so that they can more effectively monitor use and secure access to sensitive information.

Network security is usually based on limiting or blocking operations from remote systems.

Network security comprises three aspects: firewall, authentication, and authorization, as illustrated in Figure 18–1.

Figure 18–1
Security Restrictions for remote operations.

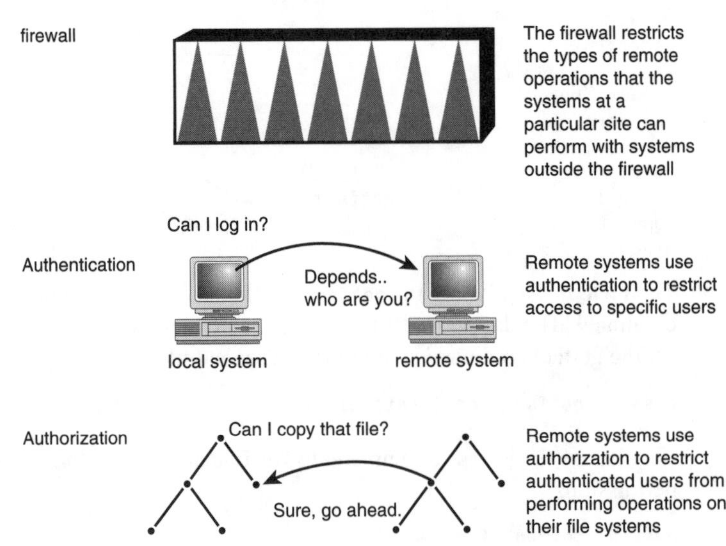
firewall
The firewall restricts the types of remote operations that the systems at a particular site can perform with systems outside the firewall
Can I log in?
Authentication
Depends.. who are you?
local system
remote system
Remote systems use authentication to restrict access to specific users
Authorization
Can I copy that file?
Sure, go ahead.
local file system
remote file system
Remote systems use authorization to restrict authenticated users from performing operations on their file systems

Firewall Systems

The purpose of creating a firewall network security system is to ensure that all of the communication between a local network and an external network conforms to your local network security policy. A network security policy can be permissive or restrictive. A permissive policy might allow access to all services unless specifically denied. A restrictive policy might deny access to all services unless specifically allowed.

You can set up a firewall system to help protect the resources in your network from outside access. A firewall system acts as a barrier between your internal network and outside networks.

The firewall has two functions:

- It acts as a gateway that passes data between the networks.
- It acts as a barrier that blocks the free passage of data to and from the network.

CAUTION! *A firewall prevents unauthorized users from accessing hosts on your network. Maintain strict and rigidly enforced security on the firewall. However, an intruder who can break into your firewall system may be able to gain access to all of the other hosts on the internal network.*

A firewall system should not have any trusted hosts. A *trusted host* is one from which a user can log in without being required to type in a password. The firewall system should not share any of its file systems or mount any file systems from other servers.

You can use ASET to make a system into a firewall and to enforce high security on a firewall system. For more information on ASET, refer to Chapter 20.

Two good reference books on firewalls are *Firewalls & Internet Security: Repelling the Wily Hacker* by Steven Cheswick and William Bellovin and *Building Internet Firewalls* by D. Brent Chapman and Elizabeth D. Zwicky. (See bibliography at the end of this book.)

Authentication and Authorization

Authentication is a way to restrict access to specific users when accessing a remote system. You can set authentication up at both the system and the network level. Once a user gains access to a remote system, *authorization* is a way to restrict operations that the user can perform on the remote system.

The types of authentication and authorization that can help protect your systems on the network against unauthorized use are listed in Table 18–10.

Table 18–10 Types of Authentication and Authorization

Type	Description
NIS+	The NIS+ name service can provide both authentication and authorization at the network level.
Remote login programs	The remote login programs (rlogin, rcp) enable users to log into a remote system over the network and use its resources. If you are a trusted host, authentication is automatic; otherwise, you are asked to authenticate yourself.
Secure RPC	Secure RPC improves the security of network environments by authenticating users who make requests on remote systems. You can use either the UNIX, DES, or Kerberos authentication system for Secure RPC.
DES Encryption	The Data Encryption Standard (DES) encryption functions use a 56-bit key to encrypt a secret key. Although DES is an encryption algorithm, it may be used as part of data authentication.
Diffie-Hellman Authentication	This authentication method is based on the capability of the sending system to use the common key to encrypt the current time, which the receiving system can decrypt and check against its current time.

Table 18–10 Types of Authentication and Authorization (continued)

Type	Description
Kerberos Version 4	Used to authenticate a user when logging in to the system.
Solstice AdminSuite	The Solstice AdminSuite product provides authentication and authorization mechanisms to remotely manage systems with the AdminSuite tools.

Monitoring Login Security Information

The following sections describe how to monitor login information in the following ways:

- Display a user's login status.
- Temporarily disable user logins.
- Save failed login attempts.

Displaying a User's Login Status

Use the `logins` command to display the status of users who are logged in. Using the `logins` command with no arguments displays a list of all user and system login accounts. Use the options listed in Table 18–11 to control the output displayed by the logins command.

Table 18–11 Options to the logins Command

Option	Description
`-a`	Add two password expiration fields to the display. The fields show how many days a password can remain unused before it automatically becomes inactive as well as the date that the password expires.
`-d`	List logins with duplicate UIDs.
`-m`	Display multiple group membership information.
`-o`	Format the output into one line of colon-separated fields.
`-p`	Display logins with no passwords.
`-s`	Display all system logins.
`-t`	Sort output by login name instead of by UID.
`-u`	Display all user logins.
`-x`	Print an extended set of information about each specified user. The extended information displays the home directory, login shell, and password aging information, each on a separate line. The password information includes password status (PS for password, NO for no password, or LK for locked). If the login is passworded, status is followed by the date the password was last changed, the number of days required between changes, and the number of days allowed before a change is required. The password aging information shows the time interval during which the user will receive a password expiration warning message at logon before the password expires.

Table 18–11 Options to the logins Command (continued)

Option	Description
`-g group`	Lists all users belonging to the group, sorted by login. You can specify multiple groups as a comma-separated list.
`-l login`	Lists the requested login. You can specify multiple logins as a comma-separated list. Depending on the name service lookup types set in `/etc/nsswitch.conf`, the information can come from the `/etc/passwd` and `/etc/shadow` files and other name services.

The `logins` command uses the following syntax:

```
/usr/bin/logins [-admopstux] [-g <group1>,<group2>...]
[-l <login1>,<login2>...]
```

You can group options together. When you group options, any login that matches any criteria is displayed. When you combine the `-l` and `-g` options, a user is listed only once, even if the user belongs to more than one of the specified groups.

NOTE. *You must be superuser to run the* `logins` *command.*

The following example shows the output of the `logins` command, which is used with no arguments:

```
castle% su
Password:
# logins
root         0        other       1        Super-User
smtp         0        root        0        Mail Daemon User
daemon       1        other       1
bin          2        bin         2
sys          3        sys         3
adm          4        adm         4        Admin
uucp         5        uucp        5        uucp Admin
nuucp        9        nuucp       9        uucp Admin
listen       37       adm         4        Network Admin
lp           71       lp          8        Line Printer Admin
winsor       1001     staff       10
ray          1002     staff       10
des          1003     staff       10
rob          1004     staff       10
nobody       60001    nobody      60001    Nobody
noaccess     60002    noaccess    60002    No Access User
nobody4      65534    nogroup     65534    SunOS 4.x Nobody
#
```

The following example displays an extended set of login status information for user `winsor`.

```
# logins -x -l winsor
winsor       1001     staff       10
                      /export/home/winsor
                      /bin/csh
```

```
                    PS 000000 -1 -1 -1
#
```

The following example shows a list of user accounts with no password.

```
# logins -p
ray            1002    staff           10
des            1003    staff           10
rob            1004    staff           10
#
```

The following example shows extended login status for all user accounts on a standalone system.

```
# logins -xu
winsor         1001    staff           10
                       /export/home/winsor
                       /bin/csh
                       PS 000000 -1 -1 -1
ray            1002    staff           10
                       /export/home/ray
                       /bin/csh
                       NP 000000 -1 -1 -1
des            1003    staff           10
                       /export/home/des
                       /bin/csh
                       NP 000000 -1 -1 -1
rob            1004    staff           10
                       /export/home/rob
                       /bin/csh
                       NP 000000 -1 -1 -1
nobody         60001   nobody          60001   Nobody
                       /
                       /sbin/sh
                       LK 082587 -1 -1 -1
noaccess       60002   noaccess        60002   No Access User
                       /
                       /sbin/sh
                       LK 082587 -1 -1 -1
nobody4        65534   nogroup         65534   SunOS 4.x Nobody
                       /
                       /sbin/sh
                       LK 082587 -1 -1 -1
#
```

Temporarily Disabling User Logins

You can temporarily disable logins to prevent new login sessions in one of two ways:

- Bringing the system to run level 0 (single-user mode)
- Creating an `/etc/nologin` file

When a system will not be available for an extended time, you can create an `/etc/nologin` file to prevent users from logging in to the system. When a user logs in to a system that has an

`/etc/nologin` file, the message in the `/etc/nologin` file is displayed and the user login is terminated. Superuser logins are not affected by the `/etc/nologin` file.

Use the following steps to create an `/etc/nologin` file:

1. Become superuser.
2. Use any editor to create a file named `/etc/nologin`.
3. Type the message that will be displayed to users when they log in to the system. If possible, include specific information about when logins will be permitted or how users can find out when they will be able to access the system again.
4. Save the changes and close the file.

The following example shows the text of a `nologin` file:

```
# cat /etc/nologin
No Logins Are Currently Permitted

The system will be unavailable until 12 noon on Friday, October 24.
#
```

Saving Failed Login Attempts

If it is important for you to track whether users are trying to log in to your user accounts, you can create a `/var/adm/loginlog` file with read and write permissions for root only. After you create the loginlog file, all failed login activity is written to this file automatically after five failed attempts. The five-try limit avoids recording failed attempts that are the result of typographical errors.

The `loginlog` file contains one entry for each failed attempt. Each entry contains the user's login name, tty device, and time of the attempt.

NOTE. *The* `loginlog` *file may grow quickly. To use the information in this file and prevent it from getting too large, check and clear its contents regularly. If this file shows a lot of activity, it may suggest that someone is trying to break into the computer system. If you regularly track information from the* `loginlog` *file, consider creating a* `cron` *entry to track and clear out the* `loginlog` *file.*

Use the following steps to create a `loginlog` file:

1. Become superuser.
2. Type **touch /var/adm/loginlog** and press Return.
3. Type **chmod 700 /var/adm/loginlog** and press Return.
4. Type **chgrp sys /var/adm/loginlog** and press Return.
5. Make sure the log works by trying to log in to the system six times with the wrong password.

6. Type **more /var/adm/loginlog** and review the output to make sure the login attempts are being logged successfully.

Sharing Files

A network server can control which files are available for sharing. It can also control which clients have access to the files and what type of access is permitted to those clients. In general, the file server can grant read/write or read-only access either to all clients or to specific clients. Access control is specified when resources are made available by using the `share` command.

A server can use the `/etc/dfs/dfstab` file to list the file systems it makes available to clients on the network. See the *Solaris System Administrator's Guide* for more information about sharing files (see bibliography at the end of this book).

Restricting Superuser (root) Access

In general, superuser on a local system is not allowed root access to file systems shared across the network. Unless the server specifically grants superuser privileges, a user who is logged in as superuser on a client cannot gain root access to files that are remotely mounted on the client. The NFS system implements this by changing the user ID (usually `60001`) of the requester to the user ID of the user named `nobody`. The access rights of user `nobody` are the same as those given to the public or to a user without credentials for a particular file. For example, if the public has only execute permission for a file, then user `nobody` can only execute that file.

An NFS server can grant superuser privileges on a shared file system on a per-host basis, using the `root=<hostname>` option to the `share` command.

Controlling and Monitoring Superuser Access

The following sections describe how to restrict and monitor superuser access in the following ways:

- Restrict superuser login to the console.
- Monitor who is using the `su` command.

Restricting Superuser Logins to the Console

The superuser account has complete control over the entire operating system. It has access to and can execute essential system programs. For this reason, there are almost no security restraints for any program that is run by superuser.

You can protect the superuser account on a system by restricting access to a specific device through the `/etc/default/login` file. For example, if superuser access is restricted to the console, root can log in to a system only from the console. If individuals remotely log in to the system to perform administrative functions, they must first log in with their user logins and then use the `su` command to become superuser.

NOTE. *Restricting superuser login to the console is the default setup when a system is installed.*

Use the following steps to restrict superuser (root) login to the console:

1. Become superuser.
2. Edit the `/etc/default/login` file and remove the # comment from the beginning of the `#CONSOLE=/dev/console` line.
3. Save the changes to the file.
4. Try to `rlogin` to the system as superuser and verify that the operation fails.

Monitoring Who Is Using the su Command

You can monitor `su` attempts with the `/etc/default/su` file. By using this file, you can enable the `/var/adm/sulog` file to monitor each time the `su` command is used to change to another user.

NOTE. *Enabling the* `/var/adm/sulog` *file to monitor* `su` *use is the default setup when a system is installed.*

The `sulog` file lists all uses of the `su` command, not only those used to switch user to superuser. The entries show the date and time the command was used, whether or not it was successful (+ or -), the port from which the command was issued, and the name of the user and the switched identity.

Use the following steps to monitor who is using the `su` command:

1. Become superuser.
2. Edit the `/etc/default/login` file and remove the remove the # comment from the beginning of the `#SULOG=/var/adm/sulog` line.
3. Save the changes to the file.
4. Use the `su` command several times and, as superuser, display the contents of the `/var/adm/sulog` file.

The following example shows the tail of the `/var/adm/sulog` file.

```
castle% su
Password:
# tail -20 /var/adm/sulog
SU 10/07 10:35 + pts/3 winsor-root
SU 10/07 15:05 + console root-daemon
SU 10/07 15:54 + console root-daemon
SU 10/07 16:28 + pts/3 winsor-root
SU 10/08 08:23 + console root-daemon
SU 10/08 09:43 + pts/3 winsor-root
SU 10/08 10:03 + pts/3 winsor-root
SU 10/08 12:34 + pts/3 winsor-des
SU 10/08 12:39 + pts/3 winsor-root
```

```
SU 10/08 12:39 + pts/3 winsor-des
SU 10/08 12:39 - pts/3 winsor-ray
SU 10/08 12:39 - pts/3 winsor-ray
SU 10/08 12:39 - pts/3 winsor-ray
SU 10/08 12:39 - pts/3 winsor-ray
SU 10/08 12:40 - pts/3 winsor-ray
SU 10/08 12:40 - pts/3 winsor-ray
SU 10/08 12:40 + pts/3 winsor-root
SU 10/08 12:41 + pts/5 winsor-root
SU 10/08 12:44 + console root-daemon
SU 10/08 12:56 + pts/3 winsor-root
#
```

Using Privileged Ports

Secure RPC is a method of providing additional security that authenticates both the host and the user making a request. For more information about Secure RPC, refer to Chapter 19, "Using Authentication Services." If you do not want to run Secure RPC, a possible substitute is the Solaris *privileged port* mechanism. A privileged port is built up by the superuser with a port number of less than 1024. After a client system has authenticated the client's credentials, it builds a connection to the server via the privileged port. The server then verifies the client credential by examining the connection's port number.

Non-Solaris clients might not, however, be able to communicate via the privileged port. If they cannot, you might see error messages such as `Weak Authentication NFS request from unprivileged port`.

Automated Security Enhancement Tool (ASET)

The ASET security package provides automated administration tools that enable you to control and monitor system security. You specify a security level—low, medium, or high— at which ASET runs. At each higher level, ASET's file control functions increase to reduce file access and tighten your system security. For more information, see Chapter 20, "Using the Automated Security Enhancement Tool (ASET)."

CHAPTER

19

Using Authentication Services

DES Encryption

Diffie-Hellman Authentication

Kerberos Version 4

The Pluggable Authentication Module (PAM) Framework

ECURE RPC IS A METHOD OF PROVIDING ADDITIONAL SECURITY THAT AUTHENTICATES THE host and the user making a request. Secure RPC uses either Diffie-Hellman or Kerberos authentication. Both of these authentication mechanisms use DES (data encryption standard) encryption. Applications that use Secure RPC include NFS and the NIS+ name service.

The NFS software enables several hosts to share files over the network. The clients have access to the file systems that the server exports to the clients. Users logged in to the client system can access the file systems by mounting them from the server. To the user on the client system, the files seem to be local. One of the most common uses of the NFS environment is to enable systems to be installed in offices while keeping all user files in a central location. Some features of the NFS system, such as the `-nosuid` mount option, can be used to prohibit the opening of devices as well as file systems.

The NFS environment can use Secure RPC to authenticate users who make requests over the network. This combination is known as *Secure NFS*. The authentication mechanism, AUTH_DH, uses DES encryption with Diffie-Hellman authentication to ensure authorized access. The AUTH_DH mechanism has also been called AUTH_DES. The AUTH_KERB4 mechanism uses DES encryption with Kerberos authentication. This mechanism has also been called AUTH_KERB.

This chapter describes the following elements of Secure RPC:

- Data Encryption Standard (DES) encryption
- Diffie-Hellman authentication
- Kerberos Version 4
- Pluggable Authentication Module (PAM)

DES Encryption

The data encryption standard (DES) functions use a 56-bit key to encrypt user data. If two credential users (or principals) know the same DES key, they can communicate in private, using the key to encipher and decipher text. DES is a relatively fast encryption mechanism. A DES chip makes the encryption even faster; if the chip is not present, though, a software implementation is substituted.

The risk of using just DES is that, with enough time, an intruder can collect enough cipher-text messages encrypted with the same key to be able to discover the key and decipher the messages. For this reason, security systems such as Secure RPC change the keys frequently.

Diffie-Hellman Authentication

The Diffie-Hellman method of authenticating a user is non-trivial for an intruder to crack. The client and the server each has its own private key (sometimes called a *secret key*) which they use together with the public key to devise a *common key*. They use the common key to communicate with each other, using an agreed-upon encryption/decryption function such as DES. This method was identified as *DES authentication* in previous Solaris releases.

Authentication is based on the capability of the sending system to use the common key to encrypt the current time, which the receiving system can decrypt and check against its current time. Because Diffie-Hellman depends on the current times matching, the keyserver program first synchronizes the time between the client and server.

The public and private keys are stored in an NIS or NIS+ database. NIS stores the keys in the public key map, and NIS+ stores the keys in the cred table. These files contain the public key and the private key for all potential users.

The system administrator is responsible for setting up NIS or NIS+ tables and generating a public key and a private key for each user. The private key is stored encrypted with the user's password. This makes the private key known only to the user.

How Diffie-Hellman Authentication Works

This section describes the series of transactions in a client-server session using DH authorization (`AUTH_DH`).

Generating the Public and Secret Keys

Some time before a transaction, the administrator runs either the `newkey` or `nisaddcred` commands that generate a public key and a secret key. Each user has a unique public key and secret key. The public key is stored in a public database; the secret key is stored in encrypted form in the same database. To change the key pair, use the `chkey` command.

Running the keylogin Command

Normally, the login password is identical to the secure RPC password. In this case, a `keylogin` is not required. If the passwords are different, the users have to log in and then do an explicit `keylogin`.

The `keylogin` program prompts the user for a secure RPC password and uses the password to decrypt the secret key. The `keylogin` program then passes the decrypted secret key to a program called the keyserver. The *keyserver* is an RPC service with a local instance on every computer. The keyserver saves the decrypted secret key and waits for the user to initiate a Secure RPC transaction with a server.

If the passwords are the same, the login process passes the secret key to the keyserver. If the passwords are required to be different and the user must always run `keylogin`, then the `keylogin` program may be included in the user's environment configuration file such as `~/.login`, `~/.cshrc`, or `~/.profile`, so that it runs automatically whenever the user logs in.

Generating the Conversion Key

When the user initiates a transaction with a server:

1. The keyserver randomly generates a conversation key.
2. The kernel uses the conversation key to encrypt the client's time stamp (among other things).
3. The keyserver looks up the server's public key in the public-key database (see the `publickey`(4) manual page).
4. The keyserver uses the client's secret key and the server's public key to create a common key.
5. The keyserver encrypts the conversation key with the common key.

First Contact with the Server

The transmission including the encrypted time stamp and the encrypted conversation key is then sent to the server. The transmission includes a credential and a verifier. The credential has three components:

- The client's Net name
- The conversation key, encrypted with the common key
- A "window," encrypted with the conversation key

The *window* is the difference the client says should be allowed between the server's clock and the client's time stamp. If the difference between the server's clock and the time stamp is greater than the window, the server rejects the client's request. Under normal circumstances, the request is not rejected because the client first synchronizes with the server before starting the RPC session.

The client's verifier contains:

- The encrypted time stamp
- An encrypted verifier of the specified window, decremented by 1

The *window verifier* is needed in case an outsider wants to impersonate a user and writes a program that, instead of filling in the encrypted fields of the credential and verifier, just stuffs in random bits. The server decrypts the conversation key into some random key and uses it to try to decrypt the window and time stamp. The result is random numbers. After a few thousand trials, however, there is a good chance that the random window/time stamp pair will pass the authentication system. The window verifier makes guessing the right credential much more difficult.

Decrypting the Conversation Key

When the server receives the transmission from the client:

1. The keyserver local to the server looks up the client's public key in the public-key database.
2. The keyserver uses the client's public key and the server's secret key to deduce the common key—the same common key computed by the client. Only the server and the client can calculate the common key because doing so requires knowing one secret key or the other.
3. The kernel uses the common key to decrypt the conversation key.
4. The kernel calls the keyserver to decrypt the client's time stamp with the decrypted conversation key.

Storing Information on the Server

After the server decrypts the client's time stamp, it stores four items of information in a credential table:

- The client's computer name
- The conversation key
- The window
- The client's time stamp

The server stores the first three items for future use. It stores the time stamp to protect against replays. The server accepts only time stamps that are chronologically greater than the last one seen, so any replayed transactions are guaranteed to be rejected.

NOTE. *Implicit in these procedures is the name of the caller, who must be authenticated in some manner. The keyserver cannot use DES authentication to do this because it would create a deadlock. To solve this problem, the keyserver stores the secret keys by UID and grants requests only to local root processes.*

Verifier Returned to the Client

The server returns a verifier to the client, which includes:

- The index ID, which the server records in its credential cache
- The client's time stamp minus 1, encrypted by the conversation key

The reason for subtracting 1 from the time stamp is to ensure that the time stamp is invalid and cannot be reused as a client verifier.

Client Authenticates the Server

The client receives the verifier and authenticates the server. The client knows that only the server could have sent the verifier because only the server knows what time stamp the client sent.

Additional Transactions

With every transaction after the first, the client returns the index ID to the server in its second transaction and sends another encrypted time stamp. The server sends back the client's time stamp minus 1, encrypted by the conversation key.

Administering Diffie-Hellman Authentication

This section describes the commands used to administer Secure RPC and provides instructions for the following tasks associated with network security:

- Restarting the keyserver
- Setting up NIS+ credentials for Diffie-Hellman authentication
- Setting up NIS credentials for Diffie-Hellman authentication
- Sharing and mounting files with Diffie-Hellman authentication

Secure RPC Commands

Table 19–1 lists manual pages that provide useful reference information about Secure RPC.

Table 19–1 Secure RPC Manual Page References

Command	Description
`secure_rpc(3N)`	Description of Secure RPC library routines for secure remote procedure calls.
`rpc(3N)`	Description of RPC library routines for secure remote procedure calls.
`attributes(5)`	Characteristics of commands, utilities, and device drivers.

Table 19–2 lists commands used to administer Diffie-Hellman authentication.

Table 19–2 Secure RPC Commands

Command	Description
`chkey`	Change user's Secure RPC key pair.
`getpublickey`	Retrieve public key.

Table 19–2 Secure RPC Commands (continued)

Command	Description
getsecretkey	Retrieve secret key.
keylogin	Decrypt and store secret key with keyserv.
keylogout	Delete stored secret key with keyserv.
keyserv	Daemon for storing private encryption keys.
login	Sign on to a system.
newkey	Create a new Diffie-Hellman pair in the public-key database.
nisaddcred	Create NIS+ credentials.
nisclient	Initialize NIS+ credentials for NIS+ principals.
publickey	Retrieve public or secret key.

Restarting the Keyserver

The keyserv daemon must be running before Diffie-Hellman authentication can work properly. Normally, the keyserver is started at boot time by the `rc2` script that runs the `/etc/rc2.d/S71rpc` script.

If the keyserv daemon dies or is not running on a system, use the following steps to restart it:

1. Become superuser.
2. Type **ps -ef | grep keyserv** and press Return. Check the output to verify that the keyserv daemon is not running.
3. Type **/usr/sbin/keyserv** and press Return.

In the following example, the `ps -ef` command is used to verify that the keyserv daemon is not running, the keyserv daemon is restarted, and the `ps -ef` command is used again to verify that it is now running.

```
castle% su
Password:
castle# ps -ef ¦ grep keyserv
    root   727   722  0 12:58:25 pts/3    0:00 grep keyserv
castle# /usr/sbin/keyserv
castle# ps -ef ¦ grep keyserv
    root   729     1  0 12:58:46 ?        0:00 /usr/sbin/keyserv
    root   733   722  0 12:58:57 pts/3    0:00 grep keyserv
castle#
```

NOTE. *If you start the keyserv daemon when it is already running, the message* `/usr/sbin/keyserv: unable to create service` *is displayed.*

Setting Up NIS+ Credentials for Diffie-Hellman Authentication

To set up Diffie-Hellman authentication for the NIS+ name service, you must set up a new key for both root and user accounts. This section describes how to set up a new key for these two accounts.

To set up a new key for root on an NIS+ client:

1. Become superuser on the client.
2. Edit the publickey entry in the `/etc/nsswitch.conf` file to read **publickey: nisplus**.
3. Type **nisinit -cH *<hostname>*** and press Return to initialize the NIS+ client.
4. Type **nisaddcred local** and press Return.
5. Type **nisaddcred des** and press Return. The client is added to the cred table.
6. When prompted, type the network password.
7. When prompted, retype the network password.
8. Type **keylogin** and press Return. If you are prompted for a password, the procedure succeeded.

The following example uses the host `castle` to set up `seachild` as an NIS+ client. You can ignore the warnings. The `keylogin` command is accepted, verifying that `seachild` is correctly set up as a secure NIS+ client.

```
# nisinit -cH castle
NIS Server/Client setup utility.
This machine is in the Castle.Abc.COM. directory.
Setting up NIS+ client ...
All done.

# nisaddcred local
# nisaddcred des
DES principal name: unix.seachild@Castle.Abc.COM (seachild.Castle.Abc,COM.)

Network password: xxx <Press Return>
Warning, password differs from login password.
Retype password: xxx <Press Return>

# keylogin
Password:
#
```

To set up a new key for an NIS+ user:

1. On the root master server, type **nisaddcred -p unix.*<UID@domainname>* -P *<username.domainname.>* des** and press Return. Note that the *username.domainname.* must end with a dot (.).

2. Rlogin to the root master server as the client, type **keylogin**, and press Return. If you are prompted for a password, the procedure succeeded.

The following example gives DES security authorization to user `ray` and connects to the system named rootmaster as login `ray` to check the connection.

```
# nisaddcred -p unix.1002@Castle.Abcv.COM -P ray.Castle.Abc.COM. des
DES principal name : unix.1002@ Castle.Abc.COM
Adding new key for unix.1002@Castle.Abc.Com (ray.Castle.Abc.COM.)

Password:
Retype password:

# rlogin rootmaster -l ray
# keylogin
Password:
#
```

Setting Up NIS Credentials for Diffie-Hellman Authentication

This section describes how to set up NIS credentials for Diffie-Hellman authentication. You must set up a new key for both root and user accounts.

To create a new key for superuser on a client:

1. Become superuser on the client.
2. Edit the publickey entry in the `/etc/nsswitch.conf` file to read **publickey: nis**.
3. Type **newkey -h *<hostname>*** and press Return. This command creates a new key pair.
4. When prompted, type the password.
5. When prompted, retype the password.

The following example sets up `seachild` as a secure NIS client.

```
# newkey -h seachild
Adding new key for unix.seachild@Castle.Abc.COM
New Password:
Retype Password:
Please wait for the database to get updated...
Your new key has been successfully stored away
#
```

Only the system administrator who is logged into the NIS server can generate a new key for a user. To create a new key for a user:

1. Log in to the NIS server as superuser.
2. Type **newkey -u *<username>*** and press Return. The system prompts for a password. You can type a generic password.
3. When prompted, type the password.

4. When prompted, retype the password.
5. Instruct the user to log in and type the **chkey -p** command.

The following example creates a newkey for user `ray`:

```
# newkey -u ray
Adding a new key for unix.1002@Castle.Abc.COM
New Password:
Retype password:
Please wait for the database to get updated...
Your new key has been successfully stored away.
#

seachild% chkey -p
Updating nis publickey database.
Reencrypting key for unix.1002@Castle.Abc.COM
Please enter the Secure-RPC password for ray:
Please enter the login password for ray:
Sending key change request to castle...
seachild%
```

Sharing and Mounting Files with Diffie-Hellman Authentication

Before you can share files from a server and mount file systems on clients with Diffie-Hellman authentication, the Diffie-Hellman publickey authentication must be enabled on the network.

To share a file system with Diffie-Hellman authentication:

1. On the server, become superuser.
2. Type **share -F nfs -o sec_dh /*<filesystem>*** and press Return.

To mount a file system with Diffie-Hellman authentication, specify the -o `sec=dh` option to the `mount` command:

1. On the client, become superuser.
2. Check to make sure the mount point is available. If not, type **mkdir *<directory-name>*** and press Return to create the mount point.
3. Type **mount -F nfs -o sec=dh *<server>*:*<resource>* *<mountpoint>*** and press Return.

Kerberos Version 4

Kerberos is an authentication system that was developed at the Massachusetts Institute of Technology. Kerberos uses DES to authenticate a user when logging in to the system. *Authentication* is based on the capability of the sending system to use the common key to encrypt the current time, which the receiving system can decrypt and check against its current time. Kerberos Version 4 is supported in the Solaris 2.6 release.

Kerberos works by authenticating the user's login password. A user enters the `kinit` command, which acquires a ticket that is valid for the time of the session (or eight hours, the default session time) from the Kerberos authentication server. When the user logs out, the ticket can be destroyed (by using the `kdestroy` command).

NOTE. *Solaris 2.6 provides the capability to connect to the Kerberos functionality. However, it does not provide the Kerberos package. You can* `ftp` *Kerberos 4 source from athena-dist. mit.edu using* ***anonymous*** *as a username and your email address as a password. The source is located in the* `pub/kerberos` *directory.*

The Kerberos software is available from MIT project Athena, and is not part of the SunOS 5.*x* software. The SunOs 5.*x* software provides:

- Commands and APIs used by the client to create, acquire, and verify tickets
- An authentication option to Secure RPC
- A client-side daemon, `kerbd`(1M)

How Kerberos Authentication Works with NFS

This section provides an overview of how the Kerberos authentication procedure works. The following process assumes that the Kerberos key distribution center (KDC) is already installed on the network, using publicly available sources from MIT project Athena.

1. The `/usr/sbin/kerbd` daemon must be running on both the NFS client and server. This daemon is normally started when needed by `inetd`. You can use the `rpcinfo` command to make sure that the `kerbd` service is registered. `kerbd` is the user-mode daemon that interfaces with the kernel RPC and the KDC. It generates and validates authentication tickets.
2. The system administrator sets up the NFS server to use Kerberos authentication. The MIT Kerberos software is used to register the principal names in the Kerberos KDC on the kerberos server. The following entries are required:
   - `root.`*<hostname>* (required for each NFS client)
   - `nfs.`*<hostname>* (required for each NFS server)
3. The user mounts the shared file system. The user on the client must get a ticket for root on the client to mount the shared file system.
4. The user logs in to the kerberos service by using the `kinit` command. The Kerberos authentication server authenticates the request and grants a ticket for the ticket-granting service.
5. The user accesses the mounted directory. The `kerbd` daemon automatically secures a ticket on behalf of the client for the NFS server exporting the file system. At this point, there are two valid tickets: the original ticket-granting ticket and one for the server.

6. The user destroys the tickets at the end of the session to prevent them from being compromised. The `kdestroy` command destroys the user's active kerberos authorization tickets by writing zeros to the file that contains the tickets. You can put the `kdestroy` command in the user's `.logout` file so that all Kerberos tickets are automatically destroyed when the user logs out of the system.
7. If tickets have been destroyed before the session has finished, the user must request a new ticket with the `kinit` command.

Administering Kerberos Version 4 Authentication

This section describes the command used to administer Kerberos and provides instructions for the following tasks associated with network security:

- Sharing and mounting files with Kerberos authentication
- Acquiring a Kerberos ticket for superuser on a client
- Logging in to the Kerberos service
- Listing Kerberos tickets
- Accessing a directory with Kerberos authentication
- Destroying a Kerberos ticket

Table 19–3 lists commands used to administer Kerberos authentication.

Table 19–3 Kerberos Commands

Command	Description
`kdestroy`	Destroy Kerberos tickets.
`kerbd`	Daemon that generates and validates Kerberos tickets for kernel RPC.
`kinit`	Log in to Kerberos authentication and authorization system.
`klist`	List currently held Kerberos tickets.
`ksrvtgt`	Fetch and store Kerberos ticket-granting ticket using a service key.

Refer to the MIT documentation for details about how to set up and administer Kerberos. Also refer to the `kerberos`(1), `kerberos`(3N), and `krb.conf`(4) manual pages for useful reference information about Kerberos.

Acquiring a Kerberos Ticket for Superuser on a Client

If the NFS file system you need to access has not been mounted, you need to acquire a ticket for superuser on the client before mounting it.

To acquire a ticket for a not-yet-mounted file system:

1. Become superuser.
2. Type **kinit root.<*hostname*>** and press Return.
3. When prompted, type the password. The `root.<hostname>` entry for the client is entered into the `/etc/srvtab` configuration file.

In the following example, `seachild` is the name of the client system:

```
# kinit root.seachild
Password:
#
```

If the `root.<hostname>` for the client is present in the `/etc/srvtab` configuration file, you can use the `ksrvtgt` command to get a ticket for superuser. In this case, you are not required to give a superuser password. Consult the MIT documentation for information on how to initialize the `/etc/srvtab` file.

To acquire a ticket for superuser when `root.<hostname>` is present in the `/etc/srvtab` configuration file:

1. Become superuser.
2. Type **ksrvtgt root.<*hostname*>** and press Return.

In the following example, a Kerberos ticket is acquired for superuser on the client `seachild`:

```
#ksrvtgt root.seachild
#
```

Sharing and Mounting Files with Kerberos Authentication

Before you can share a file system from the server and mount file systems on clients with Kerberos authentication, Kerberos Version 4 authentication must be enabled on the network.

To share a file system with Kerberos authentication, you specify the `-o sec=krb4` option to the `share` command:

1. On the server, become superuser.
2. Type **share -F nfs -o sec=krb4 /<*filesystem*>** and press Return.

To mount a file system with Kerberos authentication, you specify the `-o sec=krb4` option to the `mount` command:

1. On the client, become superuser.
2. Check to make sure the mount point exists. If not, type **mkdir <*directory-name*>** and press Return to create the mount point.
3. Type **mount -F nfs -o sec=krb4 <*server*>:<*resource*> <*mountpoint*>** and press Return.

Logging In to Kerberos Service

You log in to the Kerberos service by using the `kinit -l` *<username>* command.

To log in to the Kerberos service:

1. Type **kinit -l *<username>*** and press Return.
2. Type the number of minutes you want the Kerberos ticket to be valid.
3. Type your password.

In the following example, user `ray` logs in to Kerberos service with a ticket lifetime of 60 minutes:

```
seachild% kinit -l ray
SunOS (seachild)
Kerberos Initialization for "ray"
Kerberos ticket lifetime (minutes): 60
Password:
seachild%
```

Listing Kerberos Tickets

You list tickets by using the `klist` command. The following example shows a ticket for user `ray`.

```
seachild% klist
Ticket file: /tmp/tkt8765
Principal: ray@Castle.Abc.COM
  Issued              Expires            Principal
  Oct 10 15:15:56     Oct 10:16:15:56    krbtgt.Castle.Abc.COM@Castle.Abc.com
```

Accessing a Directory with Kerberos Authentication

You access a Kerberos mounted directory just as you would any other mounted directory: by typing **cd /*<mountpoint>***. You can list the files in the directory by using the `ls` command or list the Kerberos tickets by using the `klist` command.

Destroying a Kerberos Ticket

You destroy Kerberos tickets by using the `kdestroy` command. You should destroy Kerberos tickets when the session is over so that an unauthorized user cannot gain access to them. If you want to reinitiate Kerberos authentication after tickets are destroyed, use the `kinit` command.

The following example shows how to destroy Kerberos tickets. After the tickets are destroyed, if the user tries to change to or list a Kerberos-protected directory, the ticket server denies access.

```
seachild% kdestroy
Tickets destroyed
seachild% ls /mntkrb
```

```
Can't get Kerberos key: No ticket file (tf_util)
NSF getattr failed for server castle: RPC: Authentication error
cannot access directory /mntkrb.
seachild%
```

The Pluggable Authentication Module (PAM) Framework

PAM enables you to "plug in" new authentication technologies without changing system entry services such as login, ftp, telnet, and so on. You can also use PAM to integrate UNIX login with other security mechanisms such as DES or Kerberos. You can also plug in mechanisms for account, session, and password management by using this framework. The PAM framework enables you to choose any combination of system entry services (for example, ftp, login, telnet, or rsh) for user authentication.

PAM Module Types

PAM employs run-time pluggable modules to provide authentication for system entry services. These modules are broken down into four different types based on their function:

- The *authentication modules* provide authentication for users and enables credentials to be set, refreshed, or destroyed. They provide a valuable administration tool for user identification.
- The *account modules* check for password aging, account expiration, and access hour restrictions. After the user is identified through the authentication modules, the account modules determine if the user should be given access.
- The *session modules* manage the opening and closing of an authentication session. They can log activity or provide for clean-up after the session is over.
- The *password modules* enable changes to the actual password.

Stacking Feature

A *stacking* feature is provided to let you authenticate users through multiple services. Depending on the configuration, users can be prompted for passwords for each authentication method. The order in which the authentication services are used is determined through the PAM configuration file, `/etc.pam.conf`.

Password-Mapping Feature

The stacking method can require that a user remember several passwords. With the *password-mapping* feature, the primary password is used to decrypt the other passwords so that the user does not need to remember or enter multiple passwords. The other option is to synchronize the passwords across each authentication mechanism. Note that synchronizing passwords can increase the security risk, because the security of each mechanism is limited by the least secure password method used in the stack.

How PAM Works

The PAM software consists of a library, several modules, and a configuration file. New versions of several system entry commands or daemons that take advantage of the PAM interfaces are also included.

Figure 19–1 shows the relationship between the applications, the PAM library, the `pam.conf` file, and the PAM modules.

Figure 19–1
How PAM works.

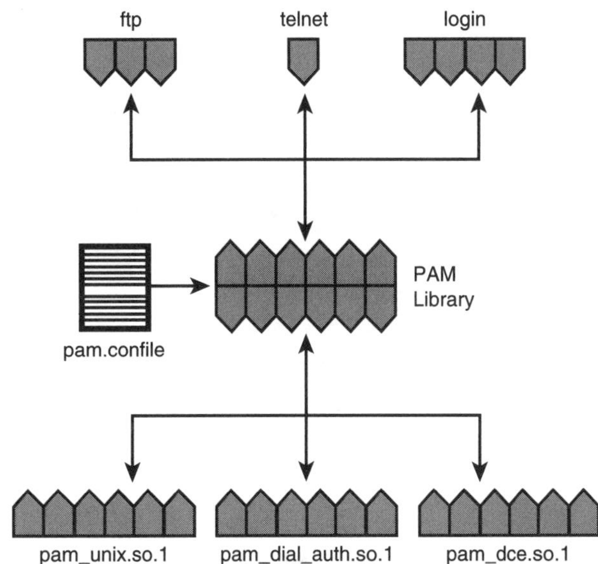

The `ftp`, `telnet`, and `login` programs use the PAM library to access the appropriate module. The `pam.conf` file defines which modules to use, and in what order they are to be used with each command. Responses from the modules are passed back through the library to the application.

PAM Library and Modules

The PAM library files found in the `/usr/lib/security` directory provide the framework to load the appropriate modules and manage the stacking process. They provide a generic structure to which all of the modules can plug in.

Each PAM module implements a specific mechanism. When setting up PAM authentication, you need to specify both the module and the module type, which defines what the module will do. More than one module type (auth, account, session, or password) may be associated with each module. The following list describes each of the PAM modules:

- The `pam_unix` module, `/usr/lib/security/pam_unix.so.1`, provides support for authentication, account management, session management, and password management.

You can use any of the four module type definitions with this module. This module uses UNIX passwords for authentication. The Solaris environment uses the `/etc/nsswitch.conf` file to control the choice of appropriate name services to get password records. For complete information, refer to the `pam_unix`(5) manual page.

- The `dial_auth` module, `/usr/lib/security/pam_dial_auth.so.1`, can be used only for authentication. This module, used mainly by the `login` command, uses data stored in the `/etc/dialups` and `/etc/d_passwd` files for authentication. For complete information refer to the `pam_dial_auth`(5) manual page.
- The `rhosts_auth` module, `/usr/lib/security/pam_rhosts_auth.so.1`, can be used only for authentication. This module, used mainly by the `rlogin` and `rsh` commands, uses data stored in the `~/.rhosts` and `/etc/host.equiv` files through `ruserok`. For compete information, refer to the `pam_rhosts_auth`(5) manual page.

PAM Configuration File

The PAM configuration file, `/etc/pam.conf`, determines the authentication services to be used and in what order they can be used. You can edit this file to choose authentication mechanisms for each system-entry application.

Each entry in the PAM configuration file has the following syntax:

```
<service_name> <module_type> <control_flag> <module_path> [<module_options>]
```

These elements are described in Table 19–4.

Table 19–4 PAM Configuration File Syntax

Element	Description
`<service_name>`	Name of the service. Use values such as ftp, login, telnet.
`<module_type>`	Module type for the service. Use one of the following values: `auth`, `account`, `session`, or `password`.
`<control_flag>`	Determines the continuation or failure semantics for the module. Use the values `required`, `requisite`, `optional`, or `sufficient`. For more information, see "Control Flags" on page 442.
`<module_path>`	Path to the library object that implements the service functionality.
`[<module_options>]`	Specific options that are passed to the service module, such as `debug` and `nowarn`. You do not need to specify module options. Refer to the manual page of the specific module for a complete list of module options.

You can add comments to the `pam.conf` file by starting the line with a pound sign (#). Use white space to delimit fields.

Each line must specify the first four elements. *<module_options>* are optional.

NOTE. *An entry in the PAM configuration file is ignored if the line has less than four fields, if an invalid value is given for* `<module_type>` *or* `<control_flag>`*, or if the named module is not found.*

Valid Service Names

Table 19–5 lists some of the valid service names, the module types that can be used with that service, and the daemon or command associated with the service name.

Several module types are not appropriate for each service. For example, the password module type is only specified to go with the `passwd` command. There is no auth module type associated with this command because it is not concerned with authentication.

Table 19–5 Valid Service Names for /etc/pam.conf

Service Name	Daemon or Command	Module Type
dtlogin	`/usr/dt/bin/dtlogin`	auth, account, session
ftp	`/usr/sbin/in.ftpd`	auth, account, session
init	`/usr/sbin/init`	session
login	`/usr/bin/login`	auth, account, session
passwd	`/usr/bin/passwd`	password
rexd	`/usr/sbin/rpc.rexd`	auth
rlogin	`/usr/sbin/in.rlogind`	auth, account, session
rsh	`/usr/sbin/in.rshd`	auth, account, session
sac	`/usr/lib/saf/sac`	session
su	`/usr/bin/su`	auth, account, session
telnet	`/usr/sbin.in.telnetd`	auth, account, session
ttymon	`/usr/lib/saf/ttymon`	session
uucp	`/usr/sbin/in.uucpd`	auth, account, session

Control Flags

You must specify one of four control flags for each entry in the `pam.conf` file to determine continuation or failure behavior from a module during authentication. The *control flags* indicate how to handle a successful or a failed attempt for each module. Even though the flags apply to all module types, the following explanation assumes that these flags are being used for authentication modules.

The control flags are:

- `required`
- `requisite`
- `optional`
- `sufficient`

The required Flag

When the `required` flag is used, the module must return success for the overall result to be successful.

- If all of the modules are labeled as `required`, then authentication through all modules must succeed for the user to be authenticated.
- If some of the modules fail, then an error value from the first failed module is reported.
- If a failure occurs for a module flagged as `required`, all modules in the stack are still tried, but `failure` is returned.
- If none of the modules are flagged as `required`, then at least one of the entries for that service must succeed for the user to be authenticated.

The requisite Flag

When the `requisite` flag is used, the module must return `success` for additional authentication to occur.

- If a module flagged as `requisite` fails, an error is immediately returned to the application, and no additional authentication is performed.
- If the stack does not include prior modules labeled as `required` that failed, then the error from this module is returned.
- If an earlier module labeled as `required` fails, the error message from the required module is returned.

The optional Flag

When the `optional` flag is used and a module fails, the overall result can be successful if another module in the stack returns `success`. Use the `optional` flag only when one success in the stack is enough for a user to be authenticated. Only use this flag if it is not important for the particular mechanism to succeed.

NOTE. *If your users need to have permission associated with a specific mechanism to get their work done, you should not label it as* `optional`.

The sufficient Flag

When the `sufficient` flag is used and the module returns `success`, skip the remaining modules in the stack, even if they are labeled as `required`. The `sufficient` flag indicates that one successful authentication is enough for the user to be granted access.

An example of the generic `/etc/pam.conf` file is shown below:

```
#ident  "@(#)pam.conf 1.19     95/11/30 SMI"
#
# PAM configuration
#
# Authentication management
#
login   auth required   /usr/lib/security/pam_unix.so.1
login   auth required   /usr/lib/security/pam_dial_auth.so.1
#
rlogin  auth sufficient /usr/lib/security/pam_rhosts_auth.so.1
rlogin  auth required   /usr/lib/security/pam_unix.so.1
#
dtlogin auth required   /usr/lib/security/pam_unix.so.1
#
rsh     auth required   /usr/lib/security/pam_rhosts_auth.so.1
other   auth required   /usr/lib/security/pam_unix.so.1
#
# Account management
#
login   account required        /usr/lib/security/pam_unix.so.1
dtlogin account required        /usr/lib/security/pam_unix.so.1
#
other   account required        /usr/lib/security/pam_unix.so.1
#
# Session management
#
other   session required        /usr/lib/security/pam_unix.so.1
#
# Password management
#
other   password required       /usr/lib/security/pam_unix.so.1
```

The generic `pam.conf` file specifies:

- When running login, authentication must succeed for both the `pam_unix` and the `pam_dial_auth` modules.
- For rlogin, authentication through the `pam_unix` module must succeed, if authentication through `pam_rhost_auth` fails.
- The `sufficient` control flag indicates that for rlogin, the successful authentication provided by the `pam_rhost_auth` module is sufficient and the next entry is ignored.
- Most of the other commands require successful authentication through the `pam_unix` module.
- Authentication for `rsh` must succeed through the `pam_rhost_auth` module.

The other service name enables a default to be set for any other commands requiring authentication that are not included in the file. The other option makes it easier to administer the file, because many commands that are using the same module can be covered using only one entry. Also, the other service name, when used as a catch-all, can ensure that each access is covered by one module. By convention, the other entry is included at the bottom of the section for each module type.

The rest of the entries in the file control the account, session, and password management.

Normally the entry for *<module_path>* is "root-relative." If the filename you enter for *<module_path>* does not begin with a slash (/), the path /usr/lib/security/ is prepended to the filename. You must use a full pathname for modules located in other directories.

You can find the values for *<module_options>* in the manual page for the specific module; for example, pam_unix(5) provides the following options:

- debug
- nowarn
- use_first_pass
- try_first_pass

If login specifies authentication through both pam_local and pam_unix, then the user is prompted to enter a password for each module. For situations in which the passwords are the same, the use_first_pass module option prompts for only one password and uses that password to authenticate the user for both modules. If the passwords are different, the authentication fails. In general, you should use this option with an optional control flag to make sure that the user can still log in, as shown in the following example:

```
# Authentication management
#
login auth required /usr/lib/security/pam_unix.so.1
login auth optional /usr/lib/security/pam_local.so.1 use_first_pass
```

If you use the try_first_pass module option instead, the local module prompts for a second password if the passwords do not match or if an error is made. If both methods of authentication are needed for a user to get access to all the tools needed, using this option could cause some confusion for the user because the user could get access with only one type of authentication.

Planning for PAM

When deciding how best to use PAM in your environment, start by focusing on the following issues:

- Determine what your needs are, especially which modules you should use.
- Identify the services that need special attention. Use other if appropriate.

- Decide on the order in which the modules should be run.
- Choose the control flag for that module.
- Choose any options needed for the module.

Consider the following suggestions before changing the configuration file:

- Use the `other` entry for each module type so that you do not have to include every application.
- Make sure to consider the security implications of the `sufficient` and `optional` control flags.
- Review the manual pages associated with the modules to understand how each module functions, what options are available, and the interactions between stacked modules.

CAUTION! *If the PAM configuration file is misconfigured or becomes corrupted, it is possible that even the superuser would not be able to log in. If the configuration file does become corrupted, you can boot in single-user mode and fix the problem because* `sulogin` *does not use PAM.*

After you change the `/etc/pam.conf` file, review it carefully while still logged in as superuser. Test all of the commands that might have been affected by your changes. For example, if you added a new module to the telnet service, use the `telnet` command and verify that the changes you made behave as expected.

Configuring PAM

This section describes how to prevent unauthorized access from remote systems, initiate PAM error reporting, and add a PAM module.

Preventing Unauthorized Access from Remote Systems with PAM

To prevent unauthorized access from remote systems with PAM, remove the rlogin `auth_rhosts_auth.so.1` entry from the `/etc/pam.conf` configuration file. Without this entry, the `~/.rhosts` files are not read during an rlogin session. Unauthenticated access to the local system from remote systems is prevented. All rlogin access requires a password, regardless of the presence or contents of any `~/.rhosts` or `/etc/hosts.equiv` files.

NOTE. *To prevent other unauthenticated access to the* `~/.rhosts` *files, remember to also disable the rsh service. The best way to disable a service is to comment out or remove the service entry from the* `/etc/inetd.conf` *file. Changing the PAM configuration file does not prevent the service from being started.*

Initiating PAM Error Reporting

You can display five different levels of PAM error reporting by adding entries to the `/etc/syslog` file:

- `auth.alert` displays messages about conditions that should be fixed immediately.
- `auth.crit` displays critical messages.
- `auth.err` displays error messages.
- `auth.info` displays informational messages.
- `auth.debug` displays debugging messages.

As with any other configuration entry in the `syslog` file, the entry consists of two tab-separated fields:

<selector> *<action>*

The *<selector>* field is one of the five levels of PAM error reporting. The *<action>* field indicates where to forward the message. Values for this field can have one of four forms:

- A filename, beginning with a leading slash, which indicates that messages specified by the selector are to be written to the specified file. The file is opened in append mode.
- A comma-separated list of usernames, which indicates that messages specified by the selector are to be written to the named users if they are logged in.
- An asterisk, which indicates that messages specified by the selector are to be written to all logged-in users.
- The name of a remote host, prefixed with an at sign (@), such as `@server`, which indicates that messages specified by the selector are to be forwarded to the syslogd on the named host.

Blank lines are ignored. Lines with a pound sign (#) as the first non-white character are treated as comments. Refer to the `syslog.conf`(4) manual page for more information.

To initiate PAM error reporting:

1. Edit the `/etc/syslog.conf` file and add a line for the *<selector>* and *<action>* you want to use for error reporting. Remember to use a tab as the separator character.
2. Restart the syslog daemon or send a `SIGHUP` signal to it to activate the PAM error reporting.

The following example displays all alert messages on the console. Critical messages are mailed to root. Informational and debug messages are added to the `/var/log/pamlog` file:

```
auth.alert	/dev/console
auth.crit	'root'
auth.info;auth.debug	/var/log/pamlog
```

Each line in the log contains a time stamp, the name of the system that generated the message, and the message itself. The `pamlog` file is capable of logging a large amount of information. Be sure to monitor the size of the log and prune it periodically to delete old information.

Adding a PAM Module

You can add new PAM modules. The `/usr/lib/security` model contains a `pam_sample.so.1` ELF executable file that you can use as a model for creating new modules.

CAUTION! *It is very important to test any changes to the* `/etc/pam.conf` *configuration file before you reboot the system to detect any misconfiguration errors. Run* `rlogin`, `su`, *and* `telnet` *to test and verify expected access results before you reboot the system. However, if the service is a daemon spawned only once when the system is booted, you may need to reboot the system before you can verify that module.*

To add a PAM module:

1. Become superuser.
2. Determine which control flags and other options you want to use.
3. Create the new module.
4. Copy the new module to `/usr/lib/security`.
5. Set permissions so that the module file is owned by `root` and permissions are set to 555.
6. Edit the `/etc/pam.conf` file and add the module to the appropriate services.

CHAPTER

20

Using Automated Security Enhancement Tool (ASET)

ASET Tasks

ASET Master Files

ASET Security Levels

How ASET Tasks Work

ASET Execution Log

ASET Reports

ASET Master Files

ASET Environment File (asetenv)

Running ASET

Restoring System Files Modified by ASET

ASET Error Messages

HE AUTOMATED SECURITY ENHANCEMENT TOOL (ASET) ENABLES YOU TO MONITOR AND control system security by automatically performing tasks that you would otherwise do manually.

ASET Tasks

ASET consists of seven tasks, each performing specific checks and adjustments to file systems:

- System files permissions verification
- System files checks
- User/group checks
- System configuration files check
- Environment check
- eeprom check
- Firewall setup

The ASET tasks tighten file permissions, check the contents of critical system files for security weaknesses, and monitor crucial areas. ASET can safeguard a network by applying the basic requirements of a firewall system to a system that serves as a gateway system.

Each task generates a report noting detected security weaknesses and changes the task has made to the system files. When run at the highest security level, ASET tries to modify all system security weaknesses. If it cannot correct a potential security problem, ASET reports the existence of the problem.

ASET Master Files

ASET uses master files for configuration. Master files, reports, and other files are available in the `/usr/aset` directory. You can change these files to suit the particular requirements of your site.

The contents of the `/usr/aset` directory are listed in Table 20–1.

Table 20–1 Contents of the /usr/aset Directory

Files and Directories	Description
`archives`	Directory ASET uses to store archive files. The `aset.restore` script uses the original files from this directory to restore a system to its pre-ASET state.

Table 20–1 Contents of the /usr/aset Directory (continued)

Files and Directories	Description
`aset`	The ASET shell script.
`aset.restore`	Script used to restore a system to its original condition before ASET was run. It also deschedules ASET if it is scheduled.
`asetenv`	Script that controls and sets ASET environment variables.
`masters`	Directory containing a list of master files that control the three levels of ASET security.
`reports`	Directory ASET uses to store reports.
`tasks`	Directory containing shell scripts and C executables that perform ASET tasks.
`tmp`	Temporary directory.
`util`	Directory containing ASET shell scripts and ELF executable utilities.

To administer ASET, if you want to change any of the ASET defaults, first you edit the `asetenv` file. Next, you initiate an ASET session at one of the three levels of security either by using the `/user/aset/aset` command interactively, or by using the aset command to put an entry into the `crontab` file to run ASET periodically. Finally, you review the contents of the reports in the `/usr/aset/reports` directory to monitor and fix any security problems reported by ASET.

CAUTION! *ASET tasks are disk-intensive and can interfere with regular system and application activities. To minimize the impact on system performance, schedule ASET to run when system activity level is lowest—for example, once every 24 or 48 hours at midnight or on weekends.*

ASET Security Levels

You can set ASET to operate at one of three security levels: low, medium, or high. At each higher level, ASET's file-control functions increase to reduce file access and heighten system security. These functions range from monitoring system security without limiting file access to users to increasingly tightening access permissions until a system is fully secured.

The following list provides more information about the three ASET security levels:

- *Low security:* This level ensures that attributes of system files are set to standard release values. ASET performs several checks and reports potential security weaknesses. At this level, ASET takes no action and does not affect system services.
- *Medium security:* This level provides adequate security control for most environments. ASET modifies some of the system file settings and parameters, restricting system access to reduce the risks from security attacks. ASET reports security weaknesses and any

modification it makes to restrict access. At this level, ASET does not affect system services.

- *High security:* This level provides a highly secure system. ASET adjusts many system files and parameter settings to minimize access permissions. Most system applications and commands continue to function normally, but at this level, security considerations take precedence over other system behavior.

NOTE. *ASET does not change the permissions of a file to make it less secure unless you downgrade the security level or intentionally revert the system to the settings that existed before running ASET.*

How ASET Tasks Work

This section describes what ASET does. You should understand each ASET task to interpret and use the reports effectively, including:

- The objective of the task
- Operations the task performs
- System components that are affected by the task

ASET report files contain messages that describe as specifically as possible any problems discovered by each ASET task. These messages can help you diagnose and correct these problems. Successful use of ASET assumes that you understand system administration and system components.

Reports are generated by the `taskstat` utility, which identifies the tasks that have been completed and the ones that are still running. Each completed task produces a report file. For a complete description of the `taskstat` utility, refer to the `taskstat`(1M) manual page.

You set up tasks and choose the files to be checked for each security level by setting environment variables in the `User Configurable Parameters` part of the `/usr/aset/asetenv` script:

```
###########################################
#                                         #
#      User Configurable Parameters       #
#                                         #
###########################################

CKLISTPATH_LOW=${ASETDIR}/tasks:${ASETDIR}/util:${ASETDIR}/masters:/etc
CKLISTPATH_MED=${CKLISTPATH_LOW}:/usr/bin:/usr/ucb
CKLISTPATH_HIGH=${CKLISTPATH_MED}:/usr/lib:/sbin:/usr/sbin:/usr/ucblib
YPCHECK=false
UID_ALIASES=${ASETDIR}/masters/uid_aliases
PERIODIC_SCHEDULE="0 0 * * *"
TASKS="firewall env sysconf usrgrp tune cklist eeprom"
```

For more information about ASET environment variables, see "ASET Environment File (asetenv)" on page 463.

System Files Permissions Verification

The `tune` task sets the permissions on system files to the security level you designate. It is run when the system is installed. If you decide later to alter the previously established levels, you must run this task again. At low security, the permissions are set to values that are appropriate for an open information-sharing environment. At medium security, the permissions are tightened to produce adequate security for most environments. At high security, they are tightened to severely restrict access.

Any modifications that this task makes to system files permissions or parameter settings are reported in the `tune.rpt` file.

System Files Checks

The `cklist` task examines system files and compares each one with a description of that file listed in a master file. The master file is created the first time ASET runs the task. The master file contains the system file settings enforced by `cklist` for the specified security level.

ASET defines a default list of directories whose files are to be checked for each security level. You can use the default list or you can modify it, specifying different directories for each level.

For each file, the following criteria are checked:

- Owner and group
- Permission bits
- Size and checksum
- Number of links
- Last modification time

Any discrepancies are reported in the `cklist.rpt` file. This file contains the results of comparing system file size, permission, and checksum values to the master file.

User/Group Checks

The `usrgrp` task checks the consistency and integrity of user accounts and groups as defined in the `passwd` and `group` files. It checks the local and NIS or NIS+ password files. NIS+ password file problems are reported but not corrected.

This task checks for the following violations:

- Duplicate names or IDs
- Entries in incorrect format
- Accounts without a password
- Invalid login directories
- The nobody account
- Null group password
- A plus sign (+) in the `/etc/passwd` file on an NIS or NIS+ server

Discrepancies are reported in the `usrgrp.rpt` file.

System Configuration Files Check

The `sysconf` task checks various system tables, most of which are in the `/etc` directory:

- `/etc/default/login`
- `/etc/hosts.equiv`
- `/etc/inetd.conf`
- `/etc/aliases`
- `/var/adm/utmp`
- `/var/adm/utmpx`
- `/.rhosts`
- `/etc/vfstab`
- `/etc/dfs/dfstab`
- `/etc/ftpusers`

ASET performs various checks and modifications on these files and reports all problems in the `sysconf.rpt` file.

Environment Check

The `env` task checks how the `PATH` and `UMASK` environment variables are set for `root` and other users in the `/.profile`, `/.login`, and `/.cshrc` files.

The results of checking the environment for security are reported in the `env.rpt` file.

eeprom Check

The `eeprom` task checks the value of the eeprom security parameter to ensure that it is set to the appropriate security level. You can set the eeprom security parameter to:

- none
- command
- full

ASET does not change the eeprom setting, but reports its recommendations in the `eeprom.rpt` file.

Firewall Setup

The `firewall` task ensures that the system can be safely used as a network relay. It protects an internal network from external public networks by setting up a dedicated system as a firewall. The firewall system separates two networks, each of which approaches the other as untrusted. The firewall setup task disables the forwarding of Internet Protocol (IP) packets and hides routing information from the external network.

The `firewall` task runs at all security levels, but takes action only at the highest level. If you want to run ASET at high security, but find that your system does not require firewall protection, you can eliminate the `firewall` task; simply remove it from the list of tasks specified by the `TASKS` environment variable in the `asetenv` file.

Any changes made by this task are reported in the `firewall.rpt` file.

ASET Execution Log

ASET generates an *execution log* whether it runs interactively or in the background. By default, ASET generates the log file on standard output. The execution log confirms that ASET ran at the designated time. It also contains any execution error messages. The `-n` option of the `aset` command directs the log to be delivered by electronic mail to a designated user. For a complete list of ASET options, refer to the `aset`(1M) manual page.

The following example shows an execution log running at low-level security:

```
castle% su
Password:
# /usr/aset/aset -l low
======= ASET Execution Log =======

ASET running at security level low

Machine = castle; Current time = 1015_09:29

aset: Using /usr/aset as working directory

Executing task list ...
        firewall
        env
        sysconf
        usrgrp
        tune
        cklist
        eeprom
```

```
All tasks executed. Some background tasks may still be running.

Run /usr/aset/util/taskstat to check their status:
     /usr/aset/util/taskstat     [aset_dir]

where aset_dir is ASET's operating directory,currently=/usr/aset.

When the tasks complete, the reports can be found in:
     /usr/aset/reports/latest/*.rpt
You can view them by:
     more /usr/aset/reports/latest/*.rpt
#
```

The log first shows the system and the time that ASET was run. Then it lists each task as it is started.

ASET invokes a background process for each of the tasks. The task is listed in the execution log when it starts. The log does not indicate when the task has been completed. To check the status of the background tasks, type **/usr/aset/util/taskstat** and press Return.

The following example shows that four tasks—`firewall`, `env`, `sysconf`, and `usrgrp`--have been completed, and that three tasks—`tune`, `cklist`, and `eeprom`—are not finished:

```
# /usr/aset/util/taskstat

Checking ASET tasks status ...
Task firewall is done.
Task env is done.
Task sysconf is done.
Task usrgrp is done.

The following tasks are done:
        firewall
        env
        sysconf
        usrgrp

The following tasks are not done:
        tune
        cklist
        eeprom
#
```

ASET Reports

All report files generated from ASET tasks are stored in subdirectories under the `/usr/aset/reports` directory. This section describes the structure of the `/usr/aset/reports` directory and provides guidelines on managing the report files.

ASET puts the report files in subdirectories that are named to reflect the time and date when the reports are generated. This structure enables you to keep an orderly set of records documenting the system status as it varies between ASET executions. You can monitor and compare the reports to determine the soundness of your system security.

The `/usr/aset/reports` directory contains a subdirectory named `latest` that is a symbolic link to the most recent set of reports generated by ASET.

The following example shows contents of the `/usr/aset/reports` directory with two subdirectories and the `latest` directory:

```
# ls -l /usr/aset/reports
total 6
drwxrwxrwx   2 root     other          512 Oct 15 09:30 1015_09:29
drwxrwxrwx   2 root     other          512 Oct 15 09:41 1015_09:41
lrwxrwxrwx   1 root     other           28 Oct 15 09:41 latest ->
/usr/aset/reports/1015_09:41
#
```

The subdirectory name indicates the date and time the reports were generated, in the format:

<monthdate_hour>:*<minute>*

where *<month>*, *<date>*, *<hour>*, and *<minute>* are all two-digit numbers. For example, `1015_09:41` represents October 15 at 9:41 a.m.

Each of the report subdirectories contains a collection of reports generated from one execution of ASET. To look at the latest reports that ASET has generated, you can always review the reports in the `/usr/aset/reports/latest` directory. The following example shows the contents of the `/usr/aset/reports/latest` directory:

```
# ls -l /usr/aset/reports/latest
total 14
-rw-rw-rw-   1 root     other          383 Oct 15 09:41 env.rpt
-rw-rw-rw-   1 root     other          622 Oct 15 09:41 execution.log
-rw-rw-rw-   1 root     other          306 Oct 15 09:41 firewall.rpt
-rw-rw-rw-   1 root     other          631 Oct 15 09:41 sysconf.rpt
-rw-rw-rw-   1 root     other           84 Oct 15 09:41 taskstatus
-rw-rw-rw-   1 root     other          114 Oct 15 09:41 tune.rpt
-rw-rw-rw-   1 root     other          256 Oct 15 09:41 usrgrp.rpt
castle#
```

NOTE. *Because ASET was not run at the highest security level, this listing does not contain the* `cklist.rpt` *and* `eeprom.rpt` *reports.*

Each report is named after the task that generates it. The complete list of reports is shown in Table 20–2 along with the task that generates the report.

Table 20–2 ASET Reports and Tasks

Report	Task
cklist.rpt	System files checklist (cklist)
eeprom.rpt	eeprom check (eeprom)

Table 20–2 ASET Reports and Tasks (continued)

Report	Task
`env.rpt`	Environment check (env)
`execution.log`	Contains messages displayed by the `taskstat` command
`firewall.rpt`	Firewall setup (firewall)
`sysconf.rpt`	System configuration files check (sysconf)
`taskstatus`	Contains messages displayed by the `taskstat` command on the status of the tasks
`tune.rpt`	System file permissions tuning (tune)
`usrgrp.rpt`	User/group checks (usrgrp)

Format of Report Files

Within each report file, messages are bracketed by a beginning and ending banner line. Sometimes a task terminates prematurely—for example, when a component of ASET is accidentally removed or damaged. In most cases, the report file contains a message near the end that indicates the reason for the premature exit.

The following example of the `usrgrp.rpt` file reports that user `rob` has no password in the `/etc/shadow` file:

```
castle# more /usr/aset/reports/latest/usrgrp.rpt

*** Begin User And Group Checking ***

Checking /etc/passwd ...

Checking /etc/shadow ...

Warning!  Shadow file, line 17, no password:
        rob:::::::

... end user check.

Checking /etc/group ...

... end group check.

*** End User And Group Checking ***
#
```

Examining and Comparing Report Files

After you run ASET the first time or when you reconfigure it, you should examine the report files closely.

Reconfiguration includes modifying the `asetenv` file or the master files in the `masters` subdirectory, or changing the security level at which ASET operates. The reports record any errors introduced when you reconfigured. By watching the reports closely, you can diagnose and solve problems as they arise.

You should routinely monitor the report files to check for security breaches. You can use the `diff` utility to compare reports.

ASET Master Files

The ASET master files—`tune.high`, `tune.low`, `tune.med`, and `uid_aliases`—are located in the `/usr/aset/masters` directory. ASET uses the master files to define security levels. The checklist files `cklist.high`, `cklist.med`, and `cklist.low` are also located in the `/usr/aset/masters` directory. The checklist files are generated when you execute ASET and are used by ASET to check file permissions.

Tune Files

The `tune.low`, `tune.med`, and `tune.high` master files define the available ASET security levels. They specify the attributes of system files at each level and are used for comparison and reference.

The `tune.high` file specifies the most restrictive level of security:

```
#
# Copyright 1990, 1991 Sun Microsystems, Inc.  All Rights Reserved.
#
#
#ident  "@(#)tune.high  1.9     94/12/07 SMI"
#
# Tune list for level high
# Format:
#       pathname mode owner group type

# The following section is from tune.low (which = Brad's tune list).
/ 02755 root root directory
/bin 00777 root bin symlink
/sbin 02775 root sys directory
/usr/sbin 02775 root bin directory
/etc 02755 root sys directory
/etc/chroot 00777 bin bin symlink
/etc/clri 00777 bin bin symlink
/etc/crash 00777 root sys symlink
/etc/cron 00777 root sys symlink
/etc/fsck 00777 bin bin symlink
/etc/fuser 00777 bin bin symlink
/etc/halt 00777 bin bin symlink
/etc/link 00777 root bin symlink
/etc/mknod 00777 bin bin symlink
/etc/mount 00777 bin bin symlink
/etc/mnttab 00644 root root file
```

```
/etc/vfstab 00664 root sys file
/etc/passwd 00644 root sys file
/etc/shadow 00400 root sys file
/etc/nsswitch.conf 00644 root sys file
/etc/resolve.conf 00644 root sys file
/etc/ncheck 00777 bin bin symlink
/etc/rmt 00777 bin bin symlink
/etc/shutdown 00777 root sys symlink
/etc/termcap 00777 bin bin symlink
/etc/umount 00777 bin bin symlink
/etc/unlink 00777 root bin symlink
/devices 02755 root sys directory
/usr 02775 root sys directory
/usr/bin 02755 root bin directory
/usr/demo 02755 root bin directory
/usr/games 02755 root bin directory
/usr/include 02755 root bin directory
/usr/kvm 02775 bin bin directory
/usr/kvm/i386 00777 bin bin symlink
/usr/kvm/iAPX286 00777 bin bin symlink
/usr/kvm/m68k 00777 bin bin symlink
/usr/kvm/mc68010 00777 bin bin symlink
/usr/kvm/mc68020 00777 bin bin symlink
/usr/kvm/sparc 00777 bin bin symlink
/usr/kvm/sun 00777 bin bin symlink
/usr/kvm/sun2 00777 bin bin symlink
/usr/kvm/sun4 00777 bin bin symlink
/usr/kvm/sun4c 00777 bin bin symlink
/usr/kvm/sun4d 00777 bin bin symlink
/usr/kvm/sun4e 00777 bin bin symlink
/usr/kvm/sun4m 00777 bin bin symlink
/usr/kvm/crash 02750 root sys file
/usr/kvm/u370 00777 bin bin symlink
/usr/kvm/u3b 00777 bin bin symlink
/usr/kvm/u3b15 00777 bin bin symlink
/usr/kvm/u3b2 00777 bin bin symlink
/usr/kvm/u3b5 00777 bin bin symlink
/usr/kvm/vax 00777 bin bin symlink
/usr/lib 02755 bin bin directory
/usr/lib/refer 02755 bin bin directory
/usr/lib/tabset 00777 bin bin symlink
/usr/man 00777 bin bin symlink
/usr/net 00775 root sys directory
/usr/old 02775 root bin directory
/usr/pub 00777 bin bin symlink
/usr/share/lib 02755 root sys directory
/usr/share/lib/tmac 02775 bin bin directory
/usr/share/src 02755 root sys directory
/usr/spool 00777 root bin symlink
/usr/src 00777 root sys symlink
/usr/tmp 00777 sys sys symlink

/usr/ucb 02775 root bin directory
/usr/ucbinclude 02755 bin bin directory
/usr/ucblib 02755 bin bin directory
/var 02755 root sys directory
#/home 02755 root sys directory
```

```
# The following section is from Beverly's list (hml.settings)
# with modifications.

/.cshrc 00600 root ? file
/.login  00600 root ? file
/.profile 00600 root ? file
/.logout 00600 root ? file
/etc/motd 00644 root sys file
/etc/syslog.pid 00640 root sys file
/etc/mail/aliases 00644 root bin file
/etc/remote 00640 bin bin file
/var/adm/utmp 644 root bin file
/var/adm/utmpx 644 root bin file
/var/adm/wtmp 664 adm adm file
/var/adm/wtmpx 664 adm adm file
/sbin/rc0 0744 root sys file
/sbin/rc1 0744 root sys file
/sbin/rc2 0744 root sys file
/sbin/rc3 0744 root sys file
/sbin/rc5 0744 root sys file
/sbin/rc6 0744 root sys file
/sbin/rcS 0744 root sys file
/etc/rc0.d 02775 root sys directory
/etc/rc1.d 02775 root sys directory
/etc/rc2.d 02775 root sys directory
/etc/rc3.d 02775 root sys directory
/etc/rc5.d 02775 root sys directory
/etc/rcS.d 02775 root sys directory
/etc/vfstab 00640 root sys file
/etc/group 00644 root sys file
/var/statmon/sm 00775 root root directory
/var/statmon/sm.bak 00775 root root directory
/var/statmon/state 00640 root root file
/platform 02755 root sys directory
/tmp 02777 root root directory
/dev/*mem 00777 root sys symlink
#/etc/rmtab 00644 root ? file
#/tmp/.getwd 00666 ? ? file

/usr/bin/* 00755 ? ? ?
/usr/ucb/* 00755 ? ? ?
/var/tmp 02777 sys sys directory
/usr/share 02755 root sys directory
/usr/include/* 00755 ? ? ?
/usr/lib/adb/* 00755 ? ? ?
/usr/share/lib/* 00755 ? ? ?
/usr/share/man/* 00755 ? ? ?
/usr/share/src/* 00755 ? ? ?
/usr/share/lib/make 02755 bin bin directory
/usr/share/lib/termcap 00644 bin bin file
/usr/share/lib/terminfo 02755 bin bin directory
/usr/share/lib/tmac 02775 bin bin directory

/dev/dump 00777 root sys symlink
/dev/dsk/* 00640 root sys file
```

```
/dev/rdsk/* 00640 root sys file
/dev 02775 root sys directory

# for security
/etc/security 02750 root sys directory
/etc/lib 02770 root sys directory
/usr/lib/security 02750 root sys directory
```

The syntax for the entries is:

<pathname> <mode> <owner> <group> <type>

The following rules apply to the entries in the `tune` files:

- You can use regular shell wildcard characters such as an asterisk (*) and a question mark (?) in the pathname for multiple references.
- *<mode>* represents the least allowable value. If the current setting is already more restrictive than the specified value, ASET does not loosen the permission settings. For example, if the specified value is 00777, the permission remains unchanged, because 00777 is always less restrictive than the current setting.

  When you decrease the security level from what it was for the previous execution, or when you want to restore the system files to the state they were in before ASET was first executed, ASET recognizes what you are doing and decreases the protection level.
- You must use names for *<owner>* and *<group>* instead of numeric IDs.
- You can use a question mark (?) in place of *<owner>*, *<group>*, and *<type>* to prevent ASET from changing the existing values of these parameters.
- *<type>* can be symlink (symbolic link), directory, or file (everything else).
- Higher security level `tune` files reset file permissions to be at least as restrictive as they are at lower levels. Also, at higher levels, additional files are added to the list.
- A file can match more than one `tune` file entry. For example, `etc/passwd` matches `etc/pass*` and `/etc*`.
- Where two entries have different permissions, the more restrictive file permission applies. In the following example, the permission of `/etc/passwd` will be set to 00755, which is the more restrictive of 00755 and 00770:

  ```
  /etc/pass* 00755 ? ? file
  /etc/* 00770 ? ? file
  ```
- If two entries have different *<owner>* or *<group>* designations, the last entry takes precedence.

You modify settings in the `tune` file by adding or deleting file entries.

NOTE. *Setting a permission to a less restrictive value than the current setting has no effect; the ASET tasks do not relax permissions unless you downgrade your system security to a lower level.*

The uid_aliases File

The uid_aliases file contains a list of multiple user accounts sharing the same ID. Normally, ASET warns about such multiple user accounts because this practice lessens accountability. You can allow for exceptions to this rule by listing the exceptions in the uid_aliases file. ASET does not report entries in the passwd file with duplicate user IDs if these entries are specified in the uid_aliases file.

The default /usr/aset/masters/uid_aliases file is:

```
#
# Copyright 1990, 1991 Sun Microsystems, Inc.  All Rights Reserved.
#
#
# sccsid = @(#) uid_aliases 1.1 1/2/91 14:39:52
#
# format:
#       uid=alias1=alias2=alias3= ...
# allows users "alias1", "aliase2", "alias3" to share the same uid.

0=+=root=checkfsys=makefsys=mountfsys=powerdown=setup=smtp=sysadm=umountfsys
1=sync=daemon
```

The default entry is to make UID 0 equivalent to user accounts root, checkfsys, makefsys, mountfsys, powerdown, setup, smpt, sysadm, and umountfsys. UID1 is equivalent to the user accounts sync and daemon.

Each entry has the format

<uid>=<alias1>=<alias2>=<alias3>-...

where *<uid>* is the shared UID number and *<aliasn>* is the name of the user account that shares the UID.

The Checklist Files

The master files cklist.high, cklist.med, and cklist.low are generated when you first execute ASET, or when you run ASET after you change the security level.

The following environment variables determine the files that are checked by this task:

- CKLISTPATH_LOW
- CKLISTPATH_MED
- CKLISTPATH_HIGH

Refer to the following section for more information about ASET environment variables.

ASET Environment File (asetenv)

The environment file asetenv contains a list of environment variables that affect ASET tasks. You can change these variables to modify ASET operation.

The default /usr/aset/asetenv file is:

```
#!/bin/sh
#
# Copyright 1990, 1991 Sun Microsystems, Inc.  All Rights Reserved.
#
#
#ident  "@(#)asetenv.sh 1.2     92/07/14 SMI"

# This is the "dot" script for ASET and should be invoked before
# running any ASET tasks.

###########################################
#                                         #
#      User Configurable Parameters       #
#                                         #
###########################################

CKLISTPATH_LOW=${ASETDIR}/tasks:${ASETDIR}/util:${ASETDIR}/masters:/etc
CKLISTPATH_MED=${CKLISTPATH_LOW}:/usr/bin:/usr/ucb
CKLISTPATH_HIGH=${CKLISTPATH_MED}:/usr/lib:/sbin:/usr/sbin:/usr/ucblib
YPCHECK=false
UID_ALIASES=${ASETDIR}/masters/uid_aliases
PERIODIC_SCHEDULE="0 0 * * *"
TASKS="firewall env sysconf usrgrp tune cklist eeprom"

###########################################
#                                         #
# ASET Internal Environment Variables     #
#                                         #
# Don't change from here on down ...      #
# there shouldn't be any reason to.       #
#                                         #
###########################################

export YPCHECK UID_ALIASES PERIODIC_SCHEDULE

# full paths of system utilites
AWK=/bin/awk
LS=/bin/ls
RM=/bin/rm
MV=/bin/mv
MKDIR=/bin/mkdir
LN=/bin/ln
SUM=/bin/sum
CUT=/bin/cut
GREP=/bin/grep
EGREP=/bin/egrep
DIFF=/bin/diff
MAIL=/bin/mail
CHGRP=/bin/chgrp
CHMOD=/bin/chmod
CHOWN=/usr/bin/chown
SORT=/bin/sort
UNIQ=/bin/uniq
YPCAT=/bin/ypcat
```

```
PS=/bin/ps
CP=/bin/cp
REALPATH=${ASETDIR}/util/realpath
ADDCKSUM=${ASETDIR}/util/addcksum
MINMODE=${ASETDIR}/util/minmode
FILE_ATTR=${ASETDIR}/util/file_attr
STR_TO_MODE=${ASETDIR}/util/str_to_mode
IS_WRITABLE=${ASETDIR}/util/is_writable
IS_READABLE=${ASETDIR}/util/is_readable
HOMEDIR=${ASETDIR}/util/homedir
SED=/bin/sed
ED=/bin/ed
CAT=/bin/cat
EXPR=/bin/expr
CRONTAB=/bin/crontab
TOUCH=/bin/touch

sysutils="AWK LS RM MV MKDIR LN SUM CUT GREP EGREP DIFF MAIL CHGRP CHMOD CHOWN
PS \
CP SORT UNIQ YPCAT REALPATH ADDCKSUM MINMODE FILE_ATTR STR_TO_MODE \
ED SED CAT IS_WRITABLE IS_READABLE HOMEDIR EXPR CRONTAB TOUCH"

progs="$AWK $LS $RM $MV $MKDIR $LN $SUM $CUT $GREP $EGREP \
$DIFF $MAIL $CHGRP $CHMOD $CHOWN $PS $CRONTAB $TOUCH \
$CP $SORT $UNIQ $YPCAT $REALPATH $ADDCKSUM $MINMODE $FILE_ATTR \
$STR_TO_MODE $ED $SED $CAT $IS_WRITABLE $IS_READABLE $HOMEDIR $EXPR"

noprog=false
for i in $progs
do
        if [ ! -x $i ]
        then
                if [ "$noprog" = "false" ]
                then
                        noprog=true
                        echo
                        echo "ASET startup unsuccessful:"
                else
                        echo "Could not find executable $i."
                fi
        fi
done
if [ "$noprog" = "true" ]
then
        echo "Unable to proceed."
        exit
fi

export $sysutils

TIMESTAMP=`date '+%m%d_%H:%M'`
QUIT="ASET: irrecoverable error -- exiting ..."

case $ASETSECLEVEL in
low)    CKLISTPATH=`echo "${CKLISTPATH_LOW}"`;;
med)    CKLISTPATH=`echo "${CKLISTPATH_MED}"`;;
```

```
high)   CKLISTPATH=`echo "${CKLISTPATH_HIGH}"`;;
*)      echo $QUIT;
        exit 3;;
esac

# Set up report directory
$RM -rf ${ASETDIR}/reports/${TIMESTAMP}
$MKDIR ${ASETDIR}/reports/${TIMESTAMP}
REPORT=${ASETDIR}/reports/${TIMESTAMP}
$RM -rf ${ASETDIR}/reports/latest
$LN -s $REPORT ${ASETDIR}/reports/latest

# temorary files directory
TMP=${ASETDIR}/tmp

export TASKS TIMESTAMP QUIT REPORT CKLISTPATH
export TMP
```

Table 20–3 lists the ASET environment variables and the values that they specify.

Table 20–3 ASET Environment Variables

Environment Variable	Default Value	Description
ASETDIR	Optional (set from shell)	ASET working directory
ASETSECLEVEL	Optional (set from shell)	Security level (low, med, high)
PERIODIC_SCHEDULE	"0 0 * * *"	Periodic schedule for running crontab entries
TASKS	"firewall env sysconf usrgrp tune cklist eeprom"	Tasks to run
UID_ALIAS	${ASETDIR}/masters/uid_aliases	Aliases file
YPCHECK	false	Extends check to NIS and NIS+
CKLISTPATH_LOW	${ASETDIR}/tasks:${ASETDIR}/util:${ASETDIR}/masters:/etc	Directory list for low security
CKLISTPATH_MED	${CKLISTPATH_LOW}:/usr/bin:/usr/ucb	Directory list for medium security
CKLISTPATH_HIGH	${CKLISTPATH_MED}:/usr/lib:/sbin:/usr/sbin:/usr/ucblib	Directory list for high security

ASET Shell Environment Variables

ASET provides two optional environment variables that you can set through a shell:

- ASETDIR specifies an ASET working directory
- ASETSECLEVEL specifies a security level at which ASET tasks are executed: low, medium, or high.

You set these environment variables in the same way you set any other shell environment variable.

From the C shell, type:

```
castle% setenv ASETDIR <pathname>
```

From the Bourne or Korn shell, type:

```
$ ASETDIR=<pathname>
$ export ASETDIR
```

PERIODIC_SCHEDULE Variable

The value of the PERIODIC_SCHEDULE variable that you set in the asetenv file follows the same format as the crontab file. You specify the variable values as a string of five fields enclosed in double quotation marks, each field separated by a space:

```
"<minutes> <hours> <day-of-month> <month> <day-of-week>"
```

Table 20–4 explains the values used for the PERIODIC_SCHEDULE variable.

Table 20–4 PERIODIC_SCHEDULE Variable Values

Variable	Value
<minutes>	Specifies start time in number of minutes after the hour, by using values from 0 through 59.
<hours>	Specifies the start time hour, by using values from 0 through 23.
<day-of-month>	Specifies the day of the month when ASET should be run, by using values from 1 through 31.
<month>	Specifies the month of the year when ASET should be run, by using values from 1 through 12.
<day-of-week>	Specifies the day of the week when ASET should be run, by using values from 0 through 6. In this scheme, Sunday is day 0.

The following rules apply:

- For any field, you can specify a list of values, each delimited by a comma.
- You can specify a value as a number or as a *range* (a pair of numbers joined by a hyphen). A range states that the ASET tasks should be executed for every time included in the range.
- You can specify an asterisk (*) as the value of any field. An asterisk specifies all possible values of the field, inclusive.

The default entry for PERIODIC_SCHEDULE executes ASET daily at midnight.

TASKS Variable

The TASKS variable in the asetenv file lists the tasks that ASET performs. The default is to list all seven tasks:

- firewall
- env
- sysconf
- usrgrp
- tune
- cklist
- eeprom

If you want to skip any of the tasks, simply remove the task from the list. To add a task, edit the asetenv file and include the task name in the quoted string following the TASK environment variable, using a space as the separator.

UID_ALIASES Variable

The UID_ALIASES variable in the asetenv file specifies which aliases file to use. If present, ASET consults this file for a list of permitted multiple aliases. The format is:

UID_ALIASES=<*pathname*>

where <*pathname*> is the full pathname of the aliases file.

The default is the uid_aliases file in the /usr/aset/masters directory.

YPCHECK Variable

The YPCHECK variable in the asetenv file extends the task of checking system tables to include NIS or NIS+ tables. The variable accepts a Boolean value, which can be set to either true or false. The default is false, confining checking to local system tables. To extend checking, edit the asetenv file and change the value for the variable to true.

CKLISTPATH_level Variable

The three checklist path variables list the directories to be checked by the checklist task.

The values for the checklist path environment variables are similar to those of shell path variables. They are a list of directory names separated by colons (:). You use an equal sign (=) to connect the variable name to its value.

Running ASET

This section describes how to run ASET either interactively or periodically.

Running ASET Interactively

You can run ASET interactively from the command line any time you want to monitor system security by using the /usr/aset/aset command. Table 20–5 lists the options to the aset command.

Table 20–5 Options to the aset Command

Option	Description
-p	Schedule aset to be executed periodically. This command adds an entry for aset to the /etc/crontab file. The option uses the value from the PERIODIC_SCHEDULE environment variable in the /usr/aset/asetenv file to define the time for execution.
-d <aset_dir>	Specify a working directory other than the default /usr/aset for ASET. ASET is installed by default in /usr/aset, which is the root directory of all ASET utilities and data files. If another directory is to be used as the ASET working directory, you can either define it with the -d option from the command line or by setting the ASETDIR environment variable before running aset. The command line option, if specified, overwrites the environment variable.
-l <sec_level>	Specify a security level (low, medium, or high) for aset to operate at. The default level is low. You can also specify the level by setting the ASETSECLEVEL environment variable before running aset. The command line option, if specified, overwrites the environment variable.
-n <user@host>	Notify <user> at system <host>. Send the output of aset to the user through email. If the option is not specified, the output is sent to the standard output. Note that this information is not the ASET report, but rather is an execution log that includes any error messages.
-u <userlist_file>	Specify a file containing a list of users for ASET to perform environment checks on. By default, ASET only checks for root. userlist_file is an ASCII text file. Each entry in the file is a line that contains only one username (login name).

To run ASET interactively:

1. Become superuser.
2. Type **/usr/aset/aset -l low | med | high [-d <*pathname*>]** and press Return. You use the -d <*pathname*> option to specify the ASET working directory if it is located somewhere else than the default /usr/aset directory.
3. Review the ASET execution log that is displayed on the screen.
4. Type **/usr/aset/util/taskstat** and press Return to verify that all tasks running in background are completed.
5. When tasks are completed, review the contents of the reports in the /usr/aset/reports/latest directory.

The following example runs ASET at low security with the default working directory. Notice that if you run the `aset` command with no arguments, the default is to run at low security level:

```
# /usr/aset/aset
======= ASET Execution Log =======

ASET running at security level low

Machine = castle; Current time = 1015_13:45

aset: Using /usr/aset as working directory

Downgrading security level:
Previous level = high; Current level = low

Executing task list ...
        firewall
        env
        sysconf
        usrgrp
        tune
        cklist
        eeprom

All tasks executed. Some background tasks may still be running.

Run /usr/aset/util/taskstat to check their status:
     /usr/aset/util/taskstat     [aset_dir]

where aset_dir is ASET's operating directory,currently=/usr/aset.

When the tasks complete, the reports can be found in:
     /usr/aset/reports/latest/*.rpt
You can view them by:
     more /usr/aset/reports/latest/*.rpt
# /usr/aset/util/taskstat


Checking ASET tasks status ...
Task firewall is done.

The following tasks are done:
        firewall

The following tasks are not done:
        env
        sysconf
        usrgrp
        tune
        cklist
        eeprom
# cd /usr/aset/reports/latest
# ls
env.rpt        firewall.rpt   taskstatus     usrgrp.rpt
execution.log  sysconf.rpt    tune.rpt
```

```
# more env.rpt

*** Begin Enviroment Check ***

Warning! umask set to umask 022 in /etc/profile - not recommended.
chmod: WARNING: can't access /tmp/tmppath.24379
Ambiguous output redirect
Can't open /tmp/tmppath.24379
Can't open /tmp/tmppath.24379
Can't open /tmp/tmppath.24379
Can't open /tmp/tmppath.24379
Can't open /tmp/tmppath.24379
cat: cannot open /tmp/tmppath.24379

*** End Enviroment Check ***
# more firewall.rpt

*** Begin Firewall Task ***

Beginning firewall.restore...

Restored ip_forwarding to previous value - 0.

Restored /usr/sbin/in.routed.

firewall.restore completed.
# more sysconf.rpt

Beginning sysconf.restore...

Restoring /etc/inetd.conf. Saved existing file in /etc/inetd.conf.asetbak.

Restoring /etc/aliases. Saved existing file in /etc/aliases.asetbak.

sysconf.restore completed.

*** Begin System Scripts Check ***

*** End System Scripts Check ***
# more tune.rpt

*** Begin Tune Task ***

Beginning tune.restore...
(This may take a while.)
# more usrgrp.rpt

Beginning usrgrp.restore...

Restoring /etc/passwd. Saved existing file in /etc/passwd.asetbak.

Restoring /etc/group. Saved existing file in /etc/group.asetbak.

Restoring /etc/shadow. Saved existing file in /etc/shadow.asetback.

usrgrp.restore completed.
```

```
*** Begin User And Group Checking ***

Checking /etc/passwd ...

Checking /etc/shadow ...

Warning!  Shadow file, line 17, no password:
        rob:::::::

... end user check.

Checking /etc/group ...

... end group check.

*** End User And Group Checking ***
```

Running ASET Periodically

To run ASET periodically, first you edit the `PERIODIC_SCHEDULE` variable in the `/usr/aset/asetenv` file, then you run the `aset -p` command which adds an ASET entry to the `crontab` file.

NOTE. *Schedule ASET to run when system demand is light. The default setting for the* `PERIODIC_SCHEDULE` *environment variable is to run ASET every 24 hours at midnight.*

To run ASET periodically:

1. Become superuser
2. Review the settings in the `/usr/aset/asetenv` file for the `PERIODIC_SCHEDULE` environment variable, and modify them as appropriate.
3. Type **/usr/aset/aset -p** and press Return. The `-p` (periodic) option edits the `crontab` file, using the values from the `asetenv` file.
4. Type **crontab -l root** and press Return to verify that the `crontab` entry for ASET has been added.

The following example uses the default values for `PERIODIC_SCHEDULE` from the `asetenv` file to schedule when ASET will run:

```
castle% su
Password:
# /usr/aset/aset -p
======= ASET Execution Log =======

ASET running at security level low

Machine = castle; Current time = 1015_14:22

aset: Using /usr/aset as working directory
```

```
ASET execution scheduled through cron.
# crontab -l root
#ident  "@(#)root       1.14    97/03/31 SMI"   /* SVr4.0 1.1.3.1       */
#
# The root crontab should be used to perform accounting data collection.
#
# The rtc command is run to adjust the real time clock if and when
# daylight savings time changes.
#
10 3 * * 0,4 /etc/cron.d/logchecker
10 3 * * 0   /usr/lib/newsyslog
15 3 * * 0 /usr/lib/fs/nfs/nfsfind
1 2 * * * [ -x /usr/sbin/rtc ] && /usr/sbin/rtc -c > /dev/null 2>&1
0 0 * * * /usr/aset/aset  -d /usr/aset
#
```

Stopping Running ASET Periodically

If you want to stop running ASET from crontab, edit the `crontab` file to remove the ASET entry.

To stop running ASET periodically:

1. Become superuser.
2. Type **crontab -e root** and press Return. A text editor window opens, displaying the contents of the `crontab` file.
3. Delete the ASET entry.
4. Save the changes and close the file.
5. Type **crontab -l root** and press Return to verify that the ASET entry is deleted.

Collecting Reports on a Server

You can collect reports from a number of client systems into a directory on the server to make comparing ASET reports easier.

To collect reports on a server:

1. Become superuser.
2. Type **cd /usr/aset** and press Return.
3. Type **mkdir *<rptdir>*** and press Return to create a report directory.
4. Type **cd *<rptdir>*** and press Return.
5. Type **mkdir *<client_rpt>*** and press Return for each client system you want to collect reports for.
6. Edit the `/etc/dfs/dfstab` file and add the `<client_rpt>` directories with read/write options:

```
share -F nfs -o rw=<client-hostname> /usr/aset/<rptdir>/<client_rpt>
```

7. Type **shareall** and press Return.
8. On each client, become superuser.
9. Type **mount *<server>*:/usr/aset/*<rptdir>*/*<client_rpt>* /usr/aset/reports** and press Return. The file system is mounted
10. On each client, also add a line to the `/etc/vfstab` file on the mount point `/usr/aset/reports`. The next time the system is booted, the reports are automatically mounted.

The following example collects ASET reports from the client `seachild` on the server `castle`:

```
castle% su
Password:
castle# cd /usr/aset
castle# mkdir all_reports
castle# cd all_reports
castle# mkdir seachild_rpt
castle# vi /etc/dfs/dfstab
share -F dfs -o rw=seachild /usr/aset/all_reports/seachild_rpt
ZZ
castle# shareall
```

On the client, `seachild`:

```
seachild% su
Password:
seachild# mount castle:/usr/aset/all_reports/seachild_rpt /usr/aset/reports
seachild# vi /etc/vfstab
castle:/usr/aset/all_reports/seachild_rpt /usr/aset/reports nfs - yes hard
ZZ
seachild#
```

Restoring System Files Modified by ASET

When ASET is executed for the first time, it saves and archives the original system files in the `/usr/aset/archive` directory. You can use the `/usr/aset/aset.restore` utility to reinstate these files. If ASET is currently scheduled for periodic execution, it also removes the line from the `crontab` entry.

Any changes made to system files are lost when you run `aset.restore`.

Use the `aset.restore` utility:

- When you want to remove ASET changes and restore the original system. If you want to deactivate ASET permanently, you can remove it from cron scheduling if the `aset` command has been added to root's `crontab`.
- After a brief period of experimenting with ASET, to restore the original system state.

- When some major functionality is not working properly and you suspect that ASET may be causing the problem.

To restore system files modified by ASET:

1. Become superuser.
2. Type **/usr/aset/aset.restore** and press Return. Informational messages are displayed while the script is restoring system files to their original state.
3. If there is an ASET crontab entry, you are prompted to ask if you want to remove it. Type **y** and press Return to remove the entry.

The following example restores system files to their pre-ASET state:

```
# /usr/aset/aset.restore

aset.restore: beginning restoration ...

Executing /usr/aset/tasks/firewall.restore

Beginning firewall.restore...

firewall.restore failed:
/usr/sbin/in.routed.asetoriginal not found.

Executing /usr/aset/tasks/sysconf.restore

Beginning sysconf.restore...

Restoring /etc/inetd.conf. Saved existing file in /etc/inetd.conf.asetbak.

Restoring /etc/aliases. Saved existing file in /etc/aliases.asetbak.

sysconf.restore completed.

Executing /usr/aset/tasks/tune.restore

Beginning tune.restore...
(This may take a while.)

tune.restore completed.

Executing /usr/aset/tasks/usrgrp.restore

Beginning usrgrp.restore...

Restoring /etc/passwd. Saved existing file in /etc/passwd.asetbak.

Restoring /etc/group. Saved existing file in /etc/group.asetbak.

Restoring /etc/shadow. Saved existing file in /etc/shadow.asetback.

usrgrp.restore completed.
```

```
Descheduling ASET from crontab file...
The following is the ASET schedule entry to be deleted:
1 2 * * * [ -x /usr/sbin/rtc ] && /usr/sbin/rtc -c > /dev/null 2>&10 0 * * *
/usr/aset/aset  -d /usr/aset
Proceed to deschedule: (y/n) y

Resetting security level from low to null.

aset.restore: restoration completed.
#
```

Note that the firewall `restore` was not successful in this example.

The `aset.restore` script does not remove files from the `/usr/aset/reports` and the `/usr/aset/archive` directories. If you want to reclaim that file system space, you may want to delete the contents of these directories.

ASET Error Messages

This section documents the error messages generated by ASET.

```
ASET failed: no mail program found.
```

ASET is directed to send the execution log to a user, but no mail program can be found. To fix the problem, install a mail program.

```
USAGE: aset [n user[@host]] in /bin mail or /usr/ucb/mail
Cannot decide current and previous security levels.
```

ASET cannot determine what the security levels are for the current and previous invocations. To fix the problem, ensure the current security level is set either through the command line option or by using the `ASETSECLEVEL` environment variable from a shell. Also, ensure that the last line of the `ASETDIR/archives/asetseclevel.arch` file correctly reflects the previous security level. If these values are not set or are incorrect, specify them correctly.

```
ASET working directory undefined.
To specify, set ASETDIR environment variable or use command line option -d
ASET startup unsuccessful.
```

The ASET working directory is not defined or is defined incorrectly. To fix the problem, use the `ASETDIR` environment variable or the `-d` command line option to correctly specify the ASET working directory and restart ASET.

```
ASET working directory $ASETDIR missing.
ASET startup unsuccessful.
```

The ASET working directory is not defined or it is defined incorrectly. This may be because the `ASETDIR` variable refers to a nonexistent directory. Ensure that the correct directory—the directory containing the ASET directory hierarchy—is referred to correctly.

```
Cannot expand $ASETDIR to full pathname.
```

ASET cannot expand the directory name given by the ASETDIR variable or the -d command line option to a full path name. To fix the problem, ensure that the directory name is correct and that it refers to an existing directory to which the user has access.

```
aset: invalid/undefined security level.
To specify, set ASESTSECLEVEL environment variable or use command line option -l,
with argument= low/med/high.
```

The security level is not defined or it is defined incorrectly. Only the values low, med, or high are acceptable. To fix the problem, use the ASETSECLEVEL variable or the -l command line option to specify one of the three values.

```
ASET environment file asetenv not found in $ASAETDIR.
ASET startup unsuccessful.
```

ASET cannot locate an asetenv file in its working directory. To fix the problem, ensure that there is an asetenv file in ASET's working directory.

```
<filename> doesn't exist or is not readable.
```

The file referred to by *<filename>* doesn't exist or is not readable. This problem can occur when using the -u option in which you can specify a file that contains a list of users whom you want to check. To fix the problem, ensure the argument to the -u option exists and is readable.

```
ASET task list TASKLIST undefined.
```

The ASET task list, which should be defined in the asetenv file, is not defined. Your asetenv file may be bad, or the entry may be missing. To fix the problem, examine your asetenv file. Ensure the task list is defined in the User Configurable section. Also check other parts of the file to ensure the file is intact. Refer to the asetenv(4) manual page for the content of a good asetenv file.

```
ASET task list TASKLIST missing.
ASET startup unsuccessful.
```

The ASET task list, which should be defined in the asetenv file, is not defined. Your asetenv file may be bad, or the entry may be missing. To fix the problem, check the User Configurable section of the asetenv file to ensure the variable is defined as in the proper format.

```
Warning! Duplicate ASET execution scheduled.
Check crontab file.
```

ASET is scheduled more than once. In other words, scheduling is requested while a schedule is already in effect. This conflict may not necessarily be an error if more than one schedule is desired. If you want more than one schedule, you should use crontab(1) scheduling. To fix the problem, check your crontab file to make sure that the correct schedule is in effect and that no duplicate crontab entries for ASET exist.

APPENDIX A

Volume Management

TARTING WITH THE SOLARIS 2.2 SYSTEM SOFTWARE, VOLUME MANAGEMENT AUTOmates the mounting of CD-ROMs and diskettes; users no longer need to have superuser permissions to mount a CD-ROM or a diskette.

NOTE. *The Solaris 2.0 and 2.1 procedures for mounting CD-ROMs and diskettes do not work for Solaris 2.2 and later releases. Volume management controls the* `/dev/dsk/c0t6d0s0` *path to a CD-ROM drive and the* `/dev/diskette` *path to the diskette drive. If you try to access a CD-ROM or diskette using these paths, an error message is displayed.*

Volume management provides users with a standard interface for dealing with diskettes and CD-ROMs. It provides three major benefits:

- Automatically mounting diskettes and CDs simplifies their use.
- Users can access diskettes and CDs without having to become superuser.
- Users on the network can gain automatic access to diskettes and CDs mounted on remote systems.

Without volume management, you mount devices manually by following these steps:

1. Insert media.
2. Become superuser.
3. Determine the location of the media device.
4. Create a mount point.
5. Make sure that you are not in the mount point directory.
6. Mount the device using the proper mount options.
7. Exit the superuser account.
8. Work with files on media.
9. Become superuser.
10. Unmount the media device.
11. Eject media.
12. Exit the superuser account.

With volume management, you mount devices automatically by following these steps:

1. Insert media.
2. For diskettes, use the `volcheck` command.

3. Work with files on media.
4. Eject media.

Volume Management Files

Volume management consists of the following elements:

- The `/usr/sbin/vold` volume management daemon
- The `/etc/vold.conf` configuration file that is used by the `vold` daemon to determine which devices to manage
- The `/etc/rmmount.conf` file that is used to configure removable media mounts as well as actions in `/usr/lib/rmmount`
- The volume daemon logs messages in the `/var/adm/vold.log` file.

The default `/etc/vold.conf` file is shown below:

```
# @(#)vold.conf 1.21     96/05/10 SMI
#
# Volume Daemon Configuration file
#

# Database to use (must be first)
db db_mem.so

# Labels supported
label dos label_dos.so floppy rmscsi pcmem
label cdrom label_cdrom.so cdrom
label sun label_sun.so floppy rmscsi pcmem

# Devices to use
use cdrom drive /dev/rdsk/c*s2 dev_cdrom.so cdrom%d
use floppy drive /dev/rdiskette[0-9] dev_floppy.so floppy%d
use pcmem drive /dev/rdsk/c*s2 dev_pcmem.so pcmem%d forceload=true
# use rmscsi drive /dev/rdsk/c*s2 dev_rmscsi.so rmscsi%d

# Actions
insert dev/diskette[0-9]/* user=root /usr/sbin/rmmount
insert dev/dsk/* user=root /usr/sbin/rmmount
eject dev/diskette[0-9]/* user=root /usr/sbin/rmmount
eject dev/dsk/* user=root /usr/sbin/rmmount
notify rdsk/* group=tty user=root /usr/lib/vold/volmissing -p

# List of file system types unsafe to eject
unsafe ufs hsfs pcfs
```

If a system has additional diskette drives, volume management automatically creates two subdirectories in `/vol/dev` for each additional drive—one to provide access to the file systems and the other to provide access to the raw device. For a second diskette drive, volume management creates directories named diskette1 and rdiskette1. For a third diskette drive, it creates directories named diskette2 and rdiskette2. And so on for additional drives.

If you want additional CD-ROM drives on a system, you must edit the /etc/vold.conf file and add the new devices to the Devices to use list. The syntax for a Devices to use entry is shown as follows:

```
use device type special shared-object symname options
```

Table A–1 describes each of the fields for the Devices to use syntax.

Table A–1 Device Control Syntax Descriptions

Field	Supported Default Values	Description
device	cdrom, floppy	The removable media device.
type	drive	The type of device—multiple or single media support.
special	/dev/dsk/c0t6 /,dev/diskette	Pathname of the device to be used in the /dev directory.
shared-object	/usr/lib/vold/*shared-object-name*	Location of the code that manages the device.
symname	cdrom0, floppy0	The symbolic name that refers to this device. The *symname* is placed in the device directory (either /cdrom or /floppy).
options	user=nobody group=nobody mode=0666	The user, group, and mode permissions for the inserted media.

The /etc/rmmount.conf file is as follows:

```
# @(#)rmmount.conf 1.3     96/05/10 SMI
#
# Removable Media Mounter configuration file.
#

# File system identification
ident hsfs ident_hsfs.so cdrom
ident ufs ident_ufs.so cdrom floppy rmscsi pcmem
ident pcfs ident_pcfs.so floppy rmscsi pcmem

# Actions
action cdrom action_filemgr.so
action floppy action_filemgr.so
action rmscsi action_filemgr.so
```

The files in the /usr/lib/vold directory are listed as follows:

```
castle% ls -1 /usr/lib/vold
db_mem.so.1
db_nis.so.1
```

```
dev_cdrom.so.1
dev_floppy.so.1
dev_pcmem.so.1
dev_rmscsi.so.1
dev_test.so.1
eject_popup
label_cdrom.so.1
label_dos.so.1
label_sun.so.1
label_test.so.1
volcancel
volmissing
volmissing_popup
volstat
castle%
```

The files in the `/usr/lib/rmmount` directory are listed as:

```
oak% ls -1 /usr/lib/rmmount
action_filemgr.so.1
action_workman.so.1
oak%
```

If you encounter problems with volume management, check the `/var/adm/vold.log` file for information. An example of this file follows:

```
oak% more /var/adm/vold.log
Tue Jun  1 17:34:24 1993 warning: dev_use: couldn't find a driver for drive cdrom
➥at /dev/dsk/cØt6
Tue Jun  1 17:39:12 1993 warning: dev_use: couldn't find a driver for drive cdrom
➥at /dev/dsk/cØt6
Tue Jun  1 18:24:24 1993 warning: dev_use: couldn't find a driver for drive cdrom
➥at /dev/dsk/cØt6
Wed Jun 23 15:Ø8:47 1993 warning: check device 36.2: device not managed
Wed Jun 23 15:Ø9:58 1993 warning: check device 36.2: device not managed
Wed Jun 23 15:11:Ø8 1993 warning: check device 36.2: device not managed
Thu Jul 15 13:51:23 1993 warning: check device 36.2: device not managed
Thu Jul 15 13:52:53 1993 warning: check device 36.2: device not managed
Thu Jul 15 14:Ø4:37 1993 warning: check device 36.2: device not managed
Thu Jul 15 14:Ø5:52 1993 warning: check device 36.2: device not managed
Thu Jul 15 14:Ø6:16 1993 warning: check device 36.2: device not managed
Wed Jul 21 16:33:33 1993 fatal: svc_tli_create: Cannot create server handleThu Jul
➥22 16:32:28 1993 warning: cdrom: /dev/rdsk/cØt6dØs2; Device busy
castle%
```

If you want to display debugging messages from the volume daemon, you can start the daemon by typing **/usr/sbin/vold -v -L 10**. With these flags set, the volume daemon logs quite a bit of information in `/var/adm/vold.log`.

Another way to gather debugging information is to run the `rmmount` command with the debug flag. To do so, edit `/etc/vold.conf` and change the lines that have `/usr/sbin/rmmount` to include the `-D` flag, as shown in the following example:

```
insert /vol*/dev/diskette[Ø-9]/* user=root /usr/sbin/rmmount -D
```

Volume Management Mount Points

Volume management automatically mounts CD-ROM file systems on the `/cdrom` mount point when you insert the media into the drive.

When you insert a diskette in the diskette drive, you must ask the system to check the diskette drive. You can check for a disk in any one of the following ways:

- From the command line, type **volcheck** and press Return.
- From the CDE front panel, click the Folders menu and then click Open Floppy.
- From the CDE File Manager File menu, choose Open Floppy.
- From the OpenWindows File Manager File menu, choose Check for Floppy.

When you use any one of these methods, the files are mounted on the `/floppy` mount point. Table A–2 describes the mount points and how volume management uses them.

Table A–2 Volume Management Mount Points

Media	Mount Point	State of Media
Diskette	`/floppy/floppy0`	Symbolic link to mounted diskette in local diskette drive
	`/floppy/`*`floppy-name`*	Mounted named diskette
	`/floppy/unnamed_floppy`	Mounted unnamed diskette
CD-ROM	`/cdrom/cdrom0`	Symbolic link to mounted CD-ROM in local CD-ROM drive
	`/cdrom/`*`CD-ROM-name`*	Mounted named CD-ROM
	`/cdrom/`*`CD-ROM-name`*`/ partition`	Mounted named CD-ROM with partitioned file system
	`/cdrom/unnamed_cdrom`	Mounted unnamed CD-ROM

If the media does not contain a file system, volume management provides block and character devices in the `/vol` file system, as shown in Table A–3.

Table A–3 Solaris 2.3 CD-ROM and Diskette Device Locations When No File System Is Present

Media	Device Location	State of Media
Diskette	`/vol/dev/diskette0/ unnamed_floppy`	Formatted unnamed diskette-block device access

Table A–3 Solaris 2.3 CD-ROM and Diskette Device Locations When No File System Is Present (continued)

Media	Device Location	State of Media
	/vol/dev/rdiskette0/unnamed_floppy	Formatted unnamed diskette—raw device access
	/vol/dev/diskette0/unlabeled	Unlabeled diskette—block diskette-raw device access
CD-ROM	/vol/dev/dsk/c0t6/unnamed_cdrom	CD-ROM—block device access
	/vol/dev/rdsk/c0t6/unnamed_cdrom	CD-ROM—raw device access

Local and Remote CD-ROMs

The following sections describe how to access files from local and remote CD-ROM drives.

Mounting a Local CD-ROM

Use the following procedure to mount a CD-ROM from a local drive:

1. Insert the CD-ROM in the CD-ROM drive. The CD-ROM is automatically mounted on the `/cdrom` mount point. If File Manager is running, a window displays the contents of the CD-ROM, as shown in Figure A–1.

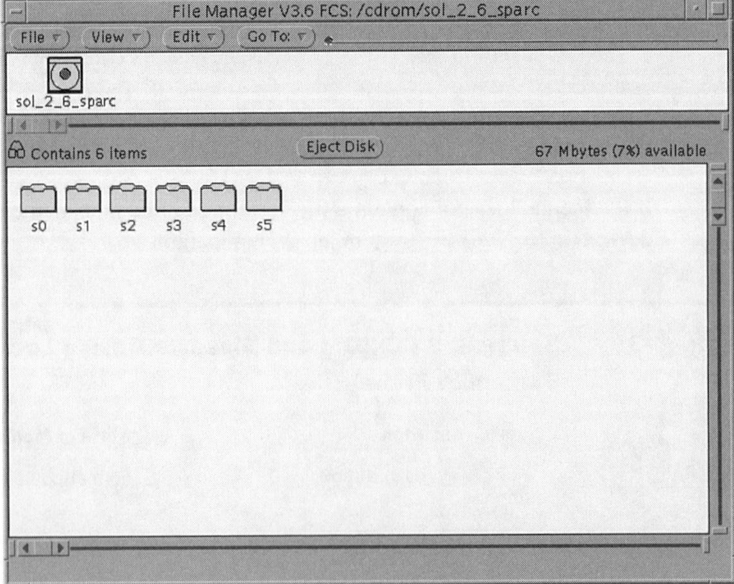

Figure A–1
The File Manager CD-ROM window.

2. To access files on the CD-ROM from a command line, type **cd /cdrom/cdrom0** and press Return.
3. Type **ls -L** and press Return. The list of files in the `/cdrom/cdrom0` directory is displayed. Use the `-L` option because some of the files on the CD may be symbolic links.

NOTE. *You can use the File Manager CD-ROM window and the command line interchangeably. For example, you can eject a CD-ROM either from a command line by typing* ***eject cdrom*** *or by clicking SELECT on the Eject button in the File Manager CD-ROM window.*

Sharing Files from a Remote CD-ROM Drive

Before you can share CD-ROM files from a command line, the `mountd` daemon must be running. On the system with the CD-ROM drive attached, type **ps -ef | grep mountd** and press Return.

If the `mountd` daemon is running, other systems can access shared files. If the `mountd` daemon is not running, you need to stop NFS services and restart them. Be sure to notify any users of the system that NFS services will be interrupted momentarily when you use the following procedure to start the `mountd` daemon:

1. Become superuser.
2. Type **/etc/rc3.d/S15nfs.server stop** and press Return. NFS services are stopped.
3. Type **/etc/rc3.d/S15nfs.server start** and press Return. NFS services are restarted and the CD files are exported.

```
oak% ps -ef ¦ grep mountd
    root  4571  4473  5 12:53:51 pts/3    0:00 grep mountd
oak% su
Password:
# /etc/rc3.d/S15nfs.server stop
# /etc/rc3.d/S15nfs.server start
```

Use the following steps to share CD files from a remote CD-ROM drive:

1. Insert the CD-ROM into the caddy and insert the caddy into the drive. The CD-ROM is mounted.
2. Become superuser on the Solaris 2.2 (or later) system with the CD-ROM drive attached.
3. Type **share -F nfs -o ro /cdrom/cdrom0** and press Return.

```
oak% su
Password:
# share -F nfs -o ro /cdrom/cdrom0
# ps -ef ¦ grep mountd
    root  4655  4473  6 12:56:05 pts/3    0:00 grep mountd
    root  4649     1 47 12:55:25 ?        0:00 /usr/lib/nfs/mountd
#
```

NOTE. *Volume management does not recognize entries in the* `/etc/dfs/dfstab` *file. With Solaris 2.3 and later releases of volume management, you can set up remote CD-ROM mounts to be automatically shared by editing the* `/etc/rmmount.conf` *file. Refer to the* `rmmount.conf` *manual page for more information.*

How to Mount Shared CD-ROM Files

You can use the `/mnt` directory as the mount point for the CD-ROM files or create another directory.

CAUTION! *Do not use the* `/cdrom` *mount point to mount local files. Volume management may interfere with accessing files on the volume management* `/cdrom` *mount point.*

Once the CD-ROM is in the remote drive and the files are shared, follow these steps to access the shared files on a local system:

1. Become superuser on the local system.
2. Type **mount *remote-system-name:/cdrom/cdrom0 /mount-point*** and press Return. The files from the remote system directory `/cdrom/cdrom0` are mounted on the `/mount-point` directory. The `cdrom0` subdirectory is symbolically linked to the actual name of the CD-ROM, which is assigned by the application vendor.

In the following example, the files from the remote system `castle` are mounted on the `/mnt` mount point.

```
oak% su
Password:
# mount castle:/cdrom/cdrom0 /mnt
# cd /mnt
# ls
SUNWssser  SUNWsssra  SUNWsssrb  SUNWsssrc  SUNWsssrd  SUNWssstr
#
```

How to Unmount Shared CD-ROM Files

When you are through using the CD-ROM files, use the following steps to unmount the remote CD-ROM:

1. On the local system, become superuser.
2. Type **cd** and press Return.
3. Type **umount */mount-point*** and press Return. The files from the remote system directory `/cdrom/cdrom0` are unmounted.

Diskettes and Volume Management

When you insert a diskette into the diskette drive, volume manager does not mount the diskette automatically; this prevents excessive reads, which can quickly wear out the diskette drive. You must use a command that checks for the presence of a diskette in the diskette drive.

Command-Line Access

Follow these steps to format a diskette from a command line:

1. Insert a diskette into the diskette drive.
2. Type **volcheck** and press Return. The system has access to the unformatted diskette.
3. Type **fdformat** and press Return to format a ufs file system or **fdformat -d** to format an MS-DOS file system.
4. When prompted, press Return to begin formatting the diskette.
5. For ufs file systems, you must also make a new file system on the diskette.
6. Become superuser.
7. Type **newfs /vol/dev/rdiskette0/unnamed_floppy** and press Return.

Follow these steps to access files on a formatted diskette:

1. Insert a formatted diskette in the diskette drive.
2. Type **volcheck** and press Return. If there is a formatted diskette in the drive, volume management mounts it on the `/floppy` mount point. If no diskette is in the drive, no error message is displayed. The volcheck command redisplays the prompt. Once the diskette is mounted on the `/floppy` mount point, you can access files on it either from the command line or from the File Manager Floppy window, which is described in the section "OpenWindows File Manager Access."
3. Type **cd /floppy** and press Return.
4. Type **ls** and press Return. The name of the diskette is displayed as the name of a directory.
5. Type **cd *diskette-name*** and press Return.
6. Type **ls** and press Return. The names of the files on the diskette are displayed. You can copy files to and from the diskette using the `cp` command.

In the following example, the diskette is not mounted, so the only directory in `/floppy` is `ms-dos_5`. After volcheck mounts the diskette, the directory with the name of the diskette is displayed. The diskette in this example contains only a `lost+found` directory.

```
oak% cd /floppy
oak% ls
ms-dos_5
oak% volcheck
oak% ls
ms-dos_5        unnamed_floppy
```

```
oak% cd unnamed_floppy
oak% ls
lost+found
oak% cp /home/winsor/Appx/appxA.doc .
oak% ls
appxA.doc lost+found
oak%
```

You cannot unmount a file system when that file system is in use by any process. If you get the message `Device busy`, a process may have its current working directory on the diskette, or some process has opened a file on the diskette. Use the `fuser` command to find out what processes are using the diskette. See the `fuser`(1M) manual page for information.

Use the following steps to eject the diskette:

1. Type **cd** and press Return. You have changed out of the `/floppy` directory.
2. Type **eject** and press Return. After a few seconds, the diskette is ejected from the drive.

OpenWindows File Manager Access

If you are running File Manager, you can use it to format a diskette, display the contents, and copy files to and from the diskette. Follow these steps to format a diskette, display its contents, and eject it:

1. Insert the diskette into the diskette drive.
2. Choose Check for Floppy from the File menu, as shown in Figure A–2.

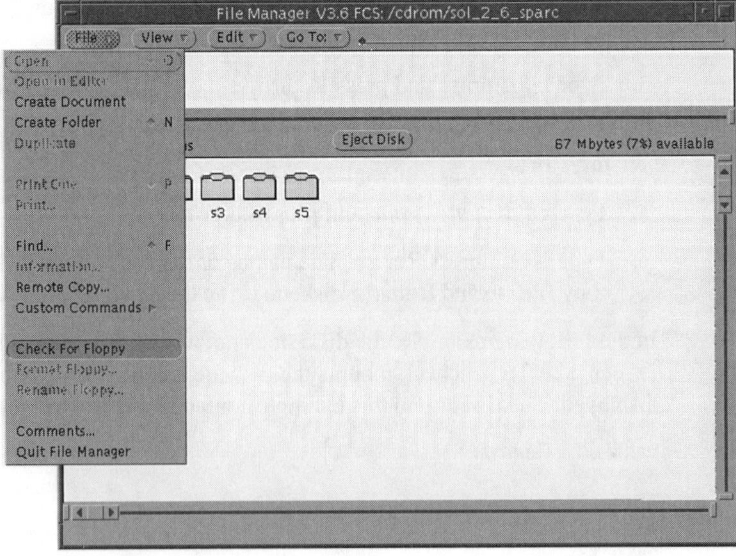

Figure A–2
Choose Check for Floppy from the File menu.

3. If the diskette is not formatted, a window is displayed, as shown in Figure A–3. Click SELECT on the Cancel & Eject button if you want to eject the diskette without formatting it.

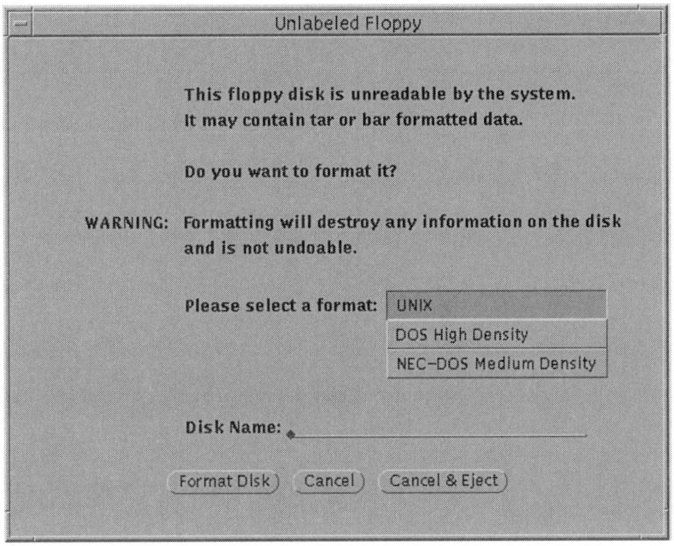

Figure A–3
The File Manager floppy format.

Unlabeled Floppy

This floppy disk is unreadable by the system.
It may contain tar or bar formatted data.

Do you want to format it?

WARNING: Formatting will destroy any information on the disk and is not undoable.

Please select a format: UNIX
DOS High Density
NEC-DOS Medium Density

Disk Name:

Format Disk Cancel Cancel & Eject

4. Click SELECT on the format you want to use and then click Format Disk. The diskette is formatted, and a new file system is created.

When the diskette is formatted and contains the file system, the File Manager Floppy window displays the contents of the diskette, as shown in Figure A–4.

NOTE. *You can drag and drop files to and from the Floppy window in the same way that you manipulate other files using the File Manager.*

To eject the diskette, click SELECT on the Eject Disk button. After a few seconds, the diskette is ejected and the File Manager Floppy window is dismissed.

CDE Front Panel Access

If you are running CDE, you can use the Folders menu on the front panel to display the contents of a floppy. Follow these steps to open a floppy from the front panel:

1. Insert a formatted or unformatted diskette into the diskette drive.

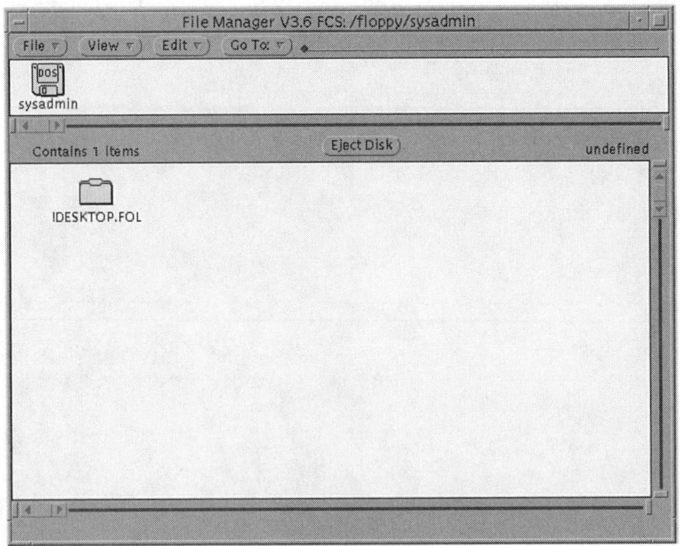

Figure A–4
The File Manager Floppy window.

2. From the front panel, open the Folders menu, shown in Figure A–5, and click Open Floppy.

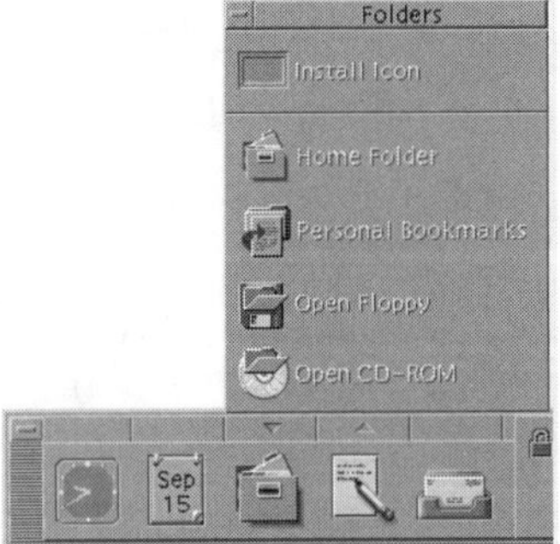

Figure A–5
The Front Panel Folders menu.

3. After the light on the CDE front panel stops flashing (about five to ten seconds), the floppy is mounted to `/floppy` and a File Manager window opens. Figure A–6 shows an example of the File Manager floppy window for a formatted floppy.

CDE File Manager Access

If you are running CDE File Manager, you can use it to format a diskette, display the contents, and copy files to and from the diskette. Follow these steps to open a diskette from the CDE File Manager:

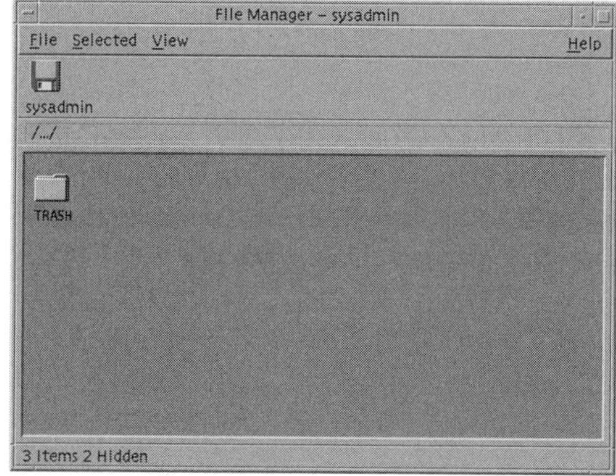

Figure A–6
The CDE File Manager floppy window.

1. Insert a formatted or unformatted diskette into the diskette drive.
2. From the File Manager File menu, shown in Figure A–7, choose Open Floppy. After the Ilight on the CDE front panel stops flashing (about five to ten seconds), the floppy is mounted to `/floppy` and a File Manager window opens.

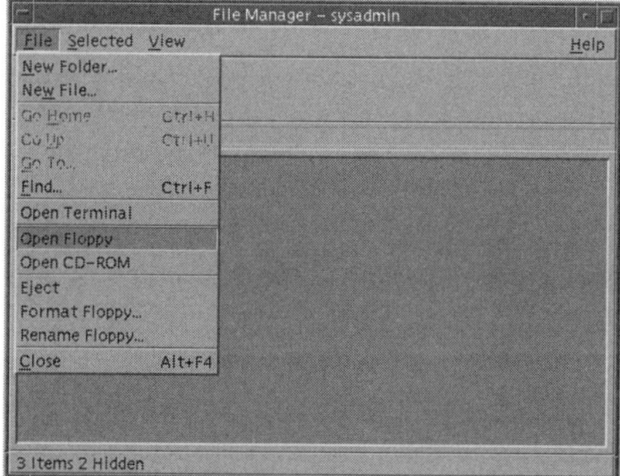

Figure A–7
The CDE File Manager menu.

3. From the File Manager File menu note that you can also format, rename, and eject the diskette by clicking the respective options.

Using the tar and cpio Commands with Diskettes

If a diskette contains `tar` or `cpio` files instead of a file system, volume management does not mount it. You cannot access files on the diskette from the old `/dev/rdiskette` device name because volume management provides access to the file system (if present), not to the device.

You can access `tar` and `cpio` files on a diskette using the symbolic link to the character cdevice for the media that is in floppy drive 0, as in the following:

`/vol/dev/aliases/floppy0`

Use the following steps to copy a file to a formatted diskette using the `tar` command:

1. Insert a formatted diskette into the diskette drive.
2. Type **volcheck** and press Return.
3. Type **tar cvf /vol/dev/aliases/floppy0** ***filename*** and press Return. The files are copied to the diskette.
4. Type **eject** and press Return. After a few seconds, the diskette is ejected.

Use the following steps to copy all `tar` files from a diskette:

1. Insert a formatted diskette into the diskette drive.
2. Change to the directory where you want to put the files.
3. Type **volcheck** and press Return. The diskette is mounted.
4. Type **tar xvf /vol/dev/aliases/floppy0** and press Return. The files are copied to the diskette.
5. Type **eject** and press Return. After a few seconds, the diskette is ejected.

Alternatively, with Solaris 2.2 (and later) systems, you can access `tar` or `cpio` files using the following device name syntax:

`/vol/dev/rfd0/`*`media-name`*

The most common *media-name* is `unlabeled`.

With Solaris 2.3, the device name syntax is changed. You access `tar` or `cpio` files using the following device name syntax:

`/vol/dev/rdiskette0/`*`media-name`*

The most frequent *media-name* for media without a file system is `unlabeled`.

For example, to copy a `tar` file to a diskette, type **tar cvf /vol/dev/rdiskette0/unlabeled** ***filename*** and press Return. To retrieve all tar files from a diskette, type **tar xvf /vol/dev/rdiskette0/unlabeled** and press Return.

Troubleshooting

From time to time, you may encounter problems with mounting diskettes (or, less frequently, a CD-ROM). If you encounter a problem, first check to find out if volume management knows about the diskette. The best way to check is to look in `/vol/dev/rdiskette0` to see if something is there. If the files are not mounted, you may have forgotten to run the `volcheck` command, or you may have a hardware problem. If references to `/vol` hang, the `/usr/sbin/vold` daemon has probably died, and you should restart it.

cIf you find a name in `/vol/dev/rdiskette0` and nothing is mounted in `/floppy/`*`media-name`*, it is likely that the data on the media is not a recognized file system. It may be a tar, cpio, or Macintosh file system. You can access these media through the block or character devices found in `/vol/dev/rdiskette0` or `/vol/dev/diskette0` and use your own tools to interpret the data on them.

Using Workman with Volume Management

Many people use the `workman` program to play music from their CD-ROM drive. Workman is not a Sun product, but it is in wide use. To use workman with volume management, add the line shown in bold to the `/etc/rmmount.conf` file. Be sure the line comes before the `action_filemgr` line.

```
# @(#)rmmount.conf 1.2     92/09/23 SMI
#
# Removable Media Mounter configuration file.
#

# File system identification
ident hsfs ident_hsfs.so cdrom
ident ufs ident_ufs.so cdrom floppy
ident pcfs ident_pcfs.so floppy

# Actions
action cdrom action_workman.so pathname
action cdrom action_filemgr.so
action floppy action_filemgr.so
```

The *`pathname`* is the name of the path where users access the workman program—for example, `/usr/apps/pkgs/exe/workman`.

When you have made this change, audio CD-ROMs are automatically detected and the workman program is started when the CD-ROM is inserted into the CD-ROM drive.

NOTE. *When you set up workman in the way described in this chapter, users should not try to start workman from the application because volume management may become confused. In addition, with Solaris 2.2 (and later) volume management, if you are using workman, you must eject the CD-ROM from the workman application. If you eject the CD-ROM from another window, workman hangs. This problem has been fixed in Solaris 2.3 system software.*

Changes with Solaris 2.3 System Software

With Solaris 2.2, you cannot automatically export CD-ROM and diskette drives or use the `/etc/vfstab` file. You must use the `share` command to export the file system after every reboot.

NOTE. *You cannot share a pcfs file system (MS-DOS formatted diskettes) with Solaris 2.2 system software.*

With Solaris 2.3 system software, a `share cdrom*` instruction is provided in the `/etc/rmmount.conf` file so that a CD-ROM is automatically shared when you insert it into the CD-ROM drive. You can specify flags in the same way as you do for the `share` command. You can also use the name of a particular piece of media, if desired. Refer to the `rmmount.conf` manual page for more details.

With Solaris 2.3, the device names for the physical device were changed to be consistent with `/dev`. In Solaris 2.2 system software, the device names are `/vol/dev/rfd0` and `/vol/dev/fd0`. With Solaris 2.3 system software, the device names are `/vol/dev/rdiskette0` and `/vol/dev/diskette0`. The symbolic link in `/vol/dev/aliases` always points to the correct device.

Disabling Volume Management

You may want to disable volume management for some users. To do so, use the following steps:

1. Become superuser.
2. Remove or rename the `/etc/rc2.d/S92volmgt` script.
3. Type **/etc/init.d/volmgt stop** and press Return.

You can disable part of volume management and leave other parts functional. You may, for example, want to automatically mount CD-ROMs, but use the Solaris 2.0 method for accessing files on a diskette. You can do so by commenting out the lines for diskettes in the `/etc/vold.conf` file, as shown:

```
# @(#)vold.conf 1.21     96/05/10 SMI
#
# Volume Daemon Configuration file
#

# Database to use (must be first)
db db_mem.so

# Labels supported
label dos label_dos.so floppy rmscsi pcmem
label cdrom label_cdrom.so cdrom
label sun label_sun.so floppy rmscsi pcmem

# Devices to use
use cdrom drive /dev/rdsk/c*s2 dev_cdrom.so cdrom%d
# use floppy drive /dev/rdiskette[0-9] dev_floppy.so floppy%d
use pcmem drive /dev/rdsk/c*s2 dev_pcmem.so pcmem%d forceload=true
# use rmscsi drive /dev/rdsk/c*s2 dev_rmscsi.so rmscsi%d
```

```
# Actions
insert dev/diskette[0-9]/* user=root /usr/sbin/rmmount
insert dev/dsk/* user=root /usr/sbin/rmmount
eject dev/diskette[0-9]/* user=root /usr/sbin/rmmount
eject dev/dsk/* user=root /usr/sbin/rmmount
notify rdsk/* group=tty user=root /usr/lib/vold/volmissing -p

# List of file system types unsafe to eject
unsafe ufs hsfs pcfs
```

APPENDIX

B

Solaris Server Intranet Extension Products

THE SOLARIS SERVER INTRANET EXTENSION 1.0 CD-ROM CONTAINS A SUITE OF PRODUCTS for system management, network services, and remote connectivity and security. Sun Microsystems automatically ships the Solaris Server Intranet Extension 1.0 CD-ROM with each server. The CD-ROM is not shipped with desktop systems. Most of the products available on this CD-ROM were previously part of the Solstice suite of tools. You can install these products on systems running Solaris 2.5.1 system software or later.

This appendix provides an overview of the products on the Solaris Server Intranet Extension CD-ROM to help you determine whether these products are useful for your system administration needs. It also lists system requirements and provides brief installation instructions for each product. If your site does not have the Solaris Server Intranet Extension CD-ROM, you can order it from your Sun sales representative or authorized reseller. You can also find information about the Solaris Server Intranet Extension products from Sun's Web page at `http://www.sun.com`.

Introducing the Solaris Server Intranet Extension Products

The products on the Solaris Server Intranet Extension CD-ROM provide functionality in three different areas:

- System management
- Network services
- Remote connectivity and security

System Management

System management capabilities are the core of any complete server offering. The Solaris Server Intranet Extension system management product set offers powerful system and network management tools for centralized, simplified management of distributed, heterogeneous environments.

The following list briefly introduces the system management products:

- *AdminSuite* software is a unified suite of tools for administering a distributed system and managing such functions as user accounts, groups, administrative data, printers, file systems, disks, and serial ports.
- *DiskSuite* software is a disk storage management tool designed to meet the demands of mission-critical business applications. DiskSuite addresses the need for increased data safety, availability, and performance. DiskSuite uses the following technologies: disk mirroring, hot spares, RAID-5, concatenation, disk striping and RAID-5, and a logging UNIX file system.

- *AutoClient* software is a desktop management application that centralizes administration, makes the desktop a field replaceable unit (FRU), eliminates software installation on desktops, and eliminates the need for desktop backups. Solstice AutoClient software reduces the cost of desktop management and is a key component of the centralized administration model.
- *Backup Utility* software is the single-server version of the Solstice Data Backup Utility that enables you to back up a single server to a single backup device and supports non-automated backup devices (single devices) in 4 mm, 8 mm, and 1/4 inch formats.

Network Services

The network services products enable Solaris to seamlessly integrate Novell, Windows, and AppleTalk clients while maintaining their native environments. In addition to basic file and printing services, Solaris adds powerful messaging, Web publishing, and Java application support that is essential to the new Web group.

The following list briefly introduces the network services products:

- *TotalNET Advanced Server (TAS)* software provides network operating system software integrated with UNIX print and application servers. You install TAS directory on to the server to enable client PC and UNIX computers to become instantaneously productive.
- *Sun Web Server* software is designed for Internet Service Providers (ISPs) and corporations whose Internet/intranet servers must be high performance, scalable, and able to handle large numbers of users and transactions.
- *Solstice Internet Mail Server (SIMS)* software is an advanced mail solution for today's Solaris workgroups. SIMS provides open, Internet-based mail built on key Internet standards such as IMAP4, POP3, SMTP, and MIME. SIMS 2.0 also includes use of five Solstice Internet Mail reference clients, which run on Solaris workstations and Microsoft Windows PCs. These clients provide the best mobile and disconnected mail client solutions available in the market today.
- *Java Interface Definition Language (IDL)* software, Sun's 100 percent pure Java Object Request Broker (ORB) system, provides the software foundation necessary to deliver enterprise client/server applications for the Internet. Applications that use Java IDL seamlessly integrate with non-Java programs and programs from other vendors. The Java IDL system is based on the latest Common Object Request Broker Architecture (CORBA) and Internet Inter ORB Protocol (IIOP) industry standards.

Remote Connectivity and Security

Whether you need to connect workgroups over leased lines or through the Internet, Solaris meets your most demanding connectivity needs and ensures that your private information remains private.

The following list briefly introduces the remote connectivity and security products:

- *Solstice PPP* software provides extended Internet connectivity for Solaris SPARC and x86 systems. With Solstice PPP, a Solaris system acts as an Internet router and supports all IP applications transparently over both leased lines and dial-up connections.
- *SunScreen SKIP* software is Sun Microsystems' implementation of Simple Key-management for Internet Protocols (SKIP). SunScreen SKIP is replacement software and upgrade software for any previous version of SKIP for Solaris. SKIP software provides encryption for your data and authentication of the IP traffic stream. SunScreen SKIP enables you to securely conduct business over both the corporate intranet and the Internet.

CD-ROM Contents

Table B–1 lists the top-level files and directories on the Intranet Extension CD-ROM.

Table B–1 Top-level Files and Directories on Solaris Server Intranet Extension CD-ROM

File/Directory	Description
`1README.html`	HTML file containing an introduction to the Solaris Server Intranet Extension products.
`AdminSuite_2.3+ AutoClient_2.1`	Directory containing packages and documentation for the AdminSuite 2.3 and AutoClient 2.1 products.
`Backup_4.2.6`	Directory containing packages and documentation for the Backup 4.2.6 product.
`Copyright`	File containing copyright information.
`DiskSuite_4.1`	Directory containing packages and documentation for the DiskSuite 4.1 product.
`JavaIDL_1.1`	Directory containing packages and documentation for the Java IDL 1.1 product.
`PPP_3.0.1`	Directory containing packages and documentation for the PPP 3.0.1 product.
`Skip_1.1.1`	Directory containing packages and documentation for the SunScreen SKIP 1.1.1 product.
`Solstice_ Internet_Mail_ Server`	Directory containing packages and documentation for the Solstice Internet Mail Server product.
`Sun_WebServer_1.0`	Directory containing packages and documentation for the Sun Web Server 1.0 product.
`Totalnet_ Advanced_Server`	Directory containing packages and documentation for the TotalNet Advanced Server product.
`autorun`	Directory containing installation scripts.
`autorun.inf`	File containing the `autorun.inf` script.
`html`	Directory containing HTML files describing the products on the CD-ROM.
`nfsc`	Directory containing installation script files.

AdminSuite

The Solstice AdminSuite 2.3 product provides a suite of graphical user interface tools and commands that you can use to perform system administration tasks.

The Solstice AdminSuite software enables you to locally or remotely manage the following:

- Important network-related system database files, such as aliases and hosts
- User accounts and groups
- File systems
- Disk slices and x86 fdisk partitions
- Terminals and modems
- Diskless and dataless clients
- AutoClient systems
- Stand-alone systems
- JavaStations
- Servers
- Printers

The Solstice AdminSuite software to perform system administration benefits you in the following ways:

- The tools and commands are faster than using numerous Solaris commands to perform the same tasks.
- System files are updated automatically without the risk of making errors by editing important system files manually.
- You can manage systems remotely from one system.

Table B–2 lists the Solstice AdminSuite tools that run under an X Window System, such as the CDE and OpenWindows environments.

Table B–2 Solstice AdminSuite Tools

AdminSuite Tool	Description
Host Manager	Use to manage system information and server support for AutoClient and stand-alone systems, diskless and dataless clients, and JavaStations.
Group Manager	Use to manage UNIX group information.

Table B–2 Solstice AdminSuite Tools (continued)

AdminSuite Tool	Description
User Manager	Use to manage user account information.
Serial Port Manager	Use to manage serial port software for terminals and modems.
Printer Manager	Use to manage printer software and configurations for print servers and clients.
Database Manager	Use to manage network-related system files such as aliases and hosts.
Storage Manager (comprised of Disk Manager and File System Manager)	Use to manage disk slices and x86 fdisk partitions on a single disk or a group of equivalent disks (Disk Manager) and file systems for a server or for a group of clients on a server (File System Manager).

AdminSuite Files and Directories on the CD

The files and directories in the `/cdrom/solaris_srvr_intranet_ext_1_0/AdminSuite_2.3+AutoClient_2.1` directory are listed in Table B–3.

Table B–3 AdminSuite Files and Directories

File/Directory	Description
`4.x`	Directory containing the SUNWhinst package. You must install this package on a server to be able to add SunOS 4.x services to support 4.x clients.
`Copyright`	File containing copyright information.
`Demo`	Directory containing animated video describing AutoClient concepts.
`Examples`	Directory containing an NIS Makefile stub used to configure automounter to support Solstice products.
`License_forms`	Directory containing license request forms used to request licenses for the Solstice AutoClient 2.1 product.
`Manuals`	Directory containing product documentation in both AnswerBook and HTML 2.0 format.
`Patches`	Directory containing x86 and SPARC patches.
`README`	Text file containing information about documentation and demo files. Note that the CD-ROM documentation paths in the README file may not be correct.
`Solaris`	Directory containing Solstice product binaries.
`admin_install`	Shell script containing the Solstice installation program.
`lic_install`	Shell script containing the license installation program used to install license servers to support the Solstice AutoClient 2.1 product.
`rm_admin`	Shell script containing a program that you can use to remove previous versions of AdminSuite (2.1) and AutoClient (1.0 and 1.0.1).

Installing Solstice AdminSuite

The following sections provide guidelines for installing Solstice AdminSuite software. For complete instructions refer to the *Solstice AdminSuite 2.3 Installation and Product Notes* documentation available in the `/cdrom/ solaris_srvr_intranet_ext_1_0/ AdminSuite_2.3+AutoClient_2.1/Manuals` directory.

Reviewing Disk Space Requirements

You need 35 MB of free disk space plus an additional 15 MB of disk space for each architecture (SPARC and X86) to perform a full installation of the Solstice AdminSuite 2.3 software on a Solstice station manager system.

NOTE. *You do not need to do a full installation of Solstice AdminSuite 2.3 on each system. You can do a complete installation on one system and use the installation program to set up other systems to access the complete Solstice AdminSuite 2.3 software installation.*

Checking Software Package Requirements

The Solstice AdminSuite 2.3 product verifies that the following software packages are installed on systems running the Solaris 2.5 or later operating environment:

- SUNWadmc (System administration core libraries)
- SUNWadmfw (System and network administration framework)
- SUNWsadml (Solstice launcher)
- SUNWmfrun (Motif runtime kit)

The SUNWsadml and SUNWmfrun software packages should be automatically installed on systems running the Solaris 2.3 and later releases. To verify that the packages are installed and available, type **pkginfo | grep <*pkgname*>** and press Return.

NOTE. *Although the Solstice AdminSuite 2.3 Installation and Product Notes documentation says that you must install these packages from the Solaris CD-ROM for Solaris 2.6, these packages may already be installed.*

The SunSoft Print Client software assumes the following Federated Naming Service (FNS) packages are already installed:

- SUNWfns
- SUNWfnspr

These packages are automatically installed by the Solstice AdminSuite installation scripts on systems running Solaris 2.3 and later releases. On systems running the Solaris 2.3 and 2.4 operating environment, you must install the SUNWlibCf package to use the SunSoft Print Client software in the NIS+ name service. You can obtain this package from the Solaris media used to originally install the system.

Removing Previously Installed AdminSuite Software

If you have installed an earlier release of the Solstice AdminSuite software (for example, Solstice AdminSuite 2.2), you must remove the old version before installing your new software.

To remove previously installed software:

1. Log in as root on the server running the old AdminSuite software.
2. Type **cd /cdrom/solaris_srvr_intranet_ext_1_0/ AdminSuite_2.3+AutoClient_2.1** and press Return.
3. Type **./rm_admin -v 2.2 -d /opt [-f]** and press Return. The `-v` option specifies the version to be removed. If you do not specify a version number, the command removes the 2.1 version from the `/export/opt` directory. The `-d` option specifies the directory where the AdminSuite software is installed. The optional `-f` option forces removal of software with no confirmation prompt.

Verifying sysadmin Group Membership

You must be a member of the sysadmin group (GID 14) to run the `admin_install` script. In addition, you must belong to the `sysadmin` group on each host you specify during installation.

To verify that you are a member of the sysadmin group, type **groups** and press Return. If the sysadmin group is listed in the output, you are a member of the group.

In the following example, the user is a member of both the `staff` and `sysadmin` groups.

```
castle% groups
staff sysadmin
castle%
```

Running the admin_install Script

To install AdminSuite and AutoClient software:

1. Log in as a member of the `sysadmin` group for the system.
2. Insert the product CD into your CD-ROM drive. If your system is running volume management, the CD is mounted automatically.
3. Type **cd /cdrom/solaris_srvr_intranet_ext_1_0/AdminSuite_2.3+AutoClient_2.1** and press Return.
4. Type **./admin_install** and press Return.
5. Follow the installation instructions displayed by the `admin_install` script. For complete instructions refer to the *Solstice AdminSuite 2.3 Installation and Product Notes* documentation available in the `/cdrom/ solaris_srvr_intranet_ext_1_0/ AdminSuite_2.3+AutoClient_2.1/Manuals` directory.

Running AdminSuite

To run AdminSuite, type **/usr/bin/solstice&** and press Return. For complete instructions on how to use AdminSuite, refer to the *Solstice AdminSuite 2.3 Administration Guide* available in the `/cdrom/solaris_srvr_intranet_ext_1_0/ AdminSuite_2.3+AutoClient_2.1/Manuals` directory.

AutoClient

An *AutoClient system* is a system that caches (locally stores copies of data as it is referenced) all of its needed system software from a server. The Solstice AutoClient product enables you to set up systems as AutoClient systems and provide centralized administration for these systems. AutoClient systems use Solaris diskless and cache file system (CacheFS) technologies.

The AutoClient technology makes administration easier, enabling system administrators to maintain many AutoClient systems from a server. You do not have to make changes on each individual system. Users may notice improved performance as well on both AutoClient systems and servers.

An AutoClient system is nearly identical to a diskless client system. Diskless client systems have no hard disk and depend on a server for its software and storage areas. Diskless clients remotely mount root (`/`), `/usr`, and `/home file` systems from a server.

An AutoClient system has the following characteristics:

- Requires 100 MB or larger local disk used for swapping and for caching its individual root (`/`) file system and the `/usr` file system from a server
- Can be set up so that it can continue to access its cache when the server is unavailable
- Relies on servers to provide other file systems and software applications
- Contains no permanent data, making it a field replaceable unit (FRU)

NOTE. *You must obtain a license for each AutoClient system you want to add to your network. For licensing information, see the Solstice AutoClient 2.1 Installation and Product Notes.*

Advantages of an AutoClient System

AutoClient technology provides many system administration advantages over existing system types.

AutoClient systems have the following advantages over diskless systems:

- Provides better overall scalability in a network environment, which could result in less network load.

- Uses less disk space on a server than a diskless system because an AutoClient system does not require any swap space on a server.
- Uses significantly less network and server bandwidth than a diskless system.

AutoClient systems have the following advantages over dataless and standalone systems:

- Require less system administration overhead. The data for an AutoClient system is on a server, which enables centralized administration. For example, with AutoClient systems need to back up only the server(s) that supports the AutoClient systems. You can also manipulate AutoClient root file systems from the server without accessing each system individually.
- Are FRUs, which makes them easy to replace if they fail.
- Are installed by setting up an AutoClient system with the Host Manager. You do not have to use the Solaris installation program to install the Solaris environment on an AutoClient system.

How an AutoClient System Works

The CacheFS technology is the important component of AutoClient systems. A *cache* is a local storage area for data. A *cached file system* is a local file system that is used to store files from a server as they are referenced. Subsequent references to the same files are accessed from the cache instead of being retrieved from the server. This functionally reduces the load on the network and the server and generally results in faster access for the AutoClient system. When the cache becomes full, space is reclaimed on a least-recently-used basis. Files that have been unreferenced from the longest time are discarded from the cache to free space for the files that are currently being referenced.

An AutoClient system uses its local disk for swap space and to cache its individual root (`/`) file system and the `/usr` file system from the server's back file system.

How an AutoClient System Cache Is Updated

An AutoClient system uses *consistency checking* to keep a cached file system synchronized with its back file system on the server.

By default, files that are updated in the server's back file systems are updated on the AutoClient system's cached file systems within 24 hours. However, if the update needs to be done sooner, you can use the `autosync` command to initiate consistency checking that updates (synchronizes) an AutoClient system's cached file systems with its server's back file systems.

Each time an AutoClient system is booted, the AutoClient system's cached file systems are checked for consistency and updated with its server's back file systems.

If you add new files to an AutoClient system, its server's back file systems are updated immediately because an AutoClient system uses a *write-through cache*. A write-through cache is one that immediately updates its back file system as data is changed or added to the cache.

NOTE. *Consistency checking for an AutoClient system is different from a system running CacheFS. AutoClient files (`/` and `/usr`) are not likely to change very often, so consistency checking does not need to be done as frequently on an AutoClient system as on a system running CacheFS.*

AutoClient Files and Directories on the CD

Refer to Table B–3 on page 502 for a list of file and directories in the `/cdrom/solaris_srvr_intranet_ext_1_0/AdminSuite_2.3+AutoClient_2.1` directory.

Installing AutoClient Software

The following sections provide guidelines for installing Solstice AutoClient software. For complete instructions refer to the *Solstice AdminSuite 2.3 Installation and Product Notes* documentation available in the `/cdrom/ solaris_srvr_intranet_ext_1_0/AdminSuite_2.3+AutoClient_2.1/Manuals` directory.

Supported Platforms and Operating Systems

You can set up both SPARC and x86 AutoClient systems on any systems running Solaris 2.4 and later system software.

AutoClient software is supported on Solaris 2.4 and later systems. If you plan on having 4.*x* clients on your server, and are running a version of Solaris later than 2.5.1, you need to manually install the SUNWhinst package that is included in the `/cdrom/solaris_srvr_intranet_ext_1_0/ AdminSuite_2.3+AutoClient_2.1/4.x` directory on the CD-ROM.

Reviewing Disk Space Requirements

You need 35 MB of free disk space for the spooled software area and an additional 7 MB of disk space for each architecture (SPARC and x86) to perform a full installation of the Solstice AutoClient 2.1 software.

Checking Software Package Requirements

The Solstice AutoClient 2.1 product verifies that the following software packages are installed on systems running the Solaris 2.5 or later operating environment:

- SUNWadmc (System administration core libraries)
- SUNWadmfw (System and network administration framework)
- SUNWsadml (Solstice launcher)

- SUNWmfrun (Motif runtime kit)

The SUNWsadml and SUNWmfrun software packages should be automatically installed on systems running the Solaris 2.3 and later releases. To verify that the packages are installed and available, type **pkginfo | grep <*pkgname*>** and press Return.

NOTE. *Although the Solstice AdminSuite 2.3 Installation and Product Notes documentation says that you must install these packages from the Solaris CD-ROM for Solaris 2.6, these packages may already be installed.*

Removing Previously Installed AutoClient Software

If you have installed an earlier release of the Solstice AutoClient software, you must remove the old version before installing your new software.

To remove previously installed software:

1. Log in as root on the server running the old AutoClient software.
2. Type **cd /cdrom/solaris_srvr_intranet_ext_1_0/ AdminSuite_2.3+AutoClient_2.1** and press Return.
3. Type **./rm_admin -a -d /opt** and press Return. The -a option specifies that you want to remove the AutoClient software. The -d option specifies the directory where the AutoClient software is installed.

Verifying sysadmin Group Membership

You must be a member of the `sysadmin` group (GID 14) to run the `admin_install` script. In addition, you must belong to the `sysadmin` group on each host you specify during installation.

To verify that you are a member of the `sysadmin` group, type **groups** and press Return. If the `sysadmin` group is listed in the output, you are a member of the group.

In the following example, the user is a member of both the `staff` and `sysadmin` groups.

```
castle% groups
staff sysadmin
castle%
```

Installing Patches

Support for automatically patching new diskless and AutoClient clients is not integrated into the AdminSuite and AutoClient tools. A command-line interface, `admclientpatch`, is provided to enable you to patch existing clients with one operation.

The AdminSuite product ships a small number of required patches for different releases of Solaris. The appropriate patches are applied as you create new clients. You can use the `admclientpatch` command to spool additional patches or you can remove patches from the spool area that you no longer need. You should, however, be careful when removing one of the patches that is shipped with Solstice AutoClient 2.1 because new clients may not work properly if a required patch is missing.

Because patches are applied automatically when you create a client, be aware that if you have existing clients, including dataless clients, that share the OS service with the new client, these existing clients now also have the patch. Use the `admclientpatch` command to be sure that all of the diskless and AutoClient systems also have the patch applied to their root file system. For dataless clients, you may need to go to each client and apply the patch to ensure that the dataless root is patched properly to match the shared OS service.

The patch also affects any dataless clients that use CacheFS and that share the OS service. You need to apply the appropriate patch to the dataless client's root for the client to work properly.

The patches are in the spool area `/opt/SUNWadmd/Patches`. The `/cdrom/ solaris_srvr_intranet_ext_1_0/AdminSuite_2.3+AutoClient_2.1/ Patches` directory on the CD-ROM contains i386 patch number 104469-06 and SPARC patch 104468-06. Refer to the `README` file in the `/cdrom/ solaris_srvr_intranet_ext_1_0/AdminSuite_2.3+AutoClient_2.1/ Patches` directories for more information.

Table B–4 lists the patches that need to be applied to the dataless client root.

Table B–4 AutoClient Patches

OS Version Number	Patch Number
Solaris 2.5 SPARC	102906-2
Solaris 2.5.1 SPARC	103006-02
Solaris 2.6 SPARC	104468-06
Solaris 2.5 i386	102939-02
Solaris 2.5.1 i386	103007-02
Solaris 2.6 i386	104469-06

Installing Solstice AdminSuite and AutoClient Software

To install AdminSuite and AutoClient software:

1. On the server, log in as a member of the `sysadmin` group.
2. Insert the product CD into your CD-ROM drive. If your system is running volume management, the CD is mounted automatically.
3. Type **cd /cdrom/solaris_srvr_intranet_ext_1_0/ AdminSuite_2.3+AutoClient_2.1** and press Return.
4. Type **./admin_install** and press Return.

5. Follow the installation instructions displayed by the admin_install script. For complete instructions refer to the *Solstice AutoClient 2.1 Installation and Product Notes* documentation available in the `/cdrom/ solaris_srvr_intranet_ext_1_0/ AdminSuite_2.3+AutoClient_2.1/Manuals` directory.

Running AutoClient

To run AutoClient, type **/usr/bin/solstice&** and press Return. For complete instructions on how to use AutoClient, refer to the *Solstice AutoClient 2.1 Administration Guide* available in the `/cdrom/solaris_srvr_intranet_ext_1_0/ AdminSuite_2.3+AutoClient_2.1/Manuals` directory.

DiskSuite

Solstice DiskSuite 4.1 is a software product that enables you to manage large numbers of disks and the file systems on those disks. Although you can use DiskSuite in many ways, most tasks include:

- Increasing storage capacity
- Increasing data availability

In some instances, DiskSuite can also improve I/O performance.

DiskSuite runs on all SPARC and x86 systems running Solaris 2.4 or later releases.

CAUTION! *If you do not use DiskSuite correctly, you can destroy data. As a minimum safety precaution, make sure you have a current backup of your data before using DiskSuite.*

DiskSuite uses virtual disks to manage physical disks and their associated data. In DiskSuite, a virtual disk is called a *metadevice*. Applications and tools accessing file systems on metadevices consider them to be functionally identical to physical disks.

DiskSuite metadevices are built from slices (disk partitions). You can build metadevices easily with the DiskSuite Tool that comes with DiskSuite. DiskSuite Tool presents you with a view of all the slices available to you. You can quickly assign slices to metadevices by dragging and dropping slices onto metadevice objects. You can also build and modify metadevices by using DiskSuite's command-line utilities.

If, for example, you want to create more storage capacity, you can use DiskSuite to make the system treat a collection of many small slices as one larger slice or device. After you have created a large metadevice from the slices, you can immediately begin using it just as any "real" slice or device.

DiskSuite can increase the reliability and availability of data by using mirrors (copied data) and RAID5 metadevices. DiskSuite's hot spares can provide another level of data availability for mirrors and RAID5 metadevices. *Hot spares* are a collection of slices that are reserved to be automatically substituted in case of slice failure in either a submirror or RAID5 metadevice.

NOTE. *Running RAID5 with DiskSuite can have a substantial impact on CPU resources.*

Once you have set up your configuration, you can use DiskSuite Tool to report on its operation. You can also use DiskSuite's SNMP trap-generating daemon so that you can work with a network monitoring console to automatically receive DiskSuite error messages.

NOTE. *Solstice DiskSuite 4.1 is not backwardly compatible with previous Online: DiskSuite 2.0.1 and 3.0 products. It is compatible with Solstice DiskSuite 4.0. If you have one of the earlier versions of Online: DiskSuite installed, you must convert your current metadevice configuration to Solstice DiskSuite 4.1.*

DiskSuite Files and Directories on the CD

Table B–5 lists the files and directories in the `/cdrom/ solaris_srvr_intranet_ext_1_0/ DiskSuite_4.1` directory.

Table B–5 DiskSuite Files and Directories

File/Directory	Description
`Manuals`	Directory containing HTML and PostScript versions of the *Solstice DiskSuite User's Guide and Reference.*
README	Text file containing information about documentation and demo files.
`copyright`	File containing copyright information.
`copyright.francais`	File containing copyright information in French.
`i386`	Directory containing x86 packages and patches.
`run_demo`	A shell script that runs the RAD demo of Solstice DiskSuite 4.1.
`scripts`	Directory containing the program to convert from Online: DiskSuite 2.0.1/3.0 to Solstice DiskSuite 4.*x*. Refer to the product notes for the proper use of this program.
`sparc`	Directory containing SPARC packages and patches.

Installing Solstice DiskSuite

The following sections provide guidelines for installing Solstice DiskSuite software. For complete instructions refer to the *Solstice DiskSuite 4.1 Installation and Product Notes* documentation available in the `/cdrom/ solaris_srvr_intranet_ext_1_0/ DiskSuite_4.1/Manuals` directory.

Reviewing Disk Space Requirements

You need 35 MB of free disk space plus an additional 15 MB of disk space for each architecture (SPARC and X86) to perform a full installation of the Solstice DiskSuite 4.1 software on a system that is set up to manage disk resources.

Choosing Software Packages

This section describes the DiskSuite packages. In addition to the DiskSuite packages, you can install the packages for Solstice AdminSuite Storage Manager, a graphical tool for administering file systems and disks. If AdminSuite 2.2 or later is already installed on your system, do not install any of the AdminSuite packages included with DiskSuite. Refer to Table B–5 for a description of the DiskSuite packages.

You must install packages in the order shown in Table B–6 for the software to function properly.

Table B–6 DiskSuite Packages

Package	Description	Required/Optional
SUNWadm5u	Solstice AdminSuite supplement for Solaris 2.3 and 2.4 releases	Required for AdminSuite Storage Manager
SUNWadm5r	Solstice AdminSuite root supplement for Solaris 2.3 and 2.4	Required for AdminSuite Storage Manager
SUNWSadmc	Solstice AdminSuite Core Methods	Required for AdminSuite Storage Manager
SUNWsadmo	Solstice AdminSuite Object	Required for AdminSuite Storage Manager
SUNWsadml	Solstice Admintool Launcher	Required for AdminSuite Storage Manager
SUNWadmsm	Solstice AdminSuite Storage Manager application	Required for AdminSuite Storage Manager
SUNWmd	The base DiskSuite product	Required
SUNWmdg	DiskSuite Tool graphical user interface	Optional but recommended
SUNWmdn	DiskSuite SNMP log daemon	Optional

Installing Solstice DiskSuite

To install DiskSuite software from the command line:

1. Insert the product CD into your CD-ROM drive. If your system is running volume management, the CD is mounted automatically. See Appendix A for information about volume management and mounting CDs.
2. Type **cd /cdrom/solaris_srvr_intranet_ext_1_0/DiskSuite_4.1/sparc | i386** and press Return.

3. Become superuser. You must be superuser to run the pkgadd command.

4. Type **pkgadd -d .** and press Return. A list of available packages is displayed and pkgadd prompts you to enter the number associated with a package. You must install packages in the order specified in Table B–6 on page 512.

```
castle# pkgadd -d .

The following packages are available:
  1  SUNWadm5r     Solstice AdminSuite root supplement for Solaris 2.3 and 2.4
                   (sparc) 6.5,REV=95.10.26.00.11
  2  SUNWadm5u     Solstice AdminSuite supplement for Solaris 2.3 and 2.4
                   (sparc) 6.5,REV=95.10.26.00.11
  3  SUNWadmsm     Solstice AdminSuite Storage Manager Application
                   (sparc) 6.6,REV=96.11.18.00.43
  4  SUNWmd        Solstice DiskSuite
                   (sparc) 4.1-FCS,REV=6.0
  5  SUNWmdg       Solstice DiskSuite Tool
                   (sparc) 4.1-FCS,REV=6.0
  6  SUNWmdn       Solstice DiskSuite Log Daemon
                   (sparc) 4.1-FCS,REV=6.0
  7  SUNWsadmc     Solstice AdminSuite Core Methods
                   (sparc) 6.6,REV=96.11.18.00.42
  8  SUNWsadml     Solstice Admintool Launcher.
                   (sparc) 6.5,REV=96.04.25.17.31
  9  SUNWsadmo     Solstice AdminSuite Object Libraries
                   (sparc) 6.6,REV=96.11.18.00.42

Select package(s) you wish to process (or 'all' to process
all packages). (default: all) [?,??,q]:
```

5. Type **2,1,7,9,8,3,4,5,6** and press Return.

6. Follow the pkgadd prompts.

7. When installation is complete, reboot the system.

8. Modify the root account PATH variable to include /usr/opt/SUNWmd/sbin.

9. Modify the root account MANPATH to include /usr/opt/SUNWmd/man.

For complete instructions and instructions on how to use Admintool to install DiskSuite packages, refer to the *Solstice DiskSuite 4.1 Installation and Product Notes* documentation available in the /cdrom/ solaris_srvr_intranet_ext_1_0/DiskSuite_4.1/Manuals directory.

For instructions on how to use DiskSuite, refer to the *Solstice DiskSuite 4.1 User's Guide* available in /cdrom/solaris_srvr_intranet_ext_1_0/ DiskSuite_4.1/Manuals directory.

Backup Utility

Solstice Backup is an easy-to-use network storage management software product. Backup performs automatic backups of files. You can also perform backups on an as-needed basis and archive project-related data for additional protection.

Backup automates the day-to-day process of backing up every computer on the network, thus protecting every system from file loss. Backup simplifies the management of backup media, gives notice of backup events, and is easy to operate and administer through an X Window System graphical user interface.

With Backup, file recovery is fast and convenient. Simply scroll through Backup's list of backed-up files and recover the files to disk. Backup even shows multiple versions of a file, backed up over time, enabling you to choose the version you want to recover. Backup provides access to these features through a graphical user interface. You can restore files to the same system or to a different one.

The optional Solstice Backup Archive Application provides the ability to take a snapshot of finished project files or directories residing on primary media, usually disk. To conserve disk space, you can choose to have archived files automatically removed from disk after Backup verifies the snapshot is safely stored on removable media.

Unlike backed-up data, the media used for storing archived data is never recycled. Archived data is preserved for as long as you need it. Archiving data associated with a finished project frees up space for current projects while assuring future access to the archived data.

Sun Microsystems offers four base versions of its data protection software, designed to meet varying needs. You can easily upgrade to more powerful and feature-rich versions as your environment changes and grows.

The following list describes the four base Backup products:

- *Solstice Backup Single Server* backs up a single file server to a single backup device connected to that server. It provides no network backup support for clients. Storage management uses preconfigured settings only. The Solstice Backup Single Server is bundled with the Solaris WorkGroup and Enterprise Servers only and is not available as a separate orderable product.
- *Solstice Backup, Server Edition* backs up a single file server to multiple backup devices connected to that server. It provides preconfigured settings and enables you to create your own configurations. It includes Solstice Backup Turbo functionality, supports the Jukebox Software Modules, Solstice Archive Application, Solstice Hierarchical Storage Management Application, Solstice Database Module for Oracle Application, and the Solstice Backup Simple Network Management Protocol module. The Server Edition supports media cloning, the process of making exact duplicates of backup tapes.
- *Solstice Backup, Network Edition* backs up a heterogeneous network of systems to one or two backup devices. It provides preconfigured settings and enables you to create your own configurations. It includes support for ten clients with the option to purchase additional client connections.
- *Solstice Backup, plus Solstice Backup Turbo* backs up a heterogeneous network of systems to a maximum of sixteen backup devices concurrently. It provides preconfigured settings and enables you to create your own configuration. It supports the Jukebox Software Module, Solstice Archive Application, Solstice Hierarchical Storage

Management Application, Solstice Database Module for Oracle Application, and the Solstice Backup Simple Network Management Protocol Module. This product supports media cloning.

You configure a backup server: a system with a backup device that automatically backs up all the systems on a network. Then you specify systems to be recognized by the server as Backup clients. You install Backup client software on those clients.

Backup Files and Directories on the CD

The files and directories in the `/cdrom/solaris_srvr_intranet_ext_1_0/ Backup_4.2.6` directory are listed in Table B–7.

Table B–7 Backup Files and Directories

File/Directory	Description
`Copyright`	File containing copyright information.
`Copyright.fr`	File containing copyright information in French.
`Manuals`	Directory containing HTML and PostScript versions of the Backup documentation.
`Solaris`	Directory containing SPARC and x86 packages and patches for Solaris.
`SunOS`	Directories containing scripts and executables for SunOS.
`silo_support`	Directory containing binaries needed to support STK ACSLS silos tape storage devices with Solstice Backup 4.2.6 for Solaris.

Installing Solstice Backup

The following sections provide guidelines for installing Backup software. For complete instructions refer to the *Solstice Backup 4.2 Installation and Maintenance Guide* documentation available in the `/cdrom/ solaris_srvr_intranet_ext_1_0/ Backup_4.2.6/Manuals` directory.

The CD contains all of the Solstice Backup software:

- Backup Administrator, Backup, and Recover programs
- Upgrade to Backup Turbo
- Support for additional client connections
- Optional Solstice Jukebox Software Module
- Optional Solstice Archive Application
- Optional Hierarchical Storage Management Application

- Optional Simple Network Management Protocol Module
- Electronic versions of the Backup documentation set for UNIX in HTML and PostScript format

Your CD-ROM contains the Backup software for a server and clients of the same hardware platform. After installing the software on your server, use the same CD to install the client software on your Backup clients.

The clients may access the Backup software over the network or have it installed locally on their hard disks. Refer to Part 3 for information about using the automounter to provide network access to the Backup software. Refer to Part 5 for information about administering application software. If you install the software locally, you need to extract and install the software on each client system.

NOTE. *Once installed, you can use Backup for 30 days. After 30 days, if you have not already done so, you must purchase the appropriate enables for the Backup products you want or the software will time-out. Once enabled, you must register the Backup software as soon as possible. If you do not register Backup, it will time-out 45 days from the date you enabled it. You will not be able to Backup any more data until you register and authorize the software.*

In summary, you must complete the following tasks to install and use Backup:

- Install Backup server software on the server
- Install Backup client software either on the server or on each client system
- Enable and register the Backup products

Reviewing Disk Space Requirements

Table B–8 lists the default locations and space needed to install the Backup software.

Table B–8 Backup Default Location and Space Requirements

Software	Location	Space Needed
Software extraction (temporary)	`/usr/tmp`	39.1 MB
Backup software	`/usr/etc`	23 MB
On-line indexes	`/usr/nsr`	Depends on data quantity
Manual pages	`/usr/man`	679 KB

To install Backup on a server, you need the following:

- A directory (suggested name `nsr_extract`) for installing the Backup software. Make sure there is enough space in the default installation directory.

- A directory on the server large enough for the Backup indexes (usually /usr/nsr). The installation script checks for space and suggests one or more locations for the indexes.
- A directory with 679 KB of disk space for the Backup on-line manual pages (for example, /usr/man).
- The system path name of the device used for extracting the Backup software. For example /cdrom for a system running SunOS 4.1.x.
- The system path name of at least one nonrewinding backup device used by the Backup server to back up and recover files. For example, enter **/dev/drst8** at the prompt for a system running SunOS 4.1.x. If you are using an optical jukebox to back up and recover data, use the raw name of the device. For example, use /dev/rsd1c instead of /dev/sd1c.

Installing Solstice DiskSuite for Solaris

To install DiskSuite software on the server:

1. Become superuser.
2. Insert the product CD into your CD-ROM drive. If your system is running volume management, the CD is mounted automatically. Refer to Appendix A for information about volume management and mounting CDs.
3. Type **cd /cdrom/solaris_srvr_intranet_ext_1_0/ Backup__4.2.6/Solaris/sparc | i386** and press Return.
4. Type **pkgadd -d .** and press Return. A list of packages is displayed.
5. Type the number of the package you want to install and press Return. If you install more than one package, separate the numbers with a comma.
6. Follow the installation instructions displayed by the pkgadd command. For complete instructions refer to the *Solstice Backup 4.2 Installation and Maintenance Guide* available in the /cdrom/ solaris_srvr_intranet_ext_1_0/Backup_4.2.6/Manuals directory.

You use the same steps to install software on client systems.

Installing Solstice DiskSuite for SunOS

To install DiskSuite software on the server:

1. Become superuser.
2. Insert the product CD into your CD-ROM drive. If you system is running volume management, the CD is mounted automatically.
3. Type **cd /cdrom/solaris_srvr_intranet_ext_1_0/Backup__4.2.6/SunOS** and press Return.
4. Type **./nsr_ize** and press Return.

5. Follow the installation instructions displayed by the `nsr_ize` script. For complete instructions refer to the *Solstice Backup 4.2 Installation and Maintenance Guide* available in the `/cdrom/ solaris_srvr_intranet_ext_1_0/Backup_4.2.6/Manuals` directory.

You use the same script to install software on client systems.

Running Backup

To run Backup, type **nwadmin&** and press Return. For complete instructions on how to use Backup, refer to the *Solstice Backup 2.3 User's Guide* available in the `/cdrom/solaris_srvr_intranet_ext_1_0/ Backup_4.2.6/Manuals` directory.

TotalNET Advanced Server (TAS)

The TotalNET Advanced Server (TAS) 5.0 software provides transparent PC to UNIX connectivity. It enables a UNIX server to act as a file, print, and application server to a variety of client PCs in a heterogeneous, networked environment. TAS gives the following PC systems access to the same UNIX file, print, and server resources through each client's familiar desktop interface:

- Macintosh
- MS-DOS
- Windows for Workgroups
- Windows 95
- Windows NT
- OS/2 Warp

TAS is organized into three realms according to clients served and available network transport protocols:

- AppleTalk Compatible Realm, for AppleTalk clients, with the AppleTalk transport
- LM-NT-OS/2 Compatible Realm, for NetBIOS clients, with either TCP/IP or NetBEUI transport
- Netware Compatible Realm, for NetWare clients, with the IPX/SPX transport

TAS provides an HTML-based tool called TotalAdmin to facilitate ease of installation, configuration, and administration. TotalAdmin enables administrators without extensive UNIX experience to use UNIX technology to meet their PC server needs. TotalAdmin also presents a single, consistent interface for managing various communication protocols used within the TAS realms.

TAS benefits the clients in a heterogeneous networked environment by enabling each client to use a familiar desktop to access server resources. To access TAS, client workstations need only the native networking software included with their operating systems. End users do not need any additional training or expertise to exploit UNIX resources because additional file and print services are presented within their particular user interface.

TAS Files and Directories on the CD

The files and directories in the `/cdrom/solaris_srvr_intranet_ext_1_0/Totalnet_Advanced_Server/solaris2_5` directory are listed in Table B–9.

Table B–9 TAS Files and Directories

File/Directory	Description
`docs`	Directory containing product documentation in both AnswerBook and HTML 2.0 format.
`i386`	Directory containing x86 packages and patches.
`solaris`	Directory containing SPARC packages and patches.

Installing Solstice TAS

The following sections provide guidelines for installing TAS software. For complete instructions refer to the *TotalNET Advanced Server Version 5.0 Release Notes* available in the `/cdrom/solaris_srvr_intranet_ext_1_0/ Totalnet_Advanced_Server/solaris2_5/docs` directory.

Upgrading from TAS 4.1.1

TAS 5.0 is a major upgrade from TAS 4.1.1 and the two versions cannot operate together. Before proceeding with an upgrade, back up your entire TAS directory and then run the `tconvert` utility. The `tconvert` utility reads the existing server configuration files, converts the information, and writes the output to the log file at `/etc/totalnet/convert`. When the installation is complete, the converted files are placed in the TotalNET home directory TNHOME.

You must run the `tconvert` program as root before existing TotalNET servers are removed, and with existing TotalNET servers shut down.

For complete instructions on upgrading from TAS 4.1.1, refer to the *TotalNET Advanced Server Version 5.0 Release Notes.*

Reviewing System Requirements

The following list describes the system requirements for installing TAS on Solaris 2.*x* SPARC or x86 systems:

- Solaris 2.4 or later operating environment on a SPARC or x86 system.
- For systems running NetBEUI or AppleTalk over Token Ring on SPARC systems, you must install the following token-ring driver patch that fixes the multicast problem: token-ring for SPARC patch #102463-03. This patch is available from SunSoft.
- For Solaris 2.5.1 and x86 systems, Driver update 6 is recommended if running either NetBEUI, IPX, or AppleTalk protocols.
- Approximately 26 MB of free disk space in the `/usr` partition.

Installing Acrobat Readers

TAS 5.0 is bundled with Adobe's Acrobat Reader, version 3.0. To install an Acrobat reader, change to the `/acroread` directory and choose the reader relevant to your platform. Follow the installation instructions in the INSTGUID.TXT file and install the reader onto the appropriate directory of the server or the client PC.

NOTE. *Although the installation instructions say that TAS 5.0 is bundled with Adobe's Acrobat Reader, version 3.0, these files are not available on the Solaris Server Intranet Extension CD-ROM. Contact your Sun sales representative for more information.*

Installing TAS

To install TAS software:

1. Log in as root at the system login prompt.
2. Insert the product CD into your CD-ROM drive. If your system is running volume management, the CD is mounted automatically. Refer to Appendix A for information about volume management and mounting CDs.
3. Type **cd /cdrom/solaris_srvr_intranet_ext_1_0/ Totalnet_Advanced_Server/ solaris2_5/sparc | i386** and press Return.
4. Type **pkgadd -d .** and press Return. A list of available packages is displayed.
5. Type the numbers of the packages you want to install, separated by commas, or press Return to install all packages.
6. Answer yes to all prompts for the remainder of the installation.
7. When the prompt is redisplayed, type **q** and press Return to quit the pkgadd program.

For complete installation instructions refer to the *TotalNET Advanced Server Version 5.0 Release Notes* available in the `/cdrom/ solaris_srvr_intranet_ext_1_0/ Totalnet_Advanced_Server/docs` directory.

Connecting to TotalAdmin

To continue installation and configuration, you must connect to TotalAdmin and access the Getting Started Guide. Follow the instructions in the *Getting Started Guide* to complete the initial configuration wizard and start the TAS server.

The port number for connecting to TotalAdmin is displayed during the installation process. Make a note of the port number because you need to use it later. If you do not see the port number, you can find it in the `/var/totalnet/tassetup.log` file.

To connect to TotalAdmin:

1. Using a Web browser, type **http://hostname:<*nnnn*>** and press Return. <*nnnn*> is the port number for TotalAdmin.
2. From the Product Selection screen, click the link for the TotalAdmin main menu.
3. At the bottom of the TAS 5.0 main menu, click the `On-line Documentation and Readers` link.
4. Click the *Getting Started Guide*. If the appropriate Acrobat Reader for your platform is installed, clicking on the link activates it. If you do not have the Acrobat Reader for your platform, refer to the *TotalNET Advanced Server Version 5.0 Release Notes* for instructions on how to install it.
5. Run either the Initial Configuration Wizard or the `tnsetup` script to complete the installation and initial configuration of TAS. Refer to the *Getting Started Guide* for instructions on running both the Initial Configuration Wizard and the `tnsetup` script.

Sun WebServer

Sun WebServer 1.0 is designed for ISPs and corporations whose Internet/intranet servers must be high performance, scalable, and able to handle large numbers of users and transactions.

The following list describes the key features of the Sun WebServer:

- SSL 3.0 and certificate-based security is provided for secure transactions.
- Extensive and flexible access control includes URL-based access control and delegation.
- Web-based administration enables you to administer the system from any Web browser on any platform.

Sun WebServer Files and Directories on the CD

The files and directories in the `/cdrom/solaris_srvr_intranet_ext_1_0/ Sun_WebServer_1.0/ Sol_2.5.1+` directory are listed in Table B–10.

Installing Sun WebServer

The following sections provide guidelines for installing Sun WebServer software. For complete instructions refer to the *Sun WebServer 1.0 Installation and Release Notes* available in the `/cdrom/ solaris_srvr_intranet_ext_1_0/Sun_WebServer_1.0/ Sol_2.5.1+/common/Docs` directory.

Table B–10 Sun WebServer Files and Directories

File/Directory	Description
`common`	Directory containing PostScript documentation files.
`i386`	Directory containing x86 packages.
`sparc`	Directory containing SPARC packages.

Reviewing System Requirements

The following list describes the system requirements for installing Sun WebServer on Solaris 2.x SPARC or x86 systems:

- **Platform:** SPARC or Intel 486 (or greater).
- **System Software:** Solaris 2.5, 2.5.1 or 2.6 system software.
- **Disk Space:** Approximately 24 MB of disk space.
- **Memory:** For SPARC systems, a minimum of 32 MB, 64 MB recommended. For x86 systems, a minimum of 16 MB, 32 MB recommended.
- **Swap space:** for SPARC systems, a minimum of 64 MB, 192 MB recommended. For x86 systems, 64 MB, 96 MB recommended.
- **Supported Web Browsers:** Sun Microsystems HotJava 1.0, Netscape Navigator 2.01 and greater, Microsoft Internet Explorer 3.0 and greater.

Installing Sun WebServer

Table B–11 describes the Sun WebServer packages:

Table B–11 Sun WebServer Packages

Package	Description
SUNWfns	Federated Naming System
SUNWhttpr	HTTP server root package
SUNWhttpu	HTTP server usr package

Table B–11 Sun WebServer Packages (continued)

Package	Description
SUNWhttpv	HTTP server var package
SUNWski	SKI 1.0 Software (User Package)
SUNWskica	SKI 1.0 Software (CA Package)
SUNWskicw	SKI 1.0 Software (Licensing Package for CA)
SUNWskimc	SKI 1.0 Software (CA Manual Page Package)
SUNWskimu	SKI 1.0 Software (CA User Manual Page Package)
SUNWssl	SSL 1.0 Software (Library Global Version)

Sun WebServer installs the packages in the default locations listed in Table B–12.:

Table B–12 Sun WebServer Package Default Locations

Description	Location
Sun Web Server HTTP daemon	/usr/lib/httpd
Server root	/var/http/demo
Documentation root	/var/http/demo/public
Configuration files	/etc/http
Admin root	/usr/http

You must always install the security tools packages to their default locations. Install the SUNWhttp packages only in custom locations.

To install Sun WebServer software:

1. Become superuser.
2. Insert the product CD into your CD-ROM drive. If your system is running volume management, the CD is mounted automatically. See Appendix A for information about volume management and mounting CDs.
3. Type **cd /cdrom/solaris_srvr_intranet_ext_1_0/ Sun_WebServer_1.0/ Sol_2.5.1+/sparc | i386/Product** and press Return.
4. Type **pkgadd -d .** and press Return. A list of available packages is displayed as follows.

```
castle# pkgadd -d .
```

```
The following packages are available:
  1  SUNWfns        Federated Naming System
                    (sparc) 11.5.1,REV=97.05.07.01.10
  2  SUNWhttpr      HTTP server root package
                    (sparc) 1.0
  3  SUNWhttpu      HTTP server user package
                    (sparc) 1.0
  4  SUNWhttpv      HTTP server var package
                    (sparc) 1.0
  5  SUNWski        SKI 1.0 Software (User Package)
                    (sparc) 1.0
  6  SUNWskica      SKI 1.0 Software (CA Package)
                    (sparc) 1.0
  7  SUNWskicw      SKI 1.0 Software (Licensing Package for CA)
                    (sparc) 1.0
  8  SUNWskimc      SKI 1.0 Software (CA Manual Page Package)
                    (sparc) 1.0
  9  SUNWskimu      SKI 1.0 Software (User Manual Page Package)
                    (sparc) 1.0
 10  SUNWssl        SSL 1.0 Software (Library Global Version)
                    (sparc) 1.0

Select package(s) you wish to process (or 'all' to process
all packages). (default: all) [?,??,q]:
```

5. Type **1,5,6,7,8,9,10,3,4,2** and press Return. You should install the packages in the order specified, with the SUNWhttpu, SUNWhttpv, and SUNWhttpr packages last because they depend on some of the other packages.

6. Follow the installation instructions displayed by the `pkgadd` command. For complete instructions refer to the *Sun WebServer 1.0 Installation and Release Notes* available in the `/cdrom/solaris_srvr_intranet_ext_1_0/ Sun_WebServer_1.0/Sol_2.5.1+/common/Docs` directory.

7. When the prompt is redisplayed, type **q** and press Return to quit the `pkgadd` program.

Running Sun WebServer

For security reasons, do not run Sun WebServer as user `root` or user `nobody`. It is a good idea to create a second user such as `http` and have the Sun WebServer HTTP daemon run under that username. To change the daemon username, you can modify the `server_user` and `cgi_user` directives in the `httpd.conf` file. For more information about Web server security issues refer to the security FAQ at: `http://www-genome.wi.mit.edu/WWW/faqs/www-security-faq.html`.

You must start Sun WebServer as `root` to run on port 80. When you start Sun WebServer as root, it binds to its ports and changes its username to whatever `server_user` is. Only user `root` can use ports below 1024. Therefore, unless you change the default port setting, you must start `httpd` as user `root` even if it runs as another user. For example, if you run `/usr/lib/hpptd` as user `http`, it won't be able to bind to port 80. Therefore, you need to run on a port above 1024.

You can change the default port setting by editing the `<install_root>/etc/http/httpd.conf` file. If you install Sun WebServer on a port other than 80, you need to designate the port number when accessing Sun WebServer with a Web browser. For example, to access server castle on port 8080, you would type **http://castle:8080/**.

To run Sun WebServer, type **/etc.init.d.httpd start** and press Return. For complete instructions on how to use Sun WebServer, refer to the *Sun WebServer v1.0 Administration Guide* available in the `/cdrom/ solaris_srvr_intranet_ext_1_0/Sun_WebServer_1.0/ Sol_2.5.1+/common/Docs` directory.

Solstice Internet Mail Server (SIMS)

Solstice Internet Mail Server (SIMS) 2.0 is composed of Internet message access protocol V4 (IMAP4) mail server for Solaris systems plus support for the following mail client systems:

- Solaris
- Microsoft Windows 3.1.*x*
- Windows 95
- Windows NT

Supported Network Communications Protocols

SIMS is an implementation of the server side of IMAP4 RFC 1730. IMAP4 is used by client mail applications to access Internet messages in distributed enterprise/Internet-wide message stores. In addition to IMAP4, SIMS 2.0 also supports the following protocols:

- Post Office Protocol v3 (POP3) server for mailbox retrieval and support of popular mail clients such as Eudora and Pegasus
- Multipurpose Internet Mail Extensions (MIME) standard for mail attachments

Supported Mail Access Models

Mail can be accessed in one of three ways:

- Online
- Off-line
- Disconnected

In the *online model*, messages remain on a server and are remotely responded to by the mail client. Online access ensures that you can easily manage a single message store, but requires remote connection while users read and compose mail.

In the *off-line model*, the mail client fetches messages from a server system to a client system—which may be a desktop or portable system—and may delete them from the server. The mail client downloads the messages where users view and respond to them at their convenience.

In the *disconnected model*, the mail client connects to the server, makes a cache copy of selected messages, then disconnects from the server. Users may read and respond to the messages off-line. The mail client can later reconnect and resynchronize message status between the server and the client message cache. A key concept of this model is that the master copies of messages remain on the mail server where manageability and security are high, but enables the remote, off-line manipulation of selected messages.

Online and disconnected operations complement each other, as users can alternate between them depending on their needs. Off-line access, however, is incompatible with either online or disconnected models because the messages on the server can be removed after downloading to the client system.

SIMS 2.0 supports disconnected computing for mobile or remote users. The network traffic load is reduced by moving the mail message format parsing to a centralized server, thereby freeing up the local mail applications to concentrate on user interface issues. Users can send and receive messages in online, off-line, or disconnected modes. SIMS works equally well in connected, high-bandwidth modes of operation as in disconnected, remote access modes, using a low-bandwidth network connection.

SIMS 2.0 listens on TCP port 143 for the mail client to send a connection request. Once the connection is established, the server responds to commands sent from the client. When a session is complete, the client sends a logout command to the server, terminating the session and closing the TCP connection.

SIMS Features

SIMS 2.0 provides the following features:

- Handles mail storage on the mail server instead of the mail client. This architecture reduces network load and provides flexibility in accessing mail remotely through a low-bandwidth connection.
- Stores and fetches messages in response to a client mail request. IMAP4 functionality enhances connection performance over low-bandwidth links by fetching message headers to the client without downloading the entire message set. Mailboxes and mail folders stay resident on the server, so users can search for specific mail attributes and then download selected messages.
- Supports management and access of multiple mailboxes. Users can name and access both Inbox and archive mail folders. Additionally, users can create, delete, list, and rename both inbox and archive message folders. Users can perform these actions on the same or on different servers; SIMS 2.0 enables users to view and move messages from one to another at the same time.

- Supports concurrent updates and access to common mailboxes and folders. Changes in mailbox state can be updated in all concurrently active mail clients.
- You can set standard and user-defined message status flags to notify mail users of changes in message status.
- Supports efficient processing of MIME attachments. Users can selectively retrieve individual attachments in messages. For example, if a two-line mail message has several large attachments, users can search for the mail attachment header and download only the one they want.
- Exchanges mail with a broad assortment of mail clients with a single system view, so users' mail looks the same from any client application.
- Supports read-only or read/write shared mailboxes and folders.

SIMS Files and Directories on the CD

The files and directories in the `/cdrom/solaris_srvr_intranet_ext_1_0/Solstice_Internet_Mail_Server` directory are listed in Table B–13.

Table B–13 AdminSuite Directories

Directory	Description
`docs`	Directory containing PostScript documentation files.
`server`	Directory containing i386 and sparc packages.

Installing SIMS 2.0

The following sections provide guidelines for installing SIMS 2.0 software. For complete instructions refer to the *Solstice Internet Mail 2.0 Installation and Configuration Guide* available in the `/cdrom/ solaris_srvr_intranet_ext_1_0/ Solstice_Internet_Mail_Server/ docs` directory.

Reviewing System Requirements

The following list describes the minimum system requirements for installing SIMS 2.0 on a Solaris host:

- Solaris 2.4 or later with a fully installed and configured sendmail program.
- A SPARC or x86 workstation.

Removing Previously Installed SIMS Software

If you have installed an earlier SIMS release, you must remove it before installing your new software.

To remove previously installed software:

1. Log in to the mail server as root or superuser.
2. Type **pkgrm SUNWimap** and press Return.
3. Answer **yes** to any questions displayed by the `pkgrm` program.

Installing SIMS Software

To install SIMS software:

1. Log in as root or superuser.
2. Insert the product CD into your CD-ROM drive. If your system is running volume management, the CD is mounted automatically. Refer to Appendix A for information about volume management and mounting CDs.
3. Type **cd /cdrom/solaris_srvr_intranet_ext_1_0/Solstice_Internet_Mail/server/ sparc | i386** and press Return.
4. Type **pkgadd -d .** and press Return. A list of packages is displayed.

```
castle# cd
/cdrom/solaris_srvr_intranet_ext_1_0/Solstice_Internet_Mail_Server/server/sparc
castle# pkgadd -d .

The following packages are available:
  1  SUNWimap      Solstice Internet Mail IMAP4 Server
                   (sparc) 2.0
  2  SUNWipop      Solstice Internet Mail POP3 Server (NL)
                   (sparc) 2.0

Select package(s) you wish to process (or 'all' to process
all packages). (default: all) [?,??,q]:
```

5. If you want only the IMAP4 server type **1** and press Return. If you also want the POP server, type **all** and press Return.
6. Answer **yes** to any questions displayed by the `pkgadd` program.
7. When the prompt is redisplayed, type **q** and press Return to quit the `pkgadd` program.

For complete instructions refer to the *Solstice Internet Mail 2.0 Installation and Configuration Guide* available in the `/cdrom/ solaris_srvr_intranet_ext_1_0/ Solstice_Internet_Mail_Server/docs` directory.

Licensing Information

SIMS 2.0 requires a license token from Sun, as described in the *Solstice Internet Mail 2.0 Installation and Configuration Guide*. The license card is included in the CD-ROM package. Contact the appropriate license center to receive your password. You can find contact information on the Web site at `http://www.sun.com/licensing`.

You install the password by using the /opt/SUNWimap/bin/simslicense utility or by manually editing the license.dat file in the /etc/opt/SUNWimap/ license_dir4 directory.

The license is a single line of text that begins with the word FEATURE and is followed by solstice.mail.imap. If you choose to manually edit the file, make sure the line is located before any other line starting with FEATURE in the file. Only the first feature of a given type is used, even if it is expired.

If you are able to log into the mail server from your mail client, the server license is activated properly.

Configuring the Mail Server

The IMAP4 and POP3 daemons are started by the inetd daemon. During the server package installation, pkgadd automatically configures the mail server by adding an entry to the following two configuration files:

- /etc/services
- /etc/inetd.conf

The /etc/services configuration file should contain the following two lines:

```
imap   143/tcp imap   #Internet Mail Access Prot
pop-3  110/tcp pop3d  #Post Office Protocol 3
```

The /etc/inetd.conf configuration file should include the following two lines:

```
imap stream tcp nowait root /opt/SUNWimap/lib/imapd imapd
pop-3 stream tcp nowait root /opt/SUNWipop/lib/ipop3d ipop3d
```

The server's inetd daemon is restarted automatically during the installation process.

If you get an error during connection, it means that the inetd daemon looked for the inetd configuration file before the configuration table was updated. To restart the inetd daemon:

1. Type **/usr/bin/ps -ef | grep inetd** and press Return. Note the PID number for inetd.
2. Type **kill -HUP <pid>** and press Return.

You also need to verify that the services entry in the /etc/nsswitch.conf file is set to files. To verify the services entry in the /etc/nsswitch.conf file:

1. Type **grep services /etc/nsswitch.conf** and press Return. The command should return services: files. The entry may also contain NIS or NIS+, but files must be the first entry.
2. If files is not the first entry, manually change the services entry by using NIS or NIS+ administration procedures. Refer to Part 2 for information about administering NIS+.

Verifying a Successful Installation

To test for a successful installation, type **telnet *<mailserver>* 143** and press Return.

If a message similar to the following is displayed, the server is installed and running:

```
* OK <mailserver> Solstice (tm) Internet Mail Server (TM) IMAP4 service - 2.0 - at
<date>
```

Java IDL

Java IDL (Interface Definition Language) is the application platform for Internet client/server computing. Java IDL, Sun's 100% Pure Java Object Request Broker (ORB) system, provides the software foundation necessary to deliver enterprise client/server applications for the Internet. Applications that use Java IDL seamlessly integrate with non-Java programs and programs from other vendors. The Java IDL system is based on the latest CORBA and IIOP industry standards.

Java IDL includes:

- 100% Pure Java Object Request Broker
- Full Internet Inter-ORB Protocol (IIOP) implementation
- CORBA 2.0 standard IDL to Java mapping
- CORBA 2.0 standard Naming Service

The Java IDL 1.1 runtime system is included with the Solaris Server Intranet Extension 1.0 CD-ROM. In addition, you can download the complete runtime and developer package from the Web site `http://www.sun.com.solaris/java-idl/ index.html`.

The developer package includes the IDL to Java compiler and related documentation for developing Java IDL applications.

Java IDL is a Java API as defined by JavaSoft. For more information, visit `http://java.sun.com/products/jdk/idl/`.

Java IDL is part of JavaSoft's platform APIs. It provides standards-based interoperability and connectivity with CORBA, the open industry standard for heterogeneous computing. As part of the Java Enterprise API set, Java IDL enables seamless interoperability and connectivity to heterogeneous enterprise information assets.

Java IDL leverages the efforts of OMG (Object Management Group)'s CORBA, IIOP, and IDL.

The Java IDL Language Mapping Specification defines the mapping from IDL to Java. The `idltojava` tool automatically generates stub code for specific remote interfaces. These stubs are ORB independent and call into ORB specific protocol modules for all data marshalling or other ORB specific operations. Java IDL also includes `nameserv`, an implementation of the CORBA (COS) name service. The portable Java ORB core which supports IIOP version 1.0 is structured to make it easy to plug in new ORB protocols.

Java IDL Files and Directories on the CD

The files and directories in the /cdrom/solaris_srvr_intranet_ext_1_0/JavaIDL_1.1/Sol_2.5.1+/common directory are listed in Table B–14.

Table B–14 AdminSuite Directories

Directory	Description
Docs	Directory containing PostScript and HTML documentation files.
Product	Directory containing the SUNWOirun package.

Installing Java IDL

The following sections provide guidelines for installing Java IDL 1.1 software. For complete instructions refer to the *Java IDL 1.1 Manual Installation Guide* available in the /cdrom/solaris_srvr_intranet_ext_1_0/ JavaIDL_1.1/Docs directory.

Reviewing System Requirements

The following list describes the minimum system requirements for installing Java IDL 1.1 on a Solaris host:

- Solaris 2.5.1 or later
- JDK 1.0.2 or later
- Clients (Microsoft Win 32) Win NT 3.5.1 or higher, Windows 95 Visual C++ 4.0 or higher
- One of the following Web browsers to run Java IDL applets: HotJava 1.0 or later, Netscape Navigator 3.0.2 or later, Microsoft Internet Explorer 3.0.2 or later

Installing Java IDL Software

To install Java IDL software:

1. Type **pkginfo SUNWjvrt** and press Return. If the JavaVM runtime environment is not installed, install it or install JDK 1.1 or later on your system.
2. Log in as root or superuser.
3. Insert the product CD into your CD-ROM drive. If your system is running volume management, the CD is mounted automatically. Refer to Appendix A for information about volume management and mounting CDs.
4. Type **cd /cdrom/solaris_srvr_intranet_ext_1_0/JavaIDL_1.1/ 2.5.1+/common/Product** and press Return.

5. Type **pkgadd -d SUNWOirun** and press Return.
6. At the prompt type **/usr/java** and press Return.
7. Answer **yes** to any questions displayed by the `pkgadd` program.
8. When the prompt is redisplayed, type **q** and press Return to quit the `pkgadd` program.

Starting the Name Server

On Solaris, you must be root to run the name server because, by default, it uses port 900 as the initial port.

To start the name server:

1. Become superuser.
2. Type **tnameserv -ORBInitialPort** and press Return.

Solstice PPP 3.0.1

Solstice point-to-point protocol (PPP) is the ideal solution for system administrators who want to:

- Set up an Internet or office server to service multiple clients.
- Set up multiple clients to access an Internet or office server.
- Enable mobile communications and telecommuting.
- Conduct frequent or bulk transfers over leased lines.
- Connect interoffice networks and distributed resources.
- Interconnect LANs over wide area networks.

Solstice PPP implements asynchronous and synchronous PPP in a single homogeneous environment. *Asynchronous PPP* enables Solaris systems to route IP traffic over public and private telephone networks and is targeted at the growing Internet client/server market. *Synchronous PPP* enables Solaris systems to route IP traffic over dedicated leased lines and is used primarily for LAN-to-LAN interconnectivity and to replace dedicated routing equipment.

Solstice PPP 3.0.1 provides software for both PPP clients and PPP servers. The Solstice PPP Client initiates connections across public and private telephone networks through a single modem link. You are authorized to install and use the Solstice PPP client on an unrestricted number of systems.

The Solstice PPP Server provides all the functionality of a PPP server, including synchronous connectivity, support for up to 512 modems, support for IP routing, and the capability to accept incoming connections. This product incorporates a floating-license system that restricts the number of Solstice PPP servers that can run concurrently. To access all of the features of the Solstice PPP server, you must purchase and obtain a license password.

Solstice PPP 3.0.1 Files and Directories on the CD

The files and directories in the `/cdrom/solaris_srvr_intranet_ext_1_0/ PPP_3.0.1` directory are listed in Table B–15.

Table B–15 AdminSuite Directories

Directory	Description
docs	Directory containing PostScript documentation files.
x86	Directory containing x86 packages.
sparc	Directory containing SPARC packages.

Installing Solstice PPP

The following sections provide guidelines for installing Solstice PPP 3.0.1 software. For complete instructions refer to *Installing and Licensing Solstice PPP 3.0.1* available in the `/cdrom/ solaris_srvr_intranet_ext_1_0/PPP_3.0.1/ docs` directory.

The following list summarizes the installation process:

1. Plan your installation to determine where to install the packages supplied with Solstice PPP and to ensure your systems meet the installation requirements.
2. Request a license password from one of the authorized Sun license distribution centers. You can skip this step if you are upgrading from a previous version of Solstice PPP, or if you are using only the Solstice PPP client software.You can obtain information about your nearest License Distribution Center from the `http://www.sun.com/licensing` Web site.
3. Install Solstice PPP packages.
4. Install the license password.
5. Configure and start Solstice PPP.

Reviewing System Requirements

The following list describes the minimum system requirements for installing Solstice PPP software:

- Solaris 2.3 or later operating environment
- X Window System window manager to use `ppptool` or the license installation tool (`lit`)

Table B–16 describes the PPP packages and lists the directory where the software is installed and the disk space requirements in MB.

Table B–16 PPP Packages

Package	Description	Directory	Space (Mbytes)
SUNWpppk	PPP device drivers	/usr	0.3
SUNWpppr	PPP configuration files	/etc	0.03
SUNWpppu	PPP daemon and user programs	/usr	1.0
SUNWppps	PPP login service	/usr	0.2
SUNWpppm	PPP man pages	N/A	
SUNWlicsw	FlexLM License System	/opt	2.5
SUNWlit	STE License Installation Tool	N/A	

The following modems have been tested and qualified for use with Solstice PPP:

- AT&T DataPort Express
- BocaModem V.34 DataFax
- Cardinal V.34/V.FC 28.8 data/fax
- Cardinal MVP288I 28.8 Kbps V.34 Fax Modem
- Hayes Accura 144B and 288V.FC
- Megahertz XJ2288 PCMCIA
- Motorola Codex 326X V.34
- MultiModem MT2834BLF
- MultiModem MT1432BF
- Olitec 288
- Practical 14400 V32bis
- SupraFaxModem 288
- USRobotics Sporter 14400
- USRobotics Sporter 288
- USRobotics Courier V.34
- Zoom V34

NOTE. *This information does not imply a support contract, commitment to continued compatibility, or warranty from Sun Microsystems, Inc. for any of the listed devices.*

Table B–17 lists synchronous serial interfaces that have been tested and qualified for use with Solstice PPP.

Table B–17 Synchronous Serial Interfaces

Serial Device	Supplier	Description
Onboard serial port (zsh)	Sun	Solaris SPARC platforms only. Supports data transfer rates of up to 19.2 Kbps (SPARC and 64 Kbps (UltraSPARC).
SunLink HSI/S (hih)	Sun	Solaris SPARC platforms only. Provides 4 high-speed synchronous serial ports. Maximum recommended data transfer rate 512 Kbps.
Express-X (expx)	SCii/Sun	Solaris x86 platforms only. An 8-bit PC/AT half-size ISA card that provides either two EIA-232-E (V24) interfaces or two EIA-449 (V11) interfaces. Supports transfer rates of up to 64 Kbps.
800S+ (tty)	Aurora	Solaris SPARC platforms only. Single width Sbus board, which provides 8 high-speed (up to 128 Kbps) synchronous serial ports. Available with either DB25 or RJ-45 connectors.

Table B–18 lists asynchronous serial interfaces that have been tested and qualified for use with Solstice PPP.

Table B–18 Asynchronous Serial Interfaces

Serial Device	Supplier	Description
Onboard serial port (tty)	Sun	Solaris SPARC platforms only. Supports data transfer rates of up to 38.4 Kbps.
800 SX (tty)	Aurora	Solaris SPARC platforms only. Single-width Sbus board, which provides 8 high-speed (up to 115.2 Kbps) asynchronous serial ports. Available with either DB25 or RJ-45 connectors.
Onboard serial port (tty)	PC supplier	Solaris x86 platforms only. Supports data transfer rates of up to 115.2 Kbps when the Driver Update 1 (DU) for these interfaces is installed.

NOTE. *The SPC board is not supported.*

Reviewing Licensing Requirements

The Solstice PPP server incorporates a floating license system. Each license entitles you to one or more *Rights To Use (RTUs)*, according to the number requested when you ordered the product. This number defines the maximum number of Solstice PPP servers that can run concurrently. You can install the software on a larger number of systems.

You can purchase additional licenses without purchasing extra copies of the software. You can add these licenses to your existing license configuration.

The systems on which you install the license daemon are called *license servers*. Each license server can handle the licenses for multiple license clients, providing the server is accessible across an existing network.

You can choose from the following possible license server configurations:

- **Single-independent license server:** This configuration is the simplest and most frequently used. The license daemon is installed on a single system and a single password is required to enable all of the associated RTUs. All clients access the same license server.
- **Multiple-independent license servers:** You can share the total number of RTUs that you purchased between multiple-independent license servers. This configuration enables you to define separate workgroups that access a subset of the total RTUs. You must obtain a unique password for each license server in your configuration.
- **Multiple-redundant license servers:** Three license servers can work together to emulate a single-independent license server. This configuration improves stability of the license system because licensed products will not shut down as long as the majority of license servers is accessible and able to communicate. A single password enables all of the RTUs.

If you are installing Solstice PPP for the first time, you must contact your nearest Sun license distribution center to obtain the passwords that enable the license system. When you contact the License Distribution Center, you need the following information:

- The product serial number which is printed on the label located on the license certificate supplied with the product.
- A description of your license server configuration (single-independent, multiple-independent, or multiple-redundant).
- The hostname and hostid of each license server.
- The number of SPARC and x86 RTUs you require.

You can obtain information about your nearest License Distribution Center from the `http://www.sun.com/licensing` Web site.

Installing PPP Software

To install PPP software:

1. Become superuser.
2. If you have a previous version of Solstice PPP installed, type **pkgrm SUNWpppk SUNWpppr SUNWpppu** and press Return to remove the packages.
3. Insert the product CD into your CD-ROM drive. If your system is running volume management, the CD is mounted automatically. Refer to Appendix A for information about volume management and mounting CDs.
4. Type **cd /cdrom/solaris_srvr_intranet_ext_1_0/PPP_3.0.1/sparc | x86** and press Return.
5. Type **pkgadd -d .** and press Return. A list of the packages is displayed.

```
castle# pkgadd -d .

The following packages are available:
  1  SUNWlicsw     FlexLM License System
                   (sparc) 4.1
  2  SUNWlit       STE License Installation Tool
                   (sparc) 3.0
  3  SUNWpppk      Solstice PPP Device Drivers
                   (sparc) 3.0.1
  4  SUNWpppm      Solstice PPP Man Pages
                   (sparc) 3.0.1
  5  SUNWpppr      Solstice PPP Configuration Files
                   (sparc) 3.0.1
  6  SUNWppps      Solstice PPP Login Service
                   (sparc) 3.0.1
  7  SUNWpppu      Solstice PPP Daemon and User Programs
                   (sparc) 3.0.1

Select package(s) you wish to process (or 'all' to process
all packages). (default: all) [?,??,q]:
```

6. Type the numbers corresponding to the packages you want to install, or press Return to install all of the packages. You can install the packages in any order.
7. Answer **yes** to any questions displayed by the `pkgadd` program.
8. When the installation is complete, type q to quit `pkgadd`.
9. Eject the CD-ROM from the drive.
10. Repeat the procedure for each system on which you want to run Solstice PPP.
11. Install the license passwords. For complete instructions, refer to *Installing and Licensing Solstice PPP 3.0.1* available in the `/cdrom/solaris_srvr/intranet_ext_1_0/PPP_3.0.1/docs` directory on the CD.

Getting Started with Solstice PPP

Once the installation is complete and license passwords are installed, Solstice PPP is ready to configure and use. You configure Solstice PPP for the first time using the `pppinit` initialization script.

Refer to *Configuring and Using Solstice PPP Clients* and *Configuring and Using Solstice PPP Servers and Routers* for detailed information on configuring and using this product.

SunScreen SKIP

SKIP (Simple Key-management for Internet Protocols) software provides encryption for your data and authentication of the IP traffic stream. SunScreen SKIP enables you to securely conduct business over both the corporate intranet and the Internet.

SunScreen SKIP provides the most flexible methods to conduct business over an intranet or the Internet with the SunScreen SKIP product line. An easy-to-install software module, SunScreen SKIP provides secure communications transparently to users without requiring any modification of existing applications.

With SunScreen SKIP:

- Telecommuters and business travelers can remotely get to their corporate network services and businesses can securely place orders with their vendors.
- Customers can confidently perform financial transactions with their bank.
- Retail businesses can process credit card transactions for their customers.

SunScreen SKIP authenticates all incoming IP traffic. It also provides integrity and privacy of your outgoing data by ensuring that it will not be altered or viewed by others while in transit. SunScreen SKIP rounds out the security solution by interoperating with the SunScreen SPF-100/100G, and SunScreen EFS products. SunScreen SKIP is available on Solaris, Windows 3.11, Windows 95, and Windows NT operating systems.

While the SPF-100, SPF-200, and EFS products provide unparalleled security and encryption capabilities with site-to-site communication, SunScreen SKIP provides customers with the ability to communicate back to the corporate network server via the SPF-100 or EFS. Thus, a secure virtual private network is created with a client/server relationship. SunScreen SKIP also has client-to-client capabilities, enabling remote users to communicate among themselves just as securely and easily as they would with a network server.

SunScreen SKIP Files and Directories on the CD

The files and directories in the `/cdrom/solaris_srvr_intranet_ext_1_0/ Skip_1.1.1` directory are listed in Table B–19.

Table B–19 AdminSuite Directories

Directory	Description
docs	Directory containing PostScript documentation files.
sparc	Directory containing the SPARC SunScreen SKIP packages.
x86	Directory containing the x86 SunScreen SKIP packages.

Installing SunScreen SKIP

The following sections provide guidelines for installing SunScreen SKIP 1.1.1 software. For complete instructions refer to the *SunScreen SKIP User's Guide* available in the `/cdrom/solaris_srvr_intranet_ext_1_0/Skip_1.1.1/docs` directory.

Reviewing System Requirements

The following list describes the minimum system requirements for installing SunScreen SKIP 1.1.1 on a Solaris host:

- Solaris 2.4 or later for SPARC or x86 platforms
- Minimum of 16 MB of RAM is required, 32 MB of RAM is recommended.
- A minimum of 6 MB of free disk space is required for installation. 3 MB of disk space is used permanently.
- One or more supported network interfaces.

SunScreen SKIP supports the following protocol versions:

- SKIP, Version 1, for SunScreen SPF-100/100G and SPF-200 compatibility.
- Any platform that has implemented SKIP as described in the ICGT Technical Reports listed in Section 1.1.2, including the SunScreen product line, except SunScreen SPF-100, which only implements SKIP, Version 1.
- Raw mode (also known as ESP/AH, manual keying, or S/WAN) for compliance with *RFC 1825: Security Architecture for the Internet Protocol.*
- SunScreen SKIP Release 1.1 is the upgrade for SKIP for Solaris, Release 1.0.

To run SunScreen SKIP you must have the Solaris SunCore software group of packages installed. This software group contains the minimum software required to boot and run the Solaris operating system. It includes some networking software and the drivers needed to run the OpenWindows environment; it does not include the OpenWindows software. If you plan to use the skiptool GUI, install the packages for OpenWindows.

In addition, you must have installed the packages listed in Table B–20.

Table B–20 System Software Packages Required to Run SunScreen SKIP

Package	Description
SUNWadmr	System & Network Administration Root
SUNWcar	Core Architecture, (Root)
SUNWcsd	Core Solaris Devices
SUNWcsr	Core Solaris, ()Root)
SUNWcsu	Core Solaris, (Usr)
SUNWdfb	Dumb Frame Buffer Device Drivers
SUNWesu	Extended System Utilities
SUNWkvm	Core Architecture, (Kvm)
SUNWlibC	SPARCompilers Bundled libC
SUNWlibms	SPARCompilers Bundled shared libm
SUNWtoo	Programming Tools
SUNWvolr	Volume Management, (Root)
SUNWvolu	Volume Management, (Usr)

Installing SunScreen SKIP Software

To install SunScreen SKIP software:

1. Become superuser.
2. Insert the product CD into your CD-ROM drive. If your system is running volume management, the CD is mounted automatically. See Appendix A for information about volume management and mounting CDs.
3. Type **cd /cdrom/solaris_srvr_intranet_ext_1_0/SKIP_1.1.1/sparc | x86** and press Return.
4. Type **pkgadd -d .** and press Return. A list of the packages is displayed.

```
castle# cd /cdrom/solaris_srvr_intranet_ext_1_0/Skip_1.1.1/sparc
castle# pkgadd -d .

The following packages are available:
  1  SICGbdcdr     SKIP Bulk Data Crypt 1.1.1 Software
                   (sparc) 1.1.1
  2  SICGcrc2      SKIP RC2 Crypto Module 1.1.1 Software
                   (sparc) 1.1.1
  3  SICGcrc4      SKIP RC4 Crypto Module 1.1.1 Software
                   (sparc) 1.1.1
  4  SICGes        SKIP End System 1.1.1 Software
                   (sparc) 1.1.1
```

```
     5  SICGkeymg      SKIP Key Manager Tools 1.1.1 Software
                       (sparc) 1.1.1
     6  SICGkisup      SKIP I-Support module 1.1.1 Software
                       (sparc) 1.1.1

  Select package(s) you wish to process (or 'all' to process
  all packages). (default: all) [?,??,q]:
```

5. At the prompt press Return to install all of the packages.
6. Answer **yes** to any questions displayed by the `pkgadd` program.
7. When the packages are installed, type **q** and press Return to quit `pkgadd`.
8. Add `/opt/SUNWicg/bin` to root's `PATH` variable.
9. Add `/opt/SUNWicg/man` to root's `MANPATH` variable.

To complete the installation you must:

- Generate and install SKIP Unsigned Diffie-Hellman (UDH) certificates or install SunCA certificates.
- Install SunScreen SKIP on your network interface.

For information on how to complete these tasks, refer to the *SunScreen SKIP User's Guide*.

Using SunScreen SKIP

SunScreen SKIP provides two interfaces that you can use for configuring and managing the SunScreen SKIP software:

- The graphical user interface tool: `skiptool`
- The command-line interface: `skiphost`

Using `skiptool` is the easiest way to set up and administer SunScreen SKIP. The GUI allows you to enable and disable access to systems, set the type of encryption used for hosts or network connections to your system and determine how to deal with unauthorized hosts that try to connect to your system. It also enables you to view the following statistics:

- Network interface
- SKIP header
- Key
- Encryption
- Authentication

To run `skiptool`, you must be able to enable access for any client to the X server for Solaris 2.*x* systems by entering the `xhost +<localhost>` command before you become root. You must be able to become root on your system.

To start `skiptool`:

1. Type **xhost +<*localhost*>** and press Return.
2. Become superuser.
3. Type **skiptool&** and press Return.

Refer to the *SunScreen SKIP User's Guide* for complete information on how to use both `skiptool` and `skiphost` commands.

GLOSSARY

access rights The four types of operations—read, modify, create, and destroy—that control access to NIS+ objects for each of the authorization rights categories.

Admintool A graphical user interface tool that you can use to manage local systems.

AutoClient system A system that caches all of its needed system software from a server.

alias An alternative name or names assigned to a program or to an electronic mail address.

application server A server set up and administered exclusively to provide application services to users over the network.

authorization rights The four categories—nobody, owner, group, and world—that control access to NIS+ tables.

Auto_home database The database that you use to add home directories to the automounter. You can access the Auto_home database using the Solstice AdminSuite Database Manager. In SunOS 4.*x* releases, this database was a file named `auto.home`.

automounter Solaris 2.*x* software that automatically mounts a directory when a user changes into it. It automatically unmounts the directory when it is no longer in use.

automount maps The local files or name service tables that the automounter consults to determine which directories to mount, which system to mount them from, and where to mount them on the user's local system.

back file system The file system on the server from which a cache file system is mounted on a client.

bang An exclamation point (!) that acts as a single-character UNIX command or as a separator between the routes of a route-based electronic mail address.

base directory The directory into which the package commands and Admintool: Packages GUI install software packages. The default base directory is `/opt`.

baud rate The transmission speed of a serial communications channel, expressed in bits per second.

Bourne shell One of the three Solaris 2.*x* command interpreters. The Bourne shell is the default user shell, and it is the shell language used to write most system administration shell scripts. See also **C shell**, **Korn shell**.

breakout box A diagnostic device that plugs into an RS-232-C cable; it is used to test whether a signal is present on each cable pin.

cache A small, fast memory area that holds the most frequently referenced portions of a larger and/or slower memory. A cache is used to increase program or system performance. Examples include a disk cache where frequently referenced disk blocks are stored in RAM and a browser cache where frequently referenced Web pages and graphics objects are stored locally on a user's computer.

CDE Common Desktop Environment. A windowing system based on the Motif graphical user interface.

CD-ROM An acronym for compact disc, read-only memory. CD-ROM is a read-only storage medium for digital data.

character terminal A serial port device that displays only letters, numbers, and other characters, such as those produced by a typewriter.

child process A process that is created by another process. The process that creates the environment for the child is called the *parent*.

client A system or program that receives system resources from a remote system—called a server—over the network.

compiler A program that translates human-readable source code into a machine-readable form in preparation for creating directly executable programs. For example, a C compiler translates a human-readable C program into a machine-readable executable program.

concatenation The combining of two or more files to create one larger file. Also, with Online: DiskSuite, the combining of separate component disks into a sequential system of disk blocks.

C shell One of the three Solaris 2.*x* command interpreters. See also **Bourne shell**, **Korn shell**.

daemon A special type of program that, once activated, carries out a specific task without any need for user intervention. Daemons typically are used to handle jobs that have been queued, such as printing, mail, and communication. Daemons are usually started when the system is booted. Because they typically are not started by a user, daemons communicate by means other than terminal I/O, such as logfiles, signals, and configuration files.

Database Manager A graphical user interface tool accessed from Solstice AdminSuite that is used to administer NIS+ tables and ufs files in the `/etc` directory.

direct map An automount map that specifies absolute paths as the mount point.

diskette A portable, nonvolatile storage medium used to store and access data magnetically. SunOS 5.*x* system software supports 3.5-inch double-sided high density (DS, HD) diskettes in raw and MS_DOS (PCFS) formats.

domain A directory structure for electronic mail addressing, network address naming, and NIS+ hierarchy naming. Within the United States, top-level Internet domains include *com* for commercial organizations, *edu* for educational organizations, *gov* for governments, *mil* for the military, *net* for networking organizations, and *org* for other organizations. *us* is used as the top-level domain for a U.S. geographical hierarchy; two-letter state codes are the second level in the geographic hierarchy, with cities, counties, or parishes following. Outside of the United States, top-level Internet domains designate the country. Subdomains designate the organization and the individual system.

domain addressing Using a domain address to specify the destination of an electronic mail message or NIS+ table.

electronic mail A set of programs that transmit mail messages from one system to another, usually over communications lines. Electronic mail is frequently referred to as *email.*

email See **electronic mail**.

environment variable A system- or user-defined variable that provides information about the operating environment to a program or shell.

exit status A numeric value assigned in a program or a shell script to indicate whether it ran successfully. An exit status of 0 usually means that the program executed successfully. Any non-zero value usually means that the program failed, but it can also indicate various conditions of success.

export See **share**.

file descriptor A set of information kept by the UNIX kernel that is related to a file opened by a process. A file descriptor is represented by an integer. The file descriptor for STDIN is 0, for STDOUT is 1, and for STDERR is 2.

file system A hierarchical arrangement of directories and files.

floppy diskette See **diskette**.

fork To copy one process into a parent process and a child process, with separate but initially identical text, data, and stack segments. See also **child** and **parent**.

fully qualified domain name A domain name that contains all of the elements needed to specify where an electronic mail message should be delivered or where an NIS+ table is located. NIS+ fully qualified domain names always have a dot at the end. See also **domain**.

gateway A connection between differing communications networks. Also a system that handles electronic mail traffic between differing communications networks.

generic top-level domain (gTLD) The seven new domains that are being added to the existing set to accommodate increased demand for domains because of the popularity of the Internet. The seven new domains are *.arts*, *.firm*, *.info*, *.nom*, *.rec*, and *.web*.

GID The group identification number used by the system to control access to information owned by other users.

group A defined collection of users on a system who can access common data.

Group database The database that you use to create new group accounts or to modify existing group accounts. You access the Group database from Solstice AdminSuite.

here document A format used within a shell script to provide a collection of data within the shell script.

home directory The part of the file system that is allocated to an individual user for private files.

Hosts database A directory service used to look up names and addresses of other hosts on a network. You access the Hosts database from the Solstice AdminSuite's Database Manager.

indirect map An automount map that contains simple pathnames as the mount point.

init states One of the seven states, or run levels, a system can be running. A system can run in only one init state at a time.

inode An entry in a predesignated area of a disk that describes where a file is located on that disk, the size of the file, when it was last used, and other identifying information.

interpreter A program that reads and executes programming commands in sequence—one by one as they are encountered. Shell scripts are an example of interpreted programs.

IP address A unique Internet address number that identifies each system or device in a network.

kernel The master program set of SunOS software that manages all of the physical resources of the computer, including file system management, virtual memory, reading and writing files to disks and tapes, scheduling of processes, and communicating over a network.

Korn shell One of the three Solaris 2.*x* command interpreters. The Korn shell is upwards-compatible with the Bourne shell and provides an expanded set of features. See also **Bourne shell**, **C shell**.

license server A server process that provides users access to software licenses to enable users to access software programs. Licenses are frequently used to enforce a license agreement, whereby a maximum number of users is permitted to run a commercial software program concurrently.

listenBSD An LP print service daemon that is run on a SunOS 5.*x* print server to listen for print requests from SunOS 4.*x* print clients on the network.

listenS5 An LP print service daemon that is run on a print server to listen for print requests from SunOS 5.*x* print clients on the network.

login name The name assigned to an individual user that controls access to a system.

mail address The name of the recipient and the location to which an electronic mail message is delivered.

mail alias See **alias**.

mailbox A file on a mailhost where mail messages are stored for a user.

mail client A system that does not provide mail spooling for its users. Mail is spooled on a mail server.

mailer A protocol that specifies the policy and mechanics used by sendmail when it delivers mail.

mailhost The main mail system on a network that receives and distributes mail outside of the network or the domain. A mailhost can also be a mail server.

mail server Any system that stores mailboxes in the `/var/mail` directory. A mail server can also serve as a mailhost.

mail services Services provided by a set of programs and daemons that transmit electronic mail messages between systems and distribute them to individual mailboxes.

master map The automount map consulted by the automounter when a system starts up. The automount map contains the default mount points `/net` and `/home` and the names of the direct and indirect maps that the automounter consults.

metadevice A logical device that is created by using the SunSoft Online: DiskSuite product to concatenate or stripe one or more disks into a single logical device unit.

modem A peripheral device that modulates a digital signal so that it can be transmitted across analog telephone lines and then demodulates the analog signal to a digital signal at the receiving end. The name is a contraction for *mod*ulate/*dem*odulate. A modem is one way to connect a UNIX workstation or PC to a remote server or network.

mount To extend a file system directory hierarchy by attaching a file system from somewhere else in the hierarchy. See **mount point**.

mount point A directory in the file system hierarchy where another file system is attached to the hierarchy.

mount table The system file (`/etc/mnttab`) that keeps track of currently mounted file systems.

namespace A hierarchical arrangement of domains and subdomains, similar to the hierarchical UNIX file system, used by NIS+ and the automounter.

NFS (network file system) The default Solaris 1.*x* and 2.*x* distributed file system that provides file sharing among systems. NFS servers can also provide kernels and swap files to diskless clients.

NIS The SunOS 4.*x* network information service.

NIS+ The Solaris 2.*x* network information service.

null modem cable A cable that swaps RS-232 Transmit and Receive signals so that the proper transmit and receive signals are communicated between two data termination equipment (DTE) devices. The RS-232 Ground signal is wired straight through.

OpenWindows A windowing system based on the OPEN LOOK® graphical user interface.

package commands The set of Solaris 2.*x* commands—`pkgadd`, `pkgask`, `pkgchk`, `pkginfo`, and `pkgrm`—that are used to install, query, and remove software packages.

parent process A process that can create a new process, called a *child*.

parse To resolve a string of characters or a series of words into component parts to determine their collective meaning. Virtually every program that accepts command input must do some sort of parsing before the commands can be acted upon. For example, the sendmail program divides an email address into its component parts to decide where to send the message.

partially qualified domain name An NIS+ domain name that specifies the local directory only and does not contain the complete domain name. For example, `hosts.org_dir` is a partially qualified domain name that specifies the hosts table in the `org_dir` directory of the default NIS+ domain. See also **domain**.

partition A discrete portion of a disk, configured using the format program. A partition is the same as a slice.

Passwd database The database that you use to add, modify, or delete user accounts. You access the Passwd database from Solstice AdminSuite's Database Manager.

path A list of directories that is searched to find a file. `PATH` is a shell environment variable used to find user commands.

path name A list of directory names, separated with slashes (/), that specifies the location of a particular file or directory.

PCFS Personal computer file system. A file system type for diskettes in MS-DOS compatible format.

port A physical connection between a peripheral device such as a terminal, printer, or modem and the device controller. Also, a logical access point on a system used to accept connections over a network.

port monitor A program that continuously watches for requests to log in or requests to access printers or files. The ttymon and listen port monitors are part of the Service Access Facility (SAF).

positional parameter A shell script notation—`$1`, `$2`, `$n`—used to access command-line arguments.

principals Individuals or systems within the NIS+ namespace that have been "registered" with the NIS+ service.

process A program in operation. See also **fork**, **child process**, **parent process**.

relay host A system that transmits to and receives mail from outside of a network or domain using the same communications protocol.

RFC Request for Comments, specifically Internet protocols and standards. RFCs are submitted to SRI-NIC, where they are assigned numbers and are distributed by electronic mail to the Internet community. The most important RFCs (through 1985) are available in a three-volume publication, *The DDN Protocol Handbook*, which is available from SRI International in Menlo Park, California. RFCs are also available online at `http://ds.internic.net/`.

root The highest level of a hierarchical system. As a login ID, the username of the system administrator or superuser who has responsibility for an entire system. Root has permissions for all users' files and processes on the system.

run level See **init state**.

SAC See **Service Access Controller**.

SAF See **Service Access Facility**.

script See **shell script**.

sendmail The mailer transport agent used by Solaris 2.*x* system software. See also **transport agent**.

server A system that provides network service, such as disk storage and file transfer or access to a database. Alternatively, a program that provides such a service. See **client**.

service A process that is started in response to a connection request.

Service Access Controller (SAC) The process that manages access to system services provided by the Service Access Facility.

Service Access Facility (SAF) The part of the system software that is used to register and monitor port activity for modems, terminals, and printers. SAF replaces `/etc/getty` as a way to control logins.

share To make a file system available (mountable) to other systems on the network. See **mount**, **NFS**.

shell The command interpreter for a user, specified in the Passwd database. The SunOS 5.*x* system software supports the Bourne (default), C, and Korn shells.

shell script A file containing a set of executable commands that are taken as input to the shell.

shell variable Local variables maintained by a shell, which are not passed on from parent to child processes.

slice An alternate name for a partition. See also **partition**.

spooling directory A directory where files are stored until they are processed.

spooling space The amount of space allocated on a print server for storing requests in a queue.

standalone system A system that has a local disk and can boot without relying on a server.

standard error The location where error messages are sent. The file descriptor for stderr is 2. The default device for stderr is the terminal screen. See **file descriptor**.

standard input The location where input is received from. The file descriptor for stdin is 0. The default device for stdin is the keyboard. See **file descriptor**.

standard output The part of a process that determines where the results of commands are displayed. The file descriptor for stdout is 1. The default device for stdout is the terminal screen.

stderr See **standard error**.

stdin See **standard input**.

stdout See **standard output**.

striping Interlacing two or more disk partitions that make a single logical slice of up to 1 terabyte. With the SunSoft Online: DiskSuite product, the addressing of blocks is interlaced on the resulting metadevice to improve performance.

superuser A user with special privileges granted if the correct password is supplied when logging in as root or using the `su` command. For example, only the superuser can edit major administrative files in the `/etc` directory. The superuser has the username root.

symbolic link A special file that contains a pointer to the name of another file or directory.

system Another name for a computer, PC, or workstation. A system can have either local or remote disks and may have additional peripheral devices, such as CD-ROM players, tape drives, diskette drives, modems, and printers.

terminfo database The database that describes the characteristics of terminal devices and printers.

third-party software Application software that is not included as part of the basic system software.

transport agent The program that is responsible for receiving and delivering email messages. The Solaris 2.*x* transport agent is sendmail.

ufs (UNIX file system) The default disk-based file system for the SunOS 5.*x* operating system.

UID number The user identification number assigned to each login name. UID numbers are used by the system to identify, by number, the owners of files and directories. The UID of root is 0.

uncommitted interface An interface in the `sendmail.cf` file that is a de facto industry standard. Uncommitted interfaces have never had a formal architectural review, and they may be subject to change.

unmount To remove a file system from a mount point so that the files are no longer accessible. See **mount**, **NFS**.

unresolved mail Mail with an address for which sendmail cannot find a recipient in your domain.

user account An account set up for an individual user in the Passwd database that specifies the user's login name, full name, password, UID, GID, login directory, and login shell.

User Account Manager A graphical user interface tool accessed from Admintool to add users to a local system. The Solstice AdminSuite User Account Manager can be used to add users to an NIS+ environment or to a local system.

user agent A program that acts as the interface between the user and the sendmail program. The user agents for SunOS 5.x system software are `/usr/bin/mail`, `/usr/bin/mailx`, `/usr/dt/bin/dtmail`, and `$OPENWINHOME/bin/ mailtool`.

value Data, either numeric or alphanumeric.

variable A name that refers to a temporary storage area in memory. A variable holds a value.

virtual file system table The file (`/etc/vfstab`) that specifies which file systems are mounted by default. Local ufs file systems and NFS file systems that are mounted automatically when a system boots are specified in this file.

virtual memory A memory management technique used by the operating system for programs that require more space in memory than can be allotted to them. The kernel moves only pages of the program currently needed into memory, while unneeded pages remain on the disk. Virtual memory extends physical memory over disk. See also **kernel**.

volume management System software available with Solaris 2.2 and later releases that mounts CD-ROM and diskettes automatically without requiring superuser permission.

wrapper A shell script installed on an application server that is used to set up the environment for that application; the wrapper then executes the application.

write-through cache A type of cache that immediately updates its data source as data is changed or added to the cache.

BIBLIOGRAPHY

General References

Coffin, Stephen. *UNIX System V Release 4: The Complete Reference.* Osborne McGraw-Hill, 1990.

Garfinkel, Simson, and Gene Spifford. *Practical UNIX Security.* O'Reilly & Associates, 1991.

Loukides, Mike. *System Performance Tuning*. O'Reilly & Associates, 1990.

Nemeth, Evi, Garth Snyder, and Scott Seebass. *UNIX System Administration Handbook.* Prentice Hall Software Series, 1989.

Rosen, Kenneth H., Richard R. Rosinski, and James M. Farber. *UNIX System V Release 4: An Introduction.* Osborne McGraw-Hill, 1990.

Stern, Hal. *Managing NFS and NIS.* O'Reilly & Associates, 1991.

Winsor, Janice. *Solaris System Administrator's Guide, Second Edition.* SunSoft Press/Macmillan Publishing, 1997.

Electronic Mail References

DDN Protocol Handbook, The. 1985. Three-volume set of RFCs, available from SRI International, 333 Ravenswood Avenue, Menlo Park, CA 94025.

Frey, Donnalyn, and Rick Adams. *!%@:: A Directory of Electronic Mail Addressing & Network,* 2nd ed. O'Reilly & Associates, 1990.

RFC 822 *Standard for the Format of ARPA INTERNET Text Messages.*

RFC 1211 Problems with Maintaining Large email Lists.

Firewall References

Chapman, D. Brent, and Elizabeth D. Zwicky, *Building Internet Firewalls.* O'Reilly& Associates, 1995.

Cheswick, Steven, and William Bellovin, *Firewalls & Internet Security: Repelling the Wily Hacker.* Addison-Wesley Publishing Company, 1996.

NIS+ Reference

Ramsey, Rick. *All About Administering NIS+, Second Edition.* SunSoft Press/Prentice Hall, 1994.

Printing Reference

PostScript Language Reference Manual. Adobe Systems Incorporated, October 1990.

Shell References

Anderson, Gail, and Paul Anderson. *The UNIX C Shell Field Guide.* Prentice Hall, 1986.

Arick, Martin R. *UNIX C Shell Desk Reference.* QED Technical Publishing Group, 1992.

Arthur, Lowell Jay. *UNIX Shell Programming,* 2nd ed. John Wiley & Sons, Inc., 1990.

Bolsky, Morris I., and David G. Korn. *The Kornshell Command and Programming Language.* Prentice Hall, 1989.

Olczak, Anatole. *The Korn Shell User & Programming Manual.* Addison-Wesley Publishing Company, 1992.

Rosenblatt, Bill. *Learning the Korn Shell.* O'Reilly & Associates, 1993.

Programming Languages

Aho, Alfred V., Brian W. Kernighan, and Peter J. Weinberger. *The AWK Programming Language.* Addison-Wesley Publishing Company, 1988.

Dougherty, Dale. *sed & awk.* O'Reilly & Associates, 1991.

INDEX

B

C

D

E

G

M

N

O

Q

R

S

T

U

V

W

X-Z